ANGRAECOID ORCHIDS

ANGRAECOID ORCHIDS

SPECIES FROM THE AFRICAN REGION

Joyce Stewart

Johan Hermans

Bob Campbell

TIMBER PRESS

Frontispiece: *Aerangis mooreana*, salmon pink form from the Comoro Islands. J. Hermans

Published in 2006 by
Timber Press, Inc.
The Haseltine Building
133 S.W. Second Avenue, Suite 450
Portland, Oregon 97204-3527, U.S.A.

www.timberpress.com

For contact information regarding editorial, marketing, sales, and distribution in the United Kingdom, see www.timberpress.co.uk.

Printed through Colorcraft Ltd., Hong Kong

Library of Congress Cataloging-in-Publication Data

Stewart, Joyce.
  Angraecoid orchids : species from the African region / Joyce Stewart,
Johan Hermans, Bob Campbell.
      p. cm.
  Includes bibliographical references and index.
  ISBN-13: 978-0-88192-788-7
  ISBN-10: 0-88192-788-0
  1. Angraecum--Africa. 2. Orchids--Africa. I. Hermans, Johan. II.
Campbell, Bob (Bob Ian Martin) III. Title.
  QK495.O64S712 2006
  584'.4--dc22   2005033768

A catalog record for this book is also available from the British Library.

To orchid enthusiasts who appreciate the angraecoids
as much as we do, in grateful acknowledgement of
the contributions of all the botanists, explorers, and
others whose work has preceded our own.

Nil posse creari de nilo.
Nothing can be created out of nothing.

LUCRETIUS (99–55 B.C.), *De Rarum Natura*, I. 155
(Translated by Bailey)

Contents

Preface

Angraecoid orchids are found mostly in the African region. They are distributed throughout the continent, south of the Sahara, and occur on all the neighbouring islands. Their vandaceous growth habit is characteristic, and many have glossy or sparkling white flowers that are scented in the evening. Some of the most spectacular species are confined to Madagascar, and I went there to look for them on a holiday in 1969. I remember it well. At the time, I had no book on the orchids of the island, and identification of the plants I saw was not easy.

An Introduction to the Cultivated Angraecoid Orchids of Madagascar by Fred E. Hillerman and Arthur W. Holst was warmly welcomed, worldwide, when it was published in 1986. It soon became a major resource for orchid growers seeking information about these exciting plants. Interest in the angraecoids continued even after the book went out of print.

In February 2002 Timber Press in Portland, Oregon, contacted me about writing a new book on the subject. Three years earlier the company had made a similar proposal. At that time I was fully employed at the Royal Horticultural Society, but I agreed to think about the idea. It might be a nice project for my approaching retirement, I thought. I knew that I could produce the text, as suggested, but my thoughts turned to the question of illustrations. Colour photographs would be essential, and as many as possible. I knew that I did not have enough. I thought of asking two friends if they would like to collaborate on the project. I had worked with Bob Campbell on *Orchids of Kenya*

(1996), and on *Orchids of Tropical Africa* (1970) more than 30 years before. I had seen some of Johan Hermans's excellent transparencies, heard him lecture on his visits to Madagascar, and read many of his publications on the orchids of that country, especially *The Orchids of Madagascar* (1999) and *Madagascan Orchids* (2006). Both men agreed to be involved, in addition to meeting other writing commitments of their own, and I am very grateful to them. So, six months later, the thoughts materialised into a contract from which this book developed. It is intended as a guide to the identification and culture of these specialised orchids.

At an early stage we had to decide what to include and what to leave out. This was a fairly easy decision because the main reason for compiling the book was to try to bring together in one place a lot of widely scattered information, published in several languages over more than two centuries. Whatever might be left out would be sure to be just the information which the reader was seeking. Therefore, we decided, we should try to include all the genera and species, as compactly as possible.

It was easy to make a list of genera from our own notes and records (Stewart 1976, Stewart and Hennessy 1981, Hermans and Hermans in Du Puy et al. 1999) and to check these against the invaluable publications of Senghas (1986) and Dressler (1981, 1993). The total genera came to approximately 47, 'approximate' because a few were considered to be synonymous by one taxonomist or another.

The task of preparing a list of species was at first daunting because the descriptions are so spread out in the literature, but it was made immeasurably easier by the appearance in January 2003 of the first parts of the World Checklist of Monocotyledons. The Orchidaceae information in it was compiled by R. Govaerts and published on the Web site of the Royal Botanic Gardens, Kew. The timing could not have been more helpful to us. We could extract the names of relevant genera and species from this huge database and make a start. Since then we have added a few species that were missing from that checklist and some that have been described since it was prepared. We have also consulted the revised version that appeared in February 2004. We hope that not too many more names will appear while this book is in press. Undoubtedly there will be some, and readers will be able to make their own additions to our text. At the time of completing the manuscript, our total is 690 species.

We had secured agreement to include several hundred colour photographs in the forthcoming book, but we knew that there were some little-known genera for which photographs would not be available. We were also asked to include some line drawings, which often can reveal more detail than photographs. But as it would take a long time to prepare new drawings, we agreed to use existing drawings. We have reproduced a few from the first book on Madagascar orchids, by L. M. Aubert du Petit Thouars (1822), and others from the archives at the Royal Botanic Gardens, Kew, and the Muséum national d'Histoire naturelle in Paris with the kind permission of the director and trustees of each institute and of the artists themselves. Johan has taken responsibility for choosing and coordinating the photographs that we all contributed and obtained from various friends, and the drawings. Our aim was to have at least one drawing to illustrate the diagnostic features of each genus, as well as a good selection of colour photographs taken in the wild habitats or in cultivation.

We have all spent time in the field in various parts of eastern and southern Africa—I spent 22 years in Kenya and South Africa, while Bob was born in Kenya and still lives there. We have also visited Madagascar (JS once, JH nine times), the Comoro Islands (JS and BC), Mauritius (JS), and Réunion (JS twice). Studying, photographing, and collecting orchids have been major hobby activities for all of us for many years, though collecting opportunities have become fewer recently. Some of the information and records obtained during this time have already been published (Stewart and Campbell 1970, 1996; Stewart and Hennessy 1981; Stewart et al. 1982; Hermans and Hermans 1999). We have drawn heavily on our experiences and observations in the field in compiling this book too.

With our spouses, we have been involved in maintaining living orchid collections over long periods: JS and her friend, Heather Campbell, each for more than 40 years, and JH and his wife, Clare, for more than 20 years. Started as study collections, especially to bring into flower plants that could not be recognised without flowers in the field, these have expanded in various ways, but they have provided invaluable insights into the biology and culture of the orchids concerned. The cultural information that is provided here is based on our experiences, but we do not pretend to know everything about growing these orchids or to have been successful every time. Additional information about the culture of angraecoid orchids can be found in the works of Hillerman and Holst (1986), Hillerman (1990, 1992), la Croix and la Croix (1997), Wodrich (1997), and in many general books on orchid growing.

Over the years we have built up extensive orchid libraries. Using the books and journals, reprints, drawings, and photographs has given us much pleasure. The books and papers we have consulted in preparing this book are listed in the References at the back of this volume. The floras that we have repeatedly referred to are listed chronologically below; more details of these are given in the References under each author's name.

Histoire particulière des plantes Orchidées recueillies sur les trois Îles Australes d'Afrique (Thouars 1822; reprint 1979)
Flore de l'Île de la Réunion (Cordemoy 1895, additions 1899)

Flora of Tropical Africa, vol. 7 (Rolfe 1897–1898)

Icones Orchidearum, 3 vols. (Bolus 1893–1896, 1911, 1913)

Flora Capensis, vol. 5, part 3 (Rolfe 1912–1913)

Flore de Madagascar, 49 Famille, *Orchidées*, vol. 2 (Perrier de la Bâthie 1941)

Flora of West Tropical Africa, ed. 2, vol. 3, part 1 (Summerhayes 1968)

The Orchids of South Central Africa (Williamson 1977)

Wild Orchids of Southern Africa (Stewart et al. 1982)

Flora of Tropical East Africa, Orchidaceae, part 3 (Cribb 1989)

Orchids of Malawi (la Croix et al. 1991)

Flore d'Afrique centrale, Orchidaceae, part 2 (Geerinck 1992)

Orchids of Kenya (Stewart and Campbell 1996)

Flora Zambesiaca, vol. 11, part 2 (la Croix and Cribb 1998)

Orchids of Southern Africa (Linder and Kurzweil 1999)

The Orchids of Madagascar (Hermans and Hermans in Du Puy et al. 1999)

Guide des Orchidées de São Tomé et Príncipe (Stévart and de Oliveira 2000)

Flore du Cameroun, 36, *Orchidacées*, vol. 3 (Szlachetko and Olszewski 2001)

Les Orchidées de Côte d'Ivoire (Perez-Vera 2003)

Field Guide to Ethiopian Orchids (Demissew et al. 2004)

Flore du Gabon, 37, Orchidaceae II (Szlachetko et al. 2004)

Madagascan Orchids (Hermans and Hermans et al. 2006)

Botanists who are still currently publishing new names, descriptions, and revisions relevant to our subject include particularly Jean Bosser in Paris, who has published a long series on Madagascar and Mascarene orchids in the journal *Adansonia* and elsewhere. Phillip Cribb at Kew has published many papers on African orchids as well as prepared several flora accounts. Both of these professional botanists have been extremely supportive of us in this project and we thank them for their time and trouble.

Many orchid growers have also published relevant books and papers, most notably, Lecoufle (1966, 1976, 1980, 1994), Hillerman and Holst (1986), Hillerman (1990, 1992), and la Croix and la Croix (1997).

In addition to the living plants and the literature records, we have also been most fortunate to study the dried collections of orchid specimens in herbaria. It is in the world's herbaria that one can find the type specimens, which represent the plants on which the names are based. We have been fortunate to spend time in the herbaria at the Royal Botanic Gardens, Kew; the Muséum national d'Histoire naturelle, Paris; the Natural History Museum, London; and the East African Herbarium, Nairobi, but we have made short visits to others and also borrowed material from yet more. We thank the directors concerned for welcoming us to their institutions over the years and for allowing us the use of their facilities. All these studies have contributed to the information presented in this book.

A new source of information has become available recently on the Internet. Several enthusiasts are setting up Web sites featuring photographs and drawings of orchids as well as text, though they sometimes have problems with the identification of their illustrations. The sites relevant to our area, which we have seen, are listed at the end of the References.

We should like to extend our most grateful thanks to all those who have helped us in various ways. Most of the photographs reproduced in this book were taken by Johan Hermans and Bob Campbell, and I want to thank them both for helping to make this such a beautiful book. We also particularly want to thank Coen Arends, Phillip Cribb, Moritz Grubenmann, Eric la Croix, L. Westra, and Jack Wubben for the loan of their excellent transparencies.

Many of the drawings have been available to us from the archives at the Royal Botanic Gardens, Kew, with the kind cooperation and assistance of Marilyn Ward, curator of illustrations. We thank her and the following artists for their permission: Andrew Brown, Maureen Church, Linda Cowan, Mary Grierson, Susan Hillier, Cherry-Anne Lavrih, H. B. Lloyd, Stella Ross-Craig, Judi Stone, Margaret Stones, S. Stuart-Smith, W. Wessel-Brand, Sue Wickison, and Graham Williamson. We are extremely grateful to the Muséum national d'Histoire naturelle, Paris, for permission to copy previously published drawings by Madagascan artist E. Razafindrakoto and by M. J. Vesque in the book by Henri Perrier de la Bâthie, and to Dariusz Szlachetko of Gdansk University for his drawing of *Taeniorrhiza gabonensis*, previously published in *Flore du Cameroun*. We thank Deborah Lambkin for a new drawing of the curious orchid *Lemurorchis madagascariensis*. We also thank Robert Dressler for permission to reproduce a drawing prepared for his *Phylogeny and Classification of the Orchid Family* (1993), adapted from a drawing I made many years earlier (Stewart 1976). A few other drawings have been reproduced from older publications in Johan's library as detailed in the captions.

We want to thank the librarians and staff in the libraries at the Royal Botanic Gardens, Kew, at the Lindley Library, Royal Horticultural Society, and at the Muséum national d'Histoire naturelle in Paris for their assistance in tracing rare publications and making them available to us for study, and for making us so welcome during our visits.

I wish to thank Johan Hermans for lending me his notes on the Madagascar species of *Aerangis*, *Aeranthes*, and *Jumellea*, and especially for reading all the text as it appeared, carefully and critically: a mighty effort. Isobyl la Croix kindly read and commented on the section on *Jumellea*, and Donald Stewart checked all the introductory parts. Many heartfelt thanks to all of them and an acknowledgement that any mistakes that have still crept through are mine.

Finally, a word of thanks is due to all the staff at Timber Press who made this book possible, especially Neal Maillet, who initiated the project, and Anna Mumford who saw it through to completion.

JOYCE STEWART
Honorary Research Associate
Royal Botanic Gardens, Kew

Introduction

Orchids with a monopodial habit of growth are perhaps the most highly evolved group in the huge family Orchidaceae. Instantly recognisable by their habit, whether or not they are in flower, they are often referred to as the vandaceous group and are classified in the tribe Vandeae. They are almost entirely restricted to the Old World (Africa, Asia, and Australia) in their distribution.

About 150 genera comprising nearly two thousand species are now recognised in the Vandeae. They are classified into three subtribes: Aeridinae, Angraecinae, and Aerangidinae.

Aeridinae, with more than 1250 species in over 100 genera, occur in Asia and Australia. Only two species, one in *Acampe* and one in *Taeniophyllum*, are found in Africa. Neither is included in the present book.

Angraecinae, with approximately 15 genera and 360 species, occur in Madagascar and Africa. Two other genera, *Campylocentrum* and *Dendrophylax* (now including *Harrisella* and *Polyradicion*, according to Carlsward et al. 2003), with approximately 80 species occur in the American continent but are omitted from this book. One species of *Angraecum* occurs in Sri Lanka.

Aerangidinae, with approximately 32 genera and 330 species, occur in Africa and Madagascar, and one species in Sri Lanka. All of these are included in this book.

Although the individual African and Madagascan genera are mostly easy to allocate to one subtribe or the other, they have many similarities. For this reason, and because of the gradual discovery and interpretation of the individual genera and species over more than 200 years, they are often discussed together, as the angraecoids, rather than as the angraecoids and the aerangids separately. Details of the species in the two subtribes form a major part of this book.

WHAT IS AN ANGRAECOID?

A brief summary of the characteristics of an angraecoid orchid might be presented as follows:

Habit perennial, epiphyte or lithophyte, rarely terrestrial.

Stem monopodial, sometimes branching, short or variously elongated.

Roots aerial, covered by velamen of the *Vanda*-type.

Leaves in two rows, conduplicate, sometimes laterally flattened, cylindric, or absent.

Inflorescence lateral, simple or branched, with one to many flowers arranged spirally, distichous, secund, or almost capitate.

Pedicel with ovary smooth or hairy, twisted or straight.

Angraecum leonis, Madagascar. J. Hermans

Angraecum magdalenae, growing as a lithophyte, central Madagascar. J. Hermans

Flowers tiny to large, sepals and petals often similar, lip usually different and spurred, sometimes conspicuously so.

Anther terminal on the column, two pollinia with definite, usually elongated stipe or stipes and one or two viscidia.

Rostellum deeply divided in Angraecinae, elongate and beak-like, though sometimes divided into two or three narrow lobes, in Aerangidinae.

Stigma entire, below the anther.

This description applies to all the species of angraecoids, but it conceals a huge amount of detail and diversity. A more extensive review of the morphological characters of the plants in the group is given later in this introduction, and individual or unique characters are pointed out in the main part of the book. A brief account of the contribution of botanists who have been involved in describing the angraecoids, since 1781 when the first one was described by a Swedish botanist, is given next.

HISTORY OF THE ANGRAECOIDS

The starting point for botanical names is the publication *Species Plantarum* (1753) by the Swedish botanist Carl Linnaeus (1707–1778). It contains 69 orchid names, mainly those of European orchids but including eight tropical species under the genus *Epidendrum*. Today, these represent eight different genera.

It was another Swedish botanist, Linnaeus's son (Carl von Linnaeus, 1741–1783, known as Linnaeus f. in botany), who was the first to describe an epiphytic orchid from Africa, predictably perhaps,

Oeoniella polystachys, growing as an epiphyte in lightly shaded forest near the seashore, eastern Madagascar. J. Hermans

as an *Epidendrum*. But *Epidendrum capense* Linnaeus f. (1781) became *Angraecum capense* (Linnaeus f.) Lindley in 1833 and then *Mystacidium capense* (Linnaeus f.) Schlechter in 1914. Along the way it had also been known as *Limodorum longicorne* Thunberg in 1794, *Mystacidium filicorne* Lindley in 1837, and *Aeranthes filicornis* (Lindley) Reichenbach f. in 1861, amongst other names. This nomenclatural 'safari' of a little epiphyte is not unique or even unusual amongst the earliest orchid introductions.

The French traveller L. M. Aubert du Petit Thouars (1758–1831) was amongst the earliest botanical explorers of Mauritius, Réunion, and Madagascar. After an adventurous life there, he returned to Paris in 1802 and published a number of books relating to his experiences. His *Histoire particulière des plantes Orchidées recueillies sur les trois Îles Australes d'Afrique* (1822) contains a general introductory essay on the orchids known at that time. The most important part of the book, however, is its collection of drawings of 110 species. These illustrate a good representation of the range of orchids native to the islands. The book is as useful today as it was when published, and fortunately it is available as a reprint. We are delighted that we have been able to reproduce a few of the illustrations from the original book.

John Lindley (1799–1865) is sometimes referred to as the 'father of orchidology' because of his great interest and huge contribution to the study of orchids, particularly those from the tropics. His *Genera and Species of Orchidaceous Plants*, published in parts between 1830 and 1840, is an extremely important account of the orchids coming into Europe up to that time and the part they played in developing his ideas about orchid classification. It is still referred to today as the starting point for the application of many orchid names (see, for example, Withner and Harding 2004). But so far as the angraecoids are concerned, relatively few were known at that time. Lindley established the genus *Microcoelia* in this account, in 1830, and included a number of species of *Angraecum* that had been published elsewhere. He enumerated the

species of *Aeranthes* (spelt *Aeranthus*), *Cryptopus*, and *Oeonia*, which he had already mentioned in *Edwards's Botanical Register* in 1824. Later, he also established the genus *Mystacidium*, in 1837, in the course of describing a collection of orchid specimens sent back to Kew from South Africa. His paper, 'West African Tropical Orchids' (1862), in which he described the specimens collected by Charles Barter and Gustav Mann also included some new and some well-known angraecoids.

The German botanist Heinrich Gustav Reichenbach (1823–1889) probably described more orchid species than any other botanist, including many from Africa and Madagascar. He is the author of the name *Listrostachys* that accommodated so many species at the end of the nineteenth century. He was also the first to propose that *Aerangis* should be separated from *Angraecum*. He will always be remembered for his unfortunate will, in which his priceless library and herbarium collection of orchid material were bequeathed to the Hof Museum in Vienna on condition that they would remain sealed for 25 years, instead of being left to Kew as had been expected.

It was another English botanist, Robert A. Rolfe (1855–1921), working at Kew, who compiled the first account of the orchids of tropical Africa (published in 1898). He classified all the orchids with a monopodial habit of growth into four genera, according to the structure of the pollinaria: *Angraecum* and *Saccolabium* (now *Acampe*) in which the pollinia have a single stipe and viscidium; *Listrostachys* in which the pollinia have two distinct stipes and a single viscidium; and *Mystacidium* in which each pollinium and its stipe is attached to a separate viscidium. This seemingly simple distinction accommodated about 120 species in the three angraecoid genera, but it was an oversimplification that did not fulfil the needs of taxonomists or orchid enthusiasts for very long.

In Germany, Fritz Kraenzlin (1847–1934) carried out monumental descriptive studies in which he proposed the names *Lemurorchis*, *Calyptrochilum*, and *Angraecopsis*. These became accepted and are still in use. Kraenzlin published a series of articles under the title 'Orchidaceae africanae', but many of the names of the species described have now been reduced to synonymy.

Henry Ridley (1855–1956) is best known for his work in Singapore and what is now Malaysia, not only with the development of the Singapore Botanic Garden, the establishment of rubber plantations and their exploitation, and many collecting expeditions in Southeast Asia, but also, after his retirement in 1912, for writing the *Flora of the Malay Peninsula* in five volumes. However, he had started his botanical career, after graduating from Oxford, as an assistant in the botany department of the British Museum, where he was in charge of monocotyledons from 1880 to 1887. A number of large collections of dried specimens came in from Madagascar during that time for which Ridley wrote detailed accounts (1883, 1885, 1886) including descriptions of many new discoveries, some of them angraecoid orchids.

In his revision of the African 'Sarcanthinae' (as he called them in 1907), the French botanist Achille Finet (1863–1913) raised the number of known genera to 11. He was probably the first botanist to look at the group as a whole. His careful and detailed drawings of material in the Paris Muséum helped to elucidate the floral characteristics of the different genera. Finet provided a key in which he was the first to draw attention to the two different shapes of the rostellum in the group as a whole and their taxonomic significance. He proposed the genus *Ancistrorhynchus* which is still accepted, but his other new genera, *Monixus*, *Rhaphidorhynchus*, and *Dicranotaenia*, have disappeared into synonymy.

By 1918, following several other publications, the German botanist Rudolf Schlechter (1872–1925) was ready to produce 'Versuch einer natürlichen Neuordnung der Afrikanischen Angraekoiden Orchidaceen' (Attempt at a Natural New Classification of the African Angraecoid Orchids) in which he enlarged the number of genera to 32 and produced a key that clearly defined characteristics of his genera. He had benefited from travels in Africa, including South Africa, Mozambique, and two

visits to Cameroon, and gained familiarity with material of the African angraecoids he collected there. His studies brought him independently, he wrote, to the same conclusion as Finet regarding the importance of the two different types of rostellum. Eight of the new genera proposed in this paper are still accepted together with seven genera of angraecoids that he established earlier or later. We should like to mention that we have found most useful the translation of Schlechter's paper by Australians H. J. Katz and J. T. Simmons, published under the auspices of the Australian Orchid Foundation, Melbourne (1986).

Although Rolfe, Finet, and Schlechter were hampered in their work by not having access to Reichenbach's material, they made great progress in describing new species. Nevertheless, some understandable duplication of names was effected at this time.

During the middle and later years of the twentieth century, many other botanists became involved in the study and description of angraecoid orchids from Africa and Madagascar. Victor Summerhayes (1897–1974) followed Rolfe at Kew and made huge contributions to our knowledge of African orchids during the 40 years he worked there, culminating in the publication of an account of the Orchidaceae in the *Flora of West Tropical Africa*, volume 3, part 1, and the *Flora of Tropical East Africa*, part 1, both in 1968 after his retirement. It was in the last of a long series of scientific papers on orchids, in 1966, that he formally published the two subtribes Angraecinae and Aerangidinae, establishing a brief diagnosis and type genus for each of them.

Chromosome counts were being made at Kew and elsewhere of a number of representative species of angraecoid genera (Jones 1967). They showed cytological support for the subdivision of the angraecoid genera on morphological grounds. Those genera where the column apex is deeply divided and the rostellum not elongated have a basic chromosome number $x = 19$, and those where the rostellum is elongated have a basic chromosome number $x = 25$. Thus it seemed worthwhile to formalise the major division in Schlechter's publication of 1918 and to allocate the genera that he had kept separate, *Aeranthes* to the Angraecinae, and *Rhipidoglossum*, *Calyptrochilum* and *Podangis* to the Aerangidinae. Other botanists at Kew have followed this arrangement, notably Cribb (in Bechtel et al. 1992). Recent studies in The Netherlands (Arends and van der Laan 1983, 1986) and counts of many more genera and species have shown that the cytological differences between the subtribes are not so clear-cut. Nevertheless, there has been widespread support for the recognition of the two groups of angraecoid orchids within the Vandeae.

The modern period of French work on the orchids of Madagascar was started by Henri Perrier de la Bâthie (1873–1958), who made his first visit to Madagascar in 1896. He collected there during the next 35 years and established a herbarium of more than 20,000 specimens, all with copious notes. He donated this collection to the Paris Muséum after his final return to France in 1930 and it formed the basis of his account of the Orchidaceae for the *Flore de Madagascar*, published in 1939 and 1941. Because of difficulties in communication at the time, he records that he did not see a number of the type specimens at Kew and at the British Museum. This unfortunate omission probably accounts for a number of misinterpretations and misapplications of names in the published work.

The two volumes were edited by Henri Humbert (1887–1967) who had initiated the *Flore de Madagascar et des Comores* in 1936. Though based in France, he undertook plant-collecting activities in many parts of the world including 10 expeditions to Madagascar between 1912 and 1960. Humbert was accompanied by other prominent botanists on some of these trips: René Viguier (1880–1931) in 1912 (to Madagascar and the Comoro Islands), Henri Perrier (1873–1958) in 1924, and René Capuron (1921–1971) in 1948, 1950, and 1955.

In 1943, the Berlin herbarium was badly damaged by bombing in the Second World War, and many specimens in the collections of Schlechter, Kraenzlin, and others were lost. Some duplicates are still available in other herbaria, notably in Paris and Kew, but this loss has undoubtedly had a considerable effect on subsequent work.

In Germany the late Karlheinz Senghas (1928–2003) is remembered for his enormous volume of work at Heidelberg that enabled him to complete the third edition of the work known as *Schlechter, Die Orchideen*. The first edition of this title had appeared in 1914, and the second edition was published posthumously in honour of Schlechter in 1927. The part of the third edition that contains the two subtribes—*Tribus Vandeae*: 48, *Subtribus Angraecinae* and 49, *Subtribus Aerangidinae* (1986, pages 959–1130)—is an invaluable summary, in German, with many illustrations of the genera we are including in this book.

Frenchman Jean Bosser first went to Madagascar as a botanist and research scientist in 1951. Returning to Paris in 1965, he continued to work on many plant families of the area, as well as orchids, and made several collecting expeditions to Madagascar, the Comoro Islands, Réunion, Mauritius, and Rodrigues. He has named and described many new species of angraecoids and revised several of the angraecoid genera. He has also encouraged and helped many younger botanists, officially and personally, including ourselves (JS and JH).

At the Royal Botanic Gardens, Kew, Phillip Cribb has had responsibility for the work on African orchids (amongst other things) since 1974. He has also visited various parts of Africa and Madagascar and made many new discoveries and descriptions. He completed the account of the Orchidaceae for the *Flora of Tropical East Africa* (part 2, 1984; part 3, 1989) and, with Isobyl la Croix, the Orchidaceae for the *Flora Zambesiaca* (part 1, 1995; part 2, 1998). He has encouraged and coordinated the work of many other botanists and amateur enthusiasts. His latest major task is the coordination of the project *Genera Orchidacearum* of which four volumes have appeared so far (Pridgeon et al. 1999, 2001, 2003, 2005). The appearance of the Vandeae in one of the later volumes is still a few years away but is eagerly awaited.

Finally, a brief mention should be made of botanists in other parts of the world who have studied angraecoid orchids recently. Dariusz Szlachetko in Poland proposed a new system of tribes and subtribes for the orchid family after dissecting and drawing thousands of flowers, especially their columns, in about 750 genera (1995). He proposed subdividing the Aerangidinae into five subtribes, retaining Aerangidinae to include *Aerangis*, *Plectrelminthus*, and *Summerhayesia*, amongst other genera, and proposing Bolusiellinae, Listrostachyinae, Calyptrochilinae, and Rhaesteriinae for the remaining genera. He also transferred *Angraecopsis* and *Cribbia* to the Angraecinae. These proposals seem to cut across the long-accepted arrangement and make some fairly similar genera rather widely separated, for example, *Diaphananthe* and *Rhipidoglossum*, *Mystacidium* and *Angraecopsis*.

Barbara Carlsward, an American botanist, examined 132 species of African monopodial orchids in 34 genera for a dissertation (2004). She made comprehensive anatomical and molecular studies. Her observations led her to suggest that the two subtribes Angraecinae and Aerangidinae should be merged and henceforth recognised as one, Angraecinae *sensu lato*! We look forward to the publication of the results of further DNA analyses that may confirm or refute either of these ideas, or offer new ones.

In the meantime, we have arranged the genera in this book according to the subdivision established by Summerhayes (1966), accepted by Garay (1972) and Senghas (1986), and slightly modified in the latest account of the classification of the Orchidaceae by Chase et al. (2003).

It is hardly surprising, in view of this long history, that some widespread orchid species have been described more than once, by different botanists in different countries. Many other orchids have several different names or have appeared in several different genera, because of changing ideas about orchid taxonomy. A list of generic names that are no longer in current use is provided here in an appendix. We have decided not to clutter the descriptive text in this book with long lists of species synonyms, although we have included a few of the most widely used ones that readers might come across in books and trade lists. Many other names, used in the distant past but largely ignored today, we have omitted. However, all synonyms can be traced by referring to the World Checklist of Monocotyledons (Govaerts 2004).

MORPHOLOGICAL CHARACTERS OF THE ANGRAECOIDS

The angraecoid orchids display a wealth of diversity in habit, size, leaf shape and structure, flower colour and form, and other characteristics. The features described here provide an introduction to the detail that follows in the individual species descriptions in the main part of this book.

The Roots

The roots of angraecoid orchids are extensive and often entirely aerial. They are clustered near the base of plants with short stems. In plants with long stems, aerial roots may arise along their whole length, interspersed amongst the leaves, sometimes regularly at each node, opposite a leaf, or irregularly. The shorter, younger, and more active roots are nearer the stem apex, and the older roots that provide the anchorage are nearer the base of the stem.

Anatomically, they have the structure typical of most orchid roots with a conspicuous velamen, a layer of air-filled cells, surrounding the cortex and central stele. Often the cortical cells contain chloroplasts and the roots are photosynthetic. This is easily seen when the velamen is filled with water after rain, and the roots become bright green. Photosynthetic roots are particularly important in the leafless orchids, such as *Microcoelia*, but are not confined to them. Usually the presence of chloroplasts can be seen in a live root at the root tip that is bright green or brownish.

Besides absorbing water and dissolved food substances, roots are important to an epiphytic orchid in fixing it to its host. A surprising length of root is required to attach even a small plant to its

Microcoelia perrieri, producing numerous photosynthetic roots in dry deciduous forest, western Madagascar. J. Hermans

plant *Taeniorrhiza*, the green roots are always flattened, as is indicated by the name. The roots are also quite flat in *Sphyrarhynchus* and some species of *Angraecopsis*.

The Stems

In all angraecoid orchids the stems grow indefinitely season after season. Throughout the group they vary much in length and may grow upwards, downwards, or horizontally. The stems bear aerial roots, leaves of various shapes, and lateral inflorescences. In the leafless genera *Microcoelia*, *Chauliodon*, and *Taeniorrhiza*, small brown scale leaves may be present.

The length of the stem determines the relative positions of the other organs and their spacing. In the genus *Aerangis* alone, the stem is very elongated in some species and hardly developed at all in others. Even greater contrasts can be found in the large genus *Angraecum*. One of the largest-flowered species in tropical Africa is *A. infundibulare* and it has a very elongated stem up to several metres, with widely spaced leaves. An aerial root and inflorescence often arise together, opposite a leaf. One of the smallest species is *A. minus*; apparently it consists of only a few tiny leaves clasping the very short stem. The roots and slender inflorescences are the most conspicuous parts of this minute plant.

Many angraecoid orchids grow in an upright position. Often they branch at the base, and new growths arise which all continue to grow so that a clump or tuft of stems is produced eventually. In many species the stem grows horizontally away from the host. Some of those that favour very shady forests, such as *Aerangis luteoalba* and *Eurychone rothschildiana*, grow in this way. Many forest-dwelling species have stems that are horizontal in the basal part and upright near the apex. These stems hold the plant away from its host assuring the leaves and flowers of ample space and fresh air. Some of the longer-stemmed plants, including various species of *Tridactyle* and *Jumellea*, grow upright at first; as they become longer and heavier they also become horizontal and eventually pendent, but usually the

host tree trunk, branch, or twig. Often the surface of the root that actually adheres to the host plant bears many minute projections, similar to the root hairs of other plants. These projections may also develop on roots that are entirely aerial, so they probably have an absorbing capability. On orchids with a scandent habit the roots may be stiffened, curled, and twisted and extensive enough to maintain the plants in a more or less upright position as the stems thread their way amongst the surrounding vegetation. These rather unusual roots can be found in *Dinklageella* and in some species of *Solenangis* and *Rangaeris*.

Orchid roots are usually round in cross section, but aerial roots often become flattened and tape-like especially, but not only, where they adhere to the host plant. A number of *Angraecum* species have flattened roots, as do some species of *Angraecopsis*. In the minute West African leafless

growing tip of the plant continues to be up-turned. In a few species of *Diaphananthe*, *Rhipidoglossum*, and *Calyptrochilum*, the stems become so long that they are almost entirely pendent. Two species of *Ypsilopus* and a number of *Angraecum* species are always completely pendent. They hang below the lower side of the branches of forest trees or parallel with their trunks.

The Leaves

The leaves of angraecoid orchids are arranged alternately in two neat rows. In species where the internodes of the stem are very short, the leaves are crowded together and have closely overlapping bases. These basal sheaths usually have an articulation zone where the leaf lamina becomes detached at the end of its useful life. The leaf sheaths are usually green, similar to the leaves, but in old plants they become brown and seem to have a purely protective function. In many species with a short stem the leaves are twisted at the base so that they are held in one plane, like a fan, clearly a device to catch the maximum amount of light in shady situations.

Most orchid leaves are green, though they encompass many different shades of green—grey, brown, red, yellow, or blue. They are often a fresher, lighter colour when young and may be glossy then. Few of the species in this group have a distinct margin or venation pattern, but in a few species of *Mystacidium*, *Diaphananthe*, *Aerangis*, and a few others, the venation provides a darker network showing through the paler surface.

In shape the leaves are nearly always longer than broad—in some species parallel-sided, thick, and fleshy, or almost like a grass leaf, in others more or less elliptic. The leaf apex, or tip, is nearly always bilobed, or pointed because one lobe is greatly reduced or absent. The shape of the lobes and the size of the sinus between them are often useful characters for identification when plants are not in flower. The leaf apex is one of the features that clearly delimits *Aerangis kotschyana* from other long-spurred, white-flowered species of this genus such as *A. verdickii* and *A. brachycarpa*.

Many orchids with long stems have much smaller and thicker leaves than those with short stems. These plants are often found growing in stronger light, higher in the forest canopy or along forest margins. In a few species, particularly those that may be exposed to extremes of temperature or strong winds, the leaves are terete (round in cross section) or only slightly channelled along the upper surface.

Another unusual feature in a few unrelated species is the occurrence of equitant leaves. Here the two upper surfaces of the leaf have become fused, forming a thick fleshy, single-bladed leaf that has no dorsal or ventral surface. This has happened in both *Angraecum distichum* and *A. leonis*. Other genera in which equitant leaves occur include *Bolusiella*, *Podangis*, and *Rangaeris*.

Leafless members of the monopodial orchids are found in many parts of the world and a few genera occur in Africa and Madagascar. *Microcoelia* is the largest and most well known, but there are also the monotypic genera *Chauliodon* and *Taeniorrhiza*, one leafless species in the genus *Solenangis*, and some seasonally leafless species in *Mystacidium*.

The Inflorescences

In all angraecoid orchids the inflorescences are borne laterally on the stem, either in the leaf axils, or below the leaves, particularly where the stem is short. The inflorescence stalk is usually green or brownish and round in cross section. It may be thicker towards the base or, more rarely, towards the tip. Occasionally it is flattened, or four-sided as in some species of *Tridactyle*. At or near the base several sheaths are usually found, rather like sterile bracts, covering and sometimes completely concealing the stalk.

The flowers are usually arranged rather regularly, in two rows, and may be very close together or widely spaced. In a few species of *Chamaeangis* and *Diaphananthe*, the flowers are borne in opposite pairs or in whorls of three or four together along the rachis. Each flower is supported by a bract that protects it when in bud and may fall off before the flower is fully developed. The bracts are often thin

Diaphananthe pellucida, densely flowered inflorescences. J. Stewart

The most common form of inflorescence in the angraecoids is the raceme, in which a number of flowers are borne along an unbranched rachis, each flower having its own stalk or pedicel that is quite distinct from the inferior ovary. This is easily seen where the ovary is winged and the pedicel flattened, as in *Angraecum leonis*. In many species of *Aerangis* and others it is less easy to distinguish the ovary and pedicel until the flowers have formed fruits, when the differentiation between the ribbed capsule and the often short and slender pedicel becomes clear. The part of the inflorescence stalk below the flowers is always referred to as the peduncle. This is particularly elongated in some species of *Angraecopsis*, but in other genera it is usually much shorter than the rachis, or flower-bearing portion of the inflorescence.

Very few inflorescences in this group take the form of a spike, in which the flowers are sessile on the rachis (that is, without a pedicel). In *Chamaeangis* and some species of *Tridactyle* the flowers may look as if they have no stalk but in fact always have a short piece of sterile tissue between the ovary and the rachis.

In the genus *Jumellea*, the inflorescence always bears a single flower, but many inflorescences are produced at each flowering season. Sometimes the peduncle is long and the flowers are carried at some distance from the stem, while in other species it is so short that the flowers appear almost sessile. The genus *Angraecum* also has a number of species with a single-flowered inflorescence (for example, those in the section *Perrierangraecum*), but in some of these the plants produce two or more flowers per inflorescence occasionally.

Finally, attention should be drawn to a few orchids where the flowers are congested on a short rachis. This makes the inflorescence look almost umbellate. In *Podangis* the rachis is rather short, though the individual pedicels hold the flowers well apart, but in *Ancistrorhynchus, Calyptrochilum,* and *Ossiculum* the pedicels are very short and the flowers appear clustered.

and may have turned black by the time the flowers open. In the genus *Cyrtorchis* the large bracts form a conspicuous part of the inflorescence. In a few species, notably but not only in the genera *Aerangis* and *Microterangis,* each flower is borne on a small cushion, a projection of the rachis, which grows out above the insertion of the bract.

Few species in the genus *Angraecum* have branching inflorescences, or panicles. *Angraecum calceolus* does so sometimes, but not invariably. A few others have curious inflorescences in the form of a short stem from which new inflorescences arise every year (for example, *A. multiflorum*). In some species this side branch is much reduced so that the inflorescences appear to emerge from the same point on the stem each year, a condition described as intervallate (for example, *A. viride*). Some *Aeranthes* species also have long, branching inflorescences though the branching is rather irregular.

Aerangis luteoalba var. *rhodosticta*, popular for its graceful white flower with a bright red column.
J. Hermans

The Flowers

Flower size varies widely amongst angraecoid orchids. Amongst the smallest flowers are those of *Microcoelia exilis*, although many others are almost equally minute. The largest are undoubtedly some of the angraecums, *Angraecum sesquipedale* and *A. sororium* in Madagascar and *A. infundibulare* in equatorial Africa. Excluding the spur, each of these predominantly white flowers has a diameter of 12 cm or more.

Colour is also extremely varied, though not very spectacular. Many species have white or whitish flowers, but green, yellow, pink, brown, or even bright orange are known. Some of the prettiest flowers have a bright red column (*Aerangis luteoalba*) or patches of red on the lip (*Oeonia rosea* and *Cryptopus elatus*). Several species are almost bi-coloured, with green or brownish sepals and petals contrasting with a white lip (*Plectrelminthus cau-*

datus). In a few genera the white flowers turn orange with age (*Cyrtorchis*, *Neobathiea*, *Rangaeris*).

Nearly all the flowers last for two or three weeks on the plant, and some remain quite fresh for a few months. Another feature that is not always recorded is their fragrance. Usually this is most noticeable in the evening, but some are fragrant by day, others at night, and some not at all.

Many of the angraecoid orchids are extremely floriferous, both in the wild and in cultivation. Up to a dozen racemes of 10–16 flowers each is not unusual on a well-grown plant of *Mystacidium capense* and many other species. Even *Jumellea* species, which produce only one flower on each inflorescence, may be covered with dozens of blooms if the plants are large enough.

Throughout the group the flower structure is rather similar. As in most orchids, there are three sepals, two petals, and a modified third petal that is the labellum or lip. The median, or dorsal sepal, is often different in shape and size from the two lateral sepals. Where the sepals and petals are all rather similar, they are often referred to collectively as tepals. Sometimes the lip is also similar to the other perianth parts, giving the whole flower a 'star-like' appearance.

The Lip or Labellum

In most angraecoid orchids, the lip with its basal outgrowth, the spur, provides the most distinctive feature of the flower. It is quite different in shape, size, and even colour from the rest of the flower.

The position of the lip and hence the presentation of the flower are variable. Usually, as in many other orchids, the flower is resupinate (that is, the ovary is twisted through 180° so that the lip is held on the lower side of the flower). In *Angraecum*, for example, many flowers have this pattern, but there are others, notably some in the section *Arachnangraecum*, where the lip is at the top of the flower. This occurs because the ovary is twisted through 360°, and not because the flower is not resupinate.

The lip is usually entire but may have several lobes, usually three. The middle lobe is usually the larger and may be pointed at its apex or retuse so that it appears to be two-lobed. *Tridactyle* species have a lip that is variously lobed, with the side lobes often fringed and conspicuous.

The base of the lip is inserted on the column, either so that it completely encloses the column, as in *Angraecum* and *Oeoniella*, or below the column, as in *Jumellea*, or even at the front of a distinct foot at the base of the column, as in *Aeranthes*.

The surface of the lip is usually smooth and sparkling, often with a central crest or keel along its inner side. This is particularly prominent in some species of *Jumellea* and *Angraecum*. In *Aerangis* a pair of ridges, or teeth, may be present at the base of the lip and in the mouth of the spur which appear to be guides for a pollinator's tongue. Hairs and callosities on the surface are rather rare, but in the genus *Beclardia* the lip is distinctly papillose. In many *Diaphananthe* species a distinct tooth-like outgrowth occurs on the surface of the lip, just in front of the entrance to the spur.

The nectary, or spur, at the base of the lip is one of the most distinctive features of the angraecoid flower. It is present in nearly all species, and a few *Aeranthes* species have two or three spurs. In the genus *Bonniera*, the spur is absent, or almost so, and the lip is very narrow, but these seem to be the only features separating this small genus from similar plants in *Angraecum*. The spurs contain nectar and vary in size and shape throughout the group. Within the genus *Aerangis*, for example, the length of the spur varies tremendously from a few millimetres in *A. hologlottis* to more than 20 cm in *A. kotschyana*. In addition, the spurs are variously swollen, bent, or twisted in shape, though many are cylindrical. In the smaller flowers the spurs may be minute. In *Microcoelia exilis*, the spur is completely globular and only 1 mm in diameter. Some little-known species of *Angraecum* also have tiny spurs. The largest known spur is probably that of *A. longicalcar*; it is quite straight and at least 40 cm long when the flowers are mature.

The Column

The smallest part of the orchid flower is usually the column at its centre. Besides housing the reproductive structures, the anther and stigma, the column provides the orchid taxonomist with several useful characters.

In the angraecoid orchids the column is a fairly stout structure with the two waxy pollinia hidden under the removable anther cap at its apex. The stigma is a sticky hollow or cavity on the lower surface of the column. Between the surface underneath the anther cap against which the pollinia lie, the clinandrium, and the stigma is a strip of sterile tissue known as the rostellum. Part of the rostellum is often modified into a sticky disc or discs called a viscidium (plural viscidia). The pollinia are attached to these viscidia by one or two stalks (stipes). The whole structure of pollinia, stipes, and viscidia forms the pollinarium.

As mentioned previously, the two subtribes of vandaceous orchids in Africa and Madagascar are

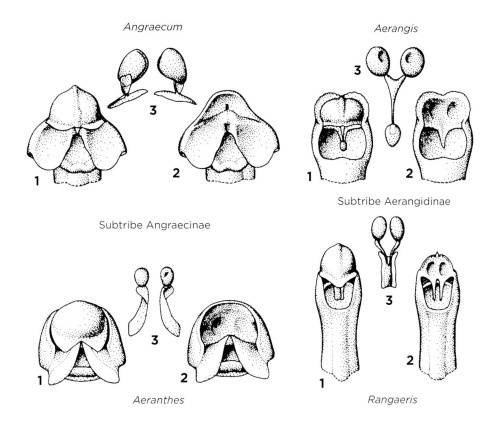

Angraecum

Aerangis

Subtribe Aerangidinae

Subtribe Angraecinae

Aeranthes

Rangaeris

A comparison of the subtribes Angraecinae (represented here by *Angraecum* and *Aeranthes*) and Aerangidinae (represented here by *Aerangis* and *Rangaeris*). 1: Column with anther in place. 2: Column with anther and pollinarium removed. 3: Pollinarium, or pollinaria. Reprinted by permission from Dressler 1993, p. 208.

delineated primarily according to the structure of the rostellum. In the subtribe Angraecinae (type genus *Angraecum*) the basal rim of the clinandrium is extended downwards like a flap or short skirt and deeply incised at its centre. The basal rim of the column appears winged and the rostellum is very abbreviated. Two pollinia are attached by one or two stipes to one or two viscidia. In the subtribe Aerangidinae (type genus *Aerangis*) the basal rim of the clinandrium is very short and entire except for a prominent, elongated rostellum at its centre. The rostellum itself may be entire or divided into two or three narrow lobes or variously expanded. Two pollinia are attached by one or two stipes to one or two viscidia.

The Ovary and Fruit

As in the rest of the orchid family, the ovary in angraecoids is behind or below the flower (inferior) and relatively undeveloped at anthesis. Some time after pollination it begins to enlarge and eventually, six weeks to several months later, it produces a fruit in the form of a capsule. The capsules vary considerably in size and shape, but details about them are little known and rarely recorded. Relatively few herbarium specimens bear fruits. Detailed study of the fruits might well reveal characters of taxonomic value at both the generic and specific level.

THE GENERA OF THE ANGRAECOID ORCHIDS

In this book, the descriptions of all the species are arranged in four chapters. The large genus *Angraecum* is presented in chapter 1, and all the other genera currently classified in the subtribe Angraecinae are presented in chapter 2 in alphabetical order. Similarly, chapter 3 contains the genus *Aerangis*, and chapter 4 includes all the other genera currently classified in the Aerangidinae, again arranged in alphabetical order for ease of reference. It is very difficult, in the absence of DNA information, to be certain about the relationships of these genera, though some are fairly obvious, and we do not wish to publish assumptions that might later prove incorrect. An alphabetical sequence does at least make the generic descriptions easy to find once one is familiar with the contents of each subtribe.

We have tried to present the information about each genus and species in a fairly uniform way. This has not always been possible because of the varied way in which historic descriptions and records have been made, and because of the lack of type specimens in some cases. We have also tried to make the text easy to read, even if this has made it a little longer. This book is not meant to be as detailed or technical a treatment as a flora, though we hope it will be as useful as many of the existing floras are in the restricted areas to which they relate.

In the Angraecinae the generic names in current use, each with its author and date of publication, are as follows:

Angraecum Bory 1804
Aeranthes Lindley 1824
Ambrella H. Perrier 1934
Bonniera Cordemoy 1899
Calyptrochilum Kraenzlin 1895
Cryptopus Lindley 1824
Jumellea Schlechter 1918
Lemurella Schlechter 1925
Lemurorchis Kraenzlin 1893
Listrostachys Reichenbach f. 1852
Neobathiea Schlechter 1925
Oeonia Lindley 1824
Oeoniella Schlechter 1918
Ossiculum P. J. Cribb & van der Laan 1986
Sobennikoffia Schlechter 1925

The Aerangidinae currently comprises the following genera:

Aerangis Reichenbach f. 1865
Ancistrorhynchus Finet 1907
Angraecopsis Kraenzlin 1900
Beclardia A. Richard 1828
Bolusiella Schlechter 1918
Cardiochilos Cribb 1977
Chamaeangis Schlechter 1915
Chauliodon Summerhayes 1943
Cribbia Senghas 1985
Cyrtorchis Schlechter 1915
Diaphananthe Schlechter 1915
Dinklageella Mansfeld 1934
Distylodon Summerhayes 1966
Eggelingia Summerhayes 1951
Eurychone Schlechter 1918
Margelliantha Cribb 1979
Microcoelia Lindley 1830
Microterangis Senghas 1986
Mystacidium Lindley 1837
Nephrangis Summerhayes 1948
Plectrelminthus Rafinesque 1836
Podangis Schlechter 1918
Rangaeris Summerhayes 1936
Rhaesteria Summerhayes 1966
Rhipidoglossum Schlechter 1918
Solenangis Schlechter 1918
Sphyrarhynchus Mansfeld 1935
Summerhayesia Cribb 1977
Taeniorrhiza Summerhayes 1943
Triceratorhynchus Summerhayes 1951
Tridactyle Schlechter 1914
Ypsilopus Summerhayes 1949

Angraecum rutenbergianum, Ibity Massif, Madagascar. J. Hermans

About 25 other generic names have been in use at various times in the past. These are now regarded as synonyms and are listed with their modern equivalents in Appendix 1.

The Accounts of the Genera

In the introduction to each genus we have given the derivation of the generic name. Some of these are made-up names commemorating various people or places; others are descriptive in origin and refer to some special character of the plants or flowers in Latin. A few, including *Angraecum*, are Latinised common names from other languages.

Each introduction also includes information about the special features of that genus. Characters by which it may be immediately recognised are noted. Some details of the history of its discovery, introduction to cultivation, and possible relationships are also given. Distribution and number of species are recorded.

In some of the larger genera the species are presented in groups that share similar features, such as flower colour, but no attempt has been made to propose relationships except in *Angraecum* where we have largely followed Garay's (1973) proposals for subdivision of the genus into sections. For reasons of space, we have not tried to prepare artificial keys for identification of all the species.

The Accounts of the Species

Almost all the descriptions follow the same pattern to make them easily comparable. In a few cases, mostly newly described species and those that are known only from a single specimen that we have not been able to see, the descriptions are much shorter. But for these we have provided references that the reader may wish to pursue in search of more information.

Following the morphological description, we have given a small amount of ecological information, particularly habitat, altitude preferences, and flowering season. All of this should be helpful to growers. We have also listed the countries where each species has been recorded, and in some cases the provinces or regions within those countries.

Finally, a few notes of interest are given. In particular, these may include a sentence or two about identification and characters that distinguish the species from others that are rather similar. There is information about people whose names are honoured in the specific epithets where we have been able to discover this. A few epithets refer to the country of origin, for example, *madagascariense*, but these are immediately recognisable by the ending of the word, *-ensis* or *-ense*. Others refer to the habitat of the plant, such as *rupicola*, 'a dweller amongst rocks', and here the word ending, *-cola*, also reveals the meaning. Many specific epithets are descriptive and derived from Latin words like *grandiflorus*, large-flowered, or Greek words like *macrophyllus*, large-leaved. We recommend reference to the invaluable *Botanical Latin* (4th edition, 1992) by the late W. T. Stearn to elucidate these.

DISTRIBUTION OF THE ANGRAECOID ORCHIDS

As currently circumscribed, the two subtribes described in this book have an interesting and complementary distribution. Most of the Angraecinae are confined to Madagascar and the neighbouring islands. Only about 50 species of *Angraecum* and two each of *Jumellea* and *Aeranthes*, perhaps 15 percent of the total, have been recorded from the African continent.

Nearly all the Aerangidinae are confined to the African continent. *Microcoelia*, *Angraecopsis*, *Chamaeangis*, and *Solenangis* have most species in Africa and one or a few each in Madagascar. *Aerangis* has more species in Africa (31) than in Madagascar (21). *Microterangis*, *Beclardia*, and *Lemurorchis* are confined to the Madagascar area. Altogether only about 18 percent of the Aerangidinae are in Madagascar.

Only four species of Aerangidinae—*Angraecopsis parviflora*, *A. trifurca*, *Microcoelia aphylla*, and *M. exilis*—and two of the Angraecinae—

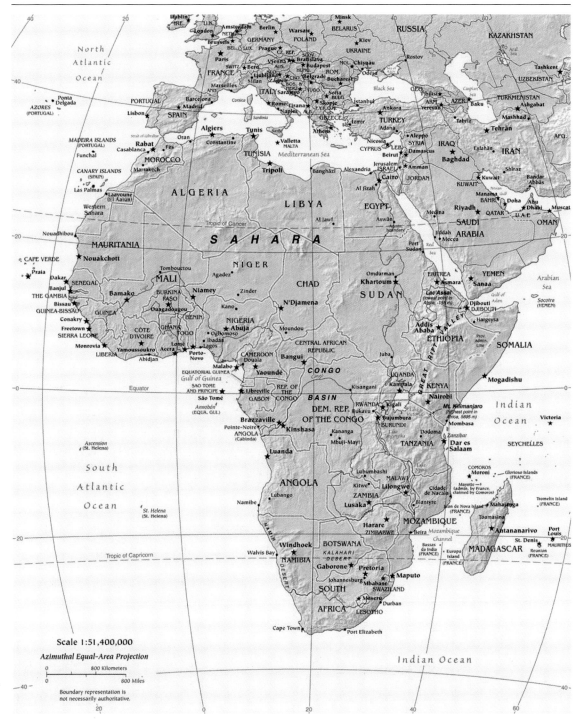

Africa. Map by U.S. Central Intelligence Agency 2002.

Angraecum calceolus and *A. eburneum*—have so far been recorded from both areas.

We have used the *Times Atlas* (2004) as the source for current names of countries in Africa. Throughout the text we have cited countries from west to east and north to south to try to give an impression of the distribution patterns of the various species. For Madagascar we have cited the same regions as those described in the account by Hermans et al. (2006).

GROWING ANGRAECOID ORCHIDS

Every book on orchids has a section on growing and it would be tedious to repeat what has already been written so many times, but some aspects of growing the angraecoid orchids need emphasis. Further details are available in the individual descriptions. A summary of the major requirements for good growing is provided here.

The most important point to bear in mind, as in the cultivation of any other special group of plants, is that the three essentials of culture—light, humidity, and temperature—should be in the correct balance with each other. Epiphytes brought down to sea level from a high altitude or moved from equatorial regions of the world to 40° latitude north or south may not grow well unless their natural growing conditions are precisely imitated in the new surroundings. Changes must be made to provide the best environmental conditions in the artificial situation of the glasshouse or windowsill. A good balance between the different features is the key to success and flowering.

Plants grow most rapidly where light, humidity, and temperature values are high, but not too high. Many orchids are naturally very slow growing and do better in cooler, less humid, and more shady conditions. Nevertheless, their natural rate of growth can often be increased in cultivation so that plants are larger, or flowers are produced twice a year instead of once, if they are maintained in well-balanced conditions.

Light

The right amount of light is extremely important. Most of the angraecoid orchids described in this book come from tropical regions. Some genera are almost all shade lovers. For example, almost all *Aerangis* species grow in well-shaded places but need more light than *Aeranthes* species. The huge genus *Angraecum* has species that can be found in full sun and others in deep shade. But it is worth remembering that strong light in Africa and Madagascar is much stronger than elsewhere. Early in the morning and late in the afternoon, and on cloudy days when the sun is completely or partly obscured, the light is greatly reduced. This is often accompanied, in the wild, by lower temperatures and mist or heavy rain, so the balance is maintained.

Day length is important for many groups of plants, but so far as the angraecoid orchids are concerned little is known of their requirements. Many of them have a distinct flowering season in the wild, which may well be related to shorter or longer days, or to the onset of the rainy season, or to a combination of both. A different balance of conditions is clearly operative.

To the experienced grower, the colour of the leaves will indicate how much light or shade a particular species prefers—dark green in the shade, yellowish green in more light—but seedlings and other glasshouse-raised plants may not show their true colours when first acquired. Under each species, in the main chapters of this book, we have tried to include details of habitat notes from herbarium specimens and personal observations, as well as other information that will indicate to the grower the best regime to try initially to grow a plant successfully.

Fresh Air and Relative Humidity

Maintaining a fresh and moving atmosphere around the plants provides the most natural environmental condition for them. In the wild, near the seashore, in forest and woodlands, on mountains and roadsides, air movement is constant. Breezes are normal and strong winds not uncommon. Normal ventilation in a glasshouse is usually not enough to provide this level of air movement for plants. Usually ventilation is carefully controlled, either to ameliorate excessive heat in summer, or to prevent the loss of too much expensively provided heat in winter. A supplementary source of air movement, such as a fan, is essential. It keeps the air moving in winter while conditions may be cool and damp, and in summer, in conjunction with more ventilation, it has a cooling effect when temperatures can soar dangerously.

As well as fans to move the air, additional devices to enhance the humidity in a glasshouse make a wonderful difference to plant growth. Some humidifiers and misters also increase air movement, but rather than drying breezes they provide humid air which is extremely beneficial to the plants.

Stagnant humid air should be avoided at all times. It is particularly dangerous if there is a large temperature gradient between day and night, as this can provide good conditions for the invasion of bacterial or fungal infections. Provided there is plenty of air movement, humidity can be maintained at 65–70 percent during the day when temperatures are in the 20–25°C range; the relative humidity will be higher at night when temperatures fall. Without extra air movement, and particularly at the lower temperatures experienced during winter in temperate climates, humidity should be much lower. As a rule, conditions that feel comfortable to a human being will be suitable for most orchids; thus dry cold is easier to bear and more successfully endured by orchids than damp cold.

Temperature

In the wild most angraecoid orchids experience changing temperatures every day. The temperature begins to rise an hour or so after sunrise, reaching its highest figure by noon, or later in the day, and falling at or before sunset to its lowest figure in the early morning hours of the next day. This regime is modified by the season, by cloud cover, and by rain and thunderstorms in the afternoons. Light, air movement, and temperature are interlinked.

It is the actual leaf temperature that is important to an orchid plant. If it is too high, growth stops, and unsightly burns may occur on the surface where strong light creates an adverse situation. But many orchids are adaptable and can accommodate themselves to the conditions the grower provides, at least within limits. Frost is usually a killer, and in very low temperatures day after day many plants will not thrive.

Perhaps the most important feature of all is the day-lift, a difference of at least 7–10°C between the minimum night and maximum day temperatures. Many growers in temperate climes rely on the sun to provide this lift during the day, but when the sun does not oblige it is very beneficial to use a supplementary source of heating. Thermostats can ensure that this is not too expensive.

Containers

Many orchid plants, and especially those purchased as seedlings, can be grown in a suitable compost mix in clay or plastic pots of appropriate size. Others thrive in the more open conditions of a rustic cedar- or teak-slatted basket, filled with a mixture of bark and other materials in the conventional way. The long aerial roots of many angraecoids need plenty of space, and the facility to drain quickly and to dry out between successive supplies of water.

Mounts

Many angraecoids grow best in cultivation if maintained in the natural way; that is, clinging to a piece of bark or a section of the limb of a tree. Almost any durable, non-resinous hardwood will make a suitable support. A branch from a living tree is better than a half-dead log from the woodpile, and those with slightly rough bark usually give good results. Wood with a very thick or rough bark is often, but not always, unsuitable as it consists of so much dead material; this can be attractive to wood lice or can quickly rot, producing large mushroom-like growths under orchid-growing conditions. A slab of bark from the cork-oak tree has almost always provided an excellent niche for an orchid in the glasshouse.

The key to success lies in the attachment. Often newly attached plants benefit from a pad of moss or osmunda fibre between the stem base and the host branch or bark slab. Others seem to do better if attached to bare bark. The plant and moss, or the plant by itself, are tied tightly to the host with nylon fishing line, copper wire, or some other resistant and durable material that is not unsightly. Some growers use sisal string or raffia twine, which look natural and have the advantage of gradually disintegrating as the plant grows onto the log or of being easily removed when no longer required. If the timing is not just right, however, the plants may become detached again just as the new roots were about to adhere to the substratum. Some of the modern 'twist-it' tapes are also easy to use and remove after a safe period.

Holes are easily drilled to attach labels and supports, or wires if the mounted plant is to be hung vertically. A group of plants established together in this way can produce a very effective display when they flower in the glasshouse.

Fixing the plants to the bark or wood is not the end of the story. The management of these freshly mounted plants is crucial during the few months that it may take for them to become established. Because the roots and therefore the plant's absorbing powers at this stage are small, and transpiration is continuous, the plants need to be kept in a very humid position. To prevent shrivelling of the leaves, often it is suggested that plants should be sprayed with water, or at least misted over, several times a day until new roots have developed. This is sometimes disastrous, especially if cold water is used, as the leaves may suffer, turn yellow, and fall off prematurely. A humid atmosphere is much less risky.

Watering, Feeding, and Drainage

Orchid plants present something of a paradox. They need moisture to maintain their turgidity and fresh air to promote growth. In their natural surroundings, the plants are soaked by heavy storms, as are surrounding mosses and ferns, but the water drains away almost immediately, and as soon as the rain stops the plants begin to dry out. The aerial roots, which swell up with water and often appear green during the rain, shrink and whiten as air replaces the moisture in their cells.

Heavy watering with quick drainage, and dry periods between successive waterings, will imi-

Eurychone rothschildiana mounted on cork oak bark. J. Stewart

tate the growing conditions of many species and promote healthy growth. Water should be supplied at the rate at which the plant can make use of it—less often in the winter or in a very humid environment. Once a week may suit some growers and their plants, but not all. Every grower needs to determine what the appropriate interval is in the conditions provided.

Angraecoid orchid plants grow slowly, so need rather little 'food' as chemicals dissolved in the water supply. 'Little and often' is a good maxim, but only during the growing period. Plant fertilisers on sale for pot plants and ornamentals need to be diluted to half or quarter the recommended strength for orchids. At these rates, if used regularly, they can be beneficial.

Resting

The host trees of most epiphytes, like the orchids themselves, grow most quickly and flower during the rainy seasons. After flowering the rate of growth slows down, and stops altogether in the dry season when there is often a complete or partial leaf fall. This allows more sun and air to reach the epiphytes and slows down their growth in turn.

Similarly in cultivation, after flowering, often accompanied by the completion of a new leaf, many plants appear to need a rest. This can be induced, in the relatively uniform conditions of a glasshouse, by increasing the light and decreasing the water supply. If this coincides with autumn and winter, and temperatures are lower, slower growth is natural. These changes are necessary to 'ripen' the new leaf and induce flowering during the following season.

Pests and Diseases

Angraecoids are not as prone to attack by pests and diseases as some other groups of orchids. Minimum hygiene and preventive measures in the glasshouse will normally be sufficient. Root tips are vulnerable to slugs and snails, and an atmosphere that is too dry may see the build-up of red spider on the underside of leaves. Patches of bacterial and

Jumellea densefoliata mounted on a piece of pine bark. J. Stewart

fungal infection may appear if air movement is insufficient, but these are easily dealt with if caught at an early stage of development. If not, they can be fatal to a leaf or indeed the plant.

Enjoyment

Successful growing usually means flower production, but a healthy and well-grown plant with richly coloured glossy leaves can also be rewarding. By attention to detail and care for the plants and their environment, growers of angraecoid orchids can have unending pleasure. Fortunately, increasing numbers of species are becoming available as laboratory-raised seedlings for anyone to try.

CHAPTER ONE

The Genus *Angraecum*

The name *Angraecum* is derived from a Malay word, *angrek*, which has been used in Southeast Asia for many different orchids. *Angraecum* was first published in 1804 by the French explorer Bory de St Vincent. He visited various islands in the western Indian Ocean from 1801 to 1802 and described *A. eburneum* in his account of these 'Voyages'. This large species grows on coral and volcanic rocks in the island of Réunion and also as an epiphyte. Similar plants with even larger flowers occur in Madagascar and the Comoro Islands, while others with smaller flowers occur in Zanzibar, Pemba Island, and near the coast in Tanzania and Kenya. Some of these plants were originally described as distinct species, but they are now treated as subspecies of the widespread and variable *A. eburneum*, the type species of the genus.

A wide range of orchids with a monopodial habit of growth was included in the genus *Angraecum* in the past. In 1918 Rudolf Schlechter reviewed this entire group and proposed many new genera, thus reducing *Angraecum* to the basis of the genus we know today. Since then many additional species have been described, and further useful reviews of all or parts of the genus have been made by Perrier de la Bâthie (1941), Summerhayes (1958), Garay (1973), and Senghas (1986). At present some 210 species are recognised. In all the species, the flowers have a concave lip that bears a nectariferous spur at its base. The lip more or less envelops the

column, which has a very short, emarginate rostellum at its apex. These characteristics are shared by many plants, both large and small, with a variety of shapes and colours of leaves and with white, green, yellowish, brown, or ochre-coloured flowers.

In this book we have followed parts of Summerhayes's revision of the *Angraecum* species occurring on the mainland of Africa (1958) and supplemented this arrangement with many of the proposals made by Garay (1973). In that study of all the names that have been published in *Angraecum*, he provided a very useful review and proposed allocating the 206 species then recognised to 19 sections.

Our treatment begins with the large-flowered plants, some of which are well known and commonly cultivated. The sections with smaller flowers, sometimes very small, are mostly less well known to orchid growers and come later in this book. Because of our familiarity with the living plants (as compared with the herbarium specimens studied by both Summerhayes and Garay, although we have studied those too) we have suggested moving a few of the species to different sections, as seems appropriate to us. Species described recently have been placed close to those that appear similar. Within each section the species from Africa and the islands in the Gulf of Guinea are described first, followed by those from Madagascar and the Comoro Islands, and finally those from the neighbouring islands of Réunion and Mauritius. The species descriptions are presented alphabetically in each group.

Angraecum sororium on the hard igneous rock of a granite inselberg, central Madagascar. J. Hermans

It should be noted that DNA studies for this genus are currently under way, and the results may provide new insight into the way in which the species are classified. Some may be transferred to other sections or even to new genera when the results of new work are coordinated and combined with information from traditional sources. Since some of the characters of various sections seem to overlap with other sections or reappear in more than one section, and some species are hard to place in any section, another review will be most welcome.

Culture

All *Angraecum* species are easy to grow in cultivation; however, it is important to know the original source of each species because individual requirements vary. The day and night temperatures that plants experience in the wild and need in cultivation may be very important for healthy growth. All the species thrive in pots or baskets with a bark-based compost mix. Some of the smaller ones also grow well mounted on slabs of wood or cork-oak bark. They all need plenty of space to allow their often lengthy and copious roots to develop and attach themselves to the substrate.

SUMMARY OF THE SECTIONS OF *ANGRAECUM*

Flowers white or partly white, large or medium-sized
    Section *Angraecum* (see pages 36–43)
    Section *Humblotiangraecum* (see pages 43–46)
    Section *Perrierangraecum* (see pages 46–62)
    Section *Hadrangis* (see pages 63–64)
    Section *Arachnangraecum* (see pages 64–76)
    Section *Pseudojumellea* (see pages 76–80)

Flowers green or yellowish green, fleshy, in short racemes
    Section *Chlorangraecum* (see pages 80–82)

Flowers white, green, yellowish green, or brownish, small to medium-sized, produced singly, rarely 2–7 per inflorescence

Section *Conchoglossum* (see pages 82–86)
Section *Angraecoides* (see pages 86–90)
Section *Filangis* (see pages 90–93)
Section *Afrangraecum* (see pages 93–96)

Flowers green or yellowish green, thin, small to medium-sized, in several- to many-flowered racemes or panicles
    Section *Gomphocentrum* (see pages 96–103)
    Section *Boryangraecum* (see pages 103–109)
    Section *Nana* (see pages 109–115)
    Section *Lepervenchea* (see pages 115–117)
    Section *Lemurangis* (see pages 117–122)

Flowers white or green, small or minute, in 1- or 2-flowered racemes
    Section *Acaulia* (see pages 122–124)
    Section *Pectinaria* (see pages 124–129)
    Section *Dolabrifolia* (see pages 129–133)

SECTION *ANGRAECUM*

In this section are large plants with leafy stems, bearing thick and fleshy leaves, with bases overlapping on the stem. The axillary inflorescences are usually several- to many-flowered in a long raceme. The white or greenish white, fleshy flowers have a long spur at the base of the lip.

Two species have been added to this section in this book: *Angraecum humberti* and *A. serpens*. Three species placed in this section by Perrier and temporarily placed here by Garay are treated as members of section *Pseudojumellea*: *A. dendrobiopsis*, *A. florulentum*, and *A. penzigianum*. Two other species seem better placed in section *Humblotiangraecum*: *A. mahavavense* and *A. potamophilum*.

Eight species are known from Madagascar, one of which (*Angraceum eburneum*) is widespread in the region with distinct subspecies in eastern tropical Africa, the Comoro Islands, and Madagascar. One species (*A. palmiforme*) described from Réunion is believed to be extinct.

Angraecum sesquipedale. From Thouars 1822, t. 67.

Angraecum crassum Thouars

Plants with upright thick stems that can be short or tall, up to 40 cm high, with leaves in 2 rows. Leaves thick and stiff, linear, unequally bilobed at the apex, 12–18 cm long, 1.5–2.5 cm wide. Inflorescence as long as the leaves, 5- to 12-flowered; pedicels and bracts short and thick. Flowers fleshy, white, turning yellow with age, up to 4 cm in diameter; sepals and petals lanceolate, acute, 18–20 mm long, lateral sepals longer and with a dorsal thickening on the midline, petals slightly smaller; lip very concave, rounded, with a short apiculus, widest in the middle; spur thick, up to 3 cm long, as long as the twisted ovary.

Angraecum eburneum, Réunion. J. Hermans

Angraecum eburneum, Seychelles. J. Hermans

Angraecum eburneum subsp. *giryamae.*
J. Hermans

Angraecum eburneum subsp. *superbum,*
Madagascar. J. Hermans

Epiphyte on tree trunks; sea level to 400 m; flowering between September and March; often self-pollinating.

Madagascar (eastern region).

Angraecum eburneum Bory

Plants large, robust, with many fleshy roots of great length; stems erect, thick, 15–100 cm long, 2–3 cm in diameter, often several close together. Leaves 6–10, succulent or leathery, usually light yellowish green, erect, ligulate, unequally bilobed at the apex, lobes rounded, 15–50 cm long, 3–7 cm wide. Inflorescences erect or ascending, 8- to 20-flowered; bracts conspicuous, blackish; pedicellate ovary twisted so that the lip is carried on the upper side of the flower. Flowers large, green with a white lip, scented in the evening; sepals reflexed, linear-lanceolate, 3–4.5 cm long, 5–10 mm wide; petals reflexed, similar to sepals; lip transversely oblong to broadly ovate, almost 3-lobed with a central apiculus between the rounded side lobes, 3–4 cm long, 2.8–4 cm wide; spur pointed behind the dorsal sepal, 4–10(–15) cm long; column fleshy, green, 5 mm long with paler rostellum lobes.

Growing near the sea on coral cliffs and as an epiphyte, and further inland as an epiphyte and on rocks; sea level to 500 m; flowering September to June.

Madagascar, Comoro Islands, Réunion, Mauritius, Seychelles, Kenya, and Tanzania.

Angraecum eburneum was described originally from Réunion and is now recognised as one variable and widespread species amongst the islands of the western Indian Ocean. However, the differences in the size of the flowers, the shape of the lip and the length of the spur, and geographical distribution are now used to recognise 4 subspecies rather than several separate species as in the past. One taxon was originally described as a variety of *A. eburneum* but is now recognised as a distinct species, *A. longicalcar* (Bosser) Senghas.

subsp. *eburneum*

Flowers smaller than those from Madagascar, larger than those from Kenya.

Growing on and amongst rocks, often in the shade of bushes, and as an epiphyte.

Réunion.

subsp. *giryamae* (Rendle) Senghas & Cribb

Flowers with the lip slightly wider than long, obscurely 3-lobed in the upper part; spur less than 6 cm long.

Epiphyte or lithophyte; sea level to 350 m; flowering July to September.

Kenya and Tanzania.

subsp. *superbum* (Thouars) H. Perrier

Syn. *Angraecum superbum* Thouars

Flowers larger than those of the other subspecies; spur up to 15 cm long.

Lithophyte and epiphyte; sea level to 500 m; flowering September to May.

Madagascar (near the east coast), Comoro Islands, and Seychelles.

subsp. *xerophilum* H. Perrier

Flowers small with a wide lip and spur 7–8 cm long.

Growing amongst rocks in dry, deciduous scrubland, isolated from other populations.

Madagascar (south-western region).

Angraecum humberti H. Perrier

Plant 20 cm high with a short thick stem, slightly flattened, 15–18 mm wide. Leaves in 2 rows, always longer than the stem, broadly linear or loriform, often conduplicate, leathery, slightly glossy, very unequally bilobed at the apex, lobes rounded, one 7–8 mm longer than the other, 12–16 cm long, 1–1.5 cm wide. Inflorescence robust, up to 20 cm long, bearing 4–8 flowers opening progressively, usually in pairs; peduncle 7–9 cm long with 2 or 3 internodes, each partly covered with a pointed sheath; bract very thin, at the base of the rachis, pedicellate ovary 4.5 cm long. Flowers greenish white with a pure white lip; sepals long-attenuate-filiform from the base to the tip, dorsal sepal 5 cm long, 5 mm wide at the base, lateral sepals larger, 7 cm long, 7 mm wide; petals similar but smaller,

4.5 cm long, 4 mm wide; lip concave, shell-shaped at the base, very attenuate-filiform with a slender acumen 3 cm long, in total 5 cm long, 2 cm wide near the base; spur funnel-shaped at the mouth, 7 mm wide, then rapidly narrowing and filiform, 13–14 cm long.

Lithophyte, growing on rocks in dry forest on the western slopes of mountains; ca. 800 m; flowering in January and February.

Madagascar (south-western region).

Named in honour of the French botanist, Henri Humbert (1887–1967), who led many expeditions to Madagascar and collected the type specimen. This species has been placed in section *Arachnangraecum* by Garay, but because of its habit and its many-flowered inflorescence, it seems to us more appropriate to place it in this section for the time being.

Angraecum longicalcar (Bosser) Senghas

Syn. *Angraecum eburneum* var. *longicalcar* Bosser

Plant large and robust with stem eventually reaching 20–50 cm long or even longer, 5–7 cm in diameter, commonly with basal side shoots. Leaves several, strap-shaped, glossy, fleshy, unevenly bilobed at the apex, V-shaped in cross section towards the base, up to 60 cm long, 8 cm wide. Inflorescences axillary, straight, to 100 cm long, 8- to 12-flowered. Flowers large, pale green with conspicuous white lip; sepals lanceolate, acute, dorsal sepal 5 cm long, 1.3 cm wide, lateral sepals slightly shorter; petals similar to sepals, 5.2 cm long, 1 cm wide; lip on the upper side of the flower, conspicuously wider than long, waxy white, with a broad keel on the upper surface towards the base, 3.2 cm long with a long acumen 1.5 cm long, 6.2–6.5 cm wide; spur pale green, straight, 30–40 cm long, 5 mm in diameter.

Epiphyte or lithophyte, amongst grasses and xerophytic vegetation and also in gallery forest; 1000–2000 m; flowering in February.

Madagascar (central regions), at a much higher altitude than the various forms of *Angraecum eburneum* that occur near the coast.

This species can always be distinguished by the shape of the lip and the spur that may reach 40 cm in length.

Angraecum protensum Schlechter

Plants with stiff upright stems, often several close together in a clump, up to 30 cm high, 6–8 mm wide, densely leaved in the upper part, covered with overlapping leaf bases below. Leaves greyish green in 2 rows, stiff and leathery, folded in the lower half and opening out flat above, unequally bilobed at the apex, 8–11 cm long, 7–10 mm wide. Inflorescences axillary, 16–19 cm long, usually 1- or 2-flowered; peduncle to 9 cm long; bracts few, small; pedicellate ovary slender, 6–8 cm long. Flowers large, 1 or 2, white, fleshy; sepals and petals oblong-lanceolate, acute, 3–4 cm long, 8 mm wide; lip ovate, concave, pointed or shortly apiculate, 4 cm long, 2.5 cm wide; spur slender, 12–15 cm long.

Lithophyte or terrestrial amongst rocks, rather resembling a smaller version of *Angraecum sororium*, which grows in the same areas; 1600–2000 m; flowering January to March.

Madagascar (central highlands).

Angraecum serpens (H. Perrier) Bosser

Plant creeping over rocks with a long stem, branched at the base, up to 50 cm long, 6–7 mm in diameter, covered by sheathing leaf bases up to 2.5 cm long which are transversely rugose. Leaves linear, narrowed at the base, 10–15 cm long, 8–15 mm wide. Inflorescence 4–5 cm long, single-flowered; peduncle 2–3 cm long with 3 sheaths in the lower half, upper part bare; bract tubular, 2.5 cm long. Flowers medium-sized; sepals lanceolate, apiculate or attenuate to the tip, dorsal sepal 2.5–3 cm long, 1 cm wide at the base, lateral sepals slightly asymmetric, dilated on the outer margin near the base; petals shorter than sepals, also asymmetric; lip narrow at the base, then dilated, apex with a long cylindrical point 12 mm long, in total 3 cm long, 8 mm wide at widest point above the base; spur 11–12 mm long, 4 mm wide at the base, then inflexed and becoming narrow.

Angraecum longicalcar. J. Hermans

Angraecum protensum. J. Hermans

Angraecum sesquipedale. J. Hermans

Angraecum sesquipedale var. *angustifolium*.
J. Hermans

Epiphyte or creeping over rocks, only collected once in humid forest; ca. 600 m; flowering in July.

Madagascar (eastern region).

Originally described in the genus *Jumellea*. Placed in this section by Garay, but rather different from all the other species here, especially in its single-flowered inflorescence.

Angraecum sesquipedale Thouars

Plants large and robust, usually with a single upright or curving stem but sometimes branched, often bare in the lower part with a fan of leaves above, up to 100 cm long but usually less, flowering from a height of 15 cm; roots extensive, dark grey, often flattened against the substrate. Leaves in 2 rows, leathery and rather bluish or greyish green, not shiny, ligulate, unequally bilobed at the apex, lobes rounded, 20–40 cm long, 6–7 cm wide. Inflorescences axillary, erect or horizontal, 1- to 3-flowered, sometimes 6-flowered; peduncle 10–12 cm long with few papery bracts. Flowers large, opening green but turning creamy white within a few days; sepals lanceolate-acuminate, fleshy, 7–11 cm long, 2–3 cm wide near the base, lateral sepals keeled on the back; petals similar but slightly falcate, 7–8 cm long, 2.5–2.8 cm wide; lip concave, pandurate, acuminate, with a ridge along the surface in front of the spur opening, 6.5–9 cm long, 3.5–4 cm at its widest part; spur thick but gradually attenuate towards the tip, 30–35 cm long; column large and fleshy with conspicuous rostellum lobes below the anther cap.

Epiphyte on the bark of large trees, rarely near the ground; between sea level and up to 100 m; flowering between May and November.

Madagascar (near the east coast).

Sometimes called the 'King of the Angraecums', this spectacular plant is a great addition to any collection when well grown. Many seed-raised plants are now available in cultivation.

var. *angustifolium* Bosser & Morat

Syn. *Angraecum bosseri* Senghas

Plants with short inflorescences 1- or 2-flowered; smaller in all features than those further north.

Terrestrial, often growing in sand.

Madagascar (Tôlañaro).

Angraecum sororium Schlechter

Plants tall and stiff when mature, often with a number of shoots around the main stem, bearing leaves in the upper part, up to 80 cm tall, 10–15 mm in diameter. Leaves in 2 upright rows, stiff, ligulate, sheathing the stem at the base, unequally bilobed at the apex, shiny bright green, 18–30 cm long, 3–4.5 cm wide. Inflorescences usually several, shorter than the leaves, 1- to 4-flowered; bracts obtuse; pedicellate ovary 4–6.5 cm long. Flowers large, pure white; sepals widest near the base, lanceolate, acute, keeled on the back, 5–6 cm long, 16 mm wide; petals somewhat falcate and slightly wider,

Angraecum sororium. J. Hermans

42

5–6 cm long, 2 cm wide; lip as long as the petals, suborbicular, acuminate, 5–6 cm long, 3–3.5 cm wide, very thickened at the apex; spur pale green, gradually tapering from a wide throat, 25–32 cm long; column white, 7 mm high.

Growing on and amongst rock outcrops in full sun though often protected by mist and low cloud; 1600–2200 m; flowering December to March.

Madagascar (central highlands).

A spectacular species that flowers rarely in a glasshouse, apparently because of the difficulty of supplying sufficient light.

SECTION *HUMBLOTIANGRAECUM*

This section has medium to large plants with stems that are scarcely developed, short, or of medium length, bearing fleshy or leathery leaves. The inflorescence is a few-flowered raceme, often with more than one flower at a time. The flowers are white or tinged with green or orange-red, fleshy, and large.

The long pedicellate ovary is often winged, and the long, slender spur emerges from a wide opening at the base of the lip.

Two species (*Angraecum mahavavense* and *A. potamophilum*) included here do not fit this description well, or indeed that of any other section, but they were placed in this section by Garay and are retained until further evidence is available to suggest where they might be placed more appropriately. We have followed Perrier in retaining *A. viguieri* in this section because its flowers are similar to those of several of the other species. The other plants in this section are generally larger than those in section *Perrierangraecum*, the flowers are borne on a long pedicel which gradually merges into the base of the ovary, and the lip is broadly funnel-shaped at the base where it merges into the spur.

Six species are recorded from Madagascar, one of which (*Angraecum leonis*) also occurs in the Comoro Islands.

Angraecum leonis, Comoro Islands. J. Hermans

Angraecum leonis (Reichenbach f.) André

Plant with a very short stem up to 10 cm long but usually less, covered by the very characteristic ensiform leaves and bearing narrow wiry roots. Leaves 4–6, falcate, the upper surfaces completely cohering, and the ventral surfaces exposed, fleshy or leathery, 10–22 cm long, 16–25 mm wide. Inflorescences 1 or 2, axillary or below the leaves, 1- to 4-flowered; bracts thin, brown, 3 mm long; pedicellate ovary 5–10 cm long, pedicel flattened and winged, ovary triquetrous. Flowers greenish at first, becoming white; sepals lanceolate, widest at the base, attenuate in the upper half, keeled on the dorsal surface and thickened at the apex, dorsal sepal 4.5–6 cm long, 7 mm wide, lateral sepals 5–6 cm long, 6–8 mm wide; petals somewhat reflexed, lanceolate, attenuate above the basal third, 4 cm long, 6 mm wide; lip broadly oval, acute, very concave, with a central ridge towards the base and in the mouth of the spur, 4–5 cm long, 2.5–3.5 cm wide; spur funnel-shaped at the mouth, then narrow and filiform, 7–9 cm long.

Epiphyte in humid forests and in deciduous forest near streams where it also grows on rocks; sea level to 1500 m; flowering November to March.

Madagascar (widespread but nowhere common) and Comoro Islands (Grande Comore).

Smaller plants with a rather different facies have been collected in central and western Madagascar, but they have not been considered taxonomically distinct. Reichenbach named this plant in honour of the French collector, Léon Humblot (1852–1914), who made great contributions to the knowledge of orchids in Madagascar and the Comoro Islands.

Angraecum magdalenae Schlechter & H. Perrier

Plant with stem concealed by overlapping leaf bases, very short, or up to 35 cm tall in very old plants, 1–2.5 cm in diameter, the main stem frequently surrounded by offshoots; roots from the base of the stem, white, 3–4 mm in diameter. Leaves 6–8 arranged in a fan shape, oblong-ligulate, unequally bilobed at the apex, contracted and folded round the stem at the base, the mid-

Angraecum magdalenae. J. Hermans

rib prominent on the ventral surface, dark green, sometimes transversely wrinkled, 25–30 cm long, 4–5 cm wide. Inflorescences arising below the leaves or axillary, 1- or 2-flowered; bracts much shorter than the pedicel, thick and fleshy, 10–15 mm long; pedicellate ovary 8–10 cm long. Flowers pure white, thick and fleshy, relatively large; sepals lanceolate, widest in the lower third, attenuate and ending in an obtuse, thickened point, dorsal sepal 4.5 cm long, 18 mm wide, lateral sepals similar but somewhat falcate, slightly keeled on the outer surface; petals ovate, wider than the sepals but of similar length, ending in a thickened point, to 4.5 cm long, 3 cm wide; lip concave, obovate, apiculate, widest in the upper half, 5 cm long, 4 cm wide; spur S-shaped, gradually narrowing from a wide, funnel-shaped mouth, 8–10 cm long.

Lithophyte or terrestrial between rocks and boulders, often shaded by *Uapaca* trees; ca. 1700 m; flowering in January.

Madagascar (central highlands).

Named in honour of Madelaine Drouhard who collected this species on Ibity Massif and grew it in Antananarivo until it flowered. In 1929 she became the wife of Henri Perrier de la Bâthie.

var. *latilabellum* Bosser

Plants and flowers larger than above and more robust.

Epiphyte in humid forest.

Madagascar (Mount Tsaratanana).

Angraecum mahavavense H. Perrier

Plant up to 15 cm high without a distinct stem, roots with uneven surface, 3–4 mm in diameter. Leaves 5 or 6, broadly linear, leathery, rigid, with a distinct keel in the middle part and V-shaped towards the base, shortly bilobed at the apex, 7–14 cm long, 11–12 mm wide. Inflorescence solitary below the leaves, with 3–5 flowers ca. 6–10 mm apart; peduncle thick and very short, 7–10 mm long; bracts short and sheathing the rachis; pedicellate ovary 2 cm long, each pedicel inserted in a groove which forms alternately on each side of the rachis, successively. Flowers white; sepals attenuate from the wide base to the acute tip, 14–15 mm long, 4–5 mm wide; petals smaller, 12–13 mm long, 3–3.5 mm wide; lip ovate, acute, 13–16 mm long, 7–10 mm wide above the base; spur with a narrow mouth, linear, 5–6 cm long.

Epiphyte on trunks of trees in humid forests; flowering in October.

Madagascar (Sambirano region in the north-west).

This species seems misplaced in this section, but does not fit well in section *Perrierangraecum* either.

Angraecum potamophilum Schlechter

Plant 12–18 cm high with a short stem 6–8 mm in diameter. Leaves 4–6, linear, thick and stiff, 12–15 cm long, 5–8 mm wide. Inflorescence pendent, ca. 5 cm long, 3- to 5-flowered; peduncle short, covered at the base with 3 or 4 short sheaths; bract as long as the internodes of the rachis which are thick and short, 4 mm long; pedicellate ovary ca. 2.5 cm long, 3-winged. Flowers white, very small for the section; sepals attenuate from the base to

tip, 17–18 mm long, 4 mm wide at the base; petals similar to the dorsal sepal, slightly shorter and narrower; lip oval-lanceolate, attenuate at the apex, 17–18 mm long, 8 mm wide below the middle; spur filiform, 8 cm long.

Epiphyte on trunks of *Eugenia* trees near a river; flowering in November.

Madagascar (western region).

Perrier comments that this small species does not fit well into any of the sections of *Angraecum*. He placed it, and the preceding species, in section *Angraecum*: Garay placed both in section *Humblotiangraecum*.

Angraecum praestans Schlechter

Plant robust, with a stem 20–30 cm long and ca. 2 cm in diameter. Leaves spaced close together, forming a fan, loriform-ligulate, thick and fleshy, unequally bilobed at the apex, 25–30 cm long, 2.2–3 cm wide. Inflorescence lax, 8- to 10-flowered;

Angraecum praestans. J. Hermans

Angraecum viguieri. J. Hermans

peduncle 15–20 cm long; bract deltoid, short; pedicellate ovary 3.5 cm long. Flowers white, rather thin, sometimes the sepals and petals greenish or yellowish and the lip white; dorsal sepal attenuate, 4.7 cm long, 7 mm wide at the base; lateral sepals similar, fused at the base on the inner side forming a collar around the spur; petals free, similar to the sepals and of equal size; lip obovate-rhomboid, widest in the upper third, with an acuminate or acute apiculus, 4 cm long, 3.2 cm wide; spur funnel-shaped at the entrance then curved and gradually filiform, 9–12.5 cm long.

Epiphyte and at the base of trees, often associated with tamarind trees, also on cliffs and in dry woods near the sea and sand dunes; sea level to 100 m; flowering November to June.

Madagascar (western and north-western regions).

Angraecum viguieri Schlechter

Plant with a short or elongated stem 15–30(–90) cm tall, ca. 1 cm in diameter; roots 3–4 mm in diameter, verrucose. Leaves 12–20 in 2 rows each nearly at right angles to the stem, widely spaced, linear-ligulate, stiff, unequally bilobed at the apex, 6–14 cm long, 8–22 mm wide. Inflorescence single-flowered, but usually several are borne at the same time; peduncle 3–5 cm long, with 2 or 3 narrow sheaths near the base; bract broadly oval-apiculate, not sheathing the pedicel, ca. 1 cm long; pedicellate ovary 3-ribbed, 3.5–4 cm long. Flowers white often variously tinged with green or rich orange-brown; sepals and petals narrowly linear-ligulate, 5.5–8.5 cm long, 5–8 mm wide only near the base; lip shell-shaped, widest at the middle, rounded towards the tip and with an acumen ca. 15 mm long, bearing a central keel on its inner surface that extends into the spur, 5–7 cm long, ca. 5 cm wide; spur broadly funnel-shaped at the mouth, narrowing beyond the ovary and gradually filiform to the tip, 10–13 cm long.

Epiphyte in humid forests; ca. 900 m; flowering October to November.

Madagascar (central region).

Seed-raised plants of this delightful species are now available and often have larger and more brightly coloured flowers than the wild plants.

SECTION *PERRIERANGRAECUM*

The small to medium-sized plants in this section have single-flowered inflorescences, rarely 2-flowered in a few species. The large flower has a conspicuous white lip and is borne on a short peduncle which is covered with 3 or 4 compressed sheaths. The pedicellate ovary often is triquetrous.

Thirty-six species are allocated to this section, mostly from Madagascar. Two species recorded in adjacent parts of Africa are dealt with first, followed by 31 from Madagascar, one of which also occurs in Mauritius. The three Réunion species come last.

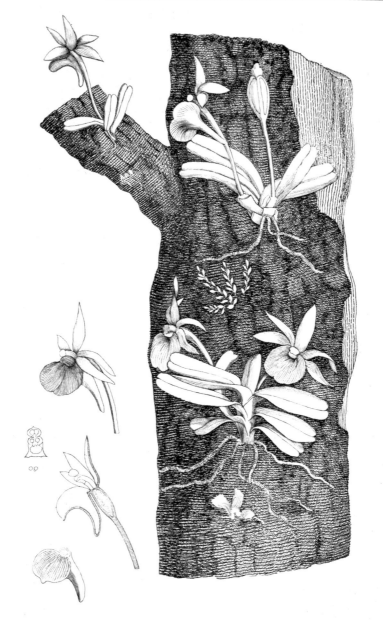

Angraecum cucullatum. From Thouars 1822, t. 48.

Species from Africa

Angraecum chimanimaniense G. Williamson

Plants with slender stems elongated to about 15 cm long, sometimes branched; roots mainly near the base of the stem 1–3 mm in diameter, verrucose. Leaves several in 2 rows, linear, obtuse at the apex, triangular in cross section to subterete, dark blue-green, 7–11 cm long, 4–6 mm wide. Inflorescence single-flowered; bract lanceolate, to 5 mm long; pedicellate ovary to 5 cm long. Flowers white, or straw coloured or pale green with a white lip, up to 7 cm in diameter; sepals narrowly lanceolate, 35–40 mm long and 5–6 mm wide; lateral sepals falcate towards the base; petals narrowly lanceolate, acute, somewhat reflexed, 35 mm long, 4 mm wide; lip narrowly ovate, long acute, concave; spur slender, gradually tapering, 10–14 cm long.

Angraecum stella-africae. E. la Croix

Epiphyte and growing on rocks under *Philippia* bushes; ca. 1800 m; flowering in December and February.

Zimbabwe (Chimanimani Mountains).

This species is superficially similar to *Angraecum cornigerum* (section *Filangis*) which grows in a very similar habitat in Réunion, where it is also rare.

Angraecum stella-africae P. J. Cribb

Plant dwarf, with erect stems 1–2 cm long; roots pale grey, slightly verrucose. Leaves 2–4(–6) in 2 rows, linear, obscurely bilobed at the apex, dark grey-green, 3.5–5 cm long, 6–8 mm wide. Inflorescences 1 or 2, arising below the leaves, single-flowered; peduncle 3–4 mm long; bract 3–4 mm long; pedicellate ovary 3–4 cm long. Flowers glistening white with green tip to the spur, large for the size of the plant but often not opening fully; sepals lanceolate, acute, spreading, 15–25 mm long, 5 mm wide; petals similar but smaller, 10–20 mm long, 3 mm wide; lip ovate, elliptic, concave, subacute, 15–26 mm long, 13–15 mm wide; spur very slender, S-shaped or coiled in bud, becoming straight and pendent, 12–15 cm long.

Epiphyte on *Uapaca* and other small trees on exposed escarpments, frequently covered in mist; 1200–1500 m; flowering in January but often self-pollinating.

Malawi, Zimbabwe, and South Africa (Limpopo).

Species from Madagascar

The large number of species in this section in Madagascar have been allocated to 4 groups in the following text, to aid identification.

Group 1. Usually more than one white flower per inflorescence; spur wide and funnel-shaped where it joins the lip, then curved backwards and forward again before straightening out, length 6–8 cm in *A. kraenzlinianum* or 9–13 cm in other species.

Group 2. One flower per inflorescence; plants of various sizes, but mostly with short stems and white flowers with a narrow spur more than 5 cm long, usually 9–12 cm long.

Group 3. Small plants whose white flowers have a spur 3–5 cm long, at least twice as long as the lip.

Group 4. Plants with longer stems and small white flowers each with a spur less than 2 cm long.

Group 1. Usually more than one white flower per inflorescence; spur wide and funnel-shaped where it joins the lip, then curved backwards and forward again before straightening out, length 6–8 cm in *Angraecum kraenzlinianum* or 9–13 cm in other species.

Angraecum aloifolium Hermans & P. J. Cribb

Plant medium-sized, with a simple, stout, erect stem to 10 cm long, 9–15 mm in diameter; roots very slender, wiry. Leaves few, narrowly ensiform, spreading, in 2 rows, very fleshy or succulent, canaliculate, pale green, the surface pitted and fissured with dark green crevices, 4.2–5 cm long, 10–12 mm wide, 7 mm wide across the upper surface. Inflorescence axillary, 1- or 2-flowered; peduncle only partly concealed by 1 or 2 bracts; bracts 4–5 mm long; pedicellate ovary 6–7 cm long, bilaterally compressed below, triquetrous above. Flowers white with green column; dorsal sepal lanceolate, acuminate, strongly keeled on the back, 22–25 mm long, 6–7 mm wide; lateral sepals very similar; petals lanceolate, acuminate, ridged along the centre on the outer surface, 17–20 mm long, 6–7 mm wide; lip elliptic, concave, strongly dilated at the base, 49–52 mm long, 15–20 mm wide; spur funnel-shaped at first, then decurved after it becomes narrow, filiform in the apical part, 8–10 cm long.

Epiphyte in dry, deciduous forests.

Madagascar (western regions).

Angraecum aloifolium. J. Hermans

Angraecum clareae. J. Hermans

Described from specimens in cultivation in Europe. The specific name refers to the leaves that superficially resemble those of certain species of *Aloe*.

Angraecum clareae Hermans, la Croix & P. J. Cribb

Plant erect or semi-pendulous, stems simple or with side growths emerging from the base, 7–8 cm long, 4–5 mm in diameter; roots slender, glabrous. Leaves 10–20, spreading, ensiform, conduplicate, fleshy-succulent, triangular in cross section, glaucous, greyish green, 25–38 mm long, 9–12 mm wide. Inflorescences often 2, each 1- or 2-flowered, sometimes with an additional, undeveloped terminal bud; peduncle fleshy, rounded and short, 5–10 mm long, the basal part naked but partly concealed by one tubular sheath 5–6 mm long; bract 3–5 mm long; pedicel flattened and winged, ovary triangular, in total pedicellate ovary ca. 45–55 mm long. Flowers sparkling white, tip of spur and column green; sepals lanceolate, acute, keeled on the back, dorsal sepal 28–30 mm long, 4–5 mm wide, lateral sepals spreading, slightly falcate, 29–32 mm long, 4–5 mm wide; petals strongly reflexed over the lateral sepals, lanceolate, acuminate, 22–30 mm long, 3–6 mm wide; lip concave, obovate, rounded at the sides, the tip apiculate and reflexed, 25–30 mm long, 15–19 mm wide, apiculus 8–10 mm long; spur funnel-shaped at the mouth, semi-erect behind the lip, then decurved and filiform, funnel 25 mm long, 6–7 mm wide with a central keel disappearing into the spur, 9–12 cm long.

Epiphyte in evergreen forest; flowering period in the wild not recorded, flowering in cultivation in UK in September.

Madagascar (eastern and central regions).

Similar to *Angraecum compactum* in some respects but always distinguished by the glaucous leaves and narrower tepals; illustrated in Hillerman and Holst (1986) as no. 80. Named for Clare Hermans.

Angraecum compactum. J. Hermans

Angraecum compactum Schlechter

Plants with short thick stems, sometimes quite elongated, up to 30 cm long or more, sometimes branched, with narrow wiry roots. Leaves 6–14, thick and somewhat succulent, dark green, with a rough or shrivelled surface, midrib well marked, ligulate, unequally bilobed at the apex, 5–10 cm long, 18–38 mm wide. Inflorescence piercing the leaf sheath on the lower part of the stem, 1- to 3-flowered; peduncle very short, 8–10 mm long, covered with 3 wide sheaths, bract wider than long, keeled along the dorsal vein; pedicellate ovary 6 cm long, the pedicel flattened and the ovary triquetrous. Flowers white, spreading, flat or with reflexed petals; sepals oblong, obtuse, 20–30 mm long, up to 12 mm wide, the laterals slightly longer and narrower; petals similar but shorter and sometimes partly reflexed; lip boat-shaped and very concave with a wide, funnel-shaped entrance to the spur, oblong, rounded at the apex with a short apiculus, 30 mm long, 26 mm wide; spur up to 10 mm wide at the entrance, gradually narrowing then bent forward below the lip finally becoming straight, 11–13 cm long.

Epiphyte in humid evergreen forests; 700–2000 m; flowering August to December.

Madagascar (central regions).

One of the largest plants in this section, with the largest flowers, sweetly scented in the evening. Very desirable in cultivation and not difficult to grow in shady, humid conditions.

Angraecum dollii Senghas

Plant pendent; stems to 40 cm long, bearing well-spaced leaves in the apical half. Leaves spreading, V-shaped in cross section, unequally bilobed at the apex, succulent, 12 cm long, 15 mm wide when flattened. Inflorescence 3 cm long, single-flowered; peduncle covered with 2 or 3 black sheaths; bract thin, brown, 5–6 mm long; ovary triangular,

Angraecum dollii. J. Hermans

ridged, 5 cm long. Flower with pale yellowish green sepals and petals, sparkling white lip; dorsal sepal lanceolate, widest at the base, 5 cm long, 10 mm wide at the base; lateral sepals similar, somewhat curved; petals similar but shorter, curved; lip concave, orbicular in the lower half with a short keel towards the base, a long attenuate acumen above, 4 cm long, 22 mm wide; spur funnel-shaped at first, then narrowing and curved through 180°, major part slender, 14 cm long.

Epiphyte in seasonally dry forest; 1000 m.

Madagascar (near Antsirabe).

Named for the collector, Hilmar Doll, an enthusiastic orchid grower in Germany.

Angraecum equitans Schlechter

Plants dwarf and compact with a stem 9–10 cm long, 8–10 mm in diameter, sometimes branched, densely covered with overlapping leaf bases, roots very fine and wiry. Leaves equitant (overlapping at the base like those of an *Iris*), spreading, somewhat curved, dark green, glossy when young becoming dull, 3–6 cm long, 11–14 mm wide. Inflorescence 1- to 3-flowered; peduncle short, entirely covered with folded sheaths; bract folded, appearing 3 mm wide; pedicellate ovary 4 cm long with 4 acute angles. Flowers white; sepals narrowly lanceolate, attenuate from the base to the tip, winged on the back, dorsal sepal 17–20 mm long, lateral sepals 20–25 mm long; petals similar to the dorsal sepal but narrower; lip concave, elliptic-acuminate, funnel-shaped at the base, 17–20 mm long, 9–15 mm wide at the middle; spur wide at the entrance, then slender, 9–11 cm long.

Epiphyte on branches of moss- and lichen-covered trees; 2000 m; flowering in December.

Madagascar (Mount Tsaratanana).

Usually described as a small, compact plant, but the type specimen (Perrier 11357) has a stem ca. 30 cm long.

Angraecum kraenzlinianum H. Perrier

Plant with short, curved, or pendent stems, 5–10 mm in diameter, bearing 11–25 leaves in 2 rows. Leaves fleshy, folded along the midrib so that the upper surfaces almost cohere and the leaves appear narrow, spreading and somewhat arching, 2.5–4 cm long, 5–7 mm wide (folded measurement), rounded at the apex. Inflorescence shorter than the leaves; peduncle very short, entirely covered by 3 short, thin, scarious sheaths; bract narrow, brown, up to 1 cm long; pedicellate ovary 3–3.5 cm long. Flowers white; sepals lanceolate, acute, keeled or winged on the back, 25–30 mm long, petals similar but without a keel on the back; lip broadly rounded, or dilated at the sides, cuspidate or subacute in front; spur 6–8 cm long, narrowing from the wide entrance to the filiform tip, first curving backward, then forward before straightening out.

Epiphyte on trees and shrubs in moss- and lichen-covered forest; 1500–2000 m; flowering in January.

Madagascar (central region).

The flowers are rather similar to others in this section but the leaves of this species are quite characteristic.

Group 2. One flower per inflorescence; plants of various sizes, but mostly with short stems and white flowers with a narrow spur more than 5 cm long, usually 9–12 cm long.

Angraecum ankeranense H. Perrier

Plant up to 15 cm high with stem 5–8 mm in diameter, bearing 5 or 6 leaves near the apex. Leaves oval-oblong, thick and leathery, folded at the base but expanded above, equally bilobed at the apex, 2–3 cm long, 11–14 mm wide. Inflorescence single-flowered, sometimes accompanied by a bracteole containing an undeveloped flower; peduncle short and thick, entirely covered by overlapping sheaths, 8 mm long; pedicellate ovary 10–12 mm long, with 3 wide wings. Flowers white; sepals lanceolate, long attenuate and pointed, 3.8 cm long, 7.5 mm wide; petals the same length but narrower, 5 mm wide; lip broadly oval, widest in the lower third, with a long acuminate tip, 3.5–3.7 cm long, 2.2 cm wide; spur cylindric, curved at the apex, ca. 8 cm long.

Epiphyte on tree trunks in mossy forest; 700–2000 m; flowering in February.

Madagascar (central region).

Angraecum bicallosum H. Perrier

Plant with stems somewhat compressed attaining 14 cm in length and 4 mm in diameter, roots smooth. Leaves short, broadly elliptic, deeply and unequally bilobed at the apex, folded near the base, 2.5 cm long, 8–11 mm wide. Inflorescence piercing the axillary sheath; peduncle very short, entirely covered with 3 or 4 sheaths of which the uppermost is folded, green and up to 1 cm long, exceeding the end of the peduncle, single-flowered; bract green, folded and keeled, 1.4 cm long, covering part of the pedicel; pedicellate ovary 2 cm long, not winged. Flowers large, the lip white, other parts yellowish orange; sepals lanceolate, gradually attenuate from the base to tip, keeled on the dorsal surface, 3 cm long, 6 mm wide; petals similar to the sepals but narrower, only 4 mm wide at the base; lip broadly oval, subacuminate-acute, almost flat, bearing 2 small (obscure) rounded calli near the base on either side of the entrance to the spur; spur cylindric, straight, gradually narrowing from the 3-mm-wide entrance to the tip, 12 cm long.

Epiphyte on tree trunks in mossy forests; ca. 1000 m; flowering in November.

Madagascar (Mount Ambre).

Angraecum breve Schlechter

Plants with a very short stem or elongating with age, up to 4 cm long with greyish green leaves in the upper part and sinuous or flattened roots 2–3 mm wide which are sometimes verrucose. Leaves stiff and leathery, rather dull, ligulate, unequally bilobed at the apex, overlapping at the base, 2–5 cm long, 5–8 mm wide. Inflorescence piercing the leaf sheath, single-flowered; peduncle 1 cm long entirely covered with 2 or 3 sheaths, slightly flattened; pedicellate ovary 2.5 cm long. Flowers pure white, or the sepals and petals pale greenish and lip white; sepals spreading, oval-lanceolate, acute, 17 mm long; petals similar but smaller, 15 mm long; lip rhomboid-elliptic, attenuate towards the base

Angraecum breve. J. Hermans

and at the apiculate tip, 18 mm long, 14 mm wide at the middle; spur slender, curved, 11 cm long, sometimes shorter.

Epiphyte on lichen-covered trees; ca. 1800 m; flowering in January.

Madagascar (Mount Tsaratanana).

Rather similar to *Angraecum rutenbergianum* in most respects but much smaller except for the spur. Flowers become yellow as they age.

Angraecum curnowianum (Reichenbach f.) Durand & Schinz

Plant with short stem and a small fan of spreading or upright leaves at the apex, up to 15 cm long, 1 cm in diameter. Leaves ca. 7, ligulate, emarginate, thick and fleshy, dark dull green and rough to the touch, 6–10(–18) cm long, ca. 2 cm wide. Inflorescence axillary, single-flowered; peduncle 3–3.5 cm long, with 2 or 3 sheaths at the base; bract obtuse, acute, 1 cm long; pedicel with ovary 4 cm long. Flowers pale greenish with a white lip, fleshy; sepals spreading, lanceolate-ligulate, acute, 2–3 cm long, 3–4(–9) mm wide; petals similar but smaller, 15(–30) mm long; lip cuneate, obovate, retuse,

apiculate, 2.5(–3) cm long, 10(–20) mm wide; spur filiform, curved, (8.5–)10 cm long.

Madagascar (exact locality not known).

This plant was named by Reichenbach in honour of Richard Curnow (d. 1896), a British traveller who collected plants for the famous orchid nursery of Low at Clapton, and later at Enfield, near London.

Angraecum didieri (Baillon ex Finet) Schlechter

Plants with a cylindrical stem 12–15 cm high, 6–7 mm in diameter; roots verrucose, up to 4 mm in diameter. Leaves 5–7, loriform, short, slightly unequally bilobed at the apex, 2–7 cm long, 6–10 mm wide. Inflorescence piercing the leaf sheath, single-flowered; peduncle very short, nearly as thick as long, covered by 2 or 3 sheaths; bract obtuse and wide, covering a third of the pedicel; pedicellate ovary 15–20 mm long, triangular with 3 wings. Flower white, or with white lip and greenish sepals, sometimes accompanied by a rudimentary second flower which does not develop; sepals attenuate from base to tip, 22–35 mm long, 5–7 mm wide, the lateral sepals a little narrower than

Angraecum didieri. J. Hermans

the dorsal sepal; petals similar but narrower; lip concave, elliptic or oval-oblong, shortly cuspidate at the apex, 23–32 mm long, ca. 20 mm wide; spur narrow at the mouth, slender, coiled at first then straightening out, 8–15 cm long.

Epiphyte in forests; 600–1500 m; flowering October to January.

Madagascar (near the east coast and in the central highlands).

This species was named for Alfred Grandidier (1836–1921) who first collected it.

Angraecum dryadum Schlechter

Plants with a distinct stem 10–15 cm long and 4–5 mm in diameter, with conspicuous sheaths and wrinkled leaf bases above and slender, glabrous roots below. Leaves 7–10 in 2 rows in the upper part of the stem, upright or spreading, oblong-ligulate but narrowing towards the base, unequally bilobed at the apex, rigid and leathery, 2–4 cm long, 5–8 mm wide at the middle. Inflorescence growing through the leaf base, single-flowered; peduncle

Angraecum dryadum. J. Hermans

covered with 3 or 4 sheaths, 5–15 mm long; bract wide and short, 4–6 mm long; pedicellate ovary ca. 2.5 cm long, flattened, ovary triquetrous. Flowers white, or the lip white with pale green sepals and petals; sepals narrowly lanceolate, acute, 3 cm long, the laterals somewhat oblique; petals similar to the sepals but often shorter; lip ovate-lanceolate, acute, concave at the base, 3 cm long, 13 mm wide at the middle; spur slender, curved, up to 10 cm long, column wider than high.

Epiphyte on small trees and bushes in forests; 1000–2000 m; flowering between October and March.

Madagascar (central region).

This species is very variable in size. The flowers are rather similar to those of *Angraecum rutenbergianum* in shape, but in addition to the differences in habitat, the plants of this species usually have much longer stems and slender, glabrous roots.

Angraecum elephantinum Schlechter

Plant with short thick stems, 10–15 cm long, ca. 8 mm in diameter; roots up to 4 mm wide, greyish white, verrucose. Leaves ligulate, leathery, thick, unequally bilobed at the apex, 7.5–12 cm long, 2–2.5 cm wide. Inflorescence very short, 1- or 2-flowered; peduncle covered with overlapping sheaths; bract obtuse; pedicellate ovary 2.5 cm long, 8 mm in diameter. Flowers white or the lip white and sepals and petals amber or peach; sepals spreading, 35–46 mm long, ca. 13 mm wide, the lateral sepals slightly narrower; petals similar in length but narrower, lanceolate-ligulate, subobtuse; lip ovate, obtuse, 3–4 cm long and 2–2.5 cm wide at the middle, close to the column at the base; spur slender, curved at first and then straight, 11 cm long.

Epiphyte; very few details of its habitat are available.

Madagascar (eastern region).

Little is known of this species; it is rather similar to *Angraecum compactum* but the flowers have narrower segments and lack the wide entrance to the spur.

Angraecum imerinense Schlechter

Plant slender with a simple, narrow stem up to 20 cm high, 2.5–3 mm in diameter, bearing glabrous, slender roots. Leaves narrow, linear, leathery but quite thin, unequally bilobed at the apex, 25–35 mm long, 2.5–3.5 mm wide. Inflorescence piercing the leaf sheath, single-flowered; peduncle 1 cm long, covered with 2 or 3 compressed sheaths; bract similar to the superior sheath; pedicellate ovary triquetrous, 2 cm long. Flower white; sepals lanceolate-ligulate, acute, 19 mm long; petals nearly equalling the sepals but less acute; lip concave, oval-elliptic, apiculate, 19 mm long, 8–9 mm wide at the middle; spur narrow, ca. 9.5 cm long.

Epiphyte in the woods on west-facing slopes; ca. 1700 m; flowering in September.

Madagascar (central region).

Angraecum lecomtei H. Perrier

Plant very small, stems not more than 5 cm high. Leaves 3–6, erect or arching, linear and very narrow, unequally bilobed at the apex, 15–35 mm long, 1–1.5 mm wide. Inflorescence arising below the leaves, single-flowered; peduncle covered entirely by 3 obtuse sheaths; bract similar to these sheaths, 4–5 mm long, sometimes with a bracteole and vestiges of an undeveloped second flower; pedicellate ovary 1–2 cm long. Flowers white, small; sepals lanceolate, tapering from the base to the tip, 10 mm long, 2.4 mm wide; petals lanceolate, acute, 9.5 mm long, 2.2 mm wide; lip broadly oval, obtuse, 12 mm long, 8 mm wide; spur slender, 3 mm wide at the mouth, 10–12 cm long.

Epiphyte on tree trunks in mossy forests; ca. 1200 m; flowering February to March.

Madagascar (central region).

A desirable, miniature orchid which, with its very narrow leaves and small white flowers, is quite distinctive. It was named for Professor P. H. Lecomte (1856–1934), a former director of the Laboratoire de Phanérogamie, Paris.

Angraecum letouzeyi Bosser

Plant very small, stems not more than 4 cm high, with verrucose roots from the base and few leaves

Angraecum lecomtei. J. Hermans

near the top. Leaves 4–5, erect, cylindric, and very narrow, pointed at the apex, 6–10 cm long, 1–1.2 mm in diameter. Inflorescence arising below the leaves, single-flowered; peduncle covered entirely by 3 or 4 obtuse sheaths; bract similar to these sheaths, 4–5 mm long; pedicel and ovary 3–4 cm long. Flowers white, small; dorsal sepal lanceolate, tapering from the base to the tip, 14–15 mm long, 2.8 mm wide; lateral sepals spreading, asymmetric at the base, keeled on the back, 15–17 mm long, 3 mm wide; petals narrowly lanceolate, acute, 13–14 mm long, 1.5–1.7 mm wide; lip concave, oval-lanceolate, without a callus on the surface, attenuate-acute at the apex, 15–16 mm long, 7 mm wide; spur slender, 6–7 cm long.

Epiphyte in shady forests; 900–1200 m; flowering in October and February.

Madagascar (on the eastern border of the central highlands).

The terete leaves and elongated tepals indicate that this species may be close to *Angraecum teretifolium* (section *Arachnangraecum*), but the small plant with peduncle covered by sheaths seems to place it in section *Perrierangraecum*. It was dedicated to the late Réné Letouzey, specialist on the flora of Cameroon and a colleague of Bosser in Paris for many years. This species is only known from 2 collections.

Angraecum litorale Schlechter

Plants small, up to 7 cm high, stem up to 2.5 cm long, 5 mm in diameter; roots slender, glabrous, not warty. Leaves 5 or 6, erect or spreading, ligulate, unequally and obtusely bilobed at the apex, 4–5.5 cm long, 5–8 mm wide. Inflorescence lateral, single-flowered; peduncle covered with 2 or 3 compressed sheaths, up to 1.3 cm long; bract oval, apiculate, much shorter than the pedicellate ovary which is triquetrous, ca. 3 cm long. Flower yellowish; sepals narrowly lanceolate, acute, ca. 2.7 cm long; lateral sepals oblique, with a thickened keel on the outer surface; petals slightly smaller and narrower than the sepals, oblique, up to 2.4 cm long; lip elliptic, long-acuminate, ca. 2.8 cm long, 1.2 cm wide; spur filiform, S-shaped, ca. 9 cm long.

Epiphyte in coastal forests; at and near sea level; flowering in October.

Madagascar (eastern region).

Said to be similar to *Angraecum rutenbergianum* but growing at a lower altitude and in a different habitat.

Angraecum obesum H. Perrier

Plant strong-growing, stem 40–50 cm tall, ca. 1 cm in diameter; roots verrucose, adhering to the stem in larger plants. Leaves 14–16 in 2 rows, spreading, ligulate, unequally bilobed at the apex, 10–12 cm long, 1.3–1.5 cm wide. Inflorescence piercing the sheath of the lower leaves, single-flowered; peduncle short, covered entirely with sheaths, the uppermost larger than the lower ones, 6–7 mm long; bract obtuse, 1 cm long; pedicellate ovary speckled with black, 1.2–1.3 cm long. Flower variable in size, sepals and petals rather thick and creamy white, lip thinner and pure white; sepals lanceolate, obtuse, dorsal sepal upright or slightly reflexed, lateral sepals spreading forwards on either side of the lip, 3–3.5 cm long, 5–8 mm wide; petals similar to the dorsal sepal but smaller, reflexed

Angraecum obesum. J. Hermans

in the upper half, 2–3 cm long, 3–6 mm wide; lip concave and broadly oval, the sides folded up at the base on either side of the column and enclosing a distinct hollow in front of the spur entrance, flattened out in front, apiculate, 2–3.4 cm long, 1.4–2 cm wide; spur cylindric, gradually narrowing towards the apex, 5–10 cm long.

Epiphyte on moss- and lichen-covered trees in forests and on rocks; 1200–1500 m; flowering January to March.

Madagascar (central region).

Angraecum oblongifolium Toilliez-Genoud & Bosser

Plant pendent, stem simple or branching, up to 20 cm long, 4 mm in diameter. Leaves many, in 2 rows, spaced close together, oblong, unequally bilobed at the apex, with rounded lobes, cordate and amplexicaul, 1.5–2 cm long, 5–10 mm wide. Inflorescence axillary, single-flowered; peduncle covered with 3 sheaths, 2–5 mm long; bracts scarious, 3–3.5 mm long; pedicellate ovary 2–2.5 cm long. Flower white, fleshy; sepals lanceolate or ovate-lanceolate, 14–17 mm long, 6–7 mm wide, lateral sepals slightly longer than dorsal sepal; petals lanceolate or ovate-lanceolate, 13–15 mm long, 5 mm wide; lip concave, broadly triangular, cordate, apiculate, 12–13 mm long, 11–12 mm wide; spur slender, gradually attenuate, 6–7 cm long.

Epiphyte in humid, highland forest.

Madagascar.

This species is difficult to place in any of the sections currently recognised and for the time being we have followed Garay (1973) in placing it here.

Angraecum palmicolum Bosser

Plants very small, stems not more than 4 cm high, with smooth roots from the base and a fan of leaves near the top. Leaves 3–6, erect, linear-cylindric, glaucous green and very narrow, pointed at the apex, with a narrow furrow along the upper surface, 3–4.5 cm long, 1 mm in diameter. Inflorescence arising below the leaves, single-flowered; peduncle 1–2 mm long, covered entirely by 2 or 3 obtuse sheaths; bract similar to these sheaths, 4–5 mm long; pedicel and ovary 1.8–2.5 cm long. Flowers with pale yellow-orange tepals, lip and spur white; dorsal sepal small, lanceolate, tapering from the base to the tip, obtuse or subacute, 12–15 mm long, 3–4 mm wide; lateral sepals spreading, asymmetric at the base, 12–18 mm long, 3.5–4.5 mm wide; petals narrowly lanceolate, acute, 11–14 mm long, 2.5–3 mm wide; lip concave, oval to suborbicular, without a callus on the surface, acute or apiculate at the apex, 11–16 mm long, 8–10 mm wide; spur slender, 10–11 cm long.

Epiphyte amongst lichens on the smooth trunks of the palm, *Chrysalidocarpus decipiens*; known from one collection, near a stream; 1300–1400 m; flowering in September.

Madagascar.

This species is rather similar to *Angraecum letouzeyi* but the glaucous foliage and smooth roots are quite different. The flower has a differently shaped lip with much longer spur.

Angraecum peyrotii Bosser

Plant with a short, robust stem 5–6 cm long, 4–5 mm in diameter, and with many smooth roots. Leaves 6–8, thick, semi-cylindric, concave on the upper surface, 10–12 cm long, 7–8 mm in diameter. Inflorescence single-flowered; peduncle thick, completely covered by thin sheaths, 1–2 cm long; bract similar to the sheaths but longer, 15–18 mm long, shorter than the ovary; ovary twisted, the angles winged, 3–3.5 cm long. Flower large, fleshy, sepals and petals pale green, lip white; sepals narrowly triangular, the laterals falcate and thickened along the midvein on the outer surface, 3.5–4.5 cm long, 5–8 mm wide; petals similar, spreading, a little smaller than the sepals; lip broadly elliptic, rounded at the base, acute, 3.5–4 cm long, 2–2.5 cm wide; spur filiform, 10–15 cm long.

Epiphyte in shady forest; ca. 1300–1500 m; flowering in September.

Madagascar.

Easily recognised by its semi-cylindric leaves; named in honour of Dr. Jean-Pierre Peyrot, a medical doctor in Madagascar, who was an amateur orchid enthusiast and discovered this plant while on a collecting trip with Bosser.

Angraecum pseudodidieri H. Perrier

Plant upright, 10–20 cm tall, 5–6 mm in diameter, with verrucose roots and 5 or 6 leaves in the apical part. Leaves thick, broadly linear, canaliculate above, almost equally bilobed at the apex, 6.5–8 cm long, 8–10 mm wide. Inflorescence axillary, single-flowered; peduncle entirely covered by dry, rigid sheaths, the upper 1 cm long and similar to the bract which is also 1 cm long; pedicellate ovary twisted, 1.5 cm long. Flower opaque, thick, yellowish sepals and petals and white lip; sepals lanceolate, attenuate from base to apex, 15 mm long, 8 mm wide; petals similar but narrower, 3.5 mm wide; lip almost flat, broadly oboval-cuspidate, 2.5 cm long, 1.8 cm wide; spur gradually narrowing from the 4-mm-wide mouth to the tip, 10–11 cm long.

Epiphyte on tree trunks in rain forest; ca. 1000 m; flowering in November.

Madagascar (Mount Ambre).

Angraecum peyrotii. J. Hermans

Angraecum rutenbergianum. J. Hermans

Angraecum rutenbergianum Kraenzlin

Plants with a very short stem or elongating with age, 4–12 cm long with greyish green leaves in the upper part and sinuous or flattened roots 2–3 mm wide which are sometimes verrucose. Leaves stiff and leathery, rather dull, ligulate, unequally bi-lobed at the apex, overlapping at the base, 2.5–6 cm long, 5–7 mm wide. Inflorescence piercing the leaf sheath, single-flowered; peduncle 5–10 mm long entirely covered with 3 or 4 sheaths; bract ca. 10 mm long; pedicellate ovary 2–3 cm long. Flowers pure white, or the sepals and petals pale greenish and lip white; sepals spreading, lanceolate, acute, 27–37 mm long, 6–6.5 mm wide; petals similar but smaller, 27–35 mm long, 3.5 mm wide; lip rhomboid-elliptic, attenuate towards the base and at the apiculate tip, 30–35 mm long, 17–18 mm wide at the middle; spur slender, curved, 11–14 cm long, sometimes shorter.

Epiphyte on trunks and branches and more often found on rocks amongst bushes or partly shaded in forest; 1500–2200 m; flowering between November and February.

Madagascar (widespread in the central regions) and Mauritius.

A very variable species, usually with shorter stems and thicker roots than *Angraecum dryadum* which also occupies a more shaded habitat; illustrated in Hillerman and Holst (1986), plate 38. Named in honour of the German plant collector and traveller, D. C. Rutenberg, who collected on the west coast of Madagascar and died there in 1878.

Angraecum sambiranoense Schlechter

Plant pendent with long slender stem to 35 cm long, 4 mm in diameter, with narrow, glabrous roots, and many leaves in the upper part. Leaves oblong-ligulate, spreading, unequally bilobed at the apex, leathery, 5–6 cm long, 1–1.3 cm wide at the middle. Inflorescence single-flowered; peduncle short, entirely covered with 2 or 3 folded sheaths, 7–10 mm long; bract apiculate, similar to the uppermost sheath; pedicellate ovary triquetrous, 25–28 mm long. Flower white, perianth spreading; sepals narrowly lanceolate, acute, 3 cm long, the laterals with a thickened keel on the outer surface; petals a little narrower and shorter than the sepals; lip lanceolate-acuminate, 3 cm long, 1 cm wide below the middle; spur 10–11 cm long, filiform, spirally twisted or undulate.

Epiphyte in forest; 700–800 m above sea level; flowering in February.

Madagascar (Sambirano valley).

Angraecum urschianum Toilliez-Genoud & Bosser

Plant very small, 2–3 cm tall, stem 3–3.5 mm in diameter, densely leafy; roots smooth, green, 1–1.5 mm in diameter. Leaves thick and fleshy with denticulate edges, punctate, folded along the midrib, unequally and obtusely bilobed, 8–23 mm long, 5–8 mm wide. Inflorescence axillary, single-flowered; peduncle short, about half covered with 3 or 4 sheaths, 6–9 mm long; bract short, ca. 3 mm long; pedicellate ovary 3.8 cm long. Flower small, pale yellowish green with a white lip; sepals lanceolate, 10–11 mm long, 3 mm wide, the laterals somewhat oblique; petals slightly shorter and narrower; lip broadly oval, triangular, widest in the lower third, 10–13 mm long, 7.5–9 mm wide; spur slender, filiform, 11–12 cm long.

Epiphyte in rain forest at moderate altitudes; flowering in September.

Madagascar (eastern region).

This species is dedicated to Eugene Ursch (1882–1962), a French collector and former Director of the Botanical and Zoological Garden at Tsimbazaza, Madagascar.

Angraecum urschianum. J. Hermans

Group 3. Small plants whose white flowers have a spur 3–5 cm long, at least twice as long as the lip.

Angraecum curvicalcar Schlechter

Plants small, with or without a short stem, 4–7 cm high; roots slender and smooth. Leaves 4 or 5, erect or spreading, linear, unequally bilobed at the apex, 3.5–6 cm long, 4–6 mm wide. Inflorescence single-flowered; peduncle ca. 3 mm long with 2 or 3 compressed sheaths; bract broadly ovate, apiculate, much shorter than the ovary; pedicellate ovary 2.5 cm long. Flowers white, spreading; sepals lanceolate-ovate, subacute, 13 mm long; petals obliquely oblong-ovate, nearly as long and wide as the sepals; lip widely rhomboid-suborbicular, concave at the base, 13 mm long, 12 mm wide; spur curved, S-shaped, slender, ca. 4 cm long.

Epiphyte amongst lichens; ca. 2000 m; flowering in January.

Madagascar (Mount Tsaratanana).

Angraecum longicaule Perrier

Plants usually small, stems 4–30 cm long and 3–4 mm in diameter. Leaves 5–12 in 2 rows near apex of stem, folded, narrowly linear, margins rough, 14–21 mm long, 2–3 mm wide. Inflorescence single-flowered; peduncle short, 3 mm long with 3 sheaths; bract thin, reddish, keeled on the back, 8 mm long; pedicel and ovary 3–5 cm long. Flower white, small; sepals oblong, narrowed from the middle towards the acute apex, dorsal sepal 12–15(–21) mm long, 6.5 mm wide, lateral sepals up to 22 mm long, 6 mm wide; petals similar to the lateral sepals, acute, up to 19.5 mm long, 4 mm wide; lip suborbicular, apiculate, 15–25 mm long, 14–18 mm wide; spur slender, filiform, 4–5 cm long.

Usually lithophytic or terrestrial amongst lichens, rock and vegetation debris, in ericaceous scrub; 500–2200 m; flowering in November-December and March.

Madagascar (mountain tops in the north-east).

Angraecum rigidifolium H. Perrier

Plants small, up to 14 cm high, stems flattened and 4–5 mm wide. Leaves in 2 rows, spreading, bent away from the stem, terminal lobes equal, 16–20 mm long, 4–5 mm wide. Inflorescences usually several, scattered along the stem, single-flowered; peduncle short, entirely covered with 4 wide, flattened sheaths; bract thin, 5 mm long; pedicellate ovary 12 mm long. Flowers white; sepals lanceolate, tapering from the base to the tip, dorsal sepal 14 mm long, 2.2 mm wide, lateral sepals falcate, 16 mm long, 3 mm wide; petals linear, 13 mm long; lip oval-lanceolate, thickened towards the pointed tip, 15 mm long, 6 mm wide at the middle; spur slender and curved, 3–3.3 cm long.

Epiphyte on mossy tree trunks; ca. 1300 m; flowering in February.

Madagascar (central regions).

Group 4. Plants with longer stems and small white flowers each with a spur less than 2 cm long.

Angraecum ambrense H. Perrier

Plant upright or pendent with stems up to 30 cm long, usually shorter, 3–4 mm wide. Leaves in 2 rows, linear, dark green, 5 cm long, 3–3.5 mm wide. Inflorescences usually several, each single-flowered; peduncle piercing the axillary sheaths, 1–2 cm long, covered with 3–4 sheaths and a short bract; pedicellate ovary 2 cm long. Flowers white; sepals narrowly lanceolate, subacute, 12 mm long, 3–4 mm wide; petals similar to sepals but more obtuse; lip narrow at the base, not surrounding the column, somewhat pandurate, 4 mm wide above the base, then narrowing and broadening again to 6 mm wide in the apical third, 12 mm long; spur cylindric, 12 mm long.

Epiphyte on moss- and lichen-covered trees; ca. 1200 m; flowering in September.

Madagascar (Mount Ambre).

Angraecum compressicaule H. Perrier

Plants with upright, rigid stems, 10–20 cm long, flattened, 3–4 mm in diameter, covered with compressed leaf bases. Leaves 5–10 in 2 rows near apex of stem, stiff, upright or arching away from the stem, linear, unequally bilobed at the apex, 2–3 cm long, 2–3 mm wide. Inflorescence axillary, single-flowered; peduncle short, covered with 3 or 4 compressed sheaths; bract 5–6 mm long; pedicellate ovary ca. 2 cm long. Flowers white; sepals lanceolate, gradually tapering from base to tip, dorsal sepal 11–13 mm long, ca. 5 mm wide, lateral sepals 13–15 mm long, 3–4 mm wide; petals similar to the sepals but wider, ca. 12 mm long, 5–5.6 mm wide; lip lanceolate from a narrow base, not surrounding the base of the column, expanded above to 8–10 mm wide, then narrowed and thickened at the apex, 15–20 mm long; spur cylindric, curved or straight, shorter than the lip, 12–15 mm long.

Epiphyte or lithophyte amongst mosses and lichens; ca. 1400 m; flowering in February.

Madagascar (central regions).

Angraecum drouhardii H. Perrier

Plants erect, 2–7 cm high, with thickened stems 6–8 mm in diameter, covered in wrinkled sheaths, bearing 5–12 leaves in 2 rows at the apex. Leaves rigid, oblong, unequally bilobed at the apex, 13–16 mm long, 5–6 mm wide. Inflorescence piercing the sheath of the leaf above it, single-flowered; peduncle entirely covered with 2 or 3 sheaths, 6–10 mm long; bract similar to the sheaths, 5 mm long; pedicellate ovary 22 mm long. Flowers pure white; sepals and petals similar, lanceolate, acute, 15 mm long, 3–4 mm wide; lip wide at the base, surrounding the column, nearly rhomboid, subacute, 16–17 mm long, 10–12 mm wide in the middle; spur slender, 18 mm long.

Epiphyte amongst mosses on tree trunks, ca. 1200 m; flowering in August.

Madagascar (Mount Ambre).

Perrier named this species after his father-in-law, Eugene-Jean Drouhard (1874–1945), who collected plants, insects, and fossils in Madagascar, particularly on Ibity Massif.

Species from Réunion and Mauritius

Angraecum borbonicum Bosser

Plant small, erect, with stem 2–5 cm long. Leaves 4–8, erect, rigid, dark green, oblong or narrowly oblong, V-shaped in cross section at the base, flat above, unequally bilobed at the round apex, 2–12 cm long, 7–15 mm wide. Inflorescence single-flowered; peduncle covered with 2 or 3 oval sheaths, 7–8 mm long, bract similar. Flower white, fleshy, rarely opening fully, or opening only for a very short time, self-pollinating; sepals and petals narrowly oval, acuminate, 2–2.3 cm long, 5–6 mm wide; lip broadly oval, apex acuminate, 2–2.3 cm long, 1.5–2 cm wide; spur slender, 6.5–7.5 cm long; fruit conspicuous and long-lasting on the plant, erect, obovoid, 3-ribbed, 4–5 cm long, 1.5–2 cm in diameter.

Epiphyte in rain forests, and also at the base of trunks of *Philippia* bushes; 700–2000 m above sea level; flowering in October.

Réunion.

This species is often found in fruit because the flowers appear to be self-pollinating. The 3-angled, erect capsules are characteristic. It has been known, in the past, as *Angraecum triquetrum* but that name has been transferred to *Jumellea* by several authors (Bosser 1988).

Angraecum cucullatum Thouars

Plants small, erect, 1–5 cm high, with thickened stems covered with old leaf bases, bearing 2–5 leaves at the apex. Leaves rigid, ligulate, V-shaped in cross section, unequally bilobed at the apex, 2–6 cm long, 5–9 mm wide. Inflorescence single-flowered; peduncle bare, slender, 3–4 cm long; pedicel 5 mm long. Flowers white; sepals linear-lanceolate, acuminate, 8–10 mm long, 3 mm wide at the base; petals similar but smaller, 7–8 mm long, 1.5–2 mm wide; lip broadly ovate or almost orbicular, cucullate, funnel-shaped, 9–15 mm long, 7–10 mm wide; spur funnel-shaped from a wide mouth, blunt at the apex, 8–12 mm long.

Epiphyte, on old tree trunks in dense forest, usually 50–100 cm above the ground; flowering December to March.

Mauritius and Réunion (some doubtful early records).

Angraecum liliodorum Frappier ex Cordemoy

Syn. *Jumellea liliodora* (Frappier ex Cordemoy) Schlechter

Plants erect, leafy in the upper part and with brown leaf sheaths towards the base, up to 10 cm long, 1 cm in diameter. Leaves in 2 rows, leathery, dark green, oblong-elliptic, narrowing slightly towards both ends, unequally bilobed at the apex, 5–6 cm long, 12–15 mm wide. Inflorescence axillary, single-flowered; pedicel with ovary twisted and 3-angled. Flowers white, lily-scented 5–6 cm in diameter; sepals and petals similar, lanceolate-linear, acute, the sepals keeled on the back along the midline, the petals slightly smaller and not keeled; lip large, cordate, acuminate or acute, ca. 3 cm long and wide; spur slender, gradually attenuate towards the tip, 5–6 cm long.

Epiphyte or on rocks in shady forests; sea level to 500 m; flowering May to July in Réunion, February to March in Mauritius.

Réunion and Mauritius.

Angraecum striatum. From Thouars 1822, t. 72.

SECTION *HADRANGIS*

In this section are medium-sized plants with short stems bearing tough, leathery leaves in a short fan. The racemose inflorescences are several-flowered. The fleshy, white flowers sometimes have a green column. The short spur is conical or saccate and emerges from a wide mouth.

Three species are known in Réunion, one of which (*Angraecum cadetii*) is also recorded from Mauritius.

Angraecum bracteosum Balfour f. & S. Moore

Plants upright, stems few to 30 cm long, closely covered with leaf bases and bearing thick greyish roots near the base, 5–7 mm in diameter. Leaves in 2 rows closely overlapping on the stem, dark green with very distinct venation, flexible, ligulate, unequally bilobed at the apex, 10–30 cm long, 4–6 cm wide. Inflorescence a tight, one-sided, upright raceme, axillary or arising between the leaf bases, held very close to the stem, bearing several flowers very closely together; bracts large and conspicuous, longer than the ovary. Flowers white, fleshy, 2–2.5 cm in diameter; sepals lanceolate, acute, slightly wider at the base than the petals; lip fleshy, saccate at the base, without a conspicuous spur; column green.

Epiphyte, widespread and fairly common locally where suitable habitats exist; 1000–1500 m; flowering January to March.

Réunion.

Angraecum cadetii Bosser

Plants robust, sometimes confused with *Angraecum bracteosum*; stems 2–15 cm long, ca. 1 cm in diameter, rooting from the base. Leaves in 2 rows, flexible, somewhat folded along the midrib, dark green above, paler below, venation prominent, 10–27 cm long, 1.5–4 cm wide. Inflorescences axillary, spreading or pendent, 5–15 cm long, bearing 2–5 flowers spaced 1–1.5 cm apart; bracts broadly oval, sheathing the base of the ovary, 8–15 mm long; ovary cylindric, 1–1.2 cm long. Flowers fleshy, pale green at first, becoming more or less white in the apical parts as they age; sepals and petals ovate, pointed at the apex, the lateral sepals keeled on the outer surface, the petals slightly smaller than sepals, 10–15 mm long, 7–9 mm wide; lip with a conical sac at the base, the limb curved and with rounded side lobes slightly developed, ca. 10 mm long and 8 mm deep.

Epiphyte in humid forests; 300–1000 m; flowering between January and March.

Réunion (on the windward side of the island) and Mauritius (in the forests in the centre of the island).

Recognised as a distinct species relatively recently and described in 1987 in honour of L. J. T. Cadet (1937–1987), a French botanist who made valuable studies of the orchids in his native Réunion.

Angraecum striatum Thouars

Plants upright, stems few to 30 cm long, closely covered with leaf bases and bearing thick greyish roots near the base, 5–7 mm in diameter. Leaves in 2 rows closely overlapping on the stem, dark green with very distinct venation, stiff, ligulate, slightly unequally bilobed at the apex, 10–25 cm long, 4–5 cm wide. Inflorescence in one-sided racemes, axillary or arising between the leaf bases, upright, slightly shorter than or as long as the leaves, bearing several widely spaced flowers; bracts conspicuous, shorter than the ovary. Flowers 5–7, white, fleshy, 1–1.5 cm in diameter; sepals lanceolate, acute, slightly wider at the base than the petals; lip fleshy, concave, with a conspicuous conical spur to 1 cm long; column green.

Epiphyte in forests, still relatively common in certain areas; 1000–1500 m; flowering in February and sometimes at other times of the year.

Réunion.

SECTION *ARACHNANGRAECUM*

The plants in this section have long stems bearing alternate leaves in 2 rows. Inflorescences arise above the leaf axil, on a long slender peduncle which is persistent after the flowers have fallen, and are usually single-flowered, occasionally 2- to 4-flowered. The medium-sized to large flowers have a large white lip that is sometimes held on the upper side of the flower; it is more or less orbicular in shape, acuminate at the apex, and has a long spur at the base.

Nineteen species are currently recognised in this section, the majority of them in Madagascar. They are presented here in 3 groups:

Group 1. Four African species with large flowers and the white lip on the lower side of the flower.

Group 2. Seven species from Madagascar and one from Africa (*Angraecum conchiferum*) with flat leaves and flowers of various sizes,

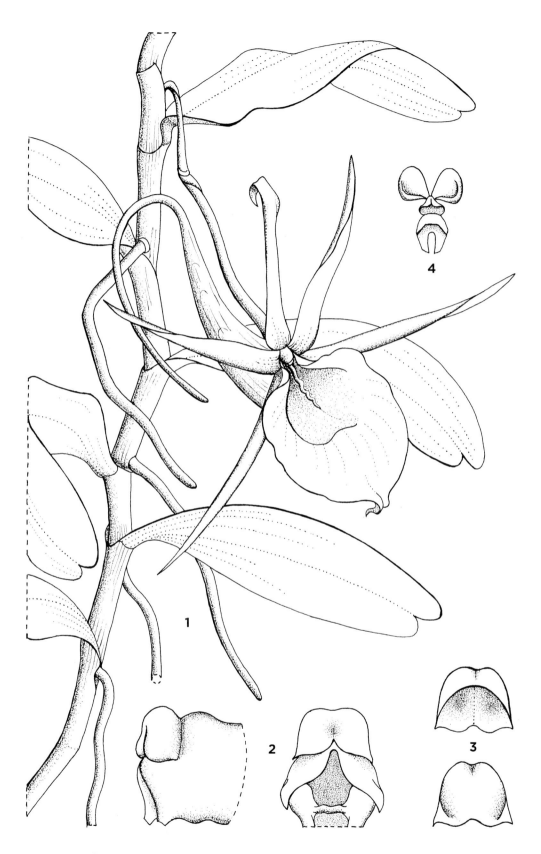

Angraecum infundibulare. 1: Habit. 2: Column. 3: Anther-cap. 4: Pollinarium.
From Cribb 1989, fig. 118. S. Hillier.

and the white lip always on the upper side of the flower.

Group 3. Seven species in Madagascar and the Comoro Islands (*Angraecum scottianum*) with very narrow leaves and the white lip usually on the upper side of the flower.

Group 1. Four species have long stems, leaves more than 1.5 cm wide, and large flowers whose white lip is on the lower side of the flower.

Angraecum birrimense Rolfe

Plants large with long stems that are upright at first and then pendent, up to 2 m long, oval in cross section and bearing numerous aerial roots, opposite the leaves. Leaves in 2 rows, thickened and rather leathery, 2–3 cm apart, elliptic, obtuse, unequally lobed at the apex, with rounded lobes, 7–14 cm long, 2–3.5 cm wide. Inflorescence single-flowered, or 2 flowers produced successively; peduncle 3–4 cm long; pedicel and ovary 3–3.5 cm long. Flowers large, greenish yellow with a white lip; sepals and petals lanceolate, acute, often with the margins reflexed, 3.5–5.5 cm long, 3–8 mm wide; lip rhomboid-orbicular, with a short apiculus, 2.5–3.5 cm wide; spur funnel-shaped from the base of the lip, then abruptly narrowed at the middle, and finally elongated and slightly swollen to the subacute apex, in total 3.5–4.7 cm long.

Epiphyte in humid forests, often in well shaded positions rather low down on trees near watercourses; flowering between May and September.

Sierra Leone eastwards to Cameroon.

Named after the place called Birrim, in Ghana.

Angraecum eichlerianum Kraenzlin

Plants with long stems up to 5 m long and numerous aerial roots opposite the leaves. Leaves in 2 rows, well spaced, oblong to elliptic, unequally

Angraecum birrimense. J. Hermans

Angraecum eichlerianum. J. Hermans

bilobed at the apex, 6–10 cm long, 1.5–4 cm wide. Inflorescence axillary, 10–20 cm long, 1- to 4-flowered. Flowers with green perianth and a white lip which is green in the centre, at the base; sepals and petals oblong to narrowly elliptic, acute, 3.5–6 cm long, 4–12 mm wide; lip broadly obovate or orbicular, the rounded sides upturned and projecting forward, apiculate, 2.5–5 cm long, 4–5 cm wide; spur funnel-shaped at first, then restricted at the middle and finally widely cylindrical, ca. 3.5 cm long.

Epiphyte in undisturbed forests.

Nigeria, Cameroon, Gabon, D.R. of Congo, Angola, and Mozambique.

Named in honour of the German botanist, A. W. Eichler.

var. *curvicalcaratum* Szlachetko & Olszewski

This varietal name has been proposed (2001) for specimens from Cameroon that have smaller flowers with a differently shaped spur which is bent through 90° at its narrowest part so that the apex points downward.

Also reported from Gabon; flowering June to August in Cameroon.

Angraecum infundibulare Lindley

Plants with long branching stems growing in clumps and bearing roots amongst the leaves. Stems bilaterally compressed, straight or branching, usually pendent with the apical part upturned, to 100 cm long but often shorter, 4–7 mm in diameter. Leaves in 2 rows, narrowly elliptic or oblanceolate, unequally bilobed at the apex, with rounded lobes, 10–22 cm long, 1.5–4 cm wide, twisted at the base and articulated to the leaf sheath. Inflorescences protruding through the sheath above the leaf axil, single-flowered; peduncle 4–7 cm long, bract elliptic-ovate, obtuse, 6 mm long; pedicel and ovary 5.5–6.5 cm long. Flower pale green with a large white lip, pale yellow inside; sepals linear-lanceolate, acuminate, margins recurved, 6–8.5 cm long, less than 1 cm wide; petals linear, slightly shorter than sepals; lip concave, ovate to oblong-ovate, with a long apiculus to 12 mm long, in total 6–8

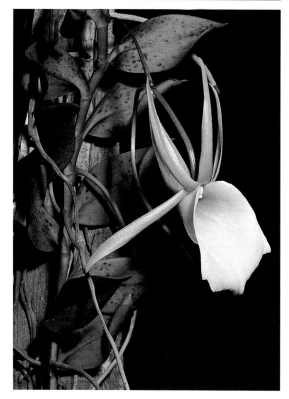

Angraecum infundibulare. B. Campbell

cm long, 5–5.5 cm wide; spur funnel-shaped at the base, curved, S-shaped and finally pendent, 16–20 cm long.

Epiphyte in warm forests where humidity is high; 1150–1300 m; flowering in June or July.

Nigeria, Príncipe, Cameroon, D.R. of Congo, Rwanda, Uganda, Kenya, and Ethiopia.

This species possesses the largest flowers amongst the African species of *Angraecum*.

Angraecum spectabile Summerhayes

Plants erect with slightly flattened stems, 24–30 cm long, 5–6 mm in diameter; roots 2.5 mm in diameter. Leaves distichous, elliptic, unequally bilobed at the apex, with rounded lobes, 7–10 cm long, 2–3 cm wide, twisted at the base and articulated to the leaf sheath. Inflorescence up to 10 cm long, single-flowered; bract ovate, obtuse, 5–6 mm long; pedicel and ovary 3–5 cm long. Flower pale green, shaded with white; sepals narrowly lanceolate, acuminate, 4.3–5 cm long, ca. 1 cm wide; petals obliquely lanceolate, acuminate, 4–4.3 cm long,

6 mm wide; lip concave, broadly obovate or obcordate, obscurely 3-lobed at the apex, an apiculus 2.5 mm long, side lobes rounded, lip in total 3.2–3.4 cm long, 4.2–4.4 cm wide; spur funnel-shaped at the base, geniculate in the middle, cylindrical in the apical part, ca. 6 cm long, 2 cm wide across the mouth.

Epiphyte and amongst rocks; 1150–1200 m; flowering in July.

Tanzania (near the town of Bukoba by Lake Victoria).

This species is close to *Angraecum eichlerianum* but has shorter and broader leaves, shorter peduncles and a broader lip with a much longer spur.

Group 2. The 'typical members' of this section have shorter stems and narrower leaves. The flowers are held on long peduncles and the round or shell-shaped lip is held on the upper side of the flower. The sepals and petals are long and narrow and may be tinted with green, yellow, brown or pink.

One species occurs in eastern Africa (and is treated first below) and the remainder in Madagascar, the Comoro Islands, and Réunion.

Angraecum conchiferum Lindley

Plants are straggling epiphytes, easily recognised by the flattened roots which have a rough, warty surface, and branching stems. Stems often somewhat flattened, up to 30 cm long but usually shorter, 3–5 mm wide, surrounded by the overlapping, black-dotted leaf sheaths. Leaves in 2 rows near apex of stem, linear, unequally bilobed at the apex, often twisted at the base so that they lie in one plane, 3–7 cm long, 5–7 mm wide. Inflorescences slender, arising opposite a leaf, 1- or 2-flowered. Flowers 4–6 cm in diameter, with a white lip and pale yellowish-green sepals and petals; dorsal sepal longer and lateral sepals wider and longer than petals, all linear-lanceolate, up to 3 cm long; lip large, orbicular with a central keel and an elongated apex, up to 12 mm wide, usually held

Angraecum conchiferum. J. Stewart

on the upper side of the flower; spur curved, 3–5 cm long.

Epiphyte in forests on isolated hills and mountains; 800–2400 m; flowering September to January.

Kenya, Tanzania, Malawi, Mozambique, Zimbabwe, and South Africa (Limpopo, KwaZulu-Natal, and Cape Province).

Angraecum ampullaceum Bosser

Plant upright with rigid stems, up to 60 cm high and ca. 8 mm in diameter. Leaves numerous, in 2 rows, contracted and folded towards the base, above a conspicuous articulation line, unequally bilobed at the apex, with rounded lobes, 8–10 cm long, 2–2.5 cm wide. Inflorescences arising above the leaf axil, 1- to 3-flowered; bract large, attenuate, ca. 12 mm long; pedicellate ovary 3.5 cm long. Flowers white; sepals narrowly lanceolate, acuminate, the acumen taking up the apical third, 3.8–4 cm long, 6–6.5 mm wide; petals a little shorter than the sepals, narrower and slightly oblique at the base; lip triangular, cordate, shortly acuminate, 2.5–3 cm long, 1.8 cm wide; spur 11–13 cm long, gradually tapering from the 5 mm wide mouth.

Epiphyte on trunks of trees; ca. 700–1400 m; flowering in November.

Madagascar (eastern and central regions).

A unique and curious feature that is only visible on the lower part of the stem, after the leaves have fallen, is the development of a resin-containing outgrowth in the axil of the peduncle. The specific epithet refers to these flask-like structures.

Angraecum arachnites Schlechter

Plant erect or ascending, up to 15 cm long; roots slender, flattened where they adhere to the substrate; stems simple or sparsely branched, densely covered with leaf bases and sheaths, ca. 2 mm in diameter. Leaves spreading, oblong-ligulate or ligulate, unequally and obtusely bilobed at the apex, margins recurved and minutely serrulate, 6–20 mm long, 2–3.5 mm wide, thin but leathery. Inflorescence axillary, longer than the leaves,

Angraecum arachnites. J. Hermans

single-flowered; bract ovate, apiculate; pedicel and ovary ca. 1.3 cm long. Flower erect, average for the section, white, but pinkish brown towards the extremities of all parts; sepals narrowly lanceolate at the base then very elongated-acuminate, ca. 4.5 cm long; lateral sepals oblique; petals shorter and narrower than the sepals, lanceolate-linear at the base, ca. 3.5 cm long; lip suborbicular, acuminate, 1.5 cm long including the acumen, 7–8 mm wide near the base; spur slender, filiform, ca. 11 cm long.

Epiphyte, widespread in evergreen, humid forests; 1380–1500 m; flowering between November and May.

Madagascar (central regions).

This is the smallest of the group of species confused with *Angraecum germinyanum* in the past. It has much smaller leaves than the other species and the flowers have a smaller, narrower lip.

Angraecum conchoglossum. J. Hermans

Angraecum germinyanum. J. Hermans

Angraecum conchoglossum Schlechter

Plants erect, much taller than 10 cm high; stem slightly compressed, densely covered with leaves, ca. 4 mm wide. Leaves spreading, oblong-ligulate, unequally and obtusely bilobed, 1.8–2.5 cm long, 6–7 mm wide. Inflorescences erect, single-flowered; bract oblong, obtuse; pedicel and ovary 1.8 cm long. Flower white; sepals spreading, narrowly lanceolate at the base and then very acuminate, ca. 4 cm long; lateral sepals similar, oblique; petals oblique at the base, narrowly lanceolate, elongate-acuminate, ca. 3.5 cm long; lip orbicular or shell-shaped, ca. 1.7 cm long and wide with an elongate acumen ca. 1.5 cm long; spur filiform below a wide mouth, ca. 11.5 cm long.

Epiphyte in evergreen forest; ca. 1000–1600 m; flowering mainly September to May.

Madagascar (widespread) and Réunion.

This plant has been widely confused with the Comorean *Angraecum germinyanum*. This is a smaller plant with a round lip that is as wide as it is long excluding the acumen at its centre. The flowers are often strongly tinged with pink or orange-brown.

Angraecum germinyanum Hooker f.

Plant scandent or pendent, usually upright in the apical part, stems slender, 30–50 cm long or longer, leafy in the upper part and bearing rather few fine, wiry roots. Leaves bright green, shiny, linear-oblong, with cordate lobes clasping the stem at the base, unequally bilobed at the apex, 5–8 cm long, 7–10 mm wide, or linear-ligulate, not stem-clasping, with a rounded, bilobed apex. Inflorescence arising opposite a leaf, single-flowered; peduncle slender, with several sheaths at the base; bract acute, very small; pedicellate ovary ca. 3 cm long. Flower white; sepals linear from a narrowly lanceolate base with a long filiform tip, 6–8 cm long, 3–4 mm wide; lateral sepals longer than dorsal sepal, curved away from the lip and pendent; petals similar but shorter, narrower than sepals, also curved; lip concave, quadrate with rounded angles, with a long acumen ca. 2.5 cm long, wider than long, 2–3 cm long, 2.5–3.5 cm wide; spur slender and curved, 10–15 cm long.

Epiphyte in humid forests; ca. 1000–2000 m; flowering at various times.

Comoro Islands.

Plants with different leaf forms have been noticed in the wild; in cultivation the longer, narrower leaves may appear on new growths while the older parts of the plants bear the shorter, ligulate leaves near the base of the stems. First discovered by Léon Humblot who collected plants for the orchid establishment of Sander and named by Sir Joseph Hooker, at F. Sander's request, in honour of Count Adrien de Germiny who had one of the best orchid collections in France at that time. This species has been confused by both Perrier (1941) and Garay (1973) with *Angraecum ramosum* which is quite different and is now placed in section *Pseudojumellea*.

Group 3. Seven species in Madagascar and one in the Comoro Islands (*Angraecum scottianum*) have very narrow leaves, some subcylindric or terete, all less than 3 mm wide. The flowers have a white lip that is usually held on the upper side of the flower.

Angraecum danguyanum H. Perrier

Plant with pendent, slender stems, 15–20 cm long, ca. 1 mm in diameter, bearing 12–14 leaves towards the apex. Leaves linear, almost semi-cylindric, recurved, 3.5–5 cm long, 1–1.2 mm wide. Inflorescence piercing the sheath of a leaf, single-flowered; bract tubular, obtuse, 2 mm long; pedicel and ovary 3–3.2 cm long. Flower white; dorsal sepal elliptic, apiculate, 15 mm long, 6 mm wide; lateral sepals falcate, longer and wider than the dorsal sepal; petals narrowly falcate, pointed, 11 mm long, 2.5 mm wide; lip broadly ovate, obtuse, 15 mm long, 12 mm wide; spur filiform from a narrow mouth, 6–7 cm long.

Epiphyte on the trunks of trees; ca. 700 m; flowering in February.

Madagascar.

Angraecum danguyanum. J. Hermans

Angraecum linearifolium. J. Hermans

Angraecum linearifolium. J. Hermans

Named in honour of Paul Danguy (1862–1942), who spent all his working life at the Muséum national d'Histoire naturelle in Paris, even in retirement. From 1909 to 1928 he curated the collections from Madagascar.

Angraecum linearifolium Garay

Plants with long slender stems up to 30 cm long and 2 mm in diameter. Leaves well spaced along the stem, ca. 1.2 cm apart, linear, perfectly cylindric with a narrow furrow on the upper side, 5–11 cm long, ca. 1 mm in diameter. Inflorescence single-flowered; bract broadly oval, 1.5–3 mm long; pedicel and ovary 2 cm long. Flower white, sepals and petals tinged with pink or brown; sepals narrowly lanceolate at the base then acute-filiform in the upper two thirds, dorsal sepal 2–4 cm long, 4 mm wide; lateral sepals longer and narrower than dorsal sepal; petals much smaller, up to 7–25 mm long, 3 mm wide; lip concave, almost circular, long

acuminate, basal part 8–12 mm long, with a conspicuous longitudinal keel on its surface, acumen ca. 15 mm long; spur pinkish brown, filiform, 9–10 cm long.

Epiphyte in shady forests at medium altitudes; 900–2000 m; flowering between October and December, and also at other times of the year.

Madagascar.

Sometimes confused with *Angraecum teretifolium*, but in *A. linearifolium* the leaves are thinner, well spaced along the stem, and the flower has a conspicuous central keel on the surface of the lip.

Angraecum mirabile Schlechter

Plants erect with many leaves on round rigid stems up to 15 cm high, 3 mm in diameter. Leaves spreading, rigid, narrowly linear, margins incurved, appearing terete, subulate, 4–5 cm long, 2.5 mm wide when spread. Inflorescence single-flowered; bract ovate, acuminate; pedicel and ovary 2 cm long. Flower medium-sized for the genus, snowy white, glabrous; sepals spreading, lanceolate at the base then becoming filiform, ca. 5 cm long; lateral sepals similar, oblique; petals spreading, oblique at the base, linear-lanceolate, filiform, ca. 3.5 cm long; lip shell-shaped or ovate-acuminate, concave, with a longitudinal keel along the centre, ca. 1.3 cm long; spur slender 11–12 cm long.

Madagascar.

The description given above is a shortened translation from the original as the type specimen no longer exists. No other specimens whose characters precisely match those in the description have yet been discovered. The collector, Laggiara, is known to have collected in the north-east of Madagascar including Île Sainte Marie in 1911 and 1913.

Angraecum popowii Braem

Plant erect, stems to 15 cm long, covered in old leaf bases. Leaves spaced close together at the apex of the stem, forming a fan, nearly terete, with a distinct groove along the upper surface, 8.5 cm long, 2 mm in diameter. Inflorescences axillary, usually several, each single-flowered; peduncle slender, 5–6 cm long, sheathed at the base; bract amplexicaul, ovate, apiculate, 7–8 mm long; pedicel and ovary 4 cm long. Flowers pale yellowish green with a white lip; sepals linear-triangular, acuminate, 3 cm long, 4–5 mm wide; petals shorter and narrower, 2.4 cm long, 4 mm wide; lip triangular, acute, with an indication of rounded side lobes at the base, 3.2 cm long, 1.4 cm wide at the base, margins slightly recurved in the apical two thirds; spur slender, 14 cm long.

Epiphyte and lithophyte in a wide area of the highlands, often in *Uapaca* woodlands; 1200–1650 m; recorded in flower at various times of the year.

Madagascar.

Originally described from a plant imported into Germany with a collection of *Jumellea teretifolia* by the nurseryman N. Popow after whom it was named. It seems to be very close to *Angraecum teretifolium* and may prove to be a form of that species when more material has been studied.

Angraecum popowii, growing in lichen forest, central Madagascar. J. Hermans

Angraecum popowii. J. Hermans

Angraecum pseudofilicornu. J. Hermans

Angraecum scottianum. J. Hermans

Angraecum pseudofilicornu H. Perrier

Plants growing in tufts with several slender stems, 10–20(–50) cm long, upright when young, becoming longer, pendent and straggling with age but upturned at the apex; roots fine, ca. 1 mm in diameter, verrucose, mostly near the base of the stems. Leaves 8–30, widely spaced, narrow, almost terete with a shallow groove on the upper surface, almost cylindric below, unequally bilobed at the apex, 3–8 cm long, ca. 3–4 mm in diameter. Inflorescence axillary, on the upper part of the stem, 1- to 3-flowered; peduncle 3–4 cm long, thickened towards the top so that at the point from which the flowers are borne it is twice as thick as near the base; bracts 6 mm long; pedicel and ovary 1–2 cm long, twisted so that the lip is held on the upper side of the flower. Flowers pinkish brown with a white lip and brownish spur; sepals ligulate, acute, 1.8–2.5 cm long, 4 mm wide at the base, dorsal sepal somewhat reflexed, lateral sepals spreading; petals

slightly shorter and narrower than the sepals; lip concave, broadly oblong, wider than long, shortly apiculate, 1.8–2.4 cm long, 2.5–3.2 cm wide; spur flattened and narrowed below the mouth, filiform, 12–15 cm long.

Epiphyte on tree trunks in humid forests; ca. 1000 m; flowering in November.

Madagascar (Mount Ambre).

Very similar to *Angraecum scottianum* but smaller in most respects.

Angraecum scottianum Reichenbach f.

Plants growing in tufts with several stems, upright when young becoming pendent and straggling with age but upturned at the apex; roots wiry, verrucose, mostly arising near the base of the stems. Leaves 8–30, narrow, terete, almost cylindric, subulate, on the apical part of the stem, 6–10 cm long, ca. 3–5 mm in diameter. Inflorescence axillary on the upper part of the stems, bearing

1–4 flowers usually opening successively, or one flower accompanied by aborted buds; peduncle 7–10 cm long, thickened towards the top; bracts 5–6 mm long; pedicel and ovary 2.5–3.5 cm long, twisted so that the lip is held on the upper side of the flower. Flowers white, the tepals sometimes tinged with green and the spur tipped with brown; sepals ligulate, acute, 2.7–3 cm long, dorsal sepal somewhat reflexed, lateral sepals spreading forwards behind the lip and with reflexed margins; petals slightly shorter and narrower; lip broadly oblong, wider than long, shortly apiculate, 2.5–2.7 cm long, 3.5–4 cm wide; spur narrowed from the mouth, filiform, 12–15 cm long.

Epiphyte on tree trunks; 400–600 m; flowering January to March.

Comoro Islands.

Named in honour of R. Scott, an orchid enthusiast at Walthamstow, near London, who was the first to flower the species in Europe in 1878. It is recorded that he received plants from Sir John Kirk who visited the Comoro Islands several times in the 1860s.

Angraecum teretifolium. J. Hermans

Angraecum sterrophyllum Schlechter

Plant upright, with rigid stems, 8–15 cm high, 4–5 mm in diameter; roots densely verrucose. Leaves stiff, ensiform, 4–4.5 cm long. Inflorescence shorter than the leaves or only a little longer, 1- or 2-flowered; bract elliptic, pointed; pedicel and ovary 17–18 mm long. Flowers white, sometimes inverted; sepals narrowly lanceolate, subacute, 15 mm long; petals narrower than the sepals; lip concave, suborbicular, apiculate, wider than long, 12 mm long, 15 mm wide; spur dilated at the mouth, then filiform, 7–8 cm long.

Epiphyte in woodlands on west-facing slopes, often on *Uapaca* trees; ca. 1500 m above sea level; flowering October to January.

Madagascar (central regions).

Angraecum teretifolium Ridley

Plants with long slender stems, more or less pendent, up to 30 cm long and 3–3.5 mm in diameter. Leaves 5–10, grouped together at the apex of the stem with short internodes, linear, perfectly cylindric with a narrow furrow on the upper side, 6–15 cm long, ca. 1 mm in diameter. Inflorescence single-flowered; bract broadly oval, keeled on the back, 5–7 mm long; pedicel and ovary 2.5–3 cm long. Flower clear green or pale yellow with a white lip; sepals narrowly lanceolate-acute, 16–27 mm long, 3.5–4 mm wide; petals narrowly lanceolate-acute to linear, 14–23 mm long, 2–2.5 mm wide; lip spreading, slightly concave at the base, ovate, acute and rather attenuate towards the apex, 16–25 mm long, 10 mm wide at the base; spur filiform, pendent, 6–11 cm long.

Epiphyte in shady forests at medium altitudes; 1200–1300 m; flowering in February and also at other times of the year.

Madagascar (rather rare).

Sometimes confused with *Angraecum linearifolium* which also has very narrow leaves but in that species they are normally well spaced along the stem. *Angraecum teretifolium* also lacks the strong keel along the centre of the lip which is such a characteristic feature of *A. linearifolium*.

Species from Réunion and Mauritius

Angraecum conchoglossum Schlechter

Also occurs in Madagascar and is described above.

Angraecum expansum Thouars

Plant erect or curved, growing in tufts, simple or branched, with rather few verrucose roots near the base of the stem. Leaves 1 cm apart, mostly near apex of stem, rigid, dark green, lanceolate, unequally bilobed at the apex, 2–3 cm long, 5–6 mm wide. Inflorescence axillary, slender, single-flowered because the lower one of 2 inside the bract aborts. Flower greenish or yellowish with white lip; sepals oval-lanceolate, acuminate, shorter than the petals; petals similar to the sepals; lip uppermost, almost square, funnel-shaped, with a wide crest along the centre, and an acumen at the apex; spur slender below the wide mouth, curving upwards, 5–6 cm long.

Epiphyte, fairly common on trees at medium to high altitudes; 1000–2000 m.

Réunion.

SECTION *PSEUDOJUMELLEA*

In this section are plants with long slender stems bearing widely spaced alternate leaves in 2 rows. The single-flowered inflorescence arises opposite a leaf base and has a long slender peduncle. The white, medium-sized flowers have a narrow lip and a slender spur. The plant habit is similar to some of those of the preceding section, and to some species of *Jumellea*, but the flowers are distinctly different with their narrow or deeply folded lip.

Seven species are allocated to this section in this book. Five are recorded from Madagascar, one of which (*Angraecum mauritianum*) is also recorded from both Mauritius and Réunion, another of which (*A. florulentum*) has been collected in the Comoro Islands, and a third (*A. ramosum*) in Réunion and Mauritius.

Angraecum coutrixii Bosser

Plant with stiff, upright stems, often branching at the base so that a number of upright stems grow close together as a dense tuft, 10–30 cm high, each stem 2–4 mm wide. Leaves in 2 rows, 3–6 mm apart, growing from basal sheaths that are persistent on the stem, erect or spreading, oblong or linear-oblong, 1.5–3 cm long, 5–10 mm wide, with a slight furrow in the centre of the upper surface. Inflorescence longer than the leaves, 1- or 2-flowered; bract concave, ovate, apiculate, 6–7 mm long; pedicellate ovary 2–3.5 cm long. Flowers white, fleshy, sepals and petals spreading so that the flower is in one plane; dorsal sepal ovate-lanceolate, obtuse or subacute, 16–19 mm long, 6–7 mm wide; lateral sepals similar but longer, 19–22 cm long, 6–7 mm wide, slightly oblique and keeled on the back; petals similar but slightly smaller, 16–18 mm long, 5–7 mm wide; lip ovate above the concave base, 17–22 mm long, 9–12 mm wide; spur slender, yellowish green, 5–5.5 cm long.

Lithophyte, sometimes growing with *Angraecum protensum* (section *Angraecum*), on quartzite rock outcrops; 1400–1650 m; flowering between January and March.

Madagascar (central regions).

Angraecum dendrobiopsis Schlechter

Plant usually pendent with long simple or branching stems, 25–60 cm long or much longer, 3–5 mm in diameter, covered by tight leaf sheaths which are sometimes glossy. Leaves widely spaced, 1–2.5 cm apart, linear-lanceolate, slightly attenuated towards base and apex, very unequally bilobed at the apex, 5–12 cm long, 5–8 mm wide. Inflorescence piercing a leaf sheath, opposite a leaf base, 4–12 cm long, 1- to 4-flowered; bracts obtuse or apiculate, about a quarter the length of the pedicel; pedicellate ovary 2–3 cm long. Flowers white, rather fleshy; sepals lanceolate, widest at the lowest third, subacuminate above, 22–27 mm long, 7 mm

Angraecum implicatum. From Thouars 1822, t. 58.

Angraecum dendrobiopsis. J. Hermans

Angraecum florulentum. J. Hermans

Angraecum florulentum.
B. Campbell

wide; lateral sepals longer than dorsal sepal, joined together at the base; petals similar but wider, 22 mm long, 8–13 mm wide; lip very concave, rhomboid-ovate, auriculate at the base where it is widest, contracted above into a short acumen 5 mm long, in total 18–20 mm long, 8–13 mm wide; spur curved round behind the flower, filiform from a 4-mm-wide mouth, 3.5–5 cm long.

Epiphyte on tree trunks in rain forest; ca. 1500–2000 m; flowering January to April.

Madagascar (Mount Tsaratanana).

Similar to *Angraecum penzigianum* but with a differently shaped lip and shorter spur.

Angraecum florulentum Reichenbach f.

Plant with elongated stems, erect at first but quickly becoming pendent, sometimes branching, covered with wrinkled leaf sheaths, somewhat flattened, 15–25 cm long or more, 5–6 mm wide. Leaves numerous, in 2 rows, 1–2 cm apart, loriform, widest at the middle, shortly unequally bilobed at the apex, fleshy, sometimes wrinkled, 4.5–7 cm long, 1–1.5 cm wide. Inflorescence arising opposite a leaf base, 2- to 4-flowered; bracts loose, widely oval-obtuse, ca. 6 mm long and wide, equalling a third or half of the internode; pedicellate ovary rather slender, 3–3.5 cm long. Flowers white, fleshy; sepals lanceolate, widest towards but above the base, attenuate to the acute apex, 20–24 mm long, 6–8 mm wide; petals similar but slightly oblique; lip on the upper side of the flower, deeply concave, lanceolate, attenuate from base to tip, 20–24 mm long, 6–8 mm wide; spur narrow, filiform, 9–10 cm long.

Epiphyte on tree trunks in highland forest; ca. 600–1000 m; flowering November to December.

Comoro Islands.

Very similar to *Angraecum penzigianum* but with narrower petals and longer spur.

Angraecum implicatum Thouars

Plant scandent or creeping with long branching stems and very long verrucose roots. Leaves widely spaced, 2–3 cm apart, oblong, unequally bilobed at the apex, with rounded lobes. Inflorescence longer than the leaves, single-flowered; bract tubular; pedicellate ovary 2–3 cm long. Flower white; sepals oval at the base then acuminate, lateral sepals narrower than dorsal and falcate, spreading; petals linear-oblong, pointed, shorter than the sepals; lip concave, suborbicular at the base, then acuminate, similar to the dorsal sepal but wider and a little shorter; spur filiform, 2–3 cm long.

Epiphyte, or creeping over the ground in shady forests; 800–1200 m; flowering in March and April.

Madagascar and Réunion.

Rather similar in habit to *Angraecum ramosum* but the leaves are more widely spaced and the flowers have a differently shaped lip.

Angraecum mauritianum (Poiret) Frappier

Plant with upright or pendent stems which are elongated and branched, somewhat flattened, very narrow at the base, 25–40 cm long or longer. Leaves numerous, in 2 rows, 15 mm apart, with

Angraecum mauritianum. J. Hermans

leaf sheaths 12–15 mm long, flattened and winged; blade oblong-lanceolate, 4.5–6 cm long, 1–1.4 cm wide, widest at the middle and tapering towards both ends, scarcely unequally bilobed at the apex. Inflorescence piercing the leaf sheath, usually single-flowered; bract shortly pointed, 5 mm long; pedicellate ovary 3–3.5 cm long. Flower pure white, rather fleshy and glossy; sepals lanceolate, attenuate towards the apex with their largest width in the lower third, 15–20 mm long, 4 mm wide, dorsal sepal a little shorter than lateral sepals which are somewhat oblique and joined at the base; petals lanceolate, narrower than the sepals, 12 mm long, 3 mm wide; lip concave, lanceolate, acute, widest towards the base, with a broad, thickened keel along its centre, as long as the sepals, 7 mm wide; spur filiform, ca. 8 cm long.

Epiphyte in forests and in regenerating scrub, often rather near the ground; 200–1400 m; flowering February to March.

Madagascar, Réunion, and Mauritius.

Angraecum penzigianum Schlechter

Plant with elongated stems, erect at first but quickly becoming pendent, sometimes branching, covered with shiny leaf sheaths, somewhat flattened, up to 50 cm long or more, 4–5 mm wide. Leaves numerous, in 2 rows, 1–2 cm apart, ligulate, fleshy or waxy, glossy, shortly unequally bilobed at the apex, 8–10 cm long, 1–1.5 cm wide. Inflorescence arising opposite a leaf base, 3-to 5-flowered; bracts loose, widely oval-obtuse, up to 10 mm long and wide; pedicellate ovary slender, ca. 4 cm long. Flowers white, fleshy; sepals lanceolate, widest towards but above the base, attenuate to the acute apex, keeled on the dorsal surface, 20–24 mm long, ca. 6 mm wide; petals similar but much wider, ca. 25 mm long, 12 mm wide; lip on the upper side of the flower, deeply concave, similar to the petals, lanceolate, with a short acumen 5 mm long, ca. 20 mm long, 8–10 mm wide; spur narrow, filiform, 5–12 cm long.

Epiphyte amongst mosses in forest; 1500–1800 m; flowering in February and March.

Madagascar (central regions).

Named in honour of Professor Penzig, a friend of Schlechter; easily distinguished from *Angraecum florulentum* by its wider petals.

Angraecum ramosum Thouars

Plant with long branching, scandent stems, often pendent or horizontal, with widely spaced leaves and finely verrucose roots. Leaves in 2 rows, ca. 1.5 cm apart, lanceolate-linear, widest near the base, then gradually narrowing, slightly unequally bilobed at the apex, 3–4 cm long, 7–8 mm wide. Inflorescence arising opposite a leaf base, single-flowered, curved; bract tubular; pedicellate ovary 3.5 cm long. Flower fleshy, white, turning yellow with age; dorsal sepal reflexed, linear, acute, 12–15 mm long, 4–5 mm wide; lateral sepals falcate, appearing to curve forward on either side of the lip, longer than the dorsal sepal; petals similar to the dorsal sepal but narrower, strongly reflexed; lip concave, parallel-sided except at the pointed tip, 15–20 mm long, 6–8 mm wide; spur very narrow, filiform, 3.5 cm long.

Growing in rain forest, forming clumps on rocks, trees and on the ground; from sea level to 1500 m; flowering in February and March.

Réunion and Mauritius.

SECTION *CHLORANGRAECUM*

The plants in this section have a very short stem, often appearing stemless, or apparently so, with a fan of large leaves. The inflorescence bears 1–3 fleshy flowers on long pedicels. The flowers are yellowish or pale green.

Two species have been recorded in Madagascar.

Angraecum ferkoanum Schlechter

Plant with a very short stem, appearing stemless. Leaves linear-ligulate, with prominent venation, unequally bilobed at the apex, 30–37 cm long, 2–2.7 cm wide. Inflorescence short, lax, 2- or 3-flowered; peduncle short; bract broadly oval-obtuse, spreading, much shorter than the ovary; pedicellate ovary very slender, 6.5–7 cm long. Flowers medium-sized, yellowish green; sepals spreading, lanceolate, subacute, 15 mm long; petals similar but a little smaller, oblique, lanceolate-ligulate, subacute, 12 mm long; lip concave, broadly oval, subcordate or rounded at the base, acuminate, 10 mm long, 10 mm wide below the middle; spur slender, curved at first and then straight, ca. 2.4 cm long.

Epiphyte; no details of habitat available.

Madagascar (eastern region).

Originally collected by the German botanist, Laggiara, who sent orchids from Île Sainte Marie and north-eastern Madagascar to Dr. Paulo Ferko from 1911 to 1913. Schlechter named this species in honour of Ferko.

Angraecum huntleyoides Schlechter
(now including *A. chloranthum* Schlechter)

Plant with a short stem up to 30 cm high. Leaves linear-ligulate, rather thin, unequally bilobed at the apex, 20–30 cm long, 2–2.5 cm wide. Inflores-

Angraecum huntleyoides. J. Hermans

Angraecum huntleyoides, growing in the crown of *Pandanus,* eastern Madagascar. J. Hermans

cence axillary, short, 1- to 3-flowered; peduncle slender, 3–5 cm long; bracts broadly oval-obtuse, spreading, much shorter than the ovary; pedicellate ovary slender, 5–10 cm long. Flowers medium-sized, pale green turning yellow with age; sepals lanceolate, subacute, 12–13 mm long; petals similar but oblique, lanceolate-ligulate, subacute, 12 mm long; lip concave, boat-shaped, broadly oval, 3-lobed in the upper half, the lateral lobes short and almost square, the mid-lobe much larger, incurved, with tiny hairs at the base of the lip, in total 9–12 mm long, 5–8 mm wide at the middle; spur slender, wide at the mouth then cylindrical, 12–20 mm long.

Epiphyte in forests, often found in the crown of *Dracaena* plants; 800–900 m; flowering in February.

Madagascar (central and eastern regions).

SECTION *CONCHOGLOSSUM*

In this section are plants with long, slender stems that are pendent or upright and scandent in habit. The inflorescence usually bears 1 or 2 flowers, often arising more than once in successive seasons from the same point on the stem (intervallate). The peduncle is quite short with 1 or 2 sheaths encircling the base. The small, thin flowers are greenish, or pinkish brown, sometimes white or yellowish.

Twelve species from various parts of Africa are allocated to this section, following the treatment of Summerhayes (1958). Some of the species are difficult to distinguish from each other, particularly in Tanzania. Many of the species seem very close to some of those in section *Angraecoides*, which for convenience in this book we have reserved for the Madagascar and Mascarene species. Further study of the limits of both of these sections and the related section *Filangis* is needed.

Angraecum angustipetalum Rendle

Plants pendent with numerous slender, elongated roots amongst the leaves; stems straight or curved, somewhat 2-edged, up to 40 cm long,

1.5–2 mm in diameter. Leaves in 2 rows, ovate or elliptic, very unequally bilobed at the apex with one lobe absent, the other to 4 mm long and acute, 4–10 cm long, 8–23 mm wide. Inflorescences arising along the stem, opposite a leaf, single-flowered. Flowers white or pale buff-coloured; sepals linear-lanceolate, acuminate, 13–18 mm long, 1.5 mm wide; petals much narrower than the sepals, almost filiform from a broader base, to 10 mm long; lip concave, ovate, 14–21 mm long, 5 mm wide; spur straight, 12–19 mm long, the last 5 mm swollen and clavate.

Epiphyte in dense evergreen forest; flowering in June and July.

Ghana, Nigeria, Cameroon, Gabon, D.R. of Congo, and Malawi.

Angraecum brevicornu Summerhayes

Plants erect with numerous slender, elongated roots amongst the leaves; stems straight or curved, somewhat 2-edged, up to 7 cm long, 1–2 mm in diameter. Leaves in 2 rows, linear, falcate, slightly leathery, often shiny, unequally and acutely bilobed at the apex, 2–5 cm long, 6–11 mm wide. Inflorescences 1 or 2 per node, arising below the roots, single-flowered; bracts lanceolate, acute, 1–2 mm long; pedicellate ovary 7 mm long. Flowers white with a faint pinkish or greenish-pink tinge; sepals lanceolate, acuminate, 8–8.5 mm long, 3–3.6 mm wide; petals elliptic-lanceolate, acuminate, 6.5–7 mm long, 2 mm wide; lip concave, ovate, acuminate, 3–4.5 mm long, 3.5 mm wide; spur straight, parallel to the ovary, ca. 2.5 mm long.

Epiphyte in lowland forest and on lemon trees at a mission station; 500–600 m; flowering in March.

Tanzania.

Angraecum cultriforme Summerhayes

Plants untidy and often pendent with numerous elongated roots amongst the leaves. Stems straight or curved, somewhat 2-edged, up to 15 cm long. Leaves in 2 rows, ligulate, falcate, very unequally bilobed at the apex, 2–6 cm long, 5–8 mm wide, usually yellowish green or pinkish green, sometimes

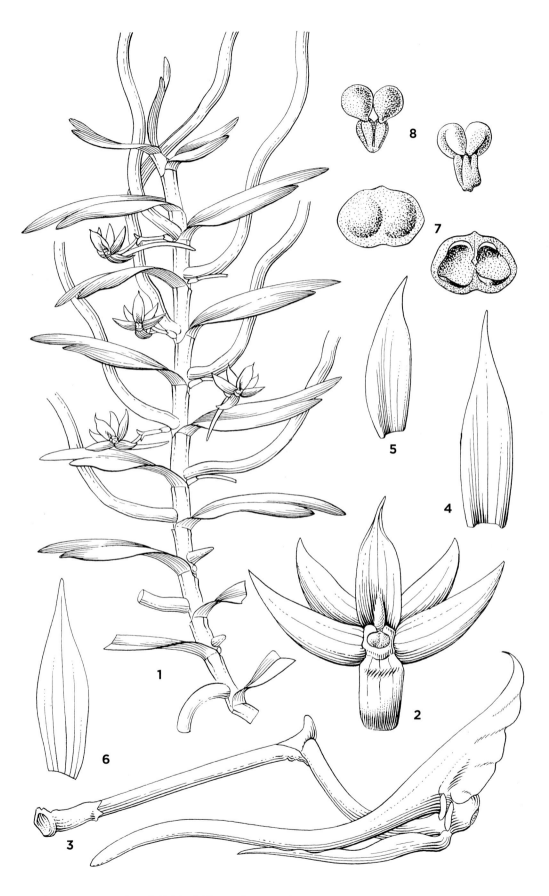

Angraecum erectum. 1: Habit. 2: Flower front. 3: Flower from side. 4: Dorsal sepal. 5: Lateral sepal. 6: Petal. 7: Anther-cap. 8: Pollinarium. From Summerhayes 1962b, t. 3592. E. M. Stones.

with darker dots. Inflorescences arising below the roots, opposite a leaf, intervallate, single-flowered, occasionally up to 4-flowered; bracts lanceolate, acute, 2–3 mm long; pedicellate ovary 6.5–10 mm long. Flowers pink, pale yellow, greenish brown or apple green; sepals linear-lanceolate, acuminate, 10–20 mm long, 3–4 mm wide; petals linear-lanceolate, acuminate, to 14 mm long, to 3 mm wide; lip recurved, ovate-lanceolate, acuminate, 8–12 mm long, 4–6 mm wide; spur straight or slightly curved, 10–25 mm long, swollen at the apex.

Epiphyte in dry evergreen forest and bushland, and in *Brachystegia* woodland; near sea level and up to 1800 m; flowering in March and July (in cultivation).

Kenya, Tanzania, Zambia, Malawi, Zimbabwe, Mozambique, and South Africa (KwaZulu-Natal).

Angraecum curvipes Schlechter

This species was described from Cameroon in 1905 but it is not included in *Flore du Cameroun* (2001). The type specimen has been destroyed, but sketches of it made by Rolfe at Kew show that this species must be allied to *Angraecum pyriforme* Summerhayes (section *Afrangraecum*). It appears to be a smaller plant with much smaller flowers than that species.

Angraecum egertonii Rendle

Plants pendent with numerous slender, elongated roots amongst the leaves. Stems straight or curved, somewhat 2-edged, up to 40 cm long, 1.5–2 mm in diameter. Leaves in 2 rows, broadly elliptic-oblong or elliptic-lanceolate, bluntly bilobed at the apex, 1.5–4.5 cm long, 8–20 mm wide. Inflorescences arising along the stem, opposite a leaf, single-flowered. Flowers white or greenish white; sepals broadly lanceolate or elliptic, acuminate, 6–11 mm long, 1.5 mm wide; petals similar to the sepals but narrower; lip concave, lanceolate-ovate, 4–7.5 mm long; spur ca. 7 mm long, swollen at the apex into an almost globoid sac.

Epiphyte in forest, near waterfalls; flowering September to November.

Southern Nigeria and Gabon.

Angraecum erectum. J. Hermans

Angraecum erectum Summerhayes

Plants erect and scrambling with numerous white roots along the stem; stems often greatly elongated, 20–60 cm high, distinctly 2-edged and covered in rather glaucous green overlapping leaf sheaths. Leaves in 2 rows, stiff and leathery, linear-lanceolate, very unequally bilobed at the apex, 3–6 cm long, 5–12 mm wide. Inflorescences arising opposite a leaf, usually immediately below a root, 1- to 2-flowered; bracts amplexicaul, 2 mm long; pedicellate ovary curved, 4–7 mm long. Flowers white, pale yellowish green or pale salmon pink, scented in the evening; sepals and petals often somewhat reflexed, lanceolate, acuminate, 10–14 mm long, 2–4 mm wide, sepals longer and wider than petals; lip lanceolate, acuminate, similar to sepals, with a linear callus in the basal half, 8–11 mm long, 3.5–4.5 mm wide; spur straight or curved, slender, 15–30 mm long.

Epiphyte and found on rocks in forests and scrub where it is seasonally dry; often found in patches of forest along rivers and dry gulleys, usually in the shade, and growing vertically amongst small trunks and branches; 1300–2350 m; flowering March to October.

Kenya, Uganda, Tanzania, and Zambia.

Angraecum lisowskianum Szlachetko & Olszewski

This species was described in 2001 from Equatorial Guinea (Rio Muni). It seems to be close to *Angraecum moandaense*, but the spur is inflated at the apex so that it appears club-shaped, the lip is shorter and wider (ovate, without a recurved apex) and the shape and size of the leaves is quite different. As yet there has been only one collection of this species, flowering in February.

Angraecum moandaense De Wildeman
(including *Angraecum chevalieri* Summerhayes)

Plants pendent with numerous slender, elongated roots amongst the leaves. Stems straight or curved, somewhat 2-edged, 6–40 cm long, 1.5–2 mm in diameter. Leaves in 2 rows, well-spaced, linear-oblong, almost parallel-sided, unequally bilobed at the apex, with rounded lobes, 4–10 cm long, 4–10 mm wide. Inflorescences axillary, arising along the stem, 5–10 cm long, 1- to 3-flowered; bracts short, ovate, acute. Flowers greenish or yellowish, with lip uppermost; sepals lanceolate, acuminate, 8–17 mm long, 1.5–3 mm wide; petals similar to the sepals but narrower; lip narrowly elliptic, acuminate, apex recurved, with a raised keel along the centre in the lower half, 8–10 mm long, 2.5–3 mm wide; spur S-shaped, 15–20 mm long, somewhat thickened in the distal half.

Epiphyte in dense forest; up to 2100 m; flowering May to July.

Guinea, Liberia, Côte d'Ivoire, Ghana, Nigeria, Equatorial Guinea (Bioco Island), Gabon, D.R. of Congo, Rwanda, and Uganda.

Angraecum moandaense. J. Hermans

Angraecum modicum Summerhayes

Plants pendent with numerous slender, elongated roots amongst the leaves. Stems straight or curved, simple or with few branches, up to 15 cm long, 1.5–2 mm in diameter. Leaves in 2 rows, narrowly linear-lanceolate, pointed, very unequally bilobed at the apex, the longer lobe to 7 mm long and acute, 3–8.5 cm long, 4–8 mm wide. Inflorescences arising along the stem, opposite a leaf, 1- to 3-flowered; bracts lanceolate, acute, 3–5 mm long; pedicellate ovary 1–1.5 cm long. Flowers pale pink or buff-coloured; sepals linear-lanceolate, acuminate, 19–23 mm long, 3 mm wide; petals lanceolate-linear, acute, 16–18 mm long, 1 mm wide; lip concave, ovate, very acute, ca. 15 mm long, 3–3.5 mm wide; spur straight, 14 mm long, slightly constricted at the middle, somewhat swollen in the apical half.

Flowering in May. No other details available.
Liberia.

Angraecum stolzii Schlechter

Plants erect or pendent with numerous slender, elongated roots amongst the leaves; stems straight or curved, somewhat 2-edged, up to 40 cm long. Leaves in 2 rows, linear, falcate, unequally and acutely bilobed at the apex, 4.5–6 cm long, 4–9 mm wide, grass green. Inflorescences arising below the roots, opposite a leaf, usually single-flowered, up to 4 from the same node; bracts ovate, acute or apiculate, 1.5–2 mm long; pedicellate ovary twisted, 4 mm long. Flowers cream or yellow-green, turning orange with age; sepals lanceolate, acuminate, 7–9 mm long, 1.5–3 mm wide; petals lanceolate, acuminate, 7–9 mm long, ca. 1.5 mm wide; lip ovate, acuminate, recurved at the apex, 5–7.5 mm long, 2.5–5 mm wide; spur straight or slightly curved, clavate, 5.5–9 mm long.

Epiphyte in montane and riverine forest; 1700–2500 m; flowering January to July.

Tanzania, Malawi, and D. R. of Congo.

This species was named for Adolf Stolz, a German missionary who collected many orchid specimens whilst living at Tukuyu, in southern Tanzania, in the early part of the last century.

Angraecum umbrosum Cribb

Plants pendent with numerous slender, elongated roots amongst the leaves. Stems straight or curved, flattened, almost winged, up to 30 cm long, 1.5–2 mm in diameter. Leaves in 2 rows, linear, falcate, unequally and acutely bilobed at the apex, 6–12 cm long, 2–4 mm wide, pale green. Inflorescences arising along the stem, opposite the leaf axils, single-flowered but often with a second bud which does not develop; pedicellate ovary 7 mm long, with a sharp bend at a point 5 mm from the base. Flowers pale yellow or yellowish green, small; sepals linear-lanceolate, acute, 6–9 mm long, 1.5–2 mm wide; petals similar but slightly shorter and narrower; lip very concave, ovate, with a central raised callus at the base, acute, 5–6 mm long, 2–3 mm wide; spur straight or slightly swollen in the apical half, 6–8 mm long.

Epiphyte in riverine and submontane forest; 1700–1900 m; flowering in April and October.

Malawi.

Usually easy to recognise by its long narrow leaves and small flowers.

Angraecum viride Kraenzlin

Plants pendent with numerous slender, elongated roots amongst the leaves. Stems straight or curved, somewhat 2-edged, up to 45 cm long, 1.5–2 mm in diameter. Leaves in 2 rows, linear-elliptic, unequally and acutely bilobed at the apex, 2–5 cm long, 4–6 mm wide, pale green. Inflorescences arising below the roots, opposite a leaf, 1- or 2-flowered, intervallate; bracts lanceolate, acuminate, 2–4 mm long; pedicellate ovary 2–2.5 mm long. Flowers green; sepals lanceolate, acuminate, 3–5 mm long; petals lanceolate, acuminate, to 4 mm long; lip concave, ovate, acuminate, 3–4 mm long, 2.5–3 mm wide; spur straight or slightly curved, clavate, 1.8–2.5 mm long.

Epiphyte in warm forest near the coast of a small area of East Africa; 300–1000 m; flowering in May.

Kenya (Shimba Hills) and Tanzania (Usambara Mountains).

SECTION *ANGRAECOIDES*

The plants in this section have long slender stems bearing small leaves in 2 rows. The inflorescence is single-flowered, rarely 2-flowered, bearing the flower on a prominent, slender peduncle, normally much longer than the internodes and with 1 or 2 sheaths at the base. In some species the inflorescences arise more than once from the same point on the stem, as in some species allocated to section *Conchoglossum*. The small flowers are green or greenish yellow, rarely white, with a cylindric or clavate spur on the lip.

Eleven species included in this section are found in Madagascar, one of which is also in Réunion, and two more of which occur only in the island of Réunion.

Species from Madagascar

These can be separated into 2 groups according to the length of the spur:

Group 1. Spur small, shorter than the sepals or equalling them in length at the most.

Group 2. Spur longer than the sepals.

Group 1. Spur small, shorter than the sepals or equalling them in length at the most.

Angraecum chermezoni H. Perrier

Plant with long branching stems, usually pendent, 20–50 cm long. Leaves numerous, lanceolate or linear, rather variable in size, tapering at both ends, 2–6 cm long, 3–5 mm wide. Inflorescences numerous, usually shorter than the leaves, single-flowered, sometimes with 2 inflorescences per leaf axil; bract 2–3 mm long, pedicel with ovary twisted, 5 mm long. Flowers yellowish; sepals ovate-lanceolate, thick and pointed, 8 mm long, 2.3 mm wide; petals lanceolate, acute, 6 mm long, 1.3 mm wide; lip triangular, dilated above a narrow base then acuminate, thick, 7 mm long, 4.5 mm wide; spur slightly enlarged towards the tip, 8 mm long.

Epiphyte on tree trunks in mossy forest; 1000 m; flowering in February.

Madagascar (eastern forests in central region).

Angraecum clavigerum Ridley

Plant small with short stems and 6–12 leaves, 5–10 cm long. Leaves rigid, ligulate, unequally bilobed at the apex, 15–25 mm long, 3–6 mm wide. Inflorescence usually longer than the leaves, single-flowered; bract very short; pedicel with ovary 6–10 mm long. Flowers white; sepals lanceolate, acute, 13–16 mm long, the lateral sepals slightly dilated and joined together at the base; petals shorter, acute, 12 mm long; lip concave, ovate-lanceolate, wide at the base and acuminate above, 11–12 mm long, 4 mm wide; spur narrow below and expanded into a rounded, club-shaped apex, 6–10 mm long.

Angraecum chermezoni. J. Hermans

Angraecum clavigerum. J. Hermans

Epiphyte in mossy forests; 1500–2000 m; flowering January to March.

Madagascar (forests in the central highlands).

Angraecum curvicaule Schlechter

Plant erect with narrow stems 35–40 cm long. Leaves linear-ligulate, 4–5 cm long, 5–6.5 mm wide. Inflorescences slender, equalling the leaves in length or a little shorter, 1- or 2-flowered; bracts small; pedicel with ovary twisted, 5 mm long. Flowers yellowish green; sepals lanceolate, acute, 7 mm long; petals linear-lanceolate, acute and almost as long as the sepals, 7 mm long; lip concave, broadly oval-apiculate, with a keel on the surface near the base, 7 mm long; spur cylindric, obtuse, 7 mm long.

Epiphyte in forests; ca. 900 m; flowering in January.

Madagascar (central region).

Angraecum rhizomaniacum Schlechter

Plant with scandent or pendent stems up to 20 cm long, 2–3 mm diameter. Leaves numerous, curved, oblong-ligulate, unequally and obtusely bilobed at the apex, 15–20 mm long, 5–8 mm wide. Inflorescences in groups of 2 or 3, much shorter than the leaves, single-flowered; bract small, oval, acute; pedicel with ovary 5 mm long. Flowers greenish white, fleshy, small; sepals oval, acute or subacuminate, 5 mm long; petals oval-lanceolate, acute, 5 mm long; lip concave, broadly rhomboid or suborbicular, shortly apiculate or subacuminate, 4.5 mm long, 5 mm wide; spur slender, cylindric, slightly inflated at the apex, 6.5 mm long.

Epiphyte in forest with lichens; ca. 2000 m; flowering in January.

Madagascar (Mount Tsaratanana).

Angraecum rostratum Ridley

Plant with long slender stems and numerous leaves, 30 cm long. Leaves lanceolate-obtuse, thickened, 18–25 mm long. Inflorescences in the axils of the uppermost leaves, longer than the leaves; pedicel with ovary 10–12 mm long. Flowers greenish; sepals broadly linear-obtuse, fleshy, 7–8 mm long; petals linear-lanceolate, thickened at the apex; lip concave, very dilate near the base, then contracted in the upper third to a sharp beak or acumen, 12 mm long; spur horizontal, at right angles to the lip, dilated into a bulbous tip, 7–10 mm long.

Epiphyte in mossy forest; ca. 1500 m.

Madagascar (central highlands).

Angraecum scalariforme H. Perrier

Plant with erect stem, rooted at the base, 15–40 cm high. Leaves numerous, in 2 rows, lanceolate, narrowing at both ends, 8–14 mm long, 1.7–2.5 mm wide. Inflorescence axillary, single-flowered; bracts thick, 3 mm long; pedicel with ovary 5–9 mm long. Flowers white; sepals 9 mm long including an acumen 4 mm long; petals narrow, 5 mm long; lip similar to sepals, with long acumen, 4 mm wide towards base, 9 mm long; spur narrow, inflated at the apex, 4 mm long.

Epilithic and on the ground amongst mosses and lichens; 1400 m; flowering in March.

Madagascar (north-eastern central region, Mount Beondroka).

Group 2. Spur longer than the sepals.

Angraecum elliotii Rolfe

Plant with elongated stems and well-spaced leaves along the stem. Leaves in 2 rows, linear or lanceolate-linear, with short, pointed lobes at the apex, 3,7–5 cm long, 6–8 mm wide. Inflorescences axillary, single-flowered; bract lanceolate-acute. Flowers white; sepals lanceolate, subacuminate, dorsal sepal 8–10 mm long, 3 mm wide, lateral sepals a little narrower; petals similar, a little shorter; lip concave, broadly oval, long acuminate, 6–8 mm long, 4 mm wide; spur inflated, 12–16 mm long.

Epiphyte in forests.

Madagascar.

Angraecum pingue Frappier ex Cordemoy
(including *Angraecum nasutum* Schlechter)

Plant with long curved stems, erect or pendent, 10–30 cm long, with numerous very slender roots mostly below the leaves. Leaves in 2 rows, thick and

Angraecum pingue. J. Hermans

Angraecum sedifolium. J. Hermans

fleshy, somewhat amplexicaul at the base, minutely bilobed at the apex, 3–6 cm long, 5–10 mm wide. Inflorescences in the axils of the upper leaves, 1- or 2-flowered; bracts short and loose; pedicel and ovary 1–2 cm long. Flowers yellowish green, the lower one often aborted; sepals reflexed, divergent, up to 15 mm long, very narrow; petals horizontal, shorter and narrower than the sepals, 12 mm long; lip hollow at the base then long acuminate, as long as the dorsal sepal; spur parallel to the ovary, gradually narrowed from the mouth, slightly swollen at the apex, 1.5–2 cm long.

Epiphyte in shady forests; 1000–2000 m; flowering in January and February.

Madagascar, Réunion, and Mauritius.

Angraecum sedifolium Schlechter

Plant erect or pendent and with many leaves, ca. 15 cm long. Leaves narrowly linear, subcylindrical, almost terete, 15–25 mm long, 1.5–2.5 mm wide.

Inflorescences shorter than the leaves, single-flowered; bract oval-apiculate; pedicel with ovary ca. 10 mm long. Flowers yellowish green, small; sepals oval-lanceolate, acuminate, 8 mm long; petals lanceolate-acuminate; lip slightly concave, broadly rhomboid below the middle, rounded at the base, then rostrate-acuminate, 7.5 mm long, 5 mm wide; spur horizontal, slender and cylindric, slightly inflated at the obtuse tip, 13 mm long.

Epiphyte in mossy forests; 2000 m; flowering December to May.

Madagascar (central highlands).

Angraecum triangulifolium Senghas

Plant erect or pendent, stems simple or branched near the base, often in tufts, to 30 cm long. Leaves numerous, closely spaced and semi-amplexicaul, narrowly triangular, rounded at the apex, 17 mm long, 7 mm wide. Inflorescences in each leaf axil, 2 or 3 at a time, much longer than the leaves; bract triangular-apiculate, 3 mm long; pedicel with ovary 10–13 mm long. Flowers yellowish, diaphanous; sepals linear-triangular, acute, with slightly reflexed margins, dorsal sepal 10–12 mm long, 2.2–2.5 mm wide, lateral sepals 9–11 mm long, 1.6–1.9 mm wide; petals linear-triangular, subulate, 8 mm long, 1–1.2 mm wide; lip lamina rounded at the base, 3 mm wide, with a narrow callus on the surface extending into the spur, triangular above, 10 mm long; spur funnel-shaped at first, then narrowing and very slender in the apical half, 2.5 cm long.

Epiphyte in forest in the hills; 1200 m.

Madagascar (near Andasibe).

Angraecum zaratananae Schlechter

Plant erect or scrambling between the host branches, unbranched. Leaves spreading or slightly recurved, ligulate, narrowing towards the base, unequally bilobed at the apex, 2–5 cm long, 4–6 mm wide. Inflorescences slightly shorter than the leaves, single-flowered; bract oval-apiculate; pedicel with ovary twisted, 8 mm long. Flowers pale, yellowish or greenish white; sepals lanceolate-subacuminate, 12 mm long; petals linear-lanceolate, acute, 10 mm long; lip slightly concave, broadly rhomboid, rostrate-acuminate, thickened along the margins, 12 mm long, 9 mm wide; spur narrow and cylindric and inflated at the apex, 4 cm long.

Epiphyte in low forest with lichens; 2000 m; flowering in January.

Madagascar (Mount Tsaratanana; always spelt with a *z* by Schlechter).

Species from Réunion

Angraecum cilaosianum (Cordemoy) Schlechter

Plants with elongated stems, usually strongly curved, to 30 cm long, 2–3 mm wide. Leaves 5 or 6 in 2 rows, near apex of stem, linear, stiff, unequally bilobed at the apex, 6–7 cm long, 6–8 mm wide. Inflorescences 1- or 2-flowered; peduncle very slender (hair-thin). Flowers greenish yellow, ca. 8 mm in diameter; sepals and petals similar, oval-lanceolate; lip slightly wider, markedly concave at the base; spur slightly swollen and slightly bent.

Epiphyte; high altitudes; flowering in October. Réunion.

Angraecum obversifolium Frappier ex Cordemoy

Plant with long curved stems, erect or pendent, 40–50 cm long, with numerous very slender roots. Leaves in 2 rows on the upper part of the stem, thin, the obverse turned upwards, falcate, minutely bilobed at the apex, 6–12 cm long, 4–8 mm wide. Inflorescences very slender, borne in the axils of the upper leaves from the same point for several years in succession, 2- to 4-flowered; bracts short and loose; pedicel and ovary short, very twisted. Flowers very small, yellowish green, up to 4 mm in diameter; sepals oval; petals smaller, lanceolate; lip hollow at the base then long acuminate, as long as the dorsal sepal; spur parallel to the ovary, as long as the lip.

Epiphyte in shady forests, fairly widespread; 1000–1800 m; flowering October to January.

Réunion.

SECTION *FILANGIS*

This section includes plants with long stems and alternate leaves in 2 rows. The inflorescence is single-flowered with a short peduncle (shorter than the internodes) and with 1 or 2 sheaths at the base. The medium-sized flowers are white or greenish white, with a long slender spur at the base of the lip.

Several of the species, and especially *Angraecum moratii*, seem similar to some that we have placed in section *Pseudojumellea* which also have white flowers with a long narrow spur. Six species are from Madagascar, one of which (*A. filicornu*) also occurs in Mauritius and Réunion, another of which (*A. meirax*) is also recorded, perhaps doubtfully, from the Comoro Islands, and a third species (*A. cornigerum*) is endemic in Réunion.

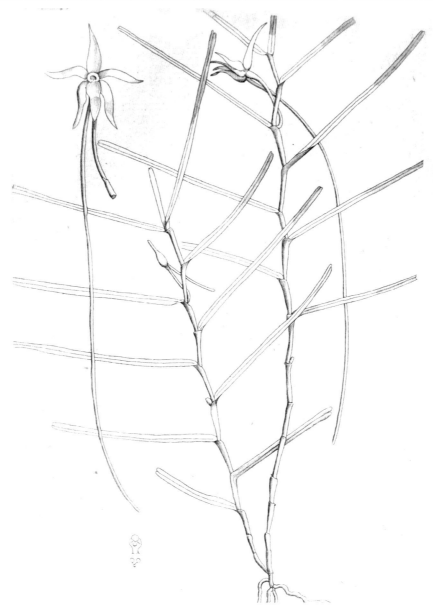

Angraecum filicornu. From Thouars 1822, t. 52.

Angraecum amplexicaule Toilliez-Genoud &
    Bosser

Plant pendent with long stem to 30 cm long,
sinuous grey roots, 3–4 mm in diameter. Leaves in
2 rows, narrowly oblong, rounded at the base and
amplexicaul, unequally bilobed at the apex, with
rounded lobes, thin, margins undulate towards the
base, 4–5.5 cm long, 1 cm wide. Inflorescence axillary, single-flowered; peduncle very short; bract
ovate, 5–6 mm long; pedicel with ovary 4 cm long.
Flowers white, fleshy; sepals ovate-lanceolate, subacute, 17 mm long, 7 mm wide; petals similar to
sepals but narrower, 16 mm long, 5–6 mm wide;
lip very concave, with a short central keel, 15 mm
long; spur S-shaped, slender, 10–11 cm long.

Epiphyte in rain forest.

Madagascar (eastern region).

Angraecum filicornu Thouars

Plants erect or pendent, often in a tuft of several stems 10–25 cm high and with numerous
verrucose roots. Leaves in 2 rows, linear, soft and

grass-like, 5–9 cm long, 1.5–4 mm wide; leaf sheaths with fine brown streaks. Inflorescences opposite a leaf-base, shorter than the leaves, single-flowered; bracts short; pedicel and ovary 20–25 mm long. Flowers white, medium-sized; sepals lanceolate, pointed, 12 mm long; petals slightly narrower; lip lanceolate or panduriform, subacute; spur filiform, 9–11 cm long.

Epiphyte in forests near the sea and up to 800 m; flowering November to June.

Madagascar (widespread along the eastern coast), Réunion, and Mauritius.

Angraecum meirax (Reichenbach f.) H. Perrier

Plants erect with a short stem up to 10 cm long. Leaves few, rigid, linear, 2.2–4.5 cm long, 3–6 mm wide. Inflorescence amongst the upper leaves, single-flowered; bract loose, obtuse, 6–8 mm long; pedicel with ovary 24–28 mm long. Flowers white; sepals narrowly lanceolate, acute, 3.2–4 cm long; petals narrower and shorter, 25–26 mm long; lip concave, oval-lanceolate, acuminate, with a conspicuous longitudinal keel on the surface in the lower half, 4 cm long, 1.2 cm wide; spur slender, 12–13 cm long.

Epiphyte in forests near the sea; flowering in October.

Madagascar (in the north-east near the lagoon at Nosy Vé) and Comoro Islands (doubtfully recorded here).

Angraecum melanostictum Schlechter

Plants erect, at the most 15 cm high, bearing many leaves with black-spotted sheaths. Leaves linear-ligulate, unequally bilobed at the apex, 5 cm long, 6–7 mm wide. Inflorescences short, single-flowered; bract oval, obtuse; pedicel with ovary slender, 33 mm long. Flowers white; sepals oblong-lanceolate, obtuse, 11 mm long; petals similar, 10 mm long; lip slightly concave, oval-lanceolate, obtuse, 9 mm long; spur slender, ca. 7 cm long.

Epiphyte in forest at low to medium elevations; flowering in March.

Madagascar (eastern and north-eastern regions).

Angraecum melanostictum. J. Hermans

Angraecum moratii Bosser

Plants with strong stems which become pendent with age, up to 50 cm long, 6–8 mm thick, somewhat flattened. Leaves in 2 rows, widely spaced, twisted to lie in the plane of the stem, thick and fleshy, unequally bilobed at the apex, 4–7.5 cm long, 1.5–2 cm wide. Inflorescences arising opposite the leaf base, 1- or 2-flowered; bracts sheathing, 4–5 mm long; pedicel with ovary twisted, 4–5 cm long. Flowers white, fleshy; dorsal sepal ovate-lanceolate, acute, 20–22 mm long; lateral sepals keeled on the back, 20–22 mm long, 8 mm wide; petals ovate, acute, 17–20 mm long, 10–11 mm wide; lip concave, narrowly oblong, apiculate, bearing a thickened cushion towards the base, 15–18 mm long, 8–9 mm wide; spur slender, pendent, 12–13 cm long.

Epiphyte in shady forests; 900 m; flowering in September.

Madagascar.

This species is named for Philippe Morat, formerly director of the Laboratoire de Phanérogamie, in Paris, who also lived in Madagascar and collected there.

Angraecum trichoplectron (Reichenbach f.) Schlechter

Plant small, up to 10 cm high. Leaves linear, soft, tapering towards the bidentate apex, 12.5 cm long, 8–9 mm wide. Flower solitary, axillary, white; sepals lanceolate, acute; petals linear-acuminate; lip broad, shell-shaped at the base, acuminate at the apex; spur 5 times longer than the ovary.

Described from a plant in cultivation in 1888. Madagascar.

Species from Réunion

Angraecum cornigerum Cordemoy

Plant erect with stems 6–8 cm long, verrucose roots only near the base. Leaves in 2 rows, dull bluish green, curved, closely spaced, fleshy, very narrow, almost terete but with a channel on the upper surface, subacute at the apex, 7.5 cm long, 2 mm wide. Inflorescence opposite a leaf, arising between 2 sheaths, single-flowered; pedicel with ovary 4 cm long. Flowers greenish or yellowish with white lip; sepals and petals spreading, narrowly lanceolate, the sepals longer and wider than the petals; lip ovate, flat with a short crest near the base, thickened at the apex; spur slender throughout, narrowing to the tip, 12–13 cm long.

Epiphyte at high altitude; can be found at the base of trunks of *Philippia* bushes.

Réunion.

Superficially this species seems very similar to *Angraecum chimanimaniense* (section *Perrierangraecum*) from Zimbabwe but is clearly distinguished by the long slender peduncle which is quite bare below the bract.

SECTION *AFRANGRAECUM*

In this section are plants with elongate, leafy stems. The axillary inflorescences sometimes have long peduncles and are 1- to 4-flowered (or more) but often with only one flower open at a time. The fleshy flowers are white with a green central spot on the labellum or yellow, yellowish green, or pale orange.

Nine species from tropical Africa are included here, some of which seem also to be close to section *Conchoglossum*. Two groups can be recognised by their flower colour:

Group 1. Flowers white or white and emerald green.

Group 2. Flowers green or yellowish green.

Group 1. Flowers white or white and emerald green.

Angraecum affine Schlechter

Plants with elongate S-shaped stems bearing leaves and roots along their length. Stems upright, somewhat compressed so that they appear flattened, 10–25 cm long. Leaves ligulate-lanceolate or oblong, unequally and obliquely bilobed at the apex, lobes rounded, 10–16 cm long, 1–2.5 cm wide. Inflorescences shorter than the leaves, slender, 3- or 4-flowered; bracts ovate, acuminate 4–5 mm long; pedicellate ovary 12–13 mm long. Flowers pale green or whitish; dorsal sepal narrowly elliptic, acuminate, 9–14 mm long, 2–5 mm wide; lateral sepals similar; petals oblong, subacute to obtuse, 9–11 mm long, 1.5–4 mm wide; lip concave, obscurely 3-lobed, 8–11 mm long, 4–6 mm wide, with a distinct longitudinal linear callus along the centre as far as the middle, the side lobes rounded, the mid-lobe recurved, linear; spur cylindric and thickened into an ellipsoid shape at the apex, 15–25 mm long.

Epiphyte, pendent or scandent in rain forest; 1500–1600 m; flowering in April.

Cameroon, Equatorial Guinea (Bioco Island), Congo, D.R. of Congo, and Uganda.

Angraecum astroarche Ridley

Plant with elongated, often pendent stems, that are flattened rather than round, almost 2-edged, up to 30 cm long. Leaves in 2 rows, widely spaced, dark green, elliptic-oblong, unequally and obtusely bilobed at the apex, 7.5–10 cm long, up to 2 cm wide. Inflorescences arising opposite the leaf base, 1- to 3-flowered but with only one flower open at a time; bracts amplexicaul, ovate, obtuse, 4–5 mm long; pedicellate ovary 1.2–1.4 cm long. Flowers white with a dark green patch around the callus on the lip; sepals linear-lanceolate to elliptic-lanceolate, acuminate, 4–5 cm long, 2.5–6 mm wide; petals slightly smaller than the sepals; lip concave, elliptic-lanceolate, acute, 1.5–3 cm long, 7 mm wide, with a longitudinal ridge-like callus in the basal half; spur slender, cylindrical, slightly swollen at the apex, 2.5 cm long.

Epiphyte; ca. 900 m.

São Tomé; perhaps extinct.

Angraecum mofakoko De Wildeman

Plants with stems bearing leaves and roots along their length. Stems upright, somewhat compressed so that they appear flattened, up to 100 cm long. Leaves well-spaced, oblong, 7–15 cm long, 1–3 cm wide. Inflorescences shorter than the leaves, slender, 1- to 3-flowered; bracts ovate, acuminate 4–5 mm long; pedicellate ovary 12–13 mm long. Flowers white and green; dorsal sepal narrowly elliptic, acuminate, 15–25 mm long, ca. 5 mm wide; lateral sepals similar but smaller, 10–20 mm long, ca. 2.5 mm wide; petals narrowly elliptic, acute, 15–20 mm long, ca. 2 mm wide; lip concave, elliptic, without a distinct longitudinal linear callus along the centre, but with undulate margins, 10–20 mm long, ca. 3.5 mm wide; spur slender, incurved at first, then reflexed, 30–35 mm long.

Epiphyte, pendent or scandent in rain forest; often near water; 1500–1600 m; flowering in April.

D.R. of Congo.

Angraecum reygaertii. J. Stewart

Angraecum reygaertii De Wildeman

Plant with elongated, often pendent stems, that are flattened rather than round, almost 2-edged, up to 50 cm long. Leaves in 2 rows, widely spaced, dark green, ligulate to oblanceolate, unequally and obtusely bilobed at the apex, 10–20 cm long, 2–3.5 cm wide. Inflorescences arising opposite the leaf base, 3- to 6-flowered but with only one flower open at a time; bracts amplexicaul, ovate, obtuse, 4–5 mm long; pedicellate ovary 1.2–1.4 cm long. Flowers white with a dark green patch around the callus on the lip; sepals linear-lanceolate to elliptic-lanceolate, acuminate, 2.5–4 cm long, 2.5–6 mm wide; petals similar; lip concave, elliptic-lanceolate, acute, 1.5–3 cm long, 6 mm wide, with a longitudinal ridge-like callus in the basal half; spur slender, slightly S-shaped or straight, 6.5–9 cm long.

Epiphyte in riverine or marshy forest, shade-loving, often rather near the ground; 1200–1250 m; flowering in March or April.

D.R. of Congo, Cameroon, and Uganda.

Similar to *Angraecum astroarche* but the slightly smaller flowers have a longer spur.

Group 2. Flowers green or yellowish green.

Angraecum claessensii De Wildeman

Plants small with an elongate stem bearing leaves and roots along its length; stems erect, somewhat compressed so that they appear flattened, 10–25 cm long. Leaves ligulate-lanceolate, falcate, unequally and obliquely bilobed at the apex, lobes rounded or acute, the smaller one sometimes absent, 6–7 cm long, 1–1.5 cm wide. Inflorescences axillary, erect, longer than the leaves, slender, 15–17 cm long, 7- to 9-flowered; bracts small, ovate, apiculate; pedicellate ovary 10–12 mm long. Flowers pale green, whitish, yellowish, or orange, small; sepals lanceolate, acuminate, 7–8 mm long, 2–2.5 mm wide; petals reflexed in the apical half, shorter and narrower than the sepals, 6–8 mm long, 1–1.5 mm wide; lip concave, 3-lobed, 6–7 mm long, 5–6 mm wide, with a narrow, longitudinal linear callus along the centre at the base, the side lobes rounded, erect on either side of the column, the mid-lobe recurved, linear acuminate; spur funnel-shaped at first, then narrowing and thickened into an ellipsoid shape at the apex, ca. 5 mm long.

Epiphyte, pendent or scandent in humid forests but well-exposed to light; 600–800 m; flowering in May or June.

Liberia, Nigeria, Côte d'Ivoire, D.R. of Congo, and Central African Republic.

Angraecum cribbianum Szlachetko & Olszewski

This recently described species (2001) appears to be very similar to *Angraecum claessensii* but with shorter inflorescences bearing only 2 flowers. The longer lip (to 12 mm) is also a distinguishing character. As yet there seems to be only one collection, from Gabon, which was discovered in flower in February.

Angraecum firthii. J. Stewart

Angraecum firthii Summerhayes

Plants with an elongate stem bearing leaves and roots along its length. Stems upright, somewhat compressed so that they appear flattened, 10–30 cm long. Leaves dark green, rather thin, oblanceolate or oblong, unequally lobed at the apex, with rounded lobes, 8–12 cm long, 1.5–2.5 cm wide. Inflorescences short, slender, 3- to 5-flowered; bracts broadly ovate, obtuse, 1.5–2 mm long; pedicellate ovary 13–16 mm long. Flowers yellowish green; dorsal sepal lanceolate, long acuminate, 13–20 mm long, 3.5–3.8 mm wide; lateral sepals similar, 14–18 mm long; petals similar but smaller, 11–13 mm long, 2–2.5 mm wide; lip somewhat 3-lobed, 12–13 mm long, 4–6 mm wide, the side lobes wide, erect, the mid-lobe recurved, linear, acuminate, 6.5 mm long; spur S-shaped, ca. 15 mm long.

Epiphyte in the warmer evergreen forests; 1450–1600 m; flowering in June.

Kenya, Uganda, and Cameroon.

Named for the late E. P. Firth of Fort Ternan, Kenya, who discovered it.

Angraecum multinominatum Rendle

Plants with an elongated stem bearing leaves and roots along its length. Stems upright, somewhat compressed so that they appear flattened, 10–30 cm long. Leaves oblanceolate or oblong, unequally bilobed at the apex, with rounded lobes, the shorter lobe often absent, 3–6 cm long, 1–2 cm wide. Inflorescences short, slender, single-flowered or bearing 2 flowers successively; bracts short. Flowers green or yellowish green, often tinged with orange, small, held with the lip on the upper side; sepals and petals broadly lanceolate, acute, 8–10 mm long; lip ovate, acute, enlarged at the base with upright lobes alongside the column, with an enlarged longitudinal callus in the basal half, 6 mm long; spur straight, narrow at the mouth then somewhat inflated in the lower third, narrowing again at the apex, 11–14 mm long.

Epiphyte in semi-deciduous woodlands, in semi-shaded situations; 200–300 m; flowering between February and April.

Guinea, Sierra Leone, Côte d'Ivoire, Ghana, Togo, Nigeria, and Gabon.

Easily recognised by its short broad leaves.

Angraecum pyriforme Summerhayes

Plants with an elongate stem bearing leaves and roots along its length. Stems upright, at least at first, becoming pendent, 10–30 cm long. Leaves in 2 rows, narrowly lanceolate or oblong, slightly unequally bilobed at the apex, the shorter lobe quite distinct, 7–11 cm long, 1–2 cm wide. Inflorescences short, slender, erect, single-flowered, or bearing 2 small flowers successively; bracts short. Flowers green or yellowish green, held with the lip on the upper side; dorsal sepal elliptic-lanceolate, subacute, 10 mm long; lateral sepals slightly curved, lanceolate, acute, 9 mm long; petals falcate, lanceolate, subacute, 8 mm long; lip ovate, acute, narrow at the base, 7.5 mm long, 4.5 mm wide; spur straight, narrow at the mouth then very narrow, swollen at the end so that it appears club-shaped, 11–12 mm long.

Epiphyte in rain forest, in semi-shaded situations at low altitudes; flowering between April and June.

Côte d'Ivoire and southern Nigeria.

Easily recognised by the short lip and characteristic shape of the spur.

SECTION *GOMPHOCENTRUM*

This section was proposed by Garay (1973) to accommodate plants with a distinct though often short stem. The inflorescences are borne in the lower leaf axils and are always several-flowered, sometimes many-flowered, sometimes paniculate. The flowers are yellowish green, rather thin, even somewhat diaphanous.

Many of these species were included in Schlechter's section *Boryangraecum* in *Flore de Madagascar* (Perrier 1941). One species (*Angraecum calceolus*) is found in Mozambique near the eastern coast of Africa and is widespread in the Madagascar region, while 15 species are restricted to Madagascar in their distribution. A further 3 species are found only in Réunion and one (*A. zeylanicum*) occurs in the Seychelles and in Sri Lanka.

Angraecum calceolus Thouars

Syns. *Angraecum anocentrum* Schlechter, *A. carpophorum* Thouars, *A. rhopaloceras* Schlechter, *A. guillauminii* H. Perrier, and many others

Plant erect, with a woody stem up to 10 cm long, and with many elongated greyish roots. Leaves up to 16, ligulate but narrowing towards the base so that they appear petiolate, very unequally bilobed at the apex, the shorter lobe almost absent, 17–22 cm long, 1.5–2.5 cm wide. Inflorescences simple or paniculate with up to 5 branches, 15–30 cm long, flowers widely spaced; bracts ca. 2 mm long; pedicel with ovary 5–6 mm long. Flowers yellow-green, thin-textured; dorsal sepal ovate-lanceolate, acute, 7–8 mm long, 2–4 mm wide; lateral sepals narrower, rather oblique, ca. 8 mm long; petals lanceolate, acuminate, 6 mm long; lip concave, ovate, acuminate, ca. 7 mm long including an acumen

Angraecum multiflorum. From Thouars 1822, t. 74.

Angraecum calceolus growing terrestrially, exposed to full sun, Southwest Madagascar. J. Hermans

2 mm long; spur narrow, slightly swollen near the apex, 12 mm long.

Epiphyte in shrubs and trees, usually near the sea; up to 100 m; flowering at various times.

Mozambique, Madagascar, Comoro Islands, Réunion, Mauritius, and Seychelles.

Angraecum calceolus. J. Hermans

Species from Madagascar and Some from Neighbouring Islands

Angraecum acutipetalum Schlechter

Plant erect, with a short stem up to 10–12 cm high. Leaves 5–9, ligulate but narrowing towards both ends, canaliculate above and keeled below, very variable in size, 4–12 cm long, 5–10 mm wide. Inflorescences shorter than the leaves, bearing 2–5 flowers close together near the apex; bracts triangular, not more than 1.5 mm long; pedicel with ovary 6 mm long. Flowers green with a white lip, small; sepals lanceolate, acute, 5.5 mm long; petals obliquely lanceolate, acute, as long as the sepals; lip concave, oval, shortly acuminate, 5 mm long; spur straight, cylindric and inflated just at the apex, 5 mm long.

Epiphyte in mossy forests and on lichen-covered trees; 1000–2000 m; flowering between September and January.

Angraecum acutipetalum. J. Hermans

Madagascar (on mountain slopes in the eastern and northern regions).

In 1941 Perrier described 2 varieties of this species with smaller flowers but did not provide diagnoses or descriptions in Latin. Thus the var. *analabeensis* Perrier and var. *ankaranae* Perrier may not be valid names.

Angraecum andringitranum Schlechter

Pendent plant with simple, rounded stems up to 40 cm long. Leaves numerous, ligulate but slightly narrowed towards the base, obliquely bilobed at the apex, leathery, 11–13 cm long, 11–13 mm wide. Inflorescences slender, much shorter than the leaves, 2- to 4-flowered; bract oval, apiculate, much shorter than the ovary; pedicel with ovary 7 mm long. Flowers greenish white, small; sepals narrowly oval, subacute, 7 mm long; petals a little shorter and much narrower than the sepals; lip concave, oval, acute, 7 mm long, 4 mm wide; spur narrow, acute, 22–25 mm long.

Epiphyte in mossy forests; ca. 1600 m; flowering in March.

Madagascar (Andringitra Massif).

Angraecum caulescens Thouars

Plant erect, with a woody stem up to 10 cm long, and with many elongated greyish roots. Leaves up to 10, dark green, ligulate but narrowing towards the base so that they appear petiolate, very unequally bilobed at the apex, the shorter lobe almost absent, 15–20 cm long, 1.5–2 cm wide. Inflorescences arising below the leaves, unbranched, bearing 3–5 flowers near the ends of each rachis, 8–12 cm long; bracts very small; pedicel with ovary 4–5 mm long. Flowers pale green, thin-textured; dorsal sepal ovate-lanceolate, 6 mm long; petals lanceolate, acuminate, 4 mm long; lip concave, ovate, acute, ca. 5 mm long; spur narrow, cylindrical, shorter than the lip.

Epiphyte in moist forests; medium altitudes.

Madagascar, Réunion, and Mauritius.

This species differs from *Angraecum calceolus* in its unbranched inflorescence and smaller flowers, and from *A. multiflorum* in its longer inflorescences, borne singly, and shorter stem.

Angraecum cornucopiae H. Perrier

Plant erect, 15–25 cm high, with slender stems 2–2.5 mm in diameter. Leaves grass-like, unequally bilobed at the apex, erect, rigid, 5–14 cm long, 4–7 mm wide. Inflorescences 2–4, arranged as in *Angraecum multiflorum*, 3–5 cm long, 1- to 7-flowered; bracts scarious, reddish, 15 mm long, 2 mm wide; pedicel with ovary 3.5 cm long, twisted below the flower. Flowers yellowish green; sepals lanceolate, 6 mm long, 2 mm wide; petals similar to the sepals, shorter and narrower, 5.5 mm long, 1 mm wide; lip concave, boat-shaped, 7 mm long, 4 mm wide; spur narrowing towards the tip, 5 mm long.

Epiphyte amongst lichens; 1500–1700 m; flowering November to December.

Madagascar (Marojejy Massif in the north-east).

Angraecum corynoceras Schlechter

Plant erect or pendent, with stems up to 25 cm long, 3 mm in diameter. Leaves many, linear, somewhat attenuate towards the base and unequally bilobed at the apex, 6–10 cm long, 5–7 mm wide. Inflorescences very slender, nearly as long as the leaves, 1- or 2-flowered; bracts oval-apiculate, much shorter than the ovary; pedicel with ovary 9 mm long. Flowers yellowish, all parts ca. 8 mm long; sepals oblong-lanceolate, dorsal sepal wider than lateral sepals; petals narrowly lanceolate, acute; lip concave, oval-subacuminate, 7.5 mm long, 4 mm wide; spur cylindric, curved, inflated at the apex, 8 mm long.

Epiphyte on trees with lichens; ca. 2000 m; flowering in January.

Madagascar (Mount Tsaratanana).

Angraecum dauphinense (Rolfe) Schlechter

Plant erect, with a distinct stem. Leaves in 2 rows, long and narrow, unequally bilobed at the apex, 12.5–18 cm long, 6–10 mm wide. Inflorescence slender, 5- to 7-flowered; bracts ovate-reni-

form, obtuse, and shortly bilobed at the apex, 1.5 mm long. Flowers small; sepals lanceolate, subacuminate, 6 mm long; petals narrower; lip broadly oval, very concave and as long as the petals; spur straight and cylindric, 6 mm long.

Epiphyte in forests. No other information available.

Madagascar (Tôlañaro).

Angraecum inapertum Thouars

Plant erect, with a very short stem. Leaves 5–7, pointed. Inflorescences arising below the leaves, single-flowered; peduncle shorter than the leaves. Flowers self-pollinating, or otherwise not opening fully; spur short and curved.

Madagascar, Réunion, and Mauritius.

Angraecum multiflorum Thouars

Plant erect, with a woody stem up to 20 cm long, and with many elongated greyish roots.

Angraecum multiflorum. J. Hermans

Leaves numerous on the upper part of the stem, oblong-lanceolate, oblique, attenuate towards both extremities, unequally bilobed at the apex, 3–8 cm long, 4–8 mm wide. Inflorescences arising annually from a short lateral axis which may become leafy at the apex after several years; bracts ca. 2 mm long; pedicel with ovary 2.5–3 mm long. Flowers 1–3, yellow, thin-textured; dorsal sepal ovate-lanceolate, acute, 3.5–5 mm long, 1.4–2.7 mm wide; lateral sepals narrower, rather oblique, united to each other at the base, 4–6 mm long; petals lanceolate, 3–4.8 mm long; lip concave, ovate, shortly acuminate, 3–5 mm long; spur curved and slightly swollen near the apex, 2–4 mm long.

Epiphyte in forests; 1000–2000 m in Réunion, at lower altitudes in Madagascar; flowering November to February.

Madagascar, Réunion, Mauritius, and Seychelles.

The curious inflorescence structure is also found in *Angraecum cornucopiae*, *A. rhizanthium*, and *A. sinuatiflorum* (section *Boryangraecum*).

Angraecum sacculatum. J. Hermans

Angraecum rhizanthium H. Perrier

Plants small and slender, up to 10–15 cm high, with stems 3 mm in diameter. Leaves erect, grass-like, linear-ligulate, 5–9 cm long, 7–8 mm wide. Inflorescences arising annually from a short lateral axis as in *Angraecum multiflorum*, erect, 1.5–6 cm long, 1- to 3-flowered; bracts 5 mm long; pedicel with ovary twisted, 5 mm long. Flowers small; sepals lanceolate, 5 mm long, 2.8 mm wide at the base; petals as long as the sepals but narrower, 1 mm wide at the base; lip concave, narrowly boat-shaped, attenuate; spur cylindric, 4 mm long.

Epiphyte in mossy forests; 1000–1500 m; flowering January to February.

Madagascar (central region, on the west slopes of Mount Marojejy).

Differs from *Angraecum multiflorum* by the shape of the lip and the short, straight spur.

Angraecum sacculatum Schlechter

Plants erect or pendent, up to 17 cm long, with a short stem up to 10 cm long and 3 mm in diameter. Leaves numerous, linear, somewhat attenuate towards the base and unequally bilobed at the apex, 3.7–6 cm long, 4–7 mm wide. Inflorescences very slender, 1- or 2-flowered; bracts oval-apiculate, very small; pedicel with ovary 3–4 mm long. Flowers yellowish, very small; sepals lanceolate, acute, 4–4.5 mm long; petals similar but a little narrower; lip concave, oval-acuminate, as long as the sepals; spur oblong, obtuse, 4 mm long.

Epiphyte in mossy forests; 1300–1800 m; flowering September to February.

Madagascar (on west-facing slopes in the centre of the island).

Angraecum tenuipes Summerhayes
(including *Angraecum ischnopus* Schlechter)

Plants usually erect, with stems up to 30 cm long, sometimes branched and bearing many leaves. Leaves linear, unequally bilobed at the apex, 5–8.5 cm long, 3–6 mm wide. Inflorescences as

Angraecum tenuipes. J. Hermans

long as the leaves, very slender, 1- to 3-flowered; bracts oval-acuminate, about as long as the ovary; pedicel with ovary 5 mm long. Flowers greenish, opaque, small; sepals oval, apiculate or acute, 5–7 mm long; petals similar, 6 mm long, 2 mm wide; lip concave, oval, acute, 6 mm long, 3 mm wide; spur as long as the lip, becoming gradually wider towards the tip, 6 mm long.

Epiphyte, amongst lichens on small trees; 1700–2500 m; flowering September to December.

Madagascar (central highlands).

Angraecum verecundum Schlechter

Plants erect or pendent, with stems up to 15–20 cm long, 4 mm in diameter. Leaves linear-ligulate, somewhat attenuate towards the base and unequally bilobed at the apex, 10–14 cm long, 8–14 mm wide. Inflorescences shorter than the leaves, 1- or 2-flowered; bracts oval, shortly apiculate, much shorter than the ovary; pedicel with ovary 10 mm

long. Flowers greenish white, all parts ca. 7 mm long; sepals oblong, subacute, lateral sepals slightly thickened along the midline of the outer surface; petals a little shorter than the sepals; lip concave, broadly oval-apiculate, bearing a small keel on the inner surface near the base, 6.5 mm long, 6 mm wide; spur subcylindric, slightly dilated towards the tip, 7.5 mm long.

Epiphyte in mossy forests on eastern slopes, ca. 2000 m; flowering in February.

Madagascar (central highlands).

Angraecum vesiculatum Schlechter

Plants erect, with stems up to 10 cm high, 5 mm in diameter. Leaves fleshy or leathery, ligulate, somewhat attenuate towards the base and unequally bilobed at the apex, 5 cm long, 7 mm wide. Inflorescences lax, as long as the leaves, 2- or 3-flowered; bracts small, oval-apiculate; pedicel with ovary 5–6 mm long. Flowers yellowish, all parts ca. 8 mm long; sepals lanceolate, acuminate; petals narrowly lanceolate, acute; lip concave, oval-elliptic, acuminate, 7 mm long, 7 mm wide; spur inflated, like a vesicle, 8 mm long.

Epiphyte in forest; ca. 2000 m; flowering in October.

Madagascar (Mount Tsaratanana).

Species from Réunion Only

Angraecum cordemoyi Schlechter

Plants small with short stems 1.5 cm long, 3–4 mm wide, rooting only from the base. Leaves 4 or 5 in 2 rows, twisted at the base so that they lie in one plane, oval or oblong, 2.5–3 cm long, 1 cm wide. Inflorescences in the axils of leaf sheaths where the leaves have fallen, very delicate, 1- or 2-flowered; peduncles up to 2.5 cm long. Flowers 8 mm in diameter, greenish white; sepals narrow, acute, dorsal sepal a little larger than lateral sepals; petals similar to the sepals; lip concave, ovate; spur cylindrical, bent, and shorter than the lip.

Epiphyte at high altitudes.

Réunion.

Angraecum crassifolium (Cordemoy) Schlechter

Plant erect with a short stem 5–7 cm long. Leaves 4 or 5 in 2 rows, oblong, slightly narrower towards the base, unequally bilobed at the apex, thick and fleshy, dark green, 8–9 cm long, 1.5–2 cm wide. Inflorescence axillary in the leaf sheath of fallen leaves, half as long as the leaves above, flexuous. Flowers unknown.

On the upper slopes of Grand Bernard; in fruit in September.

Réunion (in the north).

Angraecum undulatum (Cordemoy) Schlechter

Plant erect with short stems, 20–25 cm long. Leaves in 2 rows, well spaced, 1–1.5 cm apart, lanceolate, twisted at the base so that they lie in one plane, obliquely bilobed at the apex, margins undulate, 8 cm long, 18 mm wide. Inflorescences short, up to 2.5 cm long, 2- or 3-flowered. Flowers greenish yellow, small.

Réunion.

Species from Seychelles and Sri Lanka

Angraecum zeylanicum Lindley

Plant erect, with short stems 12–15 cm long, and with long branched roots from the lower part. Leaves few, in 2 rows, linear-oblong, flat, midrib conspicuous below, unequally bilobed at the apex, one lobe sometimes absent, 11–24 cm long, 1.3–2.4 cm wide. Inflorescences arising below the leaves, unbranched, 3.5–7.5 cm long; ovary with pedicel twisted, 7 mm long. Flowers yellowish green, 1 cm in diameter; dorsal sepal ovate-lanceolate, 5 mm long; lateral sepals lanceolate, slightly longer; petals lanceolate, acuminate, 4.8 mm long; lip concave, ovate, as wide as long, ca. 4.6 mm; spur clavate, standing erect behind the dorsal sepal, 5 mm long.

Epiphyte on trunks of trees and large shrubs in forest; sea level to 300 m; flowering in September and November.

Sri Lanka and Seychelles.

Angraecum zeylanicum. J. Hermans

SECTION *BORYANGRAECUM*

The plants in this section have short stems, sometimes apparently almost absent. The inflorescences usually bear several flowers in a loose raceme, but in some species bear only one flower. The flowers are small or medium-sized, typically larger than those in section *Nana*. Further study may reveal that some of these species should be re-allocated to other sections.

Four species are recorded in Africa, mostly near the eastern coast of the continent; nine species are recorded from Madagascar and one (*Angraecum xylopus*) from the Comoro Islands.

Angraecum pinifolium. 1: Habit. 2: Flower. 3: Lip and spur. 4: Dorsal sepal. 5: Lateral sepal. 6: Petal. 7: Column. 8: Anther. 9: Pollinarium. Reprinted by permission from Bosser 1970a, fig. 2. E. Razafindrakoto. © Publications Scientifiques du Muséum national d'Histoire naturelle, Paris.

Angraecum dives. B. Campbell

Species from Africa

Angraecum dives Rolfe

Plants erect with stems 1–5 cm long, rooting near the base. Leaves 2–10, erect, linear, bilobed at the apex, with rounded lobes, 5–20 cm long, 5–15 mm wide. Inflorescences usually many, erect or arching, 8- to 25-flowered; peduncles slender. Flowers green or yellowish green; sepals elliptic-lanceolate, acute, 5 mm long, 1.3–1.5 mm wide; petals lanceolate, acute or acuminate, recurved, 5 mm long, 1.2 mm wide; lip concave, ovate, acuminate, 4 mm long, 2.5 mm wide; spur subclavate, upcurved beside the ovary, 2–3 mm long.

Epiphyte and a lithophyte, on coral and other rocks near the coast and in coastal woodlands, usually in bright light; often found on baobab trees and also on much smaller trees and shrubs, often rather near the ground; from sea level to 80 m; flowering September to November.

Kenya, Tanzania, and Socotra Island.

Angraecum geniculatum Williamson

Plant erect with stems up to 8 cm long and roots borne along the stem. Leaves up to 9 in 2 rows, linear-ligulate, sometimes falcate, unequally bilobed at the apex, 3–4.5 cm long, 3–6 mm wide. Inflorescences arising opposite the leaves, intervallate,

1- to 3-flowered; pedicel and ovary curved, to 4 mm long. Flowers pale yellow or pale green; dorsal sepal lanceolate, acute, 3.6–5 mm long, narrow; lateral sepals longer and falcate; petals shorter and obtuse; lip concave, ovate below tapering abruptly to an acuminate tip, 4.5 mm long, 2.5 mm wide; spur wide at the mouth, tapering to a slender middle portion, then inflated at the apex, 5.5–8 mm long.

Epiphyte in dense forest; flowering in November.

Zambia.

Angraecum sacciferum Lindley

Plants very small, with stems short, almost absent, or up to 5 cm long. Leaves in a short fan or in 2 rows on either side of the stem, linear to narrowly elliptic, unequally bilobed at the apex, 1–6 cm long, 3–5 mm wide, usually twisted at the base so that they lie in one plane. Inflorescences

Angraecum sacciferum. J. Hermans

1 to several, often arising from the same point in successive years, 2- to 5-flowered. Flowers green, pedicel and ovary strongly twisted so that the lip is uppermost; sepals elliptic-oblong, 2–4 mm long, 1.5–2 mm wide; petals lanceolate, acute, 2.4–3 mm long; lip deeply concave, broadly ovate, 2.7–3.5 mm long, 3.5 mm wide; spur shortly cylindrical, truncate, to 2 mm long.

Epiphyte, widespread in upland forests where humidity is high, and on rocks by streams; 700–2400 m; flowering March to June.

São Tomé and Cameroon, eastwards to Kenya and southwards to South Africa (Limpopo, Mpumalanga, KwaZulu-Natal, Eastern Cape Province, and Cape Province).

Angraecum teres Summerhayes

Plants small with a short pendent stem less than 2 cm long. Leaves narrow, terete, always pendent but sometimes arranged in a small fan, 4–15 cm long, apiculate. Inflorescences arching or pendent, slender, up to 15 cm long, 2- to 10-flowered. Flowers greenish ochre, small; dorsal sepal ovate-lanceolate, acuminate, 7–8 mm long, 3–4 mm wide; lateral sepals lanceolate, similar to dorsal sepal but narrower; petals lanceolate, acuminate, slightly longer than sepals; lip ovate or obscurely 3-lobed, 5 mm long; spur ascending above the ovary, to 2 cm long.

Epiphyte on the boles of small trees and on large branches; rather rarely collected from only a few localities near the coast of East Africa; sea level to 200 m; flowering in March.

Kenya and northern Tanzania.

Species from Madagascar and Comoro Islands

Angraecum aviceps Schlechter

Plants small and more or less stemless, 6–7 cm high. Leaves 3 or 4, ligulate, tapering towards the apex which is unequally and obtusely bilobed, thin and papery, 5–6 cm long, 1–1.2 mm wide. Inflorescence shorter than the leaves, up to 5 cm long, 3- to 5-flowered; bracts deltoid, apiculate, very small; pedicel with ovary twisted, 6 mm long. Flowers yellowish white, thin; sepals narrowly lanceolate, acute, 7 mm long; lateral sepals keeled on the back; petals linear-lanceolate, subacuminate, 5.5 mm long; lip concave, oval at the base and rostrate above, fleshy, 6.5 mm long, 2.5 mm wide; spur horizontal, narrow beyond the wide mouth, 9–10 mm long.

Epiphyte in woods on west facing slopes; 1000 m; flowering in July.

Madagascar (northern Bemarivo Special Reserve in the north-west).

Angraecum flavidum Bosser

Plant erect with a short stem 1–1.5 cm long, bearing roots at the base that become flattened on the substratum. Leaves 3 or 4 in 2 rows, ligulate, flat, unequally bilobed at the apex, 3–5 cm long, 3–4.5 mm wide. Inflorescences slender, longer than the leaves, 2- to 4-flowered; bracts broadly oval, acute, 2–2.5 mm long; pedicel with ovary slender, twisted, 10–12 mm long. Flowers pale yellow, slightly fleshy; sepals lanceolate, subacute, 15–16 mm long, 2.5–3 mm wide; petals linear-lanceolate, acuminate, 15–16 mm long, 1.5–2 mm wide; lip concave at the base, lanceolate, acuminate, 14–15 mm long, 3–4 mm wide; spur funnel-shaped at the mouth, becoming cylindric and curved, 8–10 mm long.

Epiphyte in dry, semi-deciduous forest; 300 m; flowering in January.

Madagascar (north-eastern region).

Angraecum myrianthum Schlechter

Plants almost or quite stemless, densely covered with leaves. Leaves 7–9, linear, unequally and obtusely bilobed at the apex, 12–20 cm long, 7–9 mm wide. Inflorescences numerous, longer than the leaves, densely many-flowered; bracts hyaline, almost as long as the ovary; pedicel with ovary 2 mm long. Flowers very small, greenish white; sepals oval-lanceolate, acute, 2 mm long; petals lanceolate, acute; lip oval lanceolate, acuminate, 2 mm long; spur conical, subacute, less than 1 mm long.

Angraecum ochraceum. J. Hermans

Epiphyte on twigs of bushes in the family Didiereaceae; flowering in June.

Madagascar (south-western region near Ampanihy).

Angraecum ochraceum (Ridley) Schlechter

Plant with a short stem. Leaves narrow, linear-lanceolate, 10 cm long, 6–7 mm wide. Inflorescences single-flowered; bracts small, oval; pedicel with ovary twisted. Flowers ochreous, small; sepals lanceolate, acute; petals narrower and shorter; lip concave, boat-shaped, pointed; spur horizontal, twice as long as the lip, slender at first, then inflated in the apical third.

Epiphyte; flowering in April.

Madagascar (eastern highlands).

Angraecum pinifolium Bosser

Plant short and almost stemless, 10–15 cm high. Leaves 4–5, narrowly linear, canaliculate along the upper surface, rounded below, unequally bilobed at the apex, acute, 8–11 cm long, 1.5–2 mm wide. Inflorescence lax, arising below the leaves, shorter than the leaves, 6–10 cm long, 2- to 4-flowered; bracts green, oval, acute, 2.5–3.5 mm long; pedicel with ovary 6 mm long. Flowers yellowish green, fleshy; sepals ovate-lanceolate, 7–7.5 mm long, 3–3.5 mm wide; petals lanceolate, slightly falcate, 6 mm long, 2 mm wide; lip concave, ovate, acute, margins rounded and incurved, with a strong keel along the centre of the basal half, 4.5–5.5 mm long; spur narrow at first then inflated in the apical half, 6–6.5 mm long.

Epiphyte in shady forests; 900 m; flowering in January.

Madagascar (eastern region).

This little species looks somewhat similar to *Angraecum teres*, but the flowers are rather different with a much shorter spur.

Angraecum pumilio Schlechter

Plants small and stemless, 2–10 cm high. Leaves 3–7, thin, upright, linear-ligulate, rather variable in size, tapering towards both ends, 1.2–7.5 cm long, 2.5–7 mm wide. Inflorescences as long as the leaves or shorter, 1- or 2-flowered; bracts oval, subacute, black, 2–3 mm long; pedicel with ovary twisted, 2–7 mm long. Flowers yellowish green, small; sepals oval, subacute, 5 mm long, 3–4 mm wide; petals lanceolate, subacute, 4 mm long, 2.2 mm wide; lip concave, thick and fleshy, suborbicular, shortly acuminate, 4.5 mm long, 5 mm wide; spur wide at the mouth, then narrow, and finally inflated into an oval sac 2 mm in diameter, in total 6–7 mm long.

Epiphyte amongst lichens on ericoid shrubs; 2000–2200 m; flowering February to April.

Madagascar (Mount Tsaratanana).

Angraecum sinuatiflorum H. Perrier

Plant stemless or almost so, 12–15 cm high. Leaves erect, grass-like, 8–15 cm long, 2.5–4 mm wide. Inflorescences produced serially, as in *Angraecum multiflorum*, 2- to 5-flowered; peduncle slender; bracts inflated, apiculate, 2.5–3 mm long; pedicel with ovary curved and twisted, 3 mm long.

Flowers small; sepals all similar, oblong, apiculate, 4 mm long, 1.8 mm wide; petals narrowly linear, 3 mm long, 0.6 mm wide; lip concave, slipper-shaped, apiculate, 4 mm long, 2 mm wide; spur filiform, narrowing from a wide mouth, 13–14 mm long.

Epiphyte; flowering in September.

Madagascar (south-eastern region).

A similar inflorescence is also found in *Angraecum multiflorum*, *A. rhizanthium*, and *A. cornucopiae*, as well as in a few species in other genera.

Angraecum tamarindicolum Schlechter

Plant stemless. Leaves 3–5, ligulate or linear-ligulate, papery, unequally and obtusely bilobed at the apex, 2–5 cm long, 3.5–5 mm wide. Inflorescences usually shorter than the leaves, 1- or 2-flowered; bracts oval, apiculate, very short; pedicel with ovary twisted, 3 mm long. Flowers thin, yellowish white; sepals oval, 3 mm long; petals oblong, a little shorter than the sepals; lip concave, broadly rhomboid-oval, 3 mm long and wide; spur projecting backwards, narrow behind the wide mouth and inflated into a wide sac in the apical half, 7.5 mm long.

Epiphyte on *Tamarindus indica*; ca. 100 m; flowering in February.

Madagascar (Sambirano valley).

Angraecum vesiculiferum Schlechter

Plant small and stemless, up to 5 cm high. Leaves 3, lanceolate-ligulate, tapering towards the base and obliquely acuminate at the apex, 5 cm long, 8 mm wide. Inflorescences much shorter than the leaves, 2- or 3-flowered; bracts oval, apiculate, very short; pedicel with ovary 3 mm long. Flowers thin, small; sepals lanceolate, acute or subacuminate, 5 mm long; petals lanceolate, acuminate, recurved, and a little shorter than the sepals; lip concave, broadly oval, acuminate, 4.5 mm long, 3 mm wide; spur bent back horizontally, inflated like a vesicle, 2.5 mm long.

Epiphyte on twigs in the remnants of mossy forests; 2000 m; flowering in October.

Madagascar (eastern flanks of Mount Tsiafajavona).

Angraecum xylopus Reichenbach f.

Plants with a short, thick stem, often pendent. Leaves in 2 rows near apex of stem, subcylindric and canaliculate or almost terete, 15 cm long. Inflorescences usually several, 20–30 cm long, rigid, or flexuous towards the apex, bearing 5–9 well-spaced flowers; bracts small, oval-triangular, shorter than the ovary; pedicel with ovary ca. 12 mm long. Flowers yellowish green; sepals triangular-lanceolate, acuminate; petals a little shorter and narrower than the sepals; lip concave, lanceolate, acuminate; spur slender, 12 mm long.

Epiphyte on the trunks of trees; flowering December to January.

Comoro Islands (Grande Comore).

SECTION *NANA*

Garay (1973) proposed this section to accommodate a number of species with dwarf plants and very abbreviated stems. The tiny, thin flowers are borne in dense-flowered inflorescences that are often one-sided.

In this book we have followed Garay in allocating 20 species to this section. Four of these are found in Africa, nine in Madagascar, at least one of which also occurs in Réunion, and the remaining seven in Réunion and Mauritius. None of the species is well known in cultivation outside its country of origin. Further study of these tiny plants may reveal that the number of species in this section should be reduced by placing some names in synonymy.

Species from Africa

Angraecum chamaeanthus Schlechter

Plants diminutive only a few cm high. Stems erect, short, 1–5 mm high. Leaves 2–6, arranged in a small fan, linear or ligulate, 1–2 cm long, 1.5–2.5 mm wide, slightly bluish green. Inflorescences simple, erect or curved, 4- to 10-flowered. Flowers white or pale green, tiny, only 2–3 mm in diameter; sepals oblong or elliptic, rounded at the apex; pet-

Angraecum chamaeanthus. B. Campbell

als oblong or obovate; lip broadly ovate, obscurely 3-lobed, with a short conical spur at its base.

Usually growing as a twig epiphyte in small trees and bushes in montane forests and easily overlooked; 1400–2400 m; flowering in June.

Kenya, Tanzania, Malawi, Zambia, Zimbabwe, and South Africa (Limpopo and Mpumalanga).

Angraecum decipiens Summerhayes

Plants dwarf, only a few cm high, with short, erect stems 1–5 mm high. Leaves 2–4, arranged in a small fan, linear or ligulate, falcate, 15–35 mm long, 2.5–3.5 mm wide, rather fleshy. Inflorescences simple, curved, 5- to 15-flowered. Flowers pale green or yellowish green, tiny, only 2–4 mm in diameter; dorsal sepal elliptic or obovate, subacute to obtuse, 1.7–2.3 mm long, ca. 1 mm wide; lateral sepals obliquely elliptic-obovate, acute or subacute, ca. 2 mm long; petals elliptic, subacute to obtuse, 1.6–2 mm long; lip entire, concave, ovate, obtuse, 1.5–2.1 mm long, with a short straight, clavate spur ca. 1.5 mm long.

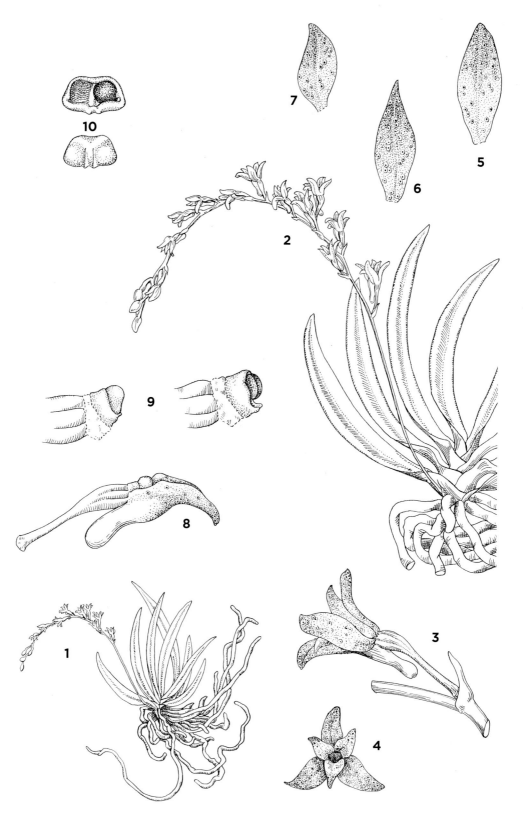

Angraecum decipiens. 1: Habit. 2: Habit, twice as large. 3: Flower, side. 4: Flower, front. 5: Dorsal sepal. 6: Lateral sepal. 7: Petal. 8: Lip and spur. 9: Column. 10: Anther-cap. From Summerhayes 1966, p. 190. M. Grierson.

Usually growing as a twig epiphyte in small trees and bushes in very shady habitats and easily overlooked; 1600–2200 m; flowering in April.

Kenya and Tanzania.

Angraecum minus Summerhayes

Plants dwarf, only a few cm high, with short, erect stems 2–10 mm high. Leaves 2–8, arranged in a small fan, suberect or arcuate, linear, 1.5–5 cm long, 1–3.8 mm wide, articulated to a leaf-sheath 6–9 mm long. Inflorescences several, arising from base of the plant, simple, erect or curved, 4- to 14-flowered; bracts ovate, sheathing at the base, 0.5–1 mm long; pedicellate ovary 1–2 mm long. Flowers white with a green spur, tiny, only 2–3 mm in diameter; sepals oblong or elliptic, rounded at the apex, lateral sepals slightly longer than dorsal sepal; petals lanceolate, acute, as long as the dorsal sepal; lip fleshy, concave, broadly ovate, obtuse, 1.4 mm long, 1.6 mm wide; spur saccate, 0.5 mm long.

Epiphyte in rain forest, and in plantations and woodlands nearby; 1000–1800 m; flowering in January, March, and August.

Tanzania, Zambia, and Zimbabwe.

Angraecum pusillum Lindley

Plants small, only a few cm high, with short, erect stems 25 mm high. Leaves grass-like, 3–10, arranged in a small fan, linear, 5–16 cm long, 2–5 mm wide, dark greyish green. Inflorescences several, arising from the base of the plant, simple, erect or curved, up to 10 cm long, bearing several to many flowers along one side; pedicels and ovary ca. 2.5 mm long. Flowers white, pale green, or yellowish, tiny, ca. 5 mm in diameter; sepals lanceolate, rounded at the apex; petals lanceolate, acuminate, similar to sepals; lip concave, broadly ovate, 1–1.6 mm long; spur saccate, 1 mm long.

Epiphyte in shady forests which are seasonally moist; flowering throughout the year.

Zimbabwe, Swaziland, and South Africa (Kwa-Zulu-Natal, Eastern Cape Province, and Cape Province).

Angraecum pusillum. J. Stewart

Species from Madagascar

Angraecum andasibeense H. Perrier

Plants small and stemless. Leaves 5–7, linear, unequally and obtusely bilobed at the apex, 3–6 cm long, 3–4 mm wide. Inflorescences numerous, arising below the leaves, 1- or 2-flowered; bracts up to 2 mm long; pedicel with ovary 5–6 mm long. Flowers yellowish; sepals broadly linear, obtuse, opaque, 4 mm long, 1 mm wide; petals thick, lanceolate-acute, 3.5 mm long, 0.8 mm wide; lip concave, oval or funnel-shaped, with a thick acumen 1.5 mm long, in total 5.5 mm long, 4 mm wide near the base; spur wide at the mouth, then narrow and pointed, 1.3 cm long.

Epiphyte in mossy forests; ca. 1000 m; flowering in February.

Madagascar (central areas near Andasibe).

Angraecum bemarivoense Schlechter

Plants very small, stemless, 4–5 cm high. Leaves 3–5, oblong or oblong-ligulate, narrowing towards the base, unequally and obtusely bilobed at the apex, to 15 mm long, 5 mm wide. Inflorescences 3–4, slender, twice as long as the leaves, bearing 7–12 flowers along one side; bracts oval-apiculate, very small; pedicel with ovary 1.25 mm long. Flowers very small, white and thin; sepals oblong-subapiculate, 1.25 mm long; petals oblique, a little shorter and narrower than the sepals; lip concave, oval, subapiculate; spur oblong, 1.35 mm long.

Epiphyte on twigs and small branches in forests; ca. 800 m; flowering in September.

Madagascar (Bemarivo Special Reserve in the north-west).

Angraecum microcharis Schlechter

Plants very small, without a stem, and 3–3.5 cm high. Leaves 4, oblique, ligulate, narrowing towards the base, unequally and obtusely bilobed at the apex, 28 mm long, 3.5–4 mm wide. Inflorescences few, erect, bearing several flowers along one side; bracts erect, oval-acute, very small; pedicel with ovary 1.25 mm long. Flowers very small, white and thin; sepals narrowly oblong, apiculate, 1.25 mm long; petals oblong-lanceolate, a little narrower than the sepals; lip broadly rhomboid, obscurely subtrilobed, 1.1 mm long, 1.25 mm wide; spur oblong-obtuse, slightly compressed, 1.25 mm long.

Epiphyte on the twigs of shrubs; 600 m; flowering in January.

Madagascar (Sambirano valley).

Angraecum muscicolum H. Perrier

Plants without a stem and up to 10 cm high. Leaves 3 or 4, shortly tapering towards both ends, 2.5–7.5 cm long, 1–3 mm wide. Inflorescences about as long as the leaves; bracts short, ca. 1 mm long; pedicel and ovary 4 mm long. Flowers 1–3; sepals oval, obtuse, 4 mm long, 1.7 mm wide, lateral sepals narrower and more pointed than dorsal sepal; petals gradually narrowing from the base, acute at the apex, 3.5 mm long, 1 mm wide at the base; lip very concave, broadly boat-shaped, rounded at the base, shortly acuminate-acute at the apex, 4 mm long, 4 mm wide; spur attenuate from the wide mouth, swollen at the apex, 3 mm long.

Epiphyte amongst mosses on tree trunks; ca. 1400 m; flowering in February.

Madagascar (central region).

Angraecum onivense H. Perrier

Plants without a stem up to 10 cm high. Leaves 7 or 8, narrowly lanceolate-linear, gradually narrowing towards both ends, very unequally and acutely lobed at the apex, 7–8.5 cm long, 3.5–4 mm wide. Inflorescences several, lax, about as long as the leaves and arising below them; bracts very small, pedicel with ovary 1.2 mm long. Flowers white, small; sepals oval-obtuse, thick, 1.8 mm long, 0.7 mm wide; petals a little smaller, 1.4 mm long, 0.7 mm wide; lip very concave, oval, obtuse, thick, 1.8 mm long, 1.3 mm wide; spur sac-like, narrow at the middle, wider at the apex, 1.4 mm long, 1.1 mm wide at the apex.

Epiphyte on tree trunks in mossy forests; 1400 m; flowering in February.

Madagascar (Andasibe, in the Onive River valley).

Angraecum perhumile H. Perrier

Plant very small, almost or quite stemless, up to 5 cm high. Leaves 3 or 4, narrow, keeled along the back, apex entire and subobtuse, 0.8–2.5 cm long, 1.3 mm wide. Inflorescences slender, longer than the leaves, 1- to 3-flowered; bracts short, obtuse; pedicel with ovary 2–2.5 mm long, twisted around the spur. Flowers with sepals oval-obtuse, lateral sepals narrower than dorsal sepal and more acute, 2 mm long, 1.2 mm wide; petals lanceolate, subacute, 1.8 mm long, 0.7 mm wide; lip very concave, wider than long, apiculate, 2.3 mm long, 3 mm wide; spur short, cylindric at the base, obtuse at the apex, 1.5 mm long.

Epiphyte on twigs in mossy forests; 1400 m; flowering in February.

Madagascar (central regions).

Angraecum muscicolum. J. Hermans

Angraecum perhumile. J. Hermans

Angraecum rubellum. J. Hermans

Angraecum tenellum. J. Hermans

Angraecum perparvulum H. Perrier

Plants very small, stemless, scarcely exceeding 1 cm in height. Leaves 4, oval, subacute, folded near the base, keeled on the outer surface towards the apex, 4.5–8 mm long, 2.2–2.5 mm long. Inflorescences usually 2; bracts 2 mm long, pointed; ovary with pedicel 2.5–3 mm long, surface warty. Flowers 2 or 3, sometimes only 2 with one aborted; sepals oval, acute, opaque, lateral sepals keeled on the back and a little longer and narrower than the dorsal, 2.5–2.8 mm long, 1.6–1.7 mm wide; petals oval, subacute, 2 mm long, 1 mm wide; lip panduriform, 2.4 mm long, 1.6 mm wide at the base, narrowing to 0.9 mm wide in the middle, 1.1 mm wide in the upper third; spur sac-like, 1.4 mm long, 1.2 mm wide.

Epiphyte on twigs in mossy forests; 1500–2000 m; flowering February to April.

Madagascar (Mounts Tsaratanana and Tsinjoarivo).

Angraecum rubellum Bosser

Plant small, more or less stemless, all parts tinted with red, 2–3 cm high. Leaves obovate to elliptic, blade twisted against the sheath to lie in one plane, rigid, with small acute lobes at the apex, slightly keeled on the back, green, more or less tinted with red, 15–22 mm long, 10–13 mm wide. Inflorescences axillary, as long as or longer than the leaves; all parts covered with red papillose hairs; bracts alternately arranged, small. Flowers fleshy, whitish or tinted pink; sepals with red papillose hairs on the outer surface, oval, acute, with a minute apiculus, 2–2.5 mm long; petals similar but shorter, and narrower, 1.7–1.8 mm long; lip concave, rounded, acute, 2.5 mm long and wide; spur slightly flattened, papillose within, 2.5–3 mm long.

Epiphyte in evergreen forests; ca. 900 m; flowering in March.

Madagascar (central highlands and eastern forests).

Angraecum tenellum (Ridley) Schlechter

Syns. *Saccolabium microphyton* Frappier ex Cordemoy, *Angraecum waterlotii* Perrier

Plant 2–3 cm high with thin leaves equitant on the stem, ca. 1.5 cm long, 4 mm wide. Inflorescences lax, 2–2.5 cm long, few-flowered. Flowers very small, white and thick, ca. 2 mm in diameter; sepals and petals ovate, obtuse; lip concave, ovate, obtuse; spur cylindrical, shorter than the ovary.

Epiphyte in semi-shade; 1000–1200 m; flowering in October.

Madagascar and Réunion.

Species from Réunion and Mauritius

These minute plants need further study.

Angraecum minutum Frappier ex Cordemoy

Plants diminutive, with fibrous roots arising from the lower part of the short stem, where leaves are arranged in a fan; stem slender, erect, 2 cm high. Leaves 5 or 6 in 2 rows, borne very close together at the base, forming a short fan, linear-lanceolate, 2–4 cm long, 2–3 mm wide. Inflorescence arising below the leaves, very slender, 2- to 4-flowered. Flowers tiny.

Epiphyte in forest; 1200 m; flowering in January and February.

Réunion.

Described by the original author as being very close to *Angraecum nanum* and perhaps not dissimilar to *A. parvulum*, originally described from Mauritius.

Angraecum nanum Frappier ex Cordemoy

Plants very small, with fibrous roots emanating from the stem below the short fan of leaves. Leaves dark green, canaliculate, 15–20 mm long, 3–4 mm wide. Inflorescence arising below the leaves, 1- to 3-flowered; bract small, one per flower. Flowers pale green, not opening fully, 3 mm in diameter; sepals oval, the lateral sepals somewhat oblique; petals smaller, lanceolate; lip fleshy, very concave, borne on the upper side of the flower; spur short, obtuse.

Epiphyte in shady forests; 2000 m; flowering in March-April.

Réunion and Mauritius.

This species is said to be very close to *Angraecum parvulum*, and perhaps not very different from *A. sacciferum* which is quite widespread in Africa.

Angraecum oberonia Finet

Plant very small, erect, stem up to 1 cm high with roots at the base. Leaves 4–6, obovate, fleshy, attenuate at the base, subobtuse and almost bilobed at the apex, 12–15 mm long, 3 mm wide. Inflorescences erect, lax, 4.5–5.2 cm long, 5- to 8-flowered. Flowers very small; sepals ovate, dorsal sepal narrow at the base, apex obtuse; lateral sepals a little longer and narrower than dorsal sepal; petals linear, falcate, obtuse; lip lamina very small, almost 3-lobed at the apex, funnel-shaped; spur a broadly conical sac, globose towards the apex.

Epiphyte; medium to high altitudes; flowering in March.

Réunion.

Angraecum parvulum Ayres ex S. Moore

Plant diminutive. Leaves narrowly linear, 2.5–5 cm long, 2 mm wide. Inflorescences as long as the leaves but arising below them, 2- or 3-flowered. Flowers pale green, about 4 mm wide; sepals longish, obtuse; petals linear, narrower than the sepals; lip concave, ovate-round, shortly acuminate; spur ellipsoid, obtuse, 2 mm long.

Réunion and Mauritius.

Similar in habit to *Angraecum sacciferum*.

Angraecum salazianum (Cordemoy) Schlechter

Plant dwarf, with a short stem ca. 1 cm high. Leaves in 2 rows along the stem, oblong, unequally bilobed at the apex, 2 cm long, 7 mm wide. Inflorescence axillary, 2- or 3-flowered. Flowers green, small; sepals and petals ovate, acute; lip a little wider.

Epiphyte; high altitudes; flowering in February.
Réunion.

Angraecum spicatum (Cordemoy) Schlechter

Plant with short, erect stems entirely covered with old leaf sheaths, rather thick, 5 mm wide. Leaves arranged in a fan, in 2 rows, narrow, somewhat thickened, unequally bilobed at the apex, subacute. Inflorescence often 2 per axil, slender, twice as long as the leaves, 4–4.5 cm long, multiflowered. Flowers unknown.

Réunion.

Angraecum viridiflorum Cordemoy ex Schlechter

Definitely the smallest species in the genus; only 1.5 cm high. Leaves 8–10 mm long, 2.5 mm wide. Inflorescences shorter than the leaves, 1- or 2-flowered. Flowers very small, whitish; sepals and petals ovate-lanceolate, ca. 2 mm long; spur slightly bent, 1 mm long.

Réunion.

Cordemoy illustrated this species in 1899 but did not describe it then.

SECTION *LEPERVENCHEA*

In this section the plants have elongated leafy stems, often pendent and branched, with small leaves in 2 rows. The inflorescences are borne in the leaf axils towards the apex of the stem and are often longer than the leaves. The rachis bears one or several flowers and is often somewhat flexuous. The small, yellowish-green flowers are thin and subdiaphanous.

Five species are currently allocated to this section from Madagascar and one (*Angraecum tenuifolium*) occurs in Réunion. It seems unlikely that many of them are in cultivation outside their country of origin.

Angraecum appendiculoides Schlechter

Plants with elongated, pendent stems, densely clothed with leaves and 2.5 mm in diameter. Leaves spreading, oval-lanceolate, cordate and clasping the stem at the base, 13–16 mm long, 6–7 mm wide. Inflorescences slender, lax, 4- to 7-flowered; bracts longer than the ovary, broadly oval-acuminate; ovary with pedicel curved and twisted, 2 mm long. Flowers greenish yellow, small, ca. 5 mm in diameter; sepals lanceolate, acute, 2.5 mm long; petals narrowly lanceolate-acuminate; lip concave, broadly oval, shortly acuminate, 2 mm long; spur straight, cylindric, 1.75 mm long.

Epiphyte, pendent in mossy forests; 1700–2000 m; flowering in November and December.

Madagascar (central regions).

Angraecum caricifolium H. Perrier

Plants with elongated, upright stems, slightly flattened, 10–25 cm long, 3–4 mm in diameter. Leaves 3–6, widely spaced, rigid, linear, canaliculate, unequally and obtusely bilobed at the apex, 5–7 cm long, 4 mm wide. Inflorescences slender, 2–6 cm long, 5- to 10-flowered; bracts very small; pedicel with ovary 3 mm long. Flowers yellowish green, small; sepals attenuate from the base to apex, 3 mm long, 1 mm wide at the base; petals similar but smaller, 2.5 mm long, 0.6 mm wide; lip concave, oval-lanceolate, narrowly attenuate above the wide base, shortly hairy on the upper surface, 3 mm long, 2.5 mm wide; spur thick, cylindric, 2.5 mm long, 1 mm wide.

Angraecum caricifolium. J. Hermans

Epiphyte on trunks in mossy forests; ca. 1400 m; flowering July to January.

Madagascar (central regions).

Angraecum musculiferum H. Perrier

Plant with upright stems, 6–30 cm long, 3–3.5 mm in diameter. Leaves numerous in 2 rows, broadly linear, unequally and obtusely bilobed at the apex, 2.5–5 cm long, 7–8 mm wide. Inflorescences numerous, piercing the leaf sheath of the upper leaves, solitary or in pairs, usually as long as the leaves, 4- to 10-flowered; bracts thin, pointed, 1.3 mm long; pedicel with ovary twisted, 3–4 mm long. Flowers yellowish; sepals oval-lanceolate, acute, 4 mm long, 1.5 mm wide; petals smaller, lanceolate, acute, 3 mm long, 0.6 mm wide; lip concave, boat-shaped, acuminate or acute, 4 mm long, 2.6 mm wide; spur cylindric, 2.5 mm long.

Epiphyte on trunks in mossy forests; 1200–1400 m; flowering between September and April.

Madagascar (Mounts Tsaratanana and Ambre).

Angraecum pauciramosum Schlechter

Plants with pendent stems of few branches, up to 15–20 cm long, 2–3 mm in diameter. Leaves numerous, ligulate or linear, unequally bilobed at the apex, 1–2 cm long, 3–4 mm wide. Inflorescences very slender, 2–4 times longer than the leaves, 4- to 7-flowered; bracts thin, about as long as the ovary; pedicel with ovary ca. 1 mm long. Flowers yellowish, tiny, ca. 4 mm in diameter; sepals lanceolate, acute, 1.5 mm long; petals narrower than the sepals; lip concave, oval, acuminate, ca. 2 mm long; spur cylindric, slightly thickened at the apex, 2 mm long.

Epiphyte in forests; ca. 800–1200 m; flowering between July and November.

Madagascar (forests along the eastern slopes).

Angraecum tenuifolium Frappier ex Cordemoy

Plants with flattened stems up to 30 cm long. Leaves linear, thin, 4–8 cm long, 2–4 mm wide. Inflorescences solitary in each leaf axil, multiflowered on a somewhat flattened rachis, as long as the leaves. Flowers yellowish green, small, 6 mm in diameter; sepals and petals ovate-lanceolate, 3 mm long; lip concave, wider than the petals; spur straight, cylindrical, as long as the ovary.

Epiphyte.

Réunion.

Angraecum tenuispica Schlechter

Plants up to 25 cm high, stems 4 mm in diameter. Leaves numerous, thin, ligulate or linear-ligulate, unequally and obtusely bilobed at the apex, 3–7 cm long, 6–8 mm wide. Inflorescences as long as the leaves, 5- to 10-flowered; bracts oval, acuminate, a little shorter than the ovary; pedicel with ovary 2.5 mm long. Flowers small; sepals lanceolate, acuminate, 2 mm long; petals a little smaller but with longer acumen; lip concave, broadly oval, shortly acuminate-obtuse, 2.25 mm long, 1.5 mm wide; spur slender, cylindric, wide at the mouth and obtuse at the apex, 2.25 mm long.

SECTION *LEMURANGIS*

The plants in this section have distinct, leafy stems that may be quite long with leaves in 2 rows. The inflorescences are borne in the axils of the upper leaves and are usually shorter than the leaves with only 1–5 small or very small flowers.

One species is known from eastern Africa, 6 from Madagascar, and 3 from Réunion. It seems unlikely that any of them are in cultivation outside their country of origin.

Angraecum humile Summerhayes

Plants very small, with elongated stems usually 1–4 cm long, straight or curved, bearing fine roots from the base. Leaves in 2 rows, equitant, very small, elliptic or oblanceolate in side view, 5–7 mm long, 2–3 mm wide. Inflorescences axillary, very short, 2- to 4-flowered. Flowers white or pale green, 2–4 mm in diameter; sepals elliptic oblong; petals similar; lip concave, ovate, acute, 1.6 mm long; spur clavate from a broad mouth, as long as the lip.

Epiphyte on mossy twigs of trees and branches, usually in the canopy of dwarf montane and riverine forest, very small and easily overlooked; 1650–2500 m; flowering August to October.

Kenya, Tanzania, and Zimbabwe.

Species from Madagascar

Angraecum alleizettei Schlechter

Plant with branching pendent stems and densely clothed with leaves, 8–20 cm long. Leaves many, obliquely recurved, leathery, oval, obtuse, rounded at the base, 6–12 mm long, 3–6 mm wide. Inflorescence as long as the leaves, 2- to 5-flowered; bracts thin, shorter than half the length of the ovary; pedicel with ovary twisted, 3–4 mm long. Flowers very small, lip on the upper side; sepals less than 2 mm long, dorsal sepal oval lanceolate, lateral sepals slightly longer and narrower, 2.2 mm long, 0.4 mm wide; petals shorter and very narrow; lip very concave, boat-shaped, oval, acute, 2 mm long; spur straight, inflated at the apex, 1.5 mm long.

Epiphyte in mossy forests, ca. 1400 m; flowering in January and July.

Madagascar (central highlands).

Angraecum baronii (Finet) Schlechter
(including *Angraecum dichaeoides* Schlechter)

Plant with slender, flattened stems, winged on the leaf sheaths, to 20 cm long. Leaves short, lanceolate, unequally and pointedly bilobed at the apex, 2 cm long, 4 mm wide. Inflorescences piercing the leaf sheath, sometimes 2-flowered; bracts cucullate; pedicel with ovary 3 mm long. Flowers small, ca. 4–6 mm in diameter; dorsal sepal oblong, 3 mm long; lateral sepals oval, acute; petals loriform, acuminate, 3 mm long; lip concave, oval, acuminate, 3 mm long; spur almost as wide as long, with an obtuse sac, 1–1.5 mm long.

Epiphyte in mossy highland forests; 1400–2500 m; flowering between September and April.

Madagascar (central highlands).

Angraecum humile. B. Campbell

Angraecum alleizettei. J. Hermans

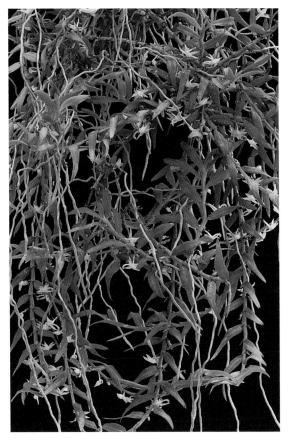

Angraecum baronii. J. Hermans

Angraecum baronii. J. Hermans

Angraecum decaryanum H. Perrier

Plant with a very long, slender stem bearing leaves spaced 6–10 mm apart. Leaves reddish, recurved, linear, keeled on the lower surface, 10–20 mm long, 1–5 mm wide. Inflorescence arising opposite a leaf base, piercing the sheath of the leaf above, less than half the length of the leaf, 1- to 4-flowered; bract broadly oval, acute, 2 mm long; pedicel with ovary ca. 3 mm long. Flowers white, small; sepals broadly oblong, subacute, 3.2 mm long, 1.5 mm wide; petals very similar to the sepals; lip oval, dilated at the base, apiculate, 3.2 mm long, 2 mm wide; spur short, narrow at the mouth and inflated into a round sac at the apex, 1.6 mm long.

Epiphyte on bushes and succulents of the family Didieraceae, in dry regions flowering in June.

Madagascar (south-western region).

Angraecum falcifolium Bosser

Plant with long flattened stems, branching, forming a network on the tree trunks, 50–60 cm long. Leaves imbricate in 2 rows, very distinctive, folded along the median vein, compressed, the lamina oval, oblong, falcate or recurved, amplexicaul, bilobed at the apex, with rounded lobes, 1.5–2 cm long, 0.8–1 cm wide. Inflorescences axillary, nearly as long as the leaves, 3- to 5-flowered; bract triangular, 2 mm long; pedicel with ovary twisted at the apex, 3 mm long. Flowers green, small; sepals lanceolate, acute, 6.5 mm long, 2 mm wide, the laterals a little narrower; petals lanceolate, acute, 5 mm long, 1.5 mm wide; lip concave, oval-lanceolate, acute, minutely papillose on the inner surface including over the central keel, in total 6 mm long, 2 mm wide; spur broadly cylindric, slightly flattened, 3 mm long.

Epiphyte in a remnant of shady forest.

Madagascar (central highlands).

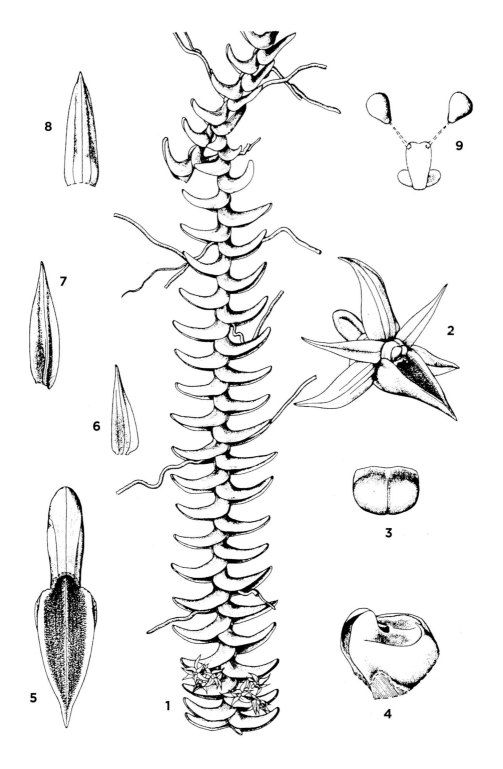

Angraecum falcifolium. 1: Habit. 2: Flower. 3: Anther from below. 4: Column. 5: Lip and spur. 6: Petal. 7: Lateral sepal. 8: Dorsal sepal. 9: Pollinarium. Reprinted by permission from Bosser 1970a, fig. 4. E. Razafindrakoto. © Publications Scientifiques du Muséum national d'Histoire naturelle, Paris.

Angraecum floribundum Bosser

Plant with a long woody stem bearing leaves throughout its length or losing its leaves towards the base, 40–60 cm long, 4–6 mm thick. Leaves many, 1–2 cm apart, the leaf sheaths keeled, ligulate, flat, dull green, narrowing slightly towards the base and unequally bilobed at the apex, 8–13 cm long, 1.5–2 cm wide. Inflorescences solitary or appearing more than once from the same point, piercing the leaf sheath, shorter than the leaves, 3–4 cm long, 1- or 2-flowered; bracts boat-shaped, compressed, 3–4 mm long; pedicel with ovary 7–8 mm long. Flowers green, fleshy; dorsal sepal ovate-lanceolate, acute, 11–13 mm long, 4–5 mm wide; lateral sepals somewhat narrower; petals lanceolate, acute, 10–11 mm long, 2.5–3.5 mm wide; lip concave, oval, rostrate, with a central papillose keel on the inner surface, 9–11 mm long, 4–5 mm wide; spur slightly curved, inflated at the apex and laterally compressed, 7–8 mm long.

Epiphyte in shady forests; 1200–1300 m; flowering in August.

Madagascar (central highlands).

Described as being rather similar to *Angraecum costatum*, from Réunion, but with much longer leaves and larger flowers.

Angraecum madagascariense (Finet) Schlechter

Plant with stems 6–10 cm high, usually pendent or curved downwards. Leaves short, spaced close together, oval, amplexicaul, obtuse, 10–13 mm long, 4.5–5 mm wide. Inflorescence half as long as the leaf, 3- or 4-flowered; bracts hyaline, obtuse, as long as the ovary; pedicel with ovary twisted, 2–2.5 mm long. Flowers very small, 1–1.5 mm apart; sepals triangular, acute, 2 mm long, 1 mm wide at the base, lateral sepals a little longer than dorsal sepal; petals narrower, 1.8 mm long, 0.6 mm wide; lip very concave, broadly oval at the base, shortly apiculate in front, 1.5 mm long; spur shorter than the ovary, cylindric and inflated at the apex, 1 mm long.

Epiphyte in humid highland forests; ca. 1500 m.

Madagascar (central highlands).

Species from Réunion

Very little material of these 3 species is available and it is hoped that further studies of them will be made in Réunion.

Angraecum costatum Frappier ex Cordemoy

Plant with erect stems, simple or branched, to 40 cm long, growing in clumps; bearing roots throughout and leaves in the upper part. Leaves alternate in 2 rows, bright green, lanceolate, unequally bilobed at the apex, 6 cm long, 1 cm wide. Inflorescences 1 or 2 in the leaf axils, intervallate; peduncle slender, usually 2-flowered but one does not develop. Flowers green, small, 5–6 mm in diameter when open; sepals oval; petals smaller, lanceolate; lip concave, boat-shaped; spur short, similar to the lip, slightly swollen towards the tip.

Epiphyte in semi-shade, common; 1200–1800 m; flowering in September and October.

Réunion.

Angraecum longinode Frappier ex Cordemoy

Plants with erect stems at least 12 cm long, bearing roots throughout their length and widely spaced leaves (up to 3 cm apart on each side of the stem). Leaves conduplicate and narrow at the base, flat in the upper half, ovate-lanceolate, pointed, 4–6 cm long, 6–12 mm wide. Inflorescences axillary, slender, single-flowered. Flower small.

Epiphyte.

Réunion.

Angraecum pseudopetiolatum Frappier ex Cordemoy

Plant with erect or perpendicular stems up to 10 cm long, and with slender roots emanating from the internodes, leafy in the upper part. Leaves in 2 rows, 15 mm apart, inserted at an acute angle, bright green, lanceolate, thick, narrow at the base and appearing almost petiolate, 3–6 cm long, 10–12 mm wide at the middle, narrowing towards the apex. Inflorescences in the leaf axils, several at a time, sometimes in horizontal groups, 1- to 3-flowered. Flowers green, small, 1–2 mm in diameter; sepals and petals oval, the petals slightly smaller than the sepals; lip shell-shaped; spur half the length of the lip, slightly curved and swollen at the apex.

Epiphyte in the forests; 1300 m above sea level; flowering in January.

Réunion.

SECTION *ACAULIA*

Garay (1973) proposed this section to accommodate a group of plants with very short stems bearing few basal leaves. The inflorescences are usually single-flowered or may bear more than one flower successively.

Five species described from Madagascar, mostly from the north of the island, have been allocated to this section by Garay. It seems unlikely that any of these species is in cultivation. They are presented here in 2 groups according to the length of the spur:

Group 1. One species has small flowers, with the spur ca. 7 mm long.

Group 2. Flowers small, with the spur 2–2.5 cm long.

Group 1. Species with spur less than 1 cm long.

Angraecum brachyrhopalon Schlechter
Plant small, 5–7 cm high. Leaves 4–5, linear, stiff, narrowing towards the base, unequally bilobed at the apex, 5 cm long, 5 mm wide. Inflorescences nearly as long as the leaves, 1- or 2-flowered; bract blackish, 2–3 mm long; pedicel with ovary twisted, 4 mm long. Flowers yellowish green, small; sepals oval, obtuse, dorsal sepal concave, 4.5–5 mm long; petals lanceolate, subacute, 3.75 mm long; lip very concave, oval, obtuse, 5–6 mm long, 3.3–4 mm wide; spur erect, at first cylindric, then expanded into a club-shaped tip, altogether 7.5 mm long.

Epiphyte in seasonally dry woods; flowering in January.

Madagascar (Sambirano valley).

Angraecum rhynchoglossum.
Reprinted by permission from Perrier 1941, fig. 64.
M. J. Vesque. © Publications Scientifiques du
Muséum national d'Histoire naturelle, Paris.

Group 2. Species with spurs more than 2 cm long.

Angraecum chaetopodum Schlechter
Plant small, slender, 4–10 cm high. Leaves 4–6, narrowly linear, stiff, pointed, 3–8 cm long, 2.5–4 mm wide. Inflorescences as long as the leaves, usu-

ally single-flowered; bract blackish, 2–3 mm long; pedicel with ovary twisted, 9–10 mm long. Flowers yellowish white, small; sepals lanceolate-ligulate, obtuse, 6 mm long; petals a little narrower; lip concave at the base, oval, shortly acuminate-rostrate, 5 mm long, 4 mm wide; spur very narrow, slightly expanded in the apical half, 20–23 mm long.

Epiphyte in mossy forests, with a herbaceous under-storey; 1200–1500 m; flowering in January.

Madagascar (Mount Tsaratanana).

Angraecum pergracile Schlechter

Plant very slender, small, to 8 cm high with the inflorescence. Leaves 3 or 4, oblong or oblanceolate-ligulate, tapering towards the base, very unequally bilobed at the apex, 4.5 cm long, 6–8 mm wide. Inflorescences usually longer than the leaves, single-flowered; bract oval, apiculate; pedicel with ovary twisted, 8–12 mm long. Flowers yellowish white, small; sepals sublanceolate-ligulate, obtuse, 7.5 mm long; petals similar but shorter, 6.5 mm long; lip concave, oval and cucullate below, attenuate-rostrate above, 6.5 mm long, 4.5 mm wide; spur narrowly subcylindric, 25 mm long.

Epiphyte on branches in seasonally dry woods; 200 m; flowering in January.

Madagascar (slopes of the Sambirano valley).

Angraecum rhynchoglossum Schlechter

Plant small, not more than 4 cm high. Leaves 3 or 4, oblong, slightly narrowed towards both ends, 11–15 mm long, 4–5 mm wide. Inflorescences as long as or longer than the leaves, single-flowered; bract pointed, 1.2 mm long; pedicel with ovary twisted, very slender, 5–6 mm long. Flowers yellowish white, lip on the upper side; sepals linear, acute, 7 mm long; petals also linear and slightly shorter; lip concave and rounded at the base, funnel-shaped at the mouth of the spur, with a long acuminate beak at the front, 6 mm long, 3 mm wide; spur narrow, 25 mm long.

Epiphyte on branches in mossy forest; ca. 1500 m; flowering between September and April.

Madagascar (central highlands).

Angraecum rhynchoglossum. J. Hermans

The description given above is based on Schlechter's original (1925), which differs in several details of the lip and spur from that given by Perrier (1941).

Angraecum setipes Schlechter

Plant 7–13 cm high. Leaves 5 or 6, lanceolate-linear, narrowing towards both ends, unequally and acutely bilobed at the apex, 3.5–11 cm long, 3–8 mm wide. Inflorescences several, 1- or 2-flowered; bract oval, acute, 3.5–4 mm long; pedicel with ovary twisted, 5 mm long. Flowers yellowish green; sepals broadly oval, acute, the laterals keeled on the back; petals oval, obtuse, 6.5 mm long; lip suborbicular or broadly rhomboid, apiculate, 7 mm long, 7 mm wide; spur horizontal, subfiliform or cylindric, scarcely thickened at the apex, 22 mm long.

Epiphyte in mossy forests; ca. 2000 m; flowering between September and February.

Angraecum setipes. J. Hermans

Madagascar (central highlands).

Apparently the flowers are rather variable in size, though the characteristic round and deep lip in this species is quite distinct.

SECTION *PECTINARIA*

In this section the plants are very distinct in appearance because of their long stems with narrow, fleshy leaves that are often flattened in a vertical plane. The white flowers are usually solitary and almost sessile in the axils of the leaves.

Four species from western Africa are described first, followed by 5 species from Madagascar and Réunion.

Species from Africa

Angraecum doratophyllum Summerhayes

Plant with pendent stems up to 50 cm long. Leaves spaced close together, oblong-lanceolate, flat, pointed, 2–4 cm long, 3–6 mm wide. Inflorescence in the leaf axil, sessile, single-flowered. Flowers white; sepals narrowly elliptic, obtuse, 11 mm long, 1.5 mm wide; petals linear, oblique or curved towards the base, 10 mm long, 1 mm wide; lip concave, suborbicular or transversely oval, apex shortly acuminate, recurved, 6.5 mm long, 7.5 mm wide; spur with a wide mouth at the base of the lip, narrowing, then recurved and inflated towards the tip, 13–14 mm long.

Epiphyte in virgin forest; ca. 1050–1200 m; flowering in November.

São Tomé.

Very similar to *Angraecum pungens* but with larger flowers that have a longer spur.

Angraecum gabonense Summerhayes

Plant with pendent stems up to 40 cm long. Leaves spaced close together, oblong to narrowly elliptic, flat, pointed, often narrowed and twisted at the base, 1–2 cm long, 2–4 mm wide. Inflorescence in the leaf axil, single-flowered; pedicel and ovary slender, 4 mm long. Flowers white; sepals oblong, subacute, 6 mm long, 1.5 mm wide; petals obliquely obovate, obtuse, 5 mm long, 2 mm wide; lip concave, suborbicular or transversely oval, apiculate or shortly acuminate, 3.5 mm long, 5 mm wide; spur narrow at first below the lip then expanded to a small globe in the apical half, ca. 3 mm long.

Epiphyte in dense forests; up to 1350 m; flowering at various times.

Cameroon, Gabon, and D.R. of Congo.

Angraecum pungens Schlechter

Plant with pendent stems up to 50 cm long. Leaves spaced close together, oblong-lanceolate, flat, pointed, narrowed at the base, 2–4 cm long, 3–6 mm wide. Inflorescence in the leaf axil, sessile, single-flowered. Flowers white; sepals narrowly

Angraecum doratophyllum. J. Hermans

Angraecum gabonense. C. Arends

Angraecum pungens. J. Hermans

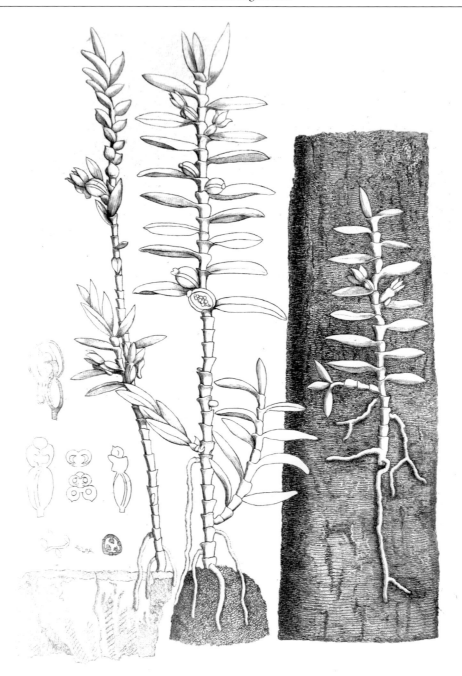

Angraecum pectinatum. From Thouars 1822, t. 51.

elliptic, obtuse, 6–7 mm long, 2 mm wide; petals obliquely and narrowly obovate, obtuse, 6–7 mm long, 2 mm wide; lip concave, suborbicular or transversely oval, apiculate or shortly acuminate, 4 mm long, 5 mm wide; spur subcylindric, pointed, 4–5 mm long.

Epiphyte in dense forest; 900–1800 m; flowering at various times.

Southern Nigeria, Cameroon, Equatorial Guinea (Bioco Island), and D.R. of Congo.

Angraecum subulatum Lindley

Plant with pendent stems up to 40 cm long, frequently branched. Leaves well spaced, subulate-terete, sharply pointed, often curved, 3–13 cm long, 1–3 mm wide. Inflorescence at the leaf base, 1- or

2-flowered; pedicel and ovary 3–4 mm long. Flowers white; sepals oblong to elliptic, subacute, 4–6 mm long, 2–2.5 mm wide; petals linear to narrowly elliptic, acute or apiculate, 4–5 mm long, 0.5–1.5 mm wide; lip concave, suborbicular, apiculate, 2–3 mm long and wide; spur subcylindric, 5 mm long.

Epiphyte in dense forests; up to 700 m; flowering in May–June and November–December.

Sierra Leone, Liberia, Côte d'Ivoire, Ghana, southern Nigeria, Cameroon, Equatorial Guinea (Bioco Island), Congo, and D.R. of Congo.

Species from Madagascar and Réunion

These are smaller plants than those described above from Africa, but they also have elongated stems, small narrow leaves and solitary white flowers that are more or less sessile.

Angraecum dasycarpum Schlechter

Plants small with upright rigid stems, simple or branched, often several in a tuft, 10 cm high; roots hairy. Leaves numerous, alternate in 2 rows, oblong, subacute, thick and fleshy, shortly apiculate, margins cartilaginous, 7–10 mm long, 4–7 mm wide. Inflorescence axillary, sessile, single-flowered; ovary covered with soft hairs, 5 mm long. Flowers white, small; sepals oblong, obtuse, 6.5 mm long; petals similar to the sepals; lip concave, oblong-ligulate, obtuse, slightly attenuate above the middle, 5.5 mm long; spur straight, held close to the ovary, 4 mm long.

Epiphyte or lithophyte in *Philippia* scrub; high elevations; flowering January to April.

Madagascar (eastern region).

Angraecum hermannii (Cordemoy) Schlechter

Plant very small, scarcely more than 3 cm high, with finely hairy roots, and with erect stems. Leaves 10 in 2 rows, spreading, elliptic, folded with a well developed dorsal keel, margins recurved, 8–12 mm long, 2.5–3.5 mm wide. Inflorescence piercing the leaf sheath, single-flowered; ovary glabrous, scarcely 2 mm long. Flower very small, white; sepals oval-oblong, thick, apiculate, 3–3.5 mm long,

Angraecum subulatum. J. Hermans

Angraecum dasycarpum. J. Hermans

2 mm wide, dorsal slightly concave; petals broadly oval, acute, thick, 2.5 mm long, 1.8 mm wide; lip concave, oval-acute, opaque, 2.5 mm long, 1.5 mm wide; spur an obtuse sac, 2 mm long, 1.2 mm wide.

Epiphyte on twigs and branches amongst mosses and lichens in forest; ca. 1200 m above sea level; flowering in February.

Madagascar (central highlands) and Réunion.

According to Garay (1973), this species is not different from *Angraecum pterophyllum* Perrier which was described much later from Madagascar.

Angraecum humblotianum (Finet) Schlechter

Plants small with upright rigid stems, simple or branched, often several in a tuft, 10–15 cm high. Leaves numerous, alternate in 2 rows, very thick and fleshy, linear-cylindric, narrow, 10–16 mm long, 1–1.5 mm wide. Inflorescence axillary, single-flowered; bract obtuse and very wide, enveloping the ovary; ovary slightly hairy, 3–4 mm long.

Flowers white, small; sepals lanceolate, dorsal sepal a little shorter than lateral sepals, obtuse, 5 mm long, 1.2 mm wide; petals a little shorter and narrower, almost linear; lip slightly concave towards the base, oval-oblong, obtuse, 5 mm long, 1.8 mm wide; spur cylindric, obtuse, 2.2–3.5 mm long.

Epiphyte; sea level to 900 m; flowering January to March.

Madagascar and Comoro Islands.

This species was named in honour of J. H. L. Humblot (1852–1914) who lived in the Comoro Islands and studied orchids there for many years.

Angraecum panicifolium H. Perrier

Plants small with pendent stems, 10–20 cm long. Leaves 5 or 6, alternate in 2 rows, well spaced near apex of stem, linear, subacute, narrow 35–38 mm long, 1.3–2.2 mm wide. Inflorescence axillary, single-flowered, sometimes accompanied by an aborted second flower; bract 2 mm long; ovary 6 mm long. Flowers white, small; dorsal sepal lan-

Angraecum humblotianum. J. Hermans

Angraecum panicifolium. J. Hermans

ceolate, slightly attenuated from the base to the tip, obtuse, 6 mm long, 2.2 mm wide; lateral sepals larger, the lower side dilated, oblique, 7–8 mm long, 2.5 mm wide; petals smaller, lanceolate, 5.5 mm long, 1.5 mm wide; lip concave, oval, appearing almost 3-lobed, obtuse, 7–8 mm long, 4 mm wide at the widest; spur slightly enlarged at the mouth then cylindric, straight, 5–6 mm long.

Epiphyte on mossy tree trunks; ca. 1000 m; flowering in February.

Madagascar (central regions).

Angraecum pectinatum Thouars

Plants small with upright rigid stems, simple or branched, often several in a tuft, 10–20 cm high. Leaves numerous, alternate in 2 rows, linear, subacute, thick and fleshy with a shallow canal on the upper surface, rounded below, 12–16 mm long, very narrow. Inflorescence axillary, single-flowered, sessile. Flowers white; sepals oblong, obtuse, 6 mm long; petals a little shorter and narrower; lip

Angraecum pectinatum. J. Hermans

similar to the sepals, almost flat but pointed; spur straight, slightly enlarged at the apex, 2 mm long.

Epiphyte, often on bare trunks and branches in humid and shady forests; from sea level to 700 m; flowering throughout the year.

Madagascar, Mauritius, and Réunion.

SECTION *DOLABRIFOLIA*

The plants in this small section are easily recognised by their elongated stems bearing laterally compressed leaves which are rather small, with closely overlapping bases. The inflorescence is usually single-flowered with a very short or scarcely developed peduncle.

Five species have been described from the warmer parts of Africa: *Angraecum podochiloides* and 4 others which are very similar to each other. The size of the flower parts, especially the spur, distinguish 3 of them from each other while the 4th, *A. poppendickianum*, may be of hybrid origin.

Angraecum aporoides Summerhayes

Plants dwarf, usually consisting of a tuft of pendent or upward-curving, flattened stems up to 40 cm long, with numerous very fine roots arising between the leaves from the lower parts of the stem. Leaves in 2 rows, glossy dark green, deciduous, bilaterally compressed, curved-elliptic or almost orbicular, obtuse in side view, with a wide groove on the upper surface extending to near the apex, 14–25 mm long, 6–10 mm wide. Inflorescences opposite the leaves, appearing axillary, shorter than the leaves, single-flowered; bracts elliptic, obtuse, 1–1.5 mm long; pedicel and ovary 7–8 mm long. Flowers white, fleshy, small, often held with the lip uppermost; sepals elliptic or oblong-elliptic, apiculate, 4–9 mm long, 2–3 mm wide; petals narrowly elliptic, obtuse, 4–6 mm long, 1.5–2 mm wide; lip concave, distinctly 3-lobed, obovate, obtuse, 2.5–4 mm long, 4–5 mm wide, lateral lobes rounded, upright on either side of the column, median lobe longer, triangular, acute; spur straight, narrowly cylindric from a wide mouth, 7 mm long.

Angraecum aporoides. 1: Habit. 2: Part plant. 3: Dorsal sepal. 4: Lateral sepal. 5: Petal. 6: Lip.
7: Ovary with column and anther. 8: Apex of column. 9: Pollinarium.
From Summerhayes 1968, fig. 398. M. Grierson.

Angraecum aporoides. C. Arends

Epiphyte on large trees in rain forest; sea level to 1300 m; flowering March to May.

Nigeria, Cameroon, Equatorial Guinea (Bioco Island), São Tomé, Príncipe, and D.R. of Congo.

Similar to *Angraecum distichum* but larger in all respects.

Angraecum bancoense Van Der Burg

Plants dwarf, usually consisting of a small tuft of flattened stems up to 15 cm long, with numerous very fine roots arising between the leaves from the lower parts of the stem. Leaves in 2 rows, glossy dark green, deciduous, bilaterally compressed, curved-elliptic or almost orbicular, obtuse in side view, without or with a very indistinct groove on the upper surface, 5–10 mm long, 3–7 mm wide. Inflorescences opposite the leaves, appearing axillary, up to 9 mm long, single-flowered; bracts elliptic, obtuse, 1–1.5 mm long; pedicel and ovary 5–6 mm long. Flowers white, small, held with the lip uppermost; dorsal sepal elliptic or oblong-elliptic, apiculate, 1.5–2 mm long, 1 mm wide; lateral sepals rounded, almost ovate, obtuse; petals narrowly elliptic; lip concave, 3-lobed, obovate, obtuse, 1 mm long, lateral lobes rounded, upright on either side of the column; spur straight, suddenly tapering near the end to a short tubular apex, 2.5–5 mm long.

Epiphyte in rain forest; flowering throughout the year.

Côte d'Ivoire (Banco Forest Reserve), Nigeria, and Cameroon.

Very similar to *Angraecum distichum* but smaller in all respects, and also differs in the details of the lateral sepals, lip and spur.

Angraecum distichum Lindley

Plants dwarf, usually consisting of a tuft of pendent or upward-curving, flattened stems up to 25 cm long, with numerous very fine roots arising between the leaves from the lower parts of the stem. Leaves in 2 rows, glossy dark green, deciduous, bilaterally compressed, curved-elliptic or almost orbicular, obtuse in side view, with a narrow groove on the upper surface reaching halfway along the

Angraecum distichum. J. Hermans

Angraecum distichum. B. Campbell

leaf, 5–11 mm long, 3–5 mm wide. Inflorescences opposite leaves, appearing axillary, up to 9 mm long, single-flowered; bracts elliptic, obtuse, 1–1.5 mm long; pedicel and ovary 5–6 mm long. Flowers white, small, often held with the lip uppermost; sepals elliptic or oblong-elliptic, apiculate, 3.5–4.5 mm long, 1.5–2 mm wide; petals similar but a little smaller; lip concave, obscurely 3-lobed, obovate, obtuse, 3–3.5 mm long, 2.8–4 mm wide, lateral lobes rounded, upright on either side of the column; spur straight or slightly upcurved, suddenly tapering near the end to an acute apex, 5.5–6 mm long.

Epiphyte in upland rain forest, on trunks and large branches in shade; 1400–1600 m; flowering between March and October, often several times in each season.

Sierra Leone eastwards to D.R. of Congo, Uganda, and Angola.

Well known in cultivation.

Angraecum podochiloides Schlechter

Plants dwarf, usually consisting of a tuft of pendent or upward-curving, flattened stems up to 60 cm long, with numerous very fine roots arising between the leaves from the lower parts of the stem. Leaves in 2 rows, glossy dark green, deciduous, bilaterally compressed, lanceolate or oblong, pointed in side view, 1–2 cm long, 2–3 mm wide. Inflorescences opposite leaves, appearing axillary, single-flowered; bracts elliptic, obtuse, 1–1.5 mm long. Flowers white, small, often held with the lip uppermost; sepals linear, obtuse, 4.5–5 mm long, 1.5–2 mm wide; petals similar but a little smaller; lip concave, sac-like, 3-lobed, obovate, obtuse, 5 mm long, 4 mm wide, lateral lobes rounded, upright on either side of the column, median lobe small, thick, subacute; spur straight, narrowly funnel-shaped, then suddenly tapering near the end to an acute apex, 4.5–6 mm long.

Epiphyte in shady places in primary rain forest; up to 1500 m; flowering between March and August.

Liberia, Côte d'Ivoire, Ghana, southern Nigeria, Cameroon, and D.R. of Congo.

Angraecum poppendickianum Szlachetko & Olszewski

This species was described in 2001 in honour of H. H. Poppendick, conservator of the Hamburg Herbarium. It appears to be intermediate between *Angraecum distichum* (similar vegetatively) and *A. aporoides* (similar to the flowers). The authors comment that the plants they have seen may be of hybrid origin. They cite one specimen from Gabon (Crystal Mountains) flowering in August, and one specimen from Cameroon.

SPECIES EXTINCT OR NOT UNDERSTOOD

Angraecum coriaceum (Swartz) Schlechter

Very little is known of the identity and characteristics of this species which is not recognised today. It has been suggested that it is very close to *Angraecum bracteosum*, but the original description, which is limited, clearly refers to a paniculate inflorescence which is not present in *A. bracteosum*.

Angraecum keniae Kraenzlin

Known only from a single herbarium specimen from the north of Kenya, which has probably been destroyed (Cribb 1989).

Angraecum palmiforme Thouars

This robust orchid is almost certainly extinct (Cadet 1989). Although described and illustrated by Thouars in 1822, it was known from only a few sites on the steep slopes of the river Saint Denis in northern Réunion and from one or 2 sites in Mauritius. Plants from all the known sites have been brought into cultivation and subsequently perished (Roberts, pers. comm.). A drawing and a few dried flowers are preserved in the Herbarium at the Royal Botanic Gardens, Kew.

Angraecum sesquisectangulum Kraenzlin

Described from 2 flowers and a bud from a plant in cultivation. No further details available.

CHAPTER TWO

Other Genera in the Subtribe Angraecinae

AERANTHES Lindley

John Lindley (1799–1865) was employed as garden clerk for the Horticultural Society of London when he established this genus in 1824. One of the most attractive species, *Aeranthes grandiflora*, flowered for the first time in England in the Society's Chiswick garden, and Lindley illustrated and described it in the *Botanical Register* (t. 817). The plant had been collected in Madagascar the previous year by the Society's collector, John Forbes (1798–1823), who died in Mozambique a few months later. Lindley derived the name from the Greek words *aer*, air or mist, and *anthos*, flower, apparently in allusion to the epiphytic habit of the plant. At the same time he also named *A. arachnitis*, which had earlier been illustrated by Thouars (1822) as *Dendrobium arachnites* from his own collections in Mauritius and Réunion.

In his description of the new genus, Lindley drew attention to the solitary, pale yellow flowers in which the column was extended at its foot into a spur and the broad lip was attached to the front edge of this spur. This defining characteristic is present in all the species so far known; in a few species the spur is very short or absent but the column foot is present. The lateral sepals are attached, at their base, to the column foot.

Although some species have indeed pale yellow or white flowers, most species have green flowers. Some of these are intensely dark green, others pale and almost translucent. They are borne mostly on long, slender peduncles, sometimes spaced far apart, or solitary, or opening successively. The plants are small or large, usually with only a short stem bearing 2 rows of leathery leaves with very unequally bilobed tips, the lobes usually rounded.

Some of the species are clearly defined and easy to recognise: *Aeranthes henrici* and *A. schlechteri*, for example, have white flowers and very long slender spurs. Others show great variation within the species, and sometimes, as in the many different plants referred to *A. ramosa*, for example, the variations are difficult to describe. Flowers for identification are best photographed, measured, and then preserved in spirit as they become easily damaged when dried.

When Perrier compiled the second part of his account of the orchids for the *Flore de Madagascar* (1941), he included 27 species of *Aeranthes*. About 50 species are now recognised, mostly in Madagascar, but others occur in Mauritius and Réunion and 2 have been described recently in Africa, from eastern Zimbabwe. There is no modern account of the genus in any one publication, and no attempt has yet been made to study the relationships of the species or to allocate them to sections within the genus. Nevertheless, all the species are immediately

Aeranthes henrici. J. Hermans

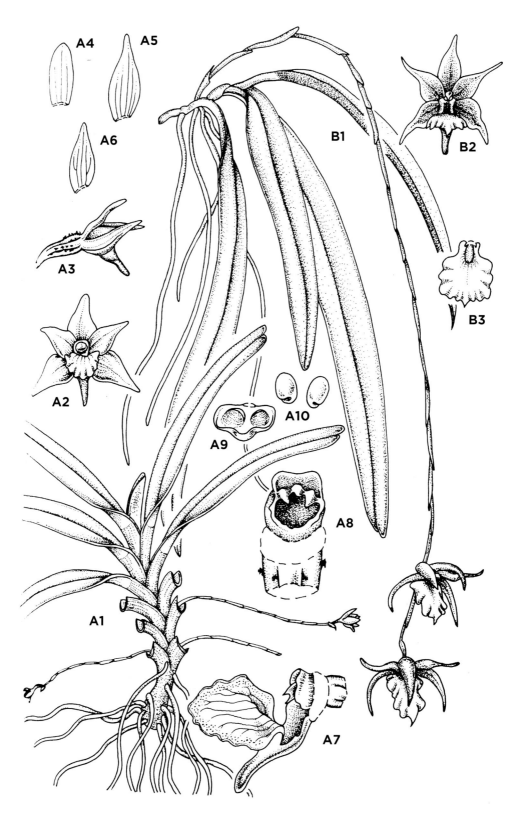

Aeranthes africana and *Aeranthes parkesii*. *Aeranthes africana*—A1: Habit. A2: Flower. A3: Bud.
A4: Dorsal sepal. A5: Lateral sepal. A6: Petal. A7: Lip and column. A8: Column. A9: Anther-cap. A10: Pollinia.
Aeranthes parkesii—B1: Habit. B2: Flower. B3: Lip. From la Croix and Cribb 1998, t. 123. J. Stone.

Aeranthes africana. J. Stewart

recognisable by their hyaline flowers and column foot as belonging to the genus *Aeranthes*.

In the following account we have dealt with the species from Africa first, followed by the species from Madagascar, and finally those from Réunion and Mauritius.

Culture

Most *Aeranthes* species are easy to grow in cultivation provided they have good drainage. They need an open growing mix with materials that retain moisture fairly well. The plants require frequent watering and a site in the shadiest part of the glasshouse in intermediate conditions of temperature and humidity. Those with long inflorescences should be moved to a high shelf when they come into flower, or grown in a hanging basket, so that the pendent inflorescences develop naturally and the flowers can be viewed to best advantage.

Species from Africa

Aeranthes africana J. Stewart

Plant small with a short woody stem covered with old leaf bases and the remains of inflorescences, 2–4 cm long. Leaves in 2 rows, linear-ligulate, unequally and obtusely bilobed at the apex, 4–7 cm long, 4–8 mm wide. Inflorescences 4–6, erect or spreading, as long as the leaves, single-flowered; peduncle slender, covered with 5–9 brownish sheaths. Flowers whitish, 10 mm in diameter; dorsal sepal ovate, shortly acuminate, 7 mm long, 3–4 mm wide; lateral sepals similar but slightly longer; petals ovate, acuminate, 4–5 mm long, 2 mm wide; lip ± rhomboid with a very small apiculus; spur straight, tapering, 3 mm long.

Epiphyte in montane forest; 1670 m; flowering November to December.

Zimbabwe (Vumba mountains).

Aeranthes parkesii G. Williamson

Plant with a short woody stem covered with old leaf bases and the remains of inflorescences, 12 mm long. Leaves 2–6 in 2 rows, lanceolate from a folded base, leathery, somewhat glaucous, 17 cm long, 1.5 cm wide. Inflorescences arising below the leaves, sometimes branched and each branch bearing one flower; peduncle slender, covered with up to 15 overlapping, sheathing bracts up to 20 mm long. Flowers translucent greenish cream, darker at the tips of the tepals; sepals ovate, acuminate, curving forwards, 20 mm long, 7 mm wide; petals ovate, acuminate, erect or recurved, 12 mm long, 7 mm wide; lip quadrate with an apical acumen 2 mm long, projecting forwards, up to 10 mm long, 10 mm wide; spur conical, to 10 mm long.

Epiphyte in riverine forest; low altitudes.

Zimbabwe.

This species is named after its collector, Duncan Parkes of Mazoe, Zimbabwe, who brought it into flower in cultivation 7 years after finding it on the Aberfoyle tea estate (Williamson 1990). It is said to be close to *Aeranthes laxiflora* Schlechter.

Species from Madagascar and Comoro Islands

As an aid to identification we have divided these species into 5 groups according to the approximate size of their flowers, dealing with the largest first. Any specimens that do not seem to fit into any of these groups may have been allocated to an adjacent group because we have seen smaller specimens.

Group 1. Flowers with very long sepals, including the acuminate tip more than 5 cm long.

Group 2. Flowers with long sepals, including the acuminate tip 3–5 cm long.

Group 3. Flowers medium-sized, with sepals 2–3 cm long.

Group 4. Flowers small, with sepals 1–2 cm long.

Group 5. Flowers very small, with sepals less than 1 cm long.

Group 1. Species with very large flowers, the sepals, including the acuminate tips, more than 5 cm long.

Aeranthes antennophora H. Perrier

Plant with a very short, erect stem a few cm long. Leaves 6 or 7, broadly ligulate, unequally bilobed at the apex, the lobes obtuse, 30–40 cm long, 2–3.5 cm wide. Inflorescence slender, pendent, laxly branched, up to 30 cm long, several-flowered, sheaths shorter than the internodes; bract 5 mm long. Flowers large, greenish white; sepals very long, acuminate, 9–12 cm long, the tail 7–8 cm long; dorsal sepal oval-oblong at the base, 10 mm long and wide; lateral sepals expanded at the front, forming a large obtuse basal lobe; petals similar to dorsal sepal but smaller, 4.5 cm long including the acumen, 8 mm wide at the base; lip broadly oval, deeply cordate at the base, 2 cm wide, narrowing to a short, filiform tail, 15–18 mm long; column foot 1 cm long; spur cylindrical or a little flattened, 13–15 mm long.

Epiphyte on moss- and lichen-covered trees in forest; ca. 1000 m; flowering in February.

Madagascar (central highlands).

This species has the longest flowers in the genus with tails on the sepals even longer than those in the following species. The inflorescences are usually shorter than the leaves.

Aeranthes caudata Rolfe

Syn. *Aeranthes imerinensis* H. Perrier

Plant with a short, erect, woody stem to 15 cm long in old specimens. Leaves 6–8, ligulate, slightly falcate, glossy green, very unequally bilobed at the apex, 20–30 cm long, 2–4 cm wide. Inflorescence arising below the leaves, paniculate, to 45 cm long, 2- to 5-flowered; peduncle wiry, with long or short branches, each with a solitary flower successively; bract small. Flowers translucent green with white on the lip; dorsal sepal ovate-lanceolate, fleshy, 2 cm long, 1.2 cm wide, narrowing abruptly into a long acumen, 5–9 cm long; lateral sepals connate with the column foot at the base, similar to dorsal sepal but lobed at the base, in total 6 cm long, 1.2 cm wide; petals smaller and thinner than dorsal sepal, 4.5 cm long, 1.1 cm wide; lip broadly obtrullate, more or less auriculate at the base, 2.5 cm long, 2 cm wide, with an apical acumen 1.5 cm long; column foot concave, 8 mm long; spur narrowly cylindrical, curved, 1 cm long.

Epiphyte in humid, evergreen forest, on trunks and branches in deep shade, often covered with mosses and leafy liverworts; 700–1500 m; flowering January to April.

Madagascar (widespread in central highlands and in the north) and Comoro Islands (Grande Comore).

This species is easily distinguished from the other large-flowered species by the very long 'tails' on the sepals and petals and by its short cylindrical spur.

Aeranthes grandiflora Lindley

Plant with a short, erect, woody stem. Leaves 5–7 in 2 rows, narrowly oblong, unequally bilobed at the apex, with rounded lobes, 15–25 cm long, 3–3.5 cm wide. Inflorescence pendent, 10–60 cm long, 1- or 2-flowered; peduncle entirely covered by overlapping sheaths. Flowers large, showy, white, yellowish white or greenish white with yellow tips to the tepals and spur; dorsal sepal oblong-ovate at the base with long acumen above, to 5 cm long, 1.4 cm wide; lateral sepals obliquely ovate below, long acuminate above, 5 cm long, 1.4 cm wide; petals ovate at the base, long acuminate, 4 cm long; lip oblong-elliptic, 2.5 cm long, auriculate at the base, acuminate, 4 cm long, 2 cm wide; column foot concave, 2 cm long; spur cylindrical at first then narrow and finally abruptly dilated at the apex, curving forward under the lip.

Epiphyte on trunks in coastal and plateau humid evergreen forest, widespread; sea level to 1200 m; flowering July to January.

Madagascar (from Antsirañana to Toliara) and Comoro Islands (Anjouan).

Aeranthes grandiflora. J. Hermans

Aeranthes henrici Schlechter

Plant robust with a very short stem and long thick roots. Leaves 4–6 in 2 rows, dark green, spreading, ligulate, leathery, unequally bilobed at the apex, margins slightly undulate, 9–24 cm long, 1.5–5.5 cm wide. Inflorescence pendent, 3- to 6-flowered; peduncle 6–15 cm long; bracts oval-obtuse, 1.5 cm long. Flowers large, showy, white, sometimes green in the base of the lip; sepals lanceolate, long-acuminate at the apex, up to 11 cm long, 2 cm wide; lateral sepals oblique, curving forwards; petals similar to the sepals, up to 9 cm long; lip wide at the base, then narrowing to a tongue-shaped central lobe which terminates in a 6-cm-long acumen, margins fimbriate or ciliate, basal part 4 cm long, 3.8 cm wide, in total 10 cm long; column foot 1 cm long, 3 cm wide, extending into the filiform spur, 11–16 cm long.

var. *henrici*

Flowers large, dorsal sepal up to 11 cm long; spur 16 cm long.

Epiphyte in humid evergreen forest; 750–1000 m; flowering in April.

Madagascar (eastern, northern, and north-western highlands).

var. *isaloensis* H. Perrier ex Hermans

Flowers smaller, dorsal sepal up to 7.5 cm long; spur 11–12 cm long.

Epiphyte in humid evergreen forest; 500–1000 m; flowering in March.

Madagascar (south-eastern highlands).

Both varieties of this species are easily recognised by their large, predominantly white flowers with a long slender spur. It was originally named for the collector, Henri Perrier de la Bâthie (1873–1958), the French botanist who made so many contributions to the study of orchids in Madagascar.

Group 2. Species with large flowers, the sepals, including the acuminate tip, 3–5 cm long.

Aeranthes angustidens H. Perrier

Plant with a very short stem or stemless. Leaves elongate, equally and obtusely bilobed at the apex, 25–32 cm long, 2–3 cm wide. Inflorescences very slender, pendent, long-lived, with short branches that each ultimately bear 2 or 3 flowers; sheaths and bracts short. Flowers green, borne at the apex of side branches; dorsal sepal lanceolate, gradually narrowing from the base to apex, 37 mm long, 7–10 mm wide; lateral sepals similar but very expanded at the front below the middle and then abruptly acuminate; petals as long as the sepals, long-acuminate above the oval base; lip subcordate at the base above the articulation with the spur, narrowing into a sharp point 12 mm long, in total to 40–45 mm long, 14–16 mm wide; column foot 12–15 mm long, extending into a cylindrical spur 12 mm long.

Epiphyte on tree trunks in humid evergreen forest; 700 m; flowering January and February.

Madagascar (eastern forests).

In this species the inflorescences can remain on the plant for several years becoming more branched and bearing additional flowers as they age.

Aeranthes crassifolia Schlechter

Plant with a short stem or stemless. Leaves 5 or 6, ligulate, fleshy or leathery, thick, 7–10 cm long, 1.3–2.3 cm wide. Inflorescences very slender, upright, simple or with 2 or 3 short branches; sheaths on the peduncle short and distant from each other. Flowers greenish, medium-sized; sepals oval or oval-oblong at the base, becoming very acuminate, 3 cm long; lateral sepals similar, slightly expanded at the front edge, above the base; petals shorter than sepals, suborbicular at the base with a few teeth at the front edge, extended into a filiform acumen, 18 mm long; lip rounded at the base, oblong-acuminate, 18 mm long, 8 mm wide; column foot widely funnel-shaped, suddenly contracted into a straight, widely cylindrical spur, 15 mm long.

Epiphyte on *Tamarindus* trees; flowering in February.

Madagascar (Sambirano valley in the north-west).

Aeranthes peyrotii Bosser

Plant with a short stem or apparently stemless. Leaves 6–8 in 2 rows, narrowly linear, slightly fleshy, glaucous green, compressed at the base to form a pseudo-petiole 2–3 cm long, in total 25–45 cm long, 0.6–1 cm wide. Inflorescences 2 or 3, pendent, 25–40 cm long, single-flowered; peduncle rigid, slender but slightly swollen at the nodes, covered with overlapping sheaths except near the base, each 7–9 mm long. Flowers green, slightly fleshy; dorsal sepal oval-lanceolate, subacuminate, 3–3.8 cm long, 6–8 mm wide near the base; lateral sepals acuminate, 3.2–4.5 cm long, 9–12 mm wide; petals lanceolate, acuminate, 2.5–3.5 cm long, 7–9 mm wide; lip rounded or subcordate at the base, flat, oblong or subpandurate with 2 basal ridges on its upper surface, acuminate, 2.2–2.8 cm long, 8–12 mm wide; column foot boat-shaped, 9–10 mm long, extending into a straight or curved spur

Aeranthes peyrotii. J. Hermans

Aeranthes ramosa, dark green form. J. Hermans

that is swollen and clavate at the end, 8–12 mm long.

Epiphyte in humid places in lowland evergreen forest; 700–1230 m; flowering January to March.

Madagascar (eastern region).

This species is easy to recognise by its long, narrow, glaucous leaves and fleshy flowers. It has a tendency to produce plantlets from the swollen nodes on the peduncles. It was named after Jean-Pierre Peyrot, a medical doctor in Madagascar, who collected the original specimen with Jean Bosser.

Aeranthes ramosa Rolfe

Syn. *Aeranthes brevivaginans* H. Perrier

Plant large, with a short stem or apparently stemless. Leaves 5–9, leathery, ligulate, almost equally bilobed at the obtuse tip, 12–28 cm long, 2.2–6 cm wide. Inflorescence pendent, very slender, 15–40 cm long, single or with few branches, bearing 1–3 flowers at the apex; peduncle thread like, dark green, sheaths few and widely spaced. Flowers olive green, sometimes with paler lip; dorsal sepal oval-lanceolate at the base, long-acuminate above, 4–5.3 cm long, 1 cm wide at the base; lateral sepals adnate to the column foot at the base, strongly expanded at the front margin to 16–23 mm wide, long-acuminate above, as long as the dorsal sepal or nearly so; petals acuminate above the oval base, in total 3.5 cm long, 1 cm wide at the base; lip subcordate at the base, oval-oblong, acuminate, 4–5 cm long, 1.6 cm wide; column foot widely boat-shaped, 1.6–2.5 cm long, extending into a spur that is narrow at the mouth, then obtuse, 1.4–2 cm long.

Epiphyte on tree trunks in humid forests, always amongst mosses, widespread in forest patches on the highland plateau; 1000–1500 m; flowering at various times throughout the year.

Madagascar.

This species is variable in size and flower colour but it is always green.

Aeranthes ramosa, pale green form. J. Hermans

Aeranthes virginalis. J. Hermans

Aeranthes schlechteri Bosser

Syns. *Neobathiea gracilis* Schlechter, *N. sambiranoensis* Schlechter

Plant with a short stem or apparently stemless, and with numerous thick, greyish-green roots at the base. Leaves 4–6 in a broad fan, ligulate, leathery and stiff, deep green, glossy, very unequally bilobed at the apex, 6–12 cm long, 1–1.8 cm wide. Inflorescence very slender, 2 or 3 times longer than the leaves, single-flowered; peduncle rigid with a few sheaths. Flowers medium-sized, white; sepals elongate, gradually acuminate from the base, 4.5–5(–6) cm long; petals narrowly linear, acuminate, above a short quadrate base, 3 cm long; lip long acuminate above the hastate blade, apparently clawed at the base, bearing 3 pubescent crests on the upper surface near the base, in total 3.2–4 cm long, 9 mm wide above the base; spur slightly expanded below the column foot, filiform, pendent, 11–13 cm long.

Epiphyte on twigs and branches of small bushes in dry forest; 90–1250 m; flowering February to March.

Madagascar (Sambirano valley and elsewhere in the north and north-west).

Jean Bosser (1969) pointed out that the type specimens of the 2 species shown as synonyms above are identical, and that the plants actually resemble closely those of the genus *Aeranthes*. The binomials *A. gracilis* and *A. sambiranoensis* had already been used for other species in *Aeranthes* so he proposed a new name for this striking species in recognition of Rudolf Schlechter who described so many plants from Madagascar.

Aeranthes virginalis D. L. Roberts

Plant with a fairly thick stem covered by foliar sheaths, roots glabrous, white, 2 mm in diameter. Leaves oblong-ligulate, pale green, up to 30 cm long, 3.6 cm wide. Inflorescence arching, branched, up to 65 cm long, several-flowered; peduncle producing plantlets at the nodes, sheaths long, dark brown, overlapping and covering much of the peduncle. Flowers pale green, diaphanous, 50 mm high, 38 mm wide; dorsal sepal erect, narrowly ovate, tapering to the base, acuminate, slightly recurved at the apex, 40–44 mm long, 9–11 mm wide; lateral sepals partly joined at the base, strongly falcate, acuminate, tips invariably crossing in front of the lip, 30–33 mm long, 12–15 mm wide; petals ovate, acuminate, spreading forward at 90º to the column, 30–33 mm long, 10 mm wide; lip ovate-triangular, acuminate, deflexed in the middle and folded against itself, 33 mm long, 16–19 mm wide; spur thickened towards the tip, 18 mm long, 3 mm wide.

Epiphyte in mossy cloud forest, 1.5–2 m above the ground; 600 m; flowering in December.

Comoro Islands (Mohéli).

This species has flowers that are slightly smaller than those of *Aeranthes caudata* and lack the long tails of that species. The lateral sepals are invariably held so that the tips cross each other.

Group 3. Species with medium-sized flowers, sepals 2–3 cm long.

Aeranthes aemula Schlechter

Syn. *Aeranthes biauriculata* H. Perrier

Plant with a very short stem or apparently stemless. Leaves 4–6, ligulate or linear, thin and leathery with prominent veins, 6–17 cm long, 0.5–1.4 cm wide. Inflorescence shorter than the leaves, upright or spreading, single-flowered or with 2 or 3 flowers on short branches; peduncle wiry with 4 or 5 distant sheaths, 40 cm long. Flowers white with yellowish tips, small, thin; dorsal sepals rounded at the base, acuminate above, 20–25 mm long, 6 mm wide at the base; lateral sepals similar but asymmetric at the base, up to 25 mm long, 6.5 mm wide; petals narrower and shorter than sepals, 12–17 mm long, 3–5 mm wide; lip broadly auriculate at the base, ovate-cordate, 9–10 mm long, 6–8 mm wide; column foot broad, extending into the wide

Aeranthes aemula. J. Hermans

mouth of the spur which is narrow below, obtuse, 8 mm long.

Epiphyte in lichen and mossy forest; 450–2000 m; flowering January to February.

Madagascar (Mount Tsaratanana and other parts of the central highlands).

Aeranthes albidiflora Toilliez-Genoud, Ursch & Bosser

Plant with a very short stem. Leaves 6 or 7 in 2 rows, ligulate, contracted towards the base, unequally and obtusely bilobed at the apex, 17–20 cm long, 1.4–1.6 cm wide. Inflorescence slender, pendent, 30 cm long, single-flowered; peduncle with 7–10 sheaths, shorter than the internodes. Flowers white, thin and transparent, sepals and petals reflexed; dorsal sepal oval lanceolate, long acuminate, 26–28 mm long, 6–7 mm wide near the base; lateral sepals similar but expanded on the front margin at the base, 29–30 mm long, 10 mm wide; petals shorter than sepals, long acuminate above the base, 16–17 mm long, 7 mm wide; lip broadly obovate, shortly apiculate (6–7 mm), 21–24 mm long, 14–15 mm wide; column foot broadly boat-shaped, 9–10 mm long; spur curving forwards below the lip, wide at the mouth, clavate at the apex, 12–13 mm long.

Epiphyte in shady forest; near sea level; flowering February to May.

Madagascar (eastern region).

Aeranthes carnosa Toilliez-Genoud, Ursch & Bosser

Plant with a short stem. Leaves 4, leathery, ligulate, unequally and obtusely bilobed at the apex, 15–32 cm long, 2–3 cm wide. Inflorescence pendulous, simple or branched, 1- to 3-flowered; peduncle rigid, sheaths 3, shorter than the internodes, 20–70 cm long. Flowers green, fleshy; dorsal sepal ovate-lanceolate, almost pandurate, subcordate at the base, acute, 21–24 mm long, 9–10 mm wide; lateral sepals larger, widened towards the base, with short obtuse apex, 23–30 mm long, 15 mm wide; petals ovate-lanceolate, smaller than sepals, with short, robust apex scarcely acuminate, 20–22 mm long, 8 mm wide; lip broadly ovate, base subcordate, apex rounded, subapiculate, 23–30 mm long, 13–18 mm wide at the upper third; column foot boat-shaped, slightly hairy within, 17–20 mm long, constricted where it descends into the spur to 2 mm in diameter; spur in total 10–12 mm long, with a narrow mouth, expanded into a globular tip, 7–8 mm long, 4–4.5 mm in diameter.

Epiphyte in humid mossy forest at low to medium altitude.

Madagascar (eastern region).

This species is characterised by the fleshy, green flowers that lack a long acumen on the sepals and petals and by the curiously shaped spur at the apex of the enlarged column foot.

Aeranthes denticulata Toilliez-Genoud, Ursch & Bosser

Plant with a very short stem or apparently stemless. Leaves 4 or 5, ligulate-oblong, leathery, unequally bilobed at the apex, with rounded lobes 8–10 mm long, midrib protuberant on lower surface, 16–22 cm long, 3.5–4 cm wide. Inflorescence pendent, slender, simple or with few branches, 1- to 5-flowered; peduncle with 13–16 blackish sheaths, shorter than the internodes, up to 1.3 m

long. Flowers green with yellow tips to the sepals and petals; dorsal sepal ovate, subacuminate, apex subobtuse, 23–26 mm long, 12–13 mm wide; lateral sepals similar but expanded on the front margin; petals broadly ovate, apex broadly acuminate, 22–24 mm long, 11–12 mm wide; lip ovate, base deeply cordate, apex acute and recurved, margins finely toothed, with 2 diverging keels on the upper surface at the base, 22–28 mm long, 18–20 mm wide; column foot boat-shaped, 15–18 mm long; spur straight, clavate, narrow at the mouth, slightly inflated above, 8–10 mm long.

Epiphyte in humid evergreen forest; 1000–1500 m; flowering July to August.

Madagascar (central parts of the eastern region).

This species can be distinguished from those with flowers of similar size by the finely toothed margin of the lip.

Aeranthes erectiflora Senghas

Plant erect with a short stem 2 cm long. Leaves 3 or 4 in 2 rows, leathery and thick, V-shaped in cross section, up to 20 cm long, 2 cm wide. Inflorescence axillary, rigid, erect, few-flowered; peduncle covered in long membranous sheaths, almost as long as the internodes, to 20 cm tall. Flowers not opening fully, diaphanous, greenish yellow, to 4.5 cm in diameter; dorsal sepal narrowly oval, long acuminate, 20 mm long, 7 mm wide; lateral sepals oblique, long acuminate, 20 mm long, 8 mm wide; petals obliquely oval at the base, 9 mm long, narrowly apiculate, in total 18 mm long, 7.5 mm wide; lip with curved, rhomboid blade with short apicule, 15 mm long, 10 mm wide; column foot boat-shaped, 10 mm long, 8 mm wide; spur with slightly bilobed apex, 10 mm long.

Epiphyte in highland forest; 1500–2000 m; flowering in September.

Madagascar (central region).

This species seems to be close to *Aeranthes longipes* but differs by the shorter sheaths that do not overlap on the peduncle, the less diaphanous flowers, and a distinctive, thickened spur.

Aeranthes filipes Schlechter

Plant with a short, slender stem. Leaves 6 or 7, linear-ligulate, 20–25 cm long, 1.8–4 cm wide. Inflorescence pendent, 1- or 2-flowered; peduncle with 2 or 3 distant sheaths, wiry, 11–20 cm long. Flowers green, variable in size, 32–48 mm high, 29–42 mm wide; dorsal sepal oval, acuminate, the acumen one-third of total length, 18–27 mm long, 8–15 mm wide; lateral sepals similar but the basal part expanded at the front margin, 20–34 mm long, 10–15 mm wide; petals elliptic, acuminate, 17–24 mm long, 7–10 mm wide; lip broadly oval, cordate at the base, acuminate, with 2 distinct calli on the upper surface near the base on either side of a gutter, 18–24 mm long, 10–15 mm wide; column foot 10 mm long and extending into the straight spur, sometimes enlarged at the apex, 12–15 mm long.

Epiphyte on trees beside rivers and waterfalls; 1000–1400 m; flowering in March.

Madagascar (central highlands).

Aeranthes filipes. J. Hermans

Aeranthes laxiflora Schlechter

Plant with a short stem hidden by the old leaf sheaths, densely leafy. Leaves 4 or 5, ligulate, fleshy, dark green, 11–17 cm long, 2–3.4 cm wide. Inflorescences short and hidden amongst the leaves, up to 10 cm long, 3- to 4-flowered; peduncle with a few distant sheaths, 4 cm long. Flowers thin, white or whitish green; dorsal sepal lanceolate, long acuminate, 25 mm long, 3 mm wide; lateral sepals similar, slightly expanded above the base on the front margin, 23 mm long, 7 mm wide; petals almost as long as sepals, broadly oval, then extending into the acumen, 21 mm long, 7 mm wide; lip broadly rhomboid-rounded, then shortly acuminate, 12–19 mm long, 8 mm wide near the middle; column foot 8 mm long, extending into the spur which curves forward becoming cylindrical, slender, 7.5–13 mm long.

Epiphyte on trunks and lianas, usually not far above the ground, in mossy forest; 1600–1800 m; flowering January to February.

Madagascar (central highlands).

This species is easily recognised by its fan of dark green leaves amongst which the white flowers are somewhat hidden.

Aeranthes leandriana Bosser

Plant with a short stem or apparently stemless. Leaves 5 or 6 in 2 rows, thick and rigid, glaucous green, linear, acutely bilobed at the apex, narrowed at the base into a short pseudo-petiole, upper surface ridged, 10–20 cm long, 5–8 mm wide. Inflorescence pendent, much shorter than or as long as the leaves, single-flowered; peduncle slender, 2.5–10 cm long, sheaths shorter than the internodes. Flowers pale green, transparent, sepals and petals projected forwards, lip held against the column; dorsal sepal oval-lanceolate, acuminate, 25–27 mm long, 8–10 mm wide at the base; lateral sepals asymmetric, broadly ovate, caudate, the front margin expanded in a rounded lobe, 27–32 mm long, 10–12 mm wide; petals oval, acuminate, 15–17 mm long, 6 mm wide; lip subrectangular, cordate at the base, apiculate, margins slightly undulate, papillose-pubescent on the upper surface at the

Aeranthes filipes, in eastern rain forest, Madagascar. J. Hermans

base, 20 mm long, 12–14 mm wide; column foot boat-shaped, 12 mm long, glabrous; spur narrow at first, curved and extended into a club-shaped tip, 10–12 mm long.

Epiphyte in humid evergreen forest on plateau; 1400–1500 m; flowering in November and December.

Madagascar (central region, near Ankazobe).

This species was named in honour of J. D. Léandri (1903–1982), a French botanist who made several expeditions to Madagascar and was eventually deputy director of the Laboratoire de Phanérogamie in Paris. It is somewhat similar to *Aeranthes albidiflora* but easily distinguished by the short peduncle and the sepals and petals projecting forwards, not reflexed.

Aeranthes longipes Schlechter

Plant apparently stemless. Leaves 6–8, lorate-linear, a little narrowed towards the tip and the base, 17–23 cm long, 1.1–1.5 cm wide. Inflorescence erect or ascending, simple or with 1 or 2 branches, to 35 cm long; peduncle robust, completely covered with pale sheaths longer than the internodes. Flowers bright green, thin, medium-sized; sepals oval, then long acuminate, 19–20 mm long, 7 mm wide; lateral sepals similar, a little expanded at the front margin above the base; petals oval, then long acuminate, 15 mm long, 7 mm wide; lip rhomboid, suborbicular, truncate at the base, apiculate, 14 mm long, 12 mm wide; spur cylindrical, obtuse, wide at the mouth, 9–13 mm long.

Epiphyte on moss- and lichen-covered trees in mossy forest; 1400 m; flowering February to March.

Madagascar (central region).

Aeranthes moratii Bosser

Plant apparently stemless. Leaves 4 or 5 in 2 rows, clear green or glaucous green, linear-oblong, unequally bilobed at the apex, midrib prominent below, 10–12 cm long, 1.5–2 cm wide. Inflorescence pendent, slender, simple or branched near the end with few flowers; peduncle thread-like with many sheaths shorter than the internodes,

Aeranthes longipes. J. Hermans

30–35 cm long. Flowers 4 or 5 in a short terminal raceme, opening successively, slightly fleshy, clear green, sepals with yellowish tips; dorsal sepal oval acuminate, 25–27 mm long, 8–9 mm wide; lateral sepals acuminate, basal lobe expanded at the front margin, 27–30 mm long, 10 mm wide at the base; petals much smaller than sepals, oval-acuminate, 16–17 mm long, 6–6.5 mm wide; lip ovate, contracted at the base into a wide claw, smooth with 2 short lateral ridges on its upper surface near the middle, 17–18 mm long, 12–13 mm wide; column foot boat-shaped, shallow, finely papillose inside; spur conical, short and wide, appearing dorso-ventrally compressed, 6–7 mm long.

Epiphyte in lowland humid forest.

Madagascar (near Antsiranana).

This species was named for the collector, Phillipe Morat, a French botanist who lived in Madagascar for some years and latterly was director of the Laboratoire de Phanérogamie in Paris. It is

Aeranthes moratii. J. Hermans

easily recognised by its thick, grey-green foliage; also the flowers have much longer sepals than petals and a characteristic short, flattened spur.

Aeranthes multinodis Bosser

Plant erect, apparently stemless. Leaves 4, linear-oblong, leathery, narrowing towards the base, unequally bilobed at the apex, with rounded lobes, 12–20 cm long, 2.5–4 cm wide. Inflorescences 1–5, pendent, slender, 1- to 3-flowered; peduncle with many nodes, completely covered by overlapping sheaths, 15–35 cm long. Flowers fleshy, pale green, yellowish at the tips, sepals recurved at the tips, dorsal sepal ovate-lanceolate, acuminate, 27–33 cm long, 8–9 mm wide, lateral sepals similar, enlarged on the front margin at the base, 25–29 mm long, 8–9 mm wide; petals broadly oval, acuminate, 22–29 mm long, 7–9 mm wide; lip rhomboid, truncate and mucronate at the apex, pubescent-papillose at the base, bearing a central ridge on the lower

half of the upper surface, margins denticulate in the apical half, 14–16 mm long, 10–12 mm wide; column foot boat-shaped, pubescent on the inside; spur cylindric, apex obtuse, 7–8 mm long.

Epiphyte in humid evergreen mossy forest; 1300–1400 m; flowering in March.

Madagascar (near Lake Tsiazompaniry).

Aeranthes nidus Schlechter

Syn. *Aeranthes pseudonidus* H. Perrier

Plant with several stems, forming dense colonies around tree trunks, stems elongated but hidden by leaf bases and sheaths. Leaves narrowly linear, narrowed towards the base to form a pseudo-petiole, 15–20 cm long, 8–10 mm wide in the middle. Inflorescences many, erect, always single-flowered, in groups of 5 or 10 along the stem, or on short, lateral, leafless branches, persistent over several years and producing flowers successively; peduncle thin, 2.5–3 cm long with few widely separated sheaths. Flowers white with the tips yellow, small, thin; dorsal sepal lanceolate, acuminate, 21 mm long, 4.5 mm wide at the base; lateral sepals longer, very slightly expanded at the front margin, 23–24 mm long; petals broadly rhomboid or suborbicular at the base, long acuminate, with a short tooth on either side at the base of the acumen, 17 mm long, 11 mm wide; lip suborbicular, a little wider than long, cordate at the base, upper surface with 2 ridges at the base, in total 17 mm long, 12 mm wide in the basal part; column foot 2 mm long; spur straight, obtuse at the apex, 10 mm long.

Epiphyte on moss- and lichen-covered trees; 1000–2000 m; flowering January to February.

Madagascar (mountains of the northern and central regions).

The habit of this species of forming large clumps is unmistakable, and the short inflorescences in groups along the stem are also characteristic (illustrated in Perrier 1941, p. 141).

Aeranthes robusta Senghas

Plant pendent with a short stem 2 cm long, and fine wiry roots. Leaves in 2 rows, spaced close together, flat, fleshy, symmetrically bilobed at the apex, 27 cm long, 4 cm wide. Inflorescences axillary, flexuose, pendent, bearing up to 10 flowers in succession; peduncle up to 50 cm long with few widely separated sheaths. Flowers not opening fully, 4.5 cm high, 3.5 cm wide, yellow green, sepals deeper green, robust and fleshy; dorsal sepal ovate, acuminate, recurved in the upper half, 27 mm long, 16 mm wide near the base; lateral sepals strongly recurved from the middle, asymmetrical, obliquely ovate, acuminate, 35 mm long, 21 mm wide; petals obliquely ovate, apiculus 12 mm long, recurved at the apex, in total 30 mm long, 16 mm wide; lip rhomboid, curved, attached to the column foot by a narrow claw, shortly apiculate, in total 30 mm long, 20 mm wide; spur linear, curved, slightly thickened at the apex, 15 mm long.

Epiphyte in montane forest; 1300–1600 m; flowering in July and September.

Madagascar (central highlands and near Andasibe).

This species seems to be somewhat similar to *Aeranthes carnosa*, except for its pendent habit.

Aeranthes sambiranoensis Schlechter

Plant apparently stemless. Leaves 3–5, narrowly linear, 23–30 cm long, 9–14 mm wide. Inflorescence erect, simple or occasionally branched, few-flowered; peduncle very thin, with 6–8 sheaths shorter than the internodes, to 33 cm long. Flowers greenish, thin; sepals ovate-lanceolate, extended in a long acumen, 24 mm long; lateral sepals a little enlarged on the front margin above the base; petals broadly oval at the base, elongated and very acuminate, 19 mm long; lip broadly oval, 3-lobed at the front, side lobes semi-oval, falcate, very obtuse, incurved, mid-lobe narrow, extended into an 8-mm-long acumen, in total 19 mm long, 10 mm wide above the middle; column foot broadly boat-shaped, 12 mm long; spur projecting forward below the lip, straight, wide at the mouth, globose at the apex, 23 mm long.

Epiphyte in seasonally dry deciduous forest and woodland; 800 m; flowering in January.

Madagascar (Sambirano valley).

Aeranthes tricalcarata H. Perrier

Plant with erect, branching stems, 20–40 cm high. Leaves many, in 2 rows, thin, broadly linear, unequally bilobed at the apex, 2–6 cm long, 6–10 mm wide. Inflorescences piercing the sheath, shorter than the leaf, single-flowered; peduncle very short, covered by sheaths, 5 mm long. Flowers green; sepals oval-lanceolate, acute, 25–27 mm long, 7 mm wide; lateral sepals a little wider at the base which is expanded at the front edge and fused to the column foot, 26 mm long, 8 mm wide; petals oval-lanceolate, narrowed from the middle to the acute tip, 21–26 mm long, 7–8 mm wide; lip broadly clawed at the base, expanded into broadly oval or suborbicular lamina, indented at the front margin, 20 mm long, 20 mm wide; column foot boat-shaped, concave, 12 mm long, expanded at the front edge into lateral lobes above the curve of the lip, the base shaped into 3 spurs and bearing a protruding, bifid crest in front of the mouth of these spurs; lateral spurs triangular, obtuse, 8 mm wide, 5 mm high; middle spur with a narrow mouth, curved forwards, gradually narrowing towards the apex, 10 mm long.

Lithophytic, growing amongst shaded rocks in a humid area; 1200 m; flowering in December.

Madagascar (southern region).

This species is easily recognised by its long stems with short inflorescences and lithophytic habit, as well as the 2 basal lobes (spurs) of the column foot that accompany the small spur attached to the lip.

Group 4. Species with small flowers, sepals 1–2 cm long.

Aeranthes bathieana Schlechter

Plant compact with a distinct stem hidden by sheaths and leaves, 5 cm long. Leaves up to 12, oblong-ligulate or oval elliptic, fleshy or leathery, unequally and obtusely bilobed at the apex, 5–6 cm long, 1.3–1.7 cm wide. Inflorescence erect, rigid, usually longer than the leaves, 1- to 4-flowered; peduncle thread-like, with 4–7 distant sheaths, 6–15 cm long. Flowers white with yellow tips, thin, small; sepals oval, then long acuminate, obtuse, 14–16 mm long, 4 mm wide; petals oval-elliptic, long acuminate, similar to sepals, 12 mm long, 3–4 mm wide; lip oval to subrectangular, truncate at the base, obtusely apiculate at the apex, bearing 2 short swollen ridges on the upper surface, 5 mm long, 4 mm wide; column foot 2.8 mm long; spur conical-cylindric, widened at the mouth, 2.5–5 mm long.

Epiphyte in mossy forest; 2000 m; flowering in February.

Madagascar (Mount Tsiafajavona).

This small species was named in honour of the collector of the first specimen, H. Perrier de la Bâthie. Schlechter (1925) noted that the sepals and petals of the white flowers are each extended into a cylindric yellow point.

Aeranthes campbelliae Hermans & Bosser

Plant small, up to 9 cm tall, with a short, flattened, leafy stem. Leaves 3–6, narrowly oblong, canaliculate, 4–6 cm long, 3–8 mm wide. Inflorescences several, axillary, 2- to 4-flowered; peduncle wiry, up to 8.5 cm long, simple or with few branches, with few sheaths partly covering the thickened nodes. Flowers greenish white, lip and tips of tepals yellowish white, 12–14 mm tall, 9–11 mm wide; dorsal sepal oblong-ovate, obtuse at the apex, 11 mm long, 3 mm wide; lateral sepals spreading, ovate, long acuminate into a tail 6 mm long, 11 mm long, 4 mm wide; petals reflexed at the apex, ovate, acuminate tail 3 mm long, 9 mm long, nearly 3 mm wide; lip broadly oval, auriculate at the base, forming 2 rounded swellings, farinose and papillose on the upper surface at the base, 4.6 mm long, 3.8 mm wide; column foot boat-shaped, very slightly inflated and continuous with the spur; spur rounded, very short, almost indistinct from the column foot.

Epiphyte.

Comoro Islands (Grande Comore).

This species was named for Heather Campbell who grew it in Nairobi for many years. It was originally collected by Jean Classen, a friend in the Kenya Orchid Society. It is somewhat similar to *Aeranthes ecalcarata*, from Madagascar, but the

Aeranthes campbelliae. J. Hermans

plants are more robust and the flowers usually larger.

Aeranthes neoperrieri Toilliez-Genoud, Ursch & Bosser

Plant with a short stem. Leaves 9 or 10, oblong-linear, unequally or nearly equally and obtusely bilobed at the apex, 9–10 cm long, 2.5 cm wide. Inflorescence slender, pendent, with 3 or 4 branches, 50–70 cm long; peduncle thread-like, dark green, branches 40 cm long, sheaths brown and much shorter than the internodes. Flowers green with darker green spur; dorsal sepal ovate, subacuminate, 15 mm long, 10 mm wide; lateral sepals similar with front margin expanded at the base to 17 mm wide and abruptly acuminate; petals subrectangular at base, obtusely acuminate, 12–13 mm long, 8 mm wide; lip subrectangular, base cordate, with 2 rounded lobes, apex triangular, acute, ending in a short incurved point, bearing 2 lateral diverging ridges on the upper surface and 1 shorter median crest, margins slightly undulating, 15 mm long, 14–15 mm wide; column foot boat-shaped, 1 cm long; spur cylindrical, wide at the mouth, then narrowing and broadened towards the tip, straight, 10 mm long.

Epiphyte in evergreen forest and mossy forest; ca. 1500 m; flowering in October.

Madagascar (eastern region).

This species is easily recognised by its attractive green flowers with wide and only shortly acuminate sepals and petals. It is another species named for Henri Perrier de la Bâthie.

Aeranthes orthopoda Toilliez-Genoud, Ursch & Bosser

Plant with a short stem or apparently stemless. Leaves 11 or 12, linear-oblong to ligulate, leathery, unequally and obtusely bilobed at the apex, 18–22 cm long, 2.2–2.9 cm wide. Inflorescence pendent, simple or branched, 30–70 cm long; peduncle slender, sheaths short. Flowers green; dorsal sepal ovate, narrowed in the apical third, subacuminate, 18 mm long, 10–11 mm wide; lateral sepals larger, obliquely ovate, apex subacuminate, 22 mm long, 12 mm wide; petals ovate-lanceolate, subacuminate, 18–20 mm long, 8–9 mm wide; lip orbicular, narrow at the base, with a short apiculus 3.5–4 mm long, 15–20 mm long, 16–21 mm wide; column foot funnel-shaped, 10 mm long; spur club-shaped, parallel to the ovary, 10–12 mm long.

Epiphyte in shady forest; no altitude or flowering information available.

Madagascar (central region, Mandraka).

Aeranthes parvula Schlechter

Plant with a short stem. Leaves 6 or 7, linear, 10–12 cm long, 5–10 mm wide. Inflorescence short, 14 cm high, often single-flowered; peduncle wiry, with 2 or 3 distant sheaths shorter than the internodes, 8 cm long. Flowers greenish white with brown, thickened tips, small; sepals oval-lanceolate, acuminate, 10–12 mm long, 3 mm wide; lateral sepals a little longer, expanded at the front margin at the base, 11.5 mm long, 4 mm wide;

petals oblong and acuminate, 8 mm long, 2 mm wide; lip subrectangular, not or slightly cordate at the base, acuminate, 8 mm long, 5 mm wide; column foot very large, expanded at the edges, 4.5 mm long; spur wide at the mouth, club-shaped, obtuse, slightly incurved, 5 mm long.

Epiphyte on *Tamarindus* trees; near sea level; flowering February to May.

Madagascar (Sambirano valley and Nosy Vé).

Aeranthes polyanthemus Ridley

Plant with a short stem to 5 cm long. Leaves narrowly ligulate, slightly bilobed, 17.5 cm long, 1.2 cm wide. Inflorescence slender and pendent, arising below the leaves from amongst the aerial roots on the elongated, 12–13 cm long, old stem bearing 7–9 flowers close together. Flowers yellowish green, almost transparent; sepals lanceolate, acuminate, dorsal sepal 16 mm long, 3 mm wide, lateral sepals with the front margin expanded at the base, 12 mm long, 5 mm wide; petals lanceolate, acuminate, 11 mm long, 3.5 mm wide; lip lanceolate, clawed at the base, subacuminate, 8 mm long, 5 mm wide; column foot deep in the centre, expanded on the margins into a small lobe; spur short, obtuse and incurved, 6–7 mm long.

Epiphyte and on wet rocks in mossy forest; 1180–1400 m; flowering in February.

Madagascar (central region).

Aeranthes setipes Schlechter

Plant small, slender, up to 7 cm high, forming small colonies by the rooting of plantlets from nodes on old inflorescences, plantlets sometimes forming instead of flowers. Leaves 5–7 per plant, linear and leathery, 4.5–8 cm long, 4–5.5 mm wide. Inflorescences spreading or pendent, often simple, sometimes with few branches, 6–14 cm long; peduncle thread-like, with few distant sheaths. Flowers greenish white, small, thin; dorsal sepal oval with a long acumen, 15 mm long, 3 mm wide; lateral sepals obliquely oval, long acuminate, 16 mm long, 4 mm wide; petals lanceolate, acuminate, 9 mm long, 3 mm wide; lip broadly rhomboid, somewhat acuminate at the front, bearing 2 obscure calli on the upper surface near the base, 10 mm long, 6 mm wide above the base; column foot extending into the spur, 4 mm long; spur conical, 5 mm long.

Epiphyte in mossy forest; 1800 m; flowering in January.

Madagascar (Mounts Tsaratanana and Marojejy).

Aeranthes subramosa Garay

Syn. *Aeranthes gracilis* Schlechter

Plant very small, stemless. Leaves 4–6, linear or linear-ligulate, fairly thick, 3.5–6 cm long, 7–9 mm wide. Inflorescences spreading or pendent, with few flowers laxly arranged, simple or with few branches, 14 cm long; peduncle with distant sheaths. Flowers whitish green, small, thin; sepals oval-lanceolate, then extended into an acumen, 14 mm long; lateral sepals expanded at the front margin near the base; petals broad at the base, then acuminate, 9 mm long; lip subrectangular, truncate at the base, rounded and apiculate at the apex, bearing 2 oblique ridges at the base on the upper surface, 5.5 mm long, 4.75 mm wide at the middle; column foot extending into the curved, forward-pointing spur, in total 6 mm long.

Epiphyte on moss- and lichen-covered trees; 2000 m; flowering January to February.

Madagascar (Mount Tsaratanana).

Garay (1972) proposed this new name for the plant Schlechter had described as *Aeranthes gracilis* (1925) because that name had already been used for a different species by Reichenbach f. in 1867. This species is said to be intermediate between *A. aemula* and *A. setipes*.

Aeranthes tenella Bosser

Plant small with a very short stem surrounded by fibrous remains of old leaf sheaths. Leaves 4 or 5 in 2 rows, oblong, flat, rounded at the base, equally bilobed at the apex, with rounded lobes, 2.5–5.5 cm long, 1–1.8 cm wide. Inflorescences 4 or 5, pendent, longer than the leaves, 5–10 cm, 1- or 2-flowered; peduncle slender, simple or few-branched, sheaths much shorter than the inter-

nodes. Flowers pale green, small, slightly fleshy; dorsal sepal lanceolate, obtuse, 18–19 mm long, 4 mm wide; lateral sepals asymmetric, oval-lanceolate, obtuse, 17–18 mm long, 6–7 mm wide; petals oval, subacuminate, 10–12 mm long, 4.5 mm wide; lip projecting forwards, rhomboid or trullate, acute at the apex, widely clawed at the base, with denticulate margins in the apical part, with loose papillae in a central mound on the upper surface at the base, extending towards the front by a central ridge, 10–12 mm long, 6–7 mm wide; column foot boat-shaped, shallow, with edges rounded or slightly incurved, inner surface papillose below the junction with the lip, 4–4.5 mm long; spur subcylindric, obtuse, broadly inflated in the apical part, 6–6.6 mm long.

Epiphyte in forest remnants; 1400–1500 m; flowering in January.

Madagascar (Mount Marojejy).

Aeranthes tropophila Bosser

Plant with a very short stem, covered with old leaf sheaths below the apical fan of leaves. Leaves 5–7 in 2 rows, linear-oblong, keeled on the lower surface, obtusely bilobed at the apex, with rounded lobes, 10–17 cm long, 1.5–1.9 cm wide. Inflorescences 3–5, very short, arising below the leaves, 2–2.5 cm long, 1- to 4-flowered; peduncle very short, completely covered with sheaths. Flowers green or white, somewhat fleshy, transparent; dorsal sepal acutely lanceolate, 11–16 mm long, 3–3.5 mm wide; lateral sepals 12–16 mm long, 4.5–5 mm wide; petals somewhat reflexed, acutely lanceolate, 10–13 mm long, 2.8–3 mm wide; lip oval to oblong, apex acute or apiculate, margins undulate in front, widely clawed at the base, with a basal, triangular, minutely papillose crest on the upper surface, 7–8 mm long, 4.5 mm wide; column foot boat-shaped, edges expanded into wide, rounded, inflexed lobes, inner surface papillose below the insertion of the lip, 4–4.5 mm long; spur cylindrical, obtuse, slightly constricted below the mouth and gradually inflated towards the tip, 5–6 mm long.

Epiphyte in seasonally dry deciduous forest and scrub overlying limestone; flowering August to October.

Madagascar (near Antsirañana).

This species is reminiscent of *Aeranthes laxiflora* in the short inflorescences borne below the leaves, but the habitat and the flowers are quite different.

Group 5. Species with very small flowers, sepals less than 1 cm long.

Aeranthes adenopoda H. Perrier

Plant small with a short stem 8–9 cm high. Leaves 7–10, lanceolate-linear, gradually narrowing towards the base, thin, 4.5–7 cm long, 5–10 mm wide. Inflorescences erect, arising below the leaves, usually several, half as long as the leaves, single-flowered, often accompanied by a second, aborted flower on a short branch; sheaths few. Flowers white or whitish green, small; dorsal sepal oval-lanceolate, subacute, 5–6 mm long, 2.5–3 mm wide; lateral sepals larger, with the front margin adnate to the column foot, 6–6.5 mm long, 2–4 mm wide; petals oval-lanceolate, acute, 4.5–5.2 mm long, 2 mm wide; lip widely obovate, obtuse and subapiculate, bearing 2 or 3 projecting keels on the upper surface, 5–6 mm long, 3.8–4.5 mm wide near the apex; column foot slightly winged, 3.5–4 mm long, 2 mm wide; spur cylindric, mouth oval, 3.5–6.5 mm long.

Epiphyte in humid forest; 1000–1300 m; flowering in January.

Madagascar (eastern region) and Réunion (Basse Vallée).

This species may be distinguished from *Aeranthes setiformis* by the smaller flowers with broader sepals, differently shaped lip, and by small blackish bristles on the ovary and exterior of the sepals.

Aeranthes ambrensis Toilliez-Genoud, Ursch & Bosser

Plant small, apparently stemless, up to 15 cm tall. Leaves 5, ligulate, unequally and obtusely bilobed at the apex, 10–12 cm long, 10–11 mm wide. Inflorescence pendent, simple or branched, bear-

Aeranthes adenopoda. J. Hermans

ing 7–9 flowers in a terminal group resembling a spike; peduncle covered with sheaths each 2.5 cm long and overlapping half of the next; floral bracts large, broadly ovate, longer than pedicellate ovary. Flowers greenish white; dorsal sepal lanceolate, subacute, 8 mm long, 3 mm wide; lateral sepals as long but distinctly widened into a lobe on the front margin, 7.5–8.5 mm long, 3–4 mm wide; petals shorter than sepals, ovate, acute, 6–6.5 mm long, 3 mm wide; lip widely ovate, concave, apex acute, recurved, bearing a central triangular ridge and a small conical callus near the base on the upper surface, 5.5–7 mm long, 3–4 mm wide; column foot 3–4 mm long, extending into a very small conical spur 1.5–2 mm long.

Epiphyte in humid forest; flowering in July.

Madagascar (Ambre Forest, near Antsirañana).

This species can be recognised by its thin, flexible leaves and long inflorescences completely covered with overlapping sheaths.

Aeranthes ecalcarata H. Perrier

Plant small with a short stem, sometimes branched, to 3 cm long. Leaves 4–6, thin, linear,

Aeranthes ecalcarata. J. Hermans

Aeranthes orophila. J. Hermans

grass-like, 3.5–12 cm long, 1–2.5 mm wide. Inflorescences emerging from the stem base, 1- to 3-flowered; peduncle wiry, with 3 or 4 small, distant sheaths, 4–10 cm long. Flowers white or pale green, widely spaced if there are several; sepals oval-lanceolate, acute, 3–5 mm long, 2–2.2 mm wide; petals oval, obtusely acuminate, 2–3 mm long, 1.5 mm wide; lip very small, almost square, base auriculate, shortly and bluntly acuminate, 1.8 mm long, 1.3 mm wide; column foot very wide and elliptic in contour, 1.8 mm long, 1.2 mm wide; spur very small, reduced to an obtuse cavity, 0.2 mm deep.

Epiphyte on moss- and lichen-covered tree trunks, widespread; 800–1750 m; flowering December to July.

Madagascar (central highlands).

This species is remarkable for its thin, grass-like leaves as well as the spur-less flowers.

Aeranthes orophila Toilliez-Genoud

Plant small with a short stem 5–10 cm high, usually several stems growing together. Leaves borne along the stem, grass-like, attenuate at both ends, canaliculate, sometimes falcate, 4–6 cm long, 3–5 mm wide. Inflorescences several, single-flowered; peduncle thread-like, with 4–7 brown sheaths that cover the internodes at the base, the upper ones shorter, 3–6 cm long. Flowers greenish white, small; dorsal sepal oval-lanceolate, 7–9 mm long, 3–5 mm wide; lateral sepals similar, subacuminate, 7–10 mm long, 3–4 mm wide; petals acuminate, 6–8 mm long, 3–5 mm wide; lip rectangular, auriculate at the base, with a small, 2-mm-long acumen at the apex, surface undulate, 6–7 mm long, 7–9 mm wide; column foot 3 mm long; spur cylindrical-conical, upright at the apex, 3–5 mm long.

Epiphyte in humid, mossy forest; 2000–2500 m; flowering November to January and in May.

Madagascar (central highlands).

Aeranthes setiformis Garay

Syn. *Aeranthes pusilla* Schlechter

Plant small, apparently stemless, 4–7 cm high. Leaves 4–7, ligulate-linear, slightly leathery, 3–5 cm long, 3–7 mm wide. Inflorescence erect or spreading, as long as the leaves or a little longer, to 45 mm long, simple or with a few short branches at the base, each branch bearing one flower; peduncle thread-like, bearing a few distant sheaths. Flowers white with a green tinge, small; sepals lanceolate-oblong, acuminate, somewhat obtuse, 7.5 mm long; lateral sepals similar but with the front margin a little expanded above the base; petals shorter, oval, very obtuse, 3.5 mm long, 3 mm wide; lip suborbicular or broadly oval, very obtuse, 3.5 mm long, 3 mm wide; column foot 2 mm long; spur wide at the mouth, curved forward, 2–3 mm long.

Epiphyte in mossy forest; 2000 m; flowering in October.

Madagascar (Mount Tsiafajavona).

Garay (1972) published this new name for the plant described as *Aeranthes pusilla* by Schlechter (1925) because that name had already been used for another species by Reichenbach f. in 1867.

Species from Réunion and Mauritius

Aeranthes adenopoda H. Perrier

This small-flowered species is described with the Madagascar species (see page 153). It has been reported recently from 800 m in Basse Vallée, Réunion.

Aeranthes arachnitis (Thouars) Lindley

Plant with a short, erect stem, covered with closely overlapping leaf bases, sometimes including many old ones. Leaves 5–7 in 2 rows, ligulate, recurved, strongly keeled on the lower surface, very unequally bilobed at the apex, 12–20 cm long, 2 cm wide. Inflorescences arising below the leaves, 1- or 2-flowered at the apex, or up to 4 flowers borne successively, 15–40 cm long; peduncle entirely covered with sheaths that are shorter or as long as the internodes. Flowers yellow-green, 5 cm in diameter across the lateral sepals; dorsal sepal with broadly ovate base, 3 cm long, 12.5 mm wide; lateral sepals larger, ovate, acuminate, with the broad base extended into a wide lobe on the front margin, 3 cm long, 18 mm wide; petals similar to the dorsal sepal but more abruptly acuminate, recurved in the upper half, 2 cm long, 7 mm wide; lip quadrate-oblong at the base, abruptly terminating in a triangular, acuminate, central lobe, notched at the base of the acuminate part, upper surface slightly pubescent, 3 cm long, 1.2 cm wide; spur a very short, inflated, obtuse sac, 8 mm long.

var. *arachnitis*

An epiphyte, or growing on rocks in open or dense shade in forest; 200–800 m; flowering from January for several months.

Réunion, Mauritius, and Madagascar (some doubtful records exist).

This species is similar to *Aeranthes grandiflora* in its growth habit, but the plants are smaller with narrower leaves and smaller flowers.

Aeranthes arachnitis. J. Hermans

var. *balfourii* S. Moore

Leaves 25 cm long; lateral sepals 3 cm long. Rodrigues Island.

This variety was named after the collector, I. B. Balfour, but seems doubtfully distinct.

Aeranthes hermannii Frappier ex Cordemoy

Plant small, with a stem up to 15 cm long. Leaves borne very close together, oblong-lanceolate, undulate, obliquely bilobed at the apex, 10–20 cm long, 2 cm wide. Inflorescence arising below the leaves, very slender, 10–20 cm long, always single-flowered, entirely covered by sheaths 2–3 cm long. Flowers medium-sized, entirely green, 4 cm in diameter; sepals oval, acuminate; lateral sepals oblique; petals narrower, united at the base, as well as the lateral sepals, with the claw of the lip; lip oboval, acuminate, biauriculate at the base, hairy at the throat; spur wide, flattened.

Epiphyte or lithophyte in forest; 400–800 m; flowering January to March.

Réunion (near town of Saint Pierre).

Aeranthes strangulata Frappier ex Cordemoy

Plant small, with a short stem enclosed in somewhat inflated leaf sheaths, a few cm high. Leaves 5–8, narrow, linear but narrowed and twisted at the base where they are articulated to the almost bulbous sheath, partly folded with distinct midrib, 6–12 cm long, 10–15 mm wide. Inflorescence sometimes branched, 12–15 cm long, bearing 1–4 flowers usually opening successively; floral bracts brown, large, ovate, inflated. Flowers green, hyaline, to 3 cm in diameter; sepals wide with short acuminate tips, 1.5 cm long; petals similar in shape but shorter and narrower, the tips somewhat recurved; lip broad and oval, curved forward in the apical half, the apical margins undulate, shortly acuminate at the apex; spur cylindrical at first, bent forward below the lip, inflated, blister-like at the apex.

Epiphyte and amongst boulders, usually amongst mosses in shady places; 500–1200 m; flowering December to May.

Réunion (in the north and south-west).

Aeranthes tenella var. *borbonica* Bosser

This variety differs from *Aeranthes tenella* by the curious way that the inflorescences are borne on short branches in bundles of 2–10, and by the peduncles that are shorter than the leaves with more nodes. The leaves and flowers are very similar to those of *A. tenella* from Madagascar.

Epiphyte in humid forest; 400–700 m; flowering in March and December.

Réunion (eastern parts of the island, above the towns of Saint Philippe and Sainte Marie) and Mauritius (a sterile specimen collected by Boivin in 1851 may be attributed to this variety).

Imperfectly Known Species

Aeranthes dentiens Reichenbach f.

This species was described from plants in cultivation in England before 1885. The pressed specimens in the herbarium at Kew consist of a single leaf and a few flowers. The flowers are said to be pale yellow-green with olive green tips; sepals and petals 2.5–4 cm long; lip cuneate or obovate, subcordate at the base. The sheaths on the peduncle are very long, but not overlapping.

According to Katz and Simmons (1986), Schlechter, who may have seen a type specimen, wrote that in habit and flower size, the species was probably best compared with *A. grandiflora*, but that it differed specifically in the more pointed tips of the sepals and petals and in the lip. The latter is distinctly dentate on both sides in front of the extended apex and the mouth of the spur is clothed with delicate, short hairs. The almost straight spur is swollen in a simple club-shape at the apex.

These specimens may have come from Madagascar or the Comoro Islands: it is hoped that they may be matched by further discoveries in due course.

AMBRELLA H. Perrier

This curious genus appears to be known only from the original collection near the Maky River

Ambrella longituba. 1: Habit. 2–3: Flower. 4: Lip and spur. 5: Dorsal sepal. 6: Petal.
7: Lateral sepal. 8. Anther-cap. Reprinted by permission from Perrier 1941, fig. 77.
M. J. Vesque. © Publications Scientifiques du Muséum national d'Histoire naturelle, Paris.

at the base of Mount Ambre in northern Madagascar. The name is apparently derived from this location. The specimen was one of Henri Perrier's own collections, and he described this monotypic genus in 1934. It is a small epiphyte with a habit somewhat similar to that of some species of *Aerangis*. It has a short stem and wide, flat leaves that are oddly thickened at the apex. The flowers are green and large for the size of the plant. The elongated lip is 3-lobed near the apex. It has inrolled margins and the inner surface is softly hairy. The short, thick column is entirely concealed within the base of the lip.

Ambrella longituba H. Perrier

Plant with a short, erect stem up to 10 cm long. Leaves 5 or 6, flat, elliptic or oboval-oblong, contracted near the base, unequally and obtusely bi-lobed at the apex, 5–9 cm long, 1.6–2.2 cm wide. Inflorescence arising below the leaves, with few sheaths, 1- to 3-flowered; peduncle 5–6 cm long; bracts wide, thin, apiculate, 6 mm long; pedicel with ovary 9–10 mm long. Flowers green, 4.5 cm long; sepals and petals similar, lanceolate, acute, 4 cm long, 6 mm wide; lip tubular at the base for 3 cm, then 3-lobed, the mid-lobe broadly oboval, 1.8 cm long, 1.3 cm wide, lateral lobes narrow, 6 mm long, 4 mm wide at the base; spur 6–7 mm wide at the mouth, narrowing below and then cylindric, curving forwards below the lip, 3.5 cm long.

Epiphyte on the branches of *Calliandra alternans*; 800 m; flowering in November.

Madagascar (Mount Ambre).

BONNIERA Cordemoy

This small genus contains 2 species that usually lack a spur at the base of the lip. It was published as a new genus by E. Jacob de Cordemoy in the second part of his account of the orchids of Réunion (1899). He named it in honour of Professor Gaston Bonnier, the editor of the *Revue General de Botanique*, in which the description appeared. The 2 species resemble various angraecums in their growth habit, particularly some of those in section *Arachnangraecum*, and it is possible that they will be transferred to the genus *Angraecum* in due course. They have been illustrated by Janine Cadet (1989), whose drawings of plants and flowers make it quite clear that 2 distinct species lacking a spur are present in Réunion, although both are now very rare.

Bonniera appendiculata (Frappier ex Boivin) Cordemoy

Plant with stems branching from the base. Leaves in 2 rows, ovate, cordate, amplexicaul, to 1 cm long, 6–8 mm wide. Inflorescence solitary, axillary, single-flowered; peduncle short and persistent, 1 cm long. Flower clear yellow, opening widely; sepals and petals almost equal, oval-lanceolate at the base, then becoming linear and filiform, 5–6 cm long; lip a little wider than the petals at the base but otherwise similar; spur absent.

Epiphyte in rain forest at medium altitudes and at the base of *Philippia* bushes.

Réunion.

Bonniera corrugata Cordemoy

Plant with upright, horizontal, or oblique stems branching from near the base, usually leafless in the lower part but bearing the old leaf sheaths and the remains of inflorescences. Leaves in 2 rows, thick, leathery, oblong, unequally and obliquely bilobed at the apex, lobes obtuse, dark green above and paler below, 3.5 cm long, 1.5 cm wide. Inflorescence solitary, axillary, single-flowered; peduncle

Bonniera appendiculata. J. Hermans

short, persistent after the flower has fallen, 1 cm long. Flower greenish white, 7 cm in diameter; sepals and petals similar, lanceolate, long and narrow above the base, acuminate; lip a little wider and concave at the base; spur absent.

Epiphyte in rain forest at high altitude; flowering in October and November.

Réunion.

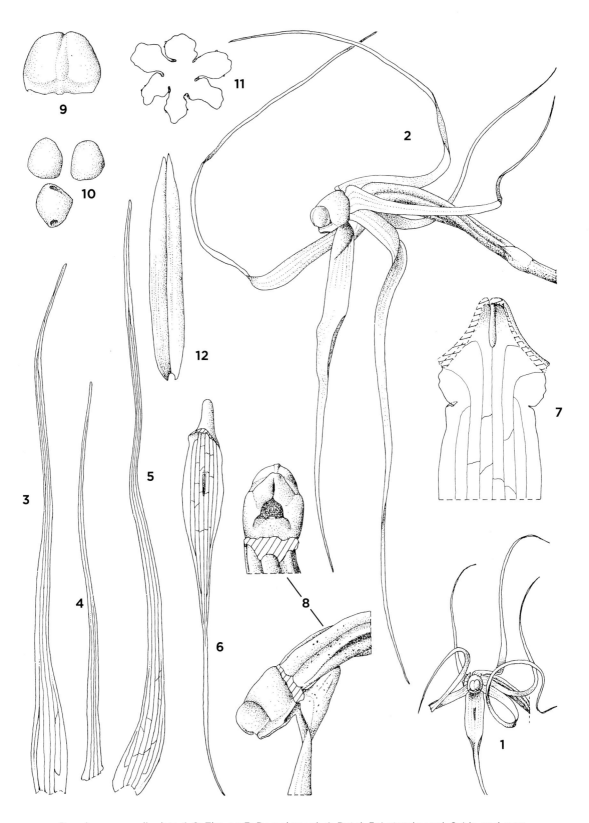

Bonniera appendiculata. 1–2: Flower. 3: Dorsal sepal. 4: Petal. 5: Lateral sepal. 6: Lip and spur. 7: Base of lip and spur. 8: Column. 9: Anther-cap. 10: Pollinia. 11: Cross section of ovary. 12: Leaf. Reprinted with permission, A. Brown. From the collections, Royal Botanic Gardens, Kew.

CALYPTROCHILUM Kraenzlin

Only 2 species are now recognised in this genus, which was established by the German botanist Fritz Kraenzlin in 1895. The name is derived from the Greek words *kalyptro*, a veil or covering, and *chilos*, lip, perhaps a reference to the way the lip sometimes appears to be concealed by the rest of the flower, or because the lip looks like a veil. Both species are immediately recognisable by the curious way that their leathery leaves are twisted at the base, so that they lie flat in one plane on either side of the stem.

Both species are widespread in the warmer parts of Africa, and *Calyptrochilum christyanum* is one of the most widespread of all African epiphytic orchids. It has smaller leaves and fewer flowers than *C. emarginatum*, which is restricted to the western side of the continent from Guinea south to Angola. The plants are a conspicuous sight in forests and large isolated trees in areas that were formerly forested, where they form huge clumps of stems like mistletoes in the shade of the canopy.

Perhaps because of their wide distribution, both species have been described under many different names. Many synonyms now exist for both entities.

Culture

These species grow well in cultivation provided the plants are kept in suitably warm and humid conditions. They can succeed in a pot but do better when mounted so that the stems can assume their normally pendent position. It is better to start with seedlings or young plants as large ones can be very difficult to get established. Whether large or small, the plants should be tied very firmly to a supporting log or piece of bark so that the new roots can gradually become attached without being damaged.

Calyptrochilum christyanum (Reichenbach f.) Summerhayes

Plants forming large clumps with long woody stems bearing many roots; stems simple, rarely

Calyptrochilum christyanum. J. Hermans

branched, 12–90 cm long. Leaves in 2 rows, ligulate, fleshy with a distinctive slightly rugose surface, 3–12 cm long, 1–2.5 cm wide. Inflorescences opposite and below leaves, 2–4 cm long; peduncle short, rachis zigzag, up to 4 cm long; bracts dark brown, lanceolate, acute, 2–4 mm long. Flowers 6–12, white, tinged with pink or apricot, spur usually greenish; sepals ovate to ovate-elliptic, 5–10 mm long, 2–4 mm wide; petals oblong-elliptic, obtuse to apiculate, 5–8 mm long, 2–3 mm wide; lip 3-lobed at the base, appearing 4-lobed because the mid-lobe is emarginate, side lobes rounded, 7–12 mm long, 7–10 mm wide; spur wide at the mouth, strongly bent and constricted in the middle, the apex inflated and at right angles to the lip, spur and lip together 1.8 cm long.

Epiphyte in tall forest trees or trees that have become isolated in areas formerly forested; sea level to 1900 m; flowering November to June.

Gambia eastwards to Sudan and Ethiopia, and south to Mozambique and Angola.

This species was named in honour of Thomas Christy who collected the type specimen in West Africa.

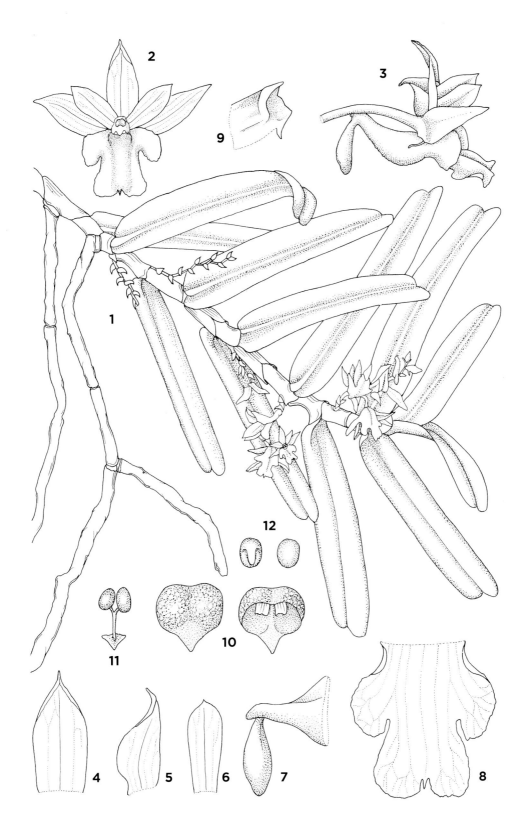

Calyptrochilum christyanum. 1: Habit. 2–3: Flower. 4: Dorsal sepal. 5: Lateral sepal. 6: Petal. 7: Spur. 8: Lip.
9: Column. 10: Anther-cap. 11: Pollinarium. 12: Pollinia. From Cribb 1989, fig. 113. S. Wickison.

Calyptrochilum emarginatum. C. Arends

Calyptrochilum emarginatum (Afzelius ex Swartz) Schlechter

Plants forming large clumps with long woody stems bearing many roots; stems simple, rarely branched, sometimes up to 2 m long. Leaves in 2 rows, ligulate, fleshy with a distinctive slightly rugose surface, 6–17 cm long, 2–5 cm wide. Inflorescences opposite and below leaves, very short and crowded with flowers; peduncle and rachis to 5 cm long; bracts orange-brown, close together 4–7 mm long. Flowers white, with yellow lip and spur; sepals and petals similar, lanceolate, acute, ca. 1 cm long; lip narrowly boat-shaped, 3-lobed at the apex, the lateral lobes large and rounded, the mid-lobe reduced to an apiculus, 7–12 mm long, 7–10 mm wide; spur wide at the mouth, recurved and briefly constricted in the middle, the apex inflated, lip and spur 2 cm long.

Epiphyte on trunks and larger branches of big trees in evergreen and deciduous rain forest; sea level to 1000 m; flowering in March and April.

Guinea to Congo and Angola.

CRYPTOPUS Lindley

This genus was established in 1824 by John Lindley when he recorded a short list of genera in the Vandeae related to *Aeranthes*, in the *Botanical Register*, t. 817. *Cryptopus elatus* was the only species of the genus known to him, and it had been illustrated by Thouars in 1822 as *Angraecum elatum*. Lindley did not give the derivation of the name *Cryptopus*, but it has been presumed to refer to the fact that the stipes and viscidia are somewhat hidden by the square side lobes of the rostellum, from the Greek *kryptos*, hidden, and *pous*, foot. In this genus the lip appears to be inserted at the front edge of the mouth of the spur, and there is no foot, as such, at the base of the column.

Cryptopus seems to be rather close to *Neobathiea* in many ways, particularly in the way the lip is related to the spur, and in the plant habit, but Bosser (1969) distinguished the 2 genera easily by their petals and spur. *Cryptopus* has very distinctive petals that are lobed in the apical part and quite different from the sepals, and the spur at the base of the lip is quite short. In *Neobathiea* the sepals and petals are similar to each other and the spur is long. It will be interesting to see if these differences continue to separate the 2 genera when DNA analysis has been carried out on these plants.

Four species of *Cryptopus* are now recognised: one (*C. elatus*) in Réunion and Mauritius, and the others in Madagascar. All are found in forest habitats in the more humid parts of the islands. The elongated stems behave as climbers, attaching themselves to twigs and branches of their hosts by their long, sometimes twisted or curled aerial roots.

Culture

These epiphytes are not easy to maintain in culture because the roots seem to require something to attach themselves to but do not thrive if potted or kept moist. Careful attachment to a cork-oak slab seems to be the best treatment. The slab needs to be hung up in a shady humid place with plenty of fresh air.

Cryptopus elatus. From Thouars 1822, t. 80.

Cryptopus brachiatus H. Perrier

Plant with slender, flexuous stems, sometimes branched, 5–10 cm long, 3–4 mm in diameter, and narrow, greyish, aerial roots. Leaves 4–8, near the apex of the stem, leathery, oblong-elliptic, obtuse, 1.5–5.6 cm long, 1–2 cm wide. Inflorescences lateral, lax, 5- to 10-flowered; peduncle rigid, erect, 2–5 cm long; bracts small, 1 mm long; pedicel with ovary 14–17 mm long. Flowers green or pale whitish green with a white lip; sepals narrowly obovate, 13–14 mm long, 4–5 mm wide; petals T-shaped, narrowly oblanceolate or linear, divided near the apex into 2 horizontal, linear lobes 8–10 mm long; lip 3-lobed, narrow at the base, basal lobes elliptic to obovate, 12 mm long, 5 mm wide, mid-lobe subquadrate at the base, deeply bifid at the apex similar to the petals, apical parts 6 mm long, 3 mm wide; spur wide at the mouth, conical, 2 cm long.

Epiphyte in humid forest; 600–1200 m; flowering February to April.

Madagascar (eastern region).

Cryptopus dissectus (Bosser) Bosser

Syn. *Cryptopus elatus* subsp. *dissectus* Bosser

Plant with tall, narrow stems 30–40 cm long, with well-distributed, wiry, greyish roots. Leaves widely spaced, ovate or oblong, bilobed at the apex, 3.5–5 cm long, 1–1.5 cm wide. Inflorescence lateral, simple, 30 cm long, bearing 8–11 well-spaced flowers; peduncle 20 cm long, stiff, sometimes divided; bracts small. Flowers yellowish green; sepals narrow below, spathulate, 11–12 mm long, 4 mm wide; petals narrow below, with 4 narrow lobes in the upper part, 1–2 mm long, in total 14–15 mm long; lip 4-lobed, basal lobes falcate, recurved, 6–8 mm long, apical lobes dissected into 4 narrow lobules, each branched at the apex, in total 15–17 mm long; spur funnel-shaped, becoming filiform, 12–13 mm long.

Epiphyte in humid forest; 500–1000 m; flowering in December.

Madagascar.

This species has the smallest flowers in the genus and the petals and lip are the most dissected of all. Bosser (1965) originally described it as a subspecies of *Cryptopus elatus* but later (1980), when he had seen more material, decided that these Madagascar plants were specifically distinct from those in the Mascarene Islands. Sadly, it is now virtually extinct in the wild.

Cryptopus elatus (Thouars) Lindley

Syns. *Angraecum elatum* Thouars, *Beclardia elata* (Thouars) A. Richard

Plant with long, sometimes sinuous stems up to 50 cm or approaching 1 m tall, 4–5 mm in diameter, with roots along the stem below the leaves. Leaves near the apex of the stem, widely spaced, oblong or elliptic, unequally bilobed at the apex, 2–7 cm long, 1.2–1.5 cm wide. Inflorescence axillary, erect, simple or with 1 or 2 branches near the base, 30–60 cm long, 7- to 13-flowered; peduncle with 3 or 4 sheaths; bracts small. Flowers creamy white, turning yellow with age, marked with red or orange at the base of the lip; sepals spathulate, 16–20 mm long; petals narrow at the base, unequally 4-lobed at the apex, 25–30 mm long; lip as long as the sepals with 4 lobes, the basal lobes small, narrow and incurved, the upper lobes diverging and separated by a short apiculus, narrow at the base and irregularly lobed at the 2 tips, 15–20 mm long; spur wide at the mouth, narrow below, 25 mm long.

Epiphyte on tree trunks and on rocks in rather open forest; sea level to 700 m.

Mauritius and Réunion.

This strange orchid was discovered by French botanist L. M. Aubert du Petit Thouars and illustrated by him in 1822.

Cryptopus paniculatus H. Perrier

Plant with a long tough stem, pendent or scrambling amongst other plants, up to 40 cm long or more, 4 mm in diameter. Leaves elliptic, obtuse at both ends, 3.5–5 cm long, 1.3–1.8 cm wide. Inflorescence paniculate, with 1–4 branches, 20–40 cm long, 3- to 10-flowered; peduncle 12–18 cm long, side branches 5–12 cm long; ovary with pedicel 1.2–1.5 cm long. Flowers milky white with 2 small red spots on the lip at the base of the column; dorsal sepal oboval, 6.5–7 mm long, 3 mm wide; lateral sepals slightly longer and narrower, dilated at the middle on the anterior side; petals broader than the sepals, somewhat anchor-shaped, widening above the middle into 2 equal, incurved lobes, 9 mm long, 12 mm wide; lip 5-lobed, mid-lobe narrowly triangular with a papillose callus near the base, 4.5 mm long, 2 mm wide, basal lobes very small and rounded, lateral lobes well developed, narrow at the base, enlarged at the apex into 2 unequal lobes, the inner part larger and incurved, 6 mm long; spur conical, 2–3 mm long.

Epiphyte in humid forests; sea level to 1000 m; flowering February to March.

Madagascar (along the eastern forested slopes).

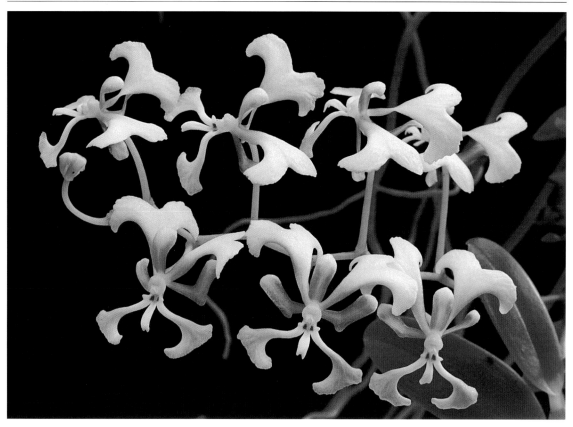

Cryptopus paniculatus. J. Hermans

JUMELLEA Schlechter

This genus of about 60 species, most of them from Madagascar, was named in honour of Henri Lucien Jumelle (1866–1935), professor of botany in Marseille, who collaborated extensively with Henri Perrier de la Bâthie but never visited Madagascar himself. All the species are easily recognised by their single-flowered inflorescences, though often more than one inflorescence is present at each flowering.

The white or cream-coloured flower that often turns bright yellow with age or after pollination is also characteristic of the genus. The dorsal sepal is upright or slightly reflexed, and distant from the lateral sepals, petals, and lip. Their posture is maintained by short outgrowths from the base of the column, described as parallel arms by Perrier, which extend forward across the mouth of the spur on either side, joined to the inner surface of the lateral sepals, but usually hidden from view by

the base of the petals. Slightly twisted and with their outer surface uppermost, these 4 perianth parts form a frame on either side of the lip. The lateral sepals are usually united at the base, enclosing the base of the spur. Unlike *Angraecum*, where the broad base of the lip enfolds the column, the lip in *Jumellea* flowers is narrow at the base, sometimes narrowed into a distinct claw, and inserted below the column. The spur is always narrow throughout its rather varied length.

No modern account of the genus *Jumellea* exists: descriptions and illustrations are somewhat scattered in the literature. It is likely that some of the species described here will be relegated to synonymy when a comparative study is made. About 42 species have been recorded from Madagascar and 5 are found in the Comoro Islands where they appear to be endemic. Ten species have been recorded in Réunion, two of which are also found in Mauritius. Only two species are known from various parts of eastern Africa. These are dealt with

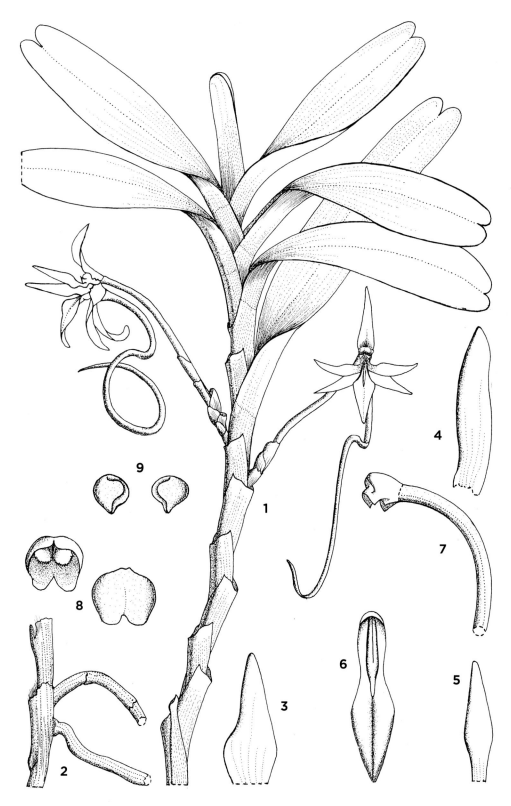

Jumellea usambarensis. 1: Habit. 2: Roots. 3: Dorsal sepal. 4: Lateral sepal. 5: Petal. 6: Lip. 7: Column. 8: Anther-cap. 9: Pollinia. From Wood 1982, p. 78. S. Hillier.

first, followed by the species from Madagascar and the Comoro Islands. The species from the Mascarene Islands come last.

Culture

Many species of *Jumellea* are easily maintained in cultivation in well-drained compost in a pot or basket. The ecological notes provided for each species should help to determine the best treatment as the environmental conditions many require are sometimes difficult to supply in combination: good drainage, high humidity, good air movement, and strong light for some of the species. Fast drainage after watering and a prolonged dry period when the plants are not in active growth are very important if the plants are to survive and flower well. It is much easier to start with laboratory-raised seedlings and grow them on than try to establish large, wild-collected plants.

Species from Africa

The 2 species recorded from Africa can be distinguished from each other by their size, *Jumellea* *usambarensis* having much larger plants, and flowers with a longer spur, than *J. walleri*.

Jumellea usambarensis J. J. Wood

Plants with long woody stems bearing many roots, leafy in the upper part; stems simple, usually growing in clusters of several stems together, 30–80 cm long. Leaves 6–10 in 2 rows, oblong-ligulate, equally or almost equally bilobed at the apex, leathery, 10–13 cm long, 1.5–2 cm wide. Inflorescences single-flowered; peduncle short, sheathed with bracts that turn black; pedicel with ovary 2.5–3 cm long. Flower white with green spur, scented in the evening; dorsal sepal ovate-elliptic, obtuse, margins undulate or crisped at the base, 13–16 mm long, 6 mm wide; lateral sepals oblong-ligulate, obtuse, 17 mm long, 4 mm wide; petals linear-ligulate, obtuse, reflexed, slightly smaller than sepals; lip rhombic, narrow at the base, with a shallow central keel, acute, 16–17 mm long, 6 mm wide; spur parallel to the ovary then bent, cylindric, sometimes coiled, 8–9 cm long.

Epiphyte in rain forest; 1600–2000 m; flowering in May and December.

Kenya, Tanzania, and Malawi.

Jumellea walleri. E. la Croix

167

Jumellea walleri (Rolfe) la Croix

Syn. *Jumellea filicornoides* (De Wildeman) Schlechter

Plants with long woody stems, leafy in the upper part; stems simple or branched, 15–40 cm long, becoming pendent when long, often forming large clumps. Leaves 6–14 in 2 rows, ligulate, unequally bilobed at the apex, fleshy or leathery, 4–13 cm long, 1–1.3 cm wide. Inflorescences single-flowered; peduncle short, sheathed with bracts that turn black; pedicel with ovary ca. 4 cm long. Flower white, scented in the evening; dorsal sepal narrowly elliptic or ligulate, obtuse, margins undulate or crisped at the base, 13–20 mm long, 3–4 mm wide; lateral sepals similar, falcate, reflexed and decurved; petals narrowly elliptic or ligulate, obtuse, reflexed, slightly smaller than sepals; lip rhombic, narrow at the base, with a shallow central keel, 16–20 mm long, 5–6 mm wide; spur parallel to the ovary then bent, cylindric, 2–3 cm long.

Epiphyte on large trees in riverine forests and occasionally on rocks; 700–1800 m; flowering in February to April.

Kenya, Tanzania, Malawi, Mozambique, Zimbabwe, and South Africa (Limpopo and KwaZulu-Natal).

Species from Madagascar

The *Jumellea* species recorded from Madagascar and the Comoro Islands have here been divided into 6 groups as an aid to identification. The species can be separated by 2 distinct growth forms: those which are rather large plants with long leaves arranged in a fan on a short stem, or apparently without a stem, or with several short stems growing together, so that at first sight there appears to be just a clump of leaves, and those with an elongated stem with the leaves closely or widely spaced in 2 rows on either side. Species with a distinct stem are further grouped into those with a rather short stem and with the leaves very close together, and those with distinctly elongated stems. The remaining species are grouped according to the length of the spur, because this is sometimes an indication of the size of the flower and is an easy character to measure. The groups are as follows:

Group 1. Plants very large, usually with a short stem, or 'stemless' and inflorescences arising around the fan of leaves (11 species).

Group 2. Plants with a rather short stem bearing small leaves very close together (3 species).

Group 3. Plants with very elongated stems; the spur at the base of the lip 15 mm long or less (10 species).

Group 4. Plants with very elongated stems; the spur 2.5–4.5 cm long (3 species).

Group 5. Plants with elongated stems; the spur 6.5–8 cm long (1 species).

Group 6. Plants with elongated stems; the spur 10 cm long or more (18 species).

Group 1. Large epiphytes, or lithophytes, with a very short stem, or described as stemless, and long leaves. Inflorescences arising around the base of the plant from old leaf axils.

Jumellea amplifolia Schlechter

Plants large and robust, up to 60 cm tall or more, with very short stems. Leaves large, erect or spreading, oblong-ligulate, 50–65 cm long, 7–9 cm wide. Inflorescences 25–30 cm long; peduncle 10–13 cm long with 3–4 cucullate sheaths; bract similar; pedicel with ovary 10–12 cm long. Flowers large, white, fleshy; sepals narrowly lanceolate, 3.5 cm long; petals similar but thinner; lip narrow below, fan-shaped above, sagittate, with a short thick keel, 3.3 cm long, 1.3 cm wide at the widest part; spur narrow, cylindric, 4.3 cm long.

Epiphyte on big trees; ca. 2000 m; flowering in January.

Madagascar (Mount Tsaratanana).

Jumellea arachnantha (Reichenbach f.) Schlechter

Plants large and robust with very short stems. Leaves large, erect or spreading, oblong-ligulate, bilobed at the apex, 45–70 cm long, 5 cm wide. Inflorescences 25–30 cm long; peduncle 11–14 cm long with 3–4 cucullate sheaths at the base, naked above; bract tubular, loose, 10–11 mm long; pedicel with ovary slender, 9–10 cm long. Flowers large, white; sepals and petals lanceolate, acuminate, 4–5 cm long; lip clawed at the base, the blade broadly lanceolate, 4–5 cm long; spur slender, 4–4.5 cm long.

Epiphyte in forest; flowering in December.

Comoro Islands (Grande Comore and Anjouan).

This species seems to have the longest inflorescences and largest flowers of this group except perhaps *Jumellea major*, which has a longer spur.

Jumellea brachycentra Schlechter

Plants large and robust, 25–40 cm tall or more; stems very short, covered with crowded old leaf sheaths. Leaves 5–7, large, erect or spreading, ligulate-linear, rather thin, 15–37 cm long, 1.4–2.5 cm wide. Inflorescences arising from the base of the plant, much shorter than the leaves; peduncle 5 cm long with 3 sheaths at the base and one halfway along; bract similar; pedicel with ovary slender, 6–7 cm long. Flowers medium-sized, white; sepals narrowly lanceolate, 2.7 cm long; petals similar, a little shorter and thinner; lip oblong, acute, slightly narrowed between the lowest third and the middle, 2.5 cm long, 9 mm wide at the widest part; spur narrow, cylindric, 12 mm long.

Epiphyte in forest; 1800–2400 m; flowering January to March.

Madagascar (central and eastern highlands).

Jumellea gladiator (Reichenbach f.) Schlechter

Plants large and robust, with very short stems. Leaves large, erect or spreading, ligulate, 45–70 cm long, 2.2–5 cm wide. Inflorescences many; peduncle 8–15 cm long with 4–5 sheaths at the base, naked above; bract 6–7 mm long; pedicel with ovary 4.5–5.5 cm long. Flower white; sepals and petals lanceolate, 2.2 cm long; petals similar but thinner; lip lanceolate, acute, rounded or obtuse at the base, 2.2 cm long, 1.3 cm wide at the widest part; spur narrow, 2.5–3.5 cm long (about half as long as the pedicellate ovary).

Epiphyte in rain forest; flowering December to March.

Comoro Islands (Grande Comore and Anjouan).

This species is often confused with *Jumellea arachnantha* and *J. sagittata* and possibly also *J. phalaenophora* but seems to be rather smaller than all the others.

Jumellea major Schlechter

Plant very large, with a short or elongated stem, upright or pendent, 40–60(–80) cm tall. Leaves near the top of the stem, large, ligulate, folded along the midline for about half the length, leathery, up to 45 cm long, 7.3 cm wide. Inflorescences piercing the leaf sheath, 18–20 cm long; peduncle with 3 apiculate sheaths, the upper sheath 15 mm long, 6–7 cm long; bract oblong, apiculate, nearly 2 cm long; pedicel with ovary 9–10 cm long. Flowers large, fleshy, pure white; sepals narrow, thick, lanceolate, acute, 4.5 cm long, 5–7 mm wide; petals linear-ligulate, acute, 4–4.2 cm long; lip gutter-shaped with a central keel at the base, blade gradually widened above, oval-lanceolate, acute, 3.5 cm long, 1.3 cm wide at the widest part; spur pendent at first then recurved, 6.5–7 cm long.

Epiphyte on trees beside streams; ca. 1500 m; flowering in March and May.

Madagascar (eastern highlands).

This plant has very distinctive, pure white flowers, probably the largest flowers in the genus.

Jumellea maxillarioides (Ridley) Schlechter

Plant large with a very short stem covered with overlapping leaf bases. Leaves leathery, dark bluish green, glossy, ligulate, bilobed at the apex, with rounded lobes, 20–25 cm long, 4–5 cm wide. Inflorescences short and thick, ca. 10 cm long; peduncle ca. 1 cm long, covered with sheaths; bract tubular;

Jumellea arachnantha. J. Hermans

Jumellea brachycentra. J. Hermans

Jumellea major. J. Hermans

Jumellea maxillarioides. J. Hermans

pedicel with ovary thick, 9 cm long. Flowers waxy, thick, ivory white, scurfy on the outer surface, ca. 5.5 cm in diameter; sepals reflexed in the upper half, narrowed from the base to tip, 3.3–3.6 cm long, 9 mm wide near the base; petals similar, but slightly thinner than the sepals, with a dorsal keel; lip similar to the sepals, 3.2 cm long, 14 mm wide; spur parallel with the ovary at first, then pendent, 3.3–4 cm long.

Large epiphytic plants and also growing on and amongst rocks; 1200–2100 m; flowering in January.

Madagascar (central highlands).

This species is quite unmistakable because of its dark green leaves and large, thick flowers each with long, pedicellate ovary.

Jumellea peyrotii Bosser

Plant large, stemless, growing in dense tufts with many old fibres around the base. Leaves 3–5, with short folded sheaths that disintegrate with age; blade linear, semi-cylindric, canaliculate, apex obtusely bilobed, 15–35 cm long, 2.5–4 mm in diameter. Inflorescences arising below the leaves, with several blackish sheaths at the base; peduncle slender, 2.5–3 cm long; bract tubular, 7 mm long; pedicel with ovary 5–6 cm long. Flower white, fleshy; sepals lanceolate, obtuse, 15–23 mm long, 4–5 mm wide; petals lanceolate, narrowly sub-acute, as long as the sepals but narrower; lip with a narrow claw at the base, canaliculate and with a small central keel, expanded above into an ovate blade then narrowed and apiculate at the apex, 20–24 mm long, 10 mm wide at the widest part; spur parallel to the ovary at the base, then pendent, 11–12 cm long.

Epiphyte in evergreen forest; 500–1000 m; flowering in February and March.

Madagascar (eastern part of the central highlands).

This species has leaves that are similar to those of *Jumellea teretifolia*, but the flowers are completely different.

Jumellea phalaenophora (Reichenbach f.) Schlechter

Plant with a very short stem. Leaves 5, ligulate, papery or parchment-like, 25 cm long, 2.5 cm wide. Inflorescences few; peduncle with 3 small sheaths at the base and 1 below the middle, 10–12.5 cm long; bract tubular, retuse. Flowers white; sepals and petals lanceolate, 25 mm long; lip shortly angular at the base, broadly oval above, acute, 25 mm long; spur filiform, 7.5 cm long.

Comoro Islands (Anjouan).

Few details are available for this plant. It seems very similar to *Jumellea arachnantha* and *J. gladiator*, which are also recorded from the Comoro Islands.

Jumellea sagittata H. Perrier

Syn. *Angraecum gracilipes* Rolfe

Plant large with a very short stem surrounded by old fibres. Leaves 5 or 6, loriform, folded at the base with a distinct dorsal keel, flat above, 25–30 cm long, 3–3.5 cm wide. Inflorescences usually pendent below the leaves; peduncle slender with several sheaths near the base and one at the middle, 11–12 cm long; bract green, 1 cm long; pedicel thicker than the peduncle, 7.5–12 cm long. Flowers white, slightly scurfy on the outside; dorsal sepal lanceolate, narrowed towards the acute tip, 3 cm long, 8 mm wide; lateral sepals longer and narrower, 4 cm long, 6 mm wide; petals similar to the dorsal sepal; lip lanceolate, clawed at the base with a prominent keel, abruptly expanded above, subauriculate, 3.6–4 cm long, 1.8–2 cm wide; spur somewhat compressed at the base, 5–6 cm long.

Epiphyte on moss- and lichen-covered trees; ca. 1400 m; flowering in January.

Madagascar (central highlands) and Comoro Islands (Grande Comore).

This species is widely cultivated and seems to be very similar to *Jumellea gladiator*.

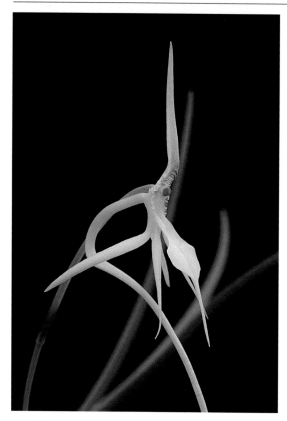

Jumellea teretifolia. J. Hermans

Jumellea teretifolia Schlechter

Plant with a short stem or stemless, up to 20 cm high. Leaves 5–7, cylindrical, rigid, subulate or subobtuse, 10–20 cm long, 2–3 mm in diameter. Inflorescences very slender, longer than the leaves; peduncle with 3 narrow sheaths below, 6–10 cm long; bract tubular, shortly acuminate, 13–15 mm long; pedicel with ovary 4.5–5 cm long. Flowers large, pure white; sepals lanceolate-linear, long acuminate, 3.5 cm long; petals linear, acuminate, slightly expanded in the middle, 3 cm long; lip narrow, clawed at the base with a short keel, then expanded to rhomboid, acuminate, 3 cm long, 7 mm wide at the middle; spur parallel to the ovary at first, then arched and pendent, 13 cm long.

Epiphyte on small trees in humid evergreen forest but usually on the drier slopes; 1300–1500 m; flowering September to December.

Madagascar (central highlands).

This species is easily recognised by its very narrow leaves, and the long, narrow parts of the large flowers.

Jumellea zaratananae Schlechter

Plant robust, up to 40 cm tall. Leaves 5 or 6, ligulate, leathery but thin, to 35 cm long, 3.5 cm wide. Inflorescences 16–20 cm long; peduncle slender, with 3 apiculate sheaths to 1 cm long; bract tubular, 1 cm long; pedicel with ovary slender, 8–10 cm long. Flowers white; sepals ligulate, narrowed towards the apex, 22 mm long; petals linear-ligulate, a little thinner than sepals; lip clawed, subligulate at the base with a short fine keel, then rhomboid-lanceolate above, acute, 23 mm long, 6 mm wide at the middle; spur filiform, pendent, 9 cm long.

Epiphyte on moss- and lichen-covered trees in mossy forest, widespread; 600–1700 m; flowering December to January.

Madagascar (central highlands).

The name of this plant is sometimes spelt *tsaratananae*, after the mountain where it was initially collected, but when he described it first, Schlechter spelt it with a *z*.

Group 2. Small plants with a short stem bearing leaves very close together.

Jumellea densefoliata Senghas

Plant small, compact, but sometimes forming large clumps, stem up to 15 cm tall, often several shorter stems close together, many dead sheaths close together at the base. Leaves 3 to several, thick, leathery, rectangular, asymmetrically bilobed at the apex, 5–7 cm long, 1–2 cm wide. Inflorescences arising amongst the dead sheaths, with 2 or 3 short sheaths at the base; peduncle 1.5–2.5 cm long; bract membranous, 5 mm long; pedicel with ovary 4–6 cm long. Flowers pale yellowish green or greenish white with white lip; dorsal sepal narrow, reflexed in the upper half, frilly at the margins near the base, 15–17 mm long, 5 mm wide; lateral sepals similar but slightly longer; petals obliquely lanceolate to slightly pandurate, with similar frilly margins near the base, 15–18 mm long, 3–4 mm wide; lip clawed at the base with a small callus in the claw and frilly margins, claw 6 mm long, 3 mm wide, broadly ovate above, 10–12 mm long and

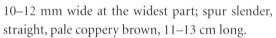

Jumellea densefoliata. J. Hermans

Jumellea gracilipes. J. Hermans

10–12 mm wide at the widest part; spur slender, straight, pale coppery brown, 11–13 cm long.

Epiphyte in light shade and on rocks, often amongst moss and lichens in *Uapaca* forest; ca. 1500–1600 m; flowering in October.

Madagascar (central highlands).

This plant is quite distinctive but the description seems similar to *Jumellea pandurata* that was described earlier.

Jumellea gracilipes Schlechter

Plants small to medium-sized, erect, apparently stemless, 15–20 cm high. Leaves erect, spreading, narrowly linear, unequally and obtusely bilobed at the apex, leathery, 14–17 cm long, 5–6 mm wide at the middle. Flowers white or pale green; sepals linear-lanceolate, 15 mm long; lateral sepals oblique, widest at the base; petals narrowly lanceolate-linear, acuminate, porrect, adnate to the column at the lower margin, subequal to the sepals; lip nar-

row below and folded into a gutter, with a slightly protruding keel at the base, cuneate, expanded above to become rhomboid-lanceolate and then acuminate, almost subulate, 18 mm long, 6 mm wide below the middle; spur narrow, with a knee-bend below the mouth, 4.5 cm long.

Epiphyte in mossy forest; 700–2000 m; flowering in May and September to November.

Madagascar (central highlands).

The description given here has been prepared from the original (Schlechter 1922). A number of different entities have been included under this name in herbaria and some publications, including those originally described as *Jumellea ambongensis* Schlechter, *J. exilipes* Schlechter, *J. imerinensis* Schlechter, and *J. unguicularis* Schlechter, but there are so many differences that they cannot all refer to the same taxon. Further study of these rather similar plants is needed, particularly in the field.

Jumellea linearipetala H. Perrier

Plant small with a very short stem up to 2 cm long. Leaves 4 or 5, thick and short, 4–7 cm long, 1 cm wide. Inflorescence arising below the leaves; peduncle short and almost covered by flattened sheaths, 1.2–2 cm long; bract obtuse, 6–7 mm long; pedicel with ovary 5 mm long. Flowers white; sepals lanceolate, linear, 16–18 mm long, 2.5–3 mm wide; petals linear, 17 mm long, 1 mm wide; lip oblanceolate, with 9 obvious veins, 17–20 mm long, 4–6 mm wide; spur curved, 10–12 mm long.

Epiphyte on trunks; flowering in February and November.

Madagascar (north-western region).

This is a very distinctive small plant with very narrow petals.

Group 3. Plants with elongated stems and small to medium-sized flowers with a spur less than 15 mm long.

Jumellea angustifolia H. Perrier

Plant with erect, rigid stems, somewhat flattened, 25–40 cm high, 6–7 mm wide. Leaves many, in 2 rows, narrowly ligulate, folded below the middle, 7–8 cm long, 8 mm wide. Inflorescences shorter than the leaves; peduncle completely covered by 2 or 3 wide sheaths, 5 mm long; bract tubular, 6 mm long; pedicel with ovary 3.5 cm long. Flowers white with green spur; dorsal sepal oval, obtuse, 13–14 mm long, 7 mm wide; lateral sepals a little narrower, expanded at the front edge below the middle; petals oval-oblong, 13–14 mm long, 7 mm wide; lip very concave, clawed at the base with a short keel in the claw, expanded above to 6 mm wide, then obtuse, 15 mm long; spur obtuse and short, 12 mm long.

Terrestrial plant in lichen-rich forest; 1400–2000 m; flowering in April.

Madagascar (northern highlands).

Jumellea anjouanensis (Finet) H. Perrier

Plant with erect or pendent stems 15–40 cm tall, rigid, flattened, 2–5 mm wide, with leaves towards the top. Leaves 5–7, folded, keeled at the back, bi-

Jumellea anjouanensis. J. Hermans

lobed at the apex, 2–4.5 cm long, 2–6 mm wide. Inflorescences axillary; peduncle covered with 2 or 3 thin sheaths, 2–3 mm long; bract partly covered with uppermost sheath, 6–8 mm long; pedicel with ovary 16–24 mm long. Flowers white; dorsal sepal oval-lanceolate, acute, 7–10 mm long, 2 mm wide; lateral sepals similar, expanded at the front edge in lower part; petals lanceolate, smaller, 6–7 mm long, 1 mm wide; lip narrowly ligulate, clawed at the base, 10 mm long; spur as long as the lip, inflated and solid at the apex, 10 mm long.

Epiphyte in humid forest; 450–1900 m; flowering in May, June, August, and November.

Comoro Islands (Anjouan and Grande Comore).

Jumellea cowanii (Ridley) Garay

Plant 15 cm tall, stem covered with old leaf sheaths and bearing leaves at the top. Leaves 4 or 5, narrow, linear, 7.5–9 cm long, 6 mm wide. Inflorescence axillary, erect; peduncle 5 mm long. Flowers white; sepals and petals similar, ovate-lanceolate; lip similar but wider; spur filiform, 12 mm long.

Epiphyte.

Madagascar (central highlands).

Jumellea cyrtoceras Schlechter

Plant erect, stem cylindric, 5 mm wide, to 15 cm tall. Leaves many, leathery, ligulate, 7–10 cm long, 8–11 mm wide near the middle. Inflorescence short; peduncle 10–13 mm long with a few sheaths; bract obtuse, 15 mm long; pedicel with ovary 2 cm long. Flower medium-sized; sepals narrowly oblong, or oblong-ligulate, obtuse, 15 mm long; petals almost as long, slightly narrower; lip clawed at the base with a shallow keel, ligulate above, subobtuse, as long as the petals; spur slender, 7–10 mm long.

Epiphyte in forest.

Madagascar (along the east coast).

Jumellea cyrtoceras. J. Hermans

Jumellea dendrobioides Schlechter

Plant erect, stem cylindrical, 4 mm in diameter, up to 40 cm tall, densely leaved. Leaves linear-ligulate, thin but leathery, 8–10 cm long, 9–12 mm wide. Inflorescences shorter than the leaves; peduncle almost covered with 3 or 4 sheaths, 12–15 mm long; bract obtuse, 10 mm long; pedicel with ovary slender, 4 cm long. Flowers medium-sized; dorsal sepal lanceolate-ligulate, obtuse, 16 mm long, 4 mm wide; lateral sepals a little smaller, 14 mm long, 3.5 mm wide; petals narrowed towards the base, 14 mm long, 4.5 mm wide; lip concave near the base with a median keel, expanded into an obovate blade, rounded, 16 mm long, 8.5 mm wide at the widest; spur slender, cylindric, 12 mm long.

Epiphyte in lichen-rich forest; ca. 2000 m; flowering in January.

Madagascar (Mount Tsaratanana).

Jumellea francoisii Schlechter

Plant erect or pendent, usually with many stems in a clump covered with greyish sheaths below the leaves, 30–60 cm long. Leaves fragrant when crushed, linear-ligulate, bilobed at the apex with rounded lobes, 8–11 cm long, 10–14 mm wide. Inflorescences usually several at a time; peduncle covered with 3 or 4 obtuse sheaths in the lower half, 6–10 mm long; bract tubular, thick, green, 8 mm long; pedicel with ovary 2–3 cm long. Flowers medium-sized, white, thick, fleshy; dorsal sepal lanceolate, slightly narrowed at the base, 18 mm long, 5 mm wide; lateral sepals fused together at the base; petals similar to dorsal sepal but shorter, 15 mm long; lip narrow and folded at the base with a fine median keel, abruptly widened above to 7 mm wide, then narrowed towards the obtuse apex, in total 16–18 mm long; spur cylindric, pendent, 12–13 mm long.

Epiphyte on tree trunks in humid evergreen forest and mossy forest; 1100–1500 m; flowering between January and May.

Madagascar (eastern highlands).

This species is sometimes confused with *Jumellea spathulata* but has longer, thinner, and more pliable leaves and different flowers with a shorter spur. In some localities the leaves are used to make an infusion similar to tea.

Jumellea hyalina H. Perrier

Plant small, stems flattened, sometimes branched, 10–15 cm long. Leaves 5–7, short, linear, rigid, folded, unequally lobed at the apex, with rounded lobes, 18–25 mm long, 5–6 mm wide. Inflorescences below the leaves, piercing the sheath; peduncle short, completely covered by 3–4 thick, keeled, sheaths, 5–6 mm long; bract similar, 6 mm long; pedicel with ovary 15–16 mm long. Flowers small, transparent, and thin; dorsal sepal oval, acute, 10 mm long, 4 mm wide; lateral sepals oblong, apiculate-acute, expanded into a wide lobe at the front edge, 11 mm long, 3.5 mm wide; petals expanded, obliquely rounded, 12 mm long, 4.5 mm wide; lip narrow in the lower half, abruptly expanded above the middle into a fan-shaped blade, broadly rounded in front with a thick, obtuse apicule, 10–11 mm long, 8 mm wide; spur cylindric, 10–11 mm long.

Epiphyte in mossy forest; 1500 m; flowering in January.

Madagascar (eastern highlands).

This species seem to be close to *Jumellea pachyra*; further study of these taxa is needed.

Jumellea marojejiensis H. Perrier

Plant with a compressed, elongated stem 5–20 cm high. Leaves 8–10, ligulate, variable in size, 2.5–8 cm long, 7–8 mm wide. Inflorescence axillary; peduncle 8–10 mm long, with one short sheath; bract reddish, 1.7 cm long; pedicel with ovary 3.7 cm long. Flower greenish white, with white lip; sepals and petals similar, 16–17 mm long; lip concave at the base, similar to sepals but apex cucullate; spur filiform 13–15 mm long.

Epiphyte in evergreen forest or mossy forest; 1400–1500 m; flowering in March or April.

Madagascar (eastern highlands).

This species seems to be rather similar to *Jumellea cyrtoceras* that was described earlier but is rather poorly known.

Jumellea hyalina. J. Hermans

Jumellea pachyceras Schlechter

Plant erect or somewhat pendent, stems 10–30 cm high. Leaves dense, linear-ligulate, unequally and obtusely bilobed, leathery, 4–6 cm long, 6–9 mm wide. Inflorescence erect; peduncle 3–7 mm long, with oblong sheaths 7 mm long; bract obtuse; pedicel with ovary 2.5 cm long. Flower medium-sized, white; dorsal sepal erect, 15 mm long; lateral sepals oblique, spreading; petals obliquely oblong-elliptic, spreading; lip obovate-elliptic, narrow at the base, widened above, subspathulate, 17 mm long, 7.5 mm wide above the middle; spur cylindric, curved, 14 mm long.

Epiphyte on moss- and lichen-covered trees; ca. 2000 m; flowering in December and January.

Madagascar (central highlands).

Jumellea pachyra (Kraenzlin) H. Perrier

Plant with a stiff, erect stem 12–30 cm high. Leaves linear-ligulate, unequally and obtusely bilobed at the apex, 2.5 cm long, 6–7 mm wide. Inflorescence short; peduncle covered with 3–4 sheaths, 4–6 mm long; pedicel with ovary 2.5–4 cm long. Flower translucent except for the spur; sepals oblong-acute, 10 mm long, 4 mm wide; petals similar but thinner, 10 mm long, 5 mm wide; lip angular at the base, thin; spur 12 mm long.

Epiphyte in forest.

Madagascar (eastern highlands).

Apparently known only from the type specimen (Hildebrandt 3988) which was also the type of *Jumellea spathulata*. The latter has larger flowers and was described much earlier. Further study of all these small-flowered species is desirable.

Group 4. Plants with elongated stems; flowers with a spur 2.5–4.5 cm long.

Jumellea bathiei Schlechter

Plant with an erect or pendent, cylindrical stem bearing many leaves, to 30 cm high. Leaves linear-ligulate, thin but leathery, 6–8 cm long, 7–11 mm wide. Inflorescence short; peduncle completely covered with sheaths, 10–15 mm long; bract similar to the upper sheath, 1 cm long; pedicel with ovary thick, 4–5 cm long. Flowers medium-sized, white, thick and fleshy but thin at the base, with green spur; sepals narrowly lanceolate, obtuse, a little expanded and thin at the base, 19–21 mm long, 7 mm wide at the base; petals similar to the sepals but slightly smaller; lip folded, narrow at the base with a central keel, expanded above to become oblanceolate, acute, 22 mm long, 7 mm wide at the widest; spur cylindrical, 35–45 mm long.

Epiphyte in mossy forest; 2400 m; flowering in March.

Madagascar (central highlands).

Jumellea ibityana Schlechter

Plant erect with many flattened stems in a clump, 15–30 cm tall. Leaves dense, ligulate, leathery and rigid, 3–4.5 cm long, 7–10 mm wide. Inflorescence as long as the leaves; peduncle short, covered with 3 sheaths, 15 mm long; bract apiculate, 1 cm long; pedicel with ovary slender, 4–5 cm long. Flowers medium-sized, white; dorsal sepal lanceolate, obtuse, somewhat expanded towards the base, 2 cm long; lateral sepals narrower; petals ligulate, slightly narrowed towards the base, 2 cm long; lip lanceolate, acute, narrower in the lower quarter with a short keel on the upper surface, 20 mm long, 6.5 mm wide; spur cylindric-filiform, 3.5 cm long.

Lithophyte on bare or slightly shaded rocks, or epiphyte amongst mosses and lichens; ca. 2000 m; flowering in March.

Madagascar (central highlands).

Jumellea spathulata (Ridley) Schlechter

Plant stout with a thick stem to 30 cm tall, covered with old leaf bases and ridged sheaths. Leaves ligulate, rather thick, unequally bilobed at the apex, 25–30 mm long, 6 mm wide. Inflorescence short, covered with 3 or 4 sheaths; bract 8 mm long; pedicel with ovary 3–3.5 cm long. Flower

Jumellea spathulata. J. Hermans

Jumellea spathulata. J. Hermans

medium-sized; sepals lanceolate, acute; petals lanceolate, spathulate, narrow at the base then expanded and shortly acute at the apex; lip oval-spathulate, obtuse; spur pendent, filiform, 25 mm long, longer than the ovary.

Epiphyte or lithophyte on rocky outcrops in forest; flowering in March.

Madagascar (eastern highlands).

This species was illustrated in Du Puy et al. (1999) as *Jumellea francoisii*.

Group 5. Plants with elongated stems; flowers arising from the same inflorescence axis for several consecutive years; lip with a spur 6.5–8 cm long.

Jumellea gregariiflora H. Perrier

Plant with many stems forming a tuft, 40–50 cm high. Leaves 5–10 at apex of stem, leathery and rigid, folded at the base, linear-ligulate above, shortly bilobed at the apex, 8–12 cm long, 8–10 mm wide. Inflorescences arising from each internode on a short axis, 6–7 cm long, bearing 3–7 flowers successively, one each season, from the apex (similar to those in *Angraecum multiflorum*); peduncle with 4 or 5 scarious sheaths at the base; bract tubular, 10–12 mm long; pedicel with ovary 3.5–4 cm long. Flowers white, all parts very narrow, opaque and thick except at the base; sepals linear-lanceolate, 20–32 mm long, 2 mm wide at the base; petals narrower, 16–18 mm long, 1 mm wide at the base; lip very narrow in the basal half, gutter-shaped, wider towards the middle and then narrowed to a long acicular point, 20–33 mm long, 3–4 mm wide at the middle; spur flattened and widened near the mouth, then filiform and pendent, 7.5–11.5 cm long.

Lithophyte on gneissic (metamorphic) rock outcrops; 1000–1150 m; flowering in November.

Madagascar (southern highlands, near the Mandrare valley).

This very floriferous lithophyte has an inflorescence style that is unique in the genus *Jumellea* but similar to that found in a few other angraecoids.

Group 6. Plants with elongated stems; flowers with a spur 10–12 cm long or more.

Jumellea ambrensis H. Perrier

Plant with several upright stems, 5–25 cm long, slightly flattened, bearing leaves at the apex. Leaves 4–6, rigid, narrowly linear or subcylindric, often recurved, dark green and scattered with small white dots, 15–23 cm long, 5 mm wide. Inflorescence piercing the leaf sheath; peduncle 4 cm long, clothed with 4 thick sheaths in the lower half, bare above; floral bract tubular, 1.7 cm long; pedicel with ovary 5 cm long. Flower white, medium-sized, rather thick; sepals lanceolate, gradually narrowed from base to apex, 4.5–5 mm wide, dorsal sepal 2 cm long, lateral sepals 2.5 cm long; petals narrowly linear-lanceolate, 2 cm long, 2.5 mm wide; lip sagittate, narrowly clawed at the base, abruptly expanded near the middle, apex acute, to 2 cm long, 8 mm wide at the middle; spur elongate, narrowing towards the apex, 12 cm long.

Epiphyte in mossy forest; 1000 m; flowering in February.

Madagascar (Mount Ambre).

This species has very distinctive almost terete leaves, somewhat similar to those of *Jumellea peyrotii* and *J. teretifolia*, but the flowers are very different from both those species.

Jumellea arborescens H. Perrier

Plant large with stems up to 1 m high, 8–10 mm in diameter, covered in old leaf bases in the lower part, leafy towards the apex. Leaves up to 20, fairly stiff, elliptic-oblong, bilobed at the apex, folded at the base, 11–14 cm long, 1.5–2.5 cm wide. Inflorescences axillary; peduncle covered below the middle with 3 or 4 loose sheaths ca. 8 mm long, 2.5–3 cm long; bract thin, brown, 9–12 mm long; pedicel with ovary 6–8 cm long. Flowers large, white, with sepals yellowing and thickened at the tips; dorsal sepal lanceolate, acuminate, 23–30 mm long, 5–6 mm wide; lateral sepals similar but narrower, somewhat falcate, reflexed, 23–30 mm long, 3–4 mm wide, joined at the base; petals linear-lanceolate, acute, deflexed, 23–29 mm long,

Jumellea arborescens. J. Hermans

2–3 mm wide; lip narrowly rhomboid, acuminate, somewhat channelled, with a channelled claw at the base 7 mm long and bearing a thick keel in the mouth of the spur, in total 24–29 mm long, 4–5.5 mm wide; spur widened below the mouth, then slender, 11–14 cm long.

Epiphyte on tree trunks in mossy forest and lithophytic; ca. 1400 m; flowering in February.

Madagascar (central highlands).

This species may be self-pollinating as plants are almost always found with capsules.

Jumellea brevifolia H. Perrier

Plant robust, 25–35 cm high, the rigid stems having short internodes. Leaves many, rigid, leathery, short, enveloping the stem at the base, strongly bilobed at the apex, with rounded lobes, 3–4 cm long, 12–13 mm wide. Inflorescences piercing the sheaths, slightly longer than the leaves; peduncle short with 2 or 3 short sheaths not covering it

completely, 10–12 mm long; bract thin, lax, 7–8 mm long; pedicel with ovary 4–5 cm long. Flowers white; dorsal sepal narrow, thick, folded at the base, 18 mm long, 4 mm wide at the base; lateral sepals flat, slightly falcate, 20–23 mm long, 3–3.5 mm wide; petals narrow, opaque, 18 mm long, 1.5 mm wide; lip narrowly clawed at the base, abruptly expanded into a triangular-acute blade above, with a protruding keel in the narrow gutter, in total 22 mm long, 7–8 mm wide at the middle; spur slender, 11 cm long.

Lithophyte on gneissic rocks in partial shade; 1500–1650 m; flowering in November.

Madagascar (south central highlands, Mount Kalambatitra).

This species is easily recognised by its closely set, short, wide leaves.

Jumellea comorensis (Reichenbach f.) Schlechter

Plant upright or pendent, stems becoming elongated and branched with age, slightly flattened, 3–4 mm wide. Leaves ligulate-linear, slightly contracted at the base, shortly bilobed at the apex, glossy, 5–9.5 cm long, 6–12 mm wide. Inflorescence piercing the sheath; peduncle short, covered with 3 flattened sheaths, the upper 10 mm long and overlapping the bract, 16–17 mm long; bract similar to sheaths, 15–16 mm long; pedicel with ovary 7.5 cm long. Flower white, opaque; sepals similar to each other, linear, 20–30 mm long, 4 mm wide; petals similar but narrowing below; lip contracted below the middle into a narrow claw with central keel, widened in the upper half, in total 3 cm long, 1 cm wide a little above the middle; spur filiform, 9–15 cm long.

Epiphyte in forest; sea level to 600 m; flowering in January, July, August, and November.

Comoro Islands (Grande Comore).

Jumellea confusa (Schlechter) Schlechter

Plant upright, sometimes pendent, with several stems arising close together, attaining 60–70 cm in height, often shorter. Leaves numerous, in 2 rows at apex of stem, leathery, folded below, linear-ligulate above, equally or almost equally lobed at the apex,

Jumellea comorensis. J. Hermans

Jumellea confusa. J. Hermans

with rounded lobes, dark green, 7–12 cm long, 10–24 mm wide. Inflorescence axillary; peduncle 2–4 cm long, covered in lower 3 quarters by 3–5 sheaths of which the upper is the longest, 10–15 mm long and thin, 2–4 cm long; bract tubular, ca. 1 cm long; pedicel with ovary 5–6 cm long. Flower white, perianth parts thick; sepals and petals lanceolate, wider above the base and narrow towards the apex, 22–30 mm long, 5–6 mm wide; petals a little shorter than sepals; lip with a narrow gutter bearing a central keel in the basal half, expanded to a rhomboid shape at the middle then narrow towards the apex, in total 22–30 mm long, 6–7 mm wide at the middle; spur slender, 12–15 cm long.

Lithophyte or epiphyte in low dense forest amongst mosses and lichens; 600–1500 m; flowering December to March.

Madagascar (eastern and central highlands).

Some published records of this species from the Comoro Islands appear likely to be misidentifications as no Comorean specimens have been located in herbaria. It is a rather variable species.

Jumellea flavescens H. Perrier

Plant erect or spreading, stems branched but not usually more than 15 cm long, with leaves near the top of each branch. Leaves 5 or 6, broadly linear, bilobed at the apex, venation visible only on the lower surface, 5–9 cm long, 8–11 mm wide. Inflorescence arising below the leaves; peduncle slender, with brown sheaths below the middle, bare above, 2–2.5 cm long; bract obtuse, 5 mm long; pedicel with ovary 4.5–5 cm long. Flower white becoming yellowish; sepals lanceolate, apex acute, 17–18 mm long, 5 mm wide; petals similar but a little shorter than the sepals, 15–16 mm long; lip oblanceolate-acute, clawed at the base, 7–8 mm wide above the middle, 2 cm long; spur 10–12 cm long.

Epiphyte on trunks in mossy forest; 600–1200 m; flowering in January and February.

Madagascar (central and eastern highlands and on Mount Ambre) and Comoro Islands (Anjouan, one record of flowering in October).

This species is similar to the following, but the plants are usually smaller and the column always green even on dried specimens.

Jumellea intricata H. Perrier

Plant with numerous erect or creeping, branching stems forming tangled masses or tufts, 20–60 cm tall. Leaves 2–7 on each stem apex, folded towards the base, flattened above, bilobed at the apex, thick and dark green, ligulate-linear, 4–11 cm long, 5–15 mm wide. Inflorescence below the leaves; peduncle slender, with 5 sheaths in the lower third, the rest bare, 3–4 cm long; bract obtuse, 7–9 mm long; pedicel with ovary 3–4 cm long. Flowers white, yellowing with age; sepals lanceolate, acute, 17–20 mm long, 3.5–4 mm wide; petals lanceolate-linear, acute, 17–19 mm long, 2.5 mm wide; lip ligulate, narrowed at the base with a prominent keel, widened above and then narrowed to a long apicule 2 mm long, in total 2 cm long, 6 mm wide at the middle; spur slender from a wide mouth, 10–12 cm long.

Epiphyte on trunks and trailing over rocks in lichen-rich forest; 1600–2000 m; flowering in November and January.

Madagascar (central and north-western highlands).

This species is similar to the preceding but forms larger, dense, tangled plants; the flowers always have an orange-brown anther cap.

Jumellea jumelleana (Schlechter) Summerhayes

Syn. *Jumellea henryi* Schlechter

Plant erect with rigid stems 12–24 cm tall. Leaves many, spaced close together, small, thick and leathery, oblong-ligulate, folded, 10–28 mm long, 5–6 mm wide. Inflorescence short; peduncle covered with 3 or 4 sheaths, the upper ones longer than the lower; bract similar to the upper sheath; pedicel with ovary 2 cm long. Flowers white, small; sepals ligulate, subacute, 13 mm long; petals similar, a little thinner; lip obovate-elliptic, with a short

Jumellea jumelleana. J. Hermans

keel in the claw, 13 mm long, 7 mm wide; spur undulate, filiform, 11–12 cm long.

Epiphyte on shrubs and in low forest canopy; 800–1500 m; flowering September to November.

Madagascar (eastern and central highlands).

Jumellea lignosa (Schlechter) Schlechter

Plant large, branching, with a rigid, woody stem up to 150 cm tall. Leaves short, 6–8 cm long, 2–2.5 cm wide. Inflorescence short; peduncle completely covered with tough sheaths, 1 cm long; bract leathery, green, overlapped by upper sheath, 15 mm long; pedicel with ovary 4.5 cm long. Flowers large, thick, white; sepals and petals narrowing from base to apex, 3–4 cm long; lip clawed at the base with a thick keel ca. 1 mm high, oval-lanceolate above and widest at the middle (10–12 mm wide), in total 3–3.2 cm long; spur filiform, 10–11 cm long.

Jumellea lignosa. J. Hermans

Lithophyte on mossy rocks and also epiphytic in highland forest amongst lichens and mosses; 700–1500 m; flowering December to February.

Madagascar (central and northern highlands).

This species seems to be rather variable and several subspecies were described by Perrier (1941), some with longer leaves and others with larger flowers with shorter spurs and a longer peduncle. It may be that some of these represent distinct species (for example, *Jumellea ferkoana* Schlechter). Further study of these robust plants is needed.

Jumellea longivaginans H. Perrier

Plant with an erect, compressed stem 10–20 cm tall, 5–8 mm wide. Leaves in 2 rows, narrowly ligulate, equally lobed at the apex, 4–9 cm long, 7–11 mm wide. Inflorescence as long as the leaves; peduncle covered by sheaths that are keeled on the back, 2–2.2 cm long; bract green, rigid, 3–4 cm long; pedicel with ovary 8 cm long. Flowers me-

dium-sized; dorsal sepal lanceolate, thick, 18 mm long, 6 mm wide; lateral sepals slightly falcate, 2 cm long, 4 mm wide; petals lanceolate, acute, narrower than dorsal sepal; lip lanceolate, narrow at the base and concave with a central, bifid keel, narrow towards the apex, 2 cm long, 7 mm wide; spur 9–10 cm long.

Epiphyte on trunks in forest; ca. 2000 m; flowering in January.

Madagascar (central and northern highlands).

This species is easily recognised by its large floral bract and long pedicel. Perrier (1938b) also described var. *grandis* based on a larger plant collected in the eastern highlands at lower altitude: this plant is taller, with larger leaves and flowers, the keel on the lower part of the lip is shorter and the spur is longer (12–13 cm).

Jumellea majalis (Schlechter) Schlechter

Plant pendent with slender branching stems up to 50 cm long. Leaves in 2 rows, linear-ligulate, bilobed at the apex, with rounded lobes, 3–7.5 cm long, 7–10 mm wide. Inflorescences amongst the leaves; peduncle completely covered by 4 sheaths, the upper ones longer than the lower, 4 cm long; bract similar to sheaths; pedicel with ovary 4–6 cm long. Flowers white, small; sepals lanceolate, dorsal sepal 20–30 mm long, 2–3 mm wide, lateral sepals 22–28 mm long, 2–3 mm wide; petals similar to sepals, 21–26 mm long, 1 mm wide; lip pandurate-ligulate, clearly contracted at the middle and again below the middle, with a single keel in the lower half, in total 24–25 mm long, 5 mm wide; spur 12–16 cm long.

Epiphyte in forest, widespread; sea level to 2000 m; flowering January to May.

Madagascar (eastern region Tôlañaro to Mount Tsaratanana).

Jumellea pandurata Schlechter

Plant erect, 20–30 cm high, sometimes branched at the base. Leaves numerous, oblong to ligulate, bilobed at the apex, dark green, rather thick, 5–8 cm long, 10–18 mm wide. Inflorescences 7–8 cm long; peduncle with 2 or 3 sheaths at the base, 1.5–

3 cm long; bract 8–15 mm long; pedicel with ovary 4.5–6 cm long. Flowers white with greenish spur, somewhat scurfy on the outer surface of the sepals and on the ovary; dorsal sepal lanceolate, acute, the margins undulate towards the base, 11–22 mm long, 2.8–4 mm wide; lateral sepals obliquely lanceolate, acute, 14–22 mm long, 2.5–4 mm wide; petals oblanceolate, acute, deflexed, 18–25 mm long, 2–2.5 mm wide; lip pandurate-lanceolate, porrect, with a narrow claw, 7–9 mm long below, the blade rhomboid, acute, in total 18–25 mm long, 5–9 mm wide; spur slender, 11–14 cm long.

Lithophytic on basalt rocks; ca. 1200 m; flowering in October.

Madagascar (central highlands).

Jumellea papangensis H. Perrier

Plant upright with a cylindrical stem bearing leaves near the apex, 15–20 cm tall, 5–6 mm in diameter. Leaves ligulate, folded at the base, unequally and obtusely bilobed at the apex, 5–8 cm long, 5–8 mm wide. Inflorescence typical for the genus; peduncle short, covered by 3 or 4 tight sheaths, the longest 11–12 mm long, 1–1.2 cm long; bract longer than the upper sheath, 1.7–2 cm long; pedicel with ovary very slender, 5–5.5 cm long. Flower small; dorsal sepal lanceolate, keeled on the back, 14 mm long, 4.5 mm wide; lateral sepals similar, slightly falcate; petals lanceolate, acute, 2 cm long, 3 mm wide; lip clawed at the base and expanded above, with a pronounced keel in the claw, in total 1.5–1.8 cm long, 9 mm wide at the middle; spur filiform, 13 cm long.

Epiphyte on *Philippia*; 1300–1700 m; flowering in December.

Madagascar (central highlands, towards the south).

This species was collected on Mount Papanga near Befotaka and, like *Jumellea longivaginans*, which occurs in similar habitats but at higher altitudes further north, it has a very long floral bract.

Jumellea porrigens Schlechter

Plant upright with a stiff, cylindrical stem, densely leaved, 10–30 cm tall, 10–12 mm in di-

ameter. Leaves linear or linear-ligulate, 5–8 cm long, 6–9 mm wide. Inflorescence 7–8 cm long; peduncle short, covered with 3 sheaths, the longest 8 mm long, 2.5 cm long; bract tubular, ca. 1 cm long; pedicel with ovary 4.5–5 cm long. Flowers small to medium-sized; sepals ligulate, obtuse, 16 mm long; petals linear, subobtuse, 16 mm long but narrower than sepals; lip oblanceolate-spathulate, almost pandurate, shortly clawed with a central ridge in the claw, expanded briefly and then contracted again before the expanded apex, 15–16 mm long, 4 mm wide in the upper third; spur filiform, 10–11 cm long.

Epiphyte in lichen-rich forest; ca. 2000 m; flowering in January.

Madagascar (Mount Tsaratanana).

Jumellea punctata H. Perrier

Plant erect with strong, slightly flattened stems, 40–50 cm tall, 5–6 mm wide. Leaf sheaths and leaf bases finely dotted with black. Leaves in 2 rows,

Jumellea punctata. J. Hermans

narrowly linear, stiff, folded towards the base, equally and obtusely lobed at the apex, 10–13 cm long, 9–13 mm wide. Inflorescences amongst the lower leaves; peduncle covered by sheaths in the lower part, 3 cm long; bract 1 cm long; pedicel with ovary 6 cm long. Flower white, opaque; sepals lanceolate, acute; dorsal sepal 27 mm long, 6 mm wide; lateral sepals 30–32 mm long, 4 mm wide; petals lanceolate, acute, 26–27 mm long, 5 mm wide; lip oval-lanceolate above the narrow claw which bears a pronounced central keel, 30 mm long, 10 mm wide above the middle; spur 10–11 cm long.

Epiphyte in humid, evergreen forest; ca. 600 m; flowering September to December.

Madagascar (eastern region).

The black dots on the old leaf sheaths and leaf bases make this species instantly recognisable.

Jumellea rigida Schlechter

Plant erect, with robust stems to 60 cm tall, 7 mm in diameter, often forming clumps. Leaves 8–10 near the apex of stems, ligulate, 8–12 cm long, 12–16 mm wide. Inflorescences axillary or below the leaves; peduncle covered with sheaths at the base, 2–2.5 cm long; bract tubular, thin, 10–12 mm long; pedicel with ovary 4.5–6.5 cm long. Flowers white, turning cream or yellow with age; sepals oblong-ligulate, subobtuse, 2 cm long; petals linear-ligulate, obtuse, 17 mm long; lip with a narrow claw at the base, expanded above into an elliptic, subacuminate blade with a fine central keel, 2 cm long, 7 mm wide in the front third; spur S-shaped, 9–10 cm long.

var. *rigida*

Stems slender. Inflorescences 7–8 cm long.

Lithophytic on rock outcrops and sometimes epiphytic; 1500–1800 m; flowering in December.

Madagascar (central highlands).

var. *altigena* Schlechter

Plants compact. Inflorescences 3–5 cm long.

Lithophyte on rock outcrops; ca. 2400 m; flowering in January.

Madagascar (southern parts of central highlands).

Jumellea similis Schlechter

Plant with slender, densely leaved stems to 55 cm tall, 6 mm in diameter. Leaves linear-ligulate, leathery but thin, 7–12 cm long, 8–10 mm wide. Inflorescence short; peduncle covered with several sheaths in the lower half, 10–20 mm long; bract tubular, thin, 12 mm long; pedicel with ovary 3 cm long. Flowers white, becoming yellow with age; sepals ligulate, subobtuse, 33–35 mm long; petals narrower and thinner, 27–29 mm long, 3 mm wide; lip with long narrow claw as long as the blade which is oval, acuminate, with a short, fine keel, in total 28 mm long, 7–12 mm wide above the middle; spur S-shaped, 11 cm long.

Epiphyte on trunks in humid evergreen forest on western slopes; ca. 1500 m; flowering in November.

Madagascar (central highlands).

This species is similar to *Jumellea confusa* but has narrower leaves and smaller flowers.

Jumellea stenoglossa H. Perrier

Plant creeping and rooting from the stem 3.5–4 mm wide. Leaves in 2 rows, oblong-lanceolate, folded at the base, 4–6 cm long, 9–10 mm wide. Inflorescence with peduncle half covered with 3 or 4 sheaths, 1.5–4.5 cm long; bract tubular, 12–15 mm long; pedicel with ovary 3–5 cm long. Flowers white; dorsal sepal linear, acute, reflexed, 2–3 mm wide at the base; lateral sepals similar, connate at the base; petals similar to the sepal but shorter, 2.5 cm long; lip thickened at the base, then with an ovate blade, in total 3 cm long, expanded part 8 mm long, 7 mm wide, then apex cylindrical, 12 mm long; spur inflexed, then filiform, 11–12 cm long.

Epiphyte in coastal forest; 20–100 m; flowering in March.

Madagascar (south-east and also on Mount Tsaratanana).

In the original description of this species (Perrier 1951) the spur is given as 11–12 mm long, but in the specimen on which the description was based the flowers have a spur 11–12 cm long.

Species from Réunion and Mauritius

Jumellea divaricata (Frappier ex Cordemoy) Schlechter

Plant with upright stems 4–8 cm long, 1 cm in diameter, bare for one-third of its length, leafy above. Leaves diverging in a fan, leathery, dark green, 3–6 cm long, 8–12 mm wide, slightly narrowed towards the base, obtuse, rather squarely bilobed at the apex. Inflorescence solitary, enclosed in 2 or 3 sheaths at the base, 25 mm long; pedicel shorter than the ovary. Flowers open, white, all tepals 15 mm long; sepals acute, dorsal sepal erect, reflexed at the apex; petals slightly smaller; lip similar to petals, acute, subobtuse, furrowed, sinuous at the margins below; spur conical, elongated, bent below the lip and then straight, pendent, thread-like.

Epiphyte in the shady forests; 500–600 m; flowering in February.

Réunion (above Saint Pierre) and Mauritius.

Jumellea fragrans. J. Stewart

Jumellea exilis (Cordemoy) Schlechter

Plant erect, with slender stems. Leaves few, widely spaced, inserted obliquely on the stem, shiny above, dull and matte below, 9 cm long, 1 cm wide. Inflorescences few, emerging from leaf sheath, slender; peduncle with 4 sheaths at the base, overlapping the bract. Flower unknown; fruit long and slender, 6 cm long.

Réunion (near Cilaos).

Jumellea fragrans (Thouars) Schlechter

Plant with upright, often branching stems, 6–10 mm in diameter, covered with wrinkled sheaths and densely leaved. Leaves linear-ligulate, almost equally bilobed at the apex, 4.5–15 cm long, 10–13 mm wide. Inflorescences axillary, shorter than the leaves; peduncle covered with 3 sheaths, the upper one longest and 1 cm long, 14–15 mm long; bract 15–17 mm long; pedicel with ovary 5–6 cm long. Flowers white; sepals and petals lanceolate, acute, 2 cm long; lip oblong-lanceolate, with a short keel on the centre of the lower quarter, 2 cm long; spur straight, 3–3.5 cm long.

Epiphyte in evergreen forest; 500–1500 m; flowering December to April.

Réunion and Mauritius.

This orchid has the vernacular name '*faham*'. The dried leaves are vanilla-scented and are used to make a tea-like infusion.

Jumellea nutans (Frappier ex Cordemoy) Schlechter

Plant with a short stem 3–6 cm high, entirely covered in old leaf sheaths. Leaves 4–5 in 2 rows, arranged in a fan, oblong, conduplicate at the base, canaliculate above and then becoming flat, obliquely bilobed at the apex, with rounded lobes, 8–12 cm long, 8–12 mm wide. Inflorescence solitary, slender, 3 cm long; peduncle with 2 or 3 sheaths at the base; pedicel with ovary 3 cm long.

Flower white nodding (facing towards the ground), 4 cm in diameter; sepals lanceolate, acute, 20 mm long, 3 mm wide; petals 14 mm long, 2 mm wide; lip shell-shaped, acuminate; spur slender, acute, cylindrical-conical, 2 cm long.

Epiphyte in forest; 1000–1500 m; flowering in February.

Réunion (Plaine des Cafres and Plaine des Palmistes).

Jumellea penicillata (Cordemoy) Schlechter

Plant erect with a short thick stem surrounded by many old fibres. Leaves in 2 rows, long, narrow, folded at the base, flattened above, bilobed at the apex, 12–14 cm long, 5–6 mm wide. Inflorescence arising below the leaves, amongst the old leaf bases.

Epiphyte on forest trees.

Réunion (Plaine des Palmistes).

This species seems to be similar to *Jumellea stenophylla*.

Jumellea recta (Thouars) Schlechter

Syn. *Jumellea recurva* (Thouars) Schlechter

Plant with long stems up to 60 cm high. Leaves in 2 rows, distantly spaced, thick and leathery in bright light, thinner and longer in shade, ligulate, equally bilobed at the apex, 7–8 cm long, 10–12 mm wide. Inflorescences usually one at a time, axillary; peduncle short, bare in the upper half; bract tubular, 5–8 mm long; pedicel with ovary 6–7 cm long. Flower white; dorsal sepal narrowly triangular, tapering, 2 cm long; lateral sepals falcate, narrower than dorsal sepal; petals similar to lateral sepals but with frilled margins near the base; lip with a wide claw bearing a central keel, lanceolate and acuminate in the upper two thirds, in total 2.5 cm long, 6–7 mm wide; spur S-shaped, 11–12 cm long.

Epiphyte at the base of forest trees and also lithophytic; 200–1000 m; flowering December to February.

Réunion (in the semi-dry areas of the north of the island and on the leeward side) and Mauritius (widespread).

Jumellea rossii Senghas

Syn. *Jumellea* sp. in Cadet (1989)

Plant erect with straight stems rooting at the base, up to 25 cm tall. Leaves in 2 rows, well spaced, ligulate-lanceolate, unequally bilobed at the apex, with rounded lobes, to 6 cm long, 1.3 cm wide. Inflorescence arising opposite the leaf base or amongst old leaf sheaths below the leaves, sometimes successively from the same point; peduncle short, covered by 3 green sheaths; bract green, 8–9 mm long; pedicel with ovary curved, 3–4 cm long. Flowers white, nodding; dorsal sepal triangular-lanceolate, straight or reflexed, 15–17 mm long, 4.5–5.5 mm wide; lateral sepals spreading, obliquely lanceolate, 15–17 mm long, 4 mm wide; petals similar but narrower; lip narrowly rhomboid, with an upright keel in the narrow basal part, 6 mm long, in total 16–18 mm long, 7 mm wide; spur curved, aligned with the ovary, 14–17 mm long.

Epiphyte in cloud forest; 1600 m.

Réunion (near Cilaos).

This species is easily recognised by the nodding flowers with a short, curved spur.

Jumellea stenophylla (Frappier ex Cordemoy) Schlechter

Plant with short, erect stems surrounded by fibrous remains from old leaf bases, 4–10 cm tall. Leaves 5 or 6, folded towards the base where the sheath is a little bulbous, flattened out above, unequally bilobed at the apex, 6–12 cm long, 4–6 mm wide. Inflorescences arising amongst the old leaf sheaths; peduncle with 2 or 3 sheaths below, bare for most of its length, 8–10 cm long; bract tubular; pedicel with ovary 4–5 cm long. Flower white; dorsal sepal narrowly triangular, acute, margins frilled at the base, 25 mm long; lateral sepals narrower, falcate; petals narrow, curved; lip narrowly clawed at the base with a central keel in the claw, abruptly expanded above, blade lanceolate or sagittate becoming long acuminate at the apex; spur straight, 10–12 cm long.

Epiphyte in shade in damp forest; 500–1000 m. Réunion.

Jumellea stipitata (Frappier ex Cordemoy) Schlechter

Plant composed of several long stems growing together in tufts, up to 90 cm long, 8–10 mm in diameter. Leaves in 2 rows, spaced close together, tips often reflexed or incurved, linear, caniculate at the base, becoming flat above, obtusely, equally bilobed at the apex, 12–18 cm long, 5–8 mm wide. Inflorescence arising opposite leaf, 7–8 cm long, enclosed by 2 or 3 sheaths at its base, single-flowered. Flowers yellowish green with a white lip, small; sepals narrow, acute; petals very narrow, acute; lip lanceolate, acute; spur slender, 8–11 cm long.

Epiphyte in forest near waterfalls and rivers; 1200 m; flowering in December.

Réunion (Saint Denis, Saint Benoît, and Plaine des Palmistes).

Jumellea triquetra (Thouars) Schlechter

Plant stemless or with very short stem covered in old leaf bases. Leaves 4–6, ligulate, folded in the lower third and clasping the stem. Inflorescences arising below the leaves, amongst the leaf bases; peduncle stout, two thirds covered in sheaths, 2 cm long; bract tubular, 8 mm long; pedicel with ovary 3–3.5 cm long. Flowers white, small and sometimes not opening fully; dorsal sepal triangular, widest near the base, tip curving forward; lateral sepals falcate, narrower and longer than dorsal sepal; petals narrow, slightly curved, as long as the lateral sepals; lip slightly narrowed below and bearing a central keel, lanceolate above the base; spur curved, close to the ovary, ca. 8 mm long.

Epiphyte in evergreen forests; 700–1500 m; flowering November to February.

Réunion.

The identity of this plant has been confused in the literature with *Angraecum borbonicum*. We have followed Summerhayes (1951c) and Bosser (1988) in our use of it here. The species is well illustrated in Benke (2004).

Imperfectly Known Species

Jumellea ophioplectron (Reichenbach f.) Schlechter

From the brief description and its nomenclatural history, this taxon could be an *Angraecum* or an *Aerangis* but is probably not a *Jumellea*. We have not been able to study the type specimen.

LEMURELLA Schlechter

Lemurella is a small genus in the Madagascar region established by Rudolf Schlechter in 1925. He did not explain the derivation of the name, but Schultes and Pease (1963) suggested that it relates to a name for the ancient landmass called *Lemuria* of which Madagascar was once a part. It may also relate to the endemic primates, known as lemurs, which are unique to the region.

Lemurella now contains 4 species with small green flowers. They are not unlike some of the smaller *Angraecum* species, but the shape of the lip is quite different, being 3-lobed, and sometimes with the mid-lobe further divided. They are also undoubtedly close to the genus *Oeonia* but can be separated from that genus by the flowers being held on the plant so that the lip is uppermost. Again, the lip has only 3 lobes, not 4 or 5, and is green like the rest of the flower. Bosser (1970b) pointed out that these 2 genera are difficult to tell apart, but nevertheless, at that time, he preferred to keep them separate. Perhaps new evidence in the future will suggest some changes at the generic level in this small group of plants.

Culture

All the plants are small and delicate and mostly grow as twig epiphytes. They seem to do best when attached to small sticks and hung in the roof of the glasshouse.

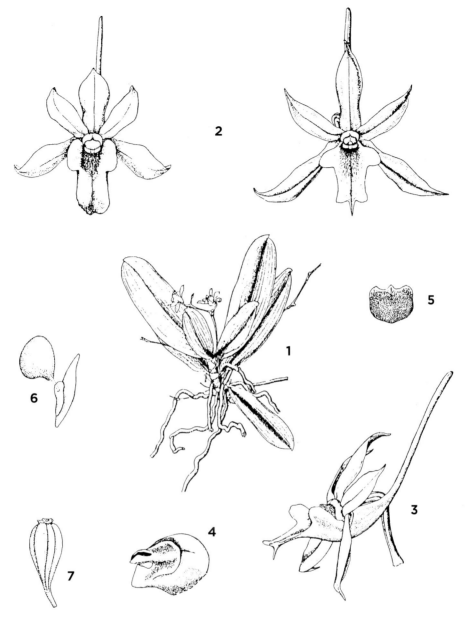

Lemurella culicifera. 1: Habit. 2–3: Flower. 4: Column. 5: Anther-cap. 6: Pollinarium. 7: Fruit. Reprinted by permission from Bosser 1970b, p. 369. E. Razafindrakoto. © Publications Scientifiques du Muséum national d'Histoire naturelle, Paris.

Lemurella culicifera (Reichenbach f.) H. Perrier

Syns. *Angraecum culiciferum* Reichenbach f., *Oeonia culicifera* (Reichenbach f.) Finet, *Lemurella ambongensis* (Schlechter) Schlechter, *Beclardia humberti* H. Perrier

Plant slender, small, stems 2–20 cm long, 3–4 mm wide. Leaves 2–12, rather variable in size and shape, oboval-oblong, oblong ligulate or oblan-ceolate-cuneiform, 2.5–10 cm long, 8–12 mm wide. Inflorescences numerous, often grouped at the same point in several successive years, 4- to 12-flowered; peduncle slender, 12–20 mm long; bracts very small; pedicel with ovary 4–8 mm long. Flowers yellowish green, small; sepals lanceolate, acute, 5 mm long, 1.5 mm wide; petals oblong, acute, 3 mm long, 1 mm wide; lip short, 3-lobed, lateral

Lemurella culicifera. J. Hermans

Lemurella pallidiflora. J. Hermans

lobes small, rounded, enclosing the column, mid-lobe square with a retuse apex and a small apiculus in the centre, thus appearing 3-lobed at the apex, lip in total 4 mm long; spur cylindric, straight, 4–8 mm long.

Epiphyte on branches and on shrubs in woods on sandy soil; sea level to 700 m; flowering October to November.

Madagascar (in seasonally dry areas in the north-west) and Comoro Islands (Grande Comore, Anjouan, and Mayotte).

The plants of this species are rather variable in size, particularly in Madagascar, and may lose their leaves in the dry season.

Lemurella pallidiflora Bosser

Plant upright with a short, simple stem 10–20 cm long. Leaves in 2 rows, fleshy, lanceolate or linear-lanceolate, twisted at the base so that they lie in the plane of the stem, unequally and acutely bilobed at the apex, 3–5 cm long, 7–15 mm wide. Inflorescence 1- or 2-flowered; peduncle slender, 8–15 mm long; bracts ovate, acute 2.5–3 mm long; pedicel with ovary 10–12 mm long. Flowers pale green, fleshy; dorsal sepal oblong-lanceolate, acute, 8–10 mm long, 4 mm wide; lateral sepals lanceolate, acuminate, spreading forwards on either side of the lip, 10–17 mm long, 3 mm wide; petals oblong, acute, recurved at the apex, 6–8 mm long, 2–2.3 mm wide; lip concave at the base, 3-lobed, lateral lobes rounded, erect, mid-lobe lanceolate, acute, recurved at the apex, lip in total 8–10 mm long; spur funnel-shaped at the mouth, then tapering, finally somewhat inflated at the apex, 1.5–2 cm long.

Epiphyte in mossy forest; 800–1200 m; flowering January to March.

Madagascar (east of Andasibe).

This species is easily separated from the others by its larger flowers, only one or 2 on each short inflorescence.

Lemurella papillosa Bosser

Plant small and slender with stem 5–6 cm long. Leaves in 2 rows, somewhat leathery, linear-oblong, twisted at the base so that they lie in the plane of the stem, 3 cm long, 7–8 mm wide. Inflorescences slender, pendent, 1- to several-flowered, pubescent or papillose, prolonged after the last flower in a slender sterile axis 1–1.5 cm long; peduncle slender, papillose, 3–5 cm long; bracts deltoid, 3–3.5 mm long; pedicel with ovary papillose, 10–12 mm long. Flowers green, fleshy, widely spaced (2–3 cm) on the inflorescence when there are several; dorsal sepal lanceolate, acute, 8 mm long, 2–3 mm wide; lateral sepals linear-lanceolate, 8 mm long, 2.5 mm wide; petals linear-lanceolate, 6 mm long, 1.7–2 mm wide; lip 3-lobed, basal lobes rounded, erect, mid-lobe lanceolate, acute, apex recurved, lip in total 5–6 mm long; spur slender, 2.5 cm long.

Epiphyte in humid, evergreen forests; 800–1000 m; flowering January to May.

Madagascar (south of Moramanga).

This species is easily recognised by the long, papillose peduncles, well-spaced flowers, and long, slender spur.

Lemurella virescens H. Perrier

Plant small with a short stem up to 5 cm long at the most. Leaves 5–7, linear, subacute, tapering towards both ends, rigid, 2.5–4 cm long, 3.5–4 mm wide. Inflorescences piercing the leaf sheath, below the leaves, simple or with a few branches, 3- or 4-flowered; peduncle very slender, 3–5 cm long; bracts very small, 1 mm long; pedicel with ovary 5–7 mm long. Flowers greenish, very small; dorsal sepal oblong, attenuate towards the base, 4 mm long, 1.7 mm wide; lateral sepals narrowly lanceolate, curved, acute, 7 mm long, 1 mm wide;

Lemurella papillosa. J. Hermans

petals narrowly deltoid, acute, 3.5 mm long, 1.4 mm wide; lip 3-lobed, the lower half funnel-shaped, thin and translucent with 2 small lateral lobes, mid-lobe opaque, oval-lanceolate, obtuse, 2.6 mm long, lip in total 5 mm long; spur wide at the mouth, quickly tapering, then inflated at the oblong apex, 1 cm long.

Epiphyte on tree trunks in mossy evergreen forests; 1000–1200 m; flowering in February.

Madagascar (eastern part of the central region).

This species has narrow, linear leaves and the smallest flowers in the genus.

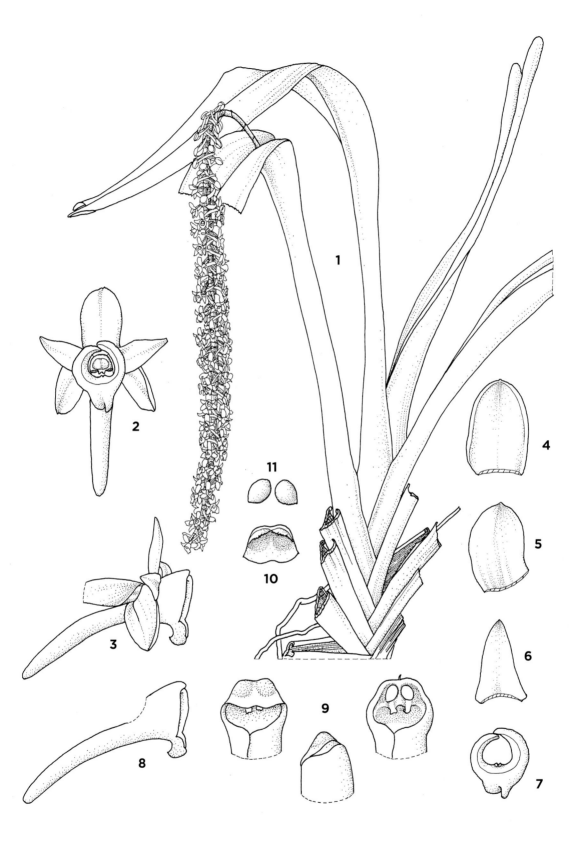

Lemurorchis madagascariensis. 1: Habit. 2–3: Flower. 4: Dorsal sepal. 5: Lateral sepal.
6: Petal. 7: Lip front. 8: Lip and spur. 9: Column. 10: Anther-cap. 11: Pollinia.
From Collection Hermans 5383, D. Lambkin (2005, unpublished).

LEMURORCHIS Kraenzlin

This strange orchid genus is represented by a single species that has been infrequently collected in central Madagascar. The genus was established by German botanist Fritz Kraenzlin in 1893, when he described a specimen collected by botanist-explorer J. M. Hildebrandt, who travelled widely in Africa and Madagascar. The generic name seems to refer to the geographic location for this orchid (see also *Lemurella*).

The habit of the plant with its long, folded leaf bases overlapping around a short stem is quite distinctive. It looks like some of the large plants of *Jumellea* and even more like a large *Phreatia*, although the leaves are quite leathery. The inflorescences are axillary and quite long, though usually shorter than the leaves, and the small white flowers are borne very close together.

Culture

This epiphyte is endemic to a small remnant of evergreen forest at about 2000 m above sea level, near Antananarivo. In a glasshouse it grows best in cool and semi-shady conditions with high atmospheric humidity. Mature plants can be quite large and are therefore best potted in compost that is free-draining and contains some moisture-retentive material. The pendent inflorescences are produced readily but abort easily when temperatures are too high and humidity is too low.

Lemurorchis madagascariensis Kraenzlin

Plant large with a short stem, reaching 30–50 cm high. Leaves 6–15, folded in the lower half and strap-shaped above, obtusely bilobed at the apex, 25–45 cm long, 2.2–3 cm wide above a leaf sheath 5–6 cm long. Inflorescences upright, shorter than the leaves, 20–30 cm long, many-flowered; peduncle rigid, 15–22 cm long; bracts conspicuous in bud, 5 mm long; pedicel with ovary very short. Flowers yellowish white, fleshy; sepals and petals free, dorsal sepal wider than others; lip short, enclosing the column, 3-lobed at the apex, side

Lemurorchis madagascariensis, Ankaratra Massif, Madagascar. J. Hermans

Lemurorchis madagascariensis. J. Hermans

lobes larger than the mid-lobe, with a fleshy callus on the surface in front of the mouth of the spur; spur with a narrow mouth, slender, curved, 8 mm long.

Epiphyte on lichen- and moss-covered trees and shrubs in mossy forests; 2000–2200 m; flowering February to March.

Madagascar (central region).

LISTROSTACHYS Reichenbach f.

This genus was established by H. G. Reichenbach in 1852. At various times a large number of species have been attributed to it, but when Rudolf Schlechter looked carefully at it during his review of all the angraecoid orchids (1918a) he found a suite of characters that demarcated the genus fairly precisely and removed many species to other genera, such as *Bolusiella* and *Cyrtorchis*.

Listrostachys as now understood contains only one species in West Africa and one in Mauritius. It is clearly recognised by the inflorescence, which is closely multi-flowered, the flowers in 2 rows, and which actually provides the name—from the Greek *listron*, spade, and *stachys*, ear. The lip is also quite distinctive, having a broad claw at its base that separates the spur entrance from the base of the column. The short, blunt spur stands at right angles to the lamina and hangs down parallel to the ovary.

Culture

The single African species is easy to grow in cultivation in warm, shady, humid conditions. It settles well in a pot of well-drained compost and seems to grow throughout the year.

Listrostachys pertusa (Lindley) Reichenbach f.

Plant with erect stems, 6–15 cm long. Leaves in 2 rows, linear-ligulate, strongly conduplicate, equally bilobed at the apex, with rounded lobes, leathery, 8–35 cm long, 1–1.7 cm wide. Inflorescences 2–4, axillary, spreading or horizontal, 10–25 cm long, multi-flowered; peduncle 2–5 cm long; bracts 1 mm long; pedicel with ovary 2–4 mm long. Flowers green on outer surface, white with small red spots at base of tepals and a purplish-green spur, small; dorsal sepal reflexed, oval, subacute, 2–4 mm long, 1.6–2 mm wide; lateral sepals spreading, obtuse, 4 mm long, 2 mm wide; petals similar, subacute, falcate, a little narrower; lip oboval, widest near the apex, apiculate, 4.5–5 mm long, 2.6–2.8 mm wide; spur emanating from the centre of the lip, inflated at the apex, 3.5–5 mm long.

Epiphyte on large branches of big trees in rain forest, protected from direct sun by the canopy; low altitudes; flowering in October and November.

Sierra Leone, Liberia, Côte d'Ivoire, Ghana, southern Nigeria, Cameroon, Príncipe, Gabon, and Congo.

Listrostachys pescatoriana (Lindley) S. Moore

Plant erect with a short, thick stem. Leaves in 2 rows, lorate, obliquely bilobed at the apex, 20–30 cm long. Inflorescence with many flowers close together, 10 cm long. Flowers small; sepals ovate, obtuse or cuspidate, 2 mm long, the outer surface clothed with short, black, glandular hairs; petals a little shorter and narrower, acute, glabrous; lip at right angles to column, nearly 4 mm long, obovate-oblong, truncate and incised at the apex, with a long, channelled claw at the base below the spur opening, nearly 4 mm long; spur nearly straight, subclavate, 4–5 mm long.

Mauritius and Réunion.

Listrostachys pertusa. L. Westra

Listrostachys pertusa. J. Wubben

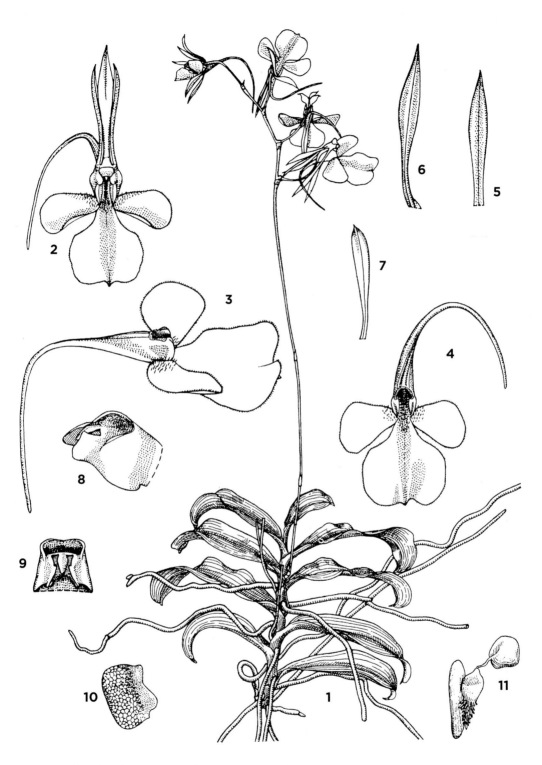

Neobathiea hirtula. 1: Habit. 2: Flower. 3–4: Lip and spur. 5: Dorsal sepal. 6: Lateral sepal. 7: Petal.
8–9: Column. 10: Anther-cap. 11: Pollinarium. Reprinted by permission from Bosser 1969, p. 543.
E. Razafindrakoto. © Publications Scientifiques du Muséum national d'Histoire naturelle, Paris.

NEOBATHIEA Schlechter

The last new genus Rudolf Schlechter described in his revision of all the African angraecoid orchids in 1918 was *Bathiea*. He proposed this name in honour of the French botanist Henri Perrier de la Bâthie (1873–1958), who had done so much to investigate the plants of Madagascar, including orchids. However, Schlechter was pre-empted in this good intention by another botanist, Drake de Castillo, who had used an almost identical name, *Bathiaea*, for a Madagascan tree genus in the family Caesalpiniaceae in 1902. To avoid confusion, Schlechter proposed a new name, *Neobathiea*, from the Greek *neos*, new, in 1925. Although *Bathiea* was originally created for a single species, *B. perrieri*, now *Neobathiea perrieri*, 4 others are now recognised and 2 species have been transferred to *Aeranthes schlechteri*. *Neobathiea* appears somewhat close to *Cryptopus* and *Oeonia*, but most of its species have much shorter stems than those 2 genera. Florally, it differs from *Cryptopus* and *Oeonia* in the small and simple sepals and petals, which are not lobed and which are often reflexed behind the column giving a characteristic appearance to the flower. Finally the lip is deeply funnel-shaped at its base, where it becomes the forward part of the spur. In 2 species the lip is entire, while in the other 3 it is 3-lobed. *Neobathiea* is also somewhat close to some species of *Aeranthes*, but in that genus the spur is attached to the foot of the column and to the lip on the anterior side only.

Most *Neobathiea* species grow in humid forests, or on mossy rocks where forest has been removed, in the highlands of central and western Madagascar. Others grow in the semi-deciduous bush and forest in western regions. All are subject to a long dry season. Thus there are ecological differences, presumably accompanied by physiological distinctions, between the species of this genus and the others just mentioned. It will be interesting to see, in due course, whether DNA analysis supports the recognition of these differences at the generic level.

Culture

All these plants grow best mounted on a cork-oak slab where drainage is good and the plants and their aerial roots dry off quickly after watering. Although they occur mostly in dry areas, which are very dry for part of the year, the plants are frequently exposed to dew and low clouds especially at night. Plants from higher altitudes require cooler conditions.

Neobathia grandidieriana (Reichenbach f.) Garay
Syn. *Neobathiea filicornu* Schlechter

Plant small with a short stem 6–15 cm high. Leaves 5 or 6, elliptic or oblanceolate, scarcely bilobed at the apex, dull green, 4–6 cm long, 1–2 cm wide. Inflorescences short and curved, 1- or 2-flowered; peduncle 2–4 cm long; pedicel with ovary 1.2–3 cm long. Flowers pale green or whitish green with a white lip, spur and column green; sepals lanceolate, acute, 13 mm long, 3 mm wide; petals similar, slightly smaller; lip entire, ovate-lanceolate, subcordate at the base, acute, 2.3–2.8 cm long, 1.3–1.6 cm wide; spur funnel-shaped at the wide mouth, becoming filiform, 12–14 cm long.

Epiphyte in humid forest on west-facing slopes; 1000–1650 m; flowering September to December.

Madagascar (central highlands) and Comoro Islands (Anjouan and Grande Comore).

Neobathia hirtula H. Perrier

Plant erect, with a short stem 2–10 cm long. Leaves 4–8, oblanceolate, narrowing from near the apex towards the base, margins undulate, 5–8.5 cm long, 1.5–1.8 cm wide. Inflorescences axillary, 13–20 cm long, 3- to 5-flowered; peduncle 10–12 cm long; bracts rigid, 4–5 mm long; pedicel with ovary 1.8–2 cm long. Flowers green with a pure white lip, sepals and petals reflexed; dorsal sepal lanceolate-linear, 15 mm long, 1 mm wide; lateral sepals fused to the petals at the base, linear, 18 mm long, 1.5 mm wide; petals oblanceolate-linear, smaller than sepals; lip deeply 3-lobed, covered with papillae on the upper surface and minutely hairy towards the

Neobathiea grandidieriana. J. Hermans

base, lateral lobes broadly oboval, 10 mm long, 6.5 mm wide, mid-lobe oboval-cuneiform, slightly retuse at the apex with a short acumen in the centre, 15 mm long, 10 mm wide; spur wide and funnel-shaped at the mouth, tapering to become filiform, 3–3.2 cm long.

var. **hirtula**

An epiphyte on branches in humid woods and semi-deciduous forest; flowering December to January.

Madagascar (north-western region).

var. **floribunda** H. Perrier ex Hermans

Described as possibly a robust form. Plants up to 30 cm long. Leaves larger than the type, 11 cm long, 2 cm wide. Inflorescences 6–10 per plant, 6- to 10-flowered. Flowers a little larger than the type in all respects.

Epiphyte in semi-deciduous forest; flowering in April.

Madagascar (Ankarafantsika in the north-west).

Neobathiea keraudrenae Toilliez-Genoud & Bosser

Plant erect, with a short stem up to 10 cm long. Leaves 4–5, arranged in a fan, fleshy, oblong-spathulate or obovate, bilobed at the apex, the lobes small, rounded, 5.5–6 cm long, 2–2.5 cm wide. Inflorescence erect or spreading, as long as the leaves, 1- or 2-flowered, sometimes formed successively on a short side branch; peduncle slender, 3.5–4.5 cm long; pedicel with ovary 2–2.8 cm long. Flowers greenish white, fleshy, rigid; sepals and petals spathulate, the claw green, white in the upper parts; dorsal sepal rounded at the apex, 10–11 mm long, 3.5–4.5 mm wide; lateral sepals a little longer and narrower, 11–12 mm long, 4 mm wide; petals similar to the sepals and a little longer, 13 mm long, 5 mm wide; lip entire, slightly cordate at the base, then becoming wider or subpandurate, truncate, 20 mm long, 12 mm wide, 7 mm wide at the apex; spur funnel-shaped at the mouth, pubescent within, slender, green, 13 cm long.

Epiphyte in shady forests; flowering in May.

Madagascar (east of Lake Alaotra).

This species is similar in its long spur to *Neobathiea perrieri* and to *N. grandidieriana*, but other details of the flowers are quite different.

Neobathiea perrieri (Schlechter) Schlechter

Syns. *Aeranthes perrieri* Schlechter, *Bathiea perrieri* (Schlechter) Schlechter

Plant small with a short stem up to 5 cm long, 5 mm in diameter. Leaves 4–6, dark glossy green, oblong-spathulate, margins undulate, 3.5–7 cm long, 1–2 cm wide. Inflorescences 6–12 cm long, 1- to 3-flowered; bracts pointed, 3–4 mm long; pedicel with ovary 2.5 cm long. Flowers white; sepals lanceolate-spathulate, narrow at the base, pointed at the apex, 22–35 mm long; petals similar to the sepals or slightly smaller; lip lanceolate, 3-lobed at the apex, lateral lobes diverging, oval, acute,

Neobathiea perrieri. J. Hermans

base of the lobes, lateral lobes oboval-cuneiform, 5 mm long and wide, mid-lobe obtriangular, narrow, emarginate at the apex and with a short thick apiculus; spur with a conspicuous aperture between the lip and column, funnel-shaped and then slender, 4–5 cm long.

Epiphyte of branches or lithophyte in deciduous forests; sea level to 350 m; flowering December to January.

Madagascar (northern and north-western regions).

OEONIA Lindley

This small genus was first described at the same time as *Cryptopus*, in 1824, though it was misspelt as *Aeonia*. Two years later, in his *Collectanea Botanica*, Lindley changed the spelling to *Oeonia*, from the Greek *oionos*, a bird of prey, presumably a reference to the flowers that have a fanciful resemblance to a bird in flight. *Oeonia volucris* was listed as an *Epidendrum* by Thouars when he discovered and illustrated it in 1822.

Five species are now recognised. All occur in Madagascar, and *Oeonia rosea* has also been collected in Réunion. The plants are somewhat similar to those of *Cryptopus* with long, scrambling, woody stems and copious grey roots almost hiding the small hard leaves. The flowers, however, are fewer and rather different. The sepals and petals are similar to each other, obovate or elliptic, and the lip is spreading, 3- to 6-lobed, and encircles the column at its base, in a similar manner to the lip in the flowers of *Angraecum*.

Culture

In the wild *Oeonia* species are twig epiphytes, generally in the canopy of a forest tree or amongst bushes along forest margins. They form miniature climbers, scrambling through the host plant. In culture, the plants are usually mounted, but they also do well in pots in suitably well-drained compost that retains moisture. The roots are brittle

mid-lobe oval, twice as big as the lateral lobes, lip in total 2.8 cm long, 2 cm wide; spur wide at the mouth, tapering, curving forward, then pendent, 7–13 cm long.

Epiphyte on shrubs in evergreen and dry forests; sea level to 350 m; flowering January to June.

Madagascar (northern and north-western regions).

Neobathiea spatulata H. Perrier

Plant with an elongated stem 5–20 cm long, with leaves at the apex. Leaves elliptic, obtuse at both ends, the terminal lobes large and unequal, 2–3.5 cm long, 1–1.5 cm wide. Inflorescences 2.5–8 cm long, 1- to 7-flowered; peduncle 3–4 cm long; bracts obtuse, 2.5–3 mm long; pedicel with ovary 1.4–1.6 cm long. Flowers white; sepals and petals spathulate, very narrow in the lower part, rounded at the apex, 14 mm long, 5 mm wide; lip deeply 3-lobed, pubescent on the upper surface near the

Oeonia volucris. From Thouars 1822, t. 81.

and easily broken when dry, but they need to be able to wander, attaching themselves as they go. Most of the species are at medium altitudes in the wild so require intermediate conditions; *O. brauniana* grows at lower altitudes and requires more warmth and humidity.

Oeonia brauniana H. Wendland & Kraenzlin

Plant with slender woody stems to 30 cm long, 3–3.5 mm in diameter. Leaves thick and fleshy, oval or oblong, variable in size, irregularly bilobed at the apex, 3.5–7.5 cm long, 1.7–2.5 cm wide. Inflorescence arising opposite a leaf base, piercing the sheath of the leaf above, 1- to 3-flowered; peduncle slender, enlarged towards the tip, 2–4.5 cm long; bracts oval, 2.5–3 mm long; pedicel with ovary 1.7–2 cm long. Flowers fleshy, yellowish green with a white lip which has a red spot at the base of each lateral lobe; sepals elliptic or oboval, rounded at the apex, 12–14 mm long, 6–9 mm wide; petals similar to the sepals, oboval, 11–14 mm long, 5–7.5 mm wide; lip 6-lobed, 2 basal lobes erect and rounded,

Oeonia brauniana var. *sarcanthoides*. J. Hermans

hiding the column, 2 lateral lobes spreading, ob-oval, rounded, 6–8 mm long, 4–7 mm wide, 1 or 2 terminal lobes oval, subacute or rounded, 6–8 mm long; spur green, flattened dorso-ventrally, 3.5–4.5 mm long.

var. *brauniana*

Lip with terminal lobes ovate, subacute or rounded at the apex, spreading.

Epiphyte in humid forests; low and medium altitudes; flowering in October.

Madagascar (northern region).

var. *sarcanthoides* (Schlechter) Bosser

Syns. *Oeoniella sarcanthoides* Schlechter, *Oeonia subacaulis* Perrier, *Lemurella sarcanthoides* (Schlechter) Senghas, *L. tricalcariformis* Perrier

Lip with a single terminal lobe that is retuse at the apex.

Epiphyte in humid forests, widespread; 500–1000 m; flowering in January and February.

Madagascar (eastern regions and in the Sambirano valley).

Oeonia curvata Bosser

Plant with slender, branched, long stems and many unbranched roots. Leaves leathery, ovate, unequally bilobed at the apex, 2 cm long, 1 cm wide. Inflorescence arising at the base of the leaf sheaths, 1- or 2-flowered; peduncle spreading, 5–7 cm long; bracts broadly ovate, 3–4 mm long. Flowers white; dorsal sepal spathulate, acute, 10 mm long, 5 mm wide; lateral sepals similar but slightly narrower; petals narrowly ovate, spathulate, acute, 10–12 mm long, 3 mm wide; lip 4-lobed, funnel-shaped at the base, side lobes broad, erect, rounded with undulate margins, terminal lobes smaller and narrower, falcate, truncate, with a narrow sinus between them, lip in total 25 mm long and wide; spur wide at the mouth, slender, cylindrical, 13–15 mm long.

Epiphyte in humid forest; 1200–1500 m.

Madagascar (Ranomafana area in the south-east).

Oeonia madagascariensis (Schlechter) Bosser

Syn. *Perrierella madagascariensis* Schlechter

Plant with a slender, pendent stem 10–25 cm long. Leaves fleshy, linear or narrowly oblong, obtuse, 1.5–3.5 cm long, 5 mm wide. Inflorescences short, single-flowered; peduncle slender, thicker towards the apex, 1–2 cm long; bracts tubular. Flower small, white or green; sepals obovate, dorsal sepal 6–8 mm long, 3 mm wide, lateral sepals rounded and slightly crenulate at the apex, 7–9 mm long, 3 mm wide; petals obovate, rounded at the apex, 5–8 mm long, 3 mm wide; lip 4-lobed, side lobes rounded or subquadrate, surrounding the column, terminal lobes rectangular with a broad sinus between them, lip in total 10–17 mm long; spur cylindrical, 15 mm long.

Epiphyte in forest; also on lichen-covered rocks; 1500–2000 m; flowering January to March.

Madagascar (Mount Tsaratanana).

Oeonia rosea Ridley

Syns. *Oeonia oncidiiflora* Kraenzlin, *O. forsythiana* Kraenzlin

Plant with long, slender stems, simple or branched. Leaves leathery, ovate or narrowly ovate, sometimes amplexicaul, apex obtuse, 2–2.5 cm long, 5 mm wide. Inflorescence erect, 3- to 7-flowered; peduncle short; pedicel with ovary 15 mm long. Flowers 10–25 mm in diameter, sepals and petals yellowish green, lip white marked with red in the base of the lip and mouth of the spur; sepals spathulate, obtuse, 10 mm long, 5 mm wide; petals oblong-spathulate, 12 mm long, 5 mm wide; lip 4-lobed, side lobes rounded surrounding the column, terminal lobes narrow at the base, large, rounded, diverging, separated by a deep sinus, lip in total 25 mm long; spur 7 mm long.

Epiphyte in humid evergreen forest; 500–2000 m; flowering September to May.

Madagascar (south-eastern forests) and Réunion (Cirque de Salazie).

Oeonia volucris (Thouars) Sprengel

Syns. *Oeonia elliotii* Rolfe, *O. humblotii* Kraenzlin

Plant erect or pendent, with a long slender stem, simple or branched. Leaves well spaced, ovate-oblong or elliptic, unequally bilobed at the apex, 2–2.6 cm long, 6–9 mm wide. Inflorescence erect, 30–40 cm long, many-flowered. Flowers white, greenish or pale yellow in the base of the lip; sepals oblong to ovate, apex acute, laterals slightly longer than dorsal sepal, 12–25 mm long; petals similar to the sepals but smaller; lip 3- to 4-lobed, obovate, side lobes erect and surrounding the column,

Oeonia rosea. J. Hermans

Oeonia volucris. J. Hermans

Oeonia rosea, in undergrowth of rain forest, eastern Madagascar. J. Hermans

mid-lobe spreading from a narrow base, rounded with a deep terminal sinus, appearing 2-lobed, lip in total 1.7–3 cm long; spur slender, cylindrical, 5 mm long.

Epiphyte in coastal forests along the east coast and inland; sea level to 1500 m; flowering March to July.

Madagascar.

Sometimes recorded as present in Mauritius and Réunion, but these records are probably mis-identifications, according to Bosser (1989). This species is rather variable in size but always recognisable by its white flowers, sometimes with a hint of yellow or pale green in the base of the lip.

OEONIELLA Schlechter

This genus was proposed by Rudolf Schlechter when he prepared his revision of all the African angraecoid orchids in 1918. Before that the most widespread species, *Oeoniella polystachys*, had been well illustrated by Thouars in 1822 as *Epidendrum polystachys*. It then acquired other synonyms, from 6 different botanists, in *Angraecum*, *Listrostachys*, *Beclardia*, *Oeonia*, *Angorchis*, and *Monixus* before coming to rest in Schlechter's new genus.

Schlechter pointed out that *Oeoniella* differed from *Angraecum*, which it rather closely resembles, in the shape of the column and in the pollinia being each attached to a long stipe. The most noticeable feature is the 3-lobed lip rolled around the column rather like a funnel with 2 rounded lateral lobes and a long, pointed mid-lobe. The short spur protrudes from a narrow mouth at the base of the lip and is shortly inflated at its tip. These features also distinguish the genus from *Oeonia*, some species of which are similar vegetatively.

Only 2 species have been recognised to date. *Oeoniella polystachys* is widespread in coastal forests of eastern Madagascar, in the Comoro Islands, Seychelles, Réunion, and Mauritius. The smaller-flowered *O. aphrodite* appears to be confined to Rodrigues Island and the Seychelles.

Oeoniella polystachys. J. Hermans

Culture

Oeoniella polystachys is well known in cultivation and is easy to maintain in the northern hemisphere in conditions appropriate for other warm-growing vandaceous plants. Bright light is essential for good flowering, and high humidity is beneficial. Plants grow well in a pot, in well-drained compost, or attached to a log or piece of cork-oak bark.

Oeoniella aphrodite (I. B. Balfour & S. Moore) Schlechter

Plant erect with elongated stems, 10–30 cm long, bearing many leaves above branching aerial roots. Leaves in 2 rows, linear-oblong or ligulate, unequally bilobed at the apex, 10–15 cm long, 8–12 mm wide. Inflorescences one to several, erect, arising opposite the leaf base, 6–20 cm long, elon-

Oeoniella polystachys. From Thouars 1822, t. 82.

gating in fruit, 10- to 16 flowered. Flowers white or pale green with white lip; sepals lanceolate, acuminate, 10–15 mm long; petals shorter, linear, acute; lip ovate-orbicular, 3-lobed, lateral lobes crenulate, embracing the column, mid-lobe narrowly linear, 4 mm long; spur short, straight or curved, not inflated, 3–5 mm long.

Lithophyte, usually in shade; sea level; flowering in June in Seychelles.

Seychelles and Rodrigues Island.

Oeoniella polystachys (Thouars) Schlechter

Syns. *Beclardia polystachya* (Thouars) Frappier, *Oeonia polystachya* (Thouars) Bentham & Hooker f.

Plant with elongated stems, at least 15–30 cm long, bearing many leaves and many aerial roots. Leaves in 2 rows, oblong, cordate or amplexicaul at the base, bilobed at the apex, with rounded lobes, 5–11 cm long, 1.5–2 cm wide. Inflorescences usually several, piercing the leaf sheath, 15–25 cm long, 7- to 15-flowered; bracts small and rounded;

pedicel with ovary 8 mm long. Flowers white or pale green with a white lip, 2–4 cm in diameter; sepals lanceolate-linear, acuminate, 12–18 mm long; petals linear, a little shorter than the sepals; lip cornet-shaped, 3-lobed, side lobes wide, sometimes with crenulated margins, mid-lobe linear, acute, very narrow, lip in total as long as the petals; spur short, with a narrow mouth, slightly inflated at the apex, 4 mm long.

Epiphyte of trunks and branches, often near the sea, on isolated trees and in lightly shaded coastal forest; sea level to 100 m; flowering August to May.

Madagascar, Comoro Islands, Seychelles, Réunion, and Mauritius.

OSSICULUM P. J. Cribb & van der Laan

This new genus caused great excitement when it was first described in 1983. The only plant known was a young seedling that had been collected by a Dutch botanist, H. J. Beentje, in Cameroon and flowered in cultivation at the University of Wageningen in The Netherlands. The plant was clearly a typical angraecoid, with an upright stem and 2 rows of fleshy leaves, but the orange-red flowers with a yellow lip were unlike any previously described angraecoid. Examination of the flowers revealed tusk-like rostellum lobes and led to the conclusion that this plant represented a genus new to science. *Ossiculum* is a translation of the Dutch word *beentje*, small bone, the name of the collector.

This orchid genus seems to be closest to *Calyptrochilum*, one species of which has a yellow lip and a spur of similar shape. It is known, so far, only from the Mungo River Forest Reserve in Cameroon. Beentje has collected several rare and inconspicuous orchids during visits to Cameroon.

Ossiculum aurantiacum P. J. Cribb & van der Laan

Plants erect with straight stems ca. 15 cm high. Leaves in 2 rows, thick and fleshy, oblong-lanceolate, obliquely and acutely or obtusely bilobed at the apex, 2–4.5 cm long, 6–10 mm wide. Inflorescences short, axillary, bearing 9–15 flowers very close together; peduncle and rachis 1.8 cm long; bracts broadly triangular, acute, 1–1.2 mm long; pedicel with ovary 2–2.5 mm long. Flowers bright orange with yellow lip, small; sepals oval-lanceolate, cuspidate, 4 mm long, 1.5 mm wide; petals obliquely oblanceolate, acuminate, 3.5 mm long, 1 mm wide; lip shell-shaped, oblong-oboval, entire, apiculate, with a fleshy callus in the throat of the spur, 4.5–5 mm long, 3 mm wide; spur swollen, parallel with the ovary, straight or slightly S-shaped, 1.5–2 mm long.

Epiphyte on thick branches of trees in primary forest.

Cameroon.

Ossiculum aurantiacum. P. J. Cribb

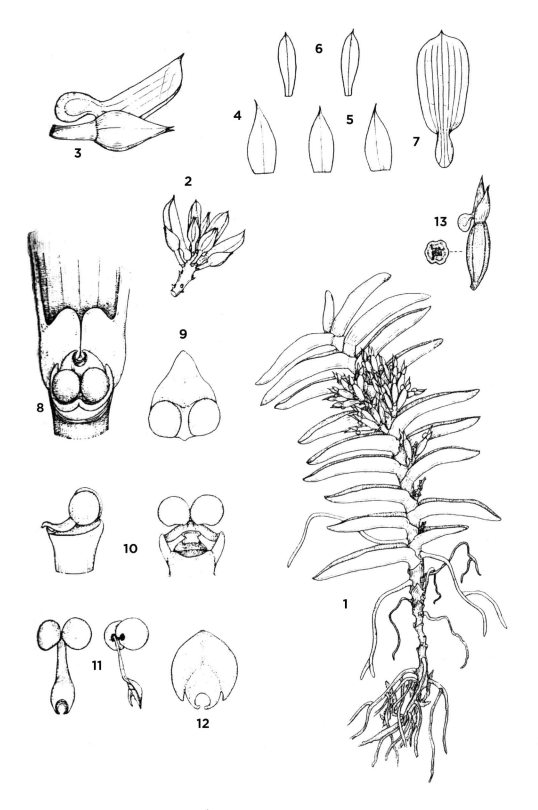

Ossiculum aurantiacum. 1: Habit. 2: Inflorescence. 3: Flower. 4–5: Sepals. 6: Petals. 7: Lip with spur.
8: Column. 9: Anther-cap. 10: Apex of column, without anther-cap. 11: Pollinarium. 12: Rostellum. 13: Fruit.
From van der Laan and Cribb 1986, p. 823. W. Wessel-Brand.

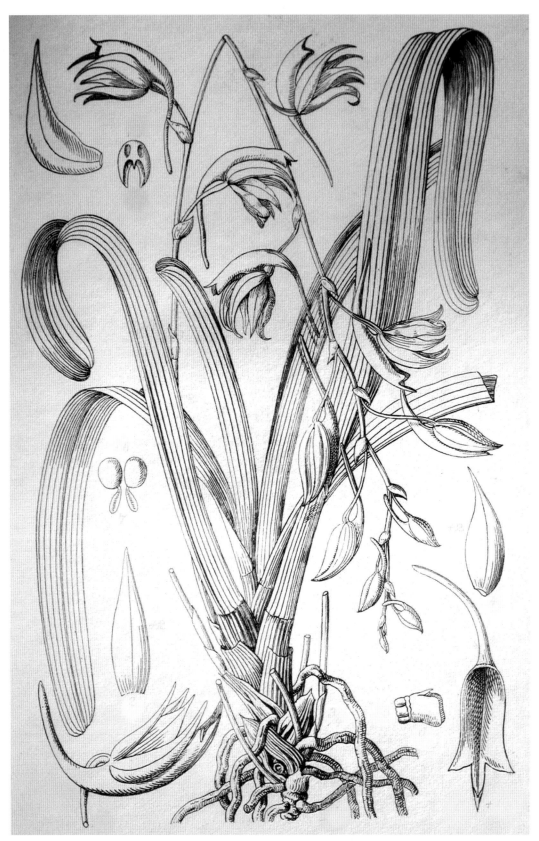

Sobennikoffia robusta. From Schlechter 1913, t. 18. R. Schlechter.

Sobennikoffia humbertiana in habitat in southwestern Madagascar. J. Hermans

SOBENNIKOFFIA Schlechter

This is one of the last orchid genera described by Rudolf Schlechter in his mammoth work on the orchids of Madagascar, *Orchidaceae Perrierianae* (1925). Schlechter proposed this new genus for 2 species formerly accommodated in *Angraecum*. They are robust plants with a funnel-shaped lip that is conspicuously 3-lobed at the apex. In the genus *Angraecum* all the species have an entire lip, sometimes with a short mucro, apiculus, or even a long acumen at the apex. Schlechter coined his new name in honour of his wife, the daughter of a Russian tea merchant. Two more species have been described since then, by Perrier de la Bâthie, both named in honour of their collector.

Culture

These attractive orchids are not well known in culture, perhaps because their environmental and cultural needs are not well understood. They are terrestrial or lithophytic plants or sometimes epiphytic on tree trunks shortly above the ground with roots running down into sandy or rocky soil. They occur in northern and western Madagascar, with one species recorded from the south-west, all in areas with a long dry season. The leaves are fleshy, or leathery, suggesting that these plants should be treated like succulents in cultivation.

Sobennikoffia fournieriana (Kraenzlin) Schlechter

Syn. *Angraecum fournierianum* Kraenzlin

Plant very robust with long, erect stems. Leaves numerous, thick and leathery, strap-shaped, unequally bilobed at the apex, with rounded lobes, 60–70 cm long, 3–5 cm wide. Inflorescences as long as the leaves. Flowers white and green; sepals and petals similar, oblong-acuminate, 4–4.5 cm long, 1.3 cm wide; lip oboval or nearly square when flattened, funnel-shaped at the base, 3-lobed at the apex, the side lobes rounded, the mid-lobe very narrow and acuminate, bearing a distinct keel along the centre towards the base, 5 cm long; spur wide at the mouth, tapering, as long as the lip or a little longer.

Described from a plant in cultivation and not known in the wild.

Sobennikoffia humbertiana H. Perrier

Plant robust with stem 15–50 cm long, 10–15 mm in diameter. Leaves 11–15 in 2 rows, near apex of stem, loriform, leathery and somewhat folded, unequally and obtusely bilobed at the apex, 15–25 cm long, 1.8–2.5 cm wide. Inflorescences axillary, longer than the leaves, 5- to 9-flowered; peduncle 9–11 cm long; bracts wide and obtuse, 6–7 mm long; pedicel with ovary 3.5 cm long. Flowers white, becoming yellowish as they fade; dorsal sepal ovate-lanceolate, attenuate, 2.5 cm long, 6 mm wide; lateral sepals curved, lanceolate and very acuminate; petals ovate-lanceolate, acuminate, 2 cm long, 7 mm wide; lip funnel-shaped, usually on the upper side of the flower, 3-lobed at the apex, side lobes small and obtuse, 4 mm long,

3 mm wide, mid-lobe linear-lanceolate, pointed, 10–12 mm long, lip in total 3–3.2 cm long, 1.5 cm wide; spur wide at the mouth, tapering, horizontal or ascending, 2–2.5 cm long.

Epiphyte in humid, evergreen forest on the plateau and lithophyte in dry forest and bush; 400–1200 m; flowering October-November.

Madagascar (south and south-west, on the plateau and near the coast).

Sobennikoffia poissoniana H. Perrier

Plant small, with a very short stem. Leaves few, ligulate, narrowing at the base to resemble a petiole, 5–10 cm long, 1.7 cm wide. Inflorescence 9 cm long, few-flowered; bracts deltoid, obtuse, 3.5 cm long. Flowers white; sepals oblong, attenuate or acute at the apex; lateral sepals somewhat dilated on the internal margin; petals shorter than the sepals, slightly dilated on the lower margin; lip 3-lobed, the lobes rounded, 5 mm wide, lip in total 2–2.3 cm long; spur cylindrical, 15–17 mm long.

Epiphyte or lithophyte in coastal vegetation; near sea level; flowering November to December.

Madagascar (northern and north-western regions).

This species is known from only 2 collections. They differ from all the other species in the very small plants, but the few flowers are said to be similar to those of *Sobennikoffia robusta*.

Sobennikoffia robusta (Schlechter) Schlechter

Syns. *Oeonia robusta* Schlechter, *Angraecum robustum* (Schlechter) Schlechter

Plant robust with stems up to 25–40 cm long, 15 mm in diameter. Leaves numerous, loriform, leathery, unequally and obtusely bilobed at the apex, 30–35 cm long, 2.5–3.5 cm wide. Inflorescences erect, up to 50 cm long, 12- to 15-flowered; bracts oval, obtuse, shorter than the ovary. Flowers white, tinged with green on the outer surface, turning yellowish as they fade; dorsal sepal recurved, lanceolate-elliptic, ca. 3.5 cm long, 1.4 cm wide; lateral sepals curved, 4 cm long, 1.2 cm wide; petals oblong, acuminate, 3.5 cm long, 1.3 cm wide; lip concave, with a pronounced keel at the centre of the inner surface, 3-lobed at the apex, the lateral

Sobennikoffia robusta, near Kinkony, Madagascar. M. Grubenmann

lobes triangular and subacute, the mid-lobe a little longer, ligulate, cuspidate at the apex, 1.5 cm long, lip in total 4.5 cm long, 2.5 cm wide; spur wide at the mouth, tapering and ascending, 4.5–5 cm long.

Terrestrial, semi-epiphytic, or epiphytic in dry woods on sandy soil, often at the foot of trees; 1500–2000 m; flowering November to January.

Madagascar (western region).

Sobennikoffia humbertiana. J. Hermans

Sobennikoffia robusta. J. Hermans

CHAPTER THREE

The Genus *Aerangis*

The name *Aerangis* was coined by H. G. Reichenbach from the Greek words *aer*, air, and *angos*, vessel, probably referring to the nectariferous spur at the base of the lip. Specimens of this genus are amongst the most attractive and highly sought-after of the white-flowered epiphytes of Africa and Madagascar. The plants vary in size and shape but most have dark green or greyish-green leaves on upright or pendent stems. The flowers are graceful, white or cream, and sometimes tinged with green or pinkish brown. Two small-flowered species in Madagascar are pale green or brownish green. There may be many flowers on each raceme, or only one or few, and often there are several inflorescences on each plant at one flowering. The flowers may appear at any time of the year but in the wild they are most common during the rainy seasons in April and May or October and November in Africa and in January and February in Madagascar and neighbouring islands.

A distinctive feature of the entire genus is the rostellum on the front of the more or less elongated column. It projects forward or downward from the base of the androclinium across the surface of the stigma. In *Aerangis fastuosa* it is so long that its tip is hidden in the spur, while in *A. monantha* and *A. punctata* it is quite straight and extends below the column across the mouth of the

spur. In other species it curves forwards so that the viscidium itself is held in a horizontal position in front of the stigma.

The genus is widespread in tropical Africa and Madagascar, although some species are very restricted in their distribution, and for many species the plants are not common even where suitable habitats exist. Thirty-one species are now recognised from continental Africa. Twenty-one are recorded from Madagascar, 5 of which are also found in the Comoro Islands and one in Réunion. One species has been recorded from several places along the coast of East Africa and in Sri Lanka.

Culture

All the species are easily maintained in cultivation. The species from higher altitudes need cooler conditions than those that occur at or near the coast. They all grow well mounted on a piece of bark or timber that is suspended in deep shade, usually in high humidity. Well-rooted plants will also do well in pots in any compost that is suitable for epiphytic plants. The hardest thing to arrange, in cultivation, is the resting season that most species enjoy after flowering and fruiting. If plants are kept dry, they will dry out too much and lose their leaves. Conversely, if they are sprayed too much,

Aerangis decaryana, on a tamarind tree, southern Madagascar. J. Hermans

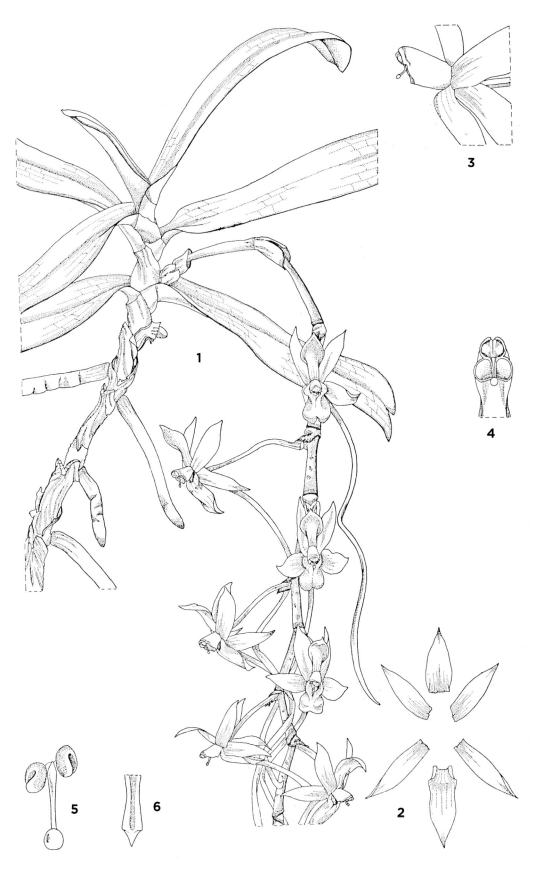

Aerangis thomsonii. 1: Habit. 2: Perianth. 3: Column and base of perianth. 4: Column. 5: Pollinarium.
6: Rostellum. From Stewart 1979, fig. 8. L. Cowan.

the roots and leaves will suffer from overwatering and the plants will die. Careful management of the plants and their environment will ensure that they are long-lived and flower prolifically.

Species from Africa

The African species are arranged here in 4 groups according to the size of the flowers, in particular the length of the spur:

Group 1. Flowers with a spur 10 cm long or more.

Group 2. Flowers with a spur 4–9 cm long.

Group 3. Plants small, flowers with a narrow lip and a spur less than 4 cm long.

Group 4. Plants small, flowers with an obovate or suborbicular lip, widest towards the apex.

These groups are not intended to indicate relationships; they are used here as an aid to identification.

Group 1: Flowers with a spur 10 cm long or more.

Aerangis bouarensis G. Chiron

Plant with a short woody stem ca. 5 cm long, closely covered with old leaf bases. Leaves 5 or 6 in 2 rows, forming a fan, medium green and black-dotted on both surfaces, oblanceolate, slightly bilobed at the apex, the sinus between the subequal lobes 5–8 mm deep, up to 21 cm long, 5.3–6 cm wide. Inflorescence axillary, with 4 or 5 flowers spaced ca. 3 cm apart, ca. 20 cm long. Flowers white, sepals and petals with pink tips and lip and spur a uniform chestnut-pink; dorsal sepal lanceolate-elliptic, acuminate, 35–36 mm long, 4 mm wide; lateral sepals similar but narrower; petals narrowly linear, acuminate, 30 mm long, 5 mm wide; lip very narrow, side margins recurved, 2 folds on the upper surface in the mouth of the spur, 36 mm long, 5 mm wide; spur straight or curved and S-shaped, 19 cm long.

Epiphyte in gallery forest along a river; 800 m; flowering in July and August.

Central African Republic (near the town of Bouar).

This species is somewhat similar to *Aerangis stelligera* and both flowers have a relatively long column (10–12 mm). *Aerangis bouarensis* has larger leaves and smaller flowers with strong pink coloration in the lip and spur while *A. stelligera* is entirely white.

Aerangis brachycarpa (A. Richard) Durand & Schinz

Plant with a woody, upright or pendent stem up to 20 cm long but usually much shorter. Leaves 4–12, alternate, 5–12 mm apart, obovate or spathulate, unequally bilobed at the apex, dark green and often black-dotted, up to 25 cm long, 2–6 cm wide near the apex. Inflorescences axillary, arching or pendent racemes up to 40 cm long, bearing 2–12 flowers in 2 rows. Flowers slender, elegant, usually pale green at first and white with a pinkish tinge when mature; tepals narrowly lanceolate, acuminate, 20–45 mm long, 4–8 mm wide near the base; dorsal sepal erect, lateral sepals and petals becoming sharply reflexed within a few days of opening; lip deflexed, 20–45 mm long, 5–10 mm wide near the base, narrowing abruptly to a long slender acumen, margins often reflexed; spur straight or slightly flexuous, 12–20 cm long.

Epiphyte in dense shade, usually rather low down on tree trunks, branches, or in the forking bases of bushes in highland forests and forest remnants; 1500–2300 m; flowering April to July, occasionally in November.

Ethiopia, Uganda, Kenya, Tanzania, Zambia, and Angola.

This is a rather variable species, both in the shape of its leaves and their apical lobes, and in the size of the flowers. In the past it was often misidentified as *Aerangis friesiorum*, which is now known to be a synonym of *A. thomsonii*. Two somewhat similar species have been described in Malawi, *A. splendida* and *A. distincta*.

Aerangis brachycarpa. B. Campbell

Aerangis coriacea. B. Campbell

Aerangis coriacea Summerhayes

Plant with a woody stem, usually short but may attain 40 cm long in old specimens. Leaves 4–many in 2 rows, ligulate or oblanceolate-ligulate, un-equally bilobed at the apex, with rounded lobes, dark green with transverse veins in a darker colour, up to 22 cm long, 2–4.5 cm wide. Inflorescences axillary, arching racemes, bearing 4–22 flowers spaced 1–3 cm apart. Flowers white, or tinged with pink or green, 3–4 cm in diameter; dorsal sepal erect, lanceolate-elliptic, margins recurved, 13–17 mm long; petals reflexed, oblanceolate-oblong, margins recurved, 13–17 mm long; lip lanceolate or oblong-lanceolate, acute at the reflexed apex, margins recurved in the middle, 14–18 mm long; spur pendulous, flexuous, narrowly cylindrical but widened and somewhat flattened in the apical half, 11–17 cm long.

Epiphyte in shady places, often near rivers, usu-ally rather low down on trunks or larger branches of trees; 1500–2300 m; flowering March through to June, usually in May.

Kenya and northern Tanzania.

Aerangis distincta. J. Hermans

Aerangis distincta J. Stewart & I. F. la Croix

Plant with a woody stem, usually short but up to 16 cm long. Leaves 3–6, rarely more, arranged in a fan in one plane, dark olive green, black-dotted, obovate or obtriangular, deeply and acutely bilobed at the apex, the lobes distinctive, the longer to 3 cm long, leaves in total 4–16 cm long, 2–5 cm wide near the apex. Inflorescences axillary, usually 2 or 3, to 27 cm long, bearing 2–5 flowers spaced 2–3 cm apart. Flowers white, often strongly tinged with pink especially towards the tips; dorsal sepal erect or arching over the column, 25–50 mm long, 7–9 mm wide; lateral sepals reflexed, oblique, 35–65 mm long, 5–7 mm wide; petals at least 10 mm shorter than lateral sepals, 25–45 mm long, 4.5–6 mm wide; lip deflexed, elliptic, strongly constricted in the lower half to a long narrow acumen, 30–45 mm long, 7–10 mm wide; spur pendent, straight, usually pink, 13–23 cm long.

Epiphyte on trunks and small branches in riverine forest or evergreen forest usually near a river; 650–1750 m; flowering December to February.

Malawi.

Aerangis gracillima (Kraenzlin) J. C. Arends & J. Stewart

Syn. *Barombia gracillima* (Kraenzlin) Schlechter

Plant with a short woody stem 3–8 cm long. Leaves 6–14, narrowly obovate, dark green, leathery, unequally and acutely or obtusely lobed at the apex, 11–24 cm long, 2.5–6 cm wide. Inflorescence pendent, up to 80 cm long, 7- to 12-flowered; pedicels long, S-shaped, upright. Flowers white with rusty red tips to the tepals or entirely pale brown or reddish, sometimes not opening fully; sepals and petals narrow, elliptic or oblanceolate, acute or acuminate, spreading or partly reflexed; dorsal sepal 35–50 mm long, 4–6 mm wide; lateral sepals narrowly linear-lanceolate, acute, 40–45 mm long, 3–5 mm wide; petals slightly shorter and narrower; lip narrowly linear-lanceolate, acuminate, 35–45 mm long, 4–6 mm wide; spur pendent, straight, slightly inflated at the apex, 18–25 cm long.

Epiphyte on trunks in shady forests with high annual rainfall and in old cocoa plantations; 470–800 m; flowering August to October.

Cameroon and Gabon.

This species is very distinctive, both by the way the flowers are held, their coloration, and by its greatly elongated slender column that is often as long as the tepals (30–40 mm).

Aerangis kotschyana (Reichenbach f.) Schlechter

Plant with a woody stem, usually short, bearing a fan of leaves in the upper part. Leaves 3–20, obovate-oblong, unequally bilobed at the apex, the shorter lobe often absent, 6–20 cm long, 2–8 cm wide. Inflorescences axillary racemes, one or several, usually arching or pendent, 10- to 20-flowered. Flowers white, sometimes tinged with pink or green when young, up to 5 cm in diameter, conspicuous; dorsal sepal erect, or arching forward over the column, elliptic-lanceolate, apiculate; lat-

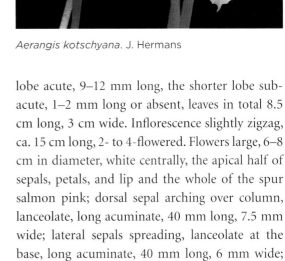

Aerangis kotschyana in habitat, Tanzania. P. J. Cribb

Aerangis kotschyana. J. Hermans

eral sepals spreading, lanceolate, apiculate; petals strongly reflexed, oblanceolate, apiculate; lip deflexed, subpandurate, apiculate, the margins often reflexed in the lower half, 2 prominent crests on the upper surface in front of the spur opening; spur curved and twisted in the lower third, 13–25 cm long.

Epiphyte in light shade, high in the tree canopy but usually on the larger branches and tree trunks, also in old bushes and smaller trees; sea level to 1500 m; flowering June to July and December to January.

Guinea eastwards to Kenya and south to Angola and Mozambique.

Hybrids with *A. verdickii* have been reported.

Aerangis maireae I. F. la Croix & J. Stewart

Plant with a short woody stem, branching at the base. Leaves ca. 5, arranged in a fan in 1 plane, obovate, unequally bilobed at the apex, the longer lobe acute, 9–12 mm long, the shorter lobe subacute, 1–2 mm long or absent, leaves in total 8.5 cm long, 3 cm wide. Inflorescence slightly zigzag, ca. 15 cm long, 2- to 4-flowered. Flowers large, 6–8 cm in diameter, white centrally, the apical half of sepals, petals, and lip and the whole of the spur salmon pink; dorsal sepal arching over column, lanceolate, long acuminate, 40 mm long, 7.5 mm wide; lateral sepals spreading, lanceolate at the base, long acuminate, 40 mm long, 6 mm wide; petals reflexed, lanceolate and acuminate, 30 mm long, 7 mm wide; lip ovate or almost orbicular at the base, then long acuminate, in total 35 mm long, 9 mm wide; spur slender, curved, forming 1 loose coil, slightly inflated at the apex, 21–22 cm long.

Epiphyte on tree trunk in forest remnant; ca. 2000 m.

Tanzania (near Njombe).

Named in honour of the collector, Maire Spurrier. This species is somewhat similar to others in this group, but can be distinguished from *Aerangis brachycarpa* and *A. distincta* by the loosely coiled, not straight spur, and by its narrower sepals, petals and lip which become abruptly narrowed into a long tapering acumen, not gradually tapering as in *A. splendida*.

Aerangis megaphylla Summerhayes

Plant with a creeping or erect stem up to 10 cm long. Leaves 6 or 7, oblanceolate or broadly lanceolate, unequally bilobed at the apex, the longer lobe acute, 5–10 mm long, the shorter lobe rounded or absent, 15–22 cm long, 3–6 cm wide. Inflorescence pendent, 15–30 cm long, bearing 5–7 widely spaced flowers. Flowers greenish white, sepals, petals and lip all narrow; dorsal sepal narrowly lanceolate, 20–27 mm long, 3–3.5 mm wide; lateral sepals deflexed, 30–35 mm long, 3–3.5 mm wide; petals reflexed, 20–22 mm long, 3–3.5 mm wide; lip lanceolate, acuminate, reflexed from a point near the middle, 25–30 mm long, 5 mm wide; spur slender, slightly inflated in the apical half, 9–10 cm long.

Epiphyte in forest; 300–1000 m; flowering June to September.

Central African Republic, Cameroon, and Equatorial Guinea (Annobón Island).

This species can be confused with *Aerangis stelligera* but has smaller flowers and the spur is never more than 10 cm long.

Aerangis somalensis (Schlechter) Schlechter

Plant with a short, upright stem. Leaves 2–6, oblong-ligulate, leathery, greyish green with a darker reticulate venation, unequally or subequally bilobed at the apex, margins thickened, 2–11 cm long, 13–34 mm wide. Inflorescences one or several, arising below the leaves, 10–20 cm long, bearing 4–17 flowers spaced 1–2 cm apart. Flowers white, sometimes tinged with pink or green, up to 2.5 cm in diameter; dorsal sepal ovate, apiculate, arching forward over the column, 8–10 mm long; lateral sepals oblique or reflexed, 9–14 mm long; petals spreading, oblong apiculate, 8–11 mm long; lip oblong-ligulate, with margins reflexed in the lower half, apiculate, 9–13 mm long; spur straight or slightly curved, 10–15 cm long.

Epiphyte on trees and at the base of branching shrubs in relict patches of woodland, along streams and near rock outcrops on prominent hills; 1000–1500 m; flowering March to April and October to November.

Ethiopia, Kenya, southern Tanzania, Malawi, Zimbabwe, and South Africa (Limpopo).

This species is sometimes confused with *Aerangis verdickii*, but it has smaller plants with greyish-green leaves that have a conspicuous reticulate venation, and the flowers are smaller, lack the distinctive ridges on the lip, and have shorter spurs.

Aerangis splendida J. Stewart & I. F. la Croix

Plant with a woody stem, to 20 cm long but usually shorter. Leaves 3–8 in 2 rows, pendent, dark glossy green, black-dotted, narrowly sheathing at the base, obovate or oblanceolate, unequally

Aerangis splendida. P. J. Cribb

bilobed at the apex, with rounded lobes, the longer lobe to 25 mm long, 12–30 cm long, 5–8 cm wide near the tip. Inflorescences pendent, to 30 cm long, bearing 2–7 flowers spaced 3–5 cm apart. Flowers white, all parts widest at the base and gradually tapering to a long narrow acumen; dorsal sepal erect, lanceolate-ovate, acuminate, 35–50 mm long, 8–12 mm wide; lateral sepals similar, spreading at first but soon reflexed, oblique; petals similar but slightly shorter; lip deflexed, obovate near the base then narrowing to a long, narrow acumen, in total 40–45 mm long, 10–14 mm wide; spur pendent, strongly curved or with a single loose coil in the middle, slightly inflated towards the apex, 20–25 cm long.

Epiphyte in deep shade in evergreen forest, usually near a river, 1000–1500 m; flowering in November and March.

Malawi and Zambia.

Aerangis stelligera Summerhayes

Plant with a woody stem, horizontal or pendent, up to 5 cm long. Leaves 3–5 in 2 rows, oblanceolate or oblong-lanceolate, unequally and acutely bilobed at the apex, the longer lobe 5–10 mm long, dark green, leathery, venation showing up when dry, 7–15 cm long, 1.5–4 cm wide. Inflorescences pendent, 10–25 cm long, bearing 3–6 flowers spaced 2–4 cm apart. Flowers white, star-shaped, all the tepals spreading or slightly reflexed, large; dorsal sepal lanceolate, acuminate, 4–5 cm long, 7 mm wide; lateral sepals similar but slightly longer and narrower; petals narrowly lanceolate, pointed, 3.7–4 cm long, 4–5 mm wide; lip similar to the tepals, narrowly lanceolate and almost caudate-acuminate, up to 4 cm long, 4.5–5 mm wide; spur narrowly cylindric, slightly inflated in the apical third but narrowing towards the tip, 20–24 cm long.

Epiphyte on shrubs and tree trunks in very shady forests; 400–1100 m; flowering June to November.

Central African Republic, Cameroon, and D.R. of Congo.

This species is somewhat similar to *Aerangis brachycarpa* but has larger flowers with longer spur

and column (10–12 mm long), and is also similar to *A. megaphylla* but has larger flowers with a spur almost twice as long.

Aerangis thomsonii (Rolfe) Schlechter

Syn. *Aerangis friesiorum* Schlechter

Plant with an elongated, woody stem 10–100 cm long, often several in close proximity. Leaves 8–20, alternate, 1–3 cm apart, ligulate, bilobed at the apex, margins entire, dark green, 8–28 cm long. Inflorescences borne at the nodes, racemes arching, bearing 4–10 flowers spaced 1.5–3.5 cm apart in 2 rows. Flowers white, erect; dorsal sepal erect, lanceolate-elliptic, cuspidate, curving forward at the apex, 22–33 mm long; lateral sepals strongly reflexed, lanceolate-elliptic, acuminate, winged on the back, 25–32 mm long; petals reflexed, oblique, lanceolate-elliptic, acute, 20–25 mm long; lip reflexed, elliptic-lanceolate, acuminate, margins recurved below, inrolled above, 20–25 mm long; spur pendulous, flexuous, cylindrical but widened and flattened in its terminal half, 10–15 cm long.

Epiphyte in shady places, usually rather low down on trunks and branches in highland forests, often overhanging streams; 1600–3000 m; flowering in March and April also in October and November.

Kenya, northern Tanzania, and eastern Uganda.

Aerangis verdickii (De Wildeman) Schlechter

Plant with a woody stem, to 5 cm long, rarely longer. Leaves 2–6 in 2 rows, sometimes deciduous in dry season, succulent or leathery, greyish or pale green sometimes with a reddish margin, oblong-ligulate, margins undulate, subequally bilobed at the apex, with acute or rounded lobes, 5–20 cm long, 2–5 cm wide. Inflorescences arising below the leaves, 20–60 cm long, bearing 4–16 flowers spaced 1.5–3.5 cm apart and closer towards the apex. Flowers white or tinged pale green; dorsal sepal arching over the column, ovate, apiculate, 11–19 mm long, 4–8 mm wide; lateral sepals spreading or deflexed, oblong-ligulate, apiculate, often falcate, 14–22 mm long, 3–8 mm wide; petals

Aerangis thomsonii. B. Campbell

reflexed, obovate-oblong, apiculate, 12–21 mm long, 3.5–8 mm wide; lip oblong-obovate or pandurate, somewhat constricted in the basal half, bearing 2 or more ridges on the upper surface at the base extending into the mouth of the spur, 11–20 mm long, 5–10 mm wide; spur flexuous, thickened in the apical half, 12–20 cm long.

var. **verdickii**

Leaves grey-green; inflorescence up to 40 cm long; sepals and petals 10–18 mm long.

Epiphyte on high branches of trees in hot dry areas or lithophytic; 100–1800 m; flowering November to January, or April to June.

Aerangis verdickii. J. Hermans

Rwanda, D.R. of Congo, Tanzania, Malawi, Zambia, Zimbabwe, Mozambique, Angola, and South Africa (Limpopo).

Hybrids with *Aerangis kotschyana* have been reported in Malawi.

var. ***rusituensis*** (Fibeck & Dare) I. F. la Croix & P. J. Cribb

Syn. *Aerangis rusituensis* Fibeck & Dare

Leaves pale or dark green; inflorescences 20–60 cm; sepals and petals 18–21 mm long.

Epiphyte in deciduous woodland; 800 m; flowering in July.

Zimbabwe (Rusitu valley).

Group 2. Flowers with a spur 4–9 cm long.

Aerangis appendiculata (De Wildeman) Schlechter

Plant with a woody stem to 5 cm long. Leaves 2–4, obovate, usually bilobed at the apex, the lobes subacute, dark green with conspicuous venation, 8–10 cm long, 2–3.5 cm wide. Inflorescence pendent, 11–22 cm long, bearing 1–10 flowers spaced 15–20 mm apart. Flowers erect, white, tinged with pink in the dorsal sepal and spur; dorsal sepal arching forward over the column, elliptic or obovate, obtuse, 5–8 mm long, 2–3.5 mm wide; lateral sepals similar, reflexed or spreading, slightly narrower than dorsal sepal; petals strongly reflexed, similar to sepals; lip elliptic-oblong, minutely apiculate, 5–8 mm long, 2.8–4.8 mm wide; spur slender, ± straight, 4–6 cm long.

Epiphyte on trunks of trees in evergreen forest, or rarely lithophytic on cliffs; 1000–2000 m; flowering November to January.

Tanzania, Malawi, Mozambique, Zambia, and Zimbabwe.

Aerangis arachnopus (Reichenbach f.) Schlechter

Plant with a woody stem up to 12 cm long. Leaves 5–9 in 2 rows, oblanceolate, obliquely and obtusely bilobed at the apex, 7–20 cm long, 2–5 cm wide in the upper half. Inflorescences slender,

Aerangis appendiculata. J. Hermans

Aerangis arachnopus. J. Hermans

pendent, 30–60 cm long, bearing 5–15 flowers spaced 3–5 cm apart. Flowers white or tinged with pinkish brown; sepals linear-lanceolate, acuminate, 14–18 mm long, 3 mm wide; petals similar but slightly shorter, sharply reflexed; lip narrowly oblong-lanceolate, acuminate, the lateral margins recurved 12–14 mm long, 3–4 mm wide; spur slender, L-shaped with the bend below the middle, 6–7 cm long.

Epiphyte in rain forest; below 1000 m; flowering October to December.

Cameroon, Gabon, Congo, D.R. of Congo, and a doubtful record from Ghana.

Aerangis biloba (Lindley) Schlechter

Plant with a woody, upright stem, to 20 cm long but usually much shorter. Leaves 4–10, alternate in 2 rows, obovate, unequally and acutely or obtusely bilobed at the apex with a shallow sinus between the lobes, dark green, glossy when young, black-

Aerangis biloba. J. Hermans

dotted, venation markedly reticulate, up to 18 cm long, 3–6 cm wide near the apex. Inflorescences axillary, pendent, 10–40 cm long, bearing 8–20 flowers spaced 1.5–2.5 cm apart. Flowers white, often tinted with pink or brown in the pedicel and spur; sepals and petals spreading, narrowly lanceolate, acute, 12–25 mm long, up to 6 mm wide; lip deflexed, oblanceolate, cuspidate, 15–25 mm long, 6–8 mm wide; spur straight or curved, usually 5–6 cm long.

Epiphyte in thickets, forest edges, woodland, and forest as well as in plantation crops and surviving on village trees; sea level to 700 m; flowering March to August.

Senegal eastwards to Cameroon.

Easily recognised by its numerous flowers that are relatively closely spaced on the inflorescence with the apical flower largest and opening first.

Aerangis carnea J. Stewart

Plant with a short woody stem up to 8 cm long. Leaves in 2 rows, dark green and glossy, oblanceolate, sometimes falcate, unequally bilobed at the apex, the lobes triangular-acute, 3–20 mm long, up to 15 cm long, 3 cm wide near the apex. Inflorescences spreading or pendent, axillary, bearing 2–7 flowers spaced 1.2–3 cm apart. Flowers pale pink with a darker spur; dorsal sepal erect or arching forward over the column, narrowly ovate, long acuminate, 33–35 mm long, 5–6 mm wide; lateral sepals reflexed or spreading, oblong-ovate below, acuminate, 35–42 mm long, 3–5 mm wide; petals reflexed, obovate, acuminate, 23–28 mm long, 3.5–4 mm wide; lip obovate, long acuminate, 27–30 mm long, 5–7 mm wide; spur slightly incurved, swollen in the apical half but narrowing towards the tip, 5.5–6.5 cm long.

Epiphyte of trunks and branches in shady forests, often near rivers; 1280–1830 m; flowering November to February.

Tanzania and Malawi.

Aerangis collum-cygni Summerhayes

Plant with a woody stem up to 10 cm long. Leaves 4–7 in 2 rows, oblanceolate, oblique, or

Aerangis carnea. J. Stewart

falcate, unequally bilobed at the apex, the longer lobe obtuse or subacute and up to 20 mm long, the shorter 2 mm long or absent, fleshy, dark green, glossy, black-dotted, 6–17 cm long, 1.5–5.5 cm wide. Inflorescences axillary or arising below the leaves, erect, horizontal or pendent, bearing 4–16 flowers spaced 1.6–3 cm apart, up to 35 cm long. Flowers pale green at first, fading to white after a few days and developing pink or pale brownish tints in the spur and tips of the tepals; dorsal sepal erect, lanceolate, acute or acuminate, 13–15 mm long, 3.5–5 mm wide; lateral sepals obliquely curved and reflexed, narrowly lanceolate, acuminate, 13.5–17 mm long, 2.5–4 mm wide; petals reflexed, lanceolate, acuminate or cuspidate, 9–15 mm long, 2.5–4 mm wide; lip deflexed, lanceolate but with the lateral margins strongly recurved, 10–14.5 mm long, 3.5–6 mm wide; spur pendent, straight or slightly incurved, gradually narrowed towards the apex, 6–7.5 cm long.

Epiphyte in moist woodlands, rain forest, and neglected plantations in areas that were formerly forested; 800–1200 m; flowering March to October.

Central African Republic, Cameroon, D.R. of Congo, Uganda, Tanzania, and Zambia.

This species is rather variable in the size of its flowers but they are larger than those of *Aerangis jacksonii* and slightly smaller than those of *A. arachnopus.*

Aerangis confusa J. Stewart

Plant with a woody stem, upright or curved with the tip upright, up to 10 cm long. Leaves 3–12, obovate or oblanceolate, widest near the unequally bilobed apex, dark green with minute black dots, 5–24 cm long, 1.5–5.5 cm wide. Inflorescences axillary, spreading or pendent, bearing 4–10 flowers spaced 1–3 cm apart in 2 rows. Flowers erect or curving forwards, pinkish or greenish white; dorsal sepal arching forward over the column, lanceolate-elliptic, 15–25 mm long; lateral sepals reflexed near the base, the tips curving forwards, lanceolate, 18–26 mm long; petals strongly reflexed, lanceolate and acuminate, 15–22 mm long; lip elliptic or lanceolate, margins recurved, 15–23 mm long; spur narrow, 4–6 cm long.

Epiphyte in shady places, usually rather low down on the trunks of small trees and bushes, usually in warmer and drier localities than *Aerangis brachycarpa* which it closely resembles when not in flower; 1600–2100 m; flowering usually April to June and October.

Kenya and northern Tanzania.

Hybrids with *A. brachycarpa*, with intermediate characters, have been reported.

Aerangis gravenreuthii (Kraenzlin) Schlechter

Plant with a woody stem up to 7 cm long. Leaves 5–10 in 2 rows, oblanceolate, unequally and acutely bilobed at the apex, 3–18 mm long, dark green with darker reticulate venation, 15 cm long, 1.5–3 cm wide. Inflorescences axillary, pendent, 10–20 cm long, bearing 2–5 flowers spaced 1–2 cm apart. Flowers erect, white, sometimes with orange-pink

Aerangis confusa. B. Campbell

flush and pink spur; dorsal sepal erect or arching forward over the column, narrowly ovate below, long acuminate, 20–32 mm long, 5–7 mm wide; lateral sepals spreading or reflexed, oblong-ovate below, acuminate, 20–35 mm long, 5–5.5 mm wide; petals reflexed, obovate below, acuminate, 15–25 mm long, 4 mm wide; lip oblong-ovate below, long acuminate, 17–25 mm long, 5 mm wide; spur curving forwards, somewhat inflated in the apical half but narrow at the apex, 4–8 cm long.

Epiphyte in very shady forests; 1500–2200 m; flowering May to October.

Equatorial Guinea (Bioco Island), Cameroon, and Tanzania.

The flowers are similar to those of *Aerangis kirkii*, which is found at low altitudes near the coast in eastern Africa, but the leaves are quite different.

Aerangis jacksonii J. Stewart

Plant with a woody stem up to 20 cm long, 10 mm in diameter. Leaves 8–15, 6 mm apart, ligulate,

Aerangis jacksonii. J. Stewart

Epiphyte in rain forest; 1200–1600 m; flowering March, May and October.

Uganda.

Plants of this species are somewhat similar to those of *Aerangis ugandensis* but the flowers are larger. The habit of producing inflorescences successively from the same flowering node has not been described in any other species of *Aerangis*.

Aerangis kirkii (Reichenbach f.) Schlechter

Plant with a woody stem, covered in closely overlapping leaf bases, up to 6 cm long. Leaves 2–7, borne very close together, oblanceolate or linear-lanceolate, the apex widely dilated, bilobed and usually curled downwards, dark green or greyish green with ridged venation, up to 15 cm long, 3 cm wide, but usually much smaller. Inflorescences one to several, arising below the leaves, bearing 2–6 flowers all facing one way. Flowers white, flat, up to 4 cm in diameter, the apical one largest and opening first; dorsal sepal erect, ovate-lanceolate, acuminate, 18–25 mm long; lateral sepals longer and narrower, spreading, 22–28 mm long; petals spreading, smaller than the sepals, 16–20 mm long; lip oblong in the lower half, acuminate or apiculate, 16–20 mm long; spur often curving forward, inflated in the lower half, 6–7.5 cm long.

linear-lanceolate or oblanceolate, often falcate, dark green, black-dotted, unequally and obtusely or subacutely bilobed at the top, the longer lobe up to 10 mm long, the shorter one often absent, up to 15 cm long, 1–2.3 cm wide. Inflorescences arising opposite a leaf, in the same place for several successive years, horizontal or arching, up to 17 cm long, bearing 4–8 flowers spaced 8–18 mm apart. Flowers white with a greenish or orange-pink suffusion; dorsal sepal erect, narrowly elliptic, acute, 10–12 mm long, 5 mm wide; lateral sepals reflexed, narrowly elliptic, 12–15 mm long, 4 mm wide; petals reflexed, narrowly elliptic, acute, 11–13 mm long, 4 mm wide; lip narrowly obovate, lateral margins recurved, apiculate, 13–15 mm long, 5 mm wide; spur deflexed or curving forwards slightly, somewhat thickened in the lower half but tapering towards the minutely bicuspidate tip, 4–5.5 cm long.

Aerangis kirkii in habitat, Tanzania. P. J. Cribb

Aerangis kirkii. B. Campbell

Aerangis montana. E. la Croix

Epiphyte in coastal bush and in riverine forest at low altitudes inland, on small trees, lianes and bushes, usually in rather dense shade; sea level to 450 m; flowering between April and June.

Kenya, Tanzania, and Mozambique.

The flowers are rather similar to those of *Aerangis gravenreuthii*, which occurs at much higher altitudes, but the leaves are quite different.

Aerangis montana J. Stewart

Plant with a woody stem up to 6 cm long, 8 mm in diameter. Leaves 2–6 in 2 rows, spreading, ligulate or oblanceolate-ligulate, lightly curved, unequally bilobed at the apex, the lobes rounded, 3–10 mm long, the shorter lobe sometimes almost absent, fleshy, dark green, 10–18 cm long, 2–2.5 cm wide. Inflorescence arising below the leaves, spreading or pendent, to 20 cm long, bearing 4–10 flowers spaced 1–3 cm apart, each on a short projection of the rachis at a point 3–5 mm above the

bract. Flowers pale green at first becoming white but the spur, pedicel and base of the tepals salmon pink; dorsal sepal erect, narrowly ovate, apiculate, 13–16 mm long, 5–7 mm wide; lateral sepals spreading, narrowly ovate, acute or apiculate, 11–15 mm long, 4–6 mm wide; petals spreading, narrowly ovate, subacute or obtuse, 11–16 mm long, 4–6 mm wide; lip similar to the tepals 11–18 mm long, 5.5–7.5 mm wide; spur projecting forwards, slightly wider in the distal half, 5–6 cm long.

Epiphyte in evergreen forest on mountains, usually growing with its roots amongst mosses and lichens in deep shade, sometimes in large, tangled masses; 1500–2400 m; flowering March to April and September to December.

Tanzania, Malawi, and Zambia.

Aerangis mystacidii (Reichenbach f.) Schlechter

Plant with a woody stem up to 4 cm long, 5 mm in diameter. Leaves 4–8 in 2 rows, oblanceolate,

Aerangis mystacidii. B. Campbell

oblong-spathulate, or shortly obovate, somewhat oblique, equally or strongly unequally bilobed at the apex, the lobes acute, obtuse, or rounded, somewhat leathery or fleshy, 4–15 cm long, 1.5–2.5 cm wide. Inflorescences arising below the leaves, horizontal or pendent, 11–30 cm long, 4- to 15-flowered, sometimes up to 24-flowered. Flowers erect or horizontal, white with a pinkish or light brown spur; dorsal sepal erect or arching forward over the column, oblong, apiculate or acute, 7–13 mm long, 2–4 mm wide; lateral sepals oblique, deflexed on either side of the lip, elliptic-oblong, apiculate, 8–14 mm long, 2.5–4 mm wide; petals nearly always strongly reflexed, oblong, subacute, 6–13 mm long, 2–4.5 mm wide; lip deflexed, oblong or ovate-oblong, obtuse or apiculate, 7–12 mm long, 3–4.5 mm wide; spur curving forwards, often somewhat enlarged in the distal half, 6–8 cm long.

Epiphyte at low levels in forest and rarely lithophytic, in deep shade along forested streams and in ravines and gorges; sea level to 1800 m; flowering March to May.

Aerangis mystacidii. J. Hermans

Aerangis calantha. J. Stewart

Tanzania, Malawi, Mozambique, Zambia, Zimbabwe, Swaziland, and South Africa.

Group 3. Small plants; flowers with a narrow lip and spur less than 4 cm long.

Aerangis calantha (Schlechter) Schlechter

Plant with a very short woody stem up to 3 cm long. Leaves 2–6, alternate, usually in 2 rows, overlapping on the stem, linear, often falcate, dark green with few black dots, unequally and shortly bilobed at the apex, 3–9 cm long, 4–8 mm wide. Inflorescence arising below the leaves or axillary, spreading or pendent, up to 12 cm long, bearing 2–10 flowers spaced 1–1.5 cm apart. Flowers white, often with pink spur; dorsal sepal erect, oblong-lanceolate, subacute, 7–12 mm long, 2–3.5 mm wide; lateral sepals similar, slightly longer and narrower, projecting forwards; petals spreading or slightly reflexed, linear-oblong, subacute, 7–10 mm long, 2–2.5 mm wide; lip oblong-lanceolate, apiculate, 7–10 mm long, 2–3.5 mm wide; spur slender, gradually tapering to the pointed tip which is often curved or hooked forwards in the lower 5–10 mm, 2.5–4 cm long.

Epiphyte in deep shade, usually on small twigs and branches, at low levels and in the canopy; found in primary forest and on plantation trees such as coffee, cocoa, and citrus where these have replaced forest; 100–1650 m; flowering times vary.

Côte d'Ivoire, Ghana, Central African Republic, Cameroon, Equatorial Guinea, D.R. of Congo, Uganda, Tanzania, and Angola.

This species has linear leaves rather like those of *Aerangis luteoalba* which grows in some of the same habitats, but it can always be recognised when in flower by the characteristic hooked tip of the spur.

Aerangis flexuosa (Ridley) Schlechter

Plant with an erect, woody stem 1–3.5 cm long. Leaves 3–5, oblanceolate, unequally bilobed at the apex, one lobe acute, 5–6 mm long, the other rounded or absent, 5–15 cm long, 1.5–3 cm wide. Inflorescences axillary or arising below the leaves, slender, horizontal or pendent, to 26 cm long, bearing 10–18 flowers spaced 8–20 mm apart. Flowers white, spreading; sepals and petals lanceolate, 10–13 mm long, 2.5–3 mm wide; lip lanceolate, acute and almost apiculate, 10–11 mm long, 2–3 mm wide; spur wide and funnel-shaped at the mouth but soon tapering to the slender tip, 19–25 mm long.

Epiphyte in evergreen forest; sea level to 700 m; flowering in December.

São Tomé.

The wide mouth of the spur and relatively long slender column (5–8 mm long) clearly distinguish this from all the other species with small flowers.

Aerangis oligantha Schlechter

Plant with an erect, woody stem up to 6 cm long. Leaves 4–8, alternate, spreading or erect, oblanceolate or narrowly spathulate, acutely bilobed at the apex, lobes 4–15 mm long, sometimes one lobe much shorter or absent, thin and leathery, dark green, to 8 cm long, 2 cm wide near the apex. Inflorescences axillary or arising below the leaves, sometimes arising from the site of previous inflorescences, usually erect, 1.5–4 cm long, bearing few to 12 flowers spaced very close together. Flowers pale green at first, becoming white, 15–18 mm in diameter; dorsal sepal lanceolate-oblong, 6–9 mm long, 3 mm wide; lateral sepals slightly falcate, 6–10 mm long, 2 mm wide; petals lanceolate-elliptic, 6–9 mm long, 3–3.5 mm wide; lip ovate, apiculate, 6–8.5 mm long, 4 mm wide; spur parallel to the ovary, slightly swollen in the apical half, 8–13 mm long.

Epiphyte on low bushes and small trees, always amongst mosses and lichens; 1800–2100 m; flowering October to December, also April to May.

Tanzania.

Aerangis oligantha. E. la Croix

This species is somewhat similar in its small, crowded flowers to *Aerangis hyaloides* from Madagascar but the flowers are always larger than in that species.

Aerangis ugandensis Summerhayes

Plant with a pendent or erect, woody stem up to 20 cm long but usually much shorter except on old plants. Leaves 4–12 in 2 rows, oblanceolate, often falcate, unequally bilobed at the apex, dark green with black dots, 5–15 cm long, 1–2 cm wide. Inflorescences 1–5, arising from the axils of the lower leaves, always pendent, 7- to 12-flowered. Flowers white or greenish, 5–12 mm apart, up to 2 cm in diameter; dorsal sepal erect, oblong-lanceolate, apiculate, 6–12 mm long; lateral sepals similar but often slightly reflexed; petals reflexed, oblong-lanceolate, acute, 6–10 mm long; lip oblong, cuspidate, 6–10 mm long; spur straight and narrow, 1–2.5 cm long.

Aerangis ugandensis. B. Campbell

Aerangis ugandensis. J. Hermans

Epiphyte in moist forests, usually in dense shade, rather low down on large tree trunks and often with the roots in a deep growth of moss; 1500–2200 m; flowering between May and July.

D.R. of Congo, Uganda, and Kenya.

Group 4. Small plants, flowers with obovate or suborbicular lip, widest towards the apex

Aerangis alcicornis (Reichenbach f.) Garay

Plant with a woody stem up to 3 cm long. Leaves 2–8, linear-oblanceolate to elliptic-oblanceolate, unequally or subequally bilobed up to 18 mm long at the apex, dark green or greyish green with much darker and distinct venation, 3.5–12 cm long, 1–2.5 cm wide. Inflorescences arising below the leaves, horizontal or somewhat pendent, 10–30 cm long, bearing 3–15 flowers spaced 8–17 mm apart and closer towards the apex. Flowers white with pink in the spur and pedicel; dorsal sepal erect, oblong-elliptic, apiculate, 10–18 mm long, 4–7 mm wide; lateral sepals similar, 10–18 mm long, 5–6 mm wide; petals elliptic, narrowed towards the base, 9–15 mm long, 5–8 mm wide; lip cuneate at the base, suborbicular or fan-shaped, sometimes apiculate, 10–20 mm long, 10–15 mm wide near the apex; spur filiform, incurved and slightly inflated towards tip, 2.5–4 cm long.

Epiphyte in thickets and montane forest, on trees, shrubs and lianes; 200–1000(–1900) m; flowering July to October.

Tanzania, Malawi, Mozambique, and at higher altitudes in Rwanda.

Aerangis hologlottis (Schlechter) Schlechter

Plant with a short woody stem up to 5 cm long in old specimens. Leaves 2–6, spaced close together, linear or narrowly oblong-ligulate, often falcate, unequally bilobed at the apex, dark green, 5–9 cm long, 7–18 mm wide. Inflorescences one to several racemes, arising below the leaves, erect, spreading or pendent, bearing 6–15 flowers spaced 5–8 mm apart. Flowers white, small, up to 10 mm in diameter; dorsal sepal narrowly elliptic, apiculate, 6–7 mm long; lateral sepals similar but narrower; petals narrowly obovate-elliptic, apiculate, 5–6 mm long, broader than sepals; lip obovate, apiculate, 5–6 mm long, 3 mm wide; spur straight, slender, 3.5–7 mm long.

Epiphyte on twigs and small branches of trees in coastal forest; 250–500 m; flowering variable, usually January or June.

Kenya, Tanzania, and Mozambique, and from the Royal Botanic Gardens, Peradeniya, Sri Lanka, where it is apparently indigenous.

Aerangis luteoalba (Kraenzlin) Schlechter

Plant with a short, inconspicuous stem 1–3 cm long except in very old plants. Leaves 2–8, usually lying in one plane, linear, ligulate or linear-lanceolate, sometimes falcate, unequally bilobed at the apex, dark green, up to 15 cm long, 6–15 mm wide. Inflorescences arising from the stem below the leaves, arching or pendent racemes, bearing 5–25 flowers in 2 rows in the upper part and all in the same plane. Flowers white or cream, 2–4 cm in diameter; sepals oblanceolate, acute, 10–15 mm long; petals obovate, equalling or a little longer than the sepals; lip obovate or rhomboid, widest above the middle, acute, 15–20 mm long, 7–15 mm wide; spur slender, incurved, 2.3–4 cm long.

var. *luteoalba*

Flowers creamy yellow throughout including the column.

Epiphyte in forest, on small twigs and branches of bushes and trees; 800–2200 m; flowering June to January.

D.R. of Congo and western Uganda.

var. *rhodosticta* (Kraenzlin) J. Stewart

Syn. *Aerangis rhodosticta* (Kraenzlin) Schlechter

Flowers cream or white with a bright red column.

Epiphyte on small twigs and branches of bushes and trees, rarely on trunks, often near rivers; 1250–2200 m; usually flowering in May or September.

Cameroon to Ethiopia and Kenya and southwards as far as south-west Tanzania and Angola.

Aerangis hologlottis. B. Campbell

*Aerangis
luteoalba* var.
rhodosticta.
J. Stewart

Species from Madagascar and Comoro Islands

Many of these species were introduced into cultivation in the nineteenth century and at that time, and later, names were misapplied to several well known species. In sorting out the taxonomy and nomenclature of these popular plants we have had a few surprises. In the account that follows, the names are used in the same way as in another recent publication (Hermans et al., 2006), and we have included here some of the most well known synonyms which have been and still are being used in horticulture.

All the species occur in Madagascar, 6 have also been found in the Comoro Islands and one, *Aerangis punctata*, has been discovered recently in Réunion. We have presented them here in 5 groups to facilitate identification:

Group 1. Plants medium-sized or large, flowers many, white or tinged pale pink, with a long spur at the base of the lip, open and star-shaped with broad tepals and lip.

Group 2. Plants sometimes rather large, some with greyish-green, succulent leaves; flowers with sepals and petals, and sometimes the lip, strongly reflexed so that the flowers appear flattened; lip with a long spur.

Group 3. Plants rather small, leaves dark green, inflorescences with many small white or whitish flowers.

Group 4. Plants rather small, with 2–6 small leaves and few large white, yellow and white, or pink-tinged flowers with a broad mouth to the spur. Three of the species are noteworthy for the long rostellum which extends downwards across the face of the stigma.

Group 5. Plants rather small, with many small pale green or yellowish green flowers.

Group 1. Plants medium-sized or large; flowers many, white or tinged pale pink with a long spur at the base of the lip. The flowers are open and star-shaped with broad tepals and lip.

Aerangis articulata (Reichenbach f.) Schlechter

Syns. *Angraecum descendens* Reichenbach f., *Aerangis calligera* (Reichenbach f.) Garay

Plant with a stout, woody stem, arching upright, bearing leaves only at the apex when long, up to 30 cm long, 10 mm in diameter. Leaves 2–11 in 2 rows, oblong, elliptic, or ligulate, unequally bilobed at the apex, the longer lobe rounded or truncate to 8 mm long, the shorter lobe often absent, dark glossy green becoming dull, paler below, smooth, margins entire, 15–23 cm long, 3–5 cm wide. Inflorescence arising below the leaves in the axils of old leaf sheaths, or axillary, up to 20 (rarely 60) cm long, bearing 2–24 flowers spaced 2–3 cm apart on short flower-bearing projections just above each bract. Flowers white, star-shaped, variable in size, the apical flower usually larger than others and opening first; dorsal sepal erect, or slightly reflexed at the apex, lanceolate, winged or keeled along the mid-line of the outer surface, acute or shortly acuminate, 1.5–3 cm long, 6–9 mm wide; lateral sepals spreading, oblique, winged on the outer surface, similar to the dorsal sepal but slightly narrower; petals similar to sepals but slightly shorter and wider; lip oblong-lanceolate, acute or shortly acuminate, 1.5–3 cm long, 6–9 mm wide; spur straight, slender, 10–15(–20) cm long on apical flowers, 8–12 cm long on lower ones.

Epiphyte on trunks and major branches of forest trees in very shady situations; sea level to 2000 m; flowering September to February.

Madagascar (eastern and northern regions) and Comoro Islands (Anjouan).

This species is easily recognised by its large, star-like (not reflexed) flowers with a short beak on the anther cap. It is sometimes confused with *Aerangis modesta* but has fewer, larger flowers with a longer spur. Perrier (1941, p. 109) misidentified this species as *A. stylosa*.

Aerangis articulata, central Madagascar. J. Hermans

Aerangis articulata. J. Hermans

Aerangis modesta. J. Hermans

Aerangis modesta (Hooker f.) Schlechter

Syn. *Aerangis crassipes* Schlechter

Plant with an arching or pendent, woody stem, to 20 cm long but usually shorter, 8 mm in diameter. Leaves 2–9 in 2 rows, oblong-elliptic, unequally bilobed at the apex, the longer lobe rounded or truncate to 6 mm long, the shorter lobe often absent, smooth, somewhat fleshy, light or dark green, to 14 cm long, 2–4 cm wide. Inflorescences axillary, to 30 cm long, bearing 7–24 flowers spaced 8–15 mm apart each on a short projection of the rachis above a bract, the apical ones usually larger than the others and opening first. Flowers white, tinged with pink or green, variable in size; sepals spreading, narrowly ovate or lanceolate, 16–22 mm long, 3–4 mm wide; petals ovate-elliptic, wider than sepals, 16–22 mm long, 6–8 mm wide; lip oblong, acute or almost apiculate, 20–24 mm long, 8–10 mm wide; spur dependent, usually incurved, 4–8(–10) cm long.

Epiphyte on the trunks and small branches of forest trees in very humid situations; 100–1500 m; flowering November to January.

Madagascar (northern and eastern regions) and Comoro Islands (Grande Comore and Anjouan).

This species is easily recognised by the long racemes of attractive, regular flowers. It appears to be similar to *Aerangis articulata* but usually has many more flowers that are rather smaller than that species with a shorter spur. Both species have a hairy column (sometimes) and a beaked anther cap.

Group 2. Plants sometimes rather large, some of them with greyish-green, succulent leaves. Flowers with sepals and petals, and sometimes the lip, strongly reflexed so that the flowers appear flattened; lip with a long spur.

Aerangis cryptodon (Reichenbach f.) Schlechter

Syns. *Rhaphidorhynchus stylosus* Finet, *Aerangis malmquistiana* Schlechter

Plant with a woody stem, often rather short or up to 8 cm long. Leaves 2–5 in 2 rows, elliptic or obovate, cuneate, unequally bilobed at the apex, the longer lobe 2–5 mm long, the shorter lobe frequently absent, fleshy, dark green, up to 15 cm long, 4.5 cm wide, usually narrower. Inflorescence slender, arching or pendent, bearing 8–20 flowers spaced 1.5–3 cm apart in 2 rows. Flowers with white petals and lip, brownish pink sepals and spur; dorsal sepal erect or parallel with the column, ligulate or lanceolate, acute, 15–18 mm long, 5–6 mm wide; lateral sepals strongly reflexed, somewhat oblique, lanceolate, acute, 15–19 mm long, 5–6 mm wide; petals reflexed, lanceolate, acute or acuminate, 13–15 mm long, 4–5 mm wide; lip deflexed in front of the spur, obovate, but narrowing above the base and with a prominent acuminate tip, bearing 2 short backwardly-pointing teeth at the point where it joins the spur, 12–16 mm long, 5–9 mm wide; spur wide at the mouth, rapidly narrowing to a slender central portion, enlarged and somewhat flattened in the apical half, 10–14 cm long.

Epiphyte in warm rain forest, some specimens recorded as lithophytic; 200–1800 m; flowering April to August.

Madagascar (eastern highlands).

This species has been confused in horticulture, in herbaria, and in the literature with the small-leaved forms of *Aerangis ellisii*, but is easily recognised by its smaller flowers that have 2 small, backward-pointing teeth on either side of the lip at the mouth of the spur, and by the 2 membranous, denticulate wings at the apex of the column (illustrated in Perrier 1941, p. 111, as *A. malmquistiana*).

Aerangis decaryana H. Perrier

Plant with an erect, woody stem up to 15 cm long. Leaves 2–6, narrowly elliptic or ligulate, unequally and shortly bilobed at the apex, margins conspicuously undulate, greyish green or dark

Aerangis decaryana. J. Hermans

green, often tinged with red, 4–10 cm long, 8–20 mm wide. Inflorescences usually several, pendulous, arising below the leaves, 8–30 cm long, bearing 4–20 flowers spaced 12–15 mm apart. Flowers white tinged pink; dorsal sepal erect or arching forward above the column, oblong or ligulate, acute, 9–18 mm long, 3.5–6 mm wide; lateral sepals reflexed, lanceolate, acute, 11–20 mm long, 3–5 mm wide; petals reflexed, ligulate, acute, 9–18 mm long, 3.5–6 mm wide; lip deflexed, narrowly pandurate, margins reflexed, subauriculate at the base, cuspidate or shortly acuminate, 10–22 mm long, 4–7 mm wide; spur parallel with the ovary at first, then pendent, 6–12 cm long.

Epiphyte on *Tamarindus*, spiny *Euphorbia* and other spiny trees in deciduous, dry forest and scrub; sea level to 900 m; flowering December to March.

Madagascar (southern and south-western regions).

This very distinctive species is easily recognised by its narrow succulent leaves with undulate margins, abundance of thick roots, and pinkish-brown, flattened spur. The flowers are rather variable in size, perhaps depending on growing conditions in its rather severe habitat; cultivated specimens seem to give the larger measurements.

Aerangis ellisii (Reichenbach f.) Schlechter

Syns. *Aerangis buyssonii* Godefroy-Lebeuf, *A. caulescens* Schlechter, *A. platyphylla* Schlechter, *A. alata* H. Perrier

Plant with a robust, woody, erect or arching and ascending stem up to 30(–60) cm long, 9–12 mm in diameter. Leaves 4–20 in 2 rows, widely spaced, ligulate, elliptic, oblong or broadly elliptic, thick and fleshy, medium green, sometimes suffused with orange throughout or at the margins, unequally bilobed at the apex, the shorter lobe usually absent, the longer 6–12 mm long, 7–25 cm long, 2–6 cm wide. Inflorescences axillary, robust, erect, horizontal or arching and finally pendent, to 30(–60) cm long, bearing 6–20 flowers on a 4- to 9-mm projection of the rachis and 1.5–2 cm apart. Flowers white, sometimes tinged with green or pinkish brown, large but variable in size; dorsal sepal erect, sometimes arching forward at the apex, broadly oblanceolate, acute, 12–25 mm long, 5–9 mm wide; lateral sepals strongly reflexed, oblique, oblanceolate, acute or cuspidate, often prominently keeled on the outer surface, 15–30 mm long, 5–7(–9) mm wide; petals similar to the lateral sepals but slightly shorter, 12–24 mm long, 6–8(–10) mm wide; lip pendent or deflexed parallel with the spur, oblanceolate or obovate, margins reflexed in the lower half, sometimes with 2 conspicuous ridges on the surface at the base running into the mouth of the spur, 12–22 mm long, 7–11(–14) mm wide; spur straight or slightly curved, 11–27 cm long.

Perrier apparently never saw the type material of *Aerangis ellisii* and used the name *A. cryptodon* for this widespread species which has been grown in France under various synonyms. *Aerangis cryptodon* is quite a different and apparently rare

Aerangis ellisii. J. Hermans

species, illustrated in *Flore de Madagascar* (1941) as *A. malmquistiana* (fig. 53).

var. *ellisii*

Flowers medium-sized, lateral sepals 15–22 mm long; spur 11–18 cm long; column large, partly adnate to the dorsal sepal, sometimes minutely hairy.

Epiphyte in forest and terrestrial amongst rocks, widespread; 300–2000 m; flowering December to May.

Madagascar (eastern and central regions).

This species is easily recognised by its long stems with many straight aerial roots, and long inflorescences of many large flowers. The plants with largest flowers have been recognised as a distinct variety, but some of the specimens seen were from cultivated plants that may have produced larger flowers in lush growing conditions.

var. **grandiflora** J. Stewart

Flowers large, lateral sepals 18–30 mm long; spur 18–27 cm long.

Epiphyte in forest and open scrub, widespread; 300–2000 m.

Madagascar (from the highlands extending eastwards).

It has been suggested that this large-flowered form may reflect the increase in size that can be obtained in cultivated plants.

Aerangis mooreana (Rolfe ex Sander) P. J. Cribb & J. Stewart

Syns. *Aerangis ikopana* Schlechter, *A. anjouanensis* Perrier

Plant with an arching or pendent woody stem, to 6 cm long. Leaves 2–6 in 2 rows, elliptic, oblong, or obovate, unequally bilobed at the apex, the shorter lobe usually absent, light green or greyish green, smooth and glossy, margins entire, 7–12 cm long, 2–3.5 cm wide. Inflorescences axillary or arising below the leaves, 15–30 cm long, bearing 10–22 flowers spaced 15–20 mm apart on a short projection just above the bract. Flowers pale pink or white with a pinkish spur; dorsal sepal arching forward over the column, ovate, obtuse, 6–12 mm long, 3–5 mm wide; lateral sepals reflexed at first then spreading, oblanceolate, 10–15 mm long, 2–4 mm wide; petals strongly reflexed, lanceolate, acute, 6–12 mm long, 2–4 mm wide; lip obovate, obtuse, projecting forward beneath the column, 8–12 mm long, 3–6 mm wide above the middle; spur slender and curved, 7–12 cm long.

Epiphyte on branches in humid forest; sea level to 600 m; flowering July to October.

Madagascar (Sambirano region) and Comoro Islands (Grande Comore and Anjouan).

This species is easily recognised by its pale pink flowers that have a small dorsal sepal and broad, obovate lip. The plants are rather similar to those of *Aerangis modesta* which grows in the same areas in Grande Comore.

Aerangis rostellaris (Reichenbach f.) H. Perrier

Syn. *Aerangis buchlohii* Senghas

Plant with a stout, woody, upright stem 2–10 cm long. Leaves 2–10 in 2 rows, narrowly elliptic, oblong or obovate, unequally bilobed at the apex, with rounded lobes, the shorter lobe often absent, thick and succulent or leathery, greyish green, the margins often distinctly and coarsely undulate, to 15 cm long, 5 cm wide. Inflorescences 1 or several, axillary or arising below the leaves, pendent, 20–35 cm long, bearing 6–15 flowers spaced 1.3–2 cm apart. Flowers white; dorsal sepal erect, incurved in the upper half, lanceolate or narrowly ovate, acuminate, 15–20 mm long, 3–6 mm wide; lateral sepals similar, strongly reflexed at first, the apical part incurved, to 19 mm long, 4 mm wide; petals narrowly oblanceolate, cuspidate, reflexed, the tips recurved, 14–18 mm long, 3–5 mm wide; lip deflexed, narrowly pandurate, cuspidate or acuminate, apex recurved, margins somewhat revolute, 16–18 mm long, 5–6 mm wide; spur parallel with

Aerangis mooreana, white form from Madagascar. J. Hermans

the lip at first, then dependent, slender or somewhat enlarged towards the tip, 9–11 cm long.

Epiphyte in humid evergreen forest.

Madagascar (Mount Ambre) and Comoro Islands (Grande Comore).

This species is easily recognised by its thick, broad leaves with undulate margins, by its medium-sized flowers with conspicuously incurved sepals and very short column (3 mm high) with long rostellum. It is smaller than *Aerangis spiculata* in every way.

Aerangis spiculata (Finet) Senghas

Syn. *Leptocentrum spiculatum* (Finet) Schlechter

Plant with a short woody stem up to 10 cm long. Leaves 2–7, elliptic-oblong, cuneate, unequally bilobed at the apex, the longer lobe 2–5 mm long, greyish or dull green, margins sometimes undulate, sometimes reddish, 10–17 cm long, 1.5–5.5 cm wide. Inflorescence stout, erect, arching or pendent, straight, 30–75 cm long, bearing 12–20 flowers, each on a short, peg-like outgrowth of the rachis, in 2 rows and spaced 2–4 cm apart. Flowers large, held with the long column (10–14 mm long) horizontal, white, tinged with pink at the tips of the sepals and in the spur; dorsal sepal erect with the tip curved forwards, narrowly lanceolate, acute, 20–28 mm long, 6 mm wide; lateral sepals oblique strongly reflexed, slightly longer and a little narrower at the base; petals reflexed, oblanceolate, acuminate or apiculate, 20–35 mm long, 6–10 mm wide; lip reflexed parallel with the spur, oblanceolate or ligulate-oblong, almost appearing trilobed at the apex which is abruptly acuminate or apiculate, with 2 parallel ridges on its surface in the mouth of the spur, 18–35 mm long, 10–15 mm wide in the distal third; spur wide at the mouth and bearing minute spicules or teeth on its inner surface, becoming slender, 16–27 cm long.

Epiphyte in moist evergreen forest; sea level to 1000 m; flowering in December.

Madagascar (northern region) and Comoro Islands (Grande Comore).

Aerangis spiculata. J. Hermans

This beautiful species has rarely been in cultivation but it is easily recognised by its large size, and especially the shape and surface of the lip and spur. It is somewhat similar to *Aerangis stylosa* in various ways but the flowers are much larger. In *Flore de Madagascar* (1941, p. 86 and fig. 51) Perrier used the earlier name *Leptocentrum spiculatum* for this species.

Aerangis stylosa (Rolfe) Schlechter

Plant with a short woody stem up to 5 cm long, 10 mm in diameter. Leaves 2–6 in 2 rows, spaced close together near apex of stem, elliptic or oblong-elliptic or obovate, cuneate to the sheathing base, unequally bilobed at the apex, the longer lobe 1–2 mm long, dull bluish green or greyish green, fleshy but thin and with a shiny surface and a red margin, up to 18 cm long, 3–6 cm wide. Inflorescences stout, usually several, arching or pendent, 30–60 cm long, bearing 9–15 flowers in 2 rows, spaced 2.5–4 cm apart, with loose sheaths and bracts. Flowers held with the elongated column (6–9 mm long) pendent or facing downwards, white, sometimes tinged with salmon pink or pale brown, the spur usually pale brown, tepals all reflexed at maturity; dorsal sepal ligulate, shortly acuminate or apiculate, the tip often curving forwards but sometimes reflexed, 18–20 mm long, 6–8 mm wide; lateral sepals oblique, ligulate, apiculate, 20–24 mm long, 6–8 mm wide; lip reflexed parallel to the spur, ligulate, apiculate, 18–22 mm long, 6–8 mm wide; spur slender, gradually tapering towards the tip and curving forwards below the flower, 10–15 cm long.

Epiphyte on trees in moist, evergreen forest, sea level to 1400 m; flowering September to May.

Madagascar (eastern and highland regions) and Comoro Islands (Grande Comore and Anjouan).

This species seems to be rather similar to *Aerangis spiculata* but always less robust and with smaller flowers. The bracts are large and loose and the rachis seems to lack the peg-like outgrowths on which the flowers are inserted in *A. spiculata*. Perrier (1941, p. 114 and fig. 54) described and illustrated this species as *A. fuscata* which is the name of a quite different species.

Group 3. Plants rather small with dark green leaves and many small white or whitish flowers on each inflorescence.

Aerangis citrata (Thouars) Schlechter

Plant with a short woody stem up to 6 cm long, often branched to form small clumps of plants. Leaves 2–8 in 2 rows, thin, dark glossy green, elliptic, oblong, lanceolate, or oblanceolate, unequally bilobed at the apex, the shorter lobe often absent, 4–16 cm long, 1–4 cm wide. Inflorescences axillary or arising below the leaves, up to 30 cm long, sometimes much longer, bearing 15–60 flowers spaced 6–10 mm apart. Flowers white, cream coloured, or almost pale yellow, variable in size; dorsal sepal small, erect or arching forward over the column, ovate, obtuse, 5–7 mm long, 3–4 mm wide; lateral sepals spreading, obliquely obovate or oblanceo-

Aerangis citrata. J. Hermans

late, obtuse, 7–10 mm long, 4–6 mm wide; petals spreading, broadly obovate or almost orbicular, usually larger than lateral sepals, 8–12 mm long, 6–8 mm wide; lip pandurate or orbicular above a narrow base, emarginate or retuse at the apex, 8–12 mm long, 6–10 mm wide; spur characteristically bent, slightly inflated in the upper third, 25–30 mm long.

Epiphyte, usually on small branches and trunks of small trees, often amongst mosses in humid, evergreen forest; sea level to 1500 m; flowering August to May.

Madagascar (eastern forests and central highlands).

This widespread species is easily recognised by its abundance of white or pale yellow flowers in which the dorsal sepal is the smallest of the perianth parts. It is easily recognised when not in flower by the very fine roots.

Aerangis concavipetala. J. Hermans

Aerangis hyaloides. J. Hermans

Aerangis concavipetala H. Perrier

Plant with an erect woody stem to 3 cm long. Leaves 3–4, obovate-oblong, obtuse and somewhat bilobed at the apex, the longer lobe twisted to the side, 8–11 cm long, 2.8–3.5 cm wide. Inflorescences 2, arising below the leaves, 20–30 cm long, bearing 12–15 flowers spaced 1–1.8 cm apart. Flowers white with clear pink venation; dorsal sepal erect, broadly ovate, minutely apiculate, 6–7 mm long, 4–5 mm wide; lateral sepals similar but slightly longer and narrower; petals concave, broadly ovate to suborbicular, cucullate, minutely apiculate, to 5 mm long, 4–5 mm wide; lip concave, ovate, cucullate, apiculate, 6–8 mm long, 5 mm wide; spur straight or slightly curved, slender, 7–9 cm long.

Epiphyte on tree trunks; flowering in June. Madagascar (Sambirano region).

Aerangis hyaloides (Reichenbach f.) Schlechter
Syn. *Aerangis pumilio* Schlechter

Plant with a short woody, erect or curved stem, often branched to form small clumps of plants, to 4 cm long. Leaves 2–8 in 2 rows, oblong, oblanceolate, elliptic, ligulate or spathulate, dark glossy green, unequally bilobed at the apex, the shorter lobe often absent, 2–6 cm long, 7–22 mm wide. Inflorescences one to many, erect, 2–6 cm long, bearing 6–20 small flowers spaced 2–5 mm apart on a stout peduncle, the apical ones opening first. Flowers white, small, hyaline but sparkling; sepals oblong-elliptic, obtuse, up to 7 mm long, 1.5–2 mm wide; petals lanceolate-elliptic, obtuse, to 6 mm long, 2 mm wide; lip elliptic to broadly lanceolate, concave, acute, 6–8 mm long, 2–3 mm wide; spur straight or curved, usually parallel with the ovary, inflated at the apex, 5–12 mm long.

Epiphyte on twigs and branches in moist forests, amongst mosses and leafy liverworts; sea level to 1100 m; flowering September to January.

Madagascar (eastern coastal areas and adjacent highlands).

This species is easily recognised by its many small flowers on short inflorescences.

Aerangis macrocentra (Schlechter) Schlechter

Syn. *Aerangis clavigera* H. Perrier

Plant with a woody, upright or pendent stem to 6 cm long, usually shorter. Leaves 4–6 in 2 rows arranged in a fan, oblong, elliptic or ligulate, unequally bilobed at the apex, the shorter lobe often absent, usually fleshy and succulent but thin, dark green or greyish green, 7–10 cm long, 2–5 cm wide. Inflorescences arising below the leaves, pendent, 8–40 cm long, bearing 12–30 flowers spaced 10–15 mm apart on a short projection of the rachis inserted above the bract. Flowers white tinged with green or pinkish brown and stronger colour in the spur and ovary, small; dorsal sepal reflexed, oblanceolate or oblong, obtuse, 7–8 mm long, up to 3 mm wide; lateral sepals reflexed oblanceolate, slightly longer and narrower than dorsal sepal; petals reflexed, obliquely oblanceolate, similar to lateral sepals; lip projecting forward under the column, then abruptly reflexed parallel with the ovary and spur, narrowly triangular or lanceolate, 8–10 mm long, 3–4 mm wide; spur curved through 90°, narrow in the basal part and much inflated in the apical third, 5–6 cm long.

Epiphyte on trees, widespread in mossy forests often rather near the ground; sea level to 2200 m; flowering March to June.

Madagascar (eastern coastal and highland forests).

Easily recognised by its short, blunt, reflexed flower parts and by the swollen spur. Non-flowering plants are sometimes confused with those of *Aerangis citrata*, but the wider, flattened roots, usually greyish-green leaves, and short projections along the rachis of old inflorescences are characteristic.

Aerangis macrocentra. J. Hermans

Aerangis ×*primulina* (Rolfe) H. Perrier

Known only from a single inflorescence removed from a cultivated plant in 1890 and preserved in the Herbarium at Kew. It was described as a probable natural hybrid between *Aerangis citrata* and *A. hyaloides*. Inflorescence similar to *A. citrata* but the flowers smaller and closer together. Flowers pale yellow with a white lip; dorsal sepal not arching forward as in *A. citrata*; lip intermediate between the putative parents in shape; spur greenish, parallel to the pedicel, 15–20 mm long.

Madagascar.

It would be interesting to try to re-make this hybrid in cultivation.

Aerangis pulchella (Schlechter) Schlechter

Plant with a woody, curved and erect stem up to 10 cm long. Leaves 5 in 2 rows, oblanceolate, unequally bilobed at the apex, the shorter lobe absent, the longer curved to one side, greyish green,

244

12–15 cm long, 2.5–5 cm wide. Inflorescences 3–4, arising below and in the axils of the leaves, bearing 12–20 flowers spaced 1–1.2 cm apart, 25–30 cm long. Flowers white; dorsal sepal ovate-oblong, obtuse or apiculate, 9–10 mm long, 3–4 mm wide; lateral sepals oblanceolate, 8–9 mm long, 3–4 mm wide; petals similar to the dorsal sepal, 8–9 mm long, 3–4 mm wide; lip elliptic, oblong, acute, 8–9 mm long, 4–5.5 mm wide; spur slender 6–7.2 cm long (all measurements from a flower dissected from a bud).

Epiphyte on branches in seasonally dry, deciduous forest and woodland; below 200 m; flowering in June.

Madagascar (Mahajanga area).

This specimen seems rather similar to some of those of *Aerangis mooreana* and may prove to be this species.

Group 4. Plants rather small, with 2–6 small leaves and few large white, yellow and white, or pink-tinged flowers with a broad mouth to the spur. Three of the species are noteworthy for the long rostellum which extends downwards across the face of the stigma.

The rostellum extends into the spur in *Aerangis fastuosa* and right across the mouth of the spur in *A. monantha* and *A. punctata*. In *A. fuscata* the rostellum is short and projects forwards as in many other species of *Aerangis*. (The epithet *curnowiana* has been used for both *A. monantha* and *A. punctata* in literature and in orchid collections in recent years, but this was originally published for an *Angraecum* and has never been validly published for an *Aerangis*.)

Aerangis fastuosa (Reichenbach f.) Schlechter
Plant with an upright, short and woody stem 0.5–6 cm long. Leaves 2–10, thick and succulent or leathery with a finely rugose upper surface, ovate, obovate orbicular or elliptic, up to 8 cm long, 3 cm wide. Inflorescences bearing 1–5 flowers spaced 1 cm apart, very short, up to 5 cm long. Flowers large for the plant, often not opening widely, pure white

Aerangis fastuosa. J. Hermans

throughout; dorsal sepal ovate-elliptic or broadly ligulate, acute, 15–30 mm long, 5–8 mm wide; lateral sepals obliquely lanceolate, 17–34 mm long, 5–7 mm wide; petals similar to dorsal sepal; lip varied, obovate, oblanceolate, or lanceolate, acute, 15–25 mm long, 4.5–11 mm wide; spur slender, sometimes coiled, 6–9 cm long.

Epiphyte on twigs and small branches in humid evergreen and seasonally dry, montane forest; 100–1500 m; flowering September to November.

Madagascar (from south-west coast to the highlands near Antananarivo).

The small plants of this rather variable species are easily recognised by their succulent or leathery leaves, large white flowers with a broad lip and very long rostellum. Several varieties have been described, in the past, and further study of these plants in the field is needed.

Aerangis fuscata (Reichenbach f.) Schlechter

Syn. *Aerangis umbonata* (Finet) Schlechter

Plant small, stemless or with a short woody stem 0.5–6 cm long. Leaves 1–7, oboval or elliptic, cuneate, unequally and bluntly bilobed at the apex, the longer lobe 2–3 mm long, the shorter often absent, smooth, dull greyish green or dark green, thin, 1.5–9 cm long, 1–3 cm wide. Inflorescences arising below the leaves, bearing 1–5 flowers spaced 3 cm apart. Flowers yellow-green or pale pinkish brown, with a white lip, 3–5 cm in diameter; dorsal sepal arching over the column, ligulate-lanceolate, 18–32 mm long, 3–5 mm wide; lateral sepals reflexed, or reflexed at first and then curving forward on either side of the lip, 20–36 mm long, 2.5–4 mm wide; petals reflexed, narrowly lanceolate, acuminate, 17–30 mm long, 3–5 mm wide; lip spreading forwards below the column, ovate-lanceolate, acuminate, 20–40 mm long, 7–12 mm wide; spur wide and funnel-shaped at the base of the lip, slender below, straight, 9–13 cm long.

Epiphyte on twigs and branches; sea level to 1500 m; flowering in October.

Madagascar (eastern and north-eastern regions).

This species has been confused with *Aerangis monantha* in the past, but photographs of well-grown plants in Hillerman and Holst (1986), plate 14, illustrate the differences very well. The short, forward-projecting rostellum is a further distinguishing character. The epithet *fuscata* has been wrongly used for several of the large-flowered species of *Aerangis* in the past.

Aerangis monantha Schlechter

Plant dwarf, almost stemless. Leaves 3–7 but often only 2, oblong-ligulate or elliptic, apex rounded, bilobed, dark, glossy green when young but becoming dull and matte with reddish margins with age, 2.5–6 cm long, 1.5 cm wide. Inflorescence short, 1-flowered, occasionally 2-flowered. Flowers large, 4–5 cm in diameter, with yellowish or pinkish sepals and petals and white lip; sepals ligulate, acute, 2–2.4 cm long, 6 mm wide; petals ligulate, acute, similar in size and shape or the pet-

als only slightly smaller than the sepals; lip obovate or ovate and long acuminate, 2–2.4 cm long, 1 cm wide; spur with a wide mouth, soon becoming narrow, elongated, slender and curved, 13 cm long.

Epiphyte on trees and shrubs; 800–1200 m; flowering in October.

Madagascar (highland and eastern regions).

This species can be recognised easily by its dull green leaves with a red margin that are bright and shiny dark green when young. The flowers are somewhat similar to those of *Aerangis punctata* but the sepals and petals are very similar to each other in shape and size and the spur is curved or coiled. Hillerman and Holst (1986, plate 12) used the incorrect name *A. curnowiana* for this species, and they also referred to it as *Aerangis* sp. no. 165 (1986, plate 14).

Aerangis punctata J. Stewart

Plant very small with short stems 1–2 cm long. Leaves 2–4, elliptic, oblong or oblong elliptic, dull greyish green punctured with minute silvery dots, apex bilobed, the lobes ending sharply on either side of the midrib, 2–3.5 cm long, 6–12 mm wide. Inflorescences arising below the leaves, 1- to 4-flowered; pedicels long. Flowers white flushed pink, sepals and petals sometimes greenish or pale brown at first, large, 2.5–3.5 cm in diameter; sepals narrowly lanceolate, acuminate, 14–20 mm long, 3–4 mm wide; petals similar, ligulate-lanceolate, but smaller, 12–16 mm long, 2–3 mm wide; lip ovate or obovate, acute, widest at the middle or in the upper half, 16–22 mm long, 7–9 mm wide; spur funnel-shaped at the mouth then narrowing abruptly and very slender, sometimes coiled in a complete circle in bud and even after opening though it usually straightens out, 10–13 cm long.

Epiphyte on shrubs and trees in highland forest and scrub; 900–1500 m; flowering December to March.

Madagascar (central highlands) and Réunion (recorded from one locality in highland forest, according to Benke 2004).

This species can be recognised easily by its silvery leaves and verrucose roots. The flowers are

Aerangis fuscata. J. Hermans

Aerangis monantha. J. Hermans

Aerangis punctata. J. Hermans

Aerangis pallidiflora. J. Hermans

somewhat similar to those of *Aerangis monantha* but the petals are always smaller than the sepals, the lip usually wider and the spur is coiled differently. Excellent photographs of plants in cultivation in the United States have been published under the incorrect name *A. curnowiana* (for example, see Fitch 2004, p. 667).

Group 5. Plants rather small; flowers many, small, pale green or yellowish green

Aerangis pallidiflora H. Perrier

Syn. *Angraecum ramulicolum* H. Perrier

Plant with a woody, erect or horizontal stem up to 3 cm long. Leaves 2–6, held horizontally like a fan all in the same plane, elliptic or broadly elliptic, minutely bilobed at the apex, folded and almost petiolate at the base, dark green, 3–7 cm long, 1–2 cm wide. Inflorescences 1–3, pendent, axillary, or arising below the leaves, bearing 7–9 flowers spaced 1–1.5 cm apart in the apical half, to 25 cm long. Flowers star-shaped, pale yellowish green; dorsal sepal erect, narrowly triangular, linguiform, acute, 7–8 mm long, 1–2 mm wide; lateral sepals similar, spreading, slightly oblique and narrower; petals spreading or slightly reflexed, as long as sepals but narrower, 1 mm wide; lip similar to dorsal sepal, lanceolate, acute, 8–9 mm long, 1.5–2 mm wide; spur slender, parallel with the ovary at first and then curved downwards, scarcely inflated in the apical third, narrow below, 2.1–2.3 cm long.

Epiphyte on mossy twigs and branches in evergreen forest; 1000–1500 m; flowering in February.

Madagascar (eastern highlands).

This species has been confused with the following but it has narrower leaves and flowers with a differently shaped spur.

Aerangis seegeri Senghas

Plant very small with a short stem 1–2 cm long. Leaves 2–4, arranged in a small fan in one plane, elliptic, folded and almost petiolate at the base, bilobed at the apex, dark green, 3.5 cm long, 2.5 cm wide. Inflorescences 1–3, axillary or arising below the leaves, pendent, bearing 6–12 flowers spaced 1 cm apart throughout or in the apical half, up to 25 cm long. Flowers star-shaped, 2 cm in diameter, pale green or yellowish green, all the parts reflexed in the upper half; sepals similar to each other narrowly triangular, 8 mm long, 1 mm wide; petals linear, long acuminate, slightly shorter than sepals, 1 mm wide; lip similar to the petals but slightly wider at the base; spur parallel with the ovary at first, then curved downwards, with a characteristic elongated, bulb-like inflation just behind the apex, 18 mm long.

Epiphyte in coastal forest; sea level to 1500 m; flowering April to June.

Madagascar (Île Sainte Marie off the east coast, and in the eastern highlands).

This species was named in honour of the orchid grower in the Botanic Garden of the University of Heidelberg. It seems very similar to *Aerangis pallidiflora* but the leaves are shorter and wider and the spur is shorter and differently shaped. The *Aerangis* sp. (Holst AER-7) described in Hillerman and Holst (1986) p. 138 appears to be this species.

Aerangis seegeri. J. Hermans

CHAPTER FOUR

Other Genera in the Subtribe Aerangidinae

ANCISTRORHYNCHUS Finet

Although Achille Finet proposed the genus *Ancistrorhynchus* in 1907, a few species had been known in cultivation much earlier. The first species was described by John Lindley in 1837 as *Angraecum clandestinum*, a plant cultivated in the nursery of Messrs. Loddiges in north London. The second was also described by Lindley, in 1862, as *Angraecum capitatum*, a plant which had been collected in southern Nigeria. Ten years later H. G. Reichenbach described another living plant, from the famous collection of W. W. Saunders, as *Listrostachys cephalotes*, pointing out its affinity with *Angraecum clandestinum*. For the first time, his description included details of the curious folded rostellum that is actually common to all 3 species. Finet apparently did not realise that these 3 species belonged to his new genus, although his drawings clearly show the rostellum and pollinarium structure, and he described 2 others, *Ancistrorhynchus brevifolius* and *A. recurvus* when he established the genus.

Rudolf Schlechter brought these together in his revision of all the angraecoid orchids in 1918. He also recognised a genus he called *Cephalangraecum*, which was similar in many respects but had congested inflorescences. Finally, V. S. Summerhayes brought these 2 genera together in 1944, when he revised the genus *Ancistrorhynchus* enumerating 12 species. He described additional species in 1954 and 1966, and other botanists have described 3 more since then, bringing the total to 17. The genus is largely tropical in distribution, mostly in western Africa, with one species extending from D.R. of Congo across to Malawi and Tanzania where 4 other species also occur.

The name of this genus is derived from the Greek words *ankistron*, hook, and *rhynchos*, snout or beak, and it alludes to the distinctive rostellum at the apex of the column. The rostellum is very long, with 2 lobes projecting downwards parallel with the column at first, then bent like an elbow in the middle, and folded back like upraised arms in the apical half. The pollinarium is correspondingly long, with one or 2 stipes and a single long, narrow viscidium. Apart from the rostellum and the small, almost capitate inflorescences in many of the species, most flowers in this genus are unremarkable. They are white, variously tinged with green, small, rarely opening fully, and not very long-lasting. Most of the plants have stiff leaves, V-shaped in cross section, and their rounded apical lobes are sometimes toothed.

Culture

Some species are awkward to accommodate, having short, erect stems and long, pendent leaves.

Mystacidium capense. J. Stewart

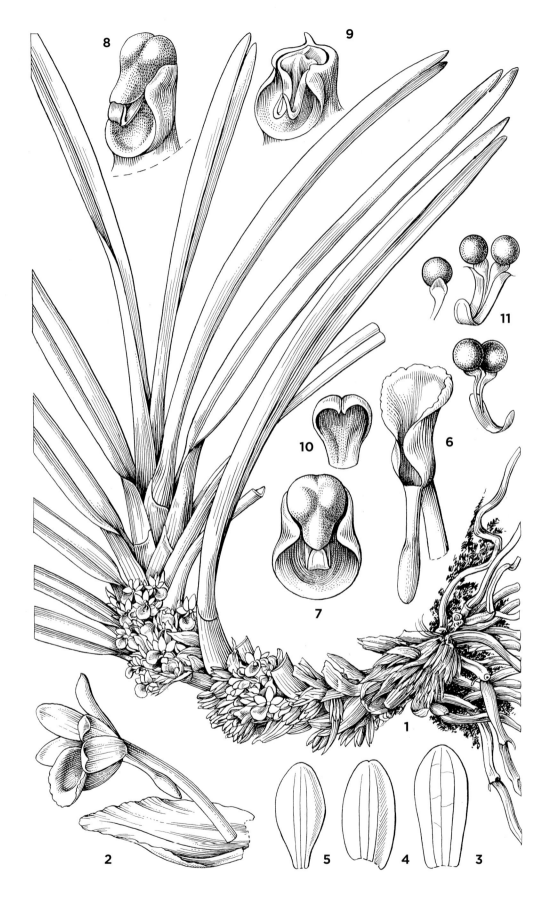

Ancistrorhynchus ovatus. 1: Habit. 2: Flower. 3: Dorsal sepal. 4: Lateral sepal. 5: Petal. 6: Lip. 7–9: Column. 10: Anther-cap. 11: Pollinarium. From Summerhayes 1947a, t. 3461. S. Ross-Craig.

Hanging pots and baskets are probably best. When well established the plants require plenty of water during the growing season and fresh, buoyant air combined with high humidity at all times. A minimum night temperature of 15°C seems to be acceptable to all of them. In the wild they are plants of dark shady forests.

Ancistrorhynchus akeassiae Perez-Vera

Plant erect or pendent with a curved stem 5–25 cm long. Leaves in 2 rows, narrowly lanceolate, rigid, unequally bilobed at the apex, the longer lobe narrow and pointed up to 2 cm long, the shorter lobe absent, 5–13 cm long, 3–12 mm wide. Inflorescences axillary, in short congested racemes 12–14 mm long, bearing 7–10 flowers produced simultaneously along the stem; bracts 1 mm long; pedicel with ovary 3–4 mm long. Flowers white, greenish on the outer surface; sepals oblong, sub-acute, 2–2.5 mm long; petals similar but narrower; lip 3-lobed, lateral lobes erect, rounded, mid-lobe cordate, recurved, margins crenulate, lip in total 5 mm long; spur S-shaped, wide at the base, then constricted, finally inflated in an egg-shaped tip, 3–4 mm long.

Epiphyte in shady, humid forests; 100–500 m; flowering in May.

Côte d'Ivoire and southern Nigeria.

Named in honour of Laurent Aké Assi, who collected the first specimen in 1966 whilst professor of botany at the University of Abidjan. This species was at first confused with *Ancistrorhynchus straussii*, which has differently shaped leaves and smaller flowers.

Ancistrorhynchus brevifolius Finet

Plant erect with a short stem, sometimes branched, up to 4 cm long. Leaves linear, unequally bilobed at the apex, 3.5 cm long, 7–8 mm wide. Inflorescence short, 12–15 mm long; bracts triangular, papery. Flowers small; dorsal sepal ovate; lateral sepals longer, triangular; petals triangular, shorter than dorsal sepal, obtuse, subfalcate; lip concave, funnel-shaped, 3-lobed at the apex, lateral lobes rounded, mid-lobe triangular, margins

thickened and erose; spur straight, apex inflated, perpendicular to the lip and as long as the ovary.

Epiphyte.

Congo.

Ancistrorhynchus capitatus (Lindley) Summerhayes

Plant suberect to pendent, with a short stem 5–25 cm long; roots 1.5–2.5 mm in diameter. Leaves 3–8, linear, unequally bilobed at the apex, each lobe with 2 or 3 sharp teeth, leathery, articulated at the base to a persistent leaf sheath 2–3 cm long, 16–32 cm long, 1.5–2 cm wide. Inflorescences capitate, dense, up to 1.5 cm long, 2.5 cm across, many-flowered; bracts papery, acute, 1 cm long; pedicel with ovary 7–9 mm long, scabrid-papillose. Flowers white with a green mark on the lip, small; sepals elliptic or oblong, obtuse, 3.5–6.5 mm long, 2–3 mm wide; petals oblong, rounded, 3–5.5 mm long, 1.5–2.5 mm wide, erose; lip concave, ovate,

Ancistrorhynchus capitatus. J. Hermans

Ancistrorhynchus capitatus. C. Arends

rounded at the apex, upcurved and undulate on margin, fleshy, 4.5–6 mm long, 3.5–5 mm wide; spur slightly incurved, inflated in the apical third, 7–11 mm long.

Epiphyte in dense evergreen forest; 100–1300 m; flowering May to October.

Sierra Leone eastwards to Uganda.

Ancistrorhynchus cephalotes (Reichenbach f.) Summerhayes

Plant erect or with a curved stem 5–20 cm long. Leaves in 2 rows, linear, slightly unequally bilobed at the apex, with rounded lobes, 7–40 cm long, 8–20 mm wide. Inflorescence axillary, capitate, many-flowered; bracts large, as long as the pedicel and ovary. Flowers white with 2 green patches on the lip; sepals narrowly oblong, obtuse, 4–7 mm long, 2–3 mm wide; petals elliptic, obtuse, 6 mm long, 3 mm wide; lip obscurely 3-lobed, cordate, 4–7 mm long, 4–9 mm wide; spur funnel-shaped at first, then narrowing and finally inflated in the apical third, straight, 6–10 mm long.

Epiphyte in evergreen or semi-deciduous forest, usually on the major branches of tall trees; flowering April to June.

Guinea to Nigeria.

Ancistrorhynchus clandestinus (Lindley) Schlechter

Plant erect or pendent with a stem 5–10 cm long; roots sometimes branching, 2–3 mm in diameter. Leaves 5–10, arranged in a fan, linear, narrow, tapering and acuminate at the bilobed apex, the lobes very unequal, articulated leaf bases 2–2.5 cm long, leaves in total 20–100 cm long, 3–25 mm wide. Inflorescences capitate, bearing many flowers successively, to 2 cm long; bracts elliptic-lanceolate, acute, 2–3 mm long; pedicel with ovary 7–9 mm long. Flowers white, the lip striped with green at the base; dorsal sepal elliptic, obtuse, 2–5.5 mm long, 1–2 mm wide; lateral sepals obliquely elliptic, obtuse, 2.5–4.7 mm long, 1.3–2.6 mm wide; petals obliquely oblong-elliptic, obtuse, 2–4 mm long, 0.6–1.4 mm wide; lip concave, obscurely 3-lobed, side lobes rounded, mid-lobe ovate with undulate margins, 4.5–9 mm long, 2–4 mm wide; spur

Ancistrorhynchus clandestinus. J. Hermans

S-shaped, wide at the mouth and swollen at the apex, 3–6 mm long.

Epiphyte in evergreen forest; 900–1100 m; flowering in March.

Sierra Leone to Uganda.

Ancistrorhynchus constrictus Szlachetko & Olszewski

Plant erect with a short stem up to 6 cm long. Leaves 4, linear-lanceolate, unequally bilobed at the apex, the lobes each with 2 teeth, 16.5 cm long, 1.3 cm wide. Inflorescence capitate, dense, 2 cm long, 10-flowered; bracts oblong or elliptic-oval, papery, 9 mm long; pedicel with ovary 10 mm long. Flowers white, the lip spotted with bright green, small; sepals oblong-oval or elliptic-oval, obtuse, 5 mm long, 2.2–2.4 mm wide; petals obliquely oblong-oval, obtuse, 5 mm long, 2 mm wide; lip concave, oblong-elliptic, rounded, 5.6 mm long, 4.3 mm wide; spur straight, narrow, slightly inflated in the apical half, 6 mm long.

Epiphyte in evergreen forest.

Cameroon.

Ancistrorhynchus crystalensis P. J. Cribb & van der Laan

Plant with an erect stem up to 6 cm long. Leaves 6–13, linear, leathery, narrowing towards the base, unequally bilobed at the apex, each lobe with 2 or 3 teeth. Inflorescence capitate, dense, 3.5 cm long, 10- to 15-flowered; pedicel with ovary 12–13 mm long. Flowers white, large for the genus, all parts scabrous on the outer surface; dorsal sepal elliptic, obtuse, concave, 9–10 mm long, 4 mm wide; lateral sepals oblong-elliptic, obtuse, 10–11 mm long, 4 mm wide; petals oblong-elliptic, obtuse, 7–8 mm long, 5 mm wide; lip obscurely 3-lobed or entire, concave, side lobes erect, transversely elliptic or semi-circular, 5–6 mm long, 8–9 mm wide; spur parallel to the ovary, curved, funnel-shaped at first, then widely cylindric, sharply constricted 4 mm from the apex and then inflated, 13–14 mm long.

Epiphyte or lithophyte; flowering in August.

Gabon.

Close to *Ancistrorhynchus capitatus*, but the flowers are larger and the longer spur is a different shape.

Ancistrorhynchus laxiflorus Mansfeld

Plant erect or spreading with a short stem 2–4 cm long; roots very long, 1.5–3 mm in diameter. Leaves 3–10, leathery, linear, unequally bilobed at the apex, with rounded lobes, articulated at the base by an acute angle to the leaf sheath 1.5–2 cm long, 13–35 cm long, 6–8 mm wide. Inflorescences dense, to 3.5 cm long, 3- to 6-flowered; bracts papery, elliptic, 8–14 mm long; pedicel with ovary 10–15 mm long. Flowers white with a green mark on the lip; dorsal sepal lanceolate, acute, 15–17 mm long, 5–6 mm wide; lateral sepals lanceolate to elliptic-lanceolate, acute or obtuse, 12.5–16 mm long, 4.5–6 mm wide; petals oblong, obtuse, 12–16 mm long, 4–5 mm wide; lip ovate, subacute to obtuse, 13–16 mm long, 8–9 mm wide; spur inflated at the wide mouth, geniculate near the apex, recurved and swollen at the apex, 9 mm long.

Epiphyte in montane forest; 1200–1600 m; flowering in November, January, and April.

Southern Tanzania.

Ancistrorhynchus metteniae (Kraenzlin) Summerhayes

Plant pendent, with a short stem 2–7 cm long; roots 2–3 mm in diameter. Leaves several, linear, unequally bilobed at the apex, each lobe with 2 teeth, articulated at the base to a leaf sheath 1–1.5 cm long, leaves in total 5–25 cm long, 7–24 mm wide. Inflorescences dense, 1.5–2 cm long, many-flowered; bracts papery, 6–10 mm long, pedicel with ovary 4–5 mm long. Flowers white with a green mark on the lip, small; dorsal sepal elliptic, obtuse, 3.5–5 mm long, 2–2.3 mm wide; lateral sepals obliquely oblong, obtuse, 4–5 mm long, 2 mm wide; petals elliptic-oblong, obtuse, 3.7–4.7 mm long, 1.7–2.5 mm wide; lip concave, broadly ovate or subcircular, obtuse, 3.5–4.5 mm long and wide; spur straight, somewhat inflated, 2.5–4 mm long.

Epiphyte in shady, evergreen forest; 900–1300 m; flowering in October.

Sierra Leone eastwards to Nigeria, also in Central African Republic, Uganda, Ethiopia, and Tanzania.

Ancistrorhynchus metteniae. J. Hermans

Ancistrorhynchus ovatus Summerhayes

Plant pendent or erect, often with a curving stem to 20 cm long; roots 1–2 mm in diameter. Leaves up to 12, linear, unequally bilobed at the apex, each lobe subacute or obscurely toothed, articulated to a leaf base 1–2.5 cm long, 7–20 cm long, 5–14 mm wide. Inflorescences capitate, dense, 1–4 cm long and wide, many-flowered; bracts ovate-lanceolate, acute 6–12 mm long; pedicel with ovary 6–8 mm long. Flowers white, small; dorsal sepal oblong-elliptic, rounded, 3.3–4.4 mm long, 1.3–2 mm wide; lateral sepals oblique, elliptic-oblong, rounded, 3.5–4.8 mm long, 1.3–2 mm wide; petals broadly elliptic-oblanceolate, rounded, 3.2–4.5 mm long, 1.3–2 mm wide; lip concave, broadly ovate, rounded, with undulate margins, 3–4.5 mm long, 2.4–3.5 mm wide; spur slender, inflated in the apical third, 4.5–6 mm long.

Epiphyte in evergreen forest; 1200–1600 m; flowering May to June.

Congo, D.R. of Congo, and Uganda.

Ancistrorhynchus parviflorus Summerhayes

Plant dwarf with a slender stem 4–5 cm long, and very narrow roots, 1 mm in diameter. Leaves up to 10 spaced along the stem, ligulate, unequally bilobed at the apex, twisted at the base and attached to leaf bases 1 cm long, 3.5–4.5 cm long, 6–7 mm wide. Inflorescences capitate, 6 mm in diameter; bracts rounded, 3 mm long; pedicel and ovary 3 mm long. Flowers white; sepals elliptic, rounded, 2.5–2.7 mm long, 1.3–1.5 mm wide; petals obovate, rounded, 2.5 mm long, 1.4 mm wide; lip concave, broadly ovate, obscurely 3-lobed, 1.8 mm long, 2.2–2.4 mm wide; spur globose, transparent, 1.2–1.3 mm long.

Epiphyte in montane evergreen forest; 850–950 m; flowering in January.

Tanzania (Usambara Mountains).

Ancistrorhynchus recurvus Finet

Plant erect with a short stem 1–6 cm long; roots narrow, 2 mm in diameter. Leaves linear, unequally bilobed at the apex, articulated to leaf bases 1–2 cm long, 14–40 cm long, 8–30 mm wide. Inflo-rescences capitate, 1.5–3 cm long; bracts 2–3 mm long; pedicel with ovary 5 mm long. Flowers white with scurfy hairs on outer surface; dorsal sepal elliptic-ovate, rounded, 3.3–3.8 mm long, 1.8–2 mm wide; lateral sepals obliquely elliptic, obtuse, 4.2 mm long, 2 mm wide; petals oblong, rounded, 3.6 mm long, 1.2 mm wide; lip 3-lobed, side lobes obscure, rounded, mid-lobe recurved, ovate, acute, 4.5–7.5 mm long, 3–4.5 mm wide; spur swollen at the mouth and at the apex, geniculate below and recurved, 4.7–6 mm long.

Epiphyte in rain forest; 1100–1300 m.

Sierra Leone eastwards to Gabon, and Uganda.

Ancistrorhynchus refractus (Kraenzlin) Summerhayes

Plant erect with a short stem up to 4 cm long; roots branching, 1.5–3 mm in diameter. Leaves 6–8, fleshy or leathery, linear, unequally and acuminately bilobed at the apex, twisted towards the apex, articulated to a leaf base 2–3 cm long, 6–40 cm long, 8–12 mm wide. Inflorescences clustered, 3–3.5 cm long; bracts ovate, 7–8 mm long; pedicel with ovary 12–14 mm long. Flowers white,

Ancistrorhynchus refractus. C. Arends

shining; sepals narrowly oblong or oblong, 10–14 mm long, 4 mm wide; petals narrowly elliptic-oblong, obtuse, 12–13 mm long, 3–4 mm wide; lip concave, obscurely 3-lobed, ovate, obtuse, 15–17 mm long, 7 mm wide; spur S-shaped, enlarged at the mouth and towards the apex, 13–17 mm long.

Epiphyte in montane evergreen forest; 900–2100 m; flowering in January, February, and May.

Tanzania (Usambara Mountains).

Apparently rather close to *Ancistrorhynchus laxiflorus*, also from Tanzania but more widespread, with wider leaves and a longer spur.

Ancistrorhynchus schumannii (Kraenzlin) Summerhayes

Plant erect with a stem up to 15 cm long. Leaves oblong, almost equally lobed at the apex, 1.5–6 cm long, 2–7.5 mm wide. Inflorescences small, 1- to 3-flowered; bracts 2–3 mm long. Flowers white; sepals and petals oboval, obtuse, 2–3 mm long, 1–1.5 mm wide; lip broadly oval, rounded, 2–3 mm long, 1.5–2.5 mm wide; spur narrow below the lip then subellipsoid, 2–2.5 mm long.

Epiphyte in dense forest.

Nigeria, Cameroon, and D.R. of Congo.

Ancistrorhynchus serratus Summerhayes

Plant with erect stems, sometimes branched, up to 10 cm long. Leaves in 2 rows, spaced close together near apex of stem, linear-ligulate, with rounded apical lobes that are irregularly serrate, 5–11 cm long, 7–10 mm wide. Inflorescences capitate, dense, 1 cm long, several- to many-flowered; bracts chaffy, shorter than the pedicel with ovary. Flowers white; sepals oblong-elliptic, 3–3.5 mm long, 1.25 mm wide; petals oblanceolate, acute, 3 mm long, 1 mm wide; lip obscurely 3-lobed, distinctly broader than long, 2.5 mm long, 4.25 mm wide; spur straight, funnel-shaped at first, then constricted, finally inflated in the apical quarter, 4–4.5 mm long.

Epiphyte in forest; ca. 1500 m; flowering in May.

Southern Nigeria, Cameroon, and Equatorial Guinea (Bioco Island).

Ancistrorhynchus straussii (Schlechter) Schlechter

Plant erect with a short stem 2.5 cm long. Leaves 5–7, linear, or linear-lanceolate, unequally bilobed at the apex, the lobes rounded, entire or finely denticulate, 5–13 cm long, 3–13 mm wide. Inflorescences capitate, dense, 5- to 14-flowered; bracts oblong-elliptic, 3–4 mm long; pedicel with ovary 4 mm long. Flowers very small, white with 2 green spots on the lip; sepals oblong-elliptic, obtuse, 2.6 mm long, 1 mm wide; petals similar to the sepals; lip concave, obscurely 3-lobed, the lobes rounded, 2.7 mm long, 3 mm wide; spur straight, inflated at the middle, narrowing towards both ends, 1.5–3.5 mm long.

Epiphyte in primary forest; 700 m.

Nigeria, Cameroon, Gabon, and D.R. of Congo.

Old records from Côte d'Ivoire have been re-identified as *Ancistrorhynchus akeassiae*.

Ancistrorhynchus tenuicaulis Summerhayes

Plants with erect or curved stems, 2–16 cm high, 2 mm in diameter, with few narrow roots, 1–2 mm in diameter. Leaves linear, clustered near apex of stem, unequally bilobed at the apex, each lobe subacute or obscurely 2-toothed, articulated to rugulose leaf bases, 2–7.2 cm long, 4–5 mm wide. Inflorescences capitate, dense, 4–5 mm long, many-flowered; bracts elliptic, obtuse, 2–3 mm long; pedicel with ovary 3 mm long. Flowers white; dorsal sepal oblong-elliptic, rounded, 1.5–3.5 mm long, 0.9–1.3 mm wide; lateral sepals obliquely elliptic-oblong, obtuse, 2–3.5 mm long, 1–1.2 mm wide; petals elliptic, rounded, 1.7–3 mm long, 0.7–1.4 mm wide; lip concave, ovate, obtuse, 1.4–2.5 mm long, 1.4–2.4 mm wide; spur globose or club-shaped, 1–2 mm long.

Epiphyte in evergreen forest; 900–1400 m; flowering April to June in Uganda and September to November in Tanzania.

D.R. of Congo, Rwanda, Uganda, Tanzania, and Malawi.

This is one of the small-flowered species, somewhat similar to *Ancistrorhynchus parviflorus* in

Tanzania and to *A. schumannii* and *A. straussii* from west and central Africa (see descriptions for all 3 species earlier in this chapter).

ANGRAECOPSIS Kraenzlin

This genus was named in 1900 by the German botanist Fritz Kraenzlin. The species he saw first, *Angraecopsis tenerrima*, looked very similar to some species of *Angraecum*, so he chose the suffix *-opsis*, having the appearance of, when creating this name. Afterwards he seems to have been uncertain about his new genus and re-described this species as *Angraecum tenerrima* in 1914. Rudolf Schlechter not only recognised the genus in 1914 and added 3 more species, but in his general revision of the angraecoid genera in 1918 he added a further 4 species. More species were described when the genus was revised by V. S. Summerhayes in 1951.

About 20 species from Africa and Madagascar are now recognised as members of this genus. At first sight it seems rather heterogeneous: *Angraecopsis tenerrima* and *A. gracillima* have attractive white flowers which set them apart from the species with many small pale green flowers. Summerhayes (1951) subdivided the genus in 3 sections, and his treatment has been followed in most recent floras. He pointed out that the genus appears to be allied to *Mystacidium*, from which it differs in the unequal sepals, almost bilobed petals, the normally 3-lobed lip, narrow mouth to the spur, and side lobes of the rostellum not being papillose or pubescent. *Angraecopsis malawiensis* does indeed look very much like a *Mystacidium*, a smaller version of *M. gracile*, perhaps. It will be interesting to learn more about the relationships of these small species via molecular studies.

In this account the species are presented in 2 groups that are fairly easy to differentiate:

Group 1. Inflorescence greatly elongated, peduncle much longer than the rachis, flowers in a tight bunch at the apex of the inflorescence (10 species).

Group 2. Flowers regularly spaced along the inflorescence, peduncle much shorter. One recently described species (*Angraecopsis hallei*) is tentatively placed in this group although, from the description, it seems more likely that it is a *Diaphananthe* (12 species).

Nineteen species occur in Africa. One (*Angraecopsis pobeguinii*) is from the Comoro Islands, and another (*A. trifurca*) occurs in the Comoro Islands and Zimbabwe, whilst one more (*A. parviflora*) occurs in Africa, Madagascar, Réunion, and Mauritius.

Culture

All the species can be maintained in cultivation. The smaller ones are much easier if they are mounted on a piece of hardwood or bark and all can be grown in this way. *Angraecopsis gracillima* also grows well in free-draining compost in a pot. The smaller species come from higher altitudes and therefore need cooler conditions at night and benefit from drying out periodically.

Group 1. Species with a long peduncle and flowers close together near the tip of the inflorescence.

Angraecopsis elliptica Summerhayes

Plant with a short erect stem 4–8 cm long. Leaves in 2 rows, curved, conduplicate at the base, flat above, elliptic-oblong or oblanceolate, unequally bilobed at the apex, the shorter lobe absent, 4–10 cm long, 1–2.5 cm wide. Inflorescence usually in the axils of old leaf sheaths, below the leaves, bearing 10–20 flowers spaced 3–4 mm apart near the apex, 4–18 cm long; bracts small, 1.5–2 mm long; pedicel with ovary very slender, 3–5 mm long. Flowers pale green, the lip sometimes tinted orange; dorsal sepal broadly lanceolate-ovate, subacute; lateral sepals oblanceolate, oblique, 3–5 mm long; petals triangular, oblique, 2–2.5 mm long,

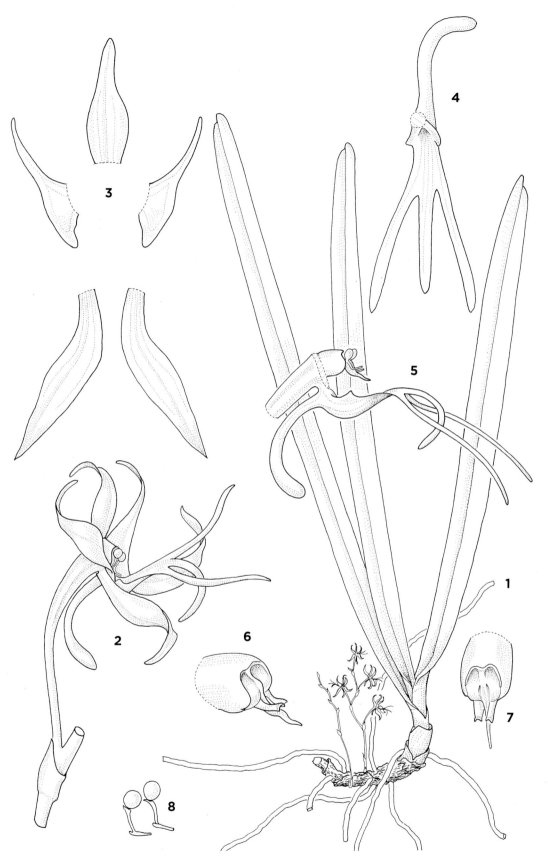

Angraecopsis cryptantha. 1: Habit. 2: Flower. 3: Sepals and petals. 4: Lip and spur. 5: Lip, column, and ovary. 6-7: Column. 8: Pollinaria. From Cribb 1996, p. 362. S. Stuart-Smith.

1.5–2 mm wide; lip 3-lobed, the side lobes narrow and half as long as the mid-lobe which is triangular, in total 3–5 mm long; spur cylindric, slightly curved or parallel with the ovary, 3–5.5 mm long.

Epiphyte in montane forests, usually in deep shade; 500–1500 m; flowering August to September.

Côte d'Ivoire to Cameroon.

Angraecopsis gassneri Williamson

Plant with a short stem; roots slender, somewhat hairy, 2 mm in diameter. Leaves 3–5 in 2 rows, ligulate, unequally bilobed at the apex, margins undulate, 15–22 cm long, 2.5–3.5 cm wide. Inflorescences 1–3, bearing up to 20 flowers close together in the apical quarter; bracts 1 mm long; pedicel with ovary curved, 15 mm long. Flowers pale green; dorsal sepal ovate, obtuse, 3 mm long, 1.8 mm wide; lateral sepals ligulate, obtuse, 9 mm long, 1 mm wide; petals ovate, acute, joined to the lateral sepals near the base, 3.5–5 mm long, 1.5–3 mm wide; lip 3-lobed to 2 mm from the base, side lobes lanceolate, obtuse, curving outwards, nearly as long as mid-lobe of similar shape, in total 6 mm long; spur slender, parallel to the ovary, 15–18 mm long.

Epiphyte on trees and on granite rocks near a waterfall, in deep moss; 1300 m; flowering in March.

Zambia.

Similar to the widespread *Angraecopsis trifurca* but distinguished by the undulate leaf margin and the longer spur.

Angraecopsis gracillima (Rolfe) Summerhayes

Plant with a short, upright or pendent stem 1–7 cm long; roots tomentose. Leaves 2–10, linear, often falcate, twisted at the base so that they lie in one plane, obtusely and bluntly bilobed at the apex, 6–15 cm long, 8–15 mm wide. Inflorescences slender, usually erect, bearing 4–20 flowers close together in the apical quarter, 5–20 cm long; bracts sheathing, 2–3 mm long; pedicel with ovary 1.7–2.7 cm long. Flowers white, usually with the lateral sepals and petals reflexed so they look very narrow;

Angraecopsis gracillima. J. Hermans

dorsal sepal ovate, up to 3 mm long; lateral sepals dependent on either side of the lip, spathulate, 7–9 mm long; petals ovate or triangular, joined to the lateral sepals for two thirds of their length, 2–5 mm long and wide; lip 3-lobed, side lobes linear and shorter than the wider mid-lobe, up to 5 mm long; spur slender and usually curved, 3–4 cm long.

Epiphyte on branches and trunks of small trees and in the canopy of evergreen forest, usually with the roots shrouded in a thin layer of moss; 1500–1850 m; flowering May to August.

D.R. of Congo, Rwanda, Uganda, Kenya, and Zambia.

Angraecopsis ischnopus (Schlechter) Schlechter

Plant with a short, erect stem to 5 cm long. Leaves 2–5, linear, ligulate or elliptic-oblong, unequally lobed at the apex, with rounded or obtuse lobes, 2–12 cm long, 4–13 mm wide. Inflorescences arising between old leaf sheaths, 3–9 cm long, up to 10-flowered; bracts amplexicaul, 2.5 mm long; pedicel with ovary slender, 2 cm long. Flowers pale green or yellowish green, small; dorsal sepal oblong oval, cucullate, 2–3.5 mm long, 1–2 mm wide; lateral sepals oblong-spathulate, subobtuse, 5–10 mm long, 2.8 mm wide; petals obliquely oval or triangular, wider than long, cohering to the lateral sepal at the base, 1.7–2.2 mm long, 2.3–3 mm wide; lip 3-lobed from the middle, side lobes linear-lanceolate, 5 mm long, mid-lobe narrowly triangular, slightly longer than side lobes, in total 8.5 mm long; spur wide at the mouth then narrowing, twisted, slightly inflated in the apical half then very acute, 12–38 mm long.

Epiphyte in montane forests; up to 1800 m; flowering August to October.

Sierra Leone, Guinea, northern Nigeria, Equatorial Guinea, and Cameroon.

Angraecopsis lisowskii Szlachetko & Oslzewski

Plant erect with a short stem 4 cm long. Leaves 6, oblong-oval or oblong-ligulate, unequally and obtusely bilobed at the apex, 14–17 cm long, 3–4 cm wide. Inflorescences lax, arising below the leaves, bearing 25–30 flowers in the apical third, 8–11(–30) cm long; bracts oval 2–2.5 mm long; pedicel with ovary slender, 7 mm long. Flowers white, small; dorsal sepal broadly oval, 1.5 mm long, 1 mm wide; lateral sepals oblong-oboval, L-shaped, 3 mm long, 1.2 mm wide; petals obliquely triangular, fused to the lateral sepals at the margin, 1.5 mm long, 1 mm wide; lip fleshy, especially at the apex, 3-lobed at the middle, side lobes very small, triangular, in total 2.5 mm long; spur narrowly cylindric in the basal half, then somewhat inflated and narrowing to the acute apex, 8 mm long.

Epiphyte, usually near the ground; 1150 m; flowering in August.

Cameroon.

Named in honour of Polish scientist Stanislaw Lisowski (1924–2002) who collected plants in Cameroon, this species has a very distinctive flower and lip.

Angraecopsis macrophylla Summerhayes

Plant pendent with a short stem 3–6 cm long. Leaves 2–4, twisted at the base so that they lie in one plane, linear to oblanceolate, falcate, acutely bilobed at the apex, 13–35 cm long, 1.4–2.2 cm wide. Inflorescences erect, bearing many flowers in the apical half, 10–20 cm long; bracts triangular, 1 mm long; pedicel with ovary 0.8–1.3 cm long. Flowers white; dorsal sepal elliptic, obtuse, 2.5 mm long, 2 mm wide; lateral sepals dependent, spathulate, rounded, 5.5 mm long, 1.7 mm wide; petals obliquely ovate-triangular, acute, 2.5 mm long, 2.7–3 mm wide; lip 3-lobed in the middle, subauriculate at the base, side lobes linear-lanceolate, 1–1.5 mm long, mid-lobe narrowly elliptic, obtuse, longer than side lobes, in total 5.5–6.5 mm long, 4 mm wide; spur incurved, cylindrical, swollen at the apex, 10–11 mm long.

Epiphyte at low levels in evergreen forest; ca. 1000 m; flowering in June.

Uganda and Ethiopia.

Angraecopsis parviflora (Thouars) Schlechter

Plant spreading or pendent, with short stems 1–3 cm long. Leaves 4–6, linear to oblanceolate, falcate, twisted at the base so that they lie in one plane, acutely bilobed at the apex, 6–20 cm long, 5–11 mm wide. Inflorescences usually several, bearing 2–8 flowers close together in the apical third, 5–10 cm long; bracts ovate-triangular, 1–1.5 mm long; pedicel with ovary 5–6 mm long. Flowers pale green; dorsal sepal ovate, obtuse, 2 mm long, 1 mm wide; lateral sepals oblanceolate, obtuse, 3.5–4 mm long, 1 mm wide; petals obliquely triangular, acute, 1.5–1.8 mm long and wide; lip 3-lobed in the middle, side lobes linear acute, slightly shorter than the mid-lobe, in total 3–3.6 mm long and wide; spur incurved, slightly inflated at the upturned apex, 5–9 mm long.

Epiphyte in lower montane forest; 600–1600 m; flowering at various times.

Côte d'Ivoire eastwards to Tanzania and south to Mozambique and Zimbabwe, Madagascar, Mauritius, and Réunion.

Angraecopsis parviflora. J. Hermans

Angraecopsis tenerrima. J. Stewart

Angraecopsis pobeguinii (Finet) Perrier

Syn. *Chamaeangis pobeguinii* (Finet) Schlechter

Plant very small with a short, erect stem to 1 cm long, 3 mm wide. Leaves 3–4, oblong or oval-oblong, flat, 8–20 mm long, 4.7 mm wide. Inflorescence slender, bearing 12–15 flowers in the apical quarter, 4–5 cm long; bracts tiny, amplexicaul; pedicel with ovary 5 mm long. Flowers very small, all perianth parts less than 3 mm long, green; dorsal sepal oval, acute; lateral sepals oblanceolate, twice as long as the dorsal sepal; petals oval, oblique, dilated or almost sublobulate on one side at the base; lip 3-lobed, side lobes very small, mid-lobe cucullate and fleshy at the apex; spur curved in a semi-circle, much inflated in the apical third, 4 mm long.

Epiphyte in montane forest; flowering in June. Comoro Islands (Grande Comore).

Angraecopsis tenerrima Kraenzlin

Plant pendent with a short stem 1–7 cm high; roots verrucose. Leaves oblanceolate to linear, falcate, unequally bilobed at the apex, with rounded lobes, twisted at the base so that they lie in one plane, 6–20 cm long, 1.4–2 cm wide. Inflorescences usually several, 7.5–20 cm long, 3- to 7-flowered; bracts amplexicaul, 2–4 mm long; pedicel with ovary 2–3 cm long. Flowers white, spur green at the apex; dorsal sepal elliptic, obtuse, 2.7–3.3 mm long, 1.6–1.8 mm wide; lateral sepals spathulate, obtuse, 8–12 mm long, 2–2.5 mm wide; petals obliquely triangular, 3 mm long, 3.8–4.6 mm wide, joined to the lateral sepals for the basal 3–5 mm; lip 3-lobed, side lobes oblanceolate, rounded at the apex, 4–5 mm long, mid-lobe lanceolate, acute, as long as the side lobes, in total 9–10 mm long, 6.5–8 mm wide; spur cylindrical, pendent, narrow from a broad mouth, 5–6 cm long.

Epiphyte at lower levels of montane forest; 400–1600 m; flowering January to May.

Tanzania.

Angraecopsis trifurca (Reichenbach f.) Schlechter

Syns. *Angraecopsis comorensis* Summerhayes, *A. thouarsii* (Finet) H. Perrier

Plant with a short, erect or pendent stem, to 1 cm long; roots slightly hairy, 1.5–2 mm in diameter. Leaves 4 or 5, linear, falcate, twisted at the base so that they lie in one plane, 12–20 cm long, ca. 1 cm wide. Inflorescence bearing 6 or 7 flowers in the apical quarter, 7–8 cm long. Flowers cream, pale green or pale brown; dorsal sepal ovate, 2.5–3.5 mm long, 1.5 mm wide; lateral sepals linear, 3–7 mm long, 1–1.5 mm wide; petals 3–4 mm long, 2.5 mm wide; lip 3-lobed in the basal half, the side lobes slightly shorter than the mid-lobe, 4–6.5 mm long; spur slender, incurved, 13–16 mm long.

Epiphyte in evergreen rain forest and on mossy rocks, in shade; ca. 1200 m; flowering in April.

Ethiopia, Zimbabwe (Chimanimani Mountains), and Comoro Islands.

Group 2. Species with small flowers, mostly regularly spaced along the inflorescence.

Angraecopsis amaniensis Summerhayes

Plant with a very short, upright or pendent stem less than 5 mm long, bearing a few leaves in the upper part, sometimes leafless, and with many long, flattened roots that are much more conspicuous than the leaves. Leaves 1–3 per stem, linear, greyish green, 1–3 cm long, 3–5 mm wide. Inflorescences slender, pendent, usually several, bearing 10–20 flowers along their length, 3–20 cm long. Flowers pale green, star-shaped, 7–10 mm in diameter; dorsal sepal elliptic, 4 mm long, up to 2 mm wide; lateral sepals linear 7–9 mm long, 1 mm wide; petals lanceolate, acute, 3–4 mm long, 1.5 mm wide; lip 3-lobed, side lobes very small, mid-lobe linear, up to 4 mm long; spur cylindrical, curved, 7–13 mm long.

On *Podocarpus* and other trees in highland forests, where it often occurs in large clumps on the trunks and main branches, also recorded from conifer plantations; 750–2100 m; flowering April and May.

Kenya, Tanzania, Malawi, Mozambique, Zambia, and Zimbabwe, at lower altitudes further south.

This species is extremely similar to *Angraecopsis breviloba* but easily distinguished from it when in flower by the longer inflorescences and longer, narrow spur. Although they are very small plants, they can be quite spectacular when bearing many inflorescences.

Angraecopsis breviloba Summerhayes

Plant with a very short, upright or pendent stem less than 5 mm long, bearing a few leaves in the upper part, sometimes leafless, and with many

Angraecopsis breviloba. B. Campbell

Angraecopsis amaniensis. B. Campbell

long, flattened roots that are much more conspicuous than the leaves. Leaves 1–3 per stem, linear-elliptic or oblanceolate, greyish green, 1–4 cm long, 3–5 mm wide. Inflorescences slender, pendent, usually several, with 10–15 flowers densely arranged along their length, 10–15 cm long. Flowers pale green or yellowish green, star-shaped, 7–10 mm in diameter; dorsal sepal elliptic, 3–5 mm long, up to 1.5 mm wide; lateral sepals similar; petals lanceolate, obtuse, 3–4 mm long, 1–1.5 mm wide; lip

obscurely 3-lobed, side lobes very small, mid-lobe lanceolate, up to 4 mm long; spur bulbous at the apex, slender below, 4–5 mm long.

On small trees and bushes, often near streams but also along ridges in montane forests, sometimes in *Citrus* plantations; 1500–2400 m; flowering May to July and November to January.

Kenya and Tanzania.

This species is similar to *Angraecopsis amaniensis* but easily distinguished from it when in flower by the shorter inflorescences and short, bulbous spur. Although they are very small plants, they can be spectacular when bearing many inflorescences.

Angraecopsis cryptantha P. J. Cribb

Plant with a short, curved stem 3–5 cm long. Leaves few, linear-sublanceolate, unequally bilobed at the apex, with rounded lobes, twisted at the base so that they lie in one plane, 12–18 cm long, 6–11 mm wide. Inflorescence short, 2–3 cm long, horizontal or pendent, 2- or 3-flowered; bracts oval-triangular, 2.5 mm long; pedicel with ovary 6–8 mm long. Flowers yellow, small; dorsal sepal oval, acuminate, reflexed in the upper half, 4.5–5 mm long, 1.5 mm wide; lateral sepals falcate, oblanceolate, acute, reflexed in the apical third, 6.5–7.5 mm long, 1.5 mm wide; petals oval, very oblique, bilobed at the base, 5.5–6.5 mm long, 1.5 mm wide; lip saccate at the base, 3-lobed below the middle, side lobes longer than the mid-lobe, all lobes linear, in total 6.5–7.5 mm long, 6.5–7.5 mm wide when spread out; spur incurved, cylindric, 4.5–5.5 mm long.

Epiphyte in montane forest; 1900–2000 m; flowering in October.

Cameroon.

Angraecopsis dolabriformis (Rolfe) Schlechter

Summerhayes (1951) wrote that this species is very close to *Angraecopsis tridens* (Lindley) Schlechter and further material may show that they are conspecific. It has broader leaves, more flowers in the inflorescence, slightly larger flowers and a longer spur than *A. tridens*, but these may be individual rather than specific differences.

São Tomé.

Angraecopsis hallei Szlachetko & Olszewski

Plant with a short squat stem 2–3 cm long. Leaves 4, elliptic-oboval, unequally and acutely bilobed at the apex, 13 cm long, 5.6 cm wide. Inflorescence lax, 10- to 15-flowered; peduncle short; bracts very small, 1 mm long; pedicel with ovary 4 mm long. Flowers greenish white, small; dorsal sepal oval, cordate, 3–3.5 mm long, 2.7 mm wide;

lateral sepals oval-lanceolate, above a narrow base, oblique, 5 mm long, 2.3 mm wide; petals obliquely oval-triangular, acute, cohering to the lateral sepals at the base, 3.8 mm long, 2.8 mm wide; lip transversely elliptic, obscurely 3-lobed, the lobes rounded or the mid-lobe subacute, a short callus at the base in front of the spur-opening, 5 mm long, 6 mm wide; spur incurved, swollen towards the apex, up to 7 mm long.

Epiphyte; flowering in October.

Gabon.

This species is named in honour of Nicolas Hallé, the French botanist who collected it. It seems most unlike all other species of *Angraecopsis* and would perhaps be better placed in the genus *Diaphananthe*, as the authors suggested.

Angraecopsis holochila Summerhayes

Plant dwarf with a short stem less than 5 mm long; flattened roots 2 mm wide. Leaves twisted at the base, linear, obtuse, 4–9 cm long, 4–6 mm wide. Inflorescences pendent, 4–5 cm long, few- to 8-flowered; bracts ovate, acute, 1–1.5 mm long; pedicel with ovary 5–10 mm long. Flowers pale green; dorsal sepal elliptic, obtuse, 3 mm long, 1.5 mm wide; lateral sepals oblanceolate, rounded, 4.5 mm long, 1.6 mm wide; petals obliquely ovate, obtuse, 3 mm long, nearly 2 mm wide; lip entire, ovate, obtuse, 3 mm long, 1.6–1.8 mm wide; spur narrow, cylindrical, slightly incurved, 14–22 mm long.

Epiphyte and on rocks, in montane forest in a ravine; 2150–2300 m; flowering May and June.

Northern Uganda and Ethiopia.

Angraecopsis lovettii P. J. Cribb

Plant dwarf with a short stem up to 5 mm long; roots wiry, 0.5 mm in diameter. Leaves twisted at the base, linear-ligulate to oblanceolate, unequally bilobed at the apex, 2–3 cm long, 3–4 mm wide. Inflorescences secund, less than 2.5 cm long, 4- to 8-flowered; bracts minute; pedicel with ovary 3–5 mm long. Flowers tiny, pale greenish white; sepals narrowly elliptic or elliptic-oblong, 3 mm long, 1 mm wide; petals oblong-elliptic, acute, 2.5 mm long, 1 mm wide; lip ovate, slightly recurved, fleshy at the apex, 2 mm long, 1 mm wide; spur slightly incurved, club-shaped, 1–2 mm long.

Epiphyte in montane forest; 2000–2300 m; flowering March and April.

Tanzania (Image Mountain).

Angraecopsis malawiensis P. J. Cribb

Plant with a very short stem; roots 1.5 mm in diameter. Leaves 2 or 3, light green with darker venation, elliptic or oblanceolate, unequally and obtusely bilobed at the apex, 1.5–2.5 cm long, 3–4 mm wide. Inflorescence bearing 4–12 equally spaced flowers, to 5 cm long; bracts sheathing, 1 mm long, set 2 mm below the point where pedicel arises, pedicel with ovary 4–5 mm long. Flowers green or yellow-green; dorsal sepal erect, lanceolate or ovate, acute or obtuse, 2 mm long, 0.5–1 mm wide; lateral sepals deflexed, obliquely linear-lanceolate, 3–4 mm long, 0.6–1 mm wide; petals triangular-ovate, 1.5 mm long, 0.5–1 mm wide; lip entire, lanceolate, acute, 2 mm long, 1 mm wide; spur slender but swollen in the middle or near the apex, 3–4 mm long.

Epiphyte on twigs and small branches in evergreen montane forest, usually in deep shade; 1700–2300 m; flowering in October.

Northern Malawi and Tanzania.

Angraecopsis parva (P. J. Cribb) P. J. Cribb

Plant dwarf with a very short stem 2–4 mm long; roots slender, terete, less than 1 mm in diameter. Leaves 2–4, twisted at the base, linear-oblanceolate, obtuse, 1.5–2 cm long, 2–4 mm wide. Inflorescences 1.5–2.5 cm long, 2- to 5-flowered; bracts minute; pedicel with ovary 2–3 mm long. Flowers tiny, greenish white; dorsal sepal elliptic, obtuse, 1.5 mm long; lateral sepals oblanceolate, acute, 2 mm long; petals obliquely elliptic, obtuse, 1.2 mm long; lip concave, ovate, shortly apiculate, fleshy and obscurely 3-lobed at the apex, 1.7 mm long, 1.3 mm wide; spur S-shaped, clavate, 1–2 mm long.

Epiphyte on twigs and branches of shrubs in montane forest, also on trunks amongst mosses; 1800–2285 m; flowering in February and April.

Southern Tanzania and northern Malawi.

Angraecopsis pusilla Summerhayes

Plant dwarf with a short stem up to 2 cm long; roots glabrous. Leaves 5–9, erect, conduplicate, linear to oblong, 1.5–5 cm long, 1.5–5 mm wide. Inflorescences axillary, slender, with 4–7 well-spaced flowers; bracts lanceolate, 1.5–2.5 mm long; pedicel with ovary 5–8 mm long. Flowers white or pale green; dorsal sepal ovate-orbicular, nearly 2 mm long; lateral sepals oblanceolate or subspathulate, curved, obtuse, 2.75 mm long, 1 mm wide; petals broadly oblique, elliptic-ovate, slightly enlarged on the lower side and joined to the lateral sepal, 2 mm long, 1.6 mm wide; lip concave, entire, broadly ovate, 2.5 mm long, 2 mm wide; spur straight, rounded at the apex, 3 mm long.

Epiphyte in montane forest, in evergreen forest, and in the bamboo zone; 1700 m; flowering in January.

Eastern D.R. of Congo.

Angraecopsis tridens (Lindley) Schlechter

Plant with short, erect stems, 1–5 cm long. Leaves 2–4 in 2 rows near apex of stem, linear or narrowly ligulate, somewhat curved, 2–12 cm long, 4–15 mm wide. Inflorescences slender, arising from the base of the stem, 4–8 cm long, few- to many-flowered; bracts small, 1 mm long; pedicel with ovary shorter than the bracts. Flowers pale or clear green; dorsal sepal oval-lanceolate, acute, 1.5–2 mm long, 1–1.5 mm wide; lateral sepals scarcely widened in the apical half, 3.5–4 mm long; petals oblong-oblanceolate, obtuse, 2–2.7 mm long, 1.5 mm wide; lip 3-lobed near the middle, side lobes slightly longer than the mid-lobe, all lobes linear-lanceolate, in total 4 mm long; spur shorter than the lip, swollen at the apex, 2–3 mm long.

Epiphyte in montane rain forest; 1250–1500 m; flowering in September.

Equatorial Guinea (Bioco Island) and Cameroon.

BECLARDIA A. Richard

The genus *Beclardia* was named in 1828 in honour of Augustine Beclard, professor of anatomy at the Faculty of Medicine in Paris, by the French botanist Achille Richard. He proposed 2 species, both of which had been illustrated by Thouars (1822). These are now considered to represent a single variable species, *B. macrostachya*, which is widespread in Madagascar, Mauritius, and Réunion. A second, more robust species has been described from Madagascar (Bosser 1997). As yet there are no records from the Comoro Islands.

Both species are small to medium-sized plants with upright stems and stiff leaves in 2 rows. The white-and-green flowers are immediately recognisable by their large, 4-lobed lip, which bears numerous warts, or coarse papillae, on its inner surface and merges gradually into the funnel-shaped spur at its base. The genus *Oeonia* also has a 4-lobed lip, but the details of the column, as well as the characteristic plant habit, are quite different in that genus.

Culture

These plants are as easy to grow as many of the other vandaceous species, but they have few roots and these are often slow to develop, so plants can be hard to establish. In the wild, they are found throughout a wide altitudinal range and can withstand a range of temperatures. However, they are usually found in semi-shaded and humid situations.

Beclardia grandiflora Bosser

Plant erect, 27–30 cm high, with a thick, slightly flattened stem and thick roots. Leaves ca. 10, loriform, conduplicate at the base, flattened above, emarginate at the apex, 27–30 cm long, 3–4 cm wide. Inflorescences to 40 cm long; peduncle with 2 short sheaths, 25 cm long; pedicel with ovary 1.5 cm long. Flowers 10–15, white; sepals oblong, obtuse, 18–24 mm long, 7–9 mm wide; petals spathulate, apiculate, narrow at the base, 22–27 mm long, 14–17 mm wide; lip with 4 rounded lobes, with hyaline hairs on the inner surface in front of the

Beclardia macrostachya. J. Hermans

spur entrance, 25–32 mm long, 20–30 mm wide; spur wide at the mouth, funnel-shaped at first, then narrowing to the middle and subcylindric below, 15 mm long.

Epiphyte in humid forests; 900–1000 m.

Madagascar (eastern region).

Plants more robust with longer leaves and larger flowers than the following species.

Beclardia macrostachya (Thouars) A. Richard

Syns. *Beclardia brachystachya* (Thouars) A. Richard, *Oeonia macrostachya* (Thouars) Lindley

Plant erect, 20–40 cm high, with a thick, slightly flattened stem and few roots. Leaves 5–12, linear-oblong, emarginate at the apex, 10–15 cm long, 1–2 cm wide. Inflorescences 20–40 cm long; peduncle with 5–7 short sheaths; pedicel with ovary 1.8 cm long. Flowers 5–12, white with green on the inner surface of the lip and at the apex of the spur; sepals oval-lanceolate, obtuse and shortly apiculate, 18–20 mm long, 7 mm wide; petals spathulate, apiculate, narrow at the base and much wider than the sepals in the apical half; lip with 4 rounded lobes, large, irregular papillae on the inner surface in front of the spur entrance, 12 mm long, 15 mm wide; spur wide at the mouth, funnel-shaped at first, then narrowing to the middle and subcylindric below, ca. 6 mm long.

Epiphyte on trunks and branches in a wide range of forest types, widespread; sea level to 2000 m; flowering between December and June.

Madagascar (eastern, central, and northern regions), Réunion, and Mauritius.

BOLUSIELLA Schlechter

When Rudolf Schlechter proposed this small genus in 1918, he pointed out that the 5 species he knew were easily recognised by their habit. They all have equitant, fleshy leaves attached to a very short stem and densely flowered inflorescences that overtop the leaves. They also have rather easily recognised small white flowers all facing in one direction, each supported by a conspicuous black bract. The in-dividual flowers often do not open fully, and on dissection they reveal a column that is appreciably swollen at the middle, and a small rostellum that is bent upwards at the apex.

The genus was named in honour of Harry Bolus (1834–1911), a Cape Town stockbroker and amateur botanist who had described the first species known (as an *Angraecum*) in 1893. His illustrated works on the orchids of South Africa (1888–1911) were a major contribution to African orchidology at the time.

Seven species and 2 subspecies of *Bolusiella* are now recorded from tropical and southern Africa. They can be distinguished from each other by characters of the leaves, inflorescences, and the shape of the lip and spur. They are found on the twigs and branches of bushes and small trees, often in rather exposed situations, and also on the mossy trunks of large trees in undisturbed rain forest.

Culture

Plants are easily maintained on small branches and twigs similar to those to which they are usually attached in the wild. They can be difficult to establish on a fresh mount in a glasshouse and need a fine medium, such as that usually used for seedlings, if grown in a pot. In the wild they mostly occur at medium or high altitudes and do best in cool conditions where the temperature drops at night.

Bolusiella alinae Szlachetko

This new species was described in 2001 from a single specimen collected in Equatorial Guinea some years earlier and named in honour of the author's wife, Alina. The plant is similar to others in the genus, but the flowers are distinctive. They are easily recognised by the spur which is bent like a knee below a wide mouth and by the small, rounded lateral lobes of the lip.

Epiphyte on a coffee bush.

Equatorial Guinea (Bioco Island).

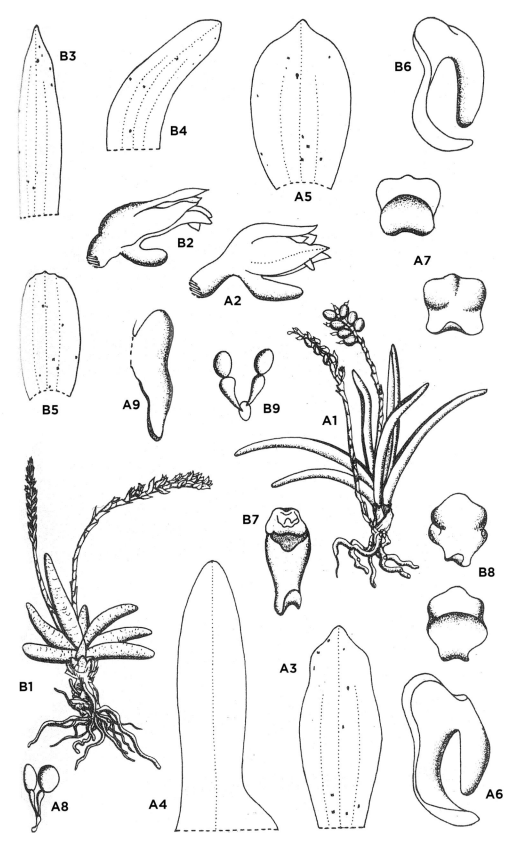

Bolusiella iridifolia and *Bolusiella maudiae*. *Bolusiella iridifolia* subsp. *iridifolia*—A1: Habit. A2: Flower. A3: Dorsal sepal. A4: Lateral sepal. A5: Petal. A6: Lip and spur. A7: Anther-cap. A8: Pollinarium. *Bolusiella iridifolia* subsp. *picea*—A9: Lip and spur. *Bolusiella maudiae*—B1: Habit. B2: Flower. B3: Dorsal sepal. B4: Lateral sepal. B5: Petal. B6: Lip and spur. B7: Column. B8: Anther-cap. B9: Pollinarium. From Cribb 1989, fig. 130. S. Hillier.

Bolusiella batesii (Rolfe) Schlechter

Plants dwarf, with an erect stem up to 2.5 cm long and very slender roots in a tuft at the base of the plant. Leaves 6–10, arranged in a fan, rigid and fleshy, glabrous, rounded at the apex, 2–6 cm long, 4–7 mm wide. Inflorescences much longer than the leaves, with many small sheaths and flowers in slender racemes, 20–25 cm long; peduncle much longer than the rachis; bracts small, brownish, 2 mm long; pedicel with ovary 2 mm long. Flowers white, very close together; tepals free, subequal, ca. 3 mm long, 0.7–1.4 mm wide; lip concave at the base, oblong-ligulate, obtuse, 3 mm long, 0.7–1.1 mm wide; spur greenish, cylindrical, curving forwards below the lip.

Epiphyte, on forest margins and on old cocoa trees; flowering October to December.

Côte d'Ivoire, Ghana, Cameroon, Equatorial Guinea (Bioco Island), Gabon, and Congo.

Bolusiella iridifolia (Rolfe) Schlechter

Plants dwarf, with a short, erect stem and very slender roots in a tuft at the base of the plant. Leaves 4–10, arranged in a fan, tapering from base to apex with a deep, V-shaped groove along the upper surface, rigid and rather fleshy, glabrous, 2–5 cm long, 1.5–5 mm wide. Inflorescences longer than the leaves, with many flowers in slender racemes, 2–6 cm long; peduncle 1 cm long; bracts small, blackish. Flowers white; tepals free, subequal, 2–3 mm long, 0.7–1.4 mm broad; lip oblong-ligulate, obtuse, 2.5–5 mm long, 0.7–1.1 mm wide; spur short, cylindrical or conical, at right angles to the lip.

Two subspecies have been recognised:

subsp. *iridifolia*

This subspecies has larger flowers with a longer and narrower spur than subsp. *picea*.

Epiphyte, on the twigs and branches of forest trees and scrub; 2300–2600 m; flowering April to July.

Kenya, Tanzania, Uganda, many parts of West Africa, and Comoro Islands (Grande Comore).

subsp. *picea* P. J. Cribb

Also widespread. The flowers are smaller with a shorter, more conical spur.

Epiphyte, on bushes and small trees near the top of the hills, often with its tuft of slender roots anchored amongst lichens; 1500 m; flowering in May.

Kenya, Tanzania, Malawi, Zambia, and Zimbabwe.

Bolusiella lebeliana Delepierre & Geerinck

This small species is close to *Bolusiella iridifolia* subsp. *picea* but said to differ in the shape of the lip which has a very short, conical but almost globular spur, 0.5 mm long.

Epiphyte in forest; flowering in February. Rwanda.

Dedicated to the missionary Jean-Paul Lebel.

Bolusiella iridifolia. J. Hermans

Bolusiella iridifolia. B. Campbell

Bolusiella maudiae. E. la Croix

Bolusiella maudiae (Bolus) Schlechter

Syn. *Bolusiella imbricata* (Rolfe) Schlechter

Plants dwarf, with a short, erect stem and very slender roots in a tuft at the base of the plant. Leaves 4–8, arranged in a fan, rigid and fleshy, straight or curved, glabrous, 1–3.5 cm long, 3–9 mm wide. Inflorescences longer than the leaves, with many flowers in slender racemes, 2–6 cm long; bracts small, blackish, as long as the flowers. Flowers white; tepals free, subequal, 3–4 mm long, 1–1.5 mm wide; lip obscurely 3-lobed, side lobes rounded, mid-lobe oblong-ligulate, 2–3 mm long, 0.7–1 mm wide; spur cylindrical, curving forward below the lip, 1.5–2 mm long.

Epiphyte, on twigs and branches of small trees and bushes in the warmer forests; 1200–1900 m; flowering June to September.

Côte d'Ivoire to Kenya, Tanzania, Malawi, Zambia, and South Africa (KwaZulu-Natal).

Bolusiella talbotii (Rendle) Summerhayes

Plants dwarf, with a short, erect stem and very slender roots in a tuft at the base of the plant. Leaves 4–7, arranged in a fan, rigid and fleshy, flattened, glabrous, 6–7 cm long, 0.8–1.2 mm wide. Inflorescences longer than the leaves, with many flowers in slender racemes, 9–10 cm long; peduncle usually shorter than the rachis; bracts small, blackish, spaced 4–5 mm apart. Flowers white; tepals free, subequal, lanceolate, subacute, 2–4 mm long; lip obscurely 3-lobed, side lobes insignificant, rounded, mid-lobe triangular, 2–3 mm long, 0.7–1 mm wide; spur cylindrical, acute, directed backwards, 2–2.5 mm long.

Epiphyte in rain forest and coffee plantations, on old mossy trunks not far above the ground; 100–1000 m; flowering May to July.

Sierra Leone, Liberia, Côte d'Ivoire, Ghana, southern Nigeria, Equatorial Guinea (Bioco and Annobón Islands).

Bolusiella zenkeri (Kraenzlin) Schlechter

This species was described from Cameroon in 1894 as *Listrostachys zenkeri* but was omitted from *Flore du Cameroun* (2001). However, the authors of that flora appear to have re-identified the specimen *Zenker* 623, the type of *Bolusiella zenkeri*, as *B. maudiae*.

CARDIOCHILOS P. J. Cribb

This genus was established in 1977 to accommodate a distinctive angraecoid orchid collected in Malawi on the Nyika Plateau. It appears to be close to the genus *Tridactyle*, but the heart-shaped lip borne on the upper side of the pale green flower makes it quite different from any species in that genus. The generic name was coined by Phillip Cribb in allusion to this feature, from the Greek *cardia*, heart, and *chilos*, lip.

The flowers are usually solitary but sometimes there are 2 per inflorescence, and the peduncle has short black hairs. In some ways this orchid resembles some of the species of *Ypsilopus* in its scabrid pedicel and ovary and bilobed rostellum, but it lacks the distinctive Y-shaped pollinarium that is characteristic of that genus. It also has certain resemblances to *Summerhayesia*. Further studies, in particular DNA analysis of all these taxa, will surely reveal their true position in the subtribe.

Cardiochilos williamsonii P. J. Cribb

Plant small, erect, up to 12 cm high, with a stem 8 cm long and with long, thick roots emanating from the lower part. Leaves in 2 rows, spreading, falcate, linear, unequally bilobed at the apex, 4–8 cm long, 3–6 mm wide. Inflorescences 3–4 cm long, 1- or 2-flowered; peduncle 1–2.5 cm long; bracts ovate to obovate, 2–3.5 mm long; pedicel with ovary scabrid, 7–13 mm long. Flowers pale green to ochreous orange; dorsal sepal elliptic, obtuse, 4 mm long, 2.2 mm wide; lateral sepals connate, obliquely falcate, elliptic, obtuse, 4.5 mm long, 2.5 mm wide; petals oblong-lanceolate, acute, 4 mm long, 2 mm wide; lip auricled at the base, cordate, shortly apiculate, 4 mm long and wide; spur slightly undulate, narrowly cylindric from a wide mouth, 13–16 mm long.

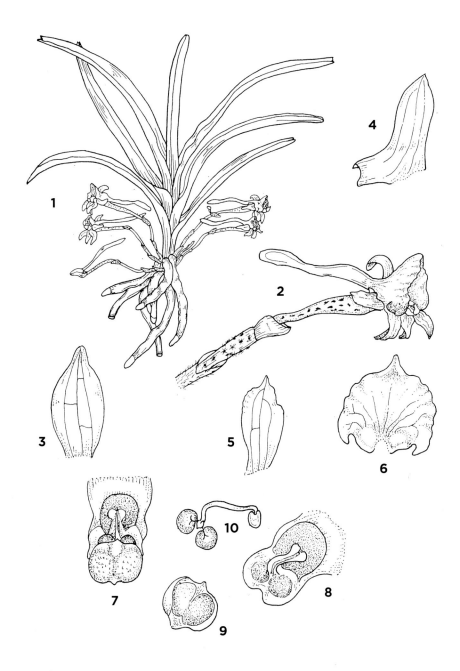

Cardiochilos williamsonii. 1: Habit. 2: Flower. 3: Dorsal sepal. 4: Lateral sepal. 5: Petal. 6: Lip. 7–8: Column. 9: Anther-cap. 10: Pollinarium. From Cribb 1977, p. 182. G. Williamson.

Epiphyte in montane and submontane forest, on *Philippia* and other shrubs, usually amongst lichens; 2200–2500 m; flowering in April.

Southern Tanzania and northern Malawi.

Named in honour of the dentist Graham Williamson who made many interesting finds in Zambia and collected this species in Malawi in 1968.

CHAMAEANGIS Schlechter

Several species were mentioned by Rudolf Schlechter when he established the genus *Chamaeangis* in 1918. He derived the name from the Greek words *chamai*, small or lowly, and *angos*, vessel, a reference to the small flowers that mostly have a swollen spur. Each flowering plant usually has several inflorescences. Normally they are longer than the leaves, and the small but colourful flowers are borne close together, sometimes in whorls.

Eleven species of *Chamaeangis* are now recognised in Africa and one in Mauritius. Six species described from Madagascar and the Comoro Islands were transferred to a new genus, *Microterangis*, by Karlheinz Senghas in 1986. Most species bear the flowers in groups of 2, 3, or more, at each node of the inflorescences, but 6 African species have only a single flower at each node. These are described first, and the single species still recorded from Mauritius and Réunion is described last.

Culture

These species are amongst the easiest epiphytic orchids to grow, either mounted on a piece of bark or placed upright in a pot. They need to be kept very well drained but respond well to frequent watering and feeding during the growing season. They flower regularly every year, sometimes more than once.

Species from Africa

Group 1. Flowers borne singly at the nodes of the inflorescence.

Chamaeangis ichneumonea (Lindley) Schlechter

Plants large with erect or pendent stems to 20 cm long. Leaves in 2 rows, curved, oblong-lanceolate, unequally bilobed at the apex, the smaller lobe sometimes absent, 17–50 cm long, 2.5–4.5 cm wide. Inflorescences pendent, arising below the leaves, 20–50 cm long, many-flowered, one flower per node; bracts clasping the rachis, broadly triangular, 1 mm long; pedicel with ovary slender, 5 mm long. Flowers cream, green, or brownish, scented at night; sepals 5–6 mm long, 2–3 mm wide; petals fleshy, finely papillose, oblong, obtuse, 5 mm long, 1.7 mm wide; lip oblong, shortly 3-lobed or 3-toothed at the apex, the side lobes often longer than the mid-lobe, 5–6 mm long, 3 mm wide; spur bent or curved, inflated in the apical part for 6–10 mm, in total 13–18 mm long.

Epiphyte; flowering June to July, also November and December.

Sierra Leone, Liberia, Ghana, southern Nigeria, Cameroon, Gabon, and Congo.

Chamaeangis lanceolata Summerhayes

Plants small with short stems, 1–5 cm long. Leaves in 2 rows, twisted at the base so that they lie in one plane, lanceolate, leathery, unequally bilobed at the apex, often with one lobe absent, 6–28 cm long, 0.7–2 cm wide. Inflorescences axillary or at the base of the stem, slender, up to 35 cm long, many-flowered, one flower per node; bracts oval, subacute, very short; pedicel with ovary slender, 5 mm long. Flowers cream at first, turning ochreous or bright orange except for the spur; sepals broadly oval-triangular, 3.5–5 mm long; petals lanceolate, acute, 2–4 mm long, 1–2 mm wide; lip broadly ovate-triangular, apiculate, 2.5–3.5 mm long, 2 mm wide; spur curved or bent, swollen in the apical 3–4 mm only, in total 12 mm long.

Epiphyte in evergreen rain forest, in deep shade; flowering in July to August or in November.

Côte d'Ivoire, southern Nigeria, Cameroon, Congo, and Gabon.

Chamaeangis letouzeyi Szlachetko & Olszewski

Plant with a short, upright stem. Leaves 3, narrowly linear-lanceolate, unequally and acutely bilobed at the apex, 18–20 cm long, 1.3–3 cm wide. Inflorescences lax, 5.5–25 cm long, 13-flowered, one flower per node; bracts pointed, 1 mm long; pedicel with ovary slender, 4–6 mm long. Flowers yellow-orange, small; dorsal sepal broadly oval, obtuse, 4 mm long, 3 mm wide; lateral sepals obliquely oblong-oval to elliptic-oval, subobtuse, 4 mm long, 2 mm wide; petals oval-triangular,

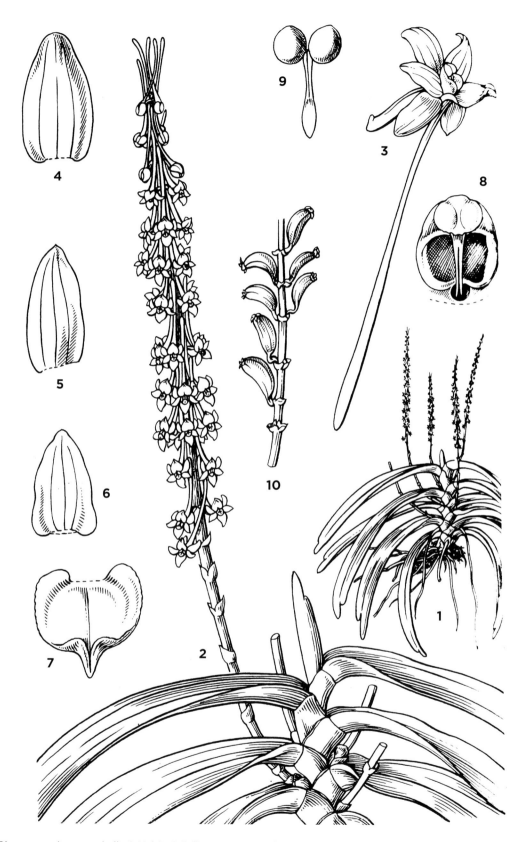

Chamaeangis sarcophylla. 1: Habit. 2: Inflorescence. 3: Flower. 4: Dorsal sepal. 5: Lateral sepal. 6: Petal. 7: Lip. 8: Column. 9: Pollinarium. 10: Fruits. From Cribb 1989, fig. 131. S. Ross-Craig.

acute, 3.2 mm long, 1.5 mm wide; lip oblong-oval, entire, very thick, 3.2 mm long, 1.5 mm wide; spur curved, cylindric, inflated near the tip only, 6 mm long.

Epiphyte in montane forest; 1800 m.

Cameroon.

Named in honour of French botanist Réné Letouzey (1918–1989), who made many plant collections in Cameroon. This species is recognised as unique by its short spur.

Chamaeangis pauciflora Perez-Vera

Plants erect with short stems 3–6 cm high. Leaves in 2 rows, spaced close together, linear, pointed, very fleshy, 10–30 cm long, 0.7–1.5 cm wide. Inflorescences pendent, below the leaves, often branched, bearing many flowers spaced 3–6 mm apart; bracts minute; pedicel with ovary curved and slender. Flowers yellowish, small; sepals narrowly lanceolate, 2–3.5 mm long; petals much smaller, acute; lip entire, reflexed at the apex, very similar to the sepals; spur slender, cylindric or slightly curved, inflated at the apical 1.5 mm only, 4.5–7 mm long.

Epiphyte in evergreen rain forest in well-shaded situations; low to medium altitude; flowering May to July.

Côte d'Ivoire.

This species is rather similar to *Chamaeangis vesicata* but can be distinguished by the branched inflorescence with widely spaced flowers borne singly at each node.

Chamaeangis thomensis (Rolfe) Schlechter

Plant with a very short stem. Leaves linear, 12–15 cm long, 12–17 mm wide. Inflorescences pendent, 30 cm long, many-flowered; bracts broadly ovate, 3 mm long; pedicel with ovary 6 mm long. Flowers pale orange, small; dorsal sepal elliptic-oblong, obtuse, 5 mm long; lateral sepals oblong, subacute; petals linear, obtuse; lip ovate, obtuse, 4 mm long; spur slightly curved, slender then subclavate, 8 mm long.

São Tomé.

Said to be close to *Chamaeangis ichneumonea* but with narrower leaves and a shorter spur.

Chamaeangis vagans (Lindley) Schlechter

Plant with long stems. Leaves elliptic, 20–25 cm long, up to 5 cm wide. Inflorescences pendent, up to 30 cm long, many-flowered; bracts short and broad; pedicel with ovary 4 mm long. Flowers pale yellow, small; sepals and petals oblong, obtuse, fleshy, 3 mm long; lip 3-dentate at the apex; spur curved or bent, inflated at the apex, 12 mm long.

Príncipe; 300–400 m.

Described by the collector as 'having the habit of a gigantic *Vanda*', and said to be very common on many islets in the Gulf of Guinea.

Group 2. Flowers mostly in groups of 2 or 3 or in whorls of 4–6 along the inflorescence.

Chamaeangis gabonensis Summerhayes

Plant with robust stems up to 5 cm high. Leaves numerous, borne very close together, long and narrow, linear or narrowly lanceolate-linear, fleshy, with upcurved margins, up to 45 cm long, 1 cm wide. Inflorescences pendent, arising below the leaves, 14–25 cm long, bearing many flowers in groups of 2 or 3 at each node; bracts very small, up to 2 mm long; pedicel with ovary slender, 4 mm long. Flowers yellowish, small; dorsal sepal ovate, apiculate, convex, 3 mm long, 2 mm wide; lateral sepals obliquely elliptic, apiculate, 5 mm long, 2 mm wide; petals lanceolate, acute, 2.5–3 mm long, 1.2 mm wide; lip oblong, widest near the base, shortly 3-lobed at the apex, 3 mm long, 1.7 mm wide; spur bent or curved, slender and slightly inflated in the apical half, 15 mm long.

Epiphyte; flowering in October.

Gabon.

This species seems to be close to *Chamaeangis vesicata* but has narrower leaves and a differently shaped lip and spur.

Chamaeangis sarcophylla. B. Campbell

Chamaeangis kloetzliana Szlachetko & Olszewski

This new species was described in 2001 from a single collection made near Nairobi, Kenya, some years earlier. It seems to be very close to *Chamaeangis vesicata*, from the published drawings, though in their text the authors compare it with *C. sarcophylla*. It is named in honour of Manfred Kloetzl, conservator of the orchid collection at the University of Hamburg.

Chamaeangis odoratissima (Reichenbach f.) Schlechter

Syn. *Chamaeangis urostachya* (Kraenzlin) Schlechter

Plants often pendent with the apical part of the stem upturned, thickened, often greatly elongated, rooting near the base, 20–45 cm long, 4–6 mm in diameter. Leaves in 2 rows, fleshy but not swollen, flat, oblanceolate, slightly falcate and drooping, unequally bilobed at the apex, 10–24 cm long, 2–3 cm wide. Inflorescences longer than the leaves, with many flowers in whorls of 2–6. Flowers yellow or yellow-green, small, 3–4 mm in diameter; sepals elliptic, obtuse, 1–2 mm long; petals round or elliptic, 1.5 mm long; lip concave, ovate, obtuse, 2 mm long; spur straight or incurved, cylindric, 5–9 mm long.

Epiphyte on large trees in forest in the warmer parts of the continent; sea level to 2300 m; flowering in April and June to December.

Sierra Leone eastwards to Kenya, and south to Malawi and Angola.

Chamaeangis sarcophylla Schlechter

Syn. *Chamaeangis orientalis* Summerhayes

Plants upright or pendent with short stems covered in overlapping leaf bases, and rooting from the base, 2–15 cm long. Leaves fleshy and swollen or rather shrunken in dry seasons, dark bluish grey, linear, falcate, unequally bilobed at the apex, 6–30 cm long, 5–25 mm wide. Inflorescences usually several, arching or upright, somewhat swollen, with many flowers in whorls of 2–4. Flowers pale apricot, orange, or salmon pink, 3–5 mm in diameter; sepals ovate to oblong-elliptic, laterals recurved, 2–3.5 mm long; petals recurved, ovate or lanceolate, obtuse, 2–3.6 mm long; lip ovate-oblong, obtuse or obscurely 3-lobed at the apex, 2–3.5 mm long; spur cylindric, 9–19 mm long, arranged parallel to the rachis.

Epiphyte, widespread in highland forests, usually high up in the tree canopy; 1500–2400 m; flowering March to July and sometimes in December.

D.R. of Congo, Rwanda, Burundi, Uganda, Kenya, Tanzania, and Malawi.

Chamaeangis vesicata (Lindley) Schlechter

Plants usually less than 10 cm high, with arching or pendent stems, rooting from the base. Leaves fleshy or coriaceous, pendent, linear, falcate, obliquely and pointedly bilobed at the apex, dull bluish green, 20–40 cm long, less than 1.5 cm wide. Inflorescences pendent, usually longer than the leaves, with many flowers in pairs. Flowers pale green or yellow with paler spurs, 3–6 mm in diameter; sepals ovate, acute, 2–3 mm long; petals lan-

Chamaeangis vesicata. J. Hermans

ceolate, acute, 2.5–3 mm long; lip ovate, subacute, 2.5–3 mm long; spur incurved, greatly swollen at the apex, 7–12 mm long.

Epiphyte, widespread in highland forests, often where there is a pronounced dry season; 1100–2200 m; flowering in March to May, also September to October.

Sierra Leone eastwards to Kenya and Tanzania.

Species from Mascarene Islands

Chamaeangis gracilis (Thouars) Schlechter

Syn. *Angraecum gracile* Thouars

Plant with a short stem. Leaves 6, lorate, long and narrow, briefly contracted at the base, articulated to a swollen leaf sheath which overlaps the stem, 33 cm long, 12 mm wide. Inflorescence as long as the leaves, 12- to 15-flowered, one flower per node; peduncle twice as long as the rachis which is slightly swollen; bracts lanceolate, 2 mm long. Flowers small; sepals and petals lanceolate, subequal; lip oval-deltoid; spur curved near the tip, as long as the pedicel and ovary.

Mauritius and Réunion.

Illustrated in Thouars (1822) as *Angraecum gracile*.

CHAULIODON Summerhayes

This monotypic genus was established by V. S. Summerhayes in 1943 when he reviewed all the leafless orchids then known in Madagascar and Africa. One specimen collected in Liberia in 1912 and another collected from southern Nigeria at about the same time seemed so different from all the others, particularly in the peculiar lip and anther structure, that he established a new genus for them. The Greek word *chauliodon* describes something with outstanding or projecting teeth and refers to the erect, pointed callus that projects upwards in front of the spur from the base of the tiny lip. Summerhayes named the only species, *C. buntingii*, after the collector who found it in Liberia.

The Swedish botanist Lars Jonsson made a detailed study of all the species of *Microcoelia* in the 1970s, in the course of which he realised that *M. deflexicalcarata*, described from Zaire (now D.R. of Congo) in 1916, should be included in the new genus *Chauliodon*, and that the specimens he saw from Zaire were in fact very similar to those studied from Liberia and Nigeria by Summerhayes. In 1979, therefore, he proposed the transfer to *Chauliodon*, where the epithet *deflexicalcaratum* takes priority over *buntingii* for the same species.

Chauliodon deflexicalcaratum (De Wildeman) Jonsson

Syns. *Chauliodon buntingii* Summerhayes, *Microcoelia deflexicalcarata* (De Wildeman) Summerhayes

Plant small with a short stem to 2 cm long and many elongated roots. Leaves absent. Inflorescences slender, usually 15–25 cm long but sometimes up to 60 cm long, many-flowered; bracts very small; pedicel with ovary slender, ca. 1 cm long. Flowers pinkish brown or white tinged with brown, 7–8 mm apart; dorsal sepal concave, oblanceolate, apiculate, 3.5–4 mm long, 2–2.5 mm wide; lateral sepals longer and wider in the upper part, almost L-shaped, 5–6 mm long, 2.5 mm wide; petals narrowly suboval, acuminate, 3–4 mm long, 1 mm wide; lip very short and acute, supporting a tooth-like, erect callus ca. 2 mm tall just in front of the spur opening; spur 3–3.5 mm wide and cup-shaped at the mouth, narrowing to just beyond the middle where it abruptly curves forward, the apical part slightly swollen, in total 12–14 mm long.

Epiphyte on trees in rain forest and on well-shaded shrubs at forest margins; flowering in July and January.

Liberia, Côte d'Ivoire, Ghana, southern Nigeria, and D.R. of Congo.

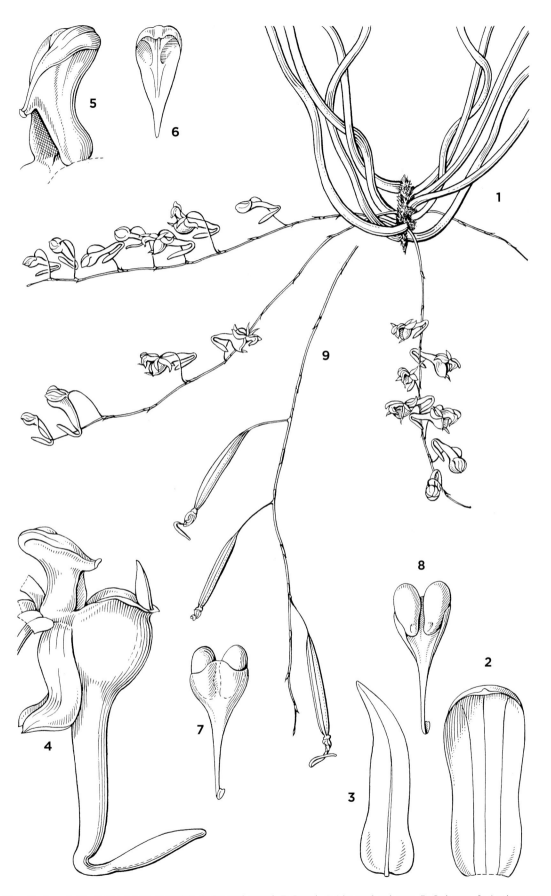

Chauliodon deflexicalcaratum. 1: Habit. 2: Dorsal sepal. 3: Petal. 4: Lip and column. 5: Column. 6: Anther-cap. 7–8: Pollinarium. 9: Fruits. From Summerhayes 1956b, t. 3566. S. Ross-Craig.

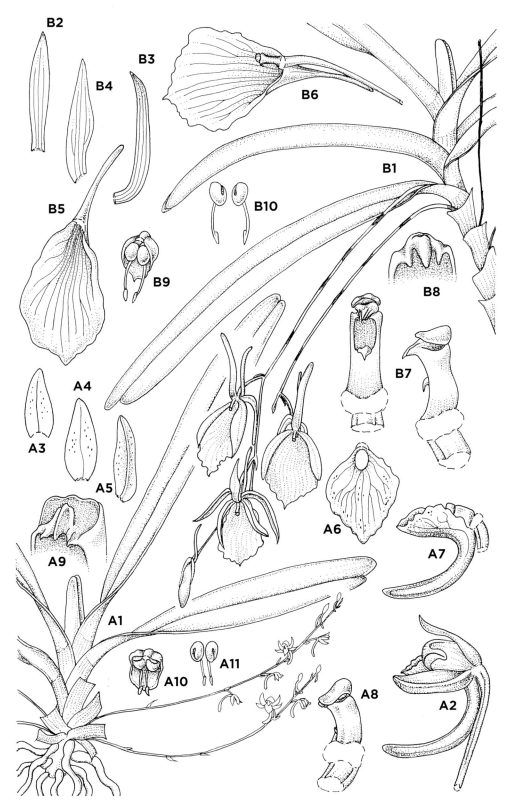

Cribbia thomensis and *C. pendula*. *Cribbia thomensis*—A1: Habit. A2: Flower. A3: Dorsal sepal. A4: Lateral sepal. A5: Petal. A6: Lip. A7: Lip and spur. A8–9: Column. A10: Anther-cap and pollinaria. A11: Pollinaria. *Cribbia pendula*—B1: Habit. B2: Dorsal sepal. B3: Lateral sepal. B4: Petal. B5–6: Lip and column. B7: Column. B8: Anther-cap. B9: Anther-cap and pollinaria. B10: Pollinaria. From Cribb and la Croix 1997, p. 746. J. Stone.

Cribbia brachyceras. B. Campbell

CRIBBIA Senghas

The genus *Cribbia* was established by Karlheinz Senghas in 1986 in honour of Phillip Cribb at the Royal Botanic Gardens, Kew. Only one species, *C. brachyceras*, was proposed at first, but 3 more have been described, one from Cameroon that seems to be quite widely distributed and two from São Tomé. *Cribbia* species are rather similar in some respects to species of *Diaphananthe* and *Mystacidium* and not all that different from some species of *Angraecopsis*. However, the known species do not fit easily into any of these genera as they are currently circumscribed and are thus kept separate in this new genus. Further work on generic limits in the Aerangidinae is long overdue.

Culture

Only *Cribbia brachyceras* is well known in cultivation. Plants are easily maintained when mounted or when placed in a pot and, because they are very

Cribbia brachyceras. J. Hermans

floriferous, are welcome additions to a collection. The plants come from the African highlands, so require cool nights with higher temperatures by day and high humidity during the growing season. Pot-grown plants need good drainage, but the compost must be water-retentive. The 3 recently described species are not yet in cultivation.

Cribbia brachyceras (Summerhayes) Senghas

Syns. *Aerangis brachyceras* Summerhayes, *Rangaeris brachyceras* (Summerhayes) Summerhayes

Plants small with short upright or arching stems, rooting at the base, up to 20 cm long. Leaves suberect or spreading, in 2 rows, linear-oblong, unequally bilobed at the apex, with rounded lobes, 8–13 cm long, 7–15 mm wide. Inflorescences usually several, suberect, with 7–15 well spaced flowers, 4–18 cm long. Flowers pale green or pale yellowish brown, almost translucent; dorsal sepal oblong-lanceolate, acute, 5–7 mm long, 1–2 mm wide; lateral sepals deflexed, linear or linear-oblanceolate, acute, 6–7.5 mm long, 1–1.5 mm wide; petals oblong or elliptic-oblong, obtuse or rounded, 5 mm long, 1.4–2 mm wide; lip entire, recurved at

tip, lanceolate, acute, 5 mm long, 3 mm wide; spur decurved, cylindric, slightly inflated towards the apex, 5–6 mm long.

Epiphyte amongst mosses on trunks and the larger branches of trees in forests; also recorded from mossy rocks; 1500–2200 m; flowering in June.

Guinea, Sierra Leone, Liberia, Nigeria, São Tomé, Cameroon, D.R. of Congo, Uganda, Kenya, Zambia, and Malawi.

Cribbia confusa P. J. Cribb

Plant small with an erect or horizontal stem, rooting at the base, 4–5 cm long. Leaves in 2 rows, conduplicate, linear-oblanceolate, unequally bilobed at the apex, 5–12 cm long, 8–12 mm wide. Inflorescences axillary or basal, spreading, rachis bearing 7–12 flowers spaced ca. 1 cm apart, 9–11 cm long; peduncle 4–5 cm long; bracts oval, acute, 3 mm long; pedicel with ovary slender, 4–6 mm long. Flowers greenish yellow; sepals lanceolate, dorsal sepal acute, 8–9 mm long, 2 mm wide, lateral sepals falcate, 7–9 mm long, 2 mm wide; petals similar to lateral sepals, acuminate, 6–8 mm long,

Cribbia confusa. J. Hermans

2 mm wide; lip entire, lanceolate, acute, 11 mm long, 3 mm wide; spur cylindric, tapering, parallel with the ovary, 5–7 mm long.

Epiphyte in humid montane forests; 600–2100 m; flowering in September, October, November, and January.

Liberia, Côte d'Ivoire, Cameroon, and São Tomé.

Probably misidentified with *Cribbia brachyceras* in the past, but distinguished from that species by the larger flowers with longer lip and shorter spur.

Cribbia pendula la Croix & P. J. Cribb

Plant small with an erect stem 7 cm long. Leaves 7–8 in 2 rows, conduplicate, ligulate-lanceolate, unequally and obtusely bilobed at the apex, 9.5–13 cm long, 15–17 mm wide. Inflorescences axillary or basal, pendent, rachis with 1–3 flowers spaced ca. 1 cm apart, up to 12 cm long; peduncle wiry, ca. 8 cm long; bracts lanceolate, acute, 3 mm long; pedicel with ovary slender, 15 mm long. Flowers translucent, pale green; dorsal sepal erect, linear, acute, 14 mm long, 2–2.5 mm wide; lateral sepals linear, reflexed, falcate, 16 mm long, 2 mm wide; petals spreading, narrowly oblanceolate, falcate, acuminate, lying along the upper margins of the lip, 14 mm long, 3 mm wide; lip obovate, apiculate, apical margins erose, 15–17 mm long, 10–12 mm wide; spur ascending, very slender, 10–11 mm long.

Epiphyte in mist forest; 2000 m.

São Tomé.

This is the most distinctive species in the genus and is characterised by its large, pale flowers with obovate lip.

Cribbia thomensis la Croix & P. J. Cribb

Plant small with an erect stem 4–5 cm long. Leaves 5 in 2 rows on upper part of stem, conduplicate, linear-oblanceolate, unequally and bluntly bilobed at the apex, 6–10 cm long, 8–10 mm wide.

Inflorescences axillary or basal, spreading, rachis with 6–10 flowers spaced ca. 1 cm apart, 6–8 cm long; peduncle 4–5 cm long; bracts oval, acute, 1–1.5 mm long; pedicel with ovary slender, 5–7 mm long. Flowers white; dorsal sepal cucullate, ovate, acute, 4 mm long, 1.5 mm wide; lateral sepals linear-lanceolate, acute, 4 mm long, 1.5 mm wide; petals lanceolate, falcate, acute, 4 mm long, 2 mm wide; lip entire, ovate, acute, 5 mm long, 3.5 mm wide; spur cylindric, incurved, slightly inflated at the apex, 8–9 mm long.

Epiphyte in montane forest; 2000–2100 m; flowering in February.

São Tomé.

This species is easily distinguished by its small white flowers.

CYRTORCHIS Schlechter

Rudolf Schlechter created the genus *Cyrtorchis* to accommodate a small group of species allied to *Angraecum arcuatum* Lindley (syn. *Listrostachys arcuata* (Lindley) Reichenbach f.). They all have lanceolate, recurved sepals and petals and a very similar lip that passes gradually into a long, curving and tapering spur. The generic name refers to these features, from the Greek *kyrtos*, a swelling or curve, and *orchis*, orchid. Although he only named 4 species of *Cyrtorchis* when he created the genus in 1914, Schlechter stated that the genus contained about 15 species altogether. Nearly 40 taxa have been described since then and about 15 species are now recognised.

The star-shaped, white or cream-coloured flowers that sometimes fade to yellow or orange as they age are characteristic. They make *Cyrtorchis* species amongst the easiest African epiphytic orchids to place in a genus, but they are some of the most difficult to identify individually. The rather stiff plants with leaves in 2 rows on either side of the stem are also characteristic of most species. Another feature is the large pale bracts that loosely enclose the flowers in bud and turn black or dark brown or are shed by the time the flowers

have opened. All the flowers are sweetly scented, particularly in the evening.

Summerhayes studied the genus when he was preparing the account of orchids in western tropical Africa for publication in 1936, and in his key he divided the species into 2 groups depending on the nature of the viscidium. In 1948 he formally published these groups as 2 distinct sections. These were revised in his paper of 1960. In section 1, *Cyrtorchis*, the viscidium consists of 2 parts, an upper hardened portion and a thin lower portion (originally called *Heterocolleticon*), and in section 2, *Homocolleticon*, the viscidium is more or less uniformly thin and hyaline. These differences are not easy to see except with a hand lens. Nevertheless, we have followed the segregation of species into these 2 sections because this separation has been widely followed in the literature. Szlachetko and Olswzewski (2001) have raised section *Homocolleticon* to generic level, but we do not believe that this treatment is justified or helpful and have not followed it.

Cyrtorchis species can be found in almost every country in tropical Africa, and it has to be admitted that knowing where a plant comes from is often a great help in trying to identify it. The type species, *C. arcuata*, was originally described by John Lindley in 1836 from material collected in south-eastern Africa by the German collector J. F. Drège (1794–1881), but is now known to be one of the most widespread African epiphytic orchids, from Sierra Leone to Kenya and from Ethiopia to the Eastern Cape in South Africa. Other species are very localised. Two species (*C. crassifolia* and *C. glaucifolia*) have light greyish-green, almost succulent foliage, and a few species, including *C. monteiroae*, have very dark green leaves. Others are more difficult to tell apart.

Culture

These plants grow as epiphytes or lithophytes in the wild and are easily maintained in cultivation. They thrive in a pot or basket of free-draining compost such as bark. Most of these plants pro-

Cyrtorchis chailluana. 1: Habit. 2–3: Column and rostellum. 4: Anther-cap. 5: Pollinarium. 6: Viscidium.
From Summerhayes 1968, fig. 402. S. Ross-Craig.

duce small branches from the lower part of the stem after some of the leaves have fallen, so that specimen plants are produced in a relatively short time. Attention must be paid to growing and resting seasons, since the plants do not need much water or nutrient when they are dormant. Smaller plants of all the species are also established easily on pieces of bark and grow well when mounted in this way.

Section *Cyrtorchis* Summerhayes

The flowers have a bipartite viscidium, the upper part saddle-shaped, thick, and hard, and the lower part hyaline.

Cyrtorchis acuminata (Rolfe) Schlechter

Plant with erect stems. Leaves oblong, shortly, obtusely, and unequally bilobed, 10–12.5 cm long, up to 4 cm wide. Inflorescences several-flowered; bracts broadly ovate, subacute, cucullate, 18–22 mm long; pedicel with ovary 3 cm long. Flowers white; sepals and petals lanceolate, acuminate, 2.5–3 cm long; lip similar, fleshy, 2–2.5 cm long; spur straight, 4–5 cm long.

Equatorial Guinea (Annobón Island) and Príncipe.

This species is very close to *Cyrtorchis arcuata* but seems to have broader leaves and the hardened part of the viscidium is broader.

Cyrtorchis arcuata (Lindley) Schlechter

Syn. *Cyrtorchis sedenii* (Reichenbach f.) Schlechter

Plants upright, often forming large clumps, with stems up to 30 cm long and thick roots with brownish tips from the basal part. Leaves in 2 rows, linear-ligulate or narrowly oblong, unequally bilobed at the apex, with rounded lobes, 12–22 cm long, 1.5–3.5 cm wide. Inflorescences axillary or below the leaves, 6–20 cm long, 5- to 14-flowered; bracts ovate, 15–33 mm long. Flowers white, tinged with green or salmon pink, fading to orange; sepals lanceolate, acuminate, recurved, 18–50 mm long, 5–7 mm wide; petals similar but shorter, 12–25

Cyrtorchis arcuata. J. Hermans

mm long; lip similar to the petals, up to 36 mm long; spur curved or S-shaped, 3–8 cm long.

Two subspecies are now recognised:

subsp. **arcuata**

Leaves usually less than 25 mm wide, dull green. Sepals 18–40 mm long; spur 3–6 cm long.

Epiphyte or lithophytic in undisturbed vegetation, usually where the plants enjoy bright sunlight such as savannah; sea level to 3000 m; flowering in March and April.

Liberia eastwards to Ethiopia and southwards to South Africa (Cape Province).

This subspecies is very variable, but attempts to subdivide it always break down when large numbers of specimens are studied.

subsp. **whytei** (Rolfe) Summerhayes

Syn. *Cyrtorchis whytei* (Rolfe) Schlechter

Leaves up to 35 mm wide, glossy dark green. Sepals 30–50 mm long; spur 6–10 cm long.

Epiphyte in mixed deciduous forest and woodland and along rivers; 750–2000 m; flowering October to December.

Sierra Leone, Liberia, Ghana, Côte d'Ivoire, and Togo; also in Zambia and Malawi.

This subspecies has larger flowers with longer spurs than the typical form. It approaches *Cyrtorchis chailluana* in these respects, but the spurs are shorter and not as slender as in that species.

Cyrtorchis aschersonii (Kraenzlin) Schlechter

Plant erect with a short stem 5–30 cm long. Leaves in 2 rows, linear, leathery, rigid, sometimes fleshy with the margins incurved, appearing almost cylindrical, equally bilobed at the apex, with rounded lobes, 8–25 cm long, 8–16 mm wide. Inflorescences axillary, half as long as the subtending leaf, 7–12 cm long, 4- to 10-flowered; bracts oval, acute, brown, 8–15 mm long, 10–14 mm apart. Flowers white, with spur and ovary tinged green, 2 cm in diameter; sepals lanceolate, acuminate, recurved in apical half, 1.5–2 cm long, 1.5–2 mm wide; petals slightly narrower and smaller, spreading; lip similar but widened at the base; spur straight or slightly sinuous, 2.5–4 cm long.

Epiphyte on the trunks and large branches of trees in rain forest, usually well-exposed to light, and in cocoa plantations; up to 1500 m; flowering April to September.

Sierra Leone, Côte d'Ivoire, Ghana, southern Nigeria, Cameroon, and Congo.

Easily recognised by its very narrow leaves and relatively small flowers.

Cyrtorchis chailluana (Hooker f.) Schlechter

Syns. *Cyrtorchis helicocalcar* Bellone, *C. letouzeyi* Szlachetko & Olszewski

Plant with long stems, usually pendent, up to 70 cm long. Leaves in 2 rows, oblong or narrowly elliptic, conduplicate at the base but flat above, unequally bilobed at the apex, with rounded lobes, 11–25 cm long, 1.9–3.5 cm wide. Inflorescences axillary or opposite a leaf base in the axil of a leaf

Cyrtorchis aschersonii. C. Arends

sheath, 12–25 cm long, 6- to 12-flowered; bracts boat-shaped, 8–25 mm long, 10–22 mm apart; pedicel with ovary 42–45 mm long. Flowers white, scented; sepals and petals acuminate, 30–50 mm long, 2.5–6 mm wide; lip acuminate, 30–50 mm long, 2.5–6 mm wide; spur straight, incurved or slightly sinuous, sometimes curled at the apex, 8.5–16 cm long.

Epiphyte in rain forest; 1150–1250 m; flowering throughout the year.

Sierra Leone and Nigeria eastwards to Gabon, D.R. of Congo, and Uganda.

This species has the largest flowers of all the species and the longest spur.

Cyrtorchis glaucifolia Summerhayes

Plant with an erect, elongated stem bearing thick fleshy roots from near the base. Leaves in 2 rows, about 15 mm apart, ligulate, conduplicate in the basal half, fleshy, pale glaucous green, unequally lobed at the apex, with rounded lobes, 6–8 cm long, 1 cm wide. Inflorescences axillary, amongst the upper leaves, 10–15 cm long, up to 6-flowered; bracts ovate, spreading, apiculate, 7–8 mm long, 6–7 mm wide; pedicel with ovary 15–25 mm long. Flowers white; dorsal sepal lanceolate, acuminate, 2 cm long, 4.5 mm wide; lateral sepals obliquely lanceolate, acuminate, 2.2–2.3 cm long, 3.5–4 mm wide; petals obliquely lanceolate, acuminate, 1.4–1.5 cm long, 4 mm wide; lip similar to the petals, recurved, 1.6 cm long, 6 mm wide; spur S-shaped, tapering to the acute apex, 4 cm long.

Epiphyte on *Xerophyta*; ca. 500 m; flowering in February and April.

Northern Mozambique.

Cyrtorchis hamata (Rolfe) Schlechter

Plant with strong erect stems, 10–50 cm long. Leaves in 2 rows, ligulate, fleshy, unequally bilobed at the apex, with rounded lobes, articulated to a persistent leaf base, 9–24 cm long, 1.5–2.5 cm wide. Inflorescences axillary, spreading or curved downwards, bearing 6–8 flowers spaced 1–1.5 cm apart, shorter than the leaves; bracts in 2 rows, broadly lanceolate, acute, brown, 10–12 mm long. Flowers white with a green spur; sepals and petals reflexed, lanceolate, acuminate, 2–3.5 cm long; lateral sepals longest; petals similar to dorsal sepal; lip lanceolate, wider at the base, acuminate, 2 cm long; spur straight or slightly S-shaped with a hooked or rolled up apex, 2–2.5 cm long.

Epiphyte in the crowns of tall trees; flowering May to August.

Côte d'Ivoire, Ghana, and Nigeria.

Somewhat similar to *Cyrtorchis arcuata* but more slender in most respects and easily recognised by the hooked end of its green spur.

Cyrtorchis neglecta Summerhayes

Plants upright, with stems 20–40 cm long. Leaves in 2 rows, suberect, linear, leathery, unequally bilobed at the apex, with rounded lobes, 8–24 cm long, 1–3 cm wide. Inflorescences axillary or below the leaves, 3–9 cm long, 4- to 10-flowered; bracts ovate, 5–11 mm long and 5–10 mm apart;

pedicel with ovary 18–22 mm long. Flowers white, tinged with salmon pink, fading to orange; sepals lanceolate, acuminate, recurved, 12–20 mm long, 4–7 mm wide; petals similar but shorter, 10–16 mm long; lip similar to the petals, up to 16 mm long; spur straight, 3–5 cm long.

Epiphyte or lithophyte in humid forest and gallery forest; sea level to 1750 m; flowering in March.

D.R. of Congo, Rwanda, Burundi, Kenya, Tanzania, and Zambia.

This species is very similar to *Cyrtorchis arcuata* but is in all respects smaller and the flowers are borne closer together than in that species. It seems to prefer more humid areas than the more widespread species and has thinner leaves.

Cyrtorchis seretii (De Wildeman) Schlechter

Syn. *Cyrtorchis erythraeae* (Rolfe) Schlechter

Plant erect or pendent with a stem up to 20 cm long. Leaves up to 14 in 2 rows, linear, conduplicate at the base, oblong, unequally bilobed at the apex, 8–16 cm long, 8–15 mm wide. Inflorescences axillary, usually shorter than the leaves, 6–12 cm long, 5- to 10-flowered; bracts ovate, subacute, 12–15 mm long, 7–11 mm apart; pedicel with ovary 26–28 mm long. Flowers white, with a greenish or pinkish spur, scented; sepals linear-lanceolate, long acuminate, 2–3 cm long, 4–6 mm wide; petals similar but shorter, 1.5–2 cm long, 4–5 mm wide; lip long acuminate, 1.7–2.5 cm long, 2.5–4.5 mm wide; spur straight or S-shaped, 5–6 cm long.

Epiphyte in shrubby savannah; 1000–1500 m; flowering May to August.

D.R. of Congo, Central African Republic, Uganda, and Ethiopia.

Named after the collector, Félix Seret.

Section *Homocolleticon* Summerhayes

The flowers have a uniform viscidium that is hyaline throughout.

Cyrtorchis brownii (Rolfe) Schlechter

Plants upright, small, usually with a single stem up to 20 cm long, thick roots with brownish tips.

Leaves in 2 rows, linear, leathery, unequally bi-lobed at the apex, with rounded lobes, 6–12 cm long, 7–15 mm wide. Inflorescences axillary or below the leaves, 3–9 cm long, 5- to 12-flowered; bracts ovate, 6–8 mm long and only 3–4 mm apart. Flowers white, tinged with green, fading to orange; sepals lanceolate, acuminate, recurved, 10–13 mm long, 2–3 mm wide; petals similar but shorter, 8–9 mm long; lip similar to the petals, up to 10 mm long; spur straight, 2–4 cm long.

Epiphyte in riverside forests; 1000–1530 m; flowering in October.

Sierra Leone to Kenya.

This is one of the smaller species. In Côte d'Ivoire, a few plants with broader leaves and very recurved sepals and petals have been recognised as a distinct variety, var. *guillaumetii* Perez-Vera (2003).

Cyrtorchis crassifolia Schlechter

Plant small with short stems to 4 cm long and with roots 5–6 mm in diameter. Leaves up to 6 in 2 rows, spaced close together, succulent, greyish green, recurved, V-shaped in cross section, 2–6 cm long, 1 cm wide. Inflorescences axillary between the lower leaves, arching, bearing 3–8 flowers spaced close together, ca. 4 cm long; bracts obtuse, 3–4 mm long; pedicel with ovary 7–12 mm long. Flowers creamy white, not opening fully, turning orange with age; sepals lanceolate, acuminate, recurved at the tips, 7–14 mm long, 2–4 mm wide; petals similar but slightly smaller, 6–10 mm long, 2.5–3.2 mm wide; lip similar to petals, 6.5–11 mm long, 3.5–5.3 mm wide; spur incurved, tapering, 1.8–3 cm long.

Epiphyte on trunks and large branches in de-ciduous woodlands, or rarely lithophytic, usually surrounded with lichens; 1200–2050 m; flowering October to December.

Tanzania, Malawi, Zambia, and Zimbabwe.

Cyrtorchis henriquesiana (Ridley) Schlechter

Plant erect with stems 3–15 cm long. Leaves many, narrowly linear, folded longitudinally, thickened, and somewhat rounded on the lower side, 15–23 cm long, 2–6 mm wide. Inflorescences axillary, shorter than the leaves, up to 6-flowered. Flowers white, becoming yellow with age, small; lip oval and acuminate, apex recurved, 10 mm long, 5 mm wide; spur 3.2 cm long.

Epiphyte or lithophyte, usually in well-lit situations; 70–370 m; recorded in flower in June, September, October, and January.

Príncipe, Equatorial Guinea (Rio Muni), and Gabon.

Easily recognised by its narrow, quill-like leaves.

Cyrtorchis injoloensis (De Wildeman) Schlechter

Plant usually pendent with stems 6–12 cm long. Leaves 8–10, linear-oblong, unequally bilobed at the apex, with rounded lobes, 22–40 cm long, 2–3 cm wide. Inflorescences dense, 22–25 cm long, many-flowered; peduncle 7–8 mm long, covered by a sheath; bracts broadly ovate, longer than the

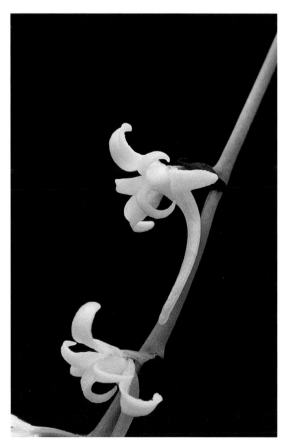

Cyrtorchis injoloensis. C. Arends

ovary; pedicel with ovary 6–7 mm long. Flowers 15–22, white; sepals lanceolate, acute to acuminate, 13–15 mm long, 4 mm wide; petals similar, 11–12 mm long, 3–3.5 mm wide; lip lanceolate, acute, 11–12 mm long, 4 mm wide; spur straight or S-shaped, 2.5–3 cm long.

Epiphyte in primary forest and relict patches; 30–1200 m; flowering in April or September.

D.R. of Congo, Uganda, and Tanzania.

This species is not well known but seems to have the largest leaves in the genus.

Cyrtorchis monteiroae (Reichenbach f.) Schlechter

Plant usually pendent with stems up to 80 cm long. Leaves in 2 rows, dark green, flat, oblanceolate or narrowly elliptic, tapering to both ends, margins often undulate, 10–20 cm long, 3–5 cm wide. Inflorescences axillary, pendent, bearing 10–20 widely spaced flowers, 18–32 cm long; peduncle slender, 5–8 cm long; bracts broadly ovate, obtuse; pedicel with ovary 13–15 mm long. Flowers white or creamy green, tinged with orange in the spur; sepals lanceolate, acuminate, 15–18 mm long, 4.5–5 mm long; petals similar, 14–15 mm long, 4–4.5 mm wide; lip lanceolate, acuminate, 14–15 mm long, 5 mm wide; spur slightly incurved, 3.5–5 cm long.

Epiphyte in forest, often near water; 550–1300 m; flowering in October and November.

Sierra Leone to Uganda and south to Angola.

Easily recognised by its long pendent stems with broad, dark green leaves and long, pendent inflorescences with widely spaced flowers.

Cyrtorchis praetermissa Summerhayes

Plants upright, with stems up to 20 cm long, bearing thick roots with brownish tips from the basal part. Leaves in 2 rows, linear, stiff, spreading, conspicuously V-shaped in cross section, unequally bilobed at the apex, with rounded lobes, 5–10 cm long, 8–12 mm wide. Inflorescences axillary or below the leaves, 6–10 cm long, 3- to 11-flowered; bracts ovate, 4–5 mm long, 3–5 mm apart. Flowers white, tinged with green, fading to orange; sepals

lanceolate, acuminate, recurved, 8–11 mm long, 2.5–5 mm wide; petals similar but shorter, 8 mm long; lip similar to the petals, up to 9 mm long; spur incurved, 2–3 cm long.

Two subspecies are now recognised:

subsp. *praetermissa*

Leaves usually V-shaped in cross section; spur straight.

Epiphyte on forest trees and shrubs in woodland, also on rocks; 1500–2300 m; flowering in May to June.

Uganda, Kenya, Tanzania, D.R. of Congo, Rwanda, Zambia, Malawi, Zimbabwe, and South Africa (Limpopo and Mpumalanga).

subsp. *zuluensis* (E. R. Harrison) H. P. Linder

Leaves flattened; spur curved outwards towards the tip.

Epiphyte in a range of forested habitats; flowering in January and February.

South Africa (KwaZulu-Natal).

Cyrtorchis ringens (Reichenbach f.) Summerhayes

Syn. *Cyrtorchis belloneorum* G. Chiron

Plant erect with a woody stem to 30 cm long; roots ca. 2 mm in diameter. Leaves usually 6–10 in 2 rows, broadly ligulate, bilobed at the apex, V-shaped near the base and flat in the upper half, leathery, olive green, 7–15 cm long, 1.2–2.3 cm wide. Inflorescences mostly below the leaves, sometimes axillary, bearing ca. 12 flowers spaced close together, 4–7 cm long; bracts pale in bud, turning brown, 5–8 mm long; pedicel with ovary 10–13 mm long. Flowers creamy white, spur sometimes pinkish or greenish; sepals lanceolate, acute, with recurved tips; dorsal sepal 9–10 mm long, 3–4 mm wide; lateral sepals 11–12 mm long, 2–3 mm wide; petals similar to sepals, 7–10 mm long, 2–4 mm wide; lip lanceolate, acuminate, apex recurved, 7–10 mm long, 3–4.5 mm wide; spur tapering, straight or slightly incurved, 2–3.3 cm long.

Epiphyte on larger branches of trees in submontane and riverine forest and in high rainfall wood-

Cyrtorchis praetermissa. B. Campbell

Cyrtorchis ringens. J. Hermans

land, often forming colonies of plants; 1000–1900 m; flowering in March and December.

Sierra Leone to Zimbabwe.

This species is variable in size but is always much smaller than *Cyrtorchis arcuata*, though both species have leaves that become flat in the upper part.

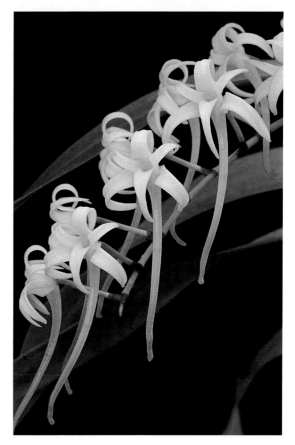

Cyrtorchis ringens. J. Hermans

DIAPHANANTHE Schlechter

The white, pale green, or yellowish flowers of most *Diaphananthe* species are not always transparent, but it was this feature which gave Rudolf Schlechter the idea for the generic name in 1914, from the Greek words *diaphanes*, transparent, and *anthos*, flower. Some of the plants grow as neat rosettes or fans, while others make rather untidy specimens in the wild, with straggling, branching stems that produce roots in many directions. The roots are often the first part to catch the eye, and when wet they exhibit characteristic white streaks along their length. The inflorescences are short or long, and they are often produced in great numbers. The flowers are mostly small but when viewed close-up they are very attractive and it is relatively easy to distinguish each species from others by the shape of the lip and spur.

Schlechter described *Rhipidoglossum* as distinct from *Diaphananthe* and other African angraecoids in 1918. *Rhipidoglossum* includes species in which each of the 2 pollinia is attached by a short stalk to its own viscidium, whereas in *Diaphananthe* 2 stipes share a single viscidium. A callus or tooth on the lip, in the mouth of the spur, has sometimes been used as a distinguishing character for *Diaphananthe*, although it is not always present, but it is also present, to some degree, in some species allocated to *Rhipidoglossum*. Senghas (1986) kept these 2 genera separate; Summerhayes (1960) and Cribb (1989) united them under *Diaphananthe*, the older name. We have followed the Senghas treatment in this book.

Some species of *Cribbia* and *Angraecopsis* also have somewhat translucent flowers and the column has a 3-lobed rostellum, but they have not been confused with any in the genus *Diaphananthe* so far. Further investigation, especially the availability of DNA information, may provide the evidence needed for a new assessment of the generic limits in this group of orchids.

At least 25 species of *Diaphananthe* have now been described from Africa. In the account below

the species are presented in 3 groups, as they were by Schlechter in 1918:

> Group 1. Flowers in opposite pairs or in whorls of 3 or 4.
>
> Group 2. Flowers alternate; stems short, up to 15 cm long in mature plants, or shorter; leaves in a rosette or crowded at the apex of the stem.
>
> Group 3. Flowers alternate; stems elongated, at least 20 cm in mature plants, leafy along most of their length.

Culture

All these species can be grown in cultivation without difficulty, though most of them grow best when mounted on a piece of bark than when planted in a pot. Due regard should be paid to the altitudinal range of each species in the wild, as some will require much cooler night temperatures than others.

Group 1. Flowers in opposite pairs or in whorls of 3 or 4.

Diaphananthe fragrantissima (Reichenbach f.) Schlechter

Plants horizontal or pendent, with stems 5–50 cm long, up to 10 mm thick, covered in old leaf bases. Leaves fleshy, pendent, linear, falcate, pointed, 15–40 cm long, 1–4 cm wide. Inflorescences usually several, pendulous, 15–60 cm long, bearing 50–100 flowers in whorls of 3 or 4; bracts sheathing, 3–5 mm long; pedicel with ovary 1–2.5 mm long. Flowers pale green, pale yellow, or white; dorsal sepal linear-triangular, acute, 8–22 mm long, 2–4 mm wide; lateral sepals slightly falcate, linear, acute, 9–11 mm long, 2–3 mm wide; petals linear to obovate, acuminate, 8–15 mm long; lip rectangular, 10–15 mm long, 6–10 mm wide, with a tooth in the mouth of the spur, 3-lobed at the apex, the mid-lobe elongated into a long-pointed

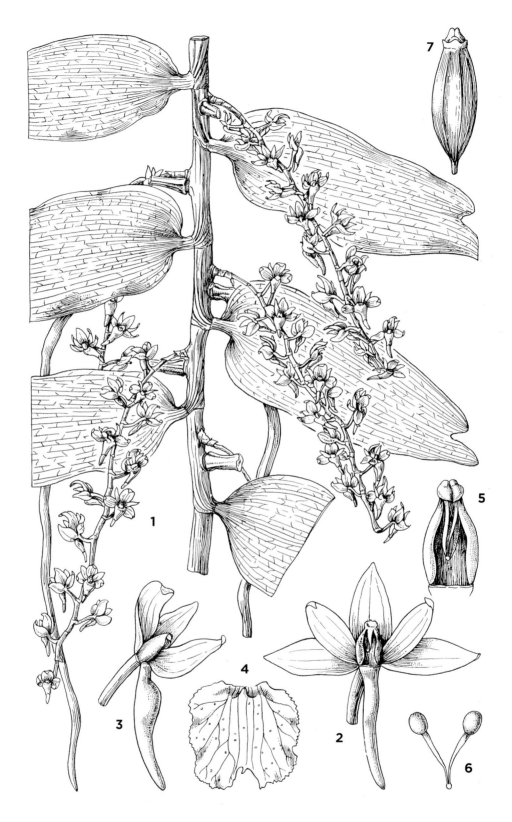

Diaphananthe bidens. 1: Habit. 2–3: Flower with lip removed. 4: Lip. 5: Column with pollinarium. 6: Pollinarium. 7: Fruit. From Summerhayes 1968, fig. 401. S. Ross-Craig.

mucro, side lobes rounded with fimbriate margins; spur bent near the base, inflated in the centre, 6–12 mm long.

Epiphyte and on rocks in the warmer forests and undisturbed bushland; 150–1500 m; flowering February to May.

Cameroon and Congo eastwards to Kenya, Sudan, and Ethiopia, and southwards to Mozambique, Zimbabwe, Angola, and South Africa (KwaZulu-Natal).

This species of *Diaphananthe* has heavy, succulent foliage and attractive flowers that are quite unmistakable.

Diaphananthe vandiformis (Kraenzlin) Schlechter

This species is recorded from Cameroon by Schlechter (1918) but is not included in *Flore du Cameroun* (2001). From Schlechter's description it appears likely that this name should be reduced to synonymy under *Diaphananthe fragrantissima*.

Diaphananthe welwitschii (Reichenbach f.) Schlechter

This species also may not be distinct from *Diaphananthe fragrantissima*. The type specimen was collected in Angola, at the same place as specimens of that species, but appears to be a smaller plant with shorter leaves and a more swollen spur—possibly just a young plant.

Group 2. Flowers alternate; stems short, up to 15 cm long in mature plants, or shorter; leaves in a rosette or crowded at the apex of the stem.

Diaphananthe alfredi Geerinck

Plant small, stem 2 cm long and 4 mm in diameter. Leaves oblong or narrowly subelliptic, acute, 9–10 cm long, 10–13 mm wide. Inflorescences 8–15 cm long; bracts ca. 4 mm long. Flowers 6–10, yellow-orange; sepals oblong, obtuse, 5 mm long, 1.5 mm wide; petals oblong, obtuse, 4 mm long, 1 mm wide; lip convex, subelliptic, obtuse, with a small triangular tooth near the base, 5 mm long, 3 mm wide; spur narrowly ellipsoidal, laterally

compressed, narrowing towards both ends, 12 mm long.

Epiphyte in montane forests; ca. 2100 m.

Burundi (Mount Teza).

The author states that this species is close to *Diaphananthe candida* Cribb (now in *Rhipidoglossum*) from Ethiopia, but that the flowers are larger. It also seems similar to *D. rohrii*.

Diaphananthe arbonnieri Geerinck

Plant with a short stem up to 4 cm long. Leaves oblong, bilobed at the apex, with rounded lobes, 8–16 cm long, 5–10 mm wide. Inflorescences up to 12 cm long, 4- to 15-flowered. Flowers white at first, becoming salmon pink; dorsal sepal elliptic, subobtuse, 7–8 mm long, 4 mm wide; lateral sepals similar but narrower, 2.5 mm wide; petals broadly elliptic, subacute, 6–7 mm long, 4–5 mm wide; lip transversely oboval, truncate, 7–8 mm long and wide; spur filiform, curved, 2.5–3 cm long.

Epiphyte in forest near a waterfall; flowering December to February.

Burundi (Mount Ngoma).

Said to be close to *Diaphananthe tenuicalcar* (now in *Rhipidoglossum*) but with larger flowers and lacking a callus on the lip.

Diaphananthe bueae (Schlechter) Schlechter

Plant small, with a short stem 2–6 cm long, 5 mm in diameter. Leaves in 2 rows, spaced close together in the upper part of the stem, lanceolate-ligulate, unequally and shortly bilobed at the apex, 8–12 cm long, 8–20 mm wide. Inflorescence axillary or below the leaves, pendent, bearing 6–10 flowers spaced 8–12 mm apart, 8–15 cm long; bracts triangular, minute. Flowers greenish yellow; sepals lanceolate, subacute or obtuse, 6–8.5 mm long, 2.5–4 mm wide; petals reflexed, lanceolate-linear, 5–8 mm long, 2 mm wide; lip narrow, ovate-elliptic, the margins rolled back, with a small tooth-like callus in the mouth of the spur, 6–9 mm long, 4 mm wide; spur cylindric, curved and upturned at the apex, 12–15 mm long.

Epiphyte in rain forest, in shaded situations amongst lichens and mosses; 1000–1700 m; flowering August to September and in February (in Uganda).

Côte d'Ivoire, Cameroon, and Uganda.

Easily recognised by its narrow lip and by the broad stipites, which are united along the inner margin and fimbriate on their outer margins.

Diaphananthe caffra (Bolus) H. P. Linder

Syns. *Mystacidium caffrum* (Bolus) Bolus, *Margelliantha caffra* (Bolus) P. J. Cribb & J. Stewart

Plants dwarf, with short, erect or creeping stems up to 2 cm long and with numerous white-streaked greyish roots. Leaves 2–4, linear-ligulate or lorate, unequally bilobed at the apex, with rounded lobes, 2.5–6.5 cm long, 5–8 mm wide. Inflorescences several, arising below the leaves, pendent, bearing 5–11 flowers spaced close together; bracts tubular, 1 mm long; pedicel with ovary 10 mm long. Flowers white with a green column apex; sepals spreading, dorsal sepal oblong-elliptic, rounded, 4.5–6 mm long, 2.5–3 mm wide, lateral sepals oblanceolate, subacute, 5–7 mm long, 1.3–3 mm wide; petals oblong-obovoid, rounded, 5–6 mm long, 1.8–3.3 mm wide; lip oblong, truncate, emarginate, with a small tooth at the entrance to the spur, 5–6 mm long, 2.5–5 mm wide; spur pendent, swollen in the apical half, 12–17 mm long.

Epiphyte on twigs and small branches in montane forest; up to 1800 m; flowering September to January.

South Africa (Limpopo, KwaZulu-Natal, and Eastern Cape Province).

Diaphananthe ceriflora Petersen

Plant with a short stem, to 4 cm long. Leaves 6, oblanceolate, articulated to the sheathing base, unequally bilobed at the apex, leathery, 31–35 cm long, 8.5–9 cm wide. Inflorescences pendent, with peduncle bearing many brownish sheaths, 22 cm long; flowering part 11 cm long bearing 21 flowers close together; bracts green. Flowers yellowish, waxy with a prominent, horizontal column; dorsal sepal ovate, acute, 13–14 mm long, 5–6 mm wide; lateral sepals similar but somewhat oblique, 14–15 mm long, 5–6 mm wide; petals similar, minutely

serrate at the apex, 12–13 mm long, 5 mm wide; lip 10–11 mm long, 20 mm wide, margins finely denticulate and deflexed, apex subretuse; spur straight, cylindric, tapering to a point 11–12 mm long.

Epiphyte on a liana above a stream; 500 m.

Cameroon.

Said to be close to *Diaphananthe kamerunensis* (now in *Rhipidoglossum*) but distinguished by the long inflorescence, half of which has no flowers, and wide leaves.

Diaphananthe divitiflora (Kraenzlin ex Gilg) Schlechter

Plant with a short erect or horizontal stem 8 cm long, 3–10 mm in diameter. Leaves narrowly obovate, almost subpetiolate, somewhat oblique, unequally bilobed at the apex, with rounded lobes, 15–20 cm long, 2–4 cm wide. Inflorescences pendent, 15–25 cm long, 15- to 25-flowered; bracts 2 mm long. Flowers whitish or pale cream; sepals narrowly oval, acuminate, 6–10 mm long, dorsal sepal 2 mm wide, lateral sepals 1.5 mm wide; petals narrowly oval, acuminate, 6–10 mm long, 1.5–2 mm wide; lip broadly oboval, bearing a bilobed crest at the base, apiculate, 6–7 mm long, 5–6 mm wide; spur subcylindric or narrowly ovoid, incurved, 5 mm long.

Epiphyte in dense forest.

D.R. of Congo and Cameroon.

Apparently close to *Diaphananthe lorifolia*, but that species usually has longer stems, slightly smaller flowers, and a different distribution.

Diaphananthe dorotheae (Rendle) Summerhayes

Plant erect, with a short stem. Leaves broadly oblanceolate, unequally acute at the apex, 10–23 cm long, 2–5 cm wide. Inflorescence 10–25 cm long, many-flowered. Flowers small; lip narrowly ovate, or elliptic, without a callus at the mouth of the spur, 6.5–8 mm long, 4–5 mm wide; spur ca. 8 mm long.

Southern Nigeria.

Diaphananthe garayana Szlachetko & Olszewski

Plant growing horizontally, stem short, up to 15 cm long. Leaves large, 12 in 2 rows, twisted at the base so that they lie in one plane, like a fan, pendent, oblanceolate, unequally bilobed at the apex, 30 cm long, 3 cm wide. Inflorescence pendent, up to 18 cm long, 10- to 25-flowered; bracts small, 2 mm long. Flowers small; sepals lanceolate, acute, 4.5–6.5 mm long, 2 mm wide; petals linear-ligulate, 3.5–5 mm long, 0.8 mm wide; lip rectangular, slightly wider towards the apex, margins denticulate in the apical half, apiculate, 4.6 mm long, 3.5 mm wide; spur narrowing gradually from a wide mouth to an acute tip, held horizontally parallel to the ovary, 6 mm long.

Epiphyte; flowering in June.

Cameroon.

Said to be close to *Diaphananthe plehniana* but has no callus on the lip and a differently shaped spur. This species was described in 2001 and named in honour of the distinguished American orchidologist, Leslie Garay.

Diaphananthe millarii (Bolus) Linder

Syn. *Mystacidium millarii* Bolus

Plant with a short, erect stem to 4 cm long. Leaves 3–10, linear-lorate to linear-oblanceolate, unequally bilobed at the apex, with rounded lobes, bright green with darker venation, 10–15 cm long, 13–18 mm wide. Inflorescences usually several, arising below the leaves, pendent, to 6 cm long, 7- to 18-flowered; bracts 1 mm long; pedicel with ovary 10 mm long. Flowers white with bright green anther cap, up to 12 mm in diameter; sepals subequal, spreading forwards, oblanceolate, 5–7 mm long, 2–3 mm wide; petals ovate, obtuse, spreading, 6 mm long, 4 mm wide; lip entire, ovate, acute, funnel-shaped, with a low callus, 6 mm long, 5 mm wide; spur wide at the mouth, tapering, acute, 2 cm long.

Diaphananthe millarii. J. Stewart

Diaphananthe millarii. J. Hermans

Epiphyte in coastal forest, usually on the underside of twigs and branches not far above the ground; sea level to 200 m; flowering December to February.

South Africa (KwaZulu-Natal and Eastern Cape Province).

Diaphananthe pellucida (Lindley) Schlechter

Plant large with a short, horizontal stem 5–12 cm long, 1 cm in diameter. Leaves large, curved, in 2 rows on upper part of stem, usually arranged in a fan, oblanceolate, subacute, unequally bilobed at the apex, the smaller lobe sometimes absent, 18–70 cm long, 2–9 cm wide. Inflorescences usually several, pendent, 30–60 cm long, densely flowered; bracts triangular, acute, 4–10 mm long; pedicel with ovary 2–3 mm long. Flowers pale yellow, white, or cream; dorsal sepal lanceolate, acute, 7–13 mm long, 3–6 mm wide; lateral sepals lanceolate, subacute, 8–16 mm long, 2.5–7 mm wide; petals linear to ovate, finely denticulate on the margins, acute, 7–17 mm long, 2.5–6.5 mm wide; lip narrow at the base, obscurely 3-lobed with a lacerate margin, bearing a small upright callus in the mouth of the spur which is accompanied by a raised fleshy rim on each side, 7.5–15 mm long, 7–18 mm wide; spur pendent, inflated in the middle, narrowing at each end, 5–14 mm long.

Epiphyte on the trunks of large trees in rain forest; 900–1800 m; flowering July to December.

West Africa, east to Uganda.

The large plants and flowers of this species are somewhat similar to those of *Diaphananthe fragrantissima*, but the flowers are always borne singly at each node, and the distribution is in the western part of the equatorial range.

Diaphananthe plehniana (Schlechter) Schlechter

Plant growing horizontally, with a short stem 2–5 cm long. Leaves large, 3–5 in 2 rows, twisted at the base so that they lie in one plane, like a fan, pendent, oblanceolate, unequally bilobed at the apex, 10–20 cm long, 1–3 cm wide. Inflorescence pendent, up to 13 cm long, 13- to 16-flowered; bracts small, 7–8 mm apart. Flowers white, cream,

Diaphananthe pellucida. J. Hermans

pink, or apricot, small; sepals lanceolate, acute, 4.5–6.5 mm long; petals linear-ligulate, 3.5–5 mm long, 1–1.5 mm wide; lip quadrangular, wider towards the base, margins denticulate, a single rounded tooth in the mouth of the spur, apiculate, 6 mm long, 3.5–5 mm wide; spur incurved, narrow near the mouth, then inflated and narrowing again towards the tip, 6 mm long.

Epiphyte in shaded situations, rain forest; low altitudes; flowering May to June.

Côte d'Ivoire, southern Nigeria, and Cameroon.

Diaphananthe rohrii (Reichenbach f.) Summerhayes

Plants with short stems, 2–5 cm long, held away from the host by the prominent roots. Leaves 2–7, dark greyish green, linear or narrowly lanceolate, falcate, unequally bilobed at the apex, 5–15 cm long, 6–22 mm wide. Inflorescences usually several, arising below the leaves, 5–17 cm long, 4- to 9-flowered; bracts 2–8 mm apart, triangular, narrow; pedicel with ovary 4 mm long. Flowers dark green or yellowish green, not transparent, 6–9 mm in diameter; dorsal sepal oblanceolate, acute, 3.5–4 mm long; lateral sepals linear to obovate, obtuse, 3–4 mm long; petals linear, obtuse, 3–4 mm long; lip ovate, acute, with an obscure tooth in the mouth of the spur, 3–4 mm long, 1.7–2.3 mm wide; spur incurved, club-shaped or cylindric, 10–12 mm long.

Epiphyte in montane forests, frequently overlooked; 2100–2800 m; flowering March to July.

Liberia to Ethiopia and south to Angola.

Diaphananthe sanfordiana Szlachetko & Olszewski

This species was described in 2001 in honour of Professor William Sanford who has made many interesting contributions to the study of orchids in Nigeria and Cameroon. It is said to be similar to *Diaphananthe pellucida* but has larger flowers in which the lip is transversely elliptic (wider than long), with a small tooth in the mouth of the spur, and the margins of the lip denticulate rather than fimbriate. So far it is known only from the type locality, north-west of Yaoundé in Cameroon.

Diaphananthe suborbicularis Summerhayes

Plant small, erect, with a stem up to 5 cm long, 4–5 mm in diameter. Leaves in 2 rows, linear-oblanceolate or narrowly oblong-lanceolate, curved, unequally and obscurely bilobed at the apex, 5–7.5 cm long, 7–13 mm wide. Inflorescences axillary, 4.5 cm long, 3- to 6-flowered; bracts small, triangular, 1–1.5 mm long; pedicel with ovary 2.5–3 mm long. Flowers spreading, pinkish or purplish; sepals ovate-lanceolate, acute, 3.5–4 mm long, 3 mm wide; petals lanceolate-oblong, subacute, 3 mm long, 1.5 mm wide; lip almost orbicular or quadrate-orbicular, with a tooth-like callus in the mouth of the spur, 4 mm long, 4.5 mm wide; spur constricted near the mouth, inflated towards the rounded tip, less than 3 mm long.

Epiphyte in cocoa plantations; flowering in October.

Ghana.

Said to be close to *Diaphananthe plehniana* but has narrower leaves and smaller flowers with an almost round lip.

Group 3. Flowers alternate; stems elongated, at least 20 cm in mature plants, leafy along most of their length.

Diaphananthe acuta (Ridley) Schlechter

Syn. *Diaphananthe subclavata* (Rolfe) Schlechter

Plant with stems up to 20 cm long. Leaves well spaced, oval or oval-oblong, 8.9–10.1 cm long, 2.2–3.7 cm wide. Inflorescences axillary, racemes 8- to 23-flowered. Flowers yellow or whitish, not opening fully; sepals and petals narrowly triangular; lip oboval, cuspidate, margins fimbriate, tooth present on surface in mouth of spur, 9.5 mm long, 7.5–9 mm wide; spur narrowing to the tip, 10 mm long.

Epiphyte on trunks and main branches of large trees in forest; 300–700 m; flowering in April.

São Tomé.

Diaphananthe bidens (Afzelius ex Swartz) Schlechter

Syn. *Diaphananthe trigonopetala* Schlechter

Plants with elongated, pendent stems up to 1 m long or more, 2–6 mm in diameter. Leaves regularly spaced in 2 rows, twisted at the base so that they lie in one plane, oblong-lanceolate to narrowly ovate, distinctly and acutely bilobed at the apex, parallel venation prominent, 5–14 cm long, 1.5–4.5 cm wide. Inflorescences pendent, 5–18 cm long, many-flowered; bracts 1–1.5 mm long; pedicel with ovary 2–5 mm long. Flowers white, pink, or yellowish pink; sepals narrowly oval, acute, 2.5–7 mm long, 1–2 mm wide; petals narrowly oval, acuminate, 2–6 mm long, 1–2 mm wide; lip reflexed towards the spur, pandurate or quadrate, with a tooth-like callus in the mouth of the spur, apicu-

Diaphananthe bidens. J. Hermans

transversely flabellate, with crenulated margins, retuse, 7 mm long, 8.5 mm wide; spur cylindric, incurved, 6–8 mm long.

Epiphyte in forest, riverside; 1800 m; flowering in March.

Rwanda and Uganda.

Dedicated to the orchid-lover Gilbert Delepierre.

Diaphananthe eggelingii P. J. Cribb

Plant with a pendent, elongated stem, ca. 10 mm in diameter. Leaves at the apex of the stem, very fleshy, oblong or oblong-lanceolate, twisted at the base so that they lie in one plane, unequally bilobed at the apex, 18–20 cm long, 2.5–2.8 cm wide. Inflorescences several in the upper part of the stem, arising opposite a leaf base, 8–16 cm long, 7- to 16-flowered; bracts sheathing, 3 mm long; pedicel with ovary 3–4 mm long. Flowers parchment white; dorsal sepal lanceolate, acute, 8–9.5 mm long, 3–3.6 mm wide; lateral sepals falcate-ovate, subacute, 7.5–9 mm long, 3–3.8 mm wide; petals elliptic, acute, 7.5 mm long, 3 mm wide; lip obscurely 3-lobed, subcordate, apiculate, margins erose, with a tooth-like outgrowth in the mouth of the spur, 7–7.5 mm long, 8–8.6 mm wide; spur pendent behind the lip, slightly inflated centrally, 8–9 mm long.

Epiphyte in rain forest; 1000 m; flowering in October.

Uganda (Impenetrable Forest).

Apparently close to *Diaphananthe lorifolia*, but the leaves are more succulent, and in the paper-white flowers the lip is broader than long.

Diaphananthe lorifolia Summerhayes

Plants with long hanging stems, 8–40 cm long. Leaves in 2 rows in the upper part, falcate, linear, unequally and obtusely bilobed at the apex, 14–25 cm long, 1–2 cm wide, twisted at the base so that they lie in one plane. Inflorescences pendent, shorter than the leaves, 7–15 cm long, 5- to 25-flowered. Flowers pale yellow, white, or pinkish; dorsal sepal lanceolate to narrowly elliptic, acute, 5–8 mm long, 2–3 mm wide; lateral sepals oblong-

late, 3–7 mm long, 2.5–6 mm wide; spur inflated and sometimes flattened laterally, 5–7 mm long.

Epiphyte on tree trunks and large branches in rain forest; 1100–1300 m; flowering throughout the year but mainly March to May.

Sierra Leone eastwards to Congo and Uganda and south to Angola.

Diaphananthe delepierreana Lebel & Geerinck

Plant with elongated stems, to 25 cm long. Leaves well spaced, broadly oblong with undulate margins, slightly leathery, unequally bilobed at the apex, with rounded lobes, 7.5–10 cm long, 2–3.5 cm wide. Inflorescences ca. 7 cm long, bearing up to 20 flowers in 2 spirals. Flowers whitish or greenish; dorsal sepal elliptic, apiculate, somewhat recurved at the apex, 4 mm long, 2.5–3 mm wide; lateral sepals oblong, obtuse, 6 mm long, 1.5–2 mm wide; petals broadly elliptic, apiculate, 4 mm long, 3.5 mm wide; lip without a tooth-like callus,

Diaphananthe lorifolia. B. Campbell

ovate, acute, 6–9 mm long, 2–3 mm wide; petals lanceolate to oblong, acute, 5–6.5 mm long, ca. 2 mm wide; lip entire, round to ovate, shortly apiculate, sometimes with a slightly fimbriate margin, with a small tooth in the mouth of the spur, 5–8 mm long and wide; spur slender, 5–9 mm long.

Epiphyte on trunks and the large lower branches of trees with a light canopy, in montane and riverine forest; 1000–2200 m; flowering throughout the year.

D.R. of Congo, Rwanda, Uganda, Sudan, Ethiopia, Kenya, and Tanzania.

Diaphananthe papagayi (Reichenbach f.) Schlechter

Plant with stems up to 40 cm long. Leaves 13–17, widely spaced, oblong, 9.5–13 cm long, 2–2.6 cm wide. Inflorescences axillary, racemes, up to 35-flowered. Flowers small; lip oblong, apiculate, margins undulate and crenulate, 5 mm long, 3 mm wide; spur cylindric, incurved, 7 mm long.

Epiphyte in shady forest; 600 m.

Príncipe (Pico Papagaio, where there has been much deforestation).

Diaphananthe sarcorhynchoides J. B. Hall

Plant with long pendent stems, up to 1 m or more long. Leaves many, in 2 rows, each spaced 1–2 cm apart, elliptic, twisted at the base so that they lie in one plane, bilobed at the apex, with rounded lobes, 6–9 cm long, 3–4 cm wide. Inflorescences arising from the base of the leaf sheath, pendent, 8–12 cm long, 8- to 14-flowered; bracts minute, 5–8 mm apart. Flowers white or pale green; sepals lanceolate, apiculate, 6–6.5 mm long; petals narrowly lanceolate, acute, 4.5 mm long; lip ovate, cordate, the margins denticulate and reflexed, minutely 3-lobed at the apex, with a tooth-like callus at the base in the mouth of the spur, 6 mm long, 7 mm wide; spur slightly inflated near the base, laterally flattened above, 7–8 mm long.

Epiphyte in forest and bush in high rainfall areas, usually in shaded situations; flowering May to June.

Côte d'Ivoire and Ghana.

DINKLAGEELLA Mansfeld

This genus was erected in 1934 in honour of the German merchant and amateur plant collector, M. J. Dinklage (1864–1935), who made many collections in West Africa, in particular in Liberia. German professor Rudolf Mansfeld (1901–1960) was the author.

Dinklageella liberica was the only species known until Summerhayes described a smaller one, *D. minor*, from Ghana and Liberia in 1960. In 2001, in the course of their work on the orchid flora of Cameroon, Polish botanists Dariusz Szlachetko and Tomasz Olszewski recognised a third species from Gabon. A fourth species has been noted in São Tomé (Stévart and Oliveira 2000) but has not yet been described.

All the plants exhibit a scandent habit, with a long slender stem bearing widely spaced leaves and many branching aerial roots. Vegetatively, they somewhat resemble *Solenangis scandens* and *Rangaeris trilobata*, but these species have quite different flowers.

Culture

All the species grow in warm West African rain forests where some rain falls in every month and humidity is always high. They are usually found along forest margins and in old plantations among bushes and rocks, the long, scandent stems climbing upwards and attached by the aerial roots. Thus in cultivation they need both high humidity and strong light in a warm glasshouse, support for the upright stems, perhaps on a tree fern pole, and plenty of water fairly regularly.

Dinklageella liberica Mansfeld

Plant with long scandent stems bearing long, branching aerial roots amongst the widely spaced leaves, up to 100 cm long or more. Leaves 2 cm apart, spreading, in 2 rows, narrowly elliptic, 1.7–3.5 cm long above a basal sheath clasping the stem, 0.8–1.5 cm wide. Inflorescences arising from the base of the leaf sheath, erect or spreading, 5–7 cm long, 3- to 6-flowered; bracts small, 4 mm long; pedicel with ovary slender, 10 mm long. Flowers white or cream, sometimes tinted with yellow or orange; sepals elliptic, obtuse, 7–8.5 mm long; petals similar but narrower; lip 3-lobed in the upper two thirds, lobes oblong, rounded, 16–17 mm long in total; spur S-shaped, narrowing from a wide mouth and slightly inflated at the apex, 2.5–3 cm long.

Epiphyte and on rocks, along forest margins and on plantation trees, often in exposed positions in humid situations; flowering October and November.

Liberia, Côte d'Ivoire, southern Nigeria, and Cameroon.

Dinklageella minor Summerhayes

Plant with scandent stems bearing long, branching aerial roots and leaves throughout its length. Leaves in 2 rows, 7–15 mm apart, spread-

Dinklageella liberica. 1: Habit. 2: Flower, section in side view. 3: Pollinarium.
From Herb. Hort. Kew, 169: 604A (1898, unpublished). H. B. Lloyd.

ing, lanceolate-ligulate, 1.3–2.7 cm long above a basal sheath clasping the stem, 5–9 mm wide. Inflorescences arising from the base of the leaf sheath, erect or spreading, 1.5–2.5 cm long, 2- or 3-flowered; bracts small, 2–3 mm long; pedicel with ovary slender, 5–6 mm long. Flowers white; sepals narrowly oblong, 5 mm long; petals linear-oblong, obtuse, 5 mm long, 1.25 mm wide; lip 3-lobed in the upper third, lobes narrowly ovate, obtuse, 6.5–7.5 mm long in total; spur much swollen from a narrow mouth, 2.5 mm long.

Liberia and Ghana.

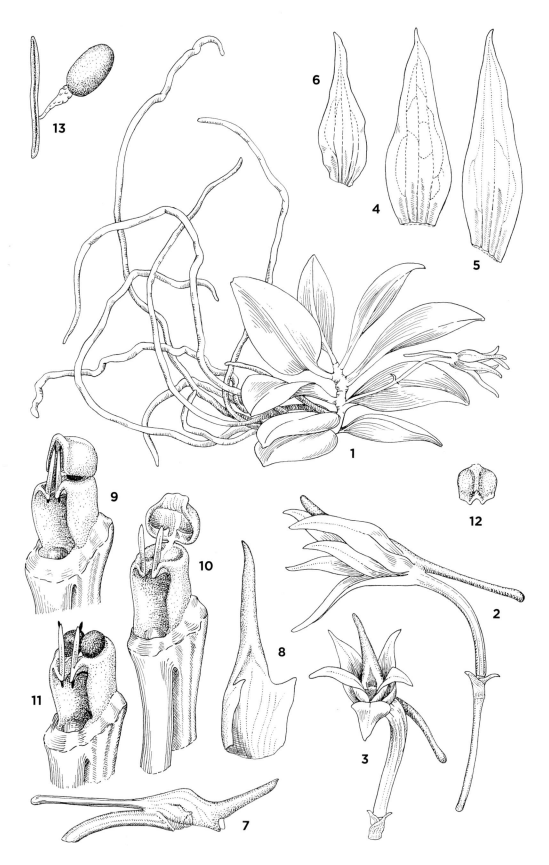

Distylodon comptum. 1: Habit. 2–3: Flower. 4: Dorsal sepal. 5: Lateral sepal. 6: Petal.
7: Flower with sepals and petals removed. 8: Lip. 9–11: Column. 12: Anther-cap. 13: Pollinarium.
From Summerhayes 1966, p. 198. M. Grierson.

Dinklageella villiersii Szlachetko & Olszewski

This species was described in 2001 from a single specimen collected by J. F. Villiers in Gabon. It seems to be very similar to *Dinklageella liberica* but a little smaller in most respects. The lip is 3-lobed from about the middle, instead of in the upper two thirds only, and the mid-lobe is truncate.

DISTYLODON Summerhayes

Distylodon is an impressive name for a tiny plant found by W. J. Eggeling in the Budongo Forest in western Uganda. It had been collected in July 1943 and grown in cultivation in Uganda until it flowered in April 1944. The complete flowering plant in liquid preservative was sent to the herbarium at the Royal Botanic Gardens at Kew, where it was eventually described in 1966. It was in fact the last new orchid genus that Victor Summerhayes published.

The characteristic feature, from which the generic name is derived, is the curious pair of pointed teeth at the front of the rostellum of this orchid. When the pollinia are removed from the apex of the short column, the most unusual rostellum is revealed: it consists of 2 erect, subulate teeth, almost fang-like. The long narrow viscidia are attached along their whole length to the edges of these teeth.

The specific epithet neatly complements the new generic name: Latin *comptum*, adorned.

Distylodon comptum Summerhayes

Plant dwarf with a short flattened stem 1.5 cm long. Leaves ovate or elliptic-lanceolate, twisted at the base so that they lie in one plane, unequally and acutely bilobed at the apex, 7–17 mm long, 4–8 mm wide. Inflorescence slender, 2.2 cm long, single-flowered; peduncle 10–18 mm long; bract ovate, acute, 3 mm long; pedicel with ovary 9 mm long. Flower pale green, not opening fully; dorsal sepal lanceolate, acute, 6.5 mm long, 2.25 mm wide; lateral sepals obliquely lanceolate, acute or acuminate, 7–8 mm long, 2 mm wide; petals lanceolate, acute or acuminate, 6–6.5 mm long, 2–2.5 mm wide; lip 3-lobed in basal half, concave at base, side lobes narrowly oblong, erect, subacute, midlobe much longer, lanceolate, acuminate, fleshy, 4–4.5 mm long, overall size of lip 6.5 mm long, 3–3.5 mm wide at base; spur narrow, cylindric, straight, 6.5–7 mm long.

Epiphyte in forest; ca. 1000 m; probably flowering in April.

Uganda.

EGGELINGIA Summerhayes

Eggelingia is another of the African epiphytic orchid genera described by Victor Summerhayes. The new genus and 2 species were described for the first time in 1951 in honour of W. J. Eggeling, who made many significant collections in Uganda where he was stationed as a forest botanist for many years.

All the species of *Eggelingia* have elongated stems, often pendent, and are easily recognised by the short pointed ligule that arises from the apex of the leaf sheath at each node, opposite the leaf. The inflorescence arises in the axil of this ligule, but the flowers are small and white. *Eggelingia* seems to be nearest to *Tridactyle* in which there are also a few species with a similar ligule.

Culture

Plants are usually found on the larger branches of evergreen rain forest trees where they are well-shaded by the canopy. In cultivation they are best planted in well-drained compost that is water-retentive and placed in a shady part of the glasshouse where they do not receive direct sunlight. Some of the species are recorded from higher altitudes in cooler forests so a pronounced drop in temperature at night is beneficial, although the temperatures should rise rapidly in the morning and stay warm throughout the day. Water should be made available frequently, interspersed with short dry periods.

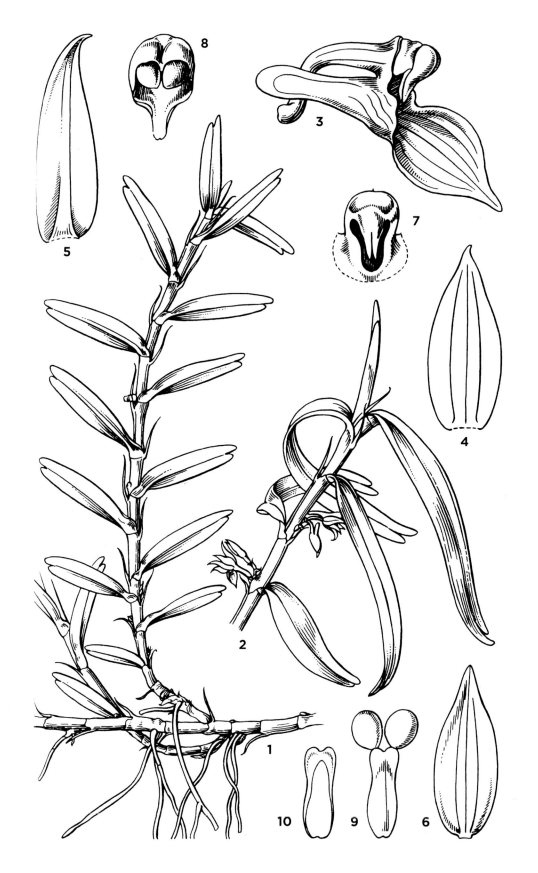

Eggelingia ligulifolia. 1: Habit. 2: Inflorescence. 3: Flower, sepals and petals removed. 4: Dorsal sepal.
5: Lateral sepal. 6: Petal. 7: Column. 8: Anther-cap with pollinia in position. 9: Pollinarium and stipes.
10: Stipes. From Cribb 1989, fig. 152. S. Ross-Craig.

Eggelingia clavata Summerhayes

Plant with slender, erect or pendent stems, often growing in dense tufts, to 35 cm long. Leaves oblong to ligulate, unequally and obtusely bilobed at the apex, 2–5 cm long, 5–9 mm wide. Inflorescences short, up to 1 cm long, 3- to 6-flowered; peduncle 3 mm long; pedicel with ovary slightly hairy, 5 mm long. Flowers whitish or yellowish; sepals and petals 3–5 mm long, 1–2 mm wide; lip concave, oval to elliptic, with 2 minute lobules at the base, acute, 3–3.5 mm long, 3 mm wide; spur briefly narrowing below the wide mouth and then inflated in the apical half, 2.5–4 mm long.

Epiphyte in dense evergreen forests, usually on the upper branches of large trees; flowering July to November.

Côte d'Ivoire, Ghana, Gabon, D.R. of Congo, Rwanda, and Malawi.

Eggelingia gabonensis P. J. Cribb & van der Laan

Plant dwarf, with very slender stems growing in tufts, 6–10 cm long. Leaves narrow, linear, acutely bilobed at the apex, twisted at the base so that they lie in one plane, articulated to a black-spotted sheathing base which bears a setose ligule 2–4 mm long, leaf lamina 1.2–4 cm long, 1–2.5 mm wide. Inflorescences opposite the leaves, 2–3 mm long, 1- or 2-flowered; peduncle very short; bracts, ovate, small; pedicel with ovary 2 mm long. Flowers white, translucent; sepals elliptic, obtuse, 3–4 mm long, 1.5 mm wide; petals elliptic, obtuse, 2.5–3 mm long, 2 mm wide; lip 3-lobed at the base, mid-lobe narrow, 3 mm long, 2.5–3 mm wide at base; spur clavate, 2 mm long.

Epiphyte; 570 m.

Cameroon and Gabon.

Much smaller than the other species in all respects, with very narrow leaves and a shorter spur.

Eggelingia ligulifolia Summerhayes

Plant with elongated, sometimes branching stems, erect or pendent, 7–45 cm long. Leaves fleshy or leathery, narrowly oblong-lanceolate, unequally bilobed at the apex, with rounded lobes, twisted at the base so that they lie in one plane, with a short, setose ligule at the apex of the basal sheath, 2–7 cm long, 4–8 mm wide. Inflorescences very short, 4–6 mm long, 2- or 3-flowered; peduncle very short;

Eggelingia ligulifolia. B. Campbell

rachis zigzag, 3 mm long; bracts triangular, acute, 1 mm long; pedicel with ovary 5 mm long. Flowers white, small; sepals lanceolate, acute, 5–7 mm long, 2–2.5 mm wide; petals oblong, obtuse, 4.5–6 mm long, 1.7–2.25 mm wide; lip entire, auriculate at the base, concave, ovate, acute, 4–6 mm long, 1.7–3.5 mm wide; spur cylindrical, tapering from a wide mouth, 4–5 mm long.

Epiphyte in rain forest and also on lava flows; 1300–2350 m; flowering August to November.

D.R. of Congo, Rwanda, and Uganda.

EURYCHONE Schlechter

This genus was established by Rudolf Schlechter in his review of all the angraecoid orchid genera published in 1918. He derived the name from the Greek words *eurys*, broad, and *chone*, funnel, which describe the distinctive lip. It lacks a callus of any kind on its surface and merges gradually with the somewhat utriculate spur.

Two species had been described before 1918, both in *Angraecum*, but Schlechter wanted to move them to a different genus because of the elongated rostellum at the front of the column. He considered the possibility of uniting these 2 species with those in the genus *Beclardia*, which also have a wide, funnel-shaped lip, but decided to keep them separate because of the very different habit of the 2 groups of plants and their different column structure.

Culture

Both species grow well in cultivation under conditions similar to those provided for *Phalaenopsis*—heavy shade, good humidity, and high temperatures with a drop at night. In pots or baskets of suitably fibrous compost the plants flower regularly, producing one or 2 short racemes from the axils of the leaves at least once a year. The spikes are somewhat shy and need to be eased away from the shelter of the leaves so that the flowers can open well. Like many other angraecoids, however, the plants grow better when firmly attached to a hardwood log or

piece of bark suspended in the glasshouse. In cultivation, they grow away from the wood at a right angle just as they grow away from their host tree or liane in the forest. The short sprays of flowers are then very accessible for viewing or for enjoying their delicate scent.

Eurychone galeandrae (Reichenbach f.) Schlechter

Plant with a short, horizontal stem 3–8 cm long. Leaves 5–7 in 2 rows, narrowly elliptic or linear, fleshy, unequally bilobed at the apex, with rounded lobes, the shorter lobe sometimes absent, 12–20 cm long, 1–2.5 cm wide. Inflorescences axillary or arising below the leaves, pendent, 8–20 cm long, 3- to 15-flowered; bracts small, 4–7 mm long; pedicel with ovary 18 mm long. Flowers all opening together, 15–20 mm apart, pale pink with brown veins in the lip and darker brown coloration in the spur; sepals and petals narrowly elliptic or lanceo-

Eurychone galeandrae. E. la Croix

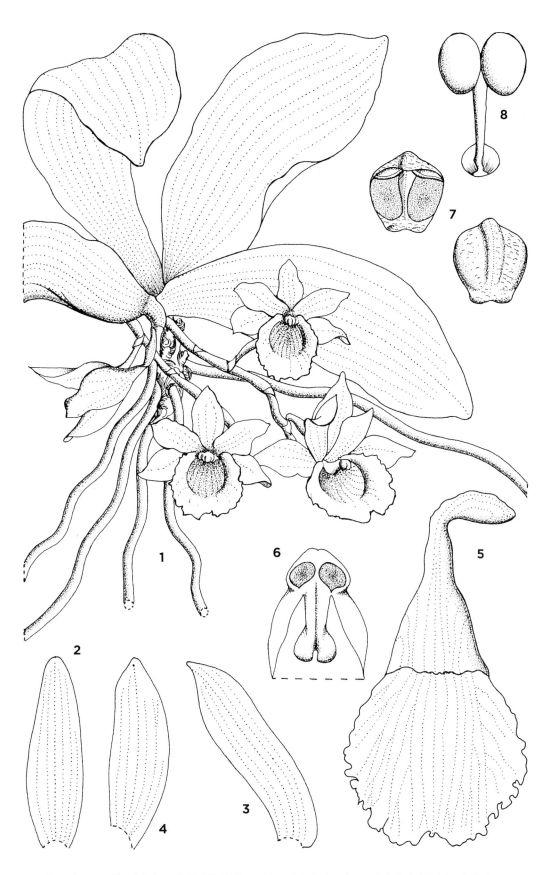

Eurychone rothschildiana. 1: Habit. 2: Dorsal sepal. 3: Lateral sepal. 4: Petal. 5: Lip. 6: Column. 7: Anther-cap. 8: Pollinarium. From Cribb 1989, fig. 145. S. Hillier.

late, the lateral sepals acute and fused at the base, the petals acute and with undulate margins, 15–23 mm long, 4 mm wide; lip funnel-shaped, 3-lobed in front, the lateral lobes large and rounded, the mid-lobe short and acute or truncate, all margins finely denticulate, 24–25 mm long, 28–30 mm wide; spur conical, narrowing to a short, slightly swollen tip which is upcurved, in total 2.5–3 cm long.

Epiphyte in rain forest and old coffee plantations; 600–700 m; flowering September and October.

Côte d'Ivoire, Gabon, Central African Republic, D.R. of Congo, and Angola.

Eurychone rothschildiana (O'Brien) Schlechter

Plant with a short horizontal stem 3–10 cm long. Leaves few, widely oboval, twisted at the base so that they lie in one plane, like a fan, leathery, unequally and acutely bilobed at the apex, 6–20 cm long, 3–7 cm wide. Inflorescences axillary or arising below the leaves, pendent, 8–10 cm long, 3- to 9-flowered; bracts oval, obtuse, 2–5 mm long; pedicel with ovary 10–12 mm long. Flowers white

Eurychone rothschildiana. J. Hermans

or cream, dark green on the interior of the lip at the base and inside the spur; dorsal sepal narrowly elliptic, obtuse, 2–2.5 cm long, 6 mm wide; lateral sepals oblique, lanceolate, acute, 2.2–3 cm long, 6 mm wide; petals oblong, acute, 1.8–2.2 cm long, 6–10 mm wide; lip entire, almost round, margins undulate, 2–2.5 cm long and wide; spur funnel-shaped from a wide mouth, abruptly narrowed and laterally compressed, then swollen for 8 mm at the apex, in total 2–2.5 cm long.

Epiphyte in well-shaded situations on tree trunks, shrubs, and lianes, usually near the ground in rain forest, also on old coffee bushes; flowering in June.

Guinea, Sierra Leone, Liberia, Côte d'Ivoire, Ghana, Nigeria, Equatorial Guinea (Bioco Island), D.R. of Congo, and Uganda.

MARGELLIANTHA P. J. Cribb

This genus of pretty little orchids was described in 1979 by Phillip Cribb. Four species are recognised at present, all immediately identifiable by the white or pale yellow flowers which are unusual amongst African orchids, many of which have reflexed parts, in remaining partly closed, or almost spherical. The name is derived from the Greek words *margelis*, pearl, and *anthos*, flower. In *Margelliantha leedalii*, the type of the genus, the resemblance to a pearl is most marked because all the tepals are a glistening white. The pearly whiteness is accentuated by the bright green anther cap at the apex of the column.

Margelliantha is undoubtedly close to some of the species currently included in *Diaphananthe*, and also to some *Mystacidium* species; however the 4 species included in *Margelliantha* here are easily recognised as distinct at first sight. Further research, particularly DNA studies, may reveal that they, or some of them, should be treated somewhat differently.

All the species grow in montane forests, often on isolated hills, where they are often enveloped in mist or low cloud while the surrounding country

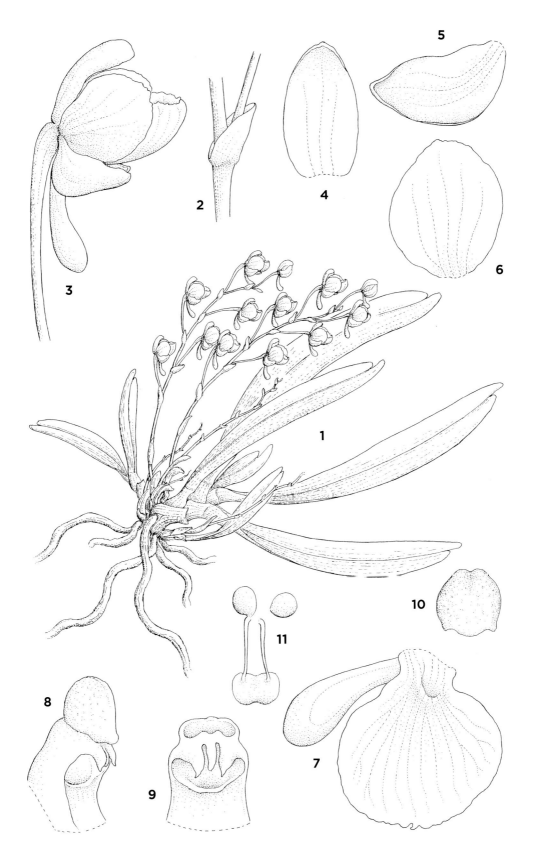

Margelliantha leedalii 1: Habit. 2: Bract. 3: Flower. 4: Dorsal sepal. 5: Lateral sepal. 6: Petal. 7: Lip. 8–9: Column. 10: Anther-cap. 11: Pollinarium. From Cribb 1989, fig. 129. M. E. Church.

may be hot and dry. The plants have their roots embedded in moss and lichens on the branches of trees and shrubs, thus occupying a special micro-habitat in places where orchids are unexpected.

Culture

Margelliantha species are not well known in cultivation. Small pots with a fine medium would probably suit them best, unless they can be established on small pieces of wood. They should be maintained in a cool, humid atmosphere.

Margelliantha burttii (Summerhayes) P. J. Cribb

Plants small, with a short stem up to 5 cm long, 5 mm in diameter. Leaves spaced close together, oblong or oboval, unequally bilobed at the apex, 10–15 cm long, 1.5–2 cm wide. Inflorescences arising below the leaves, 6–10 cm long, 6- to 10-flowered; bracts small. Flowers white; sepals subelliptic, obtuse, dorsal sepal 4–5 mm long, 2–3 mm wide, lateral sepals 5 mm long, 1.5 mm wide; petals broadly elliptic, rounded at the apex, 5–6 mm long, 4–5 mm wide; lip broadly rhomboid, 5 mm long, 8 mm wide; spur narrow, inflated at the apex, slightly incurved, ca. 10 mm long, 1.5 mm in diameter.

Epiphyte on trees in montane forest; ca 2000 m. D.R. of Congo (eastern regions) and Rwanda.

Easily distinguished from the other species in the genus by its larger leaves, as well as its geographical distribution. Daniel Geerinck (1992) prefers to retain this species in *Diaphananthe* as Victor Summerhayes originally described it.

Margelliantha clavata P. J. Cribb

Plants dwarf, stems pendent to suberect, up to 5 cm long, 3 mm in diameter. Leaves several in 2 rows, narrowly oblong, slightly falcate, twisted at the base, unequally and obtusely bilobed at the apex, 4–5 cm long, 8–10 mm wide. Inflorescences short, to 2.5 cm long, 2- to 5-flowered; peduncle wiry, 5 mm long; bracts ovate, 1–1.5 mm long; pedicel with ovary slender, 7 mm long. Flowers pale yellow-green; dorsal sepal oblong-elliptic,

rounded, 3.5 mm long, 1.5 mm wide; lateral sepals elliptic-obovate, 3–4 mm long, 1.5 mm wide; petals elliptic or almost round, obtuse, 2.5–3 mm long, 2.5 mm wide; lip broadly elliptic, 4 mm long, 5.5–6 mm wide; spur straight, inflated towards the tip, 6–7 mm long, 1–1.2 mm in diameter.

Epiphyte on twigs and small branches in montane forest; 1800–1950 m; flowering in March. Tanzania.

Margelliantha globularis P. J. Cribb

Plants small with a pendent or horizontal stem up to 3 cm long, 4 mm in diameter. Leaves 4–5 in 2 rows, ligulate, falcate, unequally and obtusely bilobed at the apex, 4–10 cm long, 6–8 mm wide. Inflorescences one or more, to 6 cm long, 5- or 6-flowered; peduncle wiry, to 3 cm long; bracts ovate-triangular, inflated, 3 mm long; pedicel with ovary slender, 11–12 mm long. Flowers campanulate, pale creamy yellow; dorsal sepal oblong-ovate, obtuse, 4 mm long, 2 mm wide; lateral sepals obliquely falcate, ovate, acute, 5 mm long, 2.5 mm wide; petals subcircular, obtuse, margins erose, 4–5 mm long, 4 mm wide; lip broadly obovate or flabellate, 5 mm long, 6 mm wide; spur subglobose, inflated, 4 mm long, 2.5–3 mm wide.

Epiphyte in montane forest; 1250 m; flowering in September.

Tanzania (Uluguru Mountains).

Margelliantha leedalii P. J. Cribb

Plants small, with thin roots at the base of short stems. Stems upright or pendent, 1.5–4 cm long, with few leaves at the apex. Leaves 3–6, ligulate, unequally bilobed at the apex, 4–8 cm long, 6–8 mm wide. Inflorescences usually several arising below the leaves, up to 7 cm long, 3- to 8-flowered. Flowers glistening white with green anther cap, only partially open; dorsal sepal ovate, obtuse, 4–5 mm long, 3 mm wide; lateral sepals falcate, obtuse, 4–5 mm long, 3 mm wide; petals obovate to almost round, obtuse, 3–4 mm long, 3 mm wide; lip flabellate, emarginate, 5–6 mm long, 6–8 mm wide; spur slightly incurved, clavate, 6–7 mm long.

Margelliantha leedalii. B. Campbell

Epiphyte on the mossy branches of trees and shrubs; ca. 1500 m; flowering in June.

Kenya and Tanzania.

MICROCOELIA Lindley

This well-known genus of African and Madagascan orchids is always easily recognised. The plants consist of a mass of grey roots arising from short stems that bear only a few brownish scale leaves. Green leaves are absent, and the genus is often described as leafless. The appearance of small white or yellow-red flowers, usually in long racemes, makes the plant more conspicuous during the flowering season. Glandular hairs are sometimes present on the outer surface of the sepals and the ovary, but this character seems rather variable. Each flower has a distinctively shaped spur at the base of the lip.

The generic name is derived from the Greek words *micros*, small, and *koilia*, abdomen. It alludes to the spur, which in the type species, *Microcoelia*

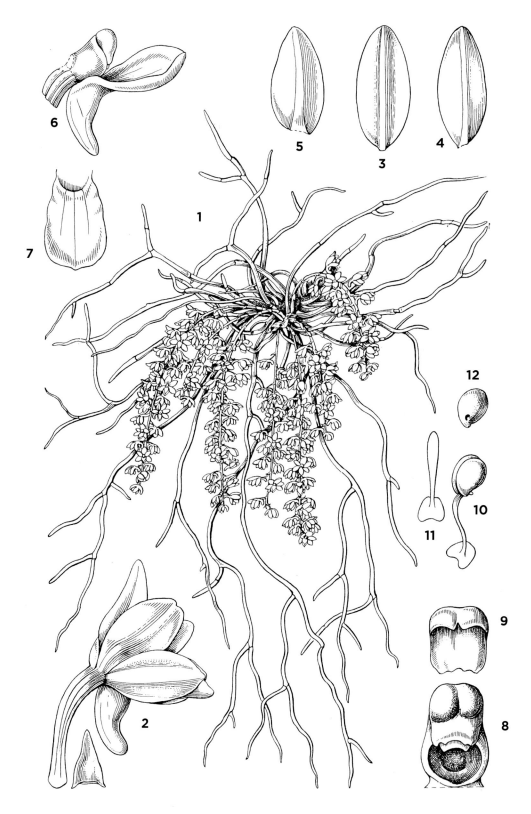

Microcoelia stolzii. 1: Habit. 2: Flower. 3: Dorsal sepal. 4: Lateral sepal. 5: Petal. 6: Column and lip. 7: Lip.
8: Column. 9: Anther-cap. 10–11: Pollinarium. 12: Pollinium. From Summerhayes 1947b, t. 3464. S. Ross-Craig.

exilis, is small and round. When he described this species in 1830, Lindley remarked that it had the smallest flowers of any orchid known to him. He had seen specimens at the Horticultural Society of London (later the Royal Horticultural Society), whose collector John Forbes had found in Madagascar during a short visit from December 1822 to January 1823.

In the past many leafless orchid species in Africa and Madagascar were described under the earliest name, *Gussonea*, established by A. Richard in 1828. But this name, under the alternative spelling, *Gussonia*, was already in use in the family Euphorbiaceae, although Rudolf Schlechter and Henri Perrier both used it for the orchids. Finet (1907) introduced a number of generic names that are no longer in use including *Dicranotaenia* for a single species of leafless orchid, *D. dahomeensis*, from Benin (known as Dahomey at that time).

Summerhayes (1936, 1943) revived the use of the name *Microcoelia* and created 2 new genera, *Encheiridion* and *Chauliodon*. The latter is still accepted as a distinct genus. *Encheiridion* was established for a species with a conspicuously long rostellum protruding from the column, *E. macrorrhynchia*. In 1954 Summerhayes described *E. leptostele*, which also has this feature, but both species were transferred to *Microcoelia* by Jonsson (1981), after studying material that was not available to Summerhayes. *Microcoelia sanfordii* is the third species with a very long rostellum.

Some 30 species of *Microcoelia* are now recognised, 22 of which have been recorded in various parts of Africa. Eleven species have been recorded from Madagascar, three of which also occur in eastern Africa. Few of the species are widespread; many have a rather distinct and localised distribution. It is likely that they have often been overlooked when not in flower.

Culture

All *Microcoelia* species survive well in cultivation provided they are not overwatered and provided they have plenty of light. The plants need to dry out well between waterings. When the weather is cooler, water should be withheld completely. In a humid glasshouse the plants can absorb sufficient moisture from the atmosphere for their limited needs.

Species from Africa

Microcoelia aphylla (Thouars) Summerhayes

Syns. *Angraecum aphyllum* Thouars, *Solenangis aphylla* (Thouars) Summerhayes

Plants scandent or pendent, climbing on twigs and branches by stiff curled roots; stems slender, up to 40 cm long, bearing roots throughout their length. Leaves absent. Inflorescences many, at intervals along the stem, bearing 8–16 flowers spaced close together, 1–2.5 cm long. Flowers white tipped with reddish brown and with a brownish spur; dorsal sepal elliptic, obtuse, 2–3 mm long; lateral sepals oblique, elliptic, obtuse, 2.5–3 mm long; petals linear-oblong, acute or obtuse, 2.5–3 mm long; lip concave, obscurely 3-lobed, side lobes erect, mid-lobe ovate, obtuse, 3 mm long, 2 mm wide; spur strongly curved and swollen at the apex, 4–5 mm long.

Epiphyte in thickets and bush; sea level to 300 m; flowering in September and October.

Kenya, Tanzania, Zanzibar, Mozambique, Zimbabwe, Madagascar, Mauritius, and Réunion.

Summerhayes made this combination in 1936 but changed his mind in 1943 when he transferred the species to *Solenangis*. Work by Carlsward (2004) indicates that the first re-interpretation of the generic affinity of this plant was more appropriate.

Microcoelia bulbocalcarata L. Jonsson

Plant with a short stem and few long, loosely attached, pendulous and sparsely branched roots to 50 cm long. Inflorescences erect, up to 4 borne simultaneously, each with ca. 6 flowers, up to 1.5 cm long; bracts sheathing, acute; pedicel smooth, 5 mm long. Flowers whitish with a dark green patch on the centre of the lip and base of sepals; dorsal sepal cucullate, elliptic, 5–6 mm long, 2.5–3.5 mm wide; lateral sepals asymmetric, elliptic, acute,

Microcoelia aphylla. J. Hermans

Microcoelia caespitosa. B. Campbell

slightly connate at the base, 5–7 mm long, 3 mm wide; petals obovate to ovate, obtuse, 4.5–6 mm long, 3–3.8 mm wide; lip scarcely 3-lobed, mid-lobe triangular, side lobes indistinct with a prominent thickening on either side of the spur mouth, 4.2–5 mm long, 2.6–3.7 mm wide; spur descending vertically, cylindrical, inflated and narrowing to a small bulbous, inflated tip, 7–10 mm long, apical inflation ca. 2 mm long.

Epiphyte on forest undergrowth in dense upland forest; 1680–1950 m; flowering in September and December.

Western Uganda and Rwanda.

Microcoelia caespitosa (Rolfe) Summerhayes

Syns. *Microcoelia bieleri* (De Wildeman) Summerhayes, *M. micropetala* (Schlechter) Summerhayes

Plant with a short stout stem, swollen at the joints with inflorescences to 10–30 mm long and with long, branching, loosely attached, pendulous roots to 90 cm long. Inflorescences erect or spreading, up to 15 borne simultaneously, each with up to 22 flowers, 3–6 cm long; bracts sheathing; pedicels terete, 5–8 mm long. Flowers white or greenish white, with a dark central green line on the sepals and a green central blotch on the lip; dorsal sepal oblong, obtuse or subacute, 2.5–3.5 mm long, 1–2 mm wide; lateral sepals asymmetric, ovate, obtuse, 3–4 mm long, 2–2.5 mm wide; petals obovate, obtuse, 2.3–3 mm long, 1.2–1.8 mm wide; lip small, indistinctly 3-lobed, mid-lobe triangular, flat, side lobes reduced to a thickening on either side of the spur mouth, 2.5–3.6 mm long, 1–2 mm wide; spur narrow at the mouth, then inflated, and tapering again in the apical half, 7–11 mm long.

Epiphyte, mostly on branches of understorey vegetation in rain forest, often near water courses; 50–1100 m; flowering mostly May to September.

Sierra Leone eastwards to Uganda.

Microcoelia corallina Summerhayes

Plant small with a mass of silvery grey roots radiating from the short stem to form a mound. Inflorescences usually several, each with up to 15 flowers, the upper flowers with much shorter pedicels than the lower ones, 2–5 cm long. Flowers white with salmon red mid-line on sepals and petals, red basal patch on lip, and column also salmon red; dorsal sepal ovate, acute, 5 mm long, 2 mm wide; lateral sepals similar but oblique, with a rounded lobe on the outer edge at the base; petals elliptic to oblong, obtuse, apiculate, 4 mm long, 2 mm wide; lip almost round, 5 mm long, 4 mm wide; spur slender at the base, tapering to an inflated apex, 6 mm long.

Epiphyte in dry hot woodland, usually growing on smooth-barked trees, on isolated hills; 200–500 m; flowering in October.

Kenya, southern Tanzania, and Malawi.

Microcoelia exilis Lindley

Plant small with a mass of silvery grey, branching roots radiating from the short stem to form a tangled, ball-shaped mass. Inflorescences arching or pendent, usually several, all densely flowered with 50–80 flowers, up to 25 cm long. Flowers white with yellowish or brownish-green spur, tiny, ca. 2 mm in diameter; dorsal sepal obovate, acute, 1 mm long; lateral sepals obliquely ovate, subacute, 1 mm long; petals ovate, obtuse, apiculate, 0.5–1 mm long; lip concave, ovate to almost round, 0.5–1 mm long; spur globose, less than 1 mm long and wide.

Usually a twig epiphyte in warmer bush, thicket, and open woodland habitats; sea level to 2000 m; flowering any time of year but mostly November to April.

D.R. of Congo, Uganda, Kenya, Tanzania, Malawi, Zambia, Mozambique, Zimbabwe, South Africa (KwaZulu-Natal), and Madagascar (southern and eastern regions).

Microcoelia globulosa (Hochstetter) L. Jonsson

Syn. *Microcoelia guyoniana* (Reichenbach f.) Summerhayes

Plant small with long silvery grey roots radiating from the short stem, often loosely attached to the host. Inflorescences usually sparse but 5–10 may appear, bearing up to 15 flowers each, 2–9

Microcoelia corallina. B. Campbell

Microcoelia exilis. J. Stewart

Microcoelia exilis. J. Hermans

Microcoelia globulosa. J. Hermans

cm long; basal bracts sheathing and with 2 hook-shaped processes opposite the flowers. Flowers white, base of tepals and ovary yellowish green, spur orange-brown at tip; dorsal sepal ovate, acute, apiculate, 2–3 mm long, 1–1.5 mm wide; lateral sepals similar or slightly narrower; petals obovate to elliptic or oblong, apiculate, 2–3 mm long, 0.8–1.2 mm wide; lip pandurate, thickened on each side of the mouth of the spur, 2–3 mm long, 1.2–1.8 mm wide; spur slender, conical, bent at right angles from the base of the lip, 2–3 mm long.

Epiphyte of twigs or small branches at the edge of thicket, patches of bush and riverine woodland; 1000–1950 m; flowering January to April and October.

Nigeria and Cameroon east to Kenya and south to Zambia and Angola.

Microcoelia hirschbergii Summerhayes

Plant small with masses of grey, sometimes flattened roots radiating from the short stem, often forming a conical mass. Inflorescences arising close together on the short stem, up to 8 borne simultaneously, each with up to 15 flowers, 15–35 mm long; bracts small, ovate, only sheathing at the extreme base. Flowers more or less erect, pure white with a greenish brown or rusty brown semi-circular band on the lip around the mouth of the spur; dorsal sepal ovate, acute, recurved, thickened along the central vein, 2.3–4 mm long, 1–2 mm wide; lateral sepals similar or slightly wider, 2.8–4 mm long, 1.3–1.8 mm wide; petals elliptic to ovate, acute, 1.4–4 mm long, 0.8–1.6 mm wide; lip 3-lobed, mid-lobe ovate, acute, more or less folded with a small conical thickening at each side of the spur mouth, side lobes small, rounded, lip in total 2–3.5 mm long, 1.7–2.9 mm wide; spur straight, slender, slightly appressed to the ovary and evenly inflated into a cylinder above, 5–6.6 mm long.

Epiphyte on small twigs and branches, often forming large colonies, in riverine forest and woodland bordering swampy ground; 750–1500 m; flowering between October and December.

Zambia and neighbouring parts of D.R. of Congo.

Microcoelia jonssonii Szlachetko & Olszewski

Plant small, upright, to 2 cm long, with many roots up to 30 cm long. Inflorescences several, up to 2 cm long, 3- to 8-flowered; bracts sheathing, small; pedicel slender, terete, 10 mm long. Flowers clear green with a white spur, small; dorsal sepal cucullate, broadly obovate or oboval-elliptic, 2.5 mm long, 1.5 mm wide; lateral sepals oblique, elliptic-oval, apiculate, 2.8 mm long, 2 mm wide; petals oblong-elliptic, concave, 2.5 mm long, 1 mm wide; lip narrowly elliptic or ligulate, acute, 3 mm long, 1 mm wide; spur cylindric and slender throughout, 8 mm long.

Epiphyte in forest; flowering in October.

Central African Republic (near Boukoko).

Named in honour of Swedish botanist Lars Jonsson, who made an important monographic study of the genus *Microcoelia*.

Microcoelia koehleri (Schlechter) Summerhayes

Syns. *Microcoelia friesii* (Schlechter) Summerhayes, *M. pachystemma* Summerhayes

Plant small, sometimes pendent, with green roots flecked with white, flattened and radiating from the short stem, often forming a small mound at right angles to the host. Inflorescences usually up to 7 borne simultaneously, each with up to 20 flowers, 2–7 cm long; basal bracts sheathing. Flowers whitish, spur orange-brown or salmon pink at the apex, anther cap orange; sepals narrowly oblong, acuminate, dorsal sepal apiculate, 5–7 mm long, 1.5–2.2 mm wide, lateral sepals slightly asymmetric, 6–8 mm long; petals ovate to narrowly ovate, apiculate, 5–6 mm long, 1.6–2 mm wide; lip large, broadly ovate, with upturned erose margins,

Microcoelia koehleri. J. Hermans

6–7 mm long, 4–5 mm wide; spur curved, slender, tapering, with a slight inflation near the apex, 6–7 mm long.

Epiphyte on twigs and branches and also occasionally on rocks in undisturbed habitats; 1000–1600 m; flowering in March and October.

Nigeria, D.R. of Congo, Rwanda, Uganda, Kenya, Tanzania, Malawi, and Zambia.

Microcoelia konduensis (De Wildeman) Summerhayes

Syn. *Microcoelia dahomeensis* (Finet) Summerhayes

Plant with short stout stems, noticeably swollen at the joints with the inflorescences, up to 5 cm long, with many crowded roots, firmly attached to the substrate, narrow and very slender at the tips, usually branched, up to 50 cm long. Inflorescences descending, up to 15 borne simultaneously, each with 15–30 flowers, 15 cm long; bracts sheathing; pedicels short, curved and twisted, 1–2 mm long. Flowers mostly twisted into a horizontal position, whitish, sepals tinged orange-brown or salmon-coloured at the base, lip white tinged with apple-green around the spur mouth, spur apex and column orange-brown or salmon-coloured; dorsal sepal cucullate, oblong to elliptic, acuminate, keeled apically, 3–5 mm long, 1–2 mm wide; lateral sepals asymmetric, narrowly ovate, curved, apiculate, 4–7 mm long, 1–2.5 mm wide; petals narrowly ovate, acute, apiculate, 2.2–6 mm long, 1–1.6 mm wide; lip large, indistinctly 3-lobed, mid-lobe spathulate, orbicular to broadly transversely elliptic, sometimes folded, erose, side lobes indistinct, thickened at the spur mouth, 5–8 mm long, 2–7 mm wide; spur distinctly incurved below the lip, inflated in the apical half, 2–5 mm long.

Epiphyte in rain forest, also in plantations and secondary vegetation; on small branches and twigs in the crown of trees; 50–500 m; flowering April to June and September to December.

Côte d'Ivoire, Ghana, Benin, Nigeria, Cameroon, D.R. of Congo, and Uganda.

Microcoelia leptostele (Summerhayes) L. Jonsson
Syn. *Encheiridion leptostele* Summerhayes

Plant erect with a stout stem to 4 cm long but more or less concealed by a dense mass of roots that are terete, up to 30 cm long. Inflorescences erect or spreading, at least 10 borne simultaneously, each with 5–10 flowers, to 4 cm long; bracts sheathing; pedicel and ovary distinct, each 2 mm long. Flowers whitish yellow; dorsal sepal cucullate, elliptic, acuminate, 8 mm long, 4–6 mm wide; lateral sepals asymmetric, oblong, apiculate, 7.5–9 mm long, 3 mm wide; petals convex, elliptic, acute, 5–7.5 mm long, 3 mm wide; lip 3-lobed, mid-lobe shortly spathulate, apiculate to 3-dentate, with a distinct hump in front of the spur mouth, side lobes raised, rounded, margins distinctly thickened, 7–9 mm long, 3.5–5 mm wide; spur flattened dorso-ventrally, incurved, with a bulbous, apical inflation, 6.5–8 mm long, bulbous part 2 mm in diameter.

Epiphyte, in rain forest and in secondary vegetation near rivers, usually in the crowns of understorey trees; 200–1000 m; flowering in March.

Central African Republic and D.R. of Congo.

Szlachetko and Olszewski (2001) have recognised 2 subspecies in Central African Republic:

subsp. ***leptostele***

Lip elliptic-oboval, widest at the middle or near the apex, the apex 3-dentate with the apical tooth smaller than those at the side.

subsp. ***cordatilabia*** Szlachetko & Olszewski

Lip entire, oval-cordate, wider near the base, the apex entire, acute or obtuse.

Microcoelia macrorrhynchia (Schlechter) Summerhayes
Syn. *Encheiridion macrorrhynchia* (Schlechter) Summerhayes

Plant with a small stem up to 3 cm long, and few, variously spreading, terete or flattened roots up to 7 cm long. Inflorescences erect to pendulous, up to 10 borne simultaneously, each with up to 20 flowers, up to 10 cm long; bracts sheathing; pedicel short, straight or twisted, to 3 mm long; ovary slightly curved, to 2 mm long. Flowers whitish, dorsal sepal, spur, and anther pale brown to orange-brown, lip white with a yellowish green spot at the base; sepals ovate, acute, dorsal sepal cucullate, 3–5 mm long, 1–2 mm wide, lateral sepals asymmetric, 3–6 mm long, 1.5–2.4 mm wide; petals asymmetric, ovate, obtuse, somewhat erose, 3–5 mm long, 1.5–3.5 mm wide; lip 3-lobed, mid-lobe spathulate, almost semi-circular in outline but emarginate in the centre, margins erose, side lobes erect, oblong, succeeded on each inner surface by a plate-like thickening that protects the spur mouth, 4.5–6 mm long, 3.6–5.8 mm wide; spur slender at first, incurved, becoming inflated at the apex with age, in total 11 mm long, inflated part 5–6 mm long.

Epiphyte, usually on smaller branches and twigs in exposed positions in rain forest, riverine forest, and old plantations; 200–1100 m; flowering February, May to June, and October to December.

Liberia, Côte d'Ivoire, Ghana, Nigeria, Cameroon, Central African Republic, Equatorial Guinea, Gabon, D.R. of Congo, Uganda, and Zambia.

Microcoelia megalorrhiza (Schlechter) Summerhayes

Plant small with long, distinctly verrucose, grey roots up to 70 cm long radiating from the short stem, often loosely attached to the host. Inflorescences usually up to 7 borne simultaneously, each with up to 20 flowers, 2–10 cm long; bracts sheathing. Flowers glistening white, spur tinged orange-brown at tip; dorsal sepal narrowly elliptic, acuminate, apiculate, 7 mm long, 2 mm wide, forming a hood with the petals; lateral sepals similar or slightly narrower, 6–9 mm long, 1.6–2 mm wide; petals similar to dorsal sepal, acuminate, 5–7 mm long, 1.8–2.4 mm wide; lip large, subspathulate, 3-lobed, side lobes thickened and upright, mid-lobe ovate, deflexed, 7–8 mm long, 2–3 mm wide; spur slender, curved, tapering to an acute apex, 8 mm long.

Microcoelia megalorrhiza. B. Campbell

Epiphyte in dry woodland, usually in the canopy of large bushes and trees; sea level to 500 m; flowering between December and March.

Kenya, Tanzania, and Malawi.

Microcoelia microglossa Summerhayes

Plant small with a stem to 3 cm long and roots loosely attached, twisting, sparingly branched up to 40 cm long. Inflorescences erect or spreading, up to 4 borne simultaneously, each with up to 10 flowers, to 5 cm long; bracts sheathing; pedicels curved, terete, to 5 mm long. Flowers whitish with a brownish median band on the sepals, spur conspicuous; sepals ovate, acute, dorsal sepal cucullate, 2.6–3 mm long, ca. 2 mm wide, lateral sepals asymmetric, 3.6 mm long, 2.3–3 mm wide; petals ovate, acute, 2.5 mm long, 1.5 mm wide; lip short,

Microcoelia microglossa. J. Stewart

Microcoelia moreauae. B. Campbell

3-lobed, mid-lobe triangular in outline, side lobes indistinct, erect, on either side of spur mouth, 2.5 mm long in total, 1.5–2 mm wide; spur cylindrical, tapering from a wide mouth to a distinctly inflated conical apex, inflation 1 mm in diameter, 18–20 mm long.

Epiphyte, usually on understorey vegetation in dense evergreen forest; 470–1070 m; flowering January to February and September to October.

Nigeria, Cameroon, D.R. of Congo, and Uganda.

Microcoelia moreauae L. Jonsson

Plant very small with silvery grey roots up to 5 cm long, radiating from the short stem, adhering closely to the bark of the host. Inflorescences up to 4 borne simultaneously, each with up to 8 flowers, 2–3 cm long; basal bracts not sheathing. Flowers white, spur green at tip; dorsal sepal oblong, obtuse, 2 mm long; lateral sepals similar but oblique, slightly longer; petals oblong, obtuse, 1.4–2 mm long; lip concave, oblong, obtuse, 1–2 mm long;

spur slender, conical, bent at right angles from the base of the lip, 1.5–2 mm long.

Epiphyte on twigs of trees and large bushes in seasonally dry montane forest; 600–1800 m; flowering August to October.

Kenya, Tanzania, Malawi, and Zimbabwe.

Microcoelia nyungwensis L. Jonsson

Plant small with a short stem up to 1 cm long, and with few slender roots that are loosely attached to the substrate, terete, branching, up to 40 cm long. Inflorescences erect or spreading, up to 7 borne simultaneously, each with up to 7 flowers, 3 cm long; bracts sheathing; pedicels distinct, up to 3 mm long. Flowers whitish; dorsal sepal cucullate, ovate to elliptic, 4–4.5 mm long, 1.6 mm wide; lateral sepals asymmetric, ovate, acute, apiculate, shortly connate at the base, 4.8–5.6 mm long, 1.8–2.3 mm wide; petals ovate, acute, 4 mm long, 1.6 mm wide; lip large, spathulate, indistinctly 3-lobed, mid-lobe broadly ovate above a basal claw, 3-dentate at the apex, side lobes reduced to a narrow thickening on either side of the spur mouth, ca. 6 mm long, 3.5 mm wide; spur slender, slightly incurved or straight, slightly inflated at the apex, 9–11 mm long.

Epiphyte on older branches in rain forest; 1950 m; flowering in March.

Rwanda (Nyungwe Forest).

Microcoelia obovata Summerhayes

Plant small, sometimes pendent, with stiff straight roots radiating from the short stem. Inflorescences erect or pendent, usually up to 10 borne simultaneously, each with up to 20 flowers, the basal bracts sheathing, 2–9 cm long. Flowers whitish, brownish at the base of tepals and spur; dorsal sepal obovate to oblong, obtuse, apiculate, 4–6 mm long, 1.2–2 mm wide; lateral sepals slightly asymmetric, oblong, acute, apiculate, reflexed apically, 5–7 mm long; petals asymmetric, oblong to obovate, apiculate, apically reflexed, 4–6 mm long, 1.3–1.8 mm wide; lip broadly obovate, folded, with a thickening on each side of the spur mouth, 5–7.5

mm long, 3–5 mm wide; spur incurved, slender, semi-circular in cross section, 3–5.5 mm long.

Epiphyte in the warm and dry woodlands and bush and on scattered trees in grassland, often growing in exposed places; sea level to 1100 m; flowering December to February.

Kenya, Tanzania, and Mozambique.

Microcoelia ornithocephala P. J. Cribb

Plant erect with a short stem and many flattened roots clinging closely to the substrate, green with white streaks, 30–40 cm long. Inflorescences 1–4 borne simultaneously, each with 5–17 flowers, 3–7 cm long; bracts sheathing; pedicel with ovary 6 mm long. Flowers khaki-beige with white lip and 2 green tubercles at the base; dorsal sepal ovate, cucullate, 5 mm long, 4 mm wide; lateral sepals obliquely ovate, spreading, 5 mm long, 2.5 mm wide; petals lanceolate, spreading, 4 mm long, 1.5 mm wide; lip obovate, or ovate, acute or apiculate, margins undulate, 6 mm long, 3 mm wide; spur C-shaped, swollen at the mouth, then narrowing again and swollen at the apex, 6 mm long.

Epiphyte in dry deciduous forest and thicket at hot, low altitudes; 480–600 m; flowering in December.

Malawi.

Microcoelia physophora (Reichenbach f.) Summerhayes

Plant small, sometimes pendent, with long roots triangular in cross section radiating from the short stem. Inflorescences erect, usually up to 6 borne simultaneously, each with up to 15 flowers, 2–9 cm long; basal bracts sheathing. Flowers white and green; sepals ovate, acute, dorsal sepal hooded, 1.5–2.5 mm long, 1–1.5 mm wide, lateral sepals slightly asymmetric, apiculate, connate below the ovary, 2–3 mm long; petals ovate, obtuse, 1.5–2.5 mm long, 0.7–1 mm wide; lip 3-lobed, mid-lobe short, obtuse, side lobes indistinct, rounded, concealing mouth of spur, 1–3 mm long, 0.5–1 mm wide; spur at right angles to ovary, tapering into a distinctly swollen egg-shaped apex, 7–10 mm long.

Microcoelia obovata. B. Campbell

Epiphyte on twigs in coastal forest; sea level to 500 m; flowering from September to December and in March.

Kenya, Tanzania, Zanzibar, and Madagascar (north and north-west coast).

Microcoelia sanfordii L. Jonsson

Syn. *Encheiridion sanfordii* (L. Jonsson) Senghas

Plant small with a very short stem and few flattened roots up to 70 cm long. Inflorescences erect or pendulous, few at a time, with up to 10 flowers each, to 7 cm long; bracts sheathing; pedicels short. Flowers whitish with green central band on lateral sepals and triangular green spot on the lip, apical part of spur and anther orange-beige; dorsal sepal cucullate, elliptic, acute, 3–6 mm long, ca. 2 mm wide; lateral sepals curved, ovate, acute, 3–6 mm long, 1–2 mm wide; petals curved, obovate, obtuse, 2.5–5 mm long, 1–2 mm wide; lip 3-lobed, mid-lobe spathulate, cordate, margin uneven, side lobes small, upright on either side of the spur

Microcoelia smithii. B. Campbell

mouth and enclosing a plate-like thickening, 2.5–4 mm long, 2–4.7 mm wide; spur long and straight at first, becoming incurved apically and with a discoid inflation at the apex, 4.5–7 mm long.

Epiphyte, mainly on the tips of branches, in riverine forest; 800–1000 m; flowering March to May.

Cameroon.

This is the third species with a very elongated rostellum, the others being *Microcoelia leptostele* and *M. macrorrhynchia*. It was named in honour of the American botanist, William Sanford, who made many contributions to the study of orchids and their ecology in Nigeria and Cameroon.

Microcoelia smithii (Rolfe) Summerhayes

Plant very small with silvery grey roots up to 12 cm long, radiating from the short stem and forming a mound that supports it away from the host. Inflorescences up to 12 borne simultaneously, each with 5–10 flowers, 2–5 cm long; basal bracts sheathing. Flowers white, spur green at tip, anther

Microcoelia stolzii. B. Campbell

cap yellow; dorsal sepal ovate, acute, 2–3 mm long; lateral sepals similar but oblique, slightly longer; petals oblong, obtuse, 1.4–2 mm long; lip concave, ovate, obtuse, 2–3 mm long; spur slender, conical, bent at right angles from the base of the lip, 1.5–2 mm long.

Epiphyte in dry deciduous forest and thicket near the coast; sea level to 600 m; flowering August and September.

Kenya, Tanzania, and Malawi.

Microcoelia stolzii (Schlechter) Summerhayes
Syn. *Microcoelia ericosma* Summerhayes

Plant small with many long silvery grey roots radiating from the short stem, forming a ball-shaped mass. Inflorescences erect or pendent, 5 or more borne simultaneously, each with up to 40 flowers, 5–12 cm long; basal bracts not sheathing. Flowers white, spur green at tip; dorsal sepal obovate to ovate, obtuse, apiculate, 2.5–3.5 mm long, 1–1.5 mm wide; lateral sepals similar or slightly narrower, oblique; petals obovate to elliptic or oblong, apiculate, 2–3 mm long, 0.8–1.2 mm wide; lip pandurate, narrowly obovate to ovate, obtuse, 3–3.5 mm long, 1.5–2 mm wide; spur tapering from the mouth then suddenly narrowed to a conical apex, 1.5–2.5 mm long.

Epiphyte on twigs and branches in forest or woodland; 1100–2300 m; flowering October to January.

Kenya, Tanzania, Malawi, Zambia, Mozambique, and Zimbabwe.

This species has been confused with *Microcoelia globulosa* (syn. *M. guyoniana*) in the past. It can be distinguished from that species by its non-sheathing bracts and much more densely flowered inflorescences.

Species from Madagascar

In the account that follows, the species are presented in 2 groups: first, those with bright yellow, orange, or reddish flowers, and secondly, those with basically white flowers.

Group 1. Flowers yellow, orange, or orange-red.

Microcoelia aurantiaca (Schlechter) Summerhayes

This species was described from Île Sainte Marie or the adjacent mainland of Madagascar in 1918, but the type specimen has been lost and the description does not match any other specimens collected from the area. Although Jonsson (1981) is doubtful of its identity, the name is included here in the hope of encouraging botanists visiting the area to search for it.

Microcoelia elliotii (Finet) Summerhayes

Plant small with short stems to 2 cm long and greyish roots bearing glandular hairs that are loosely attached to the substrate. Inflorescences erect, up to 3 borne simultaneously, each with up to 15 flowers, up to 6 cm long; bracts sheathing; pedicels orange-red, up to 8 mm long. Flowers orange-red, with glandular hairs on the pedicels and ovary and sparse on the base of the sepals and spur;

dorsal sepal hooded, elliptic, acute, 3 mm long, 1.5 mm wide; lateral sepals asymmetric, curved, ovate, connate at the base below the ovary, 3 mm long, 3 mm wide; petals oblong, acute, 2–2.5 mm long, 1–1.5 mm wide; lip indistinctly 3-lobed, mid-lobe broadly elliptic, side lobes indistinct forming a thickened rim to the spur mouth, 3.5 mm long, 2 mm wide; spur slender, curved towards the ovary, up to 10 mm long.

Epiphyte on trees in humid evergreen forest; sea level to 1300 m; flowering in January to May.

Madagascar (only recorded twice, on the Tsaratanana Massif near Antsirañana and near Tôlañaro).

Named in honour of the English collector, G. F. Scott Elliot (1862–1934), who collected the type specimen near Tôlañaro.

Microcoelia gilpinae (Reichenbach f. & S. Moore) Summerhayes

Syn. *Microcoelia melinantha* (Schlechter) Summerhayes

Plant small with short stems and few, elongated, smooth, slender roots. Inflorescences erect, spreading, 3 or 4 borne simultaneously (rarely up to 15), densely flowered with 10–20 flowers in the upper third or half, up to 4.5 cm long; pedicels straight or curved, to 9 mm long. Flowers orange-red or orange-yellow; dorsal sepal elliptic to oblong, obtuse, 2–4 mm long, 1.4–2 mm wide; lateral sepals asymmetric, ovate, acute, connate around the ovary at the base, 3–5 mm long, 2–3 mm wide; petals obovate, acute, 2.6–4 mm long, 1.5–2.6 mm wide; lip small, obovate to suborbicular, almost calceolate, 2–4 mm long, 1.2–2 mm wide; spur mouth constricted by a ring-like thickening, spur cylindrical to an obtuse or spherical apex, 5.4–9 mm long.

Epiphyte in understorey in dense rain forest, often scarcely attached to other vegetation; 200–1800 m; flowering throughout the year.

Madagascar (eastern highlands).

Named in honour of Helen Gilpin (1834–1907), a British missionary teacher in Antananarivo (1869–1895), who collected plants for herbarium

Microcoelia gilpinae. J. Hermans

Microcoelia gilpinae. J. Hermans

specimens that she sent to Kew including the type specimen of this orchid.

Group 2. Flowers basically white or whitish tinged with green or brown.

Three species with white or whitish flowers have already been described, *Microcoelia aphylla*, *M. exilis*, and *M. physophora*, as they also occur in Africa.

Microcoelia bispiculata L. Jonsson

Plant small with short stems and few, greatly elongated roots. Inflorescences few, up to 4 borne simultaneously, erect or pendulous, each with up to 15 flowers; bracts reddish brown, sheathing. Flowers horizontal, white, but brownish on the outer surface and at the apex of the spur, column, and anther; dorsal sepal ovate, acute, 4–5 mm long, 2 mm wide; lateral sepals slightly asymmet-

ric, narrowly ovate, acute, 4–5 mm long, 1.3–1.7 mm wide; petals ovate, apiculate, 3.4–4 mm long, 1.2–1.4 mm wide; lip 3-lobed, mid-lobe obovate, obtuse, side lobes small, rounded, with a spicule-shaped thickening at each side of the spur mouth, 3.6–5.5 mm long, 2–3 mm wide; spur perpendicular to the lip or inflexed apically, apex spherically inflated and then tapering to a sharp point, 4.6–6 mm long.

Epiphyte in the understorey of dense rain forest, very loosely attached to other vegetation; sea level to 1200 m; flowering between February and April.

Madagascar (north-eastern region).

Microcoelia decaryana L. Jonsson

Plant small with short stems and few to many smooth, branched, and twisted roots, which are round or triangular in cross section. Inflorescences erect, up to 17 borne simultaneously, each with up to 23 flowers, up to 5 cm long; bracts sheathing. Flowers whitish, tinged with green, up to 7 mm long; sepals elliptic, acute, dorsal sepal 2 mm long, 0.8 mm wide, lateral sepals curved, 2.5 mm long, 1.5 mm wide; petals slightly asymmetric, elliptic, acute, 2 mm long, 1 mm wide; lip obscurely 3-lobed, mid-lobe cup-shaped, broadly obovate, side lobes rounded with a ridge-like thickening on each side of the spur mouth ca. 3 mm long, 2.5 mm wide, mid-lobe 2 mm long; spur appressed to the ovary, cylindric, gradually inflated from the narrow mouth towards the obtuse apex, 4 mm long.

Epiphyte in dry bush and woodland; ca. 300 m; flowering October to December.

Madagascar (north-west in Mahajanga).

Microcoelia dolichorrhiza (Schlechter) Summerhayes

Plant small with stem up to 17 mm long and many smooth roots up to 20 cm long. Inflorescences erect, spreading, up to 4 borne simultaneously, each with 10–12 flowers, to 15 mm long; bracts small, sheathing; pedicels carmine rose, curved, 7 mm long. Flowers erect, spreading, whitish, tinged with carmine rose; dorsal sepal obovate, acute, connate to lateral sepals at the basal third, 3 mm long, 1.6 mm wide; lateral sepals asymmetric, curved, ovate, acute, connate at the base, 3.4 mm long, 3.2. mm wide; petals small, narrowly triangular, 2.5 mm long, 0.7 mm wide; lip indistinctly 3-lobed, mid-lobe narrowly triangular, 2.5 mm long, side lobes small, fleshy, occluding spur mouth; spur appressed to ovary and pedicel, straight, 5 mm long.

Epiphyte on branches in humid evergreen forest; 1000 m; flowering October to December.

Madagascar (Manongarivo Massif near Antsiråñana).

Microcoelia macrantha (H. Perrier) Summerhayes

Plant with short stems and large conical masses of coarse roots up to 50 cm long. Inflorescences erect, 5–8 borne simultaneously, each with 8–12 flowers; bracts sheathing; pedicels up to 11 mm

Microcoelia macrantha. J. Hermans

long. Flowers brilliant white but green at the base of the spur and spur mouth, horizontally oriented, up to 13 mm long; dorsal sepal oblong to obovate, 5–8 mm long, 3–5 mm wide; lateral sepals slightly asymmetric, acute, 4–8 mm long, 2–4 mm wide; petals obovate to elliptic, obtuse, 4–9 mm long, 2–5 mm wide; lip 3-lobed, mid-lobe cup-shaped, folded, emarginate, erose, side lobes rounded with a distinct thickening at each side of the spur mouth, 4–10 mm long, 3.6–11.6 mm wide when flattened; spur large, slightly incurved, flattened from the sides, apex incurved and inflated, 5.6–8.7 mm long, 1.6–2.7 mm in diameter.

Epiphyte in rain forest, often near watercourses, mostly in shady conditions on smaller branches and twigs; sea level to 1000 m; flowering January to April.

Madagascar (east coast from Antsiråñana to Tôlañaro).

Easily recognised by the large lip with an erose margin and the unique shape of the spur.

Microcoelia perrieri (Finet) Summerhayes

Plant with a short, stout stem to 55 cm long, usually shorter, with few to many simple or branched, flattened or rounded roots, spreading over the substrate. Inflorescences mostly appressed to the stem, up to 40 borne simultaneously, each with up to 26 flowers, 9 cm long; bracts sheathing; pedicels conspicuous, up to 7 mm long, with few glandular hairs at the base of the bracts and ovary. Flowers whitish, small, sepals ovate, acute, dorsal sepal 1.7–2.3 mm long, 0.9–1.4 mm wide, lateral sepals asymmetric, 2–2.8 mm long, 1.6–2.3 mm wide; petals obovate, acute, 1.2–2 mm long, 0.8–1.5 mm wide; lip 3-lobed, mid-lobe semi-orbicular when flat, side lobes rounded, cup-shaped around the spur mouth, 2.5–3 mm long, 1.4–2 mm wide; spur perpendicular to the lip, tapering into an obtusely conical apex, 5–6 mm long, swollen apex 1 mm wide.

Epiphyte or occasionally lithophytic in woodland and bush in dry areas; sea level to 500 m; flowering April to October.

Madagascar (western and north-western regions).

Microcoelia perrieri. J. Hermans

Easily recognised by its stout stems with erect and often appressed inflorescences, and by its dry habitat where it is epiphytic on the trunks of Didieraceae.

MICROTERANGIS
(Schlechter) Senghas

In his review of the angraecoid genera published in 1918, Rudolf Schlechter proposed the genus *Chamaeangis* and established 2 distinct sections within it. He classified the species then known from Africa in the section *Eu-Chamaeangis* and those from Madagascar and the Comoro Islands in section *Microterangis*. He noted, however, that it was not improbable that the latter section, later on, might be elevated to the rank of genus. This elevation was carried out by another German botanist, Karlheinz Senghas, in 1986.

In *Microterangis* (from the Greek *micros*, small, and *angos*, vessel) all the plants are small, with a short or scarcely developed stem and thin or slightly succulent leaves. Depending on the habitat, these leaves may be light or dark green. The flowers are very small and carried in long inflorescences. The pollinia have a common stipe and a single, roundish viscidium. It is not unlike some of those in the genus *Aerangis* but much smaller.

Seven species have been described in this genus—4 from the Comoro Islands and 3 from Madagascar. While those described from Madagascar appear to be distinct, it seems likely that the number of species recorded from the Comoro Islands may be reduced when more material has been examined. Reichenbach's 3 species from the Comoro Islands were named over a period of 7 years, the first being *Microterangis hildebrandtii* in 1878. *Microterangis humblotii* seems to be quite distinct, both in the colour of the flowers and in the shape of their large spur. *Microterangis hariotiana* was described by Fritz Kraenzlin in 1897 and selected as the type of the genus *Microterangis* by Senghas in 1986.

Culture

These plants are not difficult in cultivation, growing and flowering equally well in a pot containing well-drained compost or mounted on a piece of wood or cork-oak bark. Fresh air but high humidity and moderate light seem to be needed at all times. A popular plant with bright orange flowers is quite widely grown under the name *Microterangis hariotiana*.

Microterangis boutonii (Reichenbach f.) Senghas
Syns. *Angraecopsis boutonii* Reichenbach f., *Chamaeangis boutonii* (Reichenbach f.) Garay

Plant small with a short stem. Leaves few, oblong, unequally bilobed at the apex, 12 cm long, 3 cm wide. Inflorescences longer than the leaves, many-flowered; bracts very small. Flowers very small; sepals triangular; petals nearly equalling the sepals; lip wedge-shaped, 3-toothed above, the

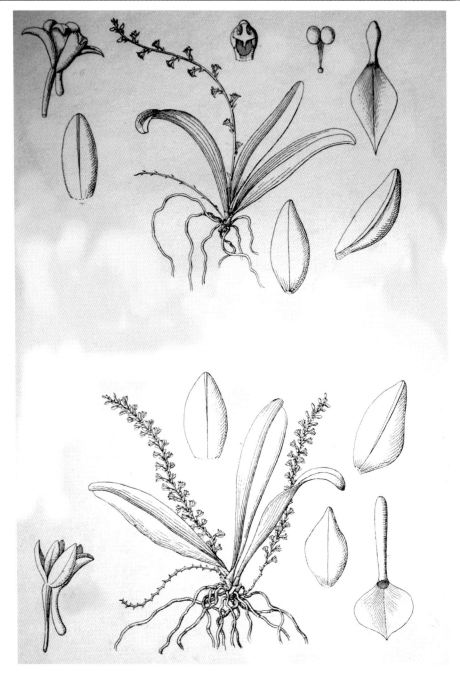

Microterangis divitiflora (top) and *Microterangis oligantha* (bottom). From Schlechter 1913, t. 22. R. Schlechter.

median tooth longer than the short side ones; spur slender, as long as the pedicellate ovary.

Epiphyte.

Comoro Islands.

Apparently named (in 1881) after L. S. Bouton (1799–1878), a Frenchman who lived in Mauritius and collected plants in the Comoro Islands in 1837 and in Madagascar in 1829 and in 1857.

Microterangis coursiana (H. Perrier) Senghas
Syn. *Chamaeangis coursiana* H. Perrier

Plant erect up to 8–16 cm high, stem 1–2 cm long. Leaves 3–4, narrowly oblanceolate, with conspicuous reticulate venation, 3.5–7.5 cm long, 1.2–2 cm wide. Inflorescences 6–12 cm long, growing annually from a perennial, leafless, lateral branch; peduncle with a few short sheaths, 1 cm long; rachis 5–7 cm long with numerous small flowers; bracts acuminate, 2 mm long. Flowers 25–35, minute, 4 mm in diameter; dorsal sepal oval, obtuse, 1.6 mm long, 1 mm wide; lateral sepals slightly narrower; petals smaller; lip broadly rhomboid, subacute, 1.5 mm long and wide; spur narrowly club-shaped, shorter than the pedicellate ovary, 2 mm long.

Epiphyte in humid highland forest; ca. 900 m; flowering in September.

Madagascar (mountains near Lake Alaotra).

Described in 1951 in honour of collector G. Cours Darne, who accompanied Perrier on several plant collecting expeditions in Madagascar. It differs from *Microterangis hariotiana* by its unusual inflorescence, with new racemes arising in a series close to the vestiges of the old ones, and by the smaller leaves and differently shaped lip.

Microterangis divitiflora. J. Hermans

Microterangis divitiflora (Schlechter) Senghas

Syn. *Chamaeangis divitiflora* (Schlechter) Schlechter

Plant almost stemless. Leaves 3–5, oblanceolate, narrowed towards the base, 6 cm long, 6–11 mm wide. Inflorescences dense, bearing many flowers spaced very close together, as long as or a little longer than the leaves. Flowers yellowish white, small; sepals and petals elliptic, obtuse, 1.75 mm long; lip almost round, shortly apiculate, ca. 1.75 mm long, 2 mm wide; spur straight, cylindric, slightly inflated towards the apex, 2 mm long.

Epiphyte in humid highland forest on calcareous rocks; flowering July to September.

Madagascar (central and north-western regions).

Microterangis hariotiana (Kraenzlin) Senghas

Syn. *Chamaeangis hariotiana* (Kraenzlin) Schlechter

Plants 10–20 cm high, stemless or with short stem at the most 4–5 cm long. Leaves 4–7, oboval-oblong, narrowing towards the base, 5–15 cm long, 1.8–4 cm wide. Inflorescences numerous, often grouped on a short, thick primary axis, with many flowers in 2 rows spaced 3–4 mm apart; peduncle 1–4 cm long, much shorter than the rachis, with a few short sheaths; rachis 10–20 cm long; bracts numerous, sheathing the rachis, wide and short. Flowers orange-ochre, very small; sepals oval-triangular, obtuse; petals narrower, acute; lip entire, subcordate, similar to the sepals; spur inflated towards the apex, 2 mm long.

Epiphyte in humid forest; sea level to 500 m; flowering August to November.

Comoro Islands (Grande Comore).

This species was selected by Karlheinz Senghas as the type of the genus. It is the name widely used for plants in cultivation but is not the earliest name applied to specimens of this genus in the Comoro Islands.

Microterangis hildebrandtii. J. Hermans

Microterangis hildebrandtii (Reichenbach f.) Senghas

Syns. *Angraecum hildebrandtii* Reichenbach f., *Chamaeangis hildebrandtii* (Reichenbach f.) Garay

Plant small-growing. Leaves ligulate, unequally bilobed. Inflorescences spreading, racemes lax. Flowers yellow-orange; sepals and petals ligulate, blunt, 2–3 mm long; lip oblong, acute; spur filiform, clavate, shorter than the ovary (Williams, 1894).

This plant was named in 1878 in honour of German collector J. M. Hildebrandt (1847–1881), who was in the Comoro Islands in 1875 and visited Madagascar in 1879–1881. It seems to be the oldest name for any of this group of plants.

Microterangis humblotii (Reichenbach f.) Senghas

Syns. *Saccolabium humblotii* Reichenbach f., *Angraecum saccolabioides* H. Perrier

Plant small. Leaves oblong, wedge-shaped at the base and unequally bilobed at the apex, 5–15 cm long, 1.5–4 cm wide. Inflorescences numerous, bearing many flowers spaced very close together, as long as the leaves; bracts triangular, often reflexed, much shorter than the ovary. Flowers pale, whitish green, small; sepals triangular, obtuse or acute; petals oblong, narrow at the base, acute; lip oblong, boat-shaped, with an obscure, short tooth on each side at the base; spur cylindric, obtuse, narrower towards the mouth, bottle-shaped, longer than the lip.

Comoro Islands (Grande Comore).

Named in honour of the French naturalist and entrepreneur, J. H. L. Humblot (1852–1914), who lived and collected in Madagascar (1881–1884) and in the Comoro Islands (1884–1914).

Microterangis oligantha (Schlechter) Senghas

Syn. *Chamaeangis oligantha* (Schlechter) Schlechter

Plant very small, almost stemless, 5–6 cm high. Leaves 4–7, elliptic-ligulate, widest at the middle, 5–6 cm long, 8–10 mm wide. Inflorescences slender, lax, bearing 8–15 flowers spaced up to 8 mm apart, 10 cm long; bracts oval, a little shorter than the ovary. Flowers with sepals oval-oblong, obtuse, 2.5 mm long; lateral sepals falcate; petals elliptic, obtuse; lip oval-lanceolate, acute, 2.5 mm long, 1.5 mm wide; spur short, globular, 1.25 mm long, shorter than the ovary and lip.

Epiphyte on twigs in humid forests; flowering in June.

Madagascar (western region).

This species seems to have slightly larger flowers than the other species, with a shorter, more globular spur.

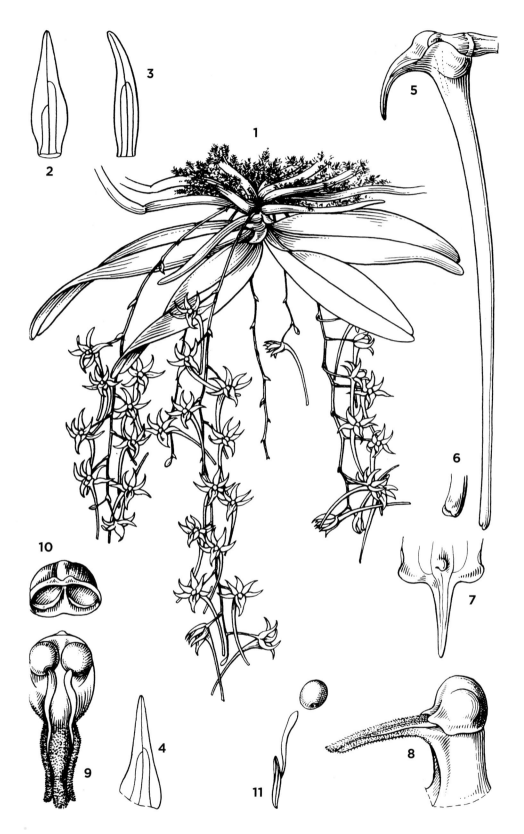

Mystacidium tanganyikense. 1: Habit. 2: Dorsal sepal. 3: Lateral sepal. 4: Petal. 5: Lip, column, and spur. 6: Apex of spur. 7: Lip lamina. 8: Column. 9: Apex of column. 10: Anther-cap. 11: Pollinarium. From Cribb 1989, fig. 148. S. Ross-Craig.

MYSTACIDIUM Lindley

The English orchidologist John Lindley (1799–1865) had limited experience of African epiphytic orchids and his name rarely appears in association with them. *Mystacidium* Lindley is an exception, though not unique.

In preparing his account published between 1830 and 1840 of all the orchid species then known, Lindley had access to many collections including some made in the previous century by C. P. Thunberg in South Africa. One of these orchid specimens had already been named *Epidendrum capense* by the younger Linnaeus, in 1781. Without looking at the column structure, Lindley transferred this species to the genus *Angraecum*, in 1833. A little later he examined specimens collected in South Africa by the German explorer and traveller J. F. Drège (1794–1881) and realised that the column structure was completely different from any other *Angraecum* that he had seen, although the habit of the plants was similar. From the front of the column, he saw the 3-lobed rostellum protruding forward, completely unprotected by the anther cap. He noticed that the outer lobes of the rostellum were papillose and longer than the smooth central lobe. He also noticed that each pollinium was borne on a long slender stipe attached to its own viscidium that nestled between the outer and central lobes, one on each side. So in 1837, when he established the genus *Mystacidium*, he was presumably alluding to the papillose rostellum lobes of this species, deriving the name from the Greek word for moustache.

The name *Mystacidium* was subsequently applied, by various botanists, to a wide range of vandaceous orchids in Africa and Madagascar, especially any that had 2 separate stipites and viscidia. But in 1918, Rudolf Schlechter re-defined the genus, noting that he had always accepted it in the narrow way it was defined by Harry Bolus in Cape Town. Schlechter included only those species whose slender spur has a slightly widened mouth which gradually becomes the lip lamina, and whose slender column has a 3-lobed rostellum with its lateral lobes being either papillose, finely toothed, or barbate. Thus the genus was reduced to about 10 species that more or less fitted this definition. New genera and re-allocations to existing genera were proposed for all the other species previously referred to *Mystacidium* by Robert Rolfe (between 1897 and 1898, and 1912 to 1913) and others.

Since that time a few of Schlechter's proposals have been superseded, and several new species have been described. Two species were transferred to the genus *Diaphananthe* (*Mystacidium caffrum* Bolus and *M. millarii* Bolus) in 1989. Ten species are currently recognised, and they are distributed along eastern Africa between Tanzania and the Western Cape Province of South Africa. Some species are periodically leafless, and all are well endowed with roots. In these 2 characters they also resemble some species of *Angraecopsis* that grow in similar habitats further north in eastern Africa.

Culture

All the species are amenable to cultivation provided they have enough roots. They grow well as mounted subjects on small branches or on pieces of cork-oak bark. The larger specimens and those which lose their leaves during a prolonged dry period do best in good light and low humidity during a resting period, usually after flowering. Most of the smaller plants require cool growing conditions and high humidity especially at night. The genus is easily divided into 2 groups according to the colour of the flowers:

Group 1. Flowers clear white, with or without a bright green anther cap.

Group 2. Flowers green, pale yellowish green, or whitish green.

Group 1. Flowers clear white, with or without a bright green anther cap.

Mystacidium brayboniae Summerhayes

Plants dwarf with short stems, 5–20 mm long. Leaves 2–5, sometimes absent at flowering time,

Mystacidium brayboniae. J. Stewart

Mystacidium capense. E. la Croix

elliptic or lorate, obscurely and unequally bilobed at the apex, 2–5 cm long, 5–10 mm wide. Inflorescences pendent, usually several racemes bearing 2–10 flowers spaced close together, 2–4 cm long; peduncle with several sheaths, 2 mm long; bracts tubular, 1–2 mm long; pedicel with ovary slender, 10–12 mm long. Flowers white, up to 2 cm in diameter; sepals subequal, dorsal sepal arching forward, narrowly oblong, acute, 8 mm long, 4 mm wide; lateral sepals narrowly elliptic-lanceolate, 10 mm long, 4 mm wide; petals erect, ovate, acute, 8 mm long, 4 mm wide; lip 3-lobed, mid-lobe triangular, acute, deflexed, side lobes porrect, 1.5 mm tall, 4–5 mm long, 3.5 mm wide; spur widely funnel-shaped at the mouth, tapering to an acute apex, 18–25 mm long.

Epiphyte in forests; flowering November to January.

South Africa (Zoutpansberg Mountains in Limpopo).

Mystacidium capense (Linnaeus f.) Schlechter

Plants small with stems 1–4 cm long. Leaves usually 4–10, ligulate, unequally and obtusely bilobed at the apex, 4–12 cm long, 10–22 mm wide. Inflorescences usually several, spreading, lax, 7–18 cm long, 7- to 15-flowered; bracts broadly ovate, tubular, 3–5 mm long; pedicel with ovary 1–2 cm long. Flowers white, 2–3 cm in diameter; sepals subequal, linear-lanceolate, acute, partly reflexed, dorsal sepal 11–14 mm long, 3.5–4 mm wide; lateral sepals suboblique, 13–17 mm long, 3–4 mm wide; petals partly reflexed, linear-lanceolate, acute, 9–13 mm long, 3–3.5 mm wide; lip 3-lobed, linear-lanceolate, acute, side lobes porrect, reflexed, mid-lobe with apical margins upcurved, 10–15 mm long, 3–4 mm wide; spur wide at the mouth, funnel-shaped, tapering to a slender apex, 3.5–6 cm long.

Epiphyte in montane and lowland forest and bush, also in dry thorn-bush and sometimes on succulent *Euphorbia* species; flowering September to January.

South Africa and Swaziland.

This species has the largest plants and flowers in the genus but is sometimes difficult to distinguish from the generally smaller *Mystacidium venosum*. These 2 species are always distinguished by their different flowering time in the wild.

Mystacidium nguruense P. J. Cribb

Plant dwarf with a short leafy stem up to 5 cm long and numerous flexuous roots. Leaves 4–5, linear, falcate, unequally and obtusely bilobed at the apex, twisted at the base, 12–18 cm long, 1.3–2 cm wide. Inflorescences pendent, one to several, 6–9 cm long, 5- to 8-flowered; peduncle and rachis very slender, wiry; bracts ovate, 1.5 mm long; pedicel with ovary slender, 8–10 mm long. Flowers white, stellate but not opening fully; dorsal sepal elliptic, acute, 7 mm long, 3.5 mm wide; lateral sepals obliquely lanceolate, acuminate, 8 mm long, 2 mm wide; petals ovate, acute, 7 mm long, 3.5 mm wide; lip ovate, shortly apiculate, obscurely 3-lobed, side lobes erect, rounded, mid-lobe broadly ovate, a narrow callus running along the midline, 7 mm long, 6 mm wide; spur narrow, tapering from a broad mouth, 20 mm long.

Epiphyte in mossy, montane forest; ca. 2000 m; flowering in February.

Tanzania.

Mystacidium pulchellum (Kraenzlin) Schlechter

Plant dwarf with a short stem to 10 mm long and many fine roots. Leaves 3–5, obovate, fleshy, unequally bilobed at the apex, with rounded lobes, 1.3–5 cm long, 4–10 mm wide. Inflorescences one to several, pendent, 4- to 7-flowered; peduncle wiry, terete; rachis zigzag, very slender; bracts ca. 6 mm apart, ovate, subacute, 1 mm long; pedicel with ovary 12–18 mm long. Flowers white with a bright green anther cap; sepals elliptic, obtuse, 6–7 mm long, 2.5–3.7 mm wide; petals obliquely ovate, subacute, 5.5–7 mm long, 3.5–5 mm wide; lip deeply concave, transversely cordate, obtuse,

4.5–5.5 mm long, 6–8 mm wide; spur tapering from a wide mouth, 15–17 mm long.

Epiphyte in upland rain forest; 1700–2400 m; flowering in December and February.

Southern Tanzania.

Mystacidium venosum Harvey ex Rolfe

Plants dwarf with a short stem and abundant roots 2–4 mm in diameter, dark grey-green with white streaks. Leaves 2–4 when present, elliptic to oblanceolate, unequally bilobed at the apex, venation distinctly darker, 1.5–6.5 cm long, 6–10 mm wide. Inflorescences pendent, usually several, bearing 4–10 flowers densely arranged; peduncle thick; bracts conspicuous but very small; pedicel with ovary slender, 9–14 mm long. Flowers white, stellate, sepals and petals slightly recurved, 15 mm in diameter; sepals subequal, reflexed to spreading, narrowly elliptic-lanceolate, acute, 7–8 mm long, 2–2.5 mm wide; lateral sepals, 8–9 mm long,

Mystacidium venosum. J. Hermans

2–3 mm wide; petals reflexed, linear-lanceolate, acute, 6–8 mm long, 1.2–2 mm wide; lip 3-lobed, mid-lobe deflexed, narrowly triangular, acute, side lobes erect on either side of the column, 1.5 mm high, 4–6 mm long, 1.5–2 mm wide; spur slender, tapering from a wide mouth, 2–4.5 cm long.

Epiphyte, often in large colonies, in woodland and riverine bush, coastal and montane forests; flowering April to July.

South Africa, Swaziland, and Mozambique.

This species is distinctive in flowering during the winter months, sometimes when leafless.

Group 2. Flowers green, pale yellowish green, or whitish green.

Mystacidium aliceae Bolus

Plants dwarf with stems 5–10 mm high. Leaves 2–5, linear-lanceolate, unequally bilobed at the apex, 2–6 cm long, 4–9 mm wide. Inflorescences spreading or pendent, usually several, 15 mm long, densely 5- to 10-flowered, bracts ovate, acute, 1 mm long; pedicel with ovary 5 mm long. Flowers shiny, yellowish green, 1 cm in diameter; sepals equal, reflexed, narrowly elliptic, 4–5 mm long, 2 mm wide; petals erect then reflexed, lanceolate, acuminate, 5 mm long, 2 mm wide; lip 3-lobed, side lobes rounded, porrect, 1 mm high, mid-lobe deflexed, acute, 3 mm long, 2 mm wide; spur tapering from a wide mouth to the narrow apex, 8–11 mm long.

Epiphyte on twigs and branches in coastal forests; up to 500 m; flowering November to March.

South Africa (KwaZulu-Natal and Eastern Cape Province).

Mystacidium flanaganii (Bolus) Bolus

Plants dwarf with stems to 10 mm tall. Leaves 3–5, lorate, or elliptic, unequally bilobed, 12–35 mm long, 3–4.5 mm wide. Inflorescences pendent, lax, usually 1–5 racemes, each with 3–8 flowers, 2–4.5 cm long; bracts ovate, acute, 1–2 mm long; pedicel with ovary 5 mm long. Flowers pale green, 7–10 mm in diameter; sepals unequal; dorsal sepal oblong-obovate, 2–3.5 mm long, ca. 1 mm wide;

lateral sepals narrowly rhomboid to oblanceolate, 2.6–5 mm long, ca. 1.5 mm wide; petals obliquely triangular, acute, 1.5–3 mm long, ca. 1 mm wide; lip 3-lobed, side lobes poorly developed, mid-lobe deflexed, acute, 1.5–2 mm long, 0.8–1 mm wide; spur tapering from a wide mouth to an acute apex, 18–25 mm long.

Epiphyte in montane and temperate forests; flowering in December and January.

South Africa.

This species is sometimes difficult to distinguish from *Mystacidium pusillum*, which is smaller in most respects, much less common, and flowers during the winter months,

Mystacidium gracile Harvey

Plants dwarf with short stems to 15 mm long from which a mass of greyish roots radiate along the host branch. Leaves tiny but rarely produced, elliptic or linear, bluish green, 1–3 cm long, 3 mm wide. Inflorescences spreading or pendent, lax, usually several, with ca. 10 flowers, 3–10 cm long; bracts tubular, 2–3 mm long; pedicel with ovary 10 mm long. Flowers pale green, up to 14 mm in diameter, all parts fleshy at the apex; dorsal sepal narrowly ovate, acute, 3–5 mm long, 1.5 mm wide; lateral sepals spreading, narrowly rhomboid, acute, 4–5 mm long, 1.5 mm wide; petals hiding the column, narrowly oblong, subacute, 3–3.5 mm long, ca. 1 mm wide; lip 3-lobed, side lobes porrect, rounded, 1 mm high, mid-lobe deflexed, narrowly triangular, 2 mm long, 0.5 mm wide; spur wide at the mouth, tapering to an acute apex, 20–25 mm long.

Epiphyte in montane and temperate forests; up to 1800 m; flowering June to October.

Zimbabwe and South Africa.

This species can be confused with *Mystacidium flanaganii* if it bears leaves, but the flowers are smaller and paler and the flowering season is different.

Mystacidium pusillum Harvey

Plants very small with stems less than 10 mm long. Leaves 1–5, elliptic or oblanceolate, unequally bilobed at the apex, with rounded lobes, 1.5–4 cm long, 4–6 mm wide. Inflorescences usually several, pendent, 1.5–3.5 cm long, 4- to 7-flowered; bracts tubular, acute, 1 mm long; pedicel with ovary 5 mm long. Flowers pale green, 5 mm in diameter; dorsal sepal erect, acute, 2.6–5 mm long, 1 mm wide; lateral sepals spreading, oblanceolate, 3–5 mm long, 1–2 mm wide; petals ovate, acute, 2–3 mm long, 1–2 mm wide; lip triangular, acute, 1 mm long, side lobes absent; spur wide at the mouth, tapering to an acute apex, 1.2–2 cm long.

Epiphyte in temperate and subtropical forests; 900–1200 m; flowering June to August.

South Africa.

This is the smallest species and flowers during the winter months.

Mystacidium tanganyikense Summerhayes

Plant dwarf with a very short stem less than 2 mm long and numerous flexuous roots. Leaves 4–5, ligulate or elliptic-lanceolate, falcate, unequally bilobed at the apex, with rounded or obtuse lobes, dark green with raised venation, 1–6 cm long, 3–9 mm wide. Inflorescences pendent, one to several, 1.5–10 cm long, up to 12-flowered; peduncle and rachis very slender, wiry; bracts 3–7 mm apart, triangular, less than 1 mm long; pedicel with ovary slender, 5–12 mm long. Flowers pale green or yellowish green; dorsal sepal recurved, lanceolate, acuminate, 5–8 mm long, 1.5–2 mm wide; lateral sepals similar; petals obliquely lanceolate, acute, 4.7–7 mm long, 1.5–2.5 mm wide; lip obscurely 3-lobed, side lobes upcurved, rounded, mid-lobe lanceolate, recurved, 4.7–6.6 mm long, 2.7–3 mm wide; spur slender, tapering from a wide mouth, 12–17 mm long.

Epiphyte in upland rain forest, also in conifer plantations, usually in moss; 1300–2500 m; flowering January and February.

Tanzania, Malawi, Zambia, and Zimbabwe.

NEPHRANGIS Summerhayes

This genus was established by Victor Summerhayes in 1948 to accommodate one species that was different from all other species of *Tridactyle* in which it had previously been placed. Although the growth habit is similar, the translucent flowers are quite different, particularly the lip with 2 rounded lobes above a narrow base from which the spur descends. The narrow, almost needle-like leaves are also quite distinctive when the plants are not in flower. In 2001 another, very similar plant was described as a second species. The name of this genus is derived from the Greek words *nephros*, kidney, and *angos*, vessel, referring to the distinctive shape of the lip lobes.

Culture

These orchids have not been grown in cultivation but should do well as mounted plants given the same treatment as the warmer-growing species of *Tridactyle*.

Nephrangis bertauxiana Szlachetko & Olszewski

This species was described in 2001 from Gabon and is known only from the type collection. It was flowering in October and is easily distinguished from *Nephrangis filiformis* by the slightly larger, pendent flowers and especially by the longer spur that has a distinct knee-bend about halfway along its length where it suddenly becomes narrower. The species is named in honour of Pierre Bertaux, conservator of the living collection of orchids in the Jardin du Luxembourg, in Paris.

Nephrangis filiformis (Kraenzlin) Summerhayes

Plants usually pendulous with elongated, slender stems, sometimes branching, to 35 cm long, leafy in the apical part, rooting at the base only. Leaves widely spaced, terete but somewhat flattened, often curved, pointed, 2–9 cm long, 1–2 mm in diameter. Inflorescences opposite the leaves, short, ca. 1 cm long, 1- to 4-flowered. Flowers translucent, pale brown or brownish green, with

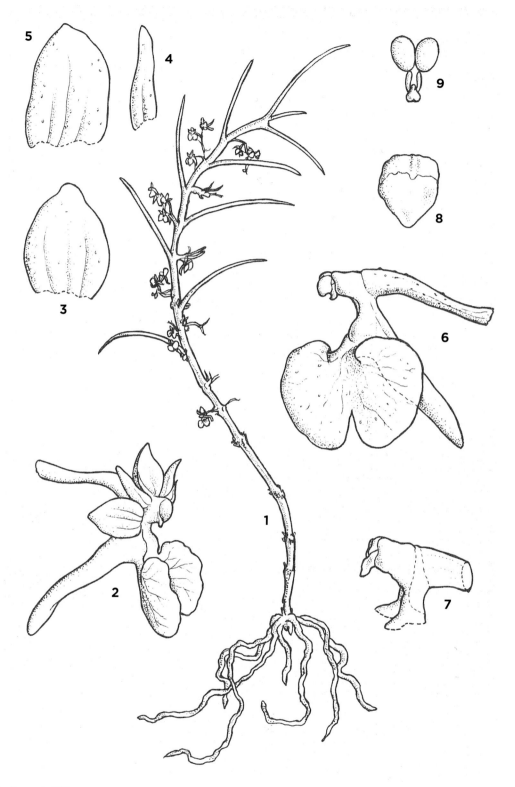

Nephrangis filiformis. 1: Habit. 2: Flower. 3: Dorsal sepal. 4: Lateral sepal. 5: Petal. 6: Column and lip. 7: Column, side view. 8: Anther-cap. 9: Pollinarium. From Cribb 1989, fig. 161. C. A. Lavrih.

a white lip; dorsal sepal ovate to almost round, obtuse, 1.5–2.5 mm long, 1.5–2 mm wide; lateral sepals similar but oblique, connate at the base; petals narrowly elliptic to linear, acute, 1.7–2.5 mm long, 0.5 mm wide; lip narrow and concave at base, abruptly spreading into 2 reniform or round lobes, total length 4–5 mm; spur narrowly conical, obtuse, sometimes bent, 4–9 mm long.

Epiphyte on branches of the canopy of woodland trees; 1500 m; flowering in June and July.

Liberia, Côte d'Ivoire, Congo, D.R. of Congo, Uganda, Kenya, Tanzania, and Zambia.

PLECTRELMINTHUS Rafinesque

This remarkable genus contains only one handsome orchid that is widespread in west tropical Africa. *Plectrelminthus* was defined in 1838 by the naturalist and author C. S. Rafinesque (1783–1840), then living in the United States. The name was derived from the Greek words *plektron*, spur, and *helminthion*, worm, in allusion to the long, thick, curved spur at the base of the lip. The epithet *bicolor*, which Rafinesque used as a species name, although appropriate, cannot be retained because Lindley had already named this species *Angraecum caudatum* when he described it, with a lovely colour plate, in *Edwards's Botanical Register* in 1836 (t. 1844). It was only in 1949 that V. S. Summerhayes regularised the situation by publishing the combination *Plectrelminthus caudatus*.

Although the long spur is a distinctive feature of this orchid, it is the large column with its conspicuous anther cap and porrect rostellum that are quite characteristic and immediately indicate that this is a member of the subtribe Aerangidinae, not an *Angraecum* at all.

Culture

This orchid is greatly sought-after in cultivation and can be maintained in warm, humid conditions with good light. The extensive roots need plenty of fresh air and good drainage, and the species is reported to thrive when loosely planted in a basket, with fern or palm fibre. Good specimens are also produced when plants are attached to pieces of bark or wood and suspended in a suitable part of the glasshouse. The combination of strong light and high humidity is essential but not always easy to achieve.

Plectrelminthus caudatus (Lindley) Summerhayes

Plant large, with an erect stem, usually 15–20 cm high but sometimes attaining 60 cm in old specimens. Leaves light yellowish green in 2 rows, closely spaced, erect or arching away from the stem, lorate or elliptic-oblong, unequally bilobed at the apex, with rounded lobes, 10–35 cm long, 1.5–3.5 cm wide. Inflorescences axillary from the lowermost leaves, horizontal at first, usually becoming pendent, 25–60 cm long, 6- to 16-flowered; rachis zigzag; bracts oval-triangular, acute,

Plectrelminthus caudatus. J. Hermans

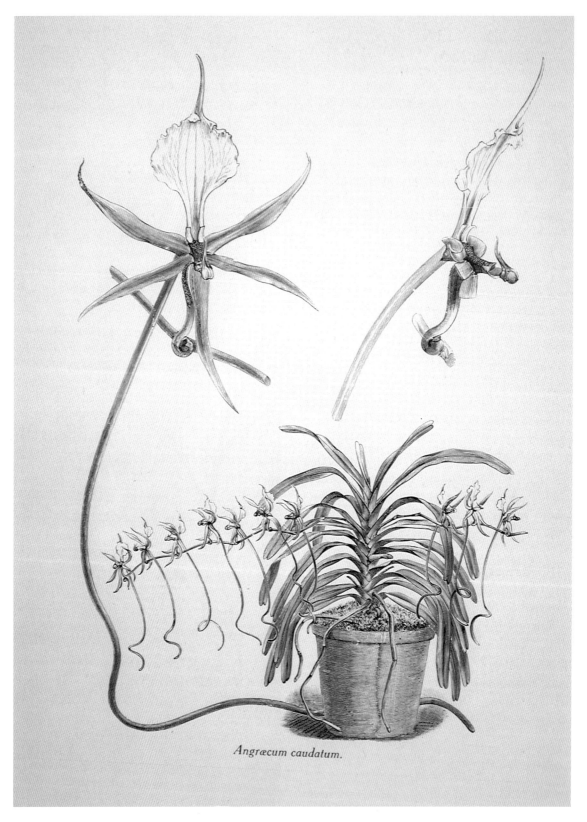

Angræcum caudatum.

Plectrelminthus caudatus. From Wilson 1915, p. 260. Apparently copied from Veitch 1891.

thin, 5 mm long; pedicel with ovary twisted at the base so that the lip is held on the upper side of the flower, 2.5 cm long. Flowers large, with white lip, tepals brown at the base and light greenish yellow towards the tips; sepals and petals similar, linear-lanceolate, acuminate, sepals 3.5–5 cm long, 5–7 mm wide; the lateral sepals united at the base behind the spur; petals 3–3.5 cm long, 4–5 mm wide; lip clawed at the base, then obcordate, 3.5–5 cm long, 1.5–2.5 cm wide, ending in a long pointed, pale green acumen 8–15 mm long; spur curved or spirally twisted, 17–25 cm long; column brown, 1.5–2 cm long, with a conspicuous anther cap and rostellum.

Epiphyte on trunks and large branches of forest trees in good light but not in direct sun, also on granitic rocks amongst grasses in heavy rainfall areas no longer forested; flowering May to October.

West Africa to Congo.

Two varieties of this species were recognised in 2001:

var. *caudatus*
Widespread in West Africa.

var. *trilobatus* Szlachetko & Olszewski
Differs from the type in having 2 extra lobes on the lip, on either side of the apex below the acumen.

Cameroon and Central African Republic.

PODANGIS Schlechter

Rudolf Schlechter created this genus in 1918 for a single species with a distinct foot at the base of the column that merges almost imperceptibly into the lip and spur (from the Greek *pous* or *podos*, foot, and *angos*, vessel). He commented that this flower resembles some of those in the subtribe Aeridinae because of this foot, but it has the pollinarium and rostellum structure of the subtribe Aerangidinae so is best placed here.

It has been suggested that the inflated tip of the spur, which somewhat resembles a foot with

Podangis dactyloceras. J. Hermans

2 toes, provided the inspiration for the generic name of this plant, but Schlechter did not explain his choice of name.

The species had already been described by Reichenbach in 1865, based on specimens collected in Angola by the Portuguese botanist and traveller Friedrich Welwitsch (1806–1872). Reichenbach called it *Listrostachys dactyloceras*, the specific epithet alluding to the finger or toe-like outgrowths that are sometimes present at the apex of the spur.

The flowers of this species are distinctive. They are translucent with a hyaline, sparkling substance that contrasts nicely with the bright green anther cap. The flowers are borne close together on pedicels of different lengths so that the inflorescence appears corymbose.

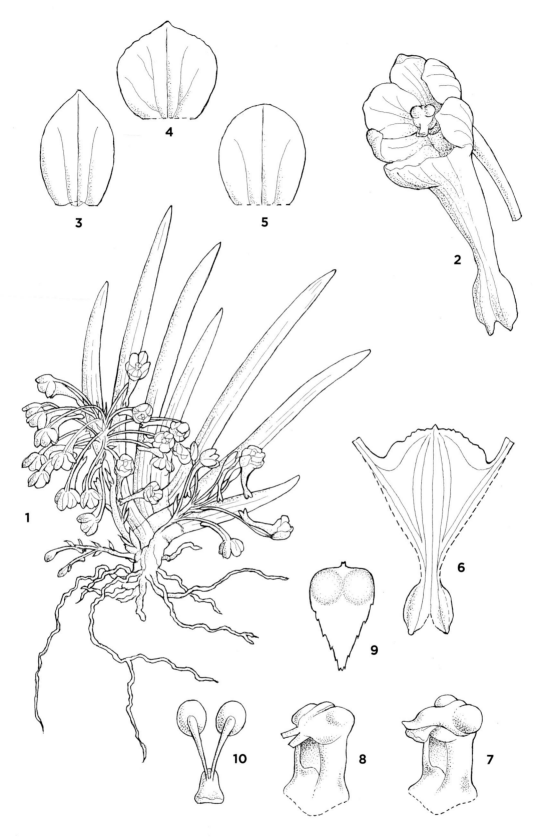

Podangis dactyloceras. 1: Habit. 2: Flower. 3: Dorsal sepal. 4: Lateral sepal. 5: Petal. 6: Lip. 7–8: Column. 9: Anther-cap. 10: Pollinarium. From Cribb 1989, fig. 112. C. A. Lavrih.

Culture

This species is easy to grow in intermediate or warm conditions with good humidity. It does well in small clay pots with a freely draining medium. It also thrives when mounted on a branch or piece of bark but is not always easy to establish in this way. Plenty of water is needed during the growing season, and a drier period during a winter rest is beneficial.

Podangis dactyloceras (Reichenbach f.) Schlechter

Plants small with erect stems to 20 cm high but usually shorter, covered by overlapping leaf bases and narrow roots. Leaves fleshy, flattened with the upper surfaces united and arranged in a fan, linear-ligulate, falcate, acute or acuminate, 4–16 cm long, 6–12 mm wide. Inflorescences axillary, below the leaves, 5- to 20-flowered; peduncle short, 1–4 cm long, rachis similar; bracts 2–5 mm long; pedicel white, slender, 2–2.5 cm long, ovary small, dark green. Flowers white, translucent, with bright green anther; sepals elliptic-oblong, obtuse, 4–5 mm long, 3–4 mm wide; petals quadrate, or broadly oblong, 5 mm long and wide; lip circular or transversely elliptic, funnel-shaped, free part 4–6 mm long, 5 mm wide; spur wide at the mouth where it merges with the lip and the foot of the column, gradually narrowing to below the middle, the tip inflated into 2 or more sacs, 9–14 mm long.

Epiphyte on branches in semi-deciduous forest and often in gallery forest along watercourses; 750–1600 m; flowering October to April.

Guinea, Sierra Leone, Côte d'Ivoire, Togo, Ghana, northern Nigeria, Cameroon, Congo, Uganda, Tanzania, and Angola.

This species can be confused with *Rangaeris rhipsalisocia* when not in flower, but it has finer roots and a different overall shape.

Podangis dactyloceras. J. Hermans

Rangaeris schliebenii. 1: Habit. 2: Inflorescence. 3: Flower. 4: Dorsal sepal. 5: Lateral sepal. 6: Petal.
7: Lip. 8: Column. 9: Anther-cap. 10: Pollinarium. From Cribb 1989, fig. 139. S. Hillier.

RANGAERIS Summerhayes

The generic name *Rangaeris* was proposed by Victor Summerhayes in 1936, initially for the species *R. muscicola* which had previously been placed in *Aerangis* on account of its conspicuous white flowers. The name *Rangaeris* is a near-anagram of *Aerangis*.

The plants of the 2 genera are very different. *Rangaeris muscicola* has stiff narrow leaves, V-shaped in cross section. In the flowers the 2 pollinia are each borne on a separate stipe but attached to a single large viscidium, instead of a shared stipe as in *Aerangis*. Summerhayes somewhat hesitantly placed *A. brachyceras* in this genus too; however, that species has green flowers with a quite different appearance and it has since been transferred to the genus *Cribbia*.

Summerhayes looked at the genus *Rangaeris* again in 1949 when he transferred *Leptocentrum amaniense* to it. In the account of *Rangaeris* in the *Flora of Tropical East Africa*, Phillip Cribb (1989) added to the genus the curiously flowered Tanzanian species previously known as *L. schliebenii*. Altogether, 6 species of *Rangaeris* are now recognised, though vegetatively they are somewhat dissimilar.

Culture

The differences in the native habitats of the various *Rangaeris* species need to be borne in mind in their cultural regime. They all grow well as mounted plants or established in a well-drained medium in a basket. It seems to be very important to prevent the roots being saturated with water for too long. Air movement and excellent drainage are the key.

Rangaeris amaniensis (Kraenzlin) Summerhayes
Syn. *Leptocentrum amaniense* (Kraenzlin) Schlechter

Plants erect, stems often branching from the leafless part and forming dense clumps, curved or pendent when very long but usually upright, bearing thick roots along their length and leaves in the upper part, 15–45 cm long. Leaves in 2 rows, folded, ligulate, unequally lobed at the apex, with rounded lobes, 4–8 cm long, 1–2 cm wide. Inflorescences arching away from stem, 6–10 cm long, 5- to 12-flowered; bracts blackish. Flowers white, green on the outer surface and in the spur, fading to yellow or orange, very variable in size; dorsal sepal lanceolate, acuminate, 1–2.5 cm long, 3–6 mm wide; lateral sepals similar, oblique; petals lanceolate, acuminate, shorter and narrower than sepals, 1–2 cm long, 2–4 mm wide; lip rhombic, somewhat 3-lobed in the middle, side lobes quadrate or rounded, mid-lobe lanceolate, 10–24 mm long, 5–11 mm wide; spur very slender, 8–16 cm long.

Epiphyte in bright situations in highland forest and also on isolated trees, occasionally on rocks; 1000–2300 m; flowering April and May, also October and November.

Kenya, Tanzania, northern Uganda, Ethiopia, and Zambia.

Rangaeris longicaudata (Rolfe) Summerhayes

Plants erect with long stems bearing leaves and many aerial roots, 30–60 cm or more long. Leaves in 2 rows, 1–2 cm apart, ligulate or lorate, sheathing the stem at the base, unequally bilobed at the apex, with rounded lobes, 6–12 cm long, 1–1.8 cm wide. Inflorescence lateral, arising opposite the base of a leaf, erect or suberect, 12–20 cm long, 3- to 8-flowered; sheaths and bracts large, dark brown, 10–15 mm long; bracts enclosing the base of the pedicels; pedicel with ovary 7–12 cm long, very slender. Flowers white; sepals lanceolate, acute, 2.5–4 cm long, 5–8 mm wide; petals similar but slightly smaller, 2–3 cm long, 5–7 mm wide; lip similar to the dorsal sepal, 1.5–2.5 cm long, 5–8 mm wide; spur straight or curved, gradually tapering from an enlarged mouth, 15–20 cm long.

Epiphyte, often growing in tufts on large branches of big trees in evergreen or semi-deciduous forest; low altitudes; flowering in November and December.

Côte d'Ivoire, southern Nigeria, and Cameroon.

Rangaeris amaniensis. J. Hermans

Rangaeris muscicola. J. Hermans

Rangaeris muscicola (Reichenbach f.)
Summerhayes

Plants erect with short stems, usually not more than 6 cm long, upright, bearing thick roots at the base and 2 rows of closely overlapping leaves. Leaves usually 4–8, arranged in a fan shape, folded, narrowly ligulate or linear, unequally lobed at the apex, with rounded lobes, dark green, 6–20 cm long, 6–12 mm wide. Inflorescences arching away from stem or almost erect, bearing 10–16 flowers in 2 rows, 6–20 cm long; bracts blackish. Flowers white, sometimes with a pinkish-orange spur, fading to yellow or orange, very variable in size; dorsal sepal ovate, acute, 7–9 mm long, 2–4 mm wide; lateral sepals similar, slightly narrower, oblique; petals obliquely elliptic or lanceolate, reflexed, acute, shorter and narrower than sepals, 6–8 mm long, 1.5–3 mm wide; lip entire, broadly ovate, acute, 6–9 mm long, 4–7 mm wide; spur very slender, 5–9 cm long.

Epiphyte in humid forests, usually growing amongst mosses on well-shaded branches, occasionally lithophytic; 1200–2200 m; flowering April to July, also in November.

Guinea eastwards to Kenya and southwards to South Africa (KwaZulu-Natal and Eastern Cape Province).

Rangaeris rhipsalisocia (Reichenbach f.)
Summerhayes
(including *Rangaeris trachypus* (Kraenzlin) Guillaumin)

Plants erect with a short stem 3–10 cm long, densely covered with old leaf bases and a few thick roots. Leaves arranged in a fan, flattened and with the upper surfaces cohering so that they appear *Iris*-like, entire and acute at the apex, 6–20 cm long, 5–10 mm wide. Inflorescences axillary or arising below the leaves, spreading or pendent, 10–15 cm long, 6- to 8-flowered, sometimes up to

Rangaeris muscicola. B. Campbell

15-flowered; bracts ovate, sheathing at the base, 3.5–5 mm long, brown; pedicel with ovary 1.5–2 cm long, densely hairy. Flowers white or cream with a greenish spur; sepals and petals lanceolate, acute; sepals 11–12 mm long, fleshy at the apex; petals less fleshy than the sepals and a little smaller; lip rhomboid-lanceolate, obscurely 3-lobed at the base, acute, fleshy, 7–8 mm long, 4 mm wide; spur tapering incurved at the apex, 9–14 mm long.

Epiphyte, usually in the forest canopy; flowering November to December.

Senegal, eastwards to Uganda and Angola.

Rangaeris schliebenii (Mansfeld) P. J. Cribb
Syn. *Leptocentrum schliebenii* Mansfeld

Plants erect, stem covered with persistent leaf bases, and roots in the lower half, 7–11 cm long. Leaves coriaceous, conduplicate, spreading or arching, linear-ligulate, unequally bilobed at the apex, with rounded lobes, 15–20 cm long, 1.7–2.5 cm wide. Inflorescences axillary, 18–27 cm long, 4- to 8-flowered; bracts brown, ovate-oblong, 8–11 mm long; pedicel with ovary 6–9 cm long. Flowers white, green on the outside with a greenish-orange spur; sepals recurved, linear, acute, 3.4–4 cm long,

353

Rangaeris rhipsalisocia. J. Hermans

3.5–4.5 mm wide; petals reflexed, linear, acuminate 3.4–3.8 cm long, 4 mm wide; lip recurved, narrowly elliptic, acuminate, margins uneven in the upper half, 3–4.2 cm long, 7–11 mm wide; spur narrow below a wide mouth, 16–19 cm long.

Epiphyte in montane and riverine forest; 400–1400 m; flowering in May and June.

Tanzania.

Apparently rare but easily distinguished from all other species by its large size and very long column (2 cm or more).

Rangaeris trilobata Summerhayes

Plants scandent, with long, slender stems 60 cm or more long, ca. 3 mm in diameter. Leaves spaced 3–5 cm apart, narrowly oblong-lanceolate, acute, shortly bilobed at the apex, 6–8 cm long, 1–2 cm wide. Inflorescences 3–5 cm long, 3- or 4-flowered; bracts broadly ovate, subacute; pedicel with ovary 1 cm long. Flowers white with salmon pink sepals; sepals lanceolate, ca. 7.5 mm long, 3 mm wide; petals narrowly lanceolate, acute, 7.5 mm long, 1.5 mm wide; lip 3-lobed, 5–9 mm long, mid-lobe lanceolate or linear, obtusely acuminate, lateral lobes much shorter, almost circular, crenulate or dentate; spur 5 cm long.

Epiphyte; flowering in May.

Southern Nigeria and Gabon.

The plants resemble those of *Solenangis scandens* and *Dinklageella liberica* with their long climbing stems and distantly placed, narrow leaves, but the flowers are typical of *Rangaeris*.

RHAESTERIA Summerhayes

This tiny orchid was collected in 1948 on the outskirts of the Impenetrable Forest near Kigezi in western Uganda. It is remarkable for the small size of the plants and for the partly united sepals and petals. It also has a broad, convex lip encircling the column at its base, and the elongated rostellum somewhat resembles the head of a hammer. In 1966 Summerhayes coined the name *Rhaesteria* in allusion to this last feature (from the Greek *rhaester*, a hammer). The single species is named after the collector W. J. Eggeling.

Rhaesteria eggelingii Summerhayes

Syn. *Angraecum petterssonianum* Geerinck

Plants dwarf with spreading or pendent stems, 6–8 cm long, 1 mm in diameter. Leaves in 2 rows, ovate or ovate-elliptic, fleshy, unequally and minutely bilobed at the apex, 10–16 mm long, 5–9 mm wide. Inflorescences slightly longer than the leaves, 2- or 3-flowered; peduncle wiry, 10–15 mm long, rachis similar but slightly zigzag; bracts very small; pedicel with ovary 2–3 mm long. Flowers yellowish; sepals and petals ovate, obtuse, united in their basal half, 2.5–3 mm long, 1.5 mm wide; lip concave, boat-shaped, 2.5 mm long, 3 mm wide; spur strongly incurved, narrow from a wide mouth, 2.5 mm long.

Epiphyte on small savannah trees in grassland in the outskirts of the forest and at higher altitudes in forest; 1300–2300 m; flowering March and September to November.

Uganda and Rwanda.

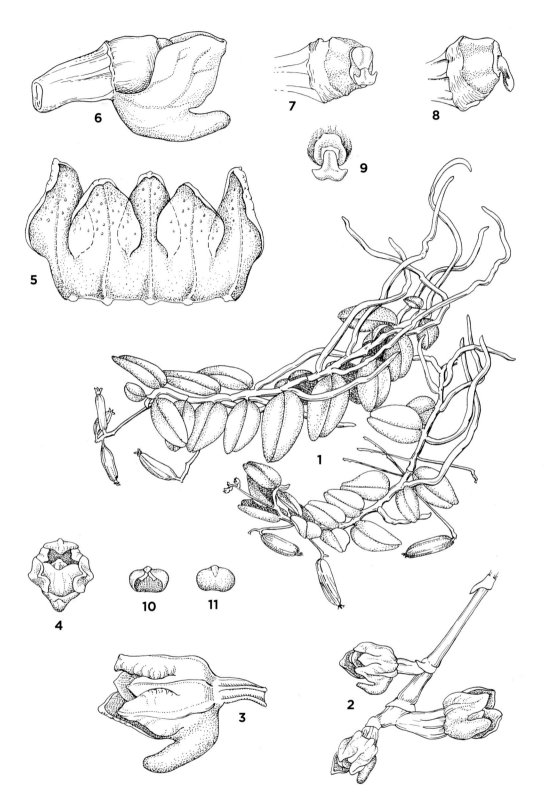

Rhaesteria eggelingii. 1: Habit. 2: Inflorescence. 3–4: Flower. 5: Sepals and petals. 6: Flower with sepals and petals removed. 7–9: Column. 10–11: Anther-cap. From Summerhayes 1966, p. 192. M. Grierson.

RHIPIDOGLOSSUM Schlechter

Many of the white, pale green, or yellowish flowers of *Rhipidoglossum* species have a fan-shaped lip, and it was this feature which gave Rudolf Schlechter the idea for the generic name in 1918, from the Greek words *rhipis*, fan, and *glossum*, tongue. Schlechter proposed *Rhipidoglossum* as distinct from *Diaphananthe* and other African angraecoids because of the way the lip was attached to a short column foot in the 5 species that he recognised.

As the number of species described has grown, to a current total of nearly 40 in *Rhipidoglossum* and 25 in *Diaphananthe*, this feature has proved to be less easily observed, and some botanists have found it difficult to distinguish positively between the 2 genera. Summerhayes, in particular, found it so difficult that he proposed to amalgamate the 2 genera (1960). However, he treated *Rhipidoglossum* as a distinct section including all those species in which each of the 2 pollinia is attached by a short stalk to its own viscidium, whereas in *Diaphananthe* one viscidium is shared by 2 separate stipes. Schlechter had not been so definitive about this feature. A callus or tooth on the lip, in the mouth of the spur, has sometimes been used as a distinguishing character for *Diaphananthe*, although it is not always present, but it is also present, to some degree, in some species of *Rhipidoglossum*. Garay (1972), Senghas (1986), and others have favoured treating the 2 genera separately and we have followed this practice in this book.

Some plants of *Rhipidoglossum* species have a short stem with the flat leaves arranged in a neat rosette or fan, while others make untidy specimens in the wild, with straggling, branching stems that produce many elongated aerial roots. The roots are often the first part to catch the eye. The inflorescences are short or long and often produced in great numbers. The flowers are generally small, but when viewed close-up they are attractive and make distinguishing the species relatively easy by details of the lip and spur.

Sarcorhynchus was also established by Schlechter in 1918 for those species with a fleshy rostellum and 4-lobed lip, but only 4 species have been assigned to it. These are currently included in *Rhipidoglossum*. Some species of *Cribbia* and *Angraecopsis* also have somewhat translucent flowers and a column with a 3-lobed rostellum, but they have not been confused with any in the genus *Rhipidoglossum* so far. Further investigation, especially the availability of DNA information, may provide the evidence needed for a new assessment of the generic limits in this group of orchids.

In the following account the species are presented in 2 groups, based on their habit:

Group 1. Stems short, usually less than 12 cm long, with leaves arranged in a rosette or fan, or, in plants with longer stems, in 2 rows along the sides of the upper part of the stem.

Group 2. Stems elongated, at least 20 cm long in mature plants, leafy along most of their length.

Culture

All these species can be grown in cultivation without difficulty, though most of them grow better when mounted on a piece of bark than when planted in a pot. Due regard should be paid to the altitudinal range of each species in the wild, as some will require much cooler night temperatures than others.

Group 1. Stems short, usually less than 12 cm long, with leaves arranged in a rosette or fan, or, in plants with longer stems, in 2 rows along the sides of the upper part of the stem.

Rhipidoglossum candidum (P. J. Cribb) Senghas

Plant small, erect, with a short stem up to 5 cm high. Leaves erect, linear, obscurely and unequally bilobed at the apex, articulated at the base, 11 cm long, 9 mm wide. Inflorescence suberect or spreading, up to 10 cm long, 6-flowered; bracts ovate, acute, 3–4 mm long, 3 mm wide. Flowers

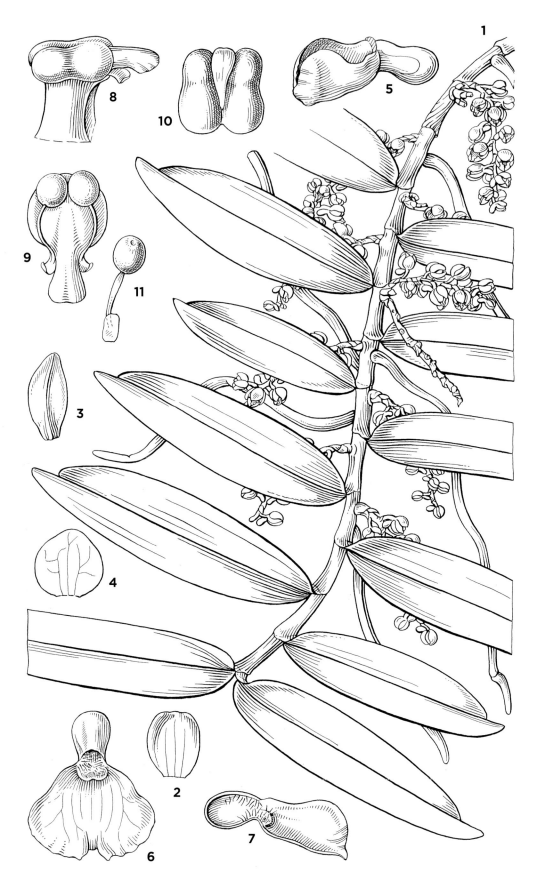

Rhipidoglossum densiflorum. 1: Habit. 2: Dorsal sepal. 3: Lateral sepal. 4: Petal. 5–6: Lip. 7: Lip section. 8–9: Column. 10: Anther-cap. 11: Pollinarium. From Summerhayes 1950, t. 3485. S. Ross-Craig.

white; dorsal sepal oblong-ovate or lanceolate, 7 mm long, 3 mm wide; lateral sepals falcate, lanceolate, subacute, 11 mm long, 2.5 mm wide; petals oblique, ovate, acute, 7 mm long, 3.5 mm wide; lip deflexed, entire, narrowly elliptic, rounded, with a minute tooth in the mouth of the spur, 10 mm long, 5 mm wide; spur cylindric, curved, slender, 3.2–3.4 cm long.

Epiphyte on *Acacia*, on rocky hillside; 2050 m; flowering in September.

Ethiopia.

Easily recognised by the white flowers with a rather narrow lip.

Rhipidoglossum cuneatum (Summerhayes) Garay

Plant small, erect, with a stem up to 5 cm long, 3–4 mm in diameter. Leaves 5, linear to oblanceolate, unequally bilobed at tip, with rounded lobes, 3–4 cm long, 5–7 mm wide. Inflorescence 9 cm long, 6- to 8-flowered; bracts conical, 1.5–2 mm long; pedicel with ovary 3 mm long, emerging from rachis 2–3 mm above the axil of the bract. Flowers pale yellowish green, small; dorsal sepal broadly elliptic, obtuse, 2.3–2.5 mm long, 2 mm wide; lateral sepals falcate, elliptic, obtuse, fused to each other at the base behind the spur, 3–3.5 mm long, 1.5–2 mm wide; petals round, obtuse, 2 mm long, 2 mm wide; lip flabellate, bilobed, 3.5–4 mm long, 2–2.5 mm wide; spur incurved, cylindric, 6–6.5 mm long.

Epiphyte in rain forest; ca. 1000 m; flowering in March.

Cameroon and Uganda.

Rhipidoglossum curvatum (Rolfe) Garay

Plant erect or horizontal, with a stem 2–4 cm long. Leaves in 2 rows, very close together, forming a fan, oblanceolate, margins undulate, unequally bilobed at the apex, with rounded lobes, the shorter lobe often absent, 4–17 cm long, 1–4.5 cm wide. Inflorescence axillary or arising below the leaves, pendent, 10–35 cm long, bearing many flowers arranged in a spiral; bracts very short, 8–12 mm apart. Flowers yellowish green, pale green, or

white, small; sepals oval, subacute, 3.5–4.5 mm long; petals similar but shorter, broadly ovate, 2.2 mm long, 2 mm wide; lip entire, ovate or nearly round, cordate, with a horizontal ridge in front of the mouth of the spur, 2.5–3 mm long; spur slender, linear or slightly curved, 10.5–16 mm long.

Epiphyte on trunks a few metres above the ground; flowering April to November.

Sierra Leone, Côte d'Ivoire, Ghana, southern Nigeria, Cameroon, and Congo.

This plant is very distinctive in flower, with its long inflorescences, but the leaves alone are superficially similar to those of *Aerangis kotschyana* and *Eurychone rothschildiana*.

Rhipidoglossum globulosocalcaratum (De Wildeman) Summerhayes

Plant erect, with a short stem 10 cm high, 2 mm in diameter. Leaves oblong, unequally bilobed at the apex, with obtuse or rounded lobes, 5–12 cm long, 3–10 mm wide. Inflorescence short, 1–2 cm long, 5- or 6-flowered; bracts small, 1 mm long; pedicel with ovary 3 mm long. Flowers whitish, very small; sepals concave, oval or oblong-elliptic, 2–2.5 mm long, 2 mm wide; petals round, oboval or broadly oval, 1.5–2 mm long, 1–2 mm wide; lip broadly oval or elliptic, without a callus, 1.5–1.7 mm long, 2.3–3 mm wide; spur constricted below the mouth, parallel to the ovary, inflated in the distal half, 1.3–2.5 mm long.

Epiphyte in rain forest; up to 2200 m.

D.R. of Congo and Rwanda.

Rhipidoglossum kamerunense (Schlechter) Garay

Plant horizontal or pendent with a short stem 6–10 cm long, 1–2 cm in diameter. Leaves 3–7, arranged in a fan, flat, narrowly elliptic or oboval, unequally and obtusely bilobed at the apex, with one lobe almost absent, 20–50 cm long, 2.5–6 cm wide. Inflorescences pendent, 20–30 cm long, 5- to 15-flowered; bracts 10–15 mm long and wide; pedicel with ovary 20–25 mm long. Flowers yellowish green, not translucent; sepals elliptic, acute, 6–10 mm wide, dorsal sepal 15–17 mm long, lateral sepals 20–23 mm long; petals broadly ovate, acute, 15–17 mm long, 10–14 mm wide; lip flabellate, obscurely 3-lobed at the apex with one tooth-like callus in the mouth of the spur, apiculate, margins erose, 18–20 mm long, 22–25 mm wide; spur subcylindric, incurved from a wide mouth, becoming slender, 12–20 mm long.

Epiphyte in marshy forests and gallery forests near rivers, usually near the ground; 1000–1150 m; flowering June to August.

Nigeria, Cameroon, D.R. of Congo, Uganda, and Zambia.

The pale or medium green flowers of this species are much larger than those of other members of the genus.

Rhipidoglossum laticalcar (J. B. Hall) Senghas

Plant erect with stems short, up to 5 cm long. Leaves elliptic or elliptic-lanceolate, lamina transversely corrugated, acute, 5–10 cm long, 1.5–3 cm wide. Inflorescences axillary and from axils of old leaf sheaths, bearing many flowers densely arranged, up to 8 cm long. Flowers translucent, green; dorsal sepal ovate, acute, 3.5–4 mm long, 3.5–4 mm wide; lateral sepals elliptic, acute, 5–5.5 mm long, 2.5–2.8 mm wide; petals obliquely ovate, acute or subacuminate, 4.3 mm long, 3.3 mm wide; lip broadly ovate, apiculate, margin smooth or denticulate, small callus in mouth of spur, 5 mm long, 7.5 mm wide; spur cylindric, incurved, inflated at the apex, 8–10 mm long, 1.5–1.9 mm wide.

Epiphyte near waterfalls; flowering May to June.

Ghana and Nigeria.

Easily recognised by the very wide spur.

Rhipidoglossum magnicalcar Szlachetko & Olszewski

Plant erect or horizontal, with a stem 2.5 cm long. Leaves 4 in 2 rows, very close together, forming a fan, oblanceolate, margins undulate, unequally bilobed at the apex, with rounded lobes, the shorter lobe often absent, 8–10 cm long, 1.8–2.2 cm wide. Inflorescence arising below the leaves, pendent,

14–15 cm long, bearing 8–10 flowers arranged in a spiral; bracts 2.5 mm long. Flowers yellowish green, pale green, or white, small; sepals oval, subacute, 4–4.5 mm long; petals similar but shorter, broadly ovate, 4 mm long, 2 mm wide; lip entire, ovate or nearly round, cordate, with a low callus in front of the mouth of the spur, 4 mm long, 3.5 mm wide; spur incurved, constricted below the mouth and then inflated, 10–11 mm long.

Epiphyte in evergreen forest; 500 m.

Gabon.

This species is said to be very similar to *Rhipidoglossum curvatum* but differs by the larger tepals and differently shaped spur.

Rhipidoglossum melianthum (P. J. Cribb) Senghas

Plant small, erect or pendent, with a stem 3–5 cm high. Leaves 3 or 4, falcate, linear, unequally bilobed at the apex, with rounded lobes, arranged in one plane so the plant appears flat, 8 cm long, 7 mm wide. Inflorescence spreading or pendent, 10 cm long, 5- to 7-flowered; peduncle slender; bracts small, triangular, acute, 2 mm long. Flowers yellow with black hairs on the pedicellate ovary; dorsal sepal oblong-ovate, obtuse, 4.5 mm long, 3 mm wide; lateral sepals decurved on either side of the spur, narrowly ovate, oblique, 5.5 mm long, 2.5 mm wide; petals round, obtuse, 3 mm long; lip oblong, fleshy, the apical third reflexed, emarginate, 2.5 mm long, 3 mm wide; spur cylindric, incurved, pendent, 1.5 cm long.

Epiphyte on small trees in montane forest; 1500–2400 m; flowering January to March and in September.

Southern Tanzania.

Rhipidoglossum mildbraedii (Kraenzlin) Garay

Plant with a short, erect stem, to 3 cm long, 2–3 mm in diameter. Leaves few, overlapping at the base and subpetiolate, linear-ligulate, unequally bilobed at the apex, with rounded lobes, 5–10 cm long, 3–5 mm wide. Inflorescence arising below the leaves, pendent, 4–5 cm long, 6- to 8-flowered; bracts oval or ovate-triangular, 2 mm long; pedicel with ovary 6–9 mm long. Flowers white, small; dorsal sepal oboval or broadly elliptic, 4–5 mm long, 3–3.5 mm wide; lateral sepals falcate, oval to elliptic, subacute, 4–5 mm long, 2.5–3 mm wide; petals oval or oval-cordate, subacute, 4–5 mm long, 3.5–4 mm wide; lip transversely elliptic, oboval, lacking a callus, 4–5 mm long, 4–6 mm wide; spur slender, recurved and somewhat inflated at the apex only, 8–10 mm long.

Epiphyte in deciduous forest; 2000–2500 m.

D.R. of Congo (Virunga Mountains).

Rhipidoglossum montanum (Piers) Senghas

Plants with short stems usually obscured by a mass of thick grey roots; stems 5–10 cm long, held away from the host by the prominent roots. Leaves 2–6, greyish green, linear or narrowly lanceolate, unequally bilobed at the apex, 1.5–6 cm long, 2–6 mm wide. Inflorescences usually several, arising below the leaves, 2–4 cm long, 4- to 9-flowered. Flowers green, yellowish green, or orange, 6–9 mm in diameter; dorsal sepal ovate, obtuse, 3.5–4 mm long; lateral sepals elliptic or ovate, obtuse, 4–5 mm long; petals round or ovate, obtuse, 3 mm long; lip concave, ovate, 3 mm long, 2.5–3 mm wide, with an obscure callus at the base; spur cylindric, slightly curved, 5 mm long.

Epiphyte on twigs and branches of bushes and trees usually amongst mosses and lichens; 2300–2750 m; recorded in flower at various times.

Kenya.

Rhipidoglossum orientale (Mansfeld) Szlachetko & Olszewski

Plant very small, erect, with a rarely branching stem, to 10 cm long, 1.5–2 mm in diameter. Leaves 5–9, linear-oblong to ligulate, slightly falcate, unequally and obtusely bilobed at the apex, 2–3.5 cm long, 3–6 mm wide. Inflorescences few, 1.5 cm long, 2- or 3-flowered; bracts ovate, acute, 1–1.5 mm long; pedicel with ovary 1–2 mm long. Flowers yellowish green, minute; dorsal sepal lanceolate-elliptic, acute, 3.5 mm long, 1.2 mm wide; lateral sepals oblong-lanceolate, acute, 3.5 mm long, 1.3 mm wide; petals lanceolate, acute, 4 mm long, 1.4 mm wide; lip concave, entire, ovate-elliptic, without a callus; spur pendent, cylindrical-clavate, 1.3–1.8 mm long.

Epiphyte in montane mist forest; ca. 1900 m; flowering in July.

Tanzania (Uluguru Mountains).

Rhipidoglossum oxycentron (P. J. Cribb) Senghas

Plant small with a short, erect or pendent stem up to 5 cm long but usually less. Leaves 2–4, ligulate, falcate, light green, 4–8 cm long, 8–12 mm wide. Inflorescences usually 2 or 3, pendent, 5 cm long, 3- to 9-flowered; bracts 1 mm long; pedicel with ovary 3 mm long. Flowers pale translucent yellow or yellow-green; dorsal sepal erect, ovate, acute, 4–5 mm long, 2.5 mm wide; lateral sepals obliquely lanceolate, 5–6 mm long, 2 mm wide; petals ovate, acute, 4–5 mm long, 3 mm wide; lip oblong or rectangular, the lower margin straight but undulate, without a callus, 4–6 mm long, 4 mm wide; spur straight behind the lip, swollen towards the apex, 4–5 mm long.

Epiphyte on tree branches and lianas in montane mist forest; 1700–2300 m; flowering February and March.

Zambia and Malawi (Nyika Plateau and Mount Zomba).

Rhipidoglossum paucifolium D. Johansson

Plant small, with a very short stem 5–10 mm long and with numerous very long, flattened roots. Leaves few, oblong or narrowly oblong, acute, shortly bilobed at the apex, dull green, to 65 mm long, 22 mm wide. Inflorescences pendent, bearing many densely arranged flowers, up to 80 mm long; peduncle to 20 mm long with a few sheaths; rachis flexuose with conspicuous bracts 1–2 mm long. Flowers pale green; dorsal sepal broadly oblong, acute, 3.5–4 mm long, 2.5–3 mm wide; lateral sepals ovate-lanceolate, acute, 4.5–5 mm long, 2 mm wide; petals triangular, acute, 3–3.5 mm long, 2.5 mm wide near the base; lip slightly recurved, convex, broadly triangular, 3-lobed, with a low crescent-shaped callus on the upper surface at the

Rhipidoglossum montanum. B. Campbell

mouth of the spur, 4–5 mm long, 6.5–7 mm wide; spur cylindric, slightly incurved, 9–10 mm long.

Epiphyte at the base of a tall tree, amongst climbers 1.5 m above the ground, close to a stream; 700 m; flowering in August.

Liberia (Mount Nimba).

Rhipidoglossum polydactylum (Kraenzlin) Garay

Plant erect with a short stem 3–25 cm long. Leaves 2–5, grouped together at apex of stem, linear-lanceolate or ligulate-elliptic, unequally and acutely bilobed at the apex, 6–17 cm long, 7–16 mm wide. Inflorescence pendent, arising below the leaves, 6–11 cm long, 5- to 9-flowered; bracts 11 mm apart, each 3 mm long; pedicel with ovary 22 mm long. Flowers white or greenish white, small; dorsal sepal concave, oblong-elliptic, obtuse, 4.5–5 mm long, 2.2–2.5 mm wide; lateral sepals slightly falcate, oblong-oboval, obtuse, 6 mm long, 2.2–2.7 mm wide; petals oval-elliptic, margins fimbriate, 4–6 mm long, 2.7–3.8 mm wide; lip 3-lobed, mid-lobe longer than side lobes, all the margins long-pectinate, with a tooth-like callus in the mouth of the spur, 5–11 mm long; spur curved and slender, twisted in the middle, 20–36 mm long.

Epiphyte on large trees amongst mosses; 1800 m; flowering in October and November.

Cameroon.

The fringed petals and pectinate lip are very characteristic features of the flower of this species.

Rhipidoglossum pulchellum (Summerhayes) Garay

Plants with short or slightly elongated stems bearing many thick grey roots. Stems 5–15 cm long with leaves towards the apex. Leaves 2–6, greyish green, leathery, oblanceolate, falcate, unequally bilobed at the apex, 3–10 cm long, 4–10 mm wide. Inflorescences usually several, pendulous, arising below the leaves, to 15 cm long, up to 12-flowered; bracts triangular 2 mm long; pedicel with ovary 2–4 mm long. Flowers pale green, cream or pale yellowish green, 1.5–2 cm in diameter; dorsal sepal ovate, obtuse or acuminate, 4–8 mm long; lateral sepals oblique, elliptic or ovate, obtuse, 5–9 mm long; petals ovate to elliptic, acute or obtuse, 4–8 mm long; lip flabellate or rectangular, obscurely 2- to 4-lobed, notched at the apex, with a tooth in the mouth of the spur, 6–9 mm long, 6–9 mm wide; spur cylindric, slightly curved, 8–14 mm long.

Two varieties have been recognised:

var. *pulchellum*

Inflorescence 6–15 cm long, 14-flowered. Lateral sepals 5.7–9.5 mm long.

Epiphyte and occasionally lithophytic on the drier slopes of montane forests, riverine bush, and woodland; 700–2500 m; flowering May, June, and November.

D.R. of Congo, Uganda, Kenya, Tanzania, Malawi, and Zambia.

var. *geniculatum* (Summerhayes) Garay

Inflorescence 10–25 cm long with many flowers. Lateral sepals 9–11 mm long and geniculate at the base, petals also with a distinctly geniculate angle at the base.

Epiphyte in rain forest; 1200–1500 m; flowering in August.

Cameroon, D.R. of Congo, and Uganda.

Rhipidoglossum stellatum (P. J. Cribb) Szlachetko & Olszewski

Plant with an erect or pendent stem 2–15 cm long, leafy in the apical part. Leaves in 2 rows but lying in one plane, narrowly oblong, falcate, unequally bilobed at the apex, with rounded lobes, 3.5–8.5 cm long, 7–9 mm wide. Inflorescences pendent, 2–4 cm long, bearing 4–7 flowers arranged in a spiral; bracts ovate, acute, 1–2 mm long; pedicel with ovary 5 mm long. Flowers yellow-green, small; sepals elliptic-lanceolate, acute, 4–5 mm long, 2 mm wide; petals lanceolate, acute, 3.8–4 mm long, 1.2 mm wide; lip recurved, lanceolate to obscurely 3-lobed at the base, acute, with a low transverse callus at the base, 4.2–5 mm long,

Rhipidoglossum pulchellum. E. la Croix

Rhipidoglossum stellatum. B. Campbell

2.5 mm wide; spur parallel with the ovary, straight, 8–13 mm long.

Epiphyte in montane forest; 1800–2400 m; flowering May to June.

Southern Tanzania.

The flowers of this species have petals resembling the mid-lobe of the lip and giving each flower a star-shaped appearance.

Group 2. Stems elongated, at least 20 cm long in mature plants, leafy along most of their length.

Rhipidoglossum adoxum (Rasmussen) Senghas

Plants with long straggling stems, 5–25 cm long. Leaves insignificant, 5–12, linear, falcate, yellowish green often flecked with dark green markings, 3.5–10 cm long, 1.5–5 mm wide. Inflorescences few and small, 2–4 cm long, 3- to 8-flowered. Flowers very small, green or yellowish green; dorsal sepal lanceolate, acute, up to 2 mm long, 1 mm wide; lat-

Rhipidoglossum adoxum. J. Hermans

eral sepals longer, to 3 mm long, 1 mm wide; petals ovate, obtuse or rounded, 2 mm long, 1.2 mm wide; lip entire, ovate, obtuse, smooth, 2 mm long and wide; spur club-shaped up to 2 mm long.

Epiphyte in upland evergreen forest; 1500–2000 m; flowering in May.

Ethiopia, Kenya, and Uganda.

Rhipidoglossum bilobatum (Summerhayes) Szlachetko & Olszewski

Plants with elongated stems and many roots in the lower part, stems usually pendent or upturned at the apex only, up to 50 cm long. Leaves up to 20 along the upper part of the stem, twisted at the base so that they lie in one plane, elliptic or oblong-elliptic, unequally bilobed at the apex, with rounded lobes, 3–10 cm long, 1.5–5 cm wide. Inflorescences usually several, often 2 or 3 from the same node in the upper part of the stem, bearing 15–30 flowers spaced close together, 5–10 cm long;

bracts 2–3 mm long; pedicel with ovary 1–1.5 mm long. Flowers fresh green or whitish; sepals oblong, obtuse, 4–7 mm long, ca. 3 mm wide; petals obovate, elliptic, obtuse, 4–5 mm long, 2–3 mm wide; lip elongated, obscurely 3-lobed, with a bilobed tooth in the mouth of the spur, 5–7 mm long, the side lobes rounded recurved, the mid-lobe deeply bilobed at its apex; spur slightly incurved, 8 mm long.

In humid forests and thickets; 1300–2200 m; flowering in April.

D.R. of Congo, Burundi, Rwanda, Uganda, and Kenya.

Rhipidoglossum brevifolium Summerhayes

Plants with long stems up to 45 cm long. Leaves many, well spaced, narrowly oblong, 3.5–5.5 cm long, 8–13 mm wide. Inflorescences arising below a root on the main stem, up to 18-flowered. Flowers greenish or whitish, translucent, small; sepals elliptic, obtuse or acute; petals wider than sepals, ovate, acute; lip orbicular, pointed or slightly bilobed at the apex, 4.5 mm long, 4 mm wide; spur cylindric, recurved, 6.5 mm long.

Epiphyte on small trees and shrubs and frequently terrestrial or scrambling about in low vegetation; 1260–1440 m; flowering in December.

São Tomé.

Rhipidoglossum densiflorum Summerhayes

Plant with long pendent stems, to 50 cm long, 3–4 mm in diameter. Leaves in 2 rows, narrowly elliptic or elliptic, oblique, unequally bilobed at the apex, twisted at the base so that they lie in one plane, 4–12 cm long, 8–25 mm wide. Inflorescences solitary or paired at the nodes, usually many at the same time, with many densely arranged flowers, 1–4 cm long; bracts 1–1.5 mm long; pedicel with ovary 2.5–3 mm long. Flowers white, yellowish, or greenish, waxy, small; dorsal sepal oblong-elliptic, obtuse, 2.2–3 mm long, 1.7–2 mm wide; lateral sepals obliquely elliptic, obtuse, 3–3.5 mm long, 1.5 mm wide; petals round, truncate or obtuse, 2–2.5 mm long and wide; lip entire, transversely oval or elliptic, with a low transverse callus at the mouth

Rhipidoglossum bilobatum. B. Campbell

of the spur, 2.7–3.7 mm long, 3.5–4.7 mm wide; spur subovoid, 2–3 mm long, 2 mm in diameter.

Epiphyte in riverine forest and montane rain forest; 1000–2000 m; flowering in September and October.

Liberia, Cameroon, Gabon, D.R. of Congo, Rwanda, Uganda, Angola, and Zambia.

Rhipidoglossum laxiflorum Summerhayes

Plant with erect or horizontal stems, 10–35 cm long. Leaves in 2 rows, 8–10 mm apart, narrowly elliptic, with small unequal lobes at the apex, 4–11 cm long, 5–10 mm wide. Inflorescences arising opposite the base of a leaf, pendent, 8–12 cm long, up to 20-flowered; bracts minute, spaced 5–8 mm apart. Flowers very small, whitish green or yellow-green; sepals lanceolate, subacute, 2–2.5 mm long; petals wider, obtuse; lip transversely orbicular, entire, funnel-shaped, with a small rounded callus in the mouth of the spur, 1.5 mm long, 3 mm wide; spur very short, narrow at the base, inflated in the apical part.

Epiphyte in humid evergreen or deciduous forest, well shaded; low to medium altitudes; flowering February to April.

Côte d'Ivoire and Ghana.

Rhipidoglossum longicalcar Summerhayes

Plant with elongated stems, erect or creeping, leaves spaced out in the apical part. Leaves linear-oblanceolate or oblanceolate, curved, unequally bilobed at the apex, sometimes the smaller lobe absent, 7–13 cm long, 6–16 mm wide. Inflorescences pendent, 5–15 cm long, many-flowered. Flowers very pale green; sepals 3–4 mm long; petals orbicular-ovate, 2.3 mm long and wide; lip quadrate, truncate in front, slightly emarginate with a small apiculus in the centre, margins irregular, 3–3.5 mm long, 2–2.5 mm wide; spur slender, 11–14 mm long.

Southern Nigeria.

This species is said to be close to *Rhipidoglossum rutilum* but is easily distinguished by the long slender spur.

Rhipidoglossum microphyllum Summerhayes

Plant with long slender stems to 20 cm long or more, branched, often growing in tangled masses with many conspicuous aerial roots, bearing leaves in apical part of the stem. Leaves up to 6, linear to oblanceolate, unequally bilobed at the apex, with rounded lobes, 6–15 mm long, 2–4 mm wide. Inflorescences usually several, arising beside the roots, secund, 2–3 cm long, few- to 5-flowered; bracts sheathing, 1 mm long; pedicel with ovary 4–5 mm long. Flowers greenish yellow; dorsal sepal oblong-elliptic, obtuse, 3 mm long, 1.5 mm wide; lateral sepals falcate, narrowly oblong, subacute, 4 mm long, 1–1.5 mm wide; petals obliquely oblong-elliptic, obtuse, 2.5–3 mm long, 1.5 mm wide; lip entire, elliptic, obtuse, 2.5–3 mm long, 1 mm wide; spur strongly incurved, slender, cylindrical, 7 mm long.

Epiphyte in montane mist forest and in old coffee plantations; 1400–2300 m; flowering in March.

Southern Tanzania and northern Malawi.

Rhipidoglossum obanense (Rendle) Summerhayes

Plant erect or semi-pendent, with stems to 20 cm long. Leaves spaced out along the apical part of the stem, oblong-lanceolate, falcate, unequally and obtusely bilobed at the apex, 6–11 cm long, 1.5–2.5 cm wide. Inflorescences bearing many flowers spaced very close together, 2–4 cm long; bracts transversely elliptic, 1 mm long; pedicel with ovary 5 mm long. Flowers greenish white; sepals oblong-oval, obtuse, 2–2.5 mm long, 1.5 mm wide; petals round or ovate, 2.25 mm long, 2 mm wide; lip transversely elliptic, retuse, lacking a callus, 1.5 mm long, 3 mm wide; spur inflated in the apical part, 2–3 mm long.

Epiphyte in humid forests.

Southern Nigeria and Cameroon.

This species seems to be very close to *Rhipidoglossum densiflorum* and numerous intermediate forms have been encountered and noted, particularly by William Sanford in *Flore du Cameroun* (2001).

Rhipidoglossum ochyrae Szlachetko & Olszewski

This species was described in 2001 in honour of Ryszard Ochyra, eminent Polish botanist. It is said to be very close to *Rhipidoglossum rutilum*, but the pedicels arise a little distance above the sheathing bracts, and the flower has an entire lip with a notch at its centre. So far this species is known only from the type locality in Cameroon.

Rhipidoglossum ovale (Summerhayes) Garay

Plant with long, pendent or erect stems to 30 cm long, 1.5–2 mm in diameter. Leaves 2–10 in the upper part of the stem, well spaced, linear, falcate, unequally bilobed at the apex, with rounded lobes, the shorter lobe absent, 2–12 cm long, 3–9 mm wide. Inflorescences pendent, 5–12 cm long, 10- to 20-flowered; bracts small, 1 mm long; pedicel with ovary 2 mm long. Flowers very small, yellowish, greenish, or brownish; dorsal sepal oval, rounded, 2.5–3 mm long, 2 mm wide; lateral sepals oblong, subobtuse, 3 mm long, 1.5 mm wide; petals oblong to elliptic, obtuse, 2 mm long, 1.5 mm wide; lip

concave, entire or obscurely 3-lobed, ovate, obtuse, without a callus, 2.3–3 mm long, 2.4–2.7 mm
wide; spur incurved, cylindrical 4–5 mm long.

Epiphyte in montane forest, often near swamps;
2100–2400 m; flowering in March.

D.R. of Congo, Burundi, Rwanda, and Uganda.

Rhipidoglossum polyanthum (Kraenzlin) Szlachetko & Olszewski

Plant erect with short stems, 5–16 cm long,
10–20 mm in diameter, leafy near the apex. Leaves
3 or more, twisted near the base to lie in one plane,
oblong-linear or linear-lanceolate, unequally and
acutely bilobed at the apex, 1.8–8 cm long, 3–13
mm wide. Inflorescences upright, arising below the
leaves, 4-flowered or more, 2–20 cm long; bracts
transversely elliptic, 1–2 mm long; pedicel with
ovary 2–3 mm long. Flowers greenish white, small;
dorsal sepal oblong or oblong-elliptic, obtuse or
rounded, 1.8–3.8 mm long, 1–1.6 mm wide; lateral sepals obliquely oblong-oval or oval-elliptic,
obtuse, 2.2–4 mm long, 1–1.8 mm wide; lip panduriform, concave at the base, 3-lobed at the apex,
thickened along the mid-line, 1.8–3.8 mm long,
1.6–2.5 mm wide; spur very small, sac-like, 1–2
mm long, 1 mm wide.

Epiphyte in montane forests, usually about 10
m above the ground; 1500–2150 m; flowering July
to November.

Cameroon and Equatorial Guinea (Bioco
Island).

Rhipidoglossum rutilum (Reichenbach f.) Schlechter

Plants pendent, often in large untidy masses
with stems 5–40 cm long, sometimes branched, often flushed reddish purple. Leaves in 2 rows along
the upper part of the stem, narrowly elliptic or
oblanceolate, unequally bilobed at the apex, 8–15
cm long, 1–3 cm wide, dull bluish green usually
flushed red or purple on the lower surface. Inflorescences often arising from the same point more
than once, 5–20 cm long, 10- to 40-flowered; bracts
sheathing, 1–2 mm long; pedicel with ovary 1–2
mm long. Flowers greenish pink or deep red, 4–8

Rhipidoglossum rutilum. J. Hermans

mm in diameter; dorsal sepal elliptic or obovate,
obtuse, 3–5 mm long; lateral sepals slightly shorter
and narrower; petals broadly ovate or round, obtuse, 2–4 mm long and wide; lip wider than long,
retuse, 1.4–3.7 mm long, 2.5–4.7 mm wide; spur
incurved, 4–7 mm long.

Epiphyte in riverine forest and more open forest
and bush, also in old coffee plantations; 100–2200
m; flowering in May and November.

Sierra Leone eastwards to Uganda and Kenya,
and southwards to Angola and Zimbabwe.

Rhipidoglossum schimperianum (A. Richard) Garay

Plant with long, pendent stems 40 cm or more
long, 3–5 mm in diameter. Leaves falcate, narrowly
oblong to oblanceolate, unequally bilobed at the
apex, with rounded lobes, twisted at the base so
that they lie in one plane, 6–14 cm long, 1.5–2.5
cm wide. Inflorescences lax, 5.5–8.5 cm long, 5- to

Rhipidoglossum rutilum, pink form. J. Hermans

10-flowered; bracts acute, 2–3.5 mm long; pedicel with ovary 2–4 mm long. Flowers white or cream, translucent; dorsal sepal ovate, acute, 5–5.6 mm long, 2.8–3.4 mm wide; lateral sepals falcate, lanceolate, acute, 7–7.5 mm long, 2 mm wide; petals obliquely triangular-ovate, acuminate, 5–5.7 mm long, 3–3.5 mm wide; lip obscurely 3-lobed in the basal half, oblong-ovate in outline, emarginate or obtuse, with a tooth-like callus at the base in the mouth of the spur, 6–7.7 mm long, 6.6–7.5 mm wide; spur incurved, slightly dilated centrally, 8–9 mm long.

Epiphyte and on rocks in montane forest; 2400–2800 m; flowering in June and July.

Ethiopia, Sudan, and northern Uganda.

Named in honour of German traveller Wilhelm Schimper (1804–1878), who made many collections in Ethiopia in the nineteenth century.

Rhipidoglossum stolzii (Schlechter) Garay

Plant with long, pendent, sometimes branching stems, 20–150 cm long, 3–5 mm in diameter. Leaves in 2 rows near apex of stem, oblong-obovate, unequally bilobed at the apex, with rounded lobes, twisted at the base, 2.5–6 cm long, 1–2 cm wide. Inflorescences 3–6.5 cm long, dense, many-flowered; bracts sheathing, 2 mm long; pedicel with ovary 7.5–10 mm long. Flowers white or pale yellow; dorsal sepal elliptic-lanceolate, acute or obtuse, 8–9 mm long, 3–4 mm wide; lateral sepals falcate, oblong-elliptic or lanceolate, acute or obtuse, 9–14 mm long, 2–3 mm wide; petals obliquely triangular-obovate, acute, 6.7–9 mm long, 4.2–7 mm wide; lip flabellate or obscurely 2- to 4-lobed, emarginate or apiculate, with a prominent tooth on the lip at the mouth of the spur, 11–12 mm long, 10–17 mm wide; spur cylindrical from a conical mouth, incurved or S-shaped, 15–21 mm long.

Epiphyte in montane forest and moist woodland, and on rocks; 200–1700 m; flowering May to July.

Tanzania, Malawi, and Zimbabwe.

Named after German missionary Adolf Stolz (1871–1917), who lived in southern Tanzania for many years and collected orchids there.

Rhipidoglossum subsimplex (Summerhayes) Garay

Plants pendent, often in large, untidy tangled masses, with stems 10–40 cm long, often branched, with leaves along upper part of stem. Leaves in 2 rows, linear, unequally bilobed at the apex, 2–5 cm long, 5–10 mm wide, yellowish green. Inflorescences below or amongst the leaves, 2–8 cm long, 5- to 12-flowered; bracts triangular, acute, 1–2.5 mm long; pedicel with ovary 2.5–3 mm long. Flowers greenish or pale yellow, 4–7 mm in diameter; dorsal sepal elliptic or oblong, obtuse, 2.7–4 mm long; lateral sepals oblong to oblong-elliptic, 3.3–4.5 mm long; petals ovate, obtuse or acute, 2.8–3.5 mm long, 1.7–2.7 mm wide; lip as wide as long, retuse, with an obscure tooth in the mouth of the spur, 2.5–3.6 mm long; spur slightly incurved, cylindrical, 4.5–7 mm long.

Rhipidoglossum tenuicalcar. B. Campbell

Epiphyte in montane forests and on forest margins, usually on the lower branches of trees; 1800–2600 m; flowering in May and June.

Uganda, Kenya, Tanzania, Malawi, and Zimbabwe.

Rhipidoglossum tanneri (P. J. Cribb) Senghas

Plants with long straggling stems 5–25 cm long. Leaves insignificant, 5–12, linear, falcate, 3–4.5 cm long, 1.5 mm wide. Inflorescences few and small, 2–3 cm long, 4- to 7-flowered; bracts ovate, acute, 1 mm long; pedicel with ovary 2–2.5 mm long. Flowers very small, bright green; dorsal sepal lanceolate, rounded to subacute, to 3.5 mm long, 1.5 mm wide; lateral sepals spreading, elliptic, rounded, 3–3.7 mm long, 1.5 mm wide; petals elliptic-ovate, acute, 3 mm long, 1.2–1.7 mm wide; lip entire, recurved, ovate, acute, smooth, with an obscure bilobed callus at the base, 2–2.5 mm long, 1.5 mm wide; spur swollen towards the apex, 4 mm long.

Epiphyte in forest; 800 m; flowering in April.

Kenya and Tanzania.

Rhipidoglossum tenuicalcar (Summerhayes) Garay

Plants pendent, often in large untidy masses, with stems 10–30 cm long, often branched. Leaves usually only 2–8 in 2 rows along the upper part of the stem, linear-lanceolate, falcate, unequally bilobed at the apex, 1–6 cm long, 5–13 mm wide, yellowish green. Inflorescences below the leaves, 1–3 cm long, up to 7-flowered; bracts sheathing, 2 mm long; pedicel with ovary 4–12 mm long. Flowers white, sweetly scented, 7–12 mm in diameter; dorsal sepal elliptic or oblong, obtuse, 4 mm long; lateral sepals oblong to oblong-elliptic, 4–5 mm long; petals ovate, obtuse or acute, 4 mm long; lip wider than long, retuse, with a tooth in the mouth of the spur, 4.5–6.5 mm long; spur slender below the wide mouth, 15–25 mm long.

Epiphyte at the edge of montane forests; 2100–2400 m; flowering in June.

Ethiopia, northern Uganda, and Kenya.

Rhipidoglossum ugandense (Rendle) Garay

Plant with elongated stems to 50 cm long, 3 mm in diameter. Leaves well spaced, linear or narrowly oblong, falcate, unequally bilobed at the apex, with rounded lobes, 6–10 cm long, 4–10 mm wide. Inflorescences several, pendent, 10–15 cm long, 10- to 20-flowered; bracts sheathing, 1–1.5 mm long; pedicel with ovary 3 mm long. Flowers yellowish green to pinkish; dorsal sepal narrowly elliptic, apiculate, 4–5 mm long, 2 mm wide; lateral sepals oblong, subapiculate, 4–6 mm long, 1.5 mm wide; petals broadly elliptic, obtuse, 3.5–5 mm long, 2.5–3 mm wide; lip broadly and transversely elliptic, notched at the apex, with a tooth-like callus in front of the spur entrance, 5–7 mm long, 6–9 mm wide; spur incurved, inflated and flattened centrally, 8–9 mm long.

Epiphyte in rain forest and gallery forests; 1500–2000 m; flowering in November.

Uganda and adjacent parts of D.R. of Congo.

Rhipidoglossum xanthopollinium (Reichenbach f.) Schlechter

Plants pendent, with stems 6–45 cm long, sometimes branched, often in large masses. Leaves in 2 rows along the upper part of the stem, linear to oblanceolate, unequally bilobed at the apex, 3–15 cm long, 5–15 mm wide, yellowish green. Inflorescences below or amongst the leaves, 8–15 cm long, 5-to 25-flowered; bracts sheathing, 1–2 mm long; pedicel with ovary 1.5–2.5 mm long. Flowers pale yellow, 5–9 mm in diameter; dorsal sepal oblong-elliptic to ovate, obtuse, 3–5 mm long; lateral sepals oblong to oblong-elliptic, 3.3–5 mm long; petals round to broadly ovate, obtuse, 2.5–4 mm long and wide; lip wider than long, retuse or 2- to 4-lobed at the apex, with a low transverse callus in the mouth of the spur, 3–4.5 mm long, 3.2–5.7 mm wide; spur slightly incurved, cylindrical, 5–7 mm long.

Epiphyte in warm humid forests; 600–1800 m; flowering in May and September.

D.R. of Congo eastwards to Kenya and south to Mozambique, Angola, and South Africa (KwaZulu-Natal).

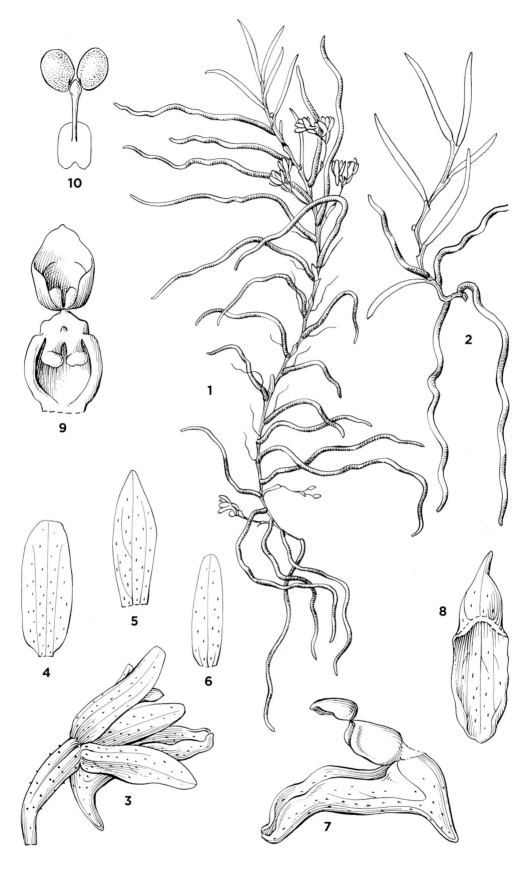

Solenangis conica. 1: Habit. 2: Leaves and roots. 3: Flower. 4: Dorsal sepal. 5: Lateral sepal. 6: Petal.
7: Lip, column, anther, and spur. 8: Lip and spur. 9: Column. 10: Pollinarium.
From Summerhayes 1967, t. 3640. E. M. Stones.

SOLENANGIS Schlechter

When Rudolf Schlechter established this genus, in 1918, he named only 2 species which did not seem to fit into any other genus—*Solenangis clavata* and *S. scandens*. Since then 3 other species have been added. All have rather long stems and, with the aid of their long roots that are often branched and curled, have adopted a scandent habit. The leaves are small or absent. The flowers are varied, very small and insignificant or quite attractive, but they all have a pollinarium in which the 2 pollinia are borne on a single stipe attached to one fairly large viscidium.

The generic name is derived from the Greek words *solen*, pipe, and *angos*, vessel, and refers to the large spur at the base of the lip. In some species the lip blade is so insignificant and the rest of the flower so small that the flower at first sight seems to consist of only a spur.

The 2 species that Schlechter recognised are widespread in West Africa. Two others, *Solenangis conica* and *S. wakefieldii*, are restricted to the eastern parts of the continent and *S. cornuta* is recorded from Madagascar and the Comoro Islands. The leafless orchid widely known as *S. aphylla*, in eastern Africa, Madagascar, Réunion, and Mauritius, is described in this book as *Microcoelia aphylla*.

Culture

These species grow easily in a suitable environment that is warm and humid throughout the year. They can be mounted on a piece of bark but grow and flower just as well when attached to a wire frame or other support. They flourish in strong light and where there is good air movement, and need to dry out well between waterings.

Solenangis clavata (Rolfe) Schlechter

Plant with long stems up to 1 m, often branched, and bearing numerous branching aerial roots. Leaves in 2 rows, widely spaced, leathery, elliptic and tapering at both ends, unequally and shortly bilobed at the apex, 2.5–5 cm long, 1–1.5 cm wide.

Inflorescences arising between the leaves, bearing 6–10 flowers spaced close together in 2 rows, short; peduncle and rachis 0.5–1.5 cm long; bracts very small; pedicel with ovary slender, 7 mm long. Flowers very small, pale greenish white with white lip and spur; sepals and petals similar, elliptic-lanceolate, obtuse, 1.5–3 mm long; lip very small, 3-lobed or consisting of rounded edges to the spur and a short apiculus; spur swollen at the mouth, tapering to the middle and slightly inflated in the apical third, 5–10 mm long.

Epiphyte, scrambling amongst bushy vegetation in rain forest and plantations, usually in well-lit situations, or lithophyte; up to 2000 m; flowering in October.

Sierra Leone, eastwards to D.R. of Congo and Rwanda.

Solenangis conica (Schlechter) L. Jonsson

Syns. *Microcoelia conica* (Schlechter) Summerhayes, *Solenangis angustifolia* Summerhayes

Plants dwarf, insignificant, scandent, climbing by prominent greyish roots; stems slender, 4–22 cm long. Leaves few, near apex of stem, narrow, *Iris*-like and slightly flattened, 13–16 mm long, 0.5–1.5 mm wide. Inflorescences usually several, arising below the roots, 10–14 mm long, 2- to 4-flowered. Flowers white or greenish white, spur green at tip; dorsal sepal ovate, 2–3 mm long, 1.3 mm wide; lateral sepals similar; petals linear, subacute, 2.5 mm long, 0.7 mm wide; lip concave, ovate, 3 mm long, 2 mm wide; spur conical, 1–2 mm long.

Twig epiphyte in montane forest with the roots and stems shrouded in lichens; 1800 m; flowering in May.

Kenya, Tanzania, Malawi, Zimbabwe, and Mozambique.

Solenangis cornuta (Reichenbach f.) Summerhayes

Plants scandent with long or short stems and many aerial roots. Leaves absent. Inflorescences straight, 7–15 cm long, 4- to 20-flowered; peduncle short; bracts very small; pedicel with ovary 4–5 mm long. Flowers white, small, ca. 5 mm in diameter; dorsal sepal very concave, widely oval, subacute, 1.2–1.3 mm long, 1 mm wide; lateral sepals larger, oblique, dilated on the anterior side, 2 mm long, 1.2 mm wide; petals oblong-lanceolate, 1–2 mm long, 0.5–0.6 mm wide; lip orbicular in front, emarginate, sometimes appearing 2-lobed, 2 mm long and wide; spur wide at the mouth, gradually narrowing to the apex, 3.5–4 mm long.

Epiphyte of twigs and branches in warm, humid woods, mostly near the sea, and on rock; sea level to 300 m; flowering September to December.

Madagascar and Comoro Islands.

Solenangis scandens (Schlechter) Schlechter

Plants scandent with long branching flexuous stems 3–4 mm in diameter and bearing many greyish-white aerial roots. Leaves widely spaced, elliptic-lanceolate, unequally and shortly bilobed at the apex, 3–7 cm long, 1–2.5 cm wide. Inflorescences opposite the leaf base, bearing 6–10 flowers spaced 5–8 mm apart; peduncle and rachis 2–9 cm long; bracts triangular, 1–2.5 mm long; pedicel with ovary slender, 13 mm long. Flowers white or cream; sepals and petals similar, oblong, obtuse, 5–7.5 mm long, 2–3.5 mm wide; lip entire, funnel-shaped, limb 6–8 mm long, 2.5–4 mm wide; spur wide at the mouth merging into the lip, narrow in the middle, and inflated into a small balloon at the apex, 2–2.5 cm long.

Epiphyte, scrambling amongst woody vegetation in rain forest, especially in well-lit situations, or lithophyte; flowering in October.

Sierra Leone and eastwards to Congo, D.R. of Congo, and Central African Republic.

Solenangis wakefieldii (Rolfe) P. J. Cribb & J. Stewart

Syn. *Tridactyle wakefieldii* (Rolfe) Summerhayes

Plants scandent, with elongated, upright or pendent stems 20–100 cm long, and with conspicuous whitish, branching, curled roots. Leaves spaced 1–3 cm apart and usually opposite a root, lanceolate or ovate, unequally and acutely bilobed at the apex, 1.5–3 cm long, 0.5–1.3 cm wide. Inflorescences spreading, one to several, bearing 4–6 well-spaced flowers, 4–6 cm long. Flowers white, sometimes with greenish spur; sepals oblong-elliptic, dorsal sepal obtuse or apiculate, 3 mm long, 1–2 mm wide, lateral sepals oblique, subacute, 4–4.5 mm long, 1.5 mm wide; petals similar to lateral sepals but 3.5 mm long; lip narrow in the basal part and 3-lobed in the apical third, 10 mm long and wide, side lobes reflexed or spreading, linear, 4–5 mm long, mid-lobe lanceolate, acute, 3 mm long; spur slender, pendent, 6–7 cm long.

Epiphyte, scrambling in coastal and lowland bush; sea level to 300 m; flowering September to November.

Kenya and Tanzania.

Solenangis wakefieldii. J. Stewart

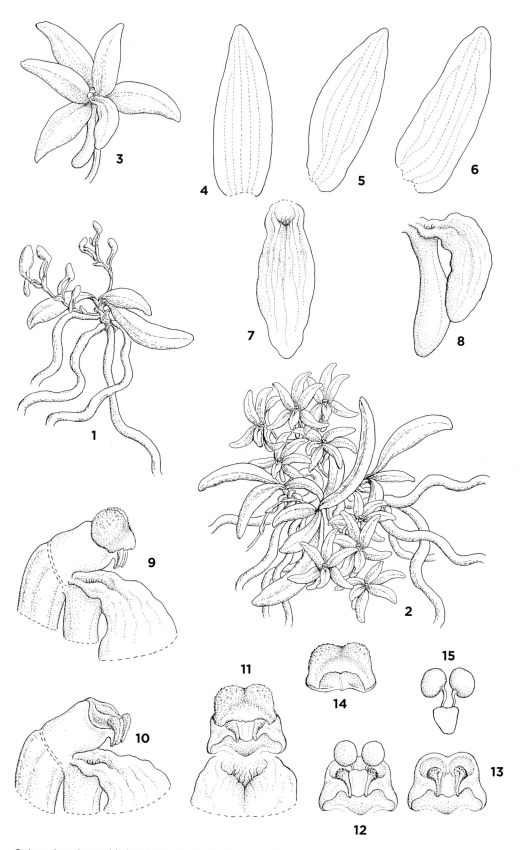

Sphyrarhynchus schliebenii. 1–2: Habit. 3: Flower. 4: Dorsal sepal. 5: Lateral sepal. 6: Petal. 7: Lip. 8: Lip and spur. 9–13: Column. 14: Anther-cap. 15: Pollinarium. From Cribb 1989, fig. 147. M. E. Church.

Sphyrarhynchus schliebenii. B. Campbell

SPHYRARHYNCHUS Mansfeld

This monotypic genus was established by German botanist Rudolf Mansfeld in 1935. It is known from a few montane sites in Tanzania and one record in central Kenya. Each plant has only a few small, glaucous leaves above a mass of flattened roots that are green when wet. They can hardly be distinguished from the 2 small species of *Angraecopsis*, with which they are often found, except when

flowering. The flowers are unexpectedly large, glistening white with a green flash on the surface of the lip. Usually there are a few flowers on each of several or many inflorescences so that the tiny plant appears to be covered in a ball of flowers.

The generic name is derived from the Greek words *sphyra*, hammer, and *rhynchos*, snout or beak, and refers to the shape of the rostellum at the apex of the column: in side view the rostellum resembles a minute hammer. The species is named in honour of H. J. Schlieben (1902–1975), a German plant collector who discovered it in Tanzania in 1935, and who later lived in South Africa where he also made many interesting collections.

Culture

This species is easily maintained in cultivation on small twigs and branches similar to those on which it is found in the wild. It has also been raised from seeds at the Royal Botanic Gardens, Kew, where the plantlets surprised everyone in the laboratory by flowering while still in the flask. The young seedlings are best established on pieces of cork-oak bark or on small pieces of hard wood. Since the species is montane, the plants thrive where the temperature drops to cool conditions at night.

Sphyrarhynchus schliebenii Mansfeld

Plants minute with a very short stem and many conspicuous flattened roots. Leaves 3–5, fleshy, linear, falcate, greyish green, 2–4 cm long, 2–5 mm wide. Inflorescences usually several, 1–3 cm long, 3- to 10-flowered. Flowers variable in size, the apical ones usually largest, glistening white with a dark green mark on the lip; dorsal sepal elliptic or lanceolate, acute, 5–15 mm long, 2–4 mm wide; lateral sepals similar, oblique; petals oblong, obtuse, 6–14 mm long, 2–4 mm wide; lip oblong or oblanceolate, subacute, 6–8 mm long, 2–4 mm wide: spur clavate, 5–8 mm long.

Epiphyte on twigs and small branches in montane evergreen forest; 900–1600 m; flowering between August and November.

Kenya and Tanzania.

Summerhayesia laurentii. C. Arends

SUMMERHAYESIA P. J. Cribb

Phillip Cribb described this genus in 1977 in honour of the late Victor S. Summerhayes (1892–1974), his predecessor at Kew. At the time it comprised 2 species, *Summerhayesia laurentii* in West Africa transferred from *Aerangis* (originally described as an *Angraecum*) and a new species, *S. zambesiaca*, collected from several localities in Zambia and Zimbabwe and illustrated by Graham Williamson (1977), an amateur botanist practising as a dentist in Zambia. Both species illustrate the generic characters: ligulate, fleshy leaves, inflorescences of several flowers in which the ovate lip is usually held on the upper side of the flower, lateral sepals which are connate enclosing the spur, and a slipper-shaped viscidium which fits neatly over the end of the pointed rostellum. Since then Belgian botanist Daniel Geerinck has described a third species from Rwanda.

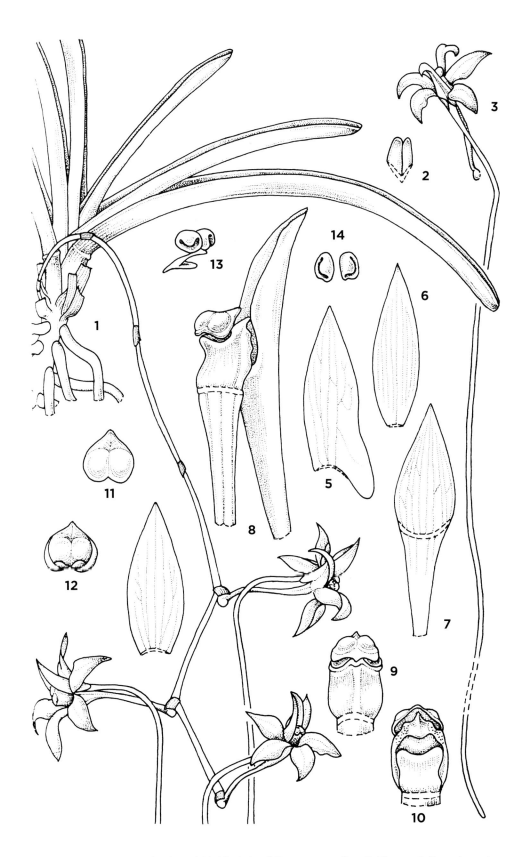

Summerhayesia zambesiaca. 1: Habit. 2: Leaf tip, cross section. 3: Flower. 4: Dorsal sepal.
5: Lateral sepal. 6: Petal. 7: Lip. 8: Column and lip, side. 9–10: Column. 11–12: Anther-cap. 13: Pollinarium.
14: Pollinia. From la Croix and Cribb 1998, t. 151. J. Stone.

Culture

All the species can be maintained in cultivation in a pot or basket of freely draining compost. They appreciate a drop in temperature at night.

Summerhayesia laurentii (De Wildeman) P. J. Cribb

Syn. *Aerangis laurentii* (De Wildeman) Schlechter

Plants erect with a short stem to 20 cm long (sometimes longer but then only leafy in the upper part) and thick roots. Leaves in 2 rows, stiff, straight or curved, conduplicate, linear, unequally bilobed at the apex, 11–25 cm long, 5–9 mm wide. Inflorescences axillary from the lower leaves, horizontal or arched, bearing many flowers spaced 10–15 mm; peduncle and rachis 15–50 cm long; bracts oval, enveloping the base of the pedicel, 1.5–2 mm long; pedicel with ovary twisted at the base, 10–15 mm long. Flowers white or cream, usually with the lip on the upper side; dorsal sepal elliptic, obtuse, 6–8 mm long, 3.5–4.5 mm wide; lateral sepals oblique, united at the base, 7–9 mm long, 4–5 mm wide; petals oblong, obtuse, 5–8 mm long, 2–3 mm wide; lip concave, oval, obtuse, fleshy, 5–8.5 mm long, 3.5–6 mm wide; spur cylindric, straight, 6–8 cm long.

Epiphyte in thick forest and plantations; flowering December to March.

Liberia, Côte d'Ivoire, Ghana, Congo, and D.R. of Congo.

Summerhayesia rwandensis Geerinck

Plants with an erect stem to 20 cm long. Leaves in 2 rows, oblong, rounded at the apex, 5–6 cm long, 8–15 mm wide. Inflorescence papillose, 6 cm long, 8-flowered; bracts ca. 3 mm long. Flowers papillose on the outer surface; dorsal sepal oval, acuminate, 5 mm long, 1.5 mm wide; lateral sepals suboval, acute, 7 mm long, 2 mm wide; petals suboval, 4 mm long, 1.5 mm wide; lip narrowly suboval, acuminate, 4 mm long, 1.5 mm wide; spur narrow, ca. 12 mm long.

Epiphyte in montane forest; 1800–2000 m. Rwanda.

Summerhayesia zambesiaca. J. Stewart

Summerhayesia zambesiaca P. J. Cribb

Plants erect, with a stem up to 20 cm long bearing thick roots from the base. Leaves 3–7 in 2 rows, linear-ligulate, conduplicate, rounded at the apex, yellowish green, 10–15 cm long, 10–12 mm wide. Inflorescence usually one, 8–15 cm long, 2- to 8-flowered; peduncle ca. 8 cm long; bracts ca. 4 mm long; pedicel and outer surface of the flower dotted with short brownish hairs, pedicel and ovary 2 cm long. Flowers yellowish white, lip paler, usually uppermost; dorsal sepal oval, obtuse, slightly concave, 13 mm long, 6 mm wide; lateral sepals oblong or suboval, united at the base behind the spur for 4 mm, 13 mm long, 6 mm wide; petals spreading, oval, 12 mm long, 5 mm wide; lip concave, oval, subauriculate at the base, 12 mm long, 6 mm wide; spur pendent, slender, 15–20 cm long.

Epiphyte on horizontal branches of tall trees, or on rocks, in hot, high rainfall areas; ca. 600 m; flowering April to May.

Malawi, Zambia, Zimbabwe, and D.R. of Congo.

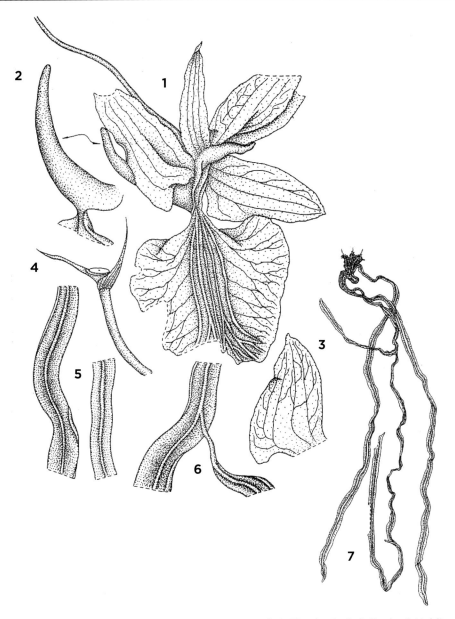

Taeniorrhiza gabonensis. 1: Flower. 2: Spur. 3: Petal. 4: Floral axis. 5–6: Roots. 7: Habit.
From Szlachetko and Olszewski 2001, p. 784. D. Szlachetko.

TAENIORRHIZA Summerhayes

This monotypic genus was described by Victor Summerhayes in 1943. It is rare and tiny but instantly recognisable by its flattened green roots to which the name refers: from the Greek *taenia*, a ribbon, also tapeworm, and *rhiza*, root. The plants are also recognised by the short stem, single-flowered inflorescence, and unique features of the column, especially the rostellum and the cup-shaped structures in which the 2 pollinia are held.

Until recently it was recorded only from Gabon, where the type specimen was collected, but Geerinck (1992) reports some sterile specimens from D.R. of Congo and one in cultivation.

Triceratorhynchus viridiflorus. B. Campbell

Taeniorrhiza gabonensis Summerhayes

Plant with a short stem up to 2 cm long, bearing many roots flattened against the host plant, green and 2-winged. Leaves absent. Inflorescences lateral, arising from the stem, 1 cm long, single-flowered; bract lanceolate-subulate, 5–8 mm long. Flower white with lilac lip; dorsal sepal oval-lanceolate, acuminate, 13–14 mm long, 7–8 mm wide; lateral sepals obliquely ovate-lanceolate, acute, 16–17 mm long, 9–11 mm wide; petals lanceolate-ligulate, acute, 13–14 mm long, 4 mm wide; lip suborbicular to oval, shortly apiculate, clawed at the base, with several thickened veins along the centre, 17–18 mm long, 19 mm wide; spur wide at the mouth, 3.5–4.5 mm wide, curved upwards behind the flower, conical, 14 mm long.

Epiphyte in forests.

Gabon and D.R. of Congo.

TRICERATORHYNCHUS
Summerhayes

This is another monotypic genus characterised by a distinctive rostellum structure that becomes visible (with a magnifying glass) when the anther cap and pollinia are removed. The rostellum has 3 distinct prongs, or horns, that protrude both up and down, the centre one shorter than the others. Summerhayes coined the name for the genus from the Greek words *tri*, three, *keras*, horn, and *rhynchos*, beak or snout.

Apart from this curious structure, the small green-flowered plants closely resemble some of the smaller species of *Angraecum* and *Angraecopsis*. The first description was made in 1951, although plants had been collected nearly 20 years earlier. They have been collected rather rarely and have probably been overlooked in the warm forests where they occur. The species has not yet been brought into cultivation.

Triceratorhynchus viridiflorus Summerhayes

Plants miniature, with numerous elongated roots and with a very short stem less than 1 cm long. Leaves suberect or spreading, linear, falcate, obscurely lobed at the apex, 1–5 cm long, 1–3 mm wide. Inflorescences arching or horizontal, longer than the leaves, to 6 cm long, up to 9-flowered; peduncle wiry, up to 2 cm long; bracts short, broadly ovate, acute; pedicel with ovary 4–5 mm long. Flowers green or yellowish green; dorsal sepal linear-lanceolate, acute, 4–5 mm long, 1 mm wide; lateral sepals obliquely linear-lanceolate, falcate, acute, 5–6 mm long, 1 mm wide; petals lanceolate, acuminate, 4–5 mm long, 1 mm wide; lip concave, obscurely 3-lobed, ovate-lanceolate, acuminate, 4–5 mm long, 3.5 mm wide, fleshy towards the apex; spur curving up above the ovary, slender, tapering, 5–8 mm long.

Epiphyte on twigs and branches in the warmer forests; 1500–1600 m; flowering in June.

Rwanda, Uganda, and Kenya.

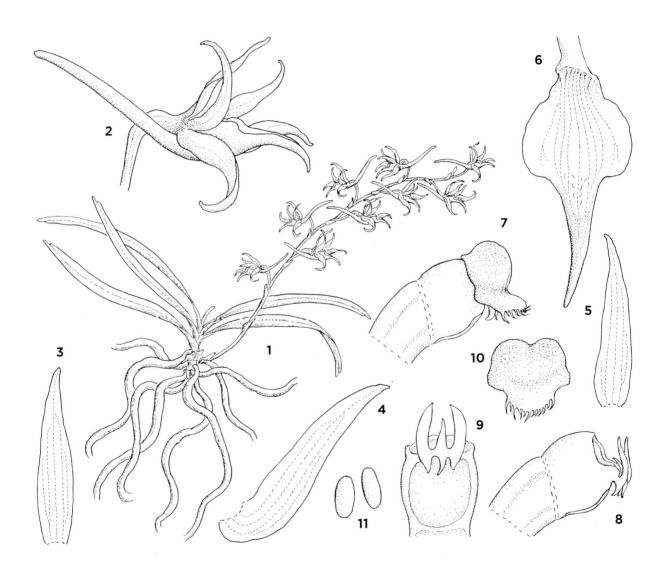

Triceratorhynchus viridiflorus. 1: Habit. 2: Flower. 3: Dorsal sepal. 4: Lateral sepal. 5: Petal. 6: Lip. 7–9: Column. 10: Anther-cap. 11: Pollinia. From Cribb 1989, fig. 151. M. E. Church.

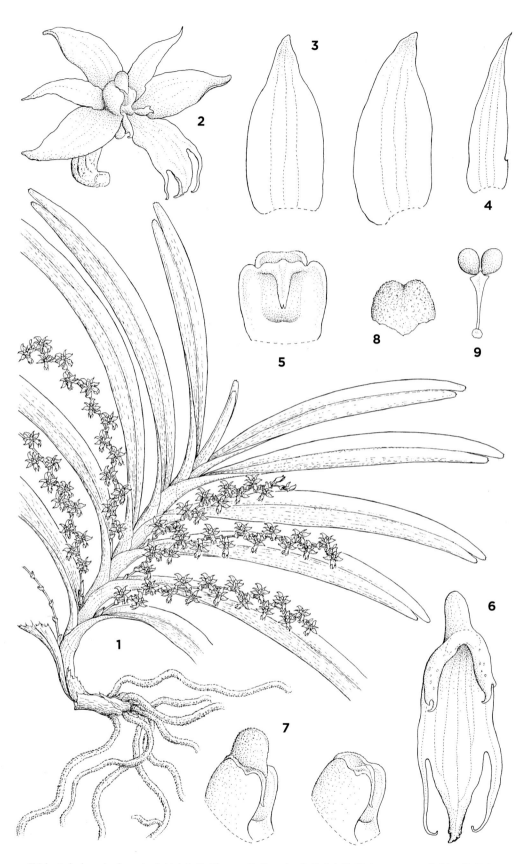

Tridactyle brevicalcarata. 1: Habit. 2: Flower. 3: Sepals. 4: Petal. 5: Column apex. 6: Lip. 7: Column. 8: Anther-cap. 9: Pollinarium. From Herb. Hort. Kew, 169: 610 (undated, unpublished). M. E. Church.

TRIDACTYLE Schlechter

The flowers of *Tridactyle* species are amongst the least showy of the African epiphytic orchids. Usually ochre brown, yellow, or green, rarely white, they are also small and mostly in few-flowered inflorescences. The sepals and petals are usually similar to each other, and the lip is the most conspicuous part of the flower. A few species have an entire lip with a pair of auricles on either side of the spur opening at the base, but typically the lip is 3-lobed as well as auriculate. Sometimes the lobes themselves, or just the lateral lobes, are further divided or fringed. The generic name is based on the overall lip structure—from the Greek words *tri-*, three, and *daktylos*, finger.

The plants of nearly all the species have long, woody stems covered in the remains of old leaf bases, often branched and growing in untidy clumps. A few are neat plants with upright stems, at least when young. Often they have distinctive roots, some thin, others quite thick, and either smooth or verrucose.

Some species are widespread throughout Africa, while others are very localised in their distribution. About 40 species are currently recognised and others will undoubtedly be described in due course. Yet other names may be reduced to synonymy as the full extent of variation within each species becomes known.

For convenience, and as an aid to identification, the species currently recognised are arranged here in 3 groups according to the length of the inflorescence and the number of flowers it bears.

Group 1. Inflorescences very short, up to 1 cm long, bearing few flowers, lip entire or with short entire lateral lobes.

Group 2. Inflorescences short to medium-sized, 1–4 cm long, bearing 3–8 flowers, sometimes more.

Group 3. Inflorescences long, usually over 4 cm long and up to 20 cm long, bearing 6 or more flowers.

Culture

All these species grow easily in cultivation whether they are mounted on a piece of bark or placed upright in a basket or pot of free-draining compost. Mature plants are often hard to establish, and it is best to start with seedlings or young plants. Providing the best conditions for their healthy growth depends on trying to emulate the environment in their native habitats. Some knowledge of the altitude and climatic conditions where the plants occur is particularly helpful.

Group 1. Plants with very short inflorescences (up to 1 cm long) with few flowers in each, lip entire or with short entire lateral lobes.

Tridactyle anthomaniaca (Reichenbach f.) Summerhayes

Plants usually pendent in large masses, with slender woody stems to 45 cm long, producing branches at right angles to the main stem and verrucose roots. Leaves fleshy, linear or narrowly oblong, unequally and obtusely bilobed at the apex, olive green, 4–8 cm long, 6–20 mm wide. Inflorescences very short, up to 1 cm long, 2- or 3-flowered. Flowers ochre or dirty orange; dorsal sepal oblong or elliptic, obtuse, 4–6 mm long, 1.5–2.5 mm wide; lateral sepals similar but oblique at the base; petals lanceolate, acute, 4–5 mm long, 1–1.8 mm wide; lip with fleshy auricles at the base by the spur mouth, entire, lanceolate, acute, 3–6 mm long, 2 mm wide; spur slender, S-shaped or straight, 10–16 mm long.

Epiphyte in the lower, warmer forests, usually on the larger branches of trees; 750–1650 m; flowering in March and April.

Sierra Leone eastwards to Kenya and south to Zimbabwe.

Tridactyle crassifolia Summerhayes

Plants with long branching stems, often pendent, to 40 cm long. Leaves many, linear-lanceolate, thick and fleshy, V-shaped in cross section, greyish green, 3–8 cm long, 6–8 mm wide. Inflorescences

Tridactyle anthomaniaca. B. Campbell

short, 1- to 3-flowered. Flowers very small, yellow; dorsal sepal oval to oblong-lanceolate, acute, 4.7–5.5 mm long, 1.7–2.5 mm wide; lateral sepals obliquely oblong-oval, acute, 3.5–6 mm long, 2–2.3 mm wide; petals obliquely oblong-lanceolate, acuminate, 4–5 mm long, 1.2–2 mm wide; lip entire except for 2 triangular auricles at the base, lanceolate or narrowly triangular, 3.7–5.6 mm long; spur straight, dilated towards the tip, 10–15 mm long.

Epiphyte in evergreen forest; flowering in August.

Ghana, Cameroon, Gabon, and D.R. of Congo.

Similar to *Tridactyle anthomaniaca* in the flowers but the thick leaves are quite different.

Triductyle eggelingii Summerhayes

Plants pendent, tufted, with stems up to 60 cm long and smooth roots. Leaves spreading, linear, unequally bilobed at the apex, 2.7–6.5 cm long, 2.5–5 mm wide. Inflorescences up to 8 mm long, 2- or 3-flowered. Flowers whitish; dorsal sepal ovate, obtuse, 4.2–4.5 mm long, 2.2–2.5 mm wide; lateral sepals oblong-ovate, obtuse, 4.3–4.6 mm long, 2.5–2.7 mm wide; petals oblong, acute, 3.8–4.3 mm long, 1.2–1.7 mm wide; lip with auricles at the base, 3-lobed in the apical half, side lobes spreading, longer than the mid-lobe, linear-tapering, fimbriate or with 2 or 3 teeth at the apex, mid-lobe triangular, in total 4–4.3 mm long, 4.3–6 mm wide; spur more or less straight, filiform, 6–7 mm long.

Epiphyte, usually on exposed trees in forest; 1600–2200 m; flowering in March.

Uganda and D.R. of Congo.

Named after the collector, W. J. Eggeling, who made many exciting discoveries while working as a forest botanist in Uganda.

Tridactyle filifolia (Schlechter) Schlechter

Syn. *Tridactyle tridentata* var. *subulifolia* Summerhayes

Plants pendent, with long slender branched stems 10–100 cm long, single or forming untidy clumps, rooting at the base. Leaves suberect or falcate, terete or grooved on the upper surface, sharply pointed, 3–12 cm long, 1–2 mm in diameter. Inflorescences very short, 2–8 mm long, 2- or 3-flowered. Flowers dingy white or ochre, small; dorsal sepal lanceolate, acute, 2–3 mm long; lateral sepals obliquely ovate, acute, 2–3 mm long; petals linear-lanceolate, smaller than the sepals; lip with 2 auricles or side lobes at the base on either side of the spur mouth and 3-lobed at the apex, lobes entire, 2–3 mm long, 1–2 mm wide; spur slender, incurved, 6–7 mm long.

Epiphyte of large branches of trees in the warmer forests; 850–1650 m; flowering in October.

Sierra Leone to Ethiopia and Kenya and south to Zambia and Malawi.

This species was formerly treated as a variety of *Tridactyle tridentata* and some botanists question its distinctness from that species.

Tridactyle inflata Summerhayes

Plants small with many stems 12–20 cm long and forming dense clumps. Leaves linear, unequally and obtusely bilobed at the apex, 5–7 cm long, 6–8 mm wide. Inflorescences up to 11 mm long, 3-flowered. Flowers pale green with orange column; dorsal sepal oblong-elliptic, obtuse, 3.5–4 mm long, 1.5–1.8 mm wide; lateral sepals obliquely oblong, obtuse, 3.7–4 mm long, 2–2.3 mm wide; petals oblong, obtuse, 3.5–3.8 mm long, 1.3–1.5 mm wide; lip flabellate, obscurely 3-lobed at the apex, auriculate at the base, side lobes triangular with several teeth on the apical margin, mid-lobe shortly triangular, in total 3 mm long, 3.1–3.3 mm wide; spur straight, clavate, 5.5 mm long.

Epiphyte on trees in mist zone on hilltop; 1600–1800 m; flowering in July.

Tanzania.

In general habit this species resembles *Tridactyle stipulata*, but it is distinguished by the lip shape and clavate spur.

Tridactyle lagosensis (Rolfe) Schlechter

Plant with slender, pendent stems up to 35 cm long. Leaves linear-lanceolate or narrowly ligulate,

Tridactyle lagosensis. C. Arends

unequally bilobed at the apex, 4–7.5 cm long, 4–9 mm wide. Inflorescences up to 6 mm long, 3- or 4-flowered. Flowers white, small; dorsal sepal elliptic-oval, obtuse, 3–4 mm long, 2 mm wide; lateral sepals obliquely oval or elliptic-oval, acute, 4–5 mm long, 2.3–3 mm wide; petals obliquely oblong or narrowly ligulate, 3–4 mm long, 1 mm wide; lip 3-lobed just below the middle, side lobes spreading, linear, acute, mid-lobe narrowly triangular or lanceolate, obtuse, in total 4.3–7 mm long, 2–3 mm wide; spur shorter than the lip, bent like a knee near the middle, with a wide mouth and slightly inflated apical part, 7–9 mm long.

Epiphyte on trunks and large branches in evergreen forest; flowering in June and July.

Nigeria and Cameroon.

Tridactyle laurentii (De Wildeman) Schlechter

Plant with narrow stems up to 40 cm long. Leaves folded longitudinally, linear to narrowly elliptic, unequally bilobed at the apex, 2.8–5 cm long, up to 2 cm wide. Inflorescence single-flowered. Flower green; sepals oblong, apiculate, 3 mm long, 1.5 mm wide; petals oblong, 2 mm long, 1 mm wide; lip with 2 auricles at the base, otherwise entire, narrowly triangular, acute, 3 mm long, 1.5 mm wide; spur straight, 8 mm long.

Two varieties have been recognised:

var. *laurentii*

Leaves linear, 2–4 cm long, 1–3 mm wide.
Epiphyte in dense evergreen forest.
D.R. of Congo.

var. *kabareensis* Geerinck

Leaves oblong or narrowly elliptic, 5–8.5 cm long, 15–20 mm wide.
Epiphyte in gallery forest; 1800 m.
D.R. of Congo (near Lakes Edward and Kivu).

Tridactyle minuta P. J. Cribb

Plant with slender, curved stems, usually pendent, with verrucose roots, leafy in the apical part. Leaves suberect, linear, grass-like, very unequally bilobed at the apex, 7.3–11.5 cm long, 1.5–3 mm

wide. Inflorescences 5–7 mm long, 3- to 5-flowered. Flowers greenish yellow with an orange column; dorsal sepal elliptic-ovate, obtuse, 2 mm long, 1.2 mm wide; lateral sepals oblong-ovate or oblong, obtuse, 1.8–2 mm long, 1–1.2 mm wide; petals elliptic, acute, 1.6 mm long, 0.7 mm wide; lip 3-lobed in the apical half, deflexed, side lobes spreading, triangular, about as large as mid-lobe, mid-lobe triangular, acute, in total 1.5 mm long, 1.8 mm wide; spur slightly incurved, clavate, 3 mm long.

Epiphyte in dwarf mist forest on steep slopes; 1400–1700 m; flowering in October and November.

Tanzania.

This species has the smallest flowers yet described in the genus.

Tridactyle muriculata (Rendle) Schlechter

Plant with a stout, branching stem to 4.5 cm long, bearing many verrucose roots. Leaves linear-oblong, broadly and obtusely bilobed at the apex, 5–6.5 cm long, 7–9 mm wide. Flowers 1.5 cm in diameter; sepals 7–7.5 mm long, 3 mm wide; petals lanceolate, 6.5 mm long, 1.5 mm wide; lip with small auricles at the base, almost entire, side lobes present as teeth, mid-lobe long and narrow, acute, 6.5 mm long, 1.5 mm wide; spur 3 cm long.

Epiphyte.

Southern Nigeria.

This species is close to *Tridactyle anthomaniaca* but separated by its slightly more slender stems, narrower leaves, and larger flowers with a much longer spur.

Tridactyle nalaensis (De Wildeman) Schlechter

Plants with slender stems up to 30 cm long. Leaves broadly oblong to subelliptic, shortly bilobed at the apex, 1–2.5 cm long, 5–6 mm wide. Inflorescence single-flowered. Flower colour unknown; sepals and petals suboval, acute, 6–7 mm long, 2 mm wide; lip with rounded auricles at the base, otherwise entire, subelliptic, acute, 6 mm long, 2.5 mm wide; spur slender, 4 cm long.

Epiphyte in dense forests.

D.R. of Congo.

Tridactyle nigrescens Summerhayes

Plants usually pendent, in masses with smooth roots; stems slender and woody, to 30 cm long, drying black. Leaves fleshy, drying black, linear, unequally and acutely bilobed at the apex, 3–7 cm long, 1–3 mm wide. Inflorescences very short, 5–6 mm long, 2- or 3-flowered. Flowers pale green or greenish yellow becoming dirty orange with age; dorsal sepal elliptic, obtuse, 3–4 mm long, 1.5–2 mm wide; lateral sepals oblong-ovate, obtuse, 3–4 mm long, 2 mm wide; petals lanceolate, acute, 3–4 mm long, 1–1.3 mm wide; lip with auricles at the base by the spur mouth, strongly 3-lobed at the apex, side lobes longer than the mid-lobe and lacerate at the apex, 2.6–4 mm long, 2 mm wide; spur slender, slightly inflated in the middle, 6–7.5 mm long.

Epiphyte; only recorded in dry highland forest, in riverine forest and on rocks above a lake; 1150–2200 m.

Uganda, Kenya, Tanzania, and D.R. of Congo.

Tridactyle oblongifolia Summerhayes

Plant small with short, few-branched stems to 8 cm long, with verrucose roots. Leaves narrowly oblong or ligulate, leathery, unequally and obtusely bilobed at the apex, twisted at the base so that they lie in one plane, 2–12 cm long, 7–17 mm wide. Inflorescences very short, to 4 mm long, 2- or 3-flowered. Flowers greenish white, turning yellow with age; dorsal sepal oblong-ovate, acute, 4.8–5.2 mm long, 1.8–2 mm wide; lateral sepals similar but oblique, 4–4.4 mm long, 2–2.5 mm wide; petals lanceolate, acuminate, 4.4–5 mm long, 1–1.2 mm wide; lip entire, lanceolate, acute, with a tooth on each side at the mouth of the spur, 3.7–4.5 mm long, 1–1.3 mm wide; spur filiform, geniculate in basal half, slightly dilated towards the apex, 13–14.5 mm long.

Epiphyte in riverine forest; 900–1300 m; flowering in November and December.

Sierra Leone, Côte d'Ivoire, Nigeria, Central African Republic, Uganda, and D.R. of Congo.

Tridactyle scottellii (Rendle) Schlechter

Plants usually pendent in large masses with smooth roots and slender woody stems to 60 cm long. Leaves grass-like, linear, unequally and obtusely bilobed, 7–18 cm long, 3.5–6 mm wide. Inflorescences very short, 3–4 mm long, 1- to 3-flowered. Flowers greenish yellow becoming dirty orange with age; dorsal sepal ovate-elliptic, acute, 4–6 mm long, 1.5–2.5 mm wide; lateral sepals similar but oblique at the base; petals lanceolate, acute, 4–5 mm long, 1–1.8 mm wide; lip with fleshy auricles at the base by the spur mouth, strongly 3-lobed at the apex, side lobes longer than the mid-lobe, 4–5 mm long, 6–7 mm wide; spur slender, straight, 9–12 mm long.

Epiphyte, widespread in highland evergreen forests; 2000–3000 m.

D.R. of Congo, Rwanda, Uganda, and Kenya.

Tridactyle stevartiana Geerinck

Inflorescences up to 1 cm long, 2- or 3-flowered. Flowers white, small; lip deeply 3-lobed; side lobes shorter than the mid-lobe and minutely denticulate along their inner margins.

Epiphyte in forest; flowering in February.
Rwanda.

This species was described in 2001 and is said to be close to *Tridactyle eggelingii* but with smaller flowers. The specific epithet honours the Belgian botanist, Tariq Stévart.

Tridactyle translucens Summerhayes

Plant with several erect stems to 20 cm long, rooting at the base. Leaves in 2 rows, ligulate or lanceolate-ligulate, unequally bilobed at the apex, very fleshy and V-shaped in cross section, 2–4 cm long, 4–8 mm wide. Inflorescences arising opposite the leaves, 6–10 mm long, 2- to 6-flowered. Flowers translucent greenish white to pale cream; dorsal sepal ovate-lanceolate, acuminate, 4 mm long, 2.5 mm wide; lateral sepals obliquely oblong-lanceolate, 4.8 mm long, 2.5 mm wide; petals oblong-lanceolate, acute, 3.5 mm long, 1.5 mm wide; lip papillose, with auricles at the base, 3-lobed at the middle, side lobes spreading, slightly fimbriate at the tips, mid-lobe triangular-ligulate, acute, in total 3.75 mm long, 3.5 mm wide; spur straight, narrow, 8.5 mm long.

Epiphyte in woodland; flowering in March.

Zambia.

Tridactyle vanderlaaniana Geerinck

Plant with slender stems up to 30 cm long. Leaves oblong, flat, shortly bilobed at the apex, 3.5–6 cm long, 10–13 mm wide. Inflorescence single-flowered. Flower colour unknown; sepals subelliptic, acute or subapiculate, 7.5 mm long, 4 mm wide; petals oblong, subobtuse, 6 mm long, 2.5 mm wide; lip with small auricles, 3-lobed at the middle, side lobes slender, acuminate, as long as the mid-lobe, mid-lobe triangular and acute, in total 9 mm long, 5 mm wide; spur curved, slender at first, inflated at the apex like a balloon, 15 mm long, 4 mm wide at the apex.

Epiphyte in dense rain forest.

D.R. of Congo.

This species was named for Frank van der Laan, an orchid specialist at the University of Wageningen, The Netherlands.

Tridactyle virgula (Kraenzlin) Schlechter

Plants with stems in tufts, curved and rarely branched, occasionally several metres long but usually 10–65 cm long, with smooth roots. Leaves linear, unequally bilobed at the apex, 9–16 cm long, 3–5 mm wide. Inflorescences 4–5 mm long, 2- to 4-flowered. Flowers greenish white or whitish; dorsal sepal ovate-elliptic, acute, 3–3.7 mm long, 1.6–2.2 mm wide; lateral sepals obliquely ovate, acute, 3.2–4 mm long, 1.9–2 mm wide; petals oblong-linear, acute, 2.5–3.6 mm long, 1–2 mm wide; lip cuneate below with fleshy auricles, 3-lobed in the apical part, side lobes spreading, short, subacute, mid-lobe slightly longer, acute, in total 2.5–3.3 mm long, 1.5–2.5 mm wide; spur decurved, slightly inflated at the apex, 8–12 mm long.

Epiphyte in undergrowth of montane forests; 1770–2500 m; flowering April to May and in September.

D.R. of Congo, Rwanda, and Uganda.

Group 2. Plants with short to medium-sized inflorescences (1–4 cm long) bearing 3–8 flowers, sometimes more.

Tridactyle brevifolia Mansfeld

Plants small, erect, with stems 6–10 cm long and with smooth roots. Leaves linear, unequally bilobed at the apex, with rounded lobes, 2–4.5 cm long, 2–4 mm wide. Inflorescences 2–3 cm long, 4- to 9-flowered. Flowers yellow-orange with reddish anther cap; dorsal sepal elliptic, obtuse, 3.5–3.7 mm long, 2 mm wide; lateral sepals obliquely ovate, obtuse, 3.5–4.2 mm long, 2.7 mm wide; petals oblong-elliptic, obtuse, 3–3.5 mm long, 1.5 mm wide; lip auriculate at the base, 3-lobed at the apex but side lobes obscure, mid-lobe oblong, 3 mm long, in total 3–3.5 mm long, 2–2.2 mm wide; spur pendent, clavate, 6–7 mm long.

Epiphyte on small trees in montane mist forest; 1650–2100 m; flowering in January and February.

Tanzania.

Tridactyle cruciformis Summerhayes

Plants usually pendent in large masses, with verrucose roots, and with slender woody stems to 60 cm long, usually upturned at the apex. Leaves grass-like, linear, unequally and acutely bilobed, 7–23 cm long, 1–2.5 mm wide, glossy green. Inflorescences 2–5 cm long, 5- to 9-flowered. Flowers pale green or greenish yellow, browning with age; dorsal sepal ovate-elliptic, obtuse, 2–3 mm long, 1.5 mm wide; lateral sepals similar but slightly longer; petals linear, acute or obtuse, 2–3 mm long, 0.5–1 mm wide; lip strongly 3-lobed at the middle, side lobes spreading, narrower than the mid-lobe, acute, 2–2.5 mm long, 1.8–3 mm wide; spur slender, incurved, 11–13 mm long.

Epiphyte in upland rainforest patches on hills; 600–2200 m; flowering in December and January.

Kenya and Tanzania.

Tridactyle flabellata P. J. Cribb

Plants erect or with curved stems 6–16 cm long, roots slender and smooth. Leaves suberect, linear, unequally bilobed at the apex, twisted at the base

Tridactyle cruciformis. B. Campbell

and attached to black-spotted leaf sheaths, 2.5–5 cm long, 2–4 mm wide. Inflorescences 1–3.7 cm long, 3- to 12-flowered. Flowers white with brown anther cap; dorsal sepal elliptic, obtuse, 2.5–4 mm long, 1.5–2 mm wide; lateral sepals obliquely oblong-elliptic, obtuse, 4–5 mm long, 2 mm wide; petals obovate, obtuse, 3 mm long, 2 mm wide; lip flabellate when flattened, erose on the apical margin, 2.5–3 mm long, 3–4 mm wide; spur slightly curved, 4–5 mm long.

Epiphyte in montane forest on steep slopes and ridge tops; 1400–1600 m; flowering in October. Tanzania.

Tridactyle fusifera Mansfeld

Plant erect with long stems and thick aerial roots. Leaves in 2 rows, ligulate or linear-ligulate, unequally bilobed at the apex, up to 18 cm long, 13 mm wide. Inflorescences axillary or below the leaves, up to 4 cm long. Flowers greenish white, small; sepals broadly lanceolate, 2–4 mm long; lateral sepals oblique and shortly connate at the base; petals linear-lanceolate, acute; lip ovate scarcely 3-lobed but with a short tooth on each side below the middle, 2–4 mm long, 2.5–3.5 mm wide; spur somewhat inflated below the narrow mouth, 6.5–8 mm long.

Epiphyte in montane rain forest on large branches and in the fork of tree trunks; 600–1500 m; flowering in February.

Sierra Leone, Liberia, Côte d'Ivoire, and Cameroon.

Tridactyle inaequilonga (De Wildeman) Schlechter

Plants with upright or pendent stems up to 30 cm long and with verrucose roots. Leaves linear, unequally and acutely bilobed at the apex, twisted at the base and attached to spotted leaf sheaths, 5–14 cm long, 4–7 mm wide. Inflorescences 8–30 mm long, 4- to 6-flowered. Flowers greenish yellow to dull orange; dorsal sepal oblong, obtuse, 3 mm long, 1.2–1.4 mm wide; lateral sepals obliquely ovate, obtuse, 3.3–5 mm long, 1.5–1.7 mm wide; petals oblong, acute, 3–4 mm long, 1 mm wide; lip 3-lobed in the middle, auriculate at the base, side lobes longer than the mid-lobe with up to 3 teeth at the front margin, mid-lobe narrowly triangular, subacute, in total 3.5–5 mm long, 5.5 mm wide; spur straight, narrow, 7–9 mm long.

Epiphyte or lithophytic in montane forest; 1250–1900 m; flowering in March and November.

D.R. of Congo, Tanzania, Malawi, and Zimbabwe.

This species seems close to *Tridactyle stipulata*.

Tridactyle lisowskii (Szlachetko) Szlachetko & Olszewski

Plant with upright or semi-pendent stems, 17–110 cm long. Leaves 3–9, linear, leathery and thick, bright green, 11.5 cm long, 1.2 cm wide. Inflorescences 3–5 cm long, 6- to 12-flowered. Flowers yellow or orange, small; dorsal sepal oval-lanceolate to triangular, acute, 5 mm long, 2 mm wide; lateral sepals obliquely lanceolate, oboval, or elliptic-lanceolate, acute, 5–5.2 mm long, 2.5–2.9 mm wide;

petals linear, linear-lanceolate to narrowly oblong, acute, margins ciliate, 4–5 mm long, 8–13 mm wide; lip auriculate at the base, the auricles small and very thick, 3-lobed in the apical third, side lobes narrow, spreading, longer than mid-lobe, ciliate along margins and with a few teeth at the apex, mid-lobe small, triangular, in total 4–6 mm long; spur straight, slightly inflated in the lower two thirds, 10–12 mm long.

Lithophyte on granite rocks, usually in exposed positions; 750–1070 m; flowering November to February.

Cameroon, Gabon, and D.R. of Congo.

This species is named after the Polish botanist, Stanislaw Lisowski (1924–2002), who collected plants in several African countries.

Tridactyle phaeocephala Summerhayes

Plant with erect or pendent stems 9–30 cm long, and smooth roots. Leaves suberect or spreading, linear, unequally bilobed at the apex, with rounded or obtuse lobes, glossy, bright green, 3–8(–14) cm long, 4–5 mm wide. Inflorescences 1–4 cm long, 3- to 7-flowered. Flowers pale green with brown anther cap; dorsal sepal oblong-elliptic, acute or obtuse, 4.8–6 mm long, 2–2.4 mm wide; lateral sepals obliquely ovate, acute or obtuse, 5 mm long, 2.4–3 mm wide; petals oblong or lanceolate, acuminate, 4.5–5.7 mm long, 1.7–1.8 mm wide; lip auriculate at the base, 3-lobed in the middle, side lobes spreading, linear, 2- to 6-lacerate at the apex, mid-lobe slightly shorter than side lobes, linear-tapering, in total 3.6–5.8 mm long, 7 mm wide; spur straight, inflated at the apex, 8–9 mm long.

Epiphyte in montane and dwarf montane forest; 2200–2400 m; flowering in January and March.

Tanzania.

This species seems close to *Tridactyle stipulata* but is distinguished by its narrower leaves, differently coloured flowers, and fimbriate side lobes of the lip.

Tridactyle stipulata (De Wildeman) Schlechter

Plant with long, branching stems, bearing a sort of needle-shaped stipule 4 mm long at the top of

Tridactyle tridentata. B. Campbell

the leaf sheath. Leaves linear-lanceolate, tapering to both ends, unequally bilobed at the apex, 9–11 cm long, 9–12 mm wide. Inflorescence a short raceme above or at the side of the 'stipule', 15 mm long, 5- or 6-flowered. Flowers white, washed with cream and rose; sepals subequal, lateral sepals a little wider than dorsal sepal, 4 mm long; petals lanceolate, as long as the sepals; lip 3-lobed, lateral lobes spreading, more slender than median lobe, auricles at the base tooth-like, 5 mm long; spur slender, 9 mm long, acute at the apex.

D.R. of Congo.

Tridactyle tridentata (Harvey) Schlechter

Syn. *Tridactyle teretifolia* Schlechter

Plants erect or pendent, single or forming untidy clumps, rooting at the base; stems branched, 10–50 cm long, robust and covered with rugulose sheaths. Leaves suberect or falcate, terete or cylindric but grooved on the upper surface, pointed, dull olive green, 6–10 cm long, 2–4 mm in diameter. Inflorescences short, 2–3 cm long, 4- or 5-flowered. Flowers green to yellow or ochre; dorsal sepal oblong-elliptic, obtuse, 4–5 mm long; lateral sepals obliquely ovate, acute, 4–5 mm long; petals falcate, lanceolate, narrower than the sepals, 3–4 mm long; lip with 2 auricles or side lobes at the base on either side of the spur mouth and 3-lobed at the apex, lobes entire, side lobes equal to or shorter than the mid-lobe, 4–5 mm long, 3–4 mm wide; spur slender, incurved, 6–9 mm long.

Epiphyte on branches of large trees in the warmer forests and woodlands; 1300–2250 m; flowering in October.

D.R. of Congo, Uganda, and Kenya southwards to South Africa (KwaZulu-Natal and Eastern Cape Province where it is lithophytic).

This species is extremely variable throughout its range. The plants always look more succulent and robust than those of *Tridactyle filifolia*, which has sometimes been treated as a variety of *T. tridentata*.

Tridactyle trimikeorum M. Dare

This species was described in 1999. It is said to be close to *Tridactyle inaequilonga*, from which it differs in its smaller stature and erect, never pendent habit with stems up to 12 cm long. The leaves are stiffer and smaller in size. The sepals are expanded and united at the base to form a sheath for the spur, and the petals are only 2.5 mm long.

Epiphyte in mid-canopy in *Brachystegia* woodland and lithophytic on boulders in exposed situations; 1600 m; flowering October to November.

Zimbabwe (Mount Buhwa).

The specific epithet is derived from the name of the 3 discoverers of this new species, Mike Dare, Mike Kimberley, and Mike Timm.

Tridactyle verrucosa P. J. Cribb

Plants with stout, erect stems 8–20 cm long bearing strongly verrucose roots. Leaves stiff, fleshy or leathery, narrowly oblong-elliptic, unequally bilobed at the apex, with rounded lobes, 3–5.3 cm long, 7–10 mm wide. Inflorescences 1–1.7(–3) cm long, 3- to 5-flowered. Flowers green or yellow with orange column; dorsal sepal lanceolate, acuminate, 5 mm long, 2 mm wide; lateral sepals similar but oblique; petals lanceolate, acuminate, 5 mm long, 1.5 mm wide; lip 3-lobed in the apical half, side lobes longer than mid-lobe, entire and thread-like or bifid at the apex, mid-lobe narrowly triangular, acute, in total 4.5–5.5 mm long, 6–7 mm wide; spur subclavate, decurved, 8–12 mm long.

Lithophytic, on rocks in exposed montane situations, and occasionally epiphytic in woodland; 1500–2200 m; flowering November to December and in March.

Tanzania and Malawi.

Tridactyle virginea P. J. Cribb & la Croix

Plant erect or trailing, stems to 40 cm long, flattened, with verrucose roots. Leaves 3–7, linear, unequally and acutely bilobed at the apex, with a hair-like ligule 5 mm long at the top of the leaf sheath opposite the leaf blade, 6–13 cm long, 7–11 mm wide. Inflorescences 1–2.7 cm long, 3- to 11-flowered. Flowers somewhat campanulate, glistening white with red anther cap; dorsal sepal ovate, acute or obtuse, 3.5–5 mm long, 1.5–2.5 mm wide; lateral sepals similar; petals elliptic to ovate, acute, 3.5–4 mm long, 1.5 mm wide; lip auriculate at the base, 3-lobed towards the apex, side lobes spreading, as long as or shorter than mid-lobe, triangular, acute, mid-lobe also triangular, acute, in total 3–4 mm long, 2–3 mm wide; spur slightly inflated in the middle, more or less parallel with the ovary, 5–7 mm long.

Epiphyte at high levels in montane forest, forming large colonies on horizontal branches; 1600–1900 m; flowering October to December.

Tanzania and Malawi.

Group 3. Plants with long inflorescences (usually over 4 cm long and up to 20 cm long) bearing 6 or more flowers.

Tridactyle armeniaca (Lindley) Schlechter

Plant with long erect stems and robust aerial roots. Leaves in 2 rows, ligulate or lanceolate-ligulate, unequally bilobed at the apex, 5–20 cm long, 1–2 cm wide. Inflorescences up to 8 cm long, 8- to 10-flowered. Flowers orange, small; sepals broadly lanceolate, acute, 2.5–4.5 mm long; lateral sepals similar but oblique, connate at the base; petals linear, lanceolate, acute; lip 3-lobed at about the middle, side lobes spreading and narrow, longer than mid-lobe, entire, mid-lobe triangular, acute, in total 2.5–4.5 mm long, 3.5–5.5 mm wide; spur

Tridactyle bicaudata. B. Campbell

distinctly swollen in the apical two thirds, 6–8.5 mm long.

Epiphyte in montane rain forest on large branches and in the forks of large trees; 600–1500 m; flowering in February.

Guinea, Sierra Leone, Liberia, Côte d'Ivoire, and Ghana.

Tridactyle bicaudata (Lindley) Schlechter

Plants upright or pendent, often forming large clumps, with woody stems 10–80 cm long, leafy only in the upper part, slightly verrucose roots mainly from the base. Leaves linear, straight or falcate, sometimes folded, unequally bilobed at the apex, with rounded lobes, 4–14 cm long, 8–15 mm wide. Inflorescences spreading, bearing 8–25 flowers in 2 rows, 3–12 cm long. Flowers ochre-orange or greenish yellow; dorsal sepal oblong-ovate, acute or apiculate, 4–6 mm long, 1.5–3 mm wide; lateral sepals obliquely ovate, acute or apiculate, 5–6.5 mm long, 2.5–3.5 mm wide; petals lanceolate, acute or obtuse, 4 mm long, 1 mm wide; lip

Tridactyle bicaudata. J. Hermans

with rhombic auricles on either side of the spur mouth, 3-lobed in the upper part, the side lobes longer than the mid-lobe and fringed, 3–6 mm long, 8–12 mm wide; spur straight, narrow, 10–16 mm long.

Two subspecies have been recognised:

subsp. *bicaudata*

Leaves thin, lax, 6–14 cm long.

Epiphyte in a wide range of undisturbed habitats, one of the commonest epiphytic orchids; sea level to 2500 m; flowering March to April and September to November.

Sierra Leone eastwards to Ethiopia and southwards to South Africa.

subsp. *rupestris* H. P. Linder

Leaves fleshy, stiffly curved, 3.5–6 cm long.

Lithophytic and only flowering in full sunlight; usually near sea level; flowering December and January.

South Africa (Eastern Cape Province and KwaZulu-Natal).

Tridactyle brevicalcarata Summerhayes

Plant with elongated stems to 30 cm long, rarely branched. Leaves many, ligulate, equally or unequally bilobed at the apex, 6–11 cm long, 7–10 mm wide. Inflorescences 2–6 cm long, many-flowered. Flowers white, small; dorsal sepal narrowly oval or elliptic oval, subacute, 2.5–3.5 mm long, 1.5 mm wide; lateral sepals obliquely oval, subacute, 3–3.5 mm long, 1.5–1.75 mm wide; petals oblong-lanceolate, acute, 2.5–3 mm long, 1 mm wide; lip auriculate at the base, 3-lobed at the middle, side lobes narrowly ligulate, spreading forward, smaller than mid-lobe, denticulate, mid-lobe triangular, acute, in total 3 mm long, 2–2.75 mm wide; spur straight, obtuse, less than 1 mm long.

Epiphyte in forests; flowering in August and October.

Ghana, Cameroon, and Gabon.

Said to resemble *Tridactyle armeniaca* but with smaller leaves and a very short spur.

Tridactyle citrina P. J. Cribb

Plant erect with short stems forming small clumps 1–9 cm high, and stout, slightly verrucose roots. Leaves 3 or 4, stiff, more or less erect, linear, unequally bilobed at the apex, with rounded lobes, slightly glaucous green, 7–14 cm long, 7–14 mm wide. Inflorescences arising near base of the stem, bearing 9–11 flowers in 2 rows all facing the same way, 7.5–11 cm long. Flowers yellow, creamy yellow, or greenish cream; dorsal sepal lanceolate, acuminate, 8–11 mm long, 2.5–4 mm wide; lateral sepals similar but somewhat oblique and with tips reflexed; petals lanceolate, acuminate, spreading, reflexed at the tips, 7–8 mm long, 2.5–3 mm wide; lip auriculate at the base, 3-lobed in the apical half, side lobes shorter than mid-lobe, obliquely spreading, mid-lobe narrowly triangular, in total 10–16 mm long, 3–5 mm wide; spur slender, 4–5 cm long.

Epiphyte on scattered trees in grassland and in woodland on mountainsides, usually on larger branches; 1360–2100 m; flowering in December.

Tanzania, Malawi, and Zambia.

Tridactyle fimbriatipetala (De Wildeman) Schlechter

Plant with long narrow stems, up to 50 cm long. Leaves narrowly elliptic or elliptic, obtuse, with rounded lobes at the apex, 8–12 cm long, 1.5–2.5 cm wide. Inflorescences 8–10 cm long, 10- to 15-flowered. Flowers pale with glandular perianth; sepals elliptic, 5–6 mm long, 2 mm wide; petals with fimbriate margins, 5 mm long, 1 mm wide; lip with acute auricles near the base and 3-lobed about the middle, side lobes as long as the mid-lobe, laciniate at the apex, mid-lobe narrowly triangular, laciniate, in total 8–11 mm long, 8 mm wide; spur slender, 2 cm long.

Epiphyte in dense forest.

D.R. of Congo.

This species is unique in the genus in having fimbriate petals.

Tridactyle furcistipes Summerhayes

Plants usually upright, often forming large clumps; stems woody, 10–20 cm long, leafy only in the upper part, rooting from the base. Leaves linear, straight or falcate, sometimes folded, unequally bilobed at the apex, with rounded lobes, 11–18 cm long, 8–15 mm wide. Inflorescences spreading, bearing 8–20 flowers in 2 rows, 4–11 cm long. Flowers greenish white or dirty cream fading to ochre-orange; sepals lanceolate, acuminate, dorsal sepal 9–12 mm long, 2–4 mm wide, lateral sepals falcate, 10–12 mm long, 2–3.5 mm wide; petals lanceolate, acuminate, 8.5–10 mm long, 2–3 mm wide; lip with rhombic auricles on either side of the spur mouth, 3-lobed in the upper part, the side lobes shorter than the mid-lobe, entire or fringed or forked at the apex, 9–12.5 mm long, 4–6 mm wide; spur straight, narrow, 14–27 mm long.

Epiphyte in highland forests and scrub at the upper edge of forests and forest margins; 2300–2850 m; flowering in March to July.

Kenya, Uganda, and Tanzania.

This species resembles *Tridactyle bicaudata* vegetatively but has much larger flowers and is usually found at higher altitudes.

Tridactyle gentilii (De Wildeman) Schlechter

Plant with robust stems 30–80 cm long and smooth roots. Leaves linear, ligulate, or oblong, obtusely bilobed at the apex, with rounded lobes, 6–20 cm long, 8–30 mm wide. Inflorescences 8–12 cm long, 7- to 15-flowered. Flowers pale green, whitish or yellowish; dorsal sepal oblong, cuspidate, 5–9 mm long, 2–4.5 mm wide; lateral sepals obliquely triangular, apiculate, 5–9 mm long, 2–5 mm wide; petals oblong, 4–8 mm long, 1–2 mm wide; lip with large basal auricles, 3-lobed at the apex, the side lobes much longer than mid-lobe, lacerate at the apex, mid-lobe triangular, in total 7.5–13 mm long, 15 mm wide; spur slender, 2.5–8 cm long.

Epiphyte in dense forest and gallery forest near rivers and swamps; 1700–2200 m; flowering in February, August, and December.

Tridactyle furcistipes. B. Campbell

Tridactyle gentilii. J. Stewart

Ghana, Nigeria, Cameroon, D.R. of Congo, Rwanda, Uganda, Zimbabwe, Zambia, Angola, and South Africa (KwaZulu-Natal).

This species is somewhat similar to *Tridactyle bicaudata* but usually has larger flowers with a much longer spur.

Tridactyle latifolia Summerhayes

Plant with robust stems 22–40 cm long, usually semi-pendent. Leaves 5 or 6, narrowly elliptic-oblong, curved, leathery, unequally bilobed at the apex, 9.5–13.5 cm long, 1.7–2.5 cm wide. Inflorescences lax, 5–11.5 cm long, 8- to 18-flowered. Flowers yellowish, small; sepals oblong-lanceolate to oblong-elliptic, dorsal sepal 4.2–6 mm long, 1.7–2 mm wide, lateral sepals oblique, 4.3–5.5 mm long, 2–2.3 mm wide; petals ligulate-lanceolate or narrowly lanceolate, 4–5.5 mm long, 1–1.2 mm wide; lip auriculate at the base, 3-lobed near the middle, side lobes longer than mid-lobe, fimbriate at the tips, mid-lobe narrowly triangular, acute, in total, 3.8–6 mm long, 9 mm wide; spur narrowly cylindric, incurved, 10–14 mm long.

Epiphyte on trees on a river bank; flowering in November.

Gabon.

According to Summerhayes (1948), this species has the widest leaves in the genus.

Tridactyle sarcodantha Mansfeld

Plant with short, suberect stem up to 5 cm long. Leaves linear, unequally bilobed at the apex, each lobe with 2 blunt teeth, 9–16.5 cm long, 1.2–1.3 cm wide. Inflorescences up to 9 cm long. Flowers fleshy, yellowish; dorsal sepal ovate-lanceolate, shortly acuminate, 9–10 mm long, 3.5 mm wide, scaly on outer surface; lateral sepals similar; pet-als triangular-lanceolate, shortly acuminate, 8 mm long, 2.5 mm wide; lip cuneate-rectangular, auriculate at the base, 3-lobed at the front, side lobes shorter than mid-lobe, spreading, mid-lobe narrowly triangular, acuminate, in total 11 mm long, 3.5 mm wide; spur incurved, slightly inflated towards the apex, 2.2 cm long.

Epiphyte in montane forest; 1800 m; flowering in March.

Tanzania.

Tridactyle tanneri P. J. Cribb

Plants small, stems short, 1–4 cm long, usually erect with long smooth roots. Leaves linear, unequally bilobed and toothed at the apex, with darker green spots or markings on pale or mid-green background, 6–10 cm long, 6–10 mm wide.

Tridactyle tanneri. B. Campbell

Inflorescences arching or pendent, 2–5 cm long, 2- to 8-flowered. Flowers green or dull yellow, scabrid on the outer surface; dorsal sepal oblong, acute, 7 mm long, 3 mm wide; lateral sepals obliquely oblong-lanceolate, acuminate, 8–9 mm long, 2.5 mm wide; petals lanceolate, acuminate, 7 mm long, 2 mm wide; lip obscurely 3-lobed in the middle, 8–9 mm long, 3–4 mm wide, auriculate at the base; spur pendent, curved at the apex, 18–20 mm long.

Epiphyte on tree trunks in deep shade in warm evergreen forest; 1200–1600 m; flowering in December and January.

Kenya and Tanzania.

With its pendent inflorescences and flowers with scabrid outer surface and Y-shaped stipes, this species might be more appropriately placed in the genus *Ypsilopus*.

Tridactyle tricuspis (Bolus) Schlechter

Plants usually small, with smooth roots growing in tangled clumps; stems upright, short, 10–20 cm long. Leaves in 2 rows, linear, arcuate, unequally bilobed at the apex, with rounded lobes, condupli-cate, 8–15 cm long, 8–12 mm wide. Inflorescences below the leaves, spreading or suberect, 4–15 cm long, bearing 7–30 flowers in 2 rows. Flowers pale green to yellow-brown; dorsal sepal lanceolate, acuminate, 6–7.5 mm long, 2–2.5 mm wide; lateral sepals obliquely lanceolate, acuminate, 6–7.5 mm long, 2 mm wide; petals lanceolate, acuminate, 5–6.5 mm long, 1.5–2 mm wide; lip 3-lobed in the apical half, cuneate at base and auriculate, side lobes short, slender, erose or bifid at tip, midlobe triangular, longer than side lobes, in total 5–8 mm long, 3.5–5 mm wide; spur slender, 12–15 mm long.

Epiphyte in forest and bush on hills; 900–2600 m; flowering in April.

Kenya southwards to South Africa (Mpumalanga, Limpopo, KwaZulu-Natal, and Eastern Cape Province), and D.R. of Congo.

Tridactyle tridactylites (Rolfe) Schlechter

Plant straggling with erect or pendent stems 40–160 cm long, roots smooth. Leaves linear, unequally and acutely bilobed at the apex, 6–21 cm

Tridactyle tridactylites. J. Hermans

long, 6–12 mm wide. Inflorescences 3–8 cm long, 6- to 15-flowered. Flowers greenish cream, straw-coloured, or yellow-green; dorsal sepal elliptic-ovate, acute, 3.5–5.3 mm long, 1.5–2.6 mm wide; lateral sepals obliquely ovate, acute, 3.7–5.6 mm long, 1.7–2.7 mm wide; petals lanceolate, acuminate, 3.6–6.0 mm long, 0.7–1.3 mm wide; lip auriculate at the base, 3-lobed in the apical part, side lobes spreading, longer than the mid-lobe, filiform, not fringed, mid-lobe triangular, in total 4–5 mm long, 5–6.5 mm wide; spur incurved, slender, 9–10 mm long.

Epiphyte in rain forest, sometimes lithophytic; 450–1800 m; flowering September to November.

Sierra Leone to Uganda and southwards to Angola and Zimbabwe.

Tridactyle truncatiloba Summerhayes

Plant with erect, spreading or pendent stems, 20–100 cm long. Leaves many in 2 rows, ligulate, oblong-ligulate, or elliptic-ligulate, unequally bilobed at the apex, with rounded lobes, 14–21 cm long, 1.2–3 cm wide. Inflorescences pendent, lax,

8–18 cm long, 6- to 9-flowered. Flowers large, white, fleshy; dorsal sepal lanceolate or lanceolate-oval, acute, 15–16 mm long, 4.5 mm wide; lateral sepals oblique, similar to dorsal sepal but with a central keel along the outer surface, 18–20 mm long, 5–5.6 mm wide; petals linear-lanceolate, acute or acuminate, curved, 16 mm long, 2–2.5 mm wide; lip with wide, toothed auricles at the base, 3-lobed at the middle, side lobes widening towards the truncate apex, denticulate along the apical margin, mid-lobe narrowly triangular, longer than side lobes, in total 20 mm long, 15 mm wide; spur slender, inflated in the apical half, 3.5–4.5 cm long.

Epiphyte; 350–550 m; flowering in November.

Gabon and Congo.

This species has the largest flowers in the genus with uniquely shaped side lobes of the lip.

Tridactyle unguiculata Mansfeld

Plant with stems up to 42 cm long. Leaves linear-ligulate, unequally bilobed at the apex, up to 15 cm long, 7 mm wide. Inflorescences up to 8 cm long, several-flowered. Flower colour not recorded; dor-

Tridactyle truncatiloba. E. la Croix

sal sepal oblong, obtuse, 8–12 mm long, 4–4.5 mm wide; lateral sepals elliptic-oblong, obtuse, 9–12 mm long, 3–5 mm wide; petals oblong-spathulate, subacute or obtuse, 8.7–12 mm long, 4–4.5 mm wide; lip broadly flabellate, cucullate, auriculate at the base, 3-lobed in the apical half, side lobes oblong-flabellate, erose-dentate on the apical margin, mid-lobe triangular, acute, in total 9 mm long, 15 mm wide; spur slender, straight, 4–5 cm long.

In mist forest; 1800 m; flowering in October. Tanzania.

YPSILOPUS Summerhayes

Summerhayes used the Greek word for the letter *y*, *upsilon*, when he named this genus of small epiphytic orchids, an allusion to the Y-shaped stipe that holds the 2 pollinia at right angles to the viscidium. Five species are now recognised, each different from the others in vegetative appearance and flowers, but all having the pollinarium he described. However, some species of *Tridactyle* have a similar pollinarium, although they have a 3-lobed lip. Further studies may reveal that the limits of these 2 genera should be re-assessed.

All the species occur in forested areas where there is a prolonged dry season. The plants have short stems with thick roots spreading widely over the host tree and often penetrating into the bark. In *Ypsilopus longifolius* and *Y. viridiflorus* the plants are curiously pendent.

Culture

All the species grow well mounted on a piece of bark. When being watered, they need a good soaking and then a dry period before being watered again. They grow best in good light where there is plenty of air movement and seem to do best where there is a pronounced drop in temperature at night.

Ypsilopus erectus (P. J. Cribb) P. J. Cribb & J. Stewart

Plant erect with a short stem to 6 cm long and with thick roots. Leaves conduplicate, sometimes recurved, linear, obtuse, 3–15 cm long, 3.5–6 mm wide. Inflorescences axillary or below the leaves, spreading or suberect, 5–20 cm long, 4- to 12-flowered; bracts ovate-triangular, 1.5–2 mm long; pedicel with ovary scabrid, 9–12 mm long. Flowers white, scabrid on the outer surface; dorsal sepal ovate, acute, 5–6.5 mm long, 3 mm wide; lateral sepals obliquely oblong-lanceolate, acute, 5–7 mm long, 2.3–3 mm wide, keeled along the outer surface; petals oblong-lanceolate, acuminate, 5–6.5 mm long, 1.5–2 mm wide; lip obscurely 3-lobed, subrhombic to lanceolate, acute, 5–6.5 mm long, 2.3–3 mm wide; spur slender, cylindrical, 3.5–5 cm long.

Epiphyte or lithophyte in seasonally dry woodland; sea level to 2100 m; flowering January to May depending on locality.

Tanzania, Malawi, Zambia, Zimbabwe, Swaziland, and South Africa (Transkei and KwaZulu-Natal).

Ypsilopus leedalii P. J. Cribb

Plant small with a short stem up to 4 cm long and thick roots. Leaves ligulate, unequally bilobed at the apex, with rounded lobes, twisted at the base so that they lie in one plane, 5–7 cm long, 8–9 mm wide. Inflorescences arising below the leaves, 4–5 cm long, 6- to 10-flowered; bracts broadly triangular, obtuse, 1.5 mm long; pedicel with ovary scabrid, 3–4 mm long. Flowers white, not opening fully; dorsal sepal oblong, obtuse, 5.5 mm long, 2.5 mm wide; lateral sepals oblique, oblong-elliptic, obtuse, 5.5–6 mm long, 2.5–3 mm wide; petals elliptic, obtuse, 5.5–6 mm long, 3 mm wide, erose on the margins; lip concave, oblong-flabellate, obtuse, 8.5–9 mm long, 5–6 mm wide; spur cylindric, tapering from a wide mouth, 13–14 mm long.

Epiphyte in montane rain forest; 2200–2300 m; flowering in March.

Southern Tanzania.

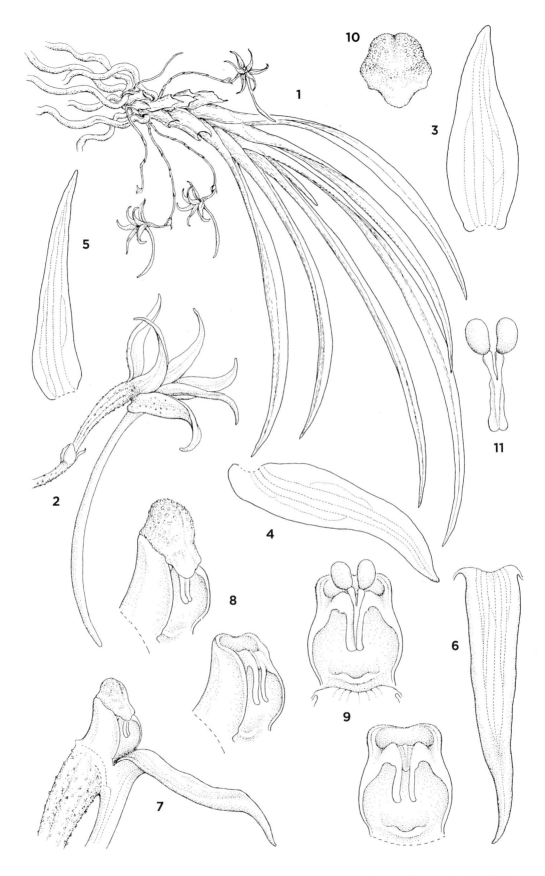

Ypsilopus viridiflorus. 1: Habit. 2: Flower. 3: Dorsal sepal. 4: Lateral sepal. 5: Petal. 6–7: Lip. 8–9: Column. 10: Anther-cap. 11: Pollinarium. From Cribb 1996, p. 418. M. E. Church.

Ypsilopus liae Delepierre & Lebel

Plants erect. Leaves broader than those of *Ypsilopus longifolius*. Inflorescences usually several, pendent, 10–30 cm long, 2- to 17-flowered. Flowers white, small; sepals and petals small; lip broad, suborbicular, 9 mm long, 8 mm wide; spur pinkish, 3 cm long.

Epiphyte in forest; 1850–2100 m; flowering in March.

Rwanda.

Dedicated to the memory of Lia Packet (1932–1989), wife of the collector Gilbert Delepierre. This species was described from a few collections in 2001. It is said to be similar to *Ypsilopus longifolius*. The chief distinguishing character of this species is the broad lip with its pinkish spur.

Ypsilopus longifolius (Kraenzlin) Summerhayes

Plants pendent with long white roots spreading from a short stem. Leaves folded, linear, acute,

Ypsilopus longifolius. B. Campbell

Ypsilopus viridiflorus. B. Campbell

greyish green, 5–25 cm long, 3–6 mm wide. Inflorescences usually several, pendent or arching, 3–8 cm long, 2- to 10-flowered. Flowers white with greenish tips to the tepals, scabrid on the outer surface; dorsal sepal ovate, acute, 6–7 mm long, 2–3 mm wide; lateral sepals oblique, ovate-lanceolate, acute, 6–9 mm long, 2–3 mm wide; petals slightly reflexed, lanceolate, acuminate, 5.5–6.5 mm long, 2–3 mm wide. Lip slightly recurved, ovate to rhombic, obscurely 3-lobed in the middle, acuminate, 6–8 mm long, 2–4 mm wide; spur slender, cylindric, 3–4 cm long.

Epiphyte on trunks and larger branches of trees in highland forests, especially rough-barked trees, and on *Grevillea* and other trees in plantations; 1450–2400 m; flowering in March and April.

Kenya and Tanzania.

Ypsilopus viridiflorus P. J. Cribb & J. Stewart

Plants pendent with a short stem and extensive grey roots. Leaves with the upper surfaces fused thus appearing bilaterally compressed, *Iris*-like, linear and tapering, 4–25 cm long, 2–5 mm wide. Inflorescences single or several, slender, 2–6 cm long, 1- or 2-flowered. Flowers pale green or yellowish green, scabrid on the outer surface; dorsal sepal lanceolate, acuminate, 7–9 mm long, 1.5–2 mm wide; lateral sepals similar, oblique at the base; petals linear-lanceolate, acuminate, 6–8 mm long, 1.5–1.8 mm wide; lip deflexed, entire, lanceolate, acuminate, 7–8 mm long, 2 mm wide; spur slender, curved or straight, 15–18 mm long.

Epiphyte on branches in mixed evergreen forest; 1500–2100 m; flowering in May.

Kenya and northern Tanzania, on Mount Kilimanjaro.

List of Generic Synonyms

This list is confined to those genera that are no longer in use and have been absorbed into another single genus. A few other names, for example, *Angorchis*, *Leptocentrum*, and *Rhaphidorhynchus*, have been used in the past for a variety of orchid species that are now allocated to several different genera.

NAMES NO LONGER IN CURRENT USE	NAMES IN USE TODAY
Aerobion Sprengel 1826	*Angraecum* Bory 1804
Azadehdelia Braem 1988	*Cribbia* Senghas 1986
Barombia Schlechter 1914	*Aerangis* Reichenbach f. 1865
Bathiea Schlechter 1918	*Neobathiea* Schlechter 1925
Cephalangraecum Schlechter 1918	*Ancistrorhynchus* Finet 1907
Crossangis Schlechter 1918	*Rhipidoglossum* Schlechter 1918
Ctenorchis K. Schumann 1901	*Angraecum* Bory 1804
Dicranotaenia Finet 1907	*Microcoelia* Lindley 1830
Encheiridion Summerhayes 1943	*Microcoelia* Lindley 1830
Gussonea A. Richard 1828	*Microcoelia* Lindley 1830 (mostly)
Holmesia Cribb 1977	*Angraecopsis* Kraenzlin 1900
Homocolleticon (Summerhayes) Szlachetko & Olszewski 2001	*Cyrtorchis* Schlechter 1914
Lepervenchea Cordemoy 1899	*Angraecum* Bory 1804
Macroplectrum Pfitzer 1889	*Angraecum* 1804
Microholmesia Cribb 1987	*Angraecopsis* Kraenzlin 1900
Monixus Finet 1907	*Angraecum* Bory 1804
Pectinaria (Bentham) Cordemoy 1899	*Angraecum* Bory 1804
Perrierella Schlechter 1925	*Oeonia* Lindley 1824
Phormangis Schlechter 1918	*Ancistrorhynchus* Finet 1907
Radinocion Ridley 1887	*Aerangis* Reichenbach f. 1865
Sarcorhynchus Schlechter 1918	*Rhipidoglossum* Schlechter 1918

Conversion Chart

Millimeters / Inches	
1 mm	$^3/_{64}$ in.
2 mm	$^3/_{32}$ in.
3 mm	$^1/_8$ in.
4 mm	$^5/_{32}$ in.
5 mm	$^3/_{16}$ in.
6 mm	$^1/_4$ in.
7 mm	$^9/_{32}$ in.
8 mm	$^5/_{16}$ in.
9 mm	$^{11}/_{32}$ in.
10 mm	$^3/_8$ in.
11 mm	$^7/_{16}$ in.
12 mm	$^1/_2$ in.
13 mm	$^{17}/_{32}$ in.
14 mm	$^9/_{16}$ in.
15 mm	$^5/_8$ in.
16 mm	$^3/_5$ in.
17 mm	$^{21}/_{32}$ in.
18 mm	$^{11}/_{16}$ in.
19 mm	$^{23}/_{32}$ in.
20 mm	$^3/_4$ in.

Centimeters / Inches	
1 cm	$^3/_8$ in.
1.5 cm	$^5/_8$ in.
2 cm	$^3/_4$ in.
2.5 cm	1 in.
3 cm	1 $^1/_8$ in.
3.5 cm	1 $^3/_8$ in.
4 cm	1 $^1/_2$ in.
4.5 cm	1 $^3/_4$ in.
5 cm	2 in.
5.5 cm	2 $^1/_4$ in.
6 cm	2 $^3/_8$ in.
6.5 cm	2 $^1/_2$ in.
7 cm	2 $^3/_4$ in.
7.5 cm	2 $^{15}/_{16}$ in.
8 cm	3 $^1/_8$ in.
8.5 cm	3 $^3/_8$ in.
9 cm	3 $^1/_2$ in.
9.5 cm	3 $^3/_4$ in.
10 cm	4 in.
10.5 cm	4 $^1/_4$ in.
11 cm	4 $^3/_8$ in.
12 cm	4 $^3/_4$ in.
13 cm	5 $^1/_8$ in.
14 cm	5 $^1/_2$ in.
15 cm	6 in.
16 cm	6 $^3/_8$ in.
17 cm	6 $^3/_4$ in.
18 cm	7 $^1/_8$ in.
19 cm	7 $^1/_2$ in.
20 cm	8 in.

Meters / Feet	
0.5 m	1 $^1/_2$ ft.
1 m	3 ft
1.5 m	5 ft.
2 m	6 $^1/_2$ ft.
2.5 m	8 ft.
3 m	10 ft.
3.5 m	11 ft.
4 m	13 ft.
4.5m	14 $^1/_2$ ft.
5 m	16 ft.
5.5 m	18 ft.
6 m	20 ft.
7 m	23 ft.
8 m	26 ft.
9 m	30 ft.
10 m	33 ft.
11 m	37 ft.
12 m	39 ft.
13 m	43 ft.
14 m	46 ft.
15 m	50 ft.
16 m	53 ft.
17 m	56 ft.
18 m	59 ft.
20 m	66 ft.
100 m	330 ft.
200 m	660 ft.
300 m	990 ft.
400 m	1320 ft.
500 m	1650 ft.
600 m	1880 ft.
700 m	2310 ft.
800 m	2640 ft.
900 m	2970 ft.
1000 m	3300 ft.

Celsius / Fahrenheit	
7°C	45°F
10°C	50°F
15°C	59°F
20°C	68°F
25°C	77°F

Glossary

The definitions of botanical terms given here are limited to the sense in which the words have been used in this book. They are illustrated in many general books on orchids, for example, Bechtel et al. (1992), Stewart and Griffiths (1995), and la Croix and la Croix (1997). Many of them could have slightly different or broader meanings in a wider botanical context.

Acumen a long slender sharp extension to another organ.

Acuminate gradually tapering to a long slender point or acumen.

Acute sharply pointed.

Amplexicaul embracing or clasping the stem.

Anther the pollen-bearing part of a stamen.

Anther cap the outer deciduous cap, or case, which covers the pollinia.

Anthesis the opening of the flower.

Apex the tip of a leaf, bract, stem, or any part of the flower.

Apical at the apex.

Apiculate ending abruptly in a sharp point.

Apiculus a short point.

Articulated jointed, separating freely by a clean scar.

Articulation line the line where a leaf will separate from the sheath.

Attenuate narrowed, tapered.

Auricle a small lobe or appendage, sometimes shaped like an ear lobe.

Auriculate eared, auricled.

Axil the angle between the upper side of a leaf, branch, or bract and the stem, or axis, from which it grows.

Axillary growing in an axil.

Axis the central, or main stem, of a plant or inflorescence.

Barbate bearded.

Bilobed divided into 2 lobes.

Bract a small leaf, or leaf-like structure, in the axil of which a flower is borne.

Bracteole a small bract.

Calceolate shaped like a slipper.

Callus (plural **Calli**) a solid protuberance caused by a mass of cells.

Campanulate bell-shaped.

Canaliculate channelled, with a longitudinal groove.

Capitate growing close together in a head.

Claw the narrow, stalk-like base of the petal or lip.

Clavate thickened at the end, club-shaped.

Column the central part of the orchid flower, formed by the union of the stamen, style, and stigma.

Conduplicate folded lengthwise, V-shaped in cross section.

Connate when the bases of 2 opposite parts are joined together.

Cordate heart-shaped.

Coriaceous leathery.

Cortex the ground tissue between the outer covering, the epidermis, and the vascular tissue.

Corymb an inflorescence that appears flat—the flowers are borne on pedicels of different lengths so that they all lie in one plane.

Corymbose like a corymb.

Crenulate scalloped, but the individual scallops or teeth small.

Cuneate, Cuneiform wedge-shaped, triangular.

Cuspidate tipped with a cusp, a sharp rigid point.

Deciduous falling off at some stage in the life of the flower or plant; not evergreen.

Deflexed bent or turned sharply downwards.

Deltoid triangular.

Dentate having a row of tooth-like outgrowths along the margin.

Denticulate toothed, but the teeth small.

Diaphanous permitting the light to show through.

Distichous arranged in 2 vertical ranks or rows on opposite sides of an axis.

Dorsal relating to the back or outer surface.

Dorsal sepal the intermediate, or odd sepal, usually at the back or upper side of the flower.

Elliptic shaped like an ellipse, narrowly oblong with regular, rounded ends.

Emarginate having a notch cut out, usually at the apical margin.

Endemic confined to a region, or country, and not occurring naturally anywhere else.

Ensiform sword-shaped.

Entire with an even margin, without teeth or divisions.

Epidermis the cellular skin or covering of a plant, often protected by a waxy outer covering or cuticle.

Epilithic growing on rocks.

Epiphyte a plant that grows on other plants but not as a parasite.

Epiphytic growing on other plants but not as a parasite

Equitant folded lengthwise so that the base of each leaf enfolds the next.

Erose as though bitten or gnawed at the edge.

Facies general appearance.

Falcate sickle-shaped.

Farinose with a mealy or floury covering.

Filiform thread-like.

Fimbriate having the margin fringed with long, narrow processes or appendages.

Flabellate fan-shaped.

Flexuose, Flexuous zigzag, bent alternately in opposite directions.

Floriferous producing many flowers.

Foot a basal extension of the column.

Geniculate abruptly bent so as to resemble a knee joint.

Genus (plural **Genera**) the smallest natural group containing distinct species.

Generic the name of a genus.

Glabrous smooth, completely lacking hairs, spines, or other projections.

Glandular possessing glands, secreting structures on the outer surface of an organ, often hair-like or pin-shaped.

Glaucous bluish green.

Globose spherical, or nearly so.

Habit the general appearance of a plant, whether prostrate, erect, climbing, or so forth.

Hyaline colourless or translucent.

Imbricate overlapping like the tiles on a roof.

Inflorescence the part of the plant bearing flowers; the arrangement of flowers on the flowering stem.

Intermediate sepal the dorsal, or odd sepal, usually uppermost in the flower.

Internode the space or portion of stem between 2 adjacent nodes.

Intervallate reappearing from the same point at intervals, for example, successive flowerings.

Keel a median, lengthwise ridge.

Keikei a small plant arising from the stem or inflorescence, rarely from a root of a mature plant.

Labellum the lip, or lowest petal of an orchid flower; usually held on the lower side of the flower and different in form from the 2 lateral petals.

Lacerate torn.

Lamina part of a leaf or petal that is expanded, usually thin and flat; the blade of a leaf.

Lanceolate lance- or spear-shaped; much longer than wide and tapering to a point at both ends.

Lateral sepals the pair of similar sepals arranged at the sides of an orchid flower.

Lax loose or distant, as opposed to tightly or densely arranged.

Liane, Liana a very elongated climber or scrambler amongst other vegetation, usually with a woody stem.

Ligulate strap-shaped.

Ligule a little tongue-like structure, usually narrow and pointed.

Limb the broad or expanded part of a petal or leaf.

Linear narrow, many times longer than wide, sides more or less parallel.

Lip the labellum, or odd petal of an orchid flower; usually held on the lower side of the flower and different in shape, colour, and size from the 2 lateral petals.

Lithophyte a plant that lives on a rock.

Lithophytic living on a rock.

Lobe a division of an organ, often round but may be of any shape.

Lobule a small lobe.

Lorate, Loriform strap-shaped.

Monocotyledons plants characterised by one seed-leaf in the embryo, and other associated features.

Monopodial a stem with a single continuous axis.

Monotypic having only one example, as in a genus with only one species.

Mucro a sharp terminal point.

Mucronate having a short sharp point, usually at the apex.

Node a point on a stem where a leaf or flower is attached.

Obcordate heart-shaped, with the widest part at the apex.

Oblanceolate lanceolate, with the widest part near the apex.

Oblong much longer than broad, with nearly parallel sides.

Oboval, Obovate reversed ovate, wider at the apical end.

Obtrullate ovate, but with angular sides (like a builder's trowel) with the widest part towards the apex.

Obtuse blunt or rounded at the end.

Orbicular round and flat.

Ovary the part of the flower that contains the ovules; in orchids it is always below the flower.

Ovate egg-shaped in outline, usually pointed at the apex, wider towards the base.

Pandurate, Panduriform fiddle-shaped.

Panicle a branching inflorescence in which all the branches bear flowers.

Paniculate having an inflorescence like a panicle.

Papilla (plural **Papillae**) a small fleshy protuberance on the surface of the leaf or flower.

Papillose bearing papillae.

Pectinate with narrow, close-set divisions, like the teeth in a comb.

Pedicel the stalk of an individual flower.

Pedicellate having a pedicel, usually used for an ovary in orchids.

Peduncle the stalk of an inflorescence.

Perennial lasting for several years, not normally perishing after flowering once.

Perianth the outer parts of an orchid flower, consisting of 6 tepals usually distinguished as 3 sepals, 2 petals, and the lip, often colourful.

Petals in orchid flowers, 2 of the 3 inner members of the perianth.

Petiolate having a petiole.

Petiole the stalk of a leaf.

Pollinarium (plural **Pollinaria**) the structure consisting of pollinia, stipe, and viscidium which is the unit of pollination in many orchids.

Pollinium (plural **Pollinia**) a body composed of many pollen grains cohering together.

Porrect directed outward and forward.

Pseudo- false, as in pseudo-petiole.

Pubescent hairy.

Punctate marked with dots, depressions, or translucent glands.

Quadrate square.

Raceme an unbranched inflorescence in which the flowers are borne on short pedicels and usually open in succession from the base upwards.

Rachis the flower-bearing portion of an inflorescence.

Recurved curved downwards or back upon itself.

Reniform kidney-shaped.

Resupinate having the lip lowermost because the pedicel or ovary is twisted through 180° during development.

Reticulate net-veined; the smallest visible veins are connected together like the meshes of a net.

Retuse having a rounded end, the centre of which is depressed or shorter than the sides.

Revolute rolled back from the edges.

Rostellum a projection from the upper edge of the stigma in front of the anther.

Rostrate with a beak, suddenly narrowed into a slender tip or point.

Rugose covered with wrinkles.

Rugulose somewhat wrinkled.

Saccate pouched or bag-shaped.

Scabrid somewhat scabrous.

Scabrous rough or gritty to the touch.

Scandent climbing.

Scarious thin, dry, and membranous, not green.

Secund having the flowers arranged apparently in one row along the side of an inflorescence.

Sepals the 3 outermost tepals of the perianth in the flower.

Serrate with forward-pointing teeth along the margin.

Serrulate serrate, but with minute teeth.

Sessile without a stalk.

Setose covered with bristles.

Sinuous wavy.

Sinus the curve or space between 2 lobes of a leaf.

Sheath the lower portion of the leaf, clasping the stem; also used for bracts which enclose the flowering stem below those which support the flowers.

Spathulate oblong, with the apical end rounded like a spatula.

Species (plural **Species**) a group of individuals that exhibit the same distinctive characters; the unit which provides the basis for classification.

Spike an unbranched inflorescence bearing sessile flowers; sometimes used in orchids for long slender racemes of many flowers.

Spreading arranged so that the tips of the parts are directed outwards, more or less horizontally.

Spur a tubular projection from one of the floral parts, usually the lip or the dorsal sepal.

Stellate star-shaped.

Stigma, Stigmatic surface the sticky area on the column that receives the pollen or pollinarium.

Stipe or **Stipes** (plural **Stipes** or **Stipites**) the stalk that connects the viscidium with the caudicles of the pollinia.

Sub- in compound words, this prefix usually indicates somewhat or almost the condition described, for example, subauriculate, subcordate, subcylindric, subglobose.

Subspecies (**Subsp.**) a subdivision of a species, usually confined to one geographical area and recognised by one or more characteristic features.

Subtribe a small group of genera that have certain characteristics in common; a smaller unit of classification than the tribe.

Subulate with a fine sharp point; awl-shaped.

Synonym another name for the same species or genus, but one which is no longer in general use.

Synonymy all that relates to synonyms.

Taxonomic pertaining to classification.

Taxonomist one who is skilled in classification.

Tepal a division of the perianth; usually used collectively or when the perianth is not markedly differentiated into sepals and petals.

Terete cylindrical, circular in cross section.

Terrestrial on or in the ground.

Tomentose densely hairy, either with many short hairs or with a matted, wool-like outgrowth of hairs.

Tribe a group of several genera that have certain characteristics in common.

Trilobed with 3 lobes or divisions.

Triquetrous 3-edged.

Trullate angular-ovate, shaped rather like a bricklayer's trowel.

Truncate straight-ended, as though cut off across the end.

Tuft, Tufted a group of leaves or stems arising very close together at the base.

Type specimen the original specimen from which a description was drawn up.

Umbel, Umbellate an inflorescence in which the diverging pedicels arise from the same point at the apex of the peduncle.

Undulate with a wavy margin or surface.

Utriculate bladder-like in appearance.

Vandaceous with a habit of growth similar to that of the genus *Vanda*, that is, monopodial with the leaves in 2 ranks.

Variety (**Var.**) a subdivision of a species that is easily recognised by its different size, colour, or other minor modification.

Velamen the absorbent epidermis of the roots of many orchids.

Venation the arrangement of the veins in a leaf, bract, or flower.

Verrucose warty.

Vesicle a small bladder.

Viscidium (plural **Viscidia**) the sticky gland attached to the pollinium, usually produced by the rostellum.

Whorl the arrangement of leaves or flowers in a circle around an axis.

References

This is a list of the books and papers we have referred to in compiling this book. It is not a complete bibliography of the literature on the angraecoid orchids of the region, and is not intended to be one. A bibliography of literature relating to orchids of Madagascar can be found in Hermans and Hermans (1999) and Hermans and Hermans et al. (2006). Other sources of information can be found by following up all these references and by referring to the World Checklist of Monocotyledons on the Kew Web site.

Arbonnier, M., and D. Geerinck. 1993. Contribution à l'étude des Orchidaceae du Burundi (part 1). *Belgian Journal of Botany* 126: 253–261.

Arends, J. C., and J. Stewart. 1989. *Aerangis gracillima*: a definitive account of a rare African orchid of Cameroon and Gabon. *Lindleyana* 4: 23–29.

Arends, J. C., and F. M. van der Laan. 1983. Cytotaxonomy of the monopodial orchids of the African and Malagasy regions. *Genetica* 62: 81–94.

Arends, J. C., and F. M. van der Laan. 1986. Cytotaxonomy of the Vandeae. *Lindleyana* 1: 33–41.

Ball, J. S. 1978. *Southern African Epiphytic Orchids*. Johannesburg: Conservation Press.

Bechtel, H., P. J. Cribb, and E. Launert. 1992. *The Manual of Cultivated Orchid Species*. 3rd ed. London: Blandford Press.

Benke, M. 2004. *La Réunion des Orchidées sauvages*. Saint Denis, Réunion: Mabé.

Bolus, H. 1893–1896, 1911, 1913. *Icones Orchidearum Austro-africanarum Extratropicarum*. 3 vols. London: Wesley and Sons.

Bory de Saint-Vincent, J. B. G. M. 1804. *Voyages dans les quatres principales îles des mers d'Afrique, fait par ordre du gouvernement, pendant les années neuf et dix de la République (1801 et 1802), avec l'histoire de la traversée du Capitaine Baudin jusqu'au Port Louis de l'île Maurice*. 3 vols. Paris: F. Buisson.

Bosser, J. 1969. Contribution à l'étude des Orchidaceae de Madagascar XI: sur les affinities des genres *Cryptopus* et *Neobathiea*. *Adansonia*, sér. 2, 9: 539–547.

Bosser, J. 1970a. Contribution à l'étude des Orchidaceae de Madagascar XII: *Jumellea* et *Angraecum* nouveaux. *Adansonia*, sér. 2, 10: 95–110.

Bosser, J. 1970b. Contribution à l'étude des Orchidaceae de Madagascar XIV: le genre *Lemurella* Schltr. *Adansonia*, sér. 2, 10: 367–373.

Bosser, J. 1971. Contribution à l'étude des Orchidaceae de Madagascar XV: Nouvelles espèces du genre *Aeranthes*. *Adansonia*, sér. 2, 11: 81–93.

Bosser, J. 1984. Contribution à l'étude des Orchidaceae de Madagascar et des Mascareignes XXI: sur l'identité du genre *Perrieriella* Schltr. *Adansonia*, sér. 4, 6: 369–372.

Bosser, J. 1987. Contribution à l'étude des Orchidaceae de Madagascar et des Mascareignes XXII: *Angraecum* sect. *Hadrangis* Schlechter aux Mascareignes. *Adansonia*, sér. 4, 9: 249–254.

Bosser, J. 1988. Contribution à l'étude des Orchidaceae de Madagascar et des Mascareignes XXIII: *Angraecum borbonicum*, espèce oubliée des Mascareignes. *Adansonia*, sér. 4, 10: 19–24.

Bosser, J. 1989a. Contribution à l'étude des Orchidaceae de Madagascar et des Mascareignes XXIV. *Adansonia*, sér. 4, 11: 29–38.

Bosser, J. 1989b. Contribution à l'étude des Orchidaceae de Madagascar ct des Mascareignes XXV: *Oeonia* Lindley. *Adansonia*, sér. 4, 11: 157–165.

Bosser, J. 1989c. Contribution à l'étude des Orchidaceae de Madagascar et des Mascareignes XXVI. *Adansonia*, sér. 4, 11: 369–382.

Bosser, J. 1997. Contribution à l'étude des Orchidaceae de Madagascar XXVII. *Adansonia*, sér. 3, 19: 181–188.

Bosser, J. 2004. Contribution à l'étude des Orchidaceae de Madagascar, des Comores et des Mascareignes XXXIII. *Adansonia*, sér. 3, 26: 53–61.

Cadet, J. 1989. *Joyaux de nos Forets: Les Orchidées de la Réunion*. Sainte Clotilde, Réunion: Janine Cadet.

Carlsward, B. S. 2004. *Molecular Systematics and Anatomy of Vandeae (Orchidaceae): The Evolution of Monopodial Leaflessness*. Ph.D. thesis, University of Florida.

Carlsward, B. S., W. M. Whitten, and N. H. Williams. 2003. Molecular phylogenetics of neotropical leafless Angraecinae (Orchidaceae): reevaluation of generic concepts. *International Journal of Plant Sciences* 164: 43–51.

Chase, M. W., K. M. Cameron, R. L. Barrett, and J. V. Freudenstein. 2003. DNA data and Orchidaceae systematics: a new phylogenetic classification. In *Orchid Conservation*, eds. K. W. Dixon, S. P. Kell, R. L. Barrett, and P. J. Cribb. 69–89. Kota Kinabalu, Sabah: Natural History Publications (Borneo).

Chiron, G., I. la Croix, and J. Stewart. 1998. Two new species of *Aerangis* from tropical Africa. *The Orchid Review* 106: 225–230.

Cordemoy, E. J. de. 1895. *Flore de l'Île de la Réunion*. Paris: Paul Klincksieck.

Cordemoy, E. J. de. 1899. Revision des Orchidées de la Réunion. *Revue Générale de Botanique* 11: 409–429.

Cribb, P. J. 1975a. A note on the identity of the Madagascan orchid *Aeranthes caudata* Rolfe. *Adansonia*, sér. 2, 15: 195–197.

Cribb, P. J. 1975b. Tab. 685, *Aeranthes caudata*, Orchidaceae. *Curtis's Botanical Magazine* 180: 117–120.

Cribb, P. J. 1977. New orchids from South Central Africa. *Kew Bulletin* 32: 137–187.

Cribb, P. J. 1979. New or little-known orchids from East Africa. *Kew Bulletin* 34: 321–340.

Cribb, P. J. 1989. *Orchidaceae*, part 3. In *Flora of Tropical East Africa*, ed. R. M. Polhill. 413–652. Rotterdam: A. A. Balkema.

Cribb, P. J. 1996. New species and records of Orchidaceae from West Africa. *Kew Bulletin* 51: 353–363.

Cribb, P. J., and J. M. Fay. 1987. Orchids of the Central African Republic: a provisional checklist. *Kew Bulletin* 42: 711–737.

Cribb, P. J., and I. la Croix. 1997. A synopsis of the genus *Cribbia* Senghas (Orchidaceae) with two new species from São Tomé. *Kew Bulletin* 52: 743–748.

Cribb, P. J., and F. Perez-Vera. 1975. A contribution to the study of the Orchidaceae of the Côte d'Ivoire. *Adansonia*, sér. 2, 15: 199–214.

Cribb, P. J., and J. Stewart. 1985. Additions to the orchid flora of tropical Africa. *Kew Bulletin* 40: 399–419.

Cribb, P. J., F. van der Laan, and J. C. Arends. 1989. Two new species of Orchidaceae from West Africa. *Kew Bulletin* 44: 479–483.

Dare, M. 1999. A new *Tridactyle* (Orchidaceae) from the *Flora Zambesiaca* region. *Excelsa* 19: 84–87.

Delepierre, G., and J.-P. Lebel. 2001. Liste des orchidées du Rwanda. *Taxonomania* 5: 5–9.

Delepierre, G., J.-P. Lebel, and D. Geerinck. 2001. Supplément à l'étude des Orchidaceae du Rwanda et des environs (III). *Taxonomania* 2: 1–10.

Demissew, S., P. Cribb, and F. Rasmussen. 2004. *Field Guide to Ethiopian Orchids*. Kew: Royal Botanic Gardens.

Dorr, L. J. 1997. *Plant Collectors in Madagascar and the Comoro Islands*. Kew: Royal Botanic Gardens.

Dressler, R. L. 1981. *The Orchids: Natural History and Classification*. Cambridge, Massachusetts: Harvard University Press.

Dressler, R. L. 1993. *Phylogeny and Classification of the Orchid Family*. Cambridge: Cambridge University Press.

Du Puy, D., P. J. Cribb, J. Bosser, J. Hermans, and C. Hermans. 1999. *The Orchids of Madagascar*. Kew: Royal Botanic Gardens.

Finet, E.-A. 1907. Classification et énumération des Orchidées africaines de la tribu des Sarcanthées, d'après les collections du Muséum de Paris. *Société Botanique de France, Mémoires* 9: 1–65, plates I–XII.

Fitch, C. M. 2004. Adaptable angraecums. *Orchids* 73: 666–671.

Garay, L. A. 1972. On the systematics of the monopodial orchids I. *Botanical Museum Leaflets* 23: 149–212.

Garay, L. A. 1973. Systematics of the genus *Angraecum* (Orchidaceae). *Kew Bulletin* 28: 495–516.

Geerinck, D. 1988. Orchidaceae. In *Flore du Rwanda*: Spermatophytes, Vol. IV, ed. G. Troupin, 505–629. Tervuren, Belgium: Musée Royal de l'Afrique Centrale.

Geerinck, D. 1992. Orchidaceae, part 2. In *Flore d'Afrique centrale*. 297–780. Meise: Jardin botanique national de Belgique.

Geerinck, D. 2003. Liste des taxons de la famille des Orchidaceae au Burundi. *Taxonomania* 9: 5–8.

Geerinck, D., G. Delepierre, and J.-P. Lebel. 1998. Supplément à l'étude des Orchidaceae du Rwanda (II). *Belgian Journal of Botany* 130: 135–138.

Govaerts, R. 2004. World Checklist of Monocotyledons Database. The Board of Trustees of the Royal Botanic Gardens, Kew. Published on the Internet; http://www.kew.org/monocotChecklist.

Gunn, M., and L. E. Codd. 1981. *Botanical Exploration of Southern Africa*. Cape Town: A. A. Balkema.

Hall, J. B. 1974. African orchids XXXIV. *Kew Bulletin* 29: 427–429.

Harrison, E. R. 1981. *Epiphytic Orchids of Southern Africa*. 2nd ed. Durban: Natal Branch of the Wildlife Society of Southern Africa.

Hermans, J., and J. Bosser. 2003. A new species of *Aeranthes* (Orchidaceae) from the Comoro Islands. *Adansonia*, sér. 3, 25: 215–217.

Hermans, J., and P. J. Cribb. 1997. A new species of *Angraecum* (Orchidaceae) from Madagascar. *The Orchid Review* 105: 108–111.

Hermans, J., and C. Hermans. 1999. Annotated bibliography. In *The Orchids of Madagascar*, D. Du Puy, P. J. Cribb, J. Bosser, J. Hermans, and C. Hermans. Kew: Royal Botanic Gardens.

Hermans, J., C. Hermans, P. J. Cribb, J. Bosser, and D. Du Puy. 2006. *Madagascan Orchids*. Kew: Royal Botanic Gardens.

Hermans, J., and I. la Croix. 2001. *Angraecum clareae* Hermans, la Croix & P. J. Cribb *sp. nov.*: A new species of *Angraecum* from Madagascar. *The Orchid Review* 109: 43–46.

Hillerman, F. 1990. *A Culture Manual for Aerangis Orchid Growers*. Grass Valley, California: Hillerman.

Hillerman, F. 1992. *A Culture Manual for Angraecoid Orchid Growers*. Grass Valley, California: Hillerman.

Hillerman, F. E., and A. W. Holst. 1986. *An Introduction to the Cultivated Angraecoid Orchids of Madagascar*. Portland: Timber Press.

Johansson, D. 1974a. Ecology of vascular epiphytes in West African rain forest. *Acta Phytogeographica Suecica* 59. Uppsala.

Johansson, D. 1974b. *Rhipidoglossum paucifolium*, a new African species of Orchidaceae. *Botaniska Notiser* 127: 149–151.

Jones, K. 1967. The chromosomes of orchids, 2. Vandeae Lindl. *Kew Bulletin* 21: 151–156.

Jonsson, L. 1979. New combinations in the African genera *Chauliodon* and *Solenangis* (Orchidaceae). *Botaniska Notiser* 132: 381–384.

Jonsson, L. 1981. A monograph of the genus *Microcoelia*. *Symbolae Botanicae Uppsalienses* 23 (4).

Katz, H. J., and J. Simmons. 1986. Attempt at a natural new classification of the African angraecoid orchids by Rudolf Schlechter. Being a translation of Versuch einer natürlichen Neuordnung der Afrikanischen Angraekoiden Orchidaceen from *Beihefte, Botanisches Centralblatt* 36: 62–181. Melbourne: Australian Orchid Foundation.

Kraenzlin, F. 1893. Orchidaceae africanae. *Botanische Jahrbücher für Systematik Pflanzengeschichte* 17: 49–68.

Kraenzlin, F. 1897. Orchidaceae africanae II. *Botanische Jahrbücher für Systematik Pflanzengeschichte* 22: 17–31.

Kraenzlin, F. 1899–1902. Orchidaceae africanae. *Botanische Jahrbücher für Systematik Pflanzengeschichte* 28: 2–179.

la Croix, I. 1998. Whatever happened to *Barombia*? *The Orchid Review* 106: 291–293.

la Croix, I., and P. J. Cribb. 1998. Orchidaceae, part 2. In *Flora Zambesiaca*, vol. 11, part 2, ed. G. V. Pope. Kew: Royal Botanic Gardens.

la Croix, I., and E. la Croix. 1997. *African Orchids in the Wild and in Cultivation*. Portland: Timber Press.

la Croix, I. F., E. A. S. la Croix, and T. M. la Croix. 1991. *Orchids of Malawi*. Rotterdam: A. A. Balkema.

la Croix, I. F., E. A. S. la Croix, T. M. la Croix, J. A. Hutson, and N. G. B. Johnston-Stewart. 1983. *Malawi Orchids*, vol. 1, *Epiphytic Orchids*. Blantyre, Malawi: National Fauna Preservation Society of Malawi.

Lecoufle, M. 1965. *Cryptopus elatus. American Orchid Society Bulletin* 34: 327–328.

Lecoufle, M. 1966. Orchids of Madagascar. In *Proceedings of the 5th World Orchid Conference*, ed. L. R. de Garmo. Long Beach, California. 233–237.

Lecoufle, M. 1976. Orchids of Madagascar. In *Proceedings of the 8th World Orchid Conference*, ed. K. Senghas. Frankfurt: D.O.G. 249–252.

Lecoufle, M. 1980. Orchids of Madagascar. In *Proceedings of the 9th World Orchid Conference*, ed. M. R. Sukshom Kashemsanta. Bangkok: Amarin Press. 169–171.

Lecoufle, M. 1994. Madagascan orchids. In *Proceedings of the 14th World Orchid Conference*. Edinburgh: HMSO. 381–382.

Linder, H. P. 1989. Notes on southern African angraecoid orchids. *Kew Bulletin* 44: 317–319.

Linder, H. P., and H. Kurzweil. 1999. *Orchids of Southern Africa*. Rotterdam: A. A. Balkema.

Lindley, J. 1830–1840. *The Genera and Species of Orchidaceous Plants*. London. Reprinted 1953. Amsterdam: Asher.

Lindley, J. 1837. Notes upon some genera and species of Orchidaceae in the collection formed by Mr. Drège, at the Cape of Good Hope. *Companion to the Botanical Magazine* 2 (19): 200–210.

Lindley, J. 1862. West African tropical orchids. *Journal of the Linnean Society, Botany* 6: 123–140.

Linnaeus, C. 1753. *Species Plantarum*. Stockholm.

Linnaeus, C. 1781. *Supplementum plantarum*. Brunswick.

Moore, S. 1877. Orchideae. In *Flora of Mauritius and the Seychelles*, ed. Baker. London: L. Reeve.

Perez-Vera, F. 2003. *Les Orchidées de Côte d'Ivoire*. Mèze, France: Collection Parthénope, éditions Biotope.

Perrier de la Bâthie, H. 1938a. Sarcanthae nouvelles ou peu connues de Madagascar. *Notulae Systematicae* 7: 29–48.

Perrier de la Bâthie, H. 1938b. Sarcanthae nouvelles ou peu connues de Madagascar. *Notulae Systematicae* 7: 49–65.

Perrier de la Bâthie, H. 1938c. Sarcanthae nouvelles ou peu connues de Madagascar. *Notulae Systematicae* 7: 105–139.

Perrier de la Bâthie, H. 1941. 49. Famille, Orchidées, vol. 2. In *Flore de Madagascar*, ed. H. Humbert. Tananarive, Madagascar: Imprimerie Officielle.

Perrier de la Bâthie, H. 1951. Orchidées de Madagascar et des Comores. Nouvelles Observations. *Notulae Systematicae* 14: 138–165.

Perrier de la Bâthie, H. 1955. Les orchidées du massif du Marojejy et des avant-monts. *Mémoires de l'Institut scientifique de Madagascar*, sér. B, biologie végétale, 6: 3–271.

Petersen, J. B. 1952. Some new or little known orchids from the Cameroons. *Botanisk Tidsskrift* 49: 160–170.

Piers, F. 1968. *Orchids of East Africa*. Lehre, Germany: J. Cramer.

Redpath, J., and P. F. Hunt. 1972. Index to African orchids I–XXX by V. S. Summerhayes. *Kew Bulletin* 27: 337–369.

Reinikka, M. A. 1972. *A History of the Orchid*. Coral Gables, Florida: University of Miami Press.

Richard, A. 1828. *Monographie des Orchidées des Îles de France et de Bourbon*. Paris.

Ridley, H. N. 1883. Descriptions and notes on new or rare monocotyledonous plants from Madagascar, with one from Angola. *Journal of the Linnean Society, Botany* 20: 329–338.

Ridley, H. N. 1885. The orchids of Madagascar. *Journal of the Linnean Society, Botany* 21: 456–523.

Ridley, H. N. 1886. On Dr. Fox's collection of orchids from Madagascar, along with some obtained by the Rev. R. Baron from the same island. *Journal of the Linnean Society, Botany* 22: 116–127.

Roberts, D. L. 2006. *Aeranthes virginalis* (Orchidaceae): a new species from the Comoro Islands. *Kew Bulletin* (in press).

Robertson, S. A. 1989. *Flowering Plants of Seychelles*. Kew: Royal Botanic Gardens.

Rolfe, R. A. 1897–1898. Orchideae. In *Flora of Tropical Africa*, vol. 7, ed. W. T. Thiselton-Dyer. Ashford: L. Reeve and Company. 12–292.

Rolfe, R. A. 1912–1913. *Flora Capensis*, vol. 5, part 3. London: L. Reeve and Company. 3–313.

Schlechter, R. 1913. Orchidacées de Madagascar—Orchidaceae Perrieranae Madagascarienses. *Annales du Musée Colonial de Marseille* 3: 148–202.

Schlechter, R. 1918a. Versuch einer natürlichen Neuordnung der Afrikanischen Angraekoiden Orchidaceen. *Beihefte, Botanisches Centralblatt* 36: 62–181.

Schlechter, R. 1918b. XLII. Orchidaceae novae et criticae. Decas LV–LVII. Additamenta ad Orchideologiam madagascarensem. *Repertorium specierum novarum regni vegetabilis* 15: 324–340.

Schlechter, R. 1924–1925. Orchidaceae Perrierianae. Ein Beitrag zur Orchideenkunde der Insel Madagaskar. *Repertorium specierum novarum regni vegetabilis, Beihefte* 33: 1–391.

Schultes, R. E., and A. S. Pease. 1963. *Generic Names of Orchids: Their Origin and Meaning*. London: Academic Press.

Segerback, L. B. 1983. *Orchids of Nigeria*. Rotterdam: A. A. Balkema.

Senghas, K. 1963. Die angraekoiden Orchideen Afrikas und Madagaskar II: die Gattung *Oeoniella*. *Die Orchidee* 14: 215–218.

Senghas, K. 1964. Sur quelques Orchidées nouvelles ou critiques de Madagascar. *Adansonia* 4: 301–314.

Senghas, K. 1967. *Jumellea rossii*: eine neue Orchidee von der Insel Réunion. *Die Orchidee* 18: 240–245.

Senghas, K. 1973. *Angraecum bosseri*: ein neuer 'Stern von Madagaskar'. *Die Orchidee* 24: 191–193.

Senghas, K. 1983. *Aerangis seegeri*: eine neue Orchidee aus Madagaskar. *Die Orchidee* 34: 23–25.

Senghas, K. 1986. 15. Tribus Vandeae, 48. Subtribus Angraecinae, 49. Subtribus Aerangidinae. In Schlechter, *Die Orchideen*, 3. Auflage, Bd. I., eds. F. G. Brieger, R. Maatsch, and K. Senghas. Berlin: Verlag Paul Parey.

Stearn, W. T. 1992. *Botanical Latin*. 4th ed. Newton Abbot: David and Charles.

Stévart, T., and F. de Oliveira. 2000. *Guide des Orchidées de São Tomé et Príncipe*. São Tomé; Ecofac.

Stewart, J. 1976. The vandaceous group in Africa and Madagascar. In *Proceedings of the 8th World Orchid Congress*, ed. K. Senghas. Frankfurt: D.O.G. 239–248.

Stewart, J. 1979. A revision of the African species of *Aerangis* (Orchidaceae). *Kew Bulletin* 34: 239–319.

Stewart, J. 1994. 110. Orchidaceae. In *Upland Kenya Wild Flowers*, 2nd ed., eds. A. D. Q. Agnew and S. Agnew. Nairobi: East Africa Natural History Society.

Stewart, J., and B. Campbell. 1970. *Orchids of Tropical Africa*. London: W. H. Allen.

Stewart, J., and B. Campbell. 1996. *Orchids of Kenya*. Winchester: St. Paul's Bibliographies.

Stewart, J., and M. Griffiths, eds. 1995. *The RHS Manual of Orchids.* London: Macmillan Press.

Stewart, J., and E. F. Hennessy. 1981. *Orchids of Africa: A Select Review.* Johannesburg: Macmillan South Africa.

Stewart, J., and I. F. la Croix. 1987. Notes on the orchids of southern tropical Africa III: *Aerangis. Kew Bulletin* 42: 215–219.

Stewart, J., H. P. Linder, E. A. Schelpe, and A. V. Hall. 1982. *Wild Orchids of Southern Africa.* Johannesburg: Macmillan South Africa.

Summerhayes, V. S. 1934. African orchids VI. *Kew Bulletin* 1934: 205–214.

Summerhayes, V. S. 1936. African orchids VIII. *Kew Bulletin* 1936: 221–239.

Summerhayes, V. S. 1937. African orchids IX. *Kew Bulletin* 1937: 457–466.

Summerhayes, V. S. 1943. African orchids XIII: The leafless angraecoid orchids. *Botanical Museum Leaflets* 11: 137–170.

Summerhayes, V. S. 1944. African orchids XIV: *Ancistrorhynchus* Finet. *Botanical Museum Leaflets* 11: 201–214.

Summerhayes, V. S. 1945a. African orchids XV. *Botanical Museum Leaflets* 11: 249–260.

Summerhayes, V. S. 1945b. African orchids XVI. *Botanical Museum Leaflets* 12: 89–116.

Summerhayes, V. S. 1947a. Tabula 3461 *Ancistrorhynchus ovatus* Summerhayes. *Hooker's Icones Plantarum* 35: t. 3461.

Summerhayes, V. S. 1947b. Tabula 3464. *Microcoelia ericosma* Summerhayes. *Hooker's Icones Plantarum* 35: t. 3464.

Summerhayes, V. S. 1948. African orchids XVIII. *Kew Bulletin* 3: 277–302.

Summerhayes, V. S. 1949. African orchids XIX. *Kew Bulletin* 4: 427–443.

Summerhayes, V. S. 1950. Tabula 3485. *Rhipidoglossum densiflorum* Summerhayes. *Hooker's Icones Plantarum* 35: t. 3485.

Summerhayes, V. S. 1951a. New orchids from Africa. *Botanical Museum Leaflets* 14: 215–239.

Summerhayes, V. S. 1951b. A revision of the genus *Angraecopsis. Botanical Museum Leaflets* 14: 240–261.

Summerhayes, V. S. 1951c. African orchids XX. *Kew Bulletin* 6: 461–475.

Summerhayes, V. S. 1956a. African orchids XXIII. *Kew Bulletin* 11: 217–236.

Summerhayes, V. S. 1956b. Tabula 3566. *Chauliodon buntingii* Summerhayes. *Hooker's Icones Plantarum* 36: t. 3566.

Summerhayes, V. S. 1958a. African orchids XXV. *Kew Bulletin* 13: 57–87.

Summerhayes, V. S. 1958b. African orchids XXVI. *Kew Bulletin* 13: 257–281.

Summerhayes, V. S. 1960. African orchids XXVII. *Kew Bulletin* 14: 126–157.

Summerhayes, V. S. 1962a. African orchids XXVIII. *Kew Bulletin* 16: 253–314.

Summerhayes, V. S. 1962b. *Angraecum erectum* Summerhayes. *Hooker's Icones Plantarum* 36: t. 3592.

Summerhayes, V. S. 1964. African orchids XXIX. *Kew Bulletin* 17: 511–561.

Summerhayes, V. S. 1966. African orchids XXX. *Kew Bulletin* 20: 165–199.

Summerhayes, V. S. 1967. *Solenangis angustifolia* Summerhayes. *Hooker's Icones Plantarum* 37: t. 3640.

Summerhayes, V. S. 1968. Orchidaceae. In *Flora of West Tropical Africa*, vol. 3, part 1, 2nd ed., ed. F. N. Hepper. London: Crown Agents.

Szlachetko, D. L. 1995. Systema Orchidalium. *Fragmenta Floristica et Geobotanica, Supplementum* 3: 1–152.

Szlachetko, D. L., and T. S. Olszewski. 2001. *Flore du Cameroun, 36, Orchidacées*, vol. 3. Yaoundé (Cameroun): Ministere de la recherche scientifique et technique.

Szlachetko, D. L., M. Sawicka, and M. Kras-Lapinska. 2004. *Flore du Gabon, 37, Orchidaceae* II. Paris: Muséum national d'Histoire naturelle, Publications Scientifiques.

Thouars, L. M. A.-A. du Petit. 1822. *Histoire particulière des plantes Orchidées recueillies sur les trois Îles Australes d'Afrique, de France, de Bourbon et de Madagascar.* Paris. Reprint 1979. Stanfordville, New York: Earl M. Coleman.

Times Atlas of the World. 2004. Compact edition. London. Times Books.

Toilliez-Genoud, J. 1958. Sur une *Aeranthes* nouvelle de Madagascar. *Naturaliste Malgache* 10: 19–20.

Toilliez-Genoud, J., and J. Bosser. 1960. Contribution à l'étude des Orchidaceae de Madagascar I. *Naturaliste Malgache* 12: 9–16.

Toilliez-Genoud, J., and J. Bosser. 1961. Contribution à l'étude des Orchidaceae de Madagascar IV: sur un *Angraecum* et un *Cynorchis* nouveaux. *Adansonia* 1: 100–105.

Toilliez-Genoud, J., and J. Bosser. 1962. Contribution à l'étude des Orchidaceae de Madagascar III: sur un *Neobathiea* et un *Cynorchis* nouveaux. *Naturaliste Malgache* 13: 25–30.

Toilliez-Genoud, J., E. Ursch, and J. Bosser. 1960. Contribution à l'étude des *Aeranthes* de Madagascar. *Notulae Systematicae* 16: 205–215.

U.S. Central Intelligence Agency. *Africa* [map]. 2002. "Perry-Castañeda Library Map Collection, University of Texas at Austin." <http://www.lib.utexas.edu/maps.africa.html> (accessed 20 September 2005).

Van der Laan, F. M., and P. J. Cribb. 1986. *Ossiculum* (Orchidaceae): a new genus from Cameroon. *Kew Bulletin* 41: 823–832.

Veitch, J. 1891. *A Manual of Orchidaceous Plants,* part 7. Chelsea: James Veitch and Sons.

Williams, B. S., and H. Williams, 1894. *The Orchid-Grower's Manual.* 7th ed. London: Victoria and Paradise Nurseries.

Williamson, G. 1977. *The Orchids of South Central Africa.* London: Dent.

Williamson, G. 1990. New orchids from the *Flora Zambesiaca* region. *Kirkia* 13: 245–252.

Wilson, G., ed. 1915. *Angraecum caudatum. The Orchid World* 5: 260.

Withner, C. L., and P. A. Harding. 2004. *The Cattleyas and Their Relatives: The Debatable Epidendrums.* Portland: Timber Press.

Wodrich, K. H. K. 1997. *Growing South African Indigenous Orchids.* Rotterdam: A. A. Balkema.

Wood, J. J. 1982. A new species of *Jumellea* (Orchidaceae) from tropical Africa. *Kew Bulletin* 37: 77–79.

Web Sites Including Information on Orchids of the Area

http://www.kew.org/monocotChecklist/default.jsp

http://www.chez.com/orchidrun (Les Orchidées de la Réunion, in French)

http://www.madaorchidee.free.fr (Madagascar et ses Orchidées, in French)

http://www.orchidspecies.com (Internet Orchid Photo Encyclopedia)

http://www.perso.wanadoo.fr/mascaorc (Le Guide des Orchidées des Mascareignes, in French)

Index of Orchid Names

Bold-faced numbers indicate pages with photographs. Italicized numbers indicate pages with drawings.